(A FAILED EMPIRE ,

THE NEW COLD WAR HISTORY

John Lewis Gaddis, editor

VLADISLAV M. ZUBOK

(A FAILED EMPIRE)

THE SOVIET UNION

IN THE COLD WAR

FROM STALIN TO

GORBACHEV

★

With a New Preface by the Author

The University of North Carolina Press

Chapel Hill

© 2007 The University of North Carolina Press
Preface to the Paperback Edition
© 2009 The University of North Carolina Press
All rights reserved
Manufactured in the United States of America
Set in Quadraat, Eagle, and Scala Sans type
by Keystone Typesetting, Inc.
The paper in this book meets the guidelines for permanence and
durability of the Committee on Production Guidelines for Book Longevity
of the Council on Library Resources.

The University of North Carolina Press has been a member
of the Green Press Initiative since 2003.

Parts of this book have been reprinted with permission in revised form from
Vladislav M. Zubok, "The Nuclear Education of Nikita Khrushchev," in *Cold War
Statesmen Confront the Bomb: Nuclear Diplomacy since 1945*, edited by John Lewis Gaddis
et al. (New York: Oxford University Press, 1999), and "Gorbachev and the End of the
Cold War: Different Perspectives on the Historical Personality," in *Cold War Endgame:
Oral History, Analysis, Debates*, edited by William C. Wohlforth (University Park:
Pennsylvania State University Press, 2003).

The Library of Congress has cataloged the original edition
of this book as follows:
Zubok, V. M. (Vladislav Martinovich)
A failed empire: the Soviet Union in the Cold War from Stalin to Gorbachev /
Vladislav M. Zubok
p. cm.—(New Cold War history)
Includes bibliographical references and index.
ISBN 978-0-8078-3098-7 (cloth : alk. paper)
ISBN 978-0-8078-5958-2 (pbk. : alk. paper)
1. Soviet Union—Politics and government—1953–1985. 2. Soviet Union—Politics and
government—1985–1991. 3. Soviet Union—Foreign relations—1945–1991. 4. Cold War.
I. Title. II. Series.
DK274.Z825 2007
947.085—dc22   2007011439

cloth   12 11 10 09 08   6 5 4 3 2
paper   13 12 11 10 09   5 4 3 2 1

For my parents

Martin and Liudmila Zubok

(CONTENTS)

A section of illustrations appears after page 154.

(PREFACE TO THE PAPERBACK EDITION)
RUSSIA'S REVENGE?

The collapse of the Soviet empire was an event of epochal geopolitical, military, ideological, and economic significance. The United States, the last superpower, became the hub of the international order. Triumphalism surged in the West. Almost all of the countries from the former Communist bloc looked toward Washington for assistance, protection, and advice. The consensus in Washington was that the countries of Eastern Europe and Russia were making a "transition" under the guidance of American consultants toward a market economy and liberal democracy. This was also the expectation in Russia.

Under American leadership, the victorious and economically prosperous West began to expand eastward, absorbing the countries of Eastern Europe, which had a traditionally strong pro-Western orientation. Even before the division of Europe ended in 1989, these countries had begun to drift covertly toward the West. The enlargement of the European Union (EU) was the most positive development in Europe after the end of the Cold War. The common European project and the desire for modernity and prosperity helped to erode historic animosities between Germany and Poland, Rumania and Hungary, and Bulgaria and Turkey that plagued the Eastern part of the continent. In the past, most of the new members had been treated as imperial provinces, satellites, or second-rate countries begging for the crumbs from the great powers' table. Some never succeeded in overcoming backwardness and poverty. Admittance into the EU gave these countries an enormous boost in morale, helping them compensate for the painful slump during their transition to a market economy. Playing by the rules and accepting Western values ensured a much smoother political transition from a post-totalitarian regime to a democracy. The integration of the "new" Europe with the "old" Europe replaced the Iron Curtain with a common space, free of protectionist and visa barriers.

After 1989, the United States acted to guarantee Europe's security. In 1996 the United States supported the admission of Poland, the Czech Republic, and Hungary into the North Atlantic Treaty Organization (NATO). From that moment on, NATO adopted the Open Door policy, inviting any European country to join its ranks. During the Cold War, the United States, in the famous phrase of Norwegian historian Geir Lundestad, had acted as the "empire by invitation."

Now NATO continued to act in this way.[1] In 2004 Bulgaria, Rumania, Slovakia, Lithuania, Latvia, and Estonia joined NATO. Sidelined after World War I and Stalinized after World War II, Central Eastern Europe and the Baltics finally got their lucky ticket.

It turned out to be a different story with the ex-Soviet Central Asian states, Belarus, Ukraine, and especially Russia. The largest successor state from the Soviet domain, the Russian Federation became recognized in 1992 as the legal successor to the Soviet Union. The new Russia inherited the Soviet Union's permanent seat on the UN Security Council but also over $100 billion in Soviet debt. Due to its size and geography, Russia did not fit into either the EU or NATO. Statesmen and diplomats in Washington, Moscow, and above all London and Berlin remembered the famous saying of Lord Ismay, the first secretary-general of NATO, that the alliance's purpose was "to keep Americans in, Russians out, and Germans down." The Clinton administration assured the Russians that this was no longer true and offered a special partnership between NATO and Russia. Russia accepted. Russia's post-Communist state was extremely weak, and its leadership appeared to be eager to join the Western order under any conditions. Soon, however, Russia's behavior began to disappoint the West.

Russia, in the eyes of many Western observers, failed to make the "transition" expected of it after the collapse of Communism. The Yeltsin government, whom the Western countries helped with lavish advice (but not much money), subjected Russia to "shock therapy" to create a market economy in one big leap, following the example of Poland and other Eastern European countries. The effects of this policy were even more traumatic and controversial than they had been in Eastern European countries. The economic reformers in the Kremlin, eager to liberate Russia from its bane of state centralism and prevent the Communist Party from returning to power, quickly privatized enormous state assets. Most of them ended up in the hands of criminal groups and a few big business oligarchs linked to the state bureaucracy. The Russian economy contracted by more than two-fifths, a greater recession than the United States had experienced in the 1930s. Whole areas of the country, including dozens of industrial conglomerates and techno-cities in the military-industrial complex, remained without funds and became blighted. The reformers failed to stop hyperinflation, and Russians, who lost their life's savings, fled from the ruble to the U.S. dollar. The extensive social services of Soviet times, from free kindergartens to free health care and paid vacations, disappeared overnight. Violent crime soared, and life expectancy plummeted from seventy to sixty-five years. Russia experienced demographic contraction of catastrophic proportions. Its science and engineering, education and culture were starving, saved only by grants from American philanthropist George Soros and a few Western foundations. During the early 1990s, 1.5 million highly educated and talented Russians emigrated for economic reasons. The Yeltsin reforms neglected not only Russian society but also state institutions. The state that emerged from the Communist collapse was very weak, could not collect taxes, and could not implement necessary market reforms effectively. Corruption swept through Russia like a tsunami. The Russian army became such a pitiful wreck that in 1994–96 it lost a war against the separatist irregulars in the mountain region of Chechnya.

Liberal economic reformers in Russia, like those in Eastern Europe, believed that, as Karl Marx had predicted, politics would follow economics and the new capitalist Russia would build a Western–type democracy. Instead, as some experts had warned, the traumatic shock of economic changes created a gigantic psychological and political backlash in Russian society against the Yeltsin regime and its "democratic" course. Unlike in Poland, the Czech Republic, or the Baltic states, where this backlash was compensated for by the strong national pro-Western consensus, in Russia the political appeal of Western liberalism collapsed, along with the political parties and leaders that advocated its advantages. There was increasing support for a strong hand to restore "order" and protect the average citizen from oligarchs and criminals. Observers began to worry about the emergence of a "Weimar Russia" and a possible cataclysmic explosion of Russian nationalism, fueled by economic frustrations and wounded imperial pride. In 1999 all of this began to affect Russia's foreign policy. Anti-Americanism grew apace: the remarkable reservoir of good feelings and positive images about the United States at the end of the Cold War disappeared in Russia's mass consciousness and among intellectual elites. Instead of emulating Americans and American society, the Russian government began to reject the "Washington consensus" that dictated shocking economic transformations and maximal political liberalization. It also questioned American wisdom and the legitimacy of its global domination.[2]

It would be an exaggeration to say that the United States "lost" Russia during the 1990s, but American policies toward Russia were to some degree responsible for Russia's growing discontent and defiance. The American superpower had prudently contained Soviet expansionism during the Cold War, wisely constructed the free world to oppose the Communist bloc, and led the enlargement of the West after the victory in the Cold War. Yet the United States did not produce any innovative vision or coherent strategy with regard to Russia. Several factors were responsible for this. First, Russia was not treated as a strategic priority. When it became clear that Communists would not return to power in Moscow, Russia disappeared from American television screens and newspapers' front pages. Developments in other regions, from China to the Middle East, grabbed American attention. Second, American politics vis-à-vis Russia looked more toward the past than toward the future. Many individuals and groups in the United States continued to look at Russia with suspicion and bias going back to the Soviet and tsarist past. They muddled images of Stalin's totalitarianism and gulags with memories of Jewish pogroms and myths of the backward Asiatic autocracy. The inept brutality of Russia's war in Chechnya revived this Russophobic imagery. And the evangelical-minded segments of American society feared that if the post-Communist Russia was not "saved for democracy," it would lapse back into the "evil empire" mode of the Soviet days.[3] By the late 1990s, when Russia was mired in anarchy and corruption, the image of Russia in American political discourse changed: it was no longer "an aspiring democracy" but rather "a looted and bankrupt zone of nuclearized anarchy" and "the world's most virulent kleptocracy."[4] After 1999, the U.S. government and media increasingly adopted an accusatory tone, blaming the Russian government for failing to follow the prescribed path toward democracy.

While critical of Russian sins and shortcomings, the United States never offered any economic incentive or morale boost to the Russian state and society. Russia never even got normal access to American markets for an absurd reason: the 1974 Congressional legislation that denied the USSR the "most-favored nation" status in trade on the issue of freedom of immigration became applicable to Russia (and still is to this day). Visa restrictions for Russian travelers and tourists became even tighter. A host of American private foundations, nongovernmental organizations, economic and political consultants, and religious missionaries operated in Russia, treating Russians in a semicolonialist fashion as subjects for their lecturing and proselytizing. In 1993–99, President Clinton cultivated a special relationship with "his friend Boris" Yeltsin.[5] The Russian reformers, however, expected much more in return for their rejection of Communism and the Soviet empire. Critics of Yeltsin's pro-Western orientation claimed that Russia got nothing from its relationship with the West and was treated like a criminal on extended probation, if not worse. With the enlargement of the EU and NATO, Russia's failure to integrate into the "new" Europe and find a place in the American international order became increasingly apparent.[6] To complicate matters further, NATO invited into its ranks former parts of the Soviet empire where anti-Soviet and anti-Communist sentiment had led to resentment of Russia and Russians. In Poland, Rumania, Latvia, and Estonia, many forgot that Russians had also been the victims of Communism and Stalinism. Many people in these countries suspected that the post-Communist Russia was just a reincarnation of the old empire. Some Eastern European and Baltic politicians believed NATO's purpose was to protect them from Russian "imperialism."

Of course, Russian political elites bore a great deal of responsibility for Russia's political and ideological distancing from the "new" Europe and the United States. The Russian political leadership began to consolidate the society around the idea of Russia's greatness instead of the discredited idea of democratic reforms. The anti-Western voices, marginal at first, slowly became mainstream. The first serious standoff between the new Russia and NATO occurred over Yugoslavia. In 1999 NATO, prodded by Washington, ignored the UN Security Council's negative vote and bombed Serbia (Yugoslavia) allegedly to prevent a genocide of the Kosovo Albanians by the Serbian army. Russians, however, perceived this action as an attack on the sovereignty of Serbia, historically a Russian ally in the Balkans. The Russian government treated the bombing campaign as a "NATO aggression." In the Russian media, pro-Western liberal voices virtually disappeared. The Russian political elites were insulted that the United States called the shots in Europe and that Russia's role in European affairs and its veto on the UN Security Council were ignored. Yeltsin's attempts to play a role in the Serbian-Kosovo settlement only revealed the extent of Russian impotence. Forgotten were American promises to Gorbachev in 1989 to build a "common European home." Increasingly, Russians, not only officials but also the broader public, gravitated toward a view that the United States and the West denied Russia a decent place in the world.[7]

These trends continued under Yeltsin's successor, Vladimir Putin. After the September 11, 2001, terrorist attack on the United States, President Putin offered immediate assistance, which facilitated the defeat of the Taliban regime in Afghanistan. The view of Russian elites, however, was that America pocketed the Russian aid and never returned the favor. Instead, the Bush administration revived the "Star Wars" missile-defense program that the end of the Cold War had seemed to bury. Washington, dominated by neoconservative voices, also announced a crusade to spread democracy around the globe that began with the most difficult place for such an endeavor, the Arab Middle East. Russian foreign policy elites, even those who had previously supported a pro-Western orientation, were outraged when the United States invaded Iraq in March 2003. From their perspective, it was a demonstration of American unilateralism at its worst. The Putin government reacted sharply when the United States began to promote and support "democratic revolutions" in Georgia, Ukraine, and Central Asia. Kremlin officials and policy analysts interpreted this strategy as a new phase in the Western game to keep Russia out.

During the 1990s, the United States did not seek to promote democracy in the ex-Soviet periphery. Instead, it focused pragmatically on the oil-rich authoritarian states of Kazakhstan and Azerbaijan, using the model Washington had supported for decades with Saudi Arabia. At the same time, the United States and Britain constructed oil pipelines that deliberately circumvented Russian territory and anchored the ex-Soviet peripheries to Western business interests. In 2003–5, however, this prudent model was abandoned in favor of messianic politics. The "colored revolutions" in Georgia and Ukraine brought to power leaders who treated Russia with hostility. The "orange revolution" in Ukraine in December 2004, although a spontaneous mass phenomenon, also became a standoff between Russia and the United States and its allies. Each side promoted its candidate for the president of Ukraine. Russia's heavy-handed involvement in the Ukrainian elections backfired. Ukraine, which by all indicators was more dysfunctional and corrupt than Russia under Yeltsin, received Western support as a "beacon of democracy."

Even some American pundits criticized the Bush foreign policy for "the pious blather about using NATO to promote democracy."[8] This "blather" was intolerable for the Kremlin under Putin. Its officials looked at the world through the goggles of newly discovered Russian-style Realpolitik. The legacy of Gorbachev's idealistic messianism and Yeltsin's romantic Westernism taught the new Russian leadership that good intentions mattered less than power. And Russia was no longer the weak and dysfunctional state it had been during the 1990s. Putin, the former KGB officer, suppressed separatism in Chechnya, strengthened the Russian state and army, and consolidated Russian society. He brushed aside the "Washington consensus" and embraced instead the "Beijing consensus": the example of the People's Republic of China showed that a strong authoritarian state, if it followed prudent policies, could harness market forces and promote fantastic economic growth.[9] The Putin administration focused on achieving this goal. Above all, the Kremlin sought to build a Chinese-style authoritarian state that controlled not only mass media and politics but also big corporations. In 2003–4, Putin sent into exile or prison the business tycoons who had mingled in politics and challenged his authority. Some of Putin's critics ended up dead. He and his entourage, KGB veterans, used the state to raid big corporations and create "national champions," state monopolies run by Putin's associates and their children. The revenues from the sale of Russian oil, gas, and other resources were rerouted to the Kremlin. Putin and his men meticulously eliminated any opportunity for mass politics that could, in their perception, be manipulated by Western forces.

Russian economic recovery began before Putin but became a miracle under his presidency. In 1999–2007, the Russian economy grew by about 7 percent annually and eventually reached its precollapse size. Real incomes and personal consumption more than doubled, hyperinflation ended, and the ruble became a stable and strong currency. While Russia failed to gain any economic role from the United States, the global economy suddenly provided it with a remarkably lucrative niche. The rapid increase in energy prices, pushed by the rapid economic growth of China, India, and other "emerging markets" around the world, generated a flood of petro-dollars to Russia's budget. As a result, the Putin Russia earned more windfall profits than the Soviet Union had received from its oil during the 1970s and early 1980s. Whereas before Putin Russia had no money to pay salaries and pensions, it now accumulated the third largest currency reserves in the world, paid off most of its foreign debt, and began to invest heavily in American and Western European bonds and securities. Social trends followed this economic recovery. The birth rate began to increase, easing the demographic catastrophe. A new multimillion-strong middle class of young educated Russians emerged who earned good salaries; spoke English; vacationed in Europe, Turkey, Egypt, India, and Thailand; owned apartments, country houses, and cars; and explored the Internet for information. This prosperity was grossly biased toward Moscow, but the rest of Russia also benefited from the construction and consumption boom. Russians had never lived as well as they did under Putin.[10]

Under Putin, Russia adopted some Soviet rituals and regalia, including Soviet patriotic propaganda about World War II. A new textbook recommended for millions of Russian high school students by the Ministry of Education praised the Soviet Union as "an example for millions of people around the world of the best and fairest society." The United States, the textbook said, had "initiated" the Cold War, and for this reason, "democratization was not an option for Stalin." The textbook explained that Mikhail Gorbachev had surrendered the Soviet empire without security guarantees and the expansion of NATO had "set a task for Moscow to pursue a more ambitious foreign policy in the post-Soviet space."[11]

Most Russians supported Putin's course and his fist-in-glove authoritarianism. The new Russian middle class did not support political opposition to the Kremlin's accumulation of wealth and power. The vast majority of Russians had learned bitter lessons from Yeltsin's big leap to "democracy" during the 1990s, and they associated Western-style reforms with misery, crime, and the collapse of state institutions. They reelected Putin by a landslide in 2004. According to the polls, the most popular concerns were stability, lowering the crime rate, and redistributing income in favor of the common people. Economic and social recovery boosted Russian national pride. In 2004, 58 percent of Russians wanted Putin to reinstate Russia as a great and respected power. They shared a nostalgia for the mythologized Soviet past, spurred on by the state-controlled electronic media. Although there are books and films in Russia that condemn Stalinism and Stalin's empire, many Russians are confused on this topic, and some even view Stalin as a positive figure in Russian history.

These two trends, the enlargement of the West and the resurgence of Russia, were bound to produce friction. In 2005, Putin summed up the NATO-Russian relationship as a partnership "in ensuring international stability" against "international terrorism." In 2006–8, however, Russia became increasingly defiant toward NATO and the United States. To complicate the situation, the integration of Russia into international economic and financial institutions was impeded by the petty frictions between Russia and its NATO neighbors. First Poland, then Lithuania and Estonia, blocked Russia's admission to the World Trade Organization. In Poland and the Baltics, as well as among anti-Moscow factions in Ukraine and Georgia, the resurgence of Russia under Putin fostered fear. The old-style security dilemma emerged. Some Eastern European leaders argued that Western Europe had become too dependent on Russian oil and gas and worried that Western European countries, especially Germany, France, and Italy, would sell them out. Eastern Europeans pushed for the construction of new oil pipelines from Asia to Europe that would bypass Russia and increase Europe's "energy independence" from Russia. On the other side, the Kremlin and an increasing number of Russians saw the Baltics, Poland, and the Czech Republic as a Russophobic belt. Putin's KGB entourage angrily rejected any responsibility of the new Russia for Soviet occupation and injustices toward those states in the past. The Russian state and the energy monopoly Gazprom obtained Germany's support for the construction of the North Current pipeline along the bottom of the Baltic Sea, avoiding the Baltic states and Poland. They also convinced Turkey, Bulgaria, and Hungary to cooperate in the construction of the South Current pipeline. Simultaneously, Putin reached exclusive agreements with the leaders of oil-rich Turkmenistan, Uzbekistan, and Kazakhstan affirming a Russian monopoly on the supplies of oil and gas to Europe. In December 2005–January 2006, a Russian-Ukrainian "gas war" erupted after Gazprom abolished price subsidies for Ukrainians and supported tough bargaining by reducing gas supplies as a form of pressure. Russia's energy monopoly, commented a leading Western expert, put it "in a stronger position relative to Western Europe than it has ever been in its history."[12] In other words, the Kremlin of Putin felt it had more leverage against the West than the Kremlin of Stalin or Brezhnev.

After the spats with Poland, the Balts, and Ukraine came the Russian-Georgian war. Tensions between Russia and Georgia, a small republic in the Southern Caucasus that was one of the fifteen Soviet successor states, had mounted since the early 1990s. The conflict intensified when the fiercely nationalistic and pro-American leader of Georgia, Mikhail Saakashvili, tried to bring his small country into NATO and restore control over the separatist ethnic enclaves, in defiance of Russia. Russia supported these enclaves, especially Abkhazia and South Ossetia, where it held peace-keeping forces according to international agreements. On August 8, 2008, the opening day of the Olympic Games in Beijing,

Georgian troops stormed into South Ossetia, killing some Russian troops and civilians. The Russian army, however, retaliated decisively, routing the Georgian troops and establishing a buffer zone on Georgian territory. In the postwar euphoria, South Ossetia and Abkhazia declared independence from Georgia, and the Russian government immediately recognized them. It looked momentarily as if a new cold war scenario was emerging. Waves of fear of the Russians spread across Eastern Europe from Ukraine and the Baltic states to Poland and Rumania. U.S. and European politicians blamed Russia for the aggression and sided with Georgia. Eastern Europeans and the Balts appealed to the "free world" to fight against "Russian imperialism." They invoked the images of the Soviet invasion of Hungary in 1956 and Czechoslovakia in 1968. The ethnic rivalries and complexities in the Southern Caucasus were ignored almost entirely. For the "new" Europe, it was the challenge of a resurgent Russian power that demanded a response.[13]

In reality, Russia and Georgia became enmeshed in the problems created by the leader of the Soviet Union, Joseph Dzhugashvili (Stalin). Born to a Georgian mother and Ossetian father, Stalin was responsible for mapping the boundaries of most of the "republics" of the Soviet Union, including the Russian Federation and Georgia. Stalin's tall statue still stands in Gori, Georgia. His countrymen maintain his museum and have preserved the cabin in which he was born and the train car in which he traveled from Moscow to Berlin in 1945 to negotiate with Franklin Roosevelt and Winston Churchill about the future of the world. Stalin's borders for Georgia, like those for Russia, were arbitrary, based on the principles of divide and conquer. Stalinist cartography in the Caucasus operated in the same way as Western colonial cartography in Africa and Asia. It lumped major "nationalities" together and divided smaller ethnic groups, including the Ossetians, half of whom lived in Russia and the other half of whom held an "ethnic autonomy" in Georgia. After the Soviet Union collapsed, Georgia's nationalists used armed force to try to liquidate the "autonomy" of the Ossetians and other ethnic minorities and drive them out of Georgia. In response, the irregular military from the Northern Caucasus, with the aid of Russian arms, counterattacked the Georgians and defeated them. The long and bloody saga of the internal ethnic strife did not attract the world's attention at the time. In 2008, however, it was a different matter since it occurred against the background of a NATO-Russian standoff. Eastern European countries and Britain called for sanctions against Russia. As this edition is going to the print, prudent restraint prevails in Western Europe and Washington but fears remain that earthquakes along the Russia-NATO fault line have not yet ended.

The complacency and triumphalism that accompanied the end of the Cold War were poor guides into the twenty-first century. The EU and NATO under American leadership performed well in Eastern Europe, responding to the will of people in that region to become part of the Western liberal project. Yet the United States lacked a vision with regard to Russia. Ultimately, American policy making concerning Russia fell victim to the messianic behavior that had led the United States astray several times during the Cold War. American policies toward Russia became a hostage to the historical fears of some American allies. Bad memories, mistrust, and insecurity—ghosts from the past—haunted the post-Soviet world. These fears appeared to be validated when Putin's Russia challenged the United States–led world order, built without Russia's involvement and understanding.

Fears of Russia restoring the Soviet empire, widespread among its smaller neighbors, are exaggerated. Russia will never become the Soviet Union again. It is a much smaller country, in both geography and population. Its military budget is a fraction of the American one. True, the pendulum in Russia has swung from semi-anarchy to authoritarian centralism. Russia became, under the slogan of "order," an openly corporatist-bureaucratic state. Yet the Russian state and society avoided the worst pitfalls. It did not collapse into nuclear-armed anarchy, did not degrade into virulent nationalism, and consolidated its sovereignty, except in Chechnya, by peaceful means. The country became a booming "emerging market," often compared to China, India, and Brazil. From 1999 to 2006, the value of traded Russian stocks rose from $74 billion to $1 trillion. In sharp contrast to Cold War times, Russia does not want a separation from the West and has much to lose from a crisis of global capitalism. It wants to be a partner with the "new" Europe and is prepared to use tough bargaining for better terms. Culturally, Russia is torn between European identity and nationalist pride.[14] In the longer term, the former factor is more important. Russian society, especially in urban and sophisticated Moscow, St. Petersburg, and other major cities, is increasingly linked to Europe and to the rest of the world through business and travel. Russian leaders, elites, and a good deal of society consider Russia a great European power. Russia joined the Bologna system of European education. Russian state corporations seek to buy European economic assets. Even the Kremlin uses its state-corporative mechanisms to rig the global economic game in its favor, not to undermine the West.[15]

For all of its bravado, Russia remains a developing country with huge unsolved problems. The Russian state and society still have to address rampant corruption, inadequate transportation and infrastructure, the historical neglect of law, an appalling attitude toward the environment, and much more. The Russian state and policies are guided by the whims and calculations of leaders. This means that Russian leadership can produce, without any checks and balances, disastrous policy choices and stagnation in the future. Russian economic power rests on a shaky foundation of high energy prices. The enormous flow of oil revenues have already produced the "Dutch disease," a combination of an overvalued ruble and inflationary pressures that stifles the competitiveness of Russian industries and agriculture. From a global perspective, Russian recovery is not as impressive as in other post-Soviet states, from Estonia and Belarus to Armenia, Kazakhstan, and Uzbekistan. Russia's economic growth is dwarfed by the Chinese and Indian economic miracles.[16]

In a geopolitical sense, Russia managed to recover as a regional power in Europe and Asia, but its success was the result of favorable global trends rather than its own efforts or far-reaching reforms. In addition to new demands for energy from China and India that gave Russia new opportunities, Russia's trump card was the erroneous American policies. It is fair to say that neither the Clinton administration nor the Bush administration got it right and both were driven by ideological messianism and emotional politics, not strategic wisdom. A growing number of analysts began to write about the decline of American hegemony and the rise of the multipolar "post-American world," spearheaded by a resurgent China and other regional powers.[17] The Kremlin and the Russian political class took these prognoses seriously; they bolstered the legitimacy of Russia's greater role in the world. They managed to convince a great segment of Russian society that the only way to get a fat slice of globalization's pie was to be tough and strong. This gave Russia a psychological boost in the short run but left it without a strategy and a viable coalition of partners. In fact, Russia's use of Western language of "humanitarian intervention" in the collision with Georgia indicates that the Kremlin cannot, even if it wanted to, come up with a new imperialist paradigm. For all of its new hubris, Russia runs great risks if it collides with the United States and the West over the Caucasus, Central Asia, or Ukraine. The good relations with the United States will remain indispensable for Russia's modernization and security.[18] For these reasons, one may hope that the next cohort of Russian political elites will reverse the anti-American trend and lead Russia's integration into the democratic Europe.

The rise of the new Russia cannot lead to another "cold war" between Russia and the West. It can, however, produce accidental spirals of tension conducive to a 1914 scenario of "the Guns of August," when ethnic minefields from the imperial past, animosity between a big country and a small neighbor, and imperial pride created an explosive international chemistry. American leadership should think twice about becoming the dog whose tail is wagged by nationalist firebrands posing as pro-Western "democrats." Prudent, patient, and visionary American leadership should ensure that Russia's rise and its relapse into a "realist" mode will not threaten peace and stability in Europe. American military "shields" and bases, the further hasty enlargement of NATO, and shallow proselytizing for democracy would not be sufficient or wise strategies for dealing with the Russian Question. Not every claim of Russia's "special interests" should be met with spasmodic accusations of "imperialism." The U.S. leadership should seek a prudent balance between managing Russia's rise as a regional power, assuaging Eastern European fears, and overcoming the historic prejudices between Russia and the "new" Europe.

NOTES

1. Geir Lundestad, "Empire by Invitation? The United States and Western Europe, 1945–1952," *Journal of Peace Research* 23, no. 3 (September 1986): 263–77, and *The United States and Western Europe since 1945: From Empire by Invitation to Transatlantic Drift* (London: Oxford University Press, 2003).

2. Anders Aslund, *Russia's Capitalist Revolution: Why Market Reform Succeeded and Democracy Failed* (Washington, D.C.: Peterson Institute, 2007), and *How Capitalism Was Built: The Transformation of Central and Eastern Europe, Russia, and Central Asia* (New York: Cambridge University Press, 2007); Eric Shiraev and Vladislav Zubok, *Anti-Americanism in Russia: From Stalin to Putin* (New York: Palgrave, 2000).

3. David Fogelson, *The American Mission and the "Evil Empire": The Crusade for a "Free Russia" since 1881* (New York: Cambridge University Press, 2007).

4. Andrei Shleifer and Daniel Treisman, "A Normal Country," *Foreign Affairs* 83, no. 2 (March–April 2004). For a voluminous criticism of Russian reforms, see Peter Reddaway and Dmitry Glinsky, *Tragedy of Russia's Reforms: Market Bolshevism against Democracy* (Washington, D.C.: U.S. Institute of Peace, 2001).

5. Strobe Talbott, *The Russia Hand: A Memoir of Presidential Diplomacy* (New York: Random House, 2003).

6. Dimitry K. Simes, *After the Collapse: Russia Seeks Its Place as a Great Power* (New York: Simon and Schuster, 1999).

7. Shiraev and Zubok, *Anti-Americanism in Russia*, chapter 6; Lev Gudkov, *Negative Identity: Essays, 1997–2002* (Moscow: Novoie Literaturnoie Obozreniie, VTSIOM-A, 2004).

8. Michael Mandelbaum, quoted in Thomas L. Freedman, "What Did We Expect?" *New York Times*, August 19, 2008.

9. On the "Beijing consensus," see Vladimir Popov, "Shock Therapy versus Gradualism Reconsidered: Lessons from Transition Economies after 15 Years of Reform," *Comparative Economic Studies* 49 (2007): 1–31.

10. Vladimir Popov, "Resurgent Russian Economy: Putin's Policy without Putin," *International Journal* 63, no. 2 (Spring 2008): 254.

11. A. A. Danilov, *Istoriia Rossii, 1945–2008* (Moscow: Prosveshcheniie, 2008); Arkady Ostrovsky, "Flirting with Stalin," *Prospect*, no. 150 (September 2008): 30.

12. Claire Bigg, "Russia: NATO Chief in Moscow for Talks with Putin," at <http://

www.globalsecurity.org/wmd./library/news/russia/2005/russia_050624_rferloi.htm>;
Marshall I. Goldman, *Petrostate: Putin, Power, and the New Russia* (New York: Oxford University Press, 2008), 180.

13. See, for instance, Simon Sebag Montefiore, "Another Battle in the 1000 Year Russia-Georgia Grudge Match," *The Times* (London), August 12, 2008.

14. James Billington, *Russia: In Search of Itself* (Baltimore: Johns Hopkins University Press, 2004).

15. Douglas W. Blum, ed., *Russia and Globalization: Identity, Security, and Society in an Era of Change* (Washington, D.C.: Woodrow Wilson Center Press, 2008).

16. Vladimir Shlapentokh with Joshua Woods, *Contemporary Russia as a Feudal Society* (New York: Palgrave, 2007); Popov, "Resurgent Russian Economy."

17. Fareed Zakaria, *The Post-American World* (New York: W. W. Norton, 2008). This view was only recently the domain of the New Left. See Giovanni Arrighi, *Adam Smith in Beijing: Lineages of the Twenty-first Century* (London: Verso, 2007).

18. Dmitri Trenin, *Getting Russia Right* (Washington, D.C.: Carnegie Endowment for International Peace, 2007).

(PREFACE)

This book explores the motives that drove the Soviet Union in the Cold War, a global confrontation with the United States and its allies. The opening of archives in Russia and other countries of the onetime Communist bloc provides fascinating opportunities to write about the Soviet past. The abundance of sources on domestic politics and social and cultural developments behind the former iron curtain is astounding. One can now examine Politburo deliberations, read hour-by-hour cable correspondence between Communist leaders, observe how impulses from above trickled down into the bureaucracy, and even read the private journals of Communist apparatchiks. A series of critical oral history projects brought together veterans of the decision-making process and provided the emotional background that is missing in the bureaucratic paperwork.

With all these sources, it became possible to write about the Cold War not just as a clash of great powers and as an accumulation of deadly weaponry. Above all, every history is the story of people and their motives, hopes, crimes, illusions, and mistakes. The Soviet Cold War had many fronts and dimensions—from Checkpoint Charlie in Berlin to Moscow kitchens, where dissidents spoke about Communism "with a human face," from the Politburo in the Kremlin to students' dorms. It was a war of nerves and resources, but above all it was a struggle of ideas and values.[1] Also, truly international comparative studies have become possible, an intellectual accomplishment that helps place Soviet policies and behavior in a larger perspective—the context of *empire*. Recently, scholars have done a great deal of research illuminating the leverage of the Kremlin's allies and satellites upon Soviet international behavior. Some of the most striking findings in the "new" Cold War historiography reveal how the People's Republic of China, North Korea, East Germany, Cuba, Afghanistan, and various other clients affected Moscow's motives, plans, and calculations.[2]

These expanding horizons and new methodological challenges shaped this book. A Russian scholar by nationality and training, I have lived and worked in the United States since the early 1990s. Months of research in Russian, American, and other archives, participation in numerous international scholarly conferences, and exchanges with colleagues, friends, and critics have greatly influenced the last fifteen years of my life. My participation in the CNN twenty-four-part television project on Cold War history was a new experience that alerted me to the significance of perceptions, images, and collective imagination. Finally, teaching at Temple University continues to remind me that the lessons and experience of the past do not pass automatically to new generations. Without constant exploration, discussion, and revision, the lessons and experience of the Cold War become boring statistics. It is challenging, but necessary, to address this bygone confrontation between the two great superpowers and explain how it shaped the modern world.

This book continues the exploration I started with Constantine Pleshakov more than a decade ago.[3] My conceptual framework for explaining Soviet motives and behavior remains the same. It is a revolutionary-imperial paradigm. Security and power were the primary objectives for Stalin and his successors. These leaders used all available methods of power politics and diplomacy to promote Soviet state interests in a competitive world. At the same time, Stalin's and his successors' foreign policy motivations cannot be separated from *how they thought* and *who they were*. The leaders of the Soviet Union, as well as Soviet elites and millions of Soviet citizens, were the inheritors of the great and tragic revolution and were motivated by a messianic ideology. It is impossible to explain Soviet motives in the Cold War without at least trying to understand how the Soviet leaders, elites, and people understood the world and themselves. One way to approach this problem is to look at Soviet ideology. Another way to understand Soviet motives is to look at the Soviet experience, especially the impact of World War II. A third way is to examine the lives of Soviet leaders and the elites, as well as the cultural factors that shaped them.

The book consists of ten chapters, organized around the major developments, policies, and leaders on the Soviet side of the Cold War. Chapter 1 explores the enormous impact of World War II on the Soviet political class and general public and explains how the wartime experience was translated into a quest not only for security but also for geopolitical dominance and external empire. Chapter 2 explains why Stalin's policies, so remarkably successful in building the Soviet empire, shattered the fragile postwar cooperation among the great powers and helped launch the Cold War. Chapter 3 uses the case study of Soviet policies in Germany to highlight the confrontation between the Kremlin's geopolitical designs and the realities and dynamics of Soviet empire in Central Europe. Chapter 4 analyzes the changes in Soviet foreign policy after Stalin's death that resulted not only from the new ideological and geopolitical aims of the new leadership but also from Soviet domestic politics. Chapter 5 explores the impact of the thermonuclear revolution and new ballistic missile technologies on Soviet national security thinking, focusing especially on Khrushchev's unique contribution to the most dangerous crises of the Cold War.

Chapter 6 is very important, as it introduces the theme of the social and

cultural transformation of Soviet elites and society away from Stalinism. It analyzes the romanticism and optimism of the de-Stalinization period and also the
first cracks in the Cold War home front and the emergence of a new generation,
the "men and women of the sixties," a phenomenon that would echo powerfully
twenty-five years later under Mikhail Gorbachev. Chapter 7 looks at the Soviet
motives for détente, with special emphasis on Leonid Brezhnev's personal motivation and involvement. Chapter 8 describes Soviet perceptions of détente's decline and the road that brought Soviet troops to Afghanistan. Chapter 9 deals
with the power transition from the Kremlin's old guard to Mikhail Gorbachev
and the cohort of "men and women of the sixties." In the final chapter, which
focuses on various interpretations of the end of the Cold War and collapse of the
Soviet Union, I offer my own explanation, emphasizing the extraordinary role of
Gorbachev's personality and his romantic ideology of "new thinking."

The study of such an event-packed period of history obviously cannot hope to
be complete in a single volume. To make amends for any oversight on my part I
refer readers to many great books and articles that cover in-depth the history of
the Cold War from a truly international perspective. I hope this book will compensate for its omissions of some events and the superficial treatment of others
with its scope and devotion to major themes. The omission I regret most, however, is the lack of a systematic review of Soviet economic and financial history.
The last chapters of the book make it clear that the nature of the economic
malaise of the 1970s and 1980s during and following Brezhnev's regime and the
political class's inability to deal with it greatly contributed to the decline of Soviet
global influence and ultimately became one of the major causes of Soviet collapse. Also, a deeper study of Soviet military thinking and the military-industrial
complex would have undoubtedly allowed me to turn many hunches and tentative
hypotheses about Soviet international behavior into solid conclusions. Thus, the
best book is the one that is still to be written.

This book would not have been possible without strong encouragement, unflagging support, and vital inspiration from numerous friends and colleagues. My
great fortune is to have belonged for many years to the international network of
Cold War scholars. The Cold War International History Project at the Woodrow
Wilson Center for International Scholars was at the center of this network. My
CWIHP "veteran" t-shirt remembers many conferences where I presented my
research and enriched it with insights and input from the network of international scholarship. CWIHP leaders James G. Hershberg, David Wolff, and
Christian Ostermann provided me with criticism and advice, editorial assistance,
and prompt access to newly available archival sources. I also express my heartfelt

thanks to Melvyn Leffler, Jeffrey Brooks, William C. Wohlforth, James Blight, Philip Brenner, Archie Brown, Jack Matlock, Robert English, Raymond Garthoff, Leo Gluchowsky, Mark Kramer, Jacques Lévesque, Odd Arne Westad, Norman Naimark, Victor Zaslavsky, and Eric Shiraev for sharing with me ideas, documents, and critical comments. Mel Leffler showed me the results of his most recent research on American foreign policy. Chen Jian, a leading Chinese American historian with whom I share a birthday, enlightened me on many nuances in the relationship between the "big brother" (the USSR) and the People's Republic of China.

I began research on this book when I worked at the National Security Archive, a unique nongovernmental think tank and library, now based at George Washington University. Thomas S. Blanton, Malcolm Byrne, William Burr, Will Ferrogiaro, Peter Kornbluh, Sue Bechtel, and Svetlana Savranskaya helped me to combine research with the great adventure of discovering new evidence on the Cold War from various archives around the world. Since 2001, the history department of Temple University has provided me with a new academic home and the place where academics meet students, their most natural "customers." Richard Immerman convinced me that some parallels between U.S. and Soviet decision making and actions, especially in the third world, were not just figments of my imagination. My other colleagues, especially James Hilty, Howard Spodek, Jay B. Lockenour, David Farber, Petra Goedde, and Will Hitchcock, gave me encouragement, human and professional. Ralph Young broadened my mind with his stories on how the Soviet threat was perceived by Americans during the 1950s and 1960s.

This book would have been unthinkable without the support and advice of numerous scholars and archivists in Russia, among them Vladimir Pechatnov, Sergei Mironenko, Oleg Naumov, Alexander Chubaryan, Natalia Yegorova, Natalia G. Tomilina, Tatiana Goryaeva, Zoia Vodopianova, Oleg Skvortsov, Yuri Smirnov, Leonid Gibiansky, Elena Zubkova, and Rudolf Pikhoia. Sergei Kudryashov, the editor of Istochnik, continually expressed interest in my research. The president of Georgia, Eduard Shevardnadze, found time for an interview and authorized access to the Presidential Archive in Georgia. I am deeply thankful to the staffs of the Gorbachev Foundation, the Russian State Archive for Social and Political History, the Archive of the Foreign Ministry of the Russian Federation, the Russian State Archive for Contemporary History, the Central Archive of Public Movements of Moscow, the Presidential Archive of Georgia, and the State Archives of Armenia for being patient with my endless requests. Russian Cold War veterans taught me, among many things, to evaluate documents in personal and historical context. I am especially grateful to Anatoly Chernyaev, Anatoly Dobrynin, Georgy

Shakhnazarov, Karen Brutents, Georgy Arbatov, Georgy Kornienko, Nikolai Detinov, Victor Starodubov, Victor Sukhodrev, Rostislav Sergeev, Yegor Ligachev, Sergo Mikoyan, David Sturua, Oleg Troyanovsky, and Alexander N. Yakovlev. Oleg Skvortsov provided the transcripts of his interviews with some veterans of the Gorbachev administration, conducted in the framework of the Oral History Project on the End of the Cold War, under the auspices of the National Security Archive and the Institute for General History, Russian Academy of Science.

The grants from the Carnegie Corporation of New York funded my research activities in Russia, Georgia, and Armenia. At various stages of my work, Jochen Laufer, Michael Lemke, Michael Thumann, Geir Lundestad, Olav Njolstad, Csaba Bekes, Alfred Rieber, Istvan Rev, Leopoldo Nuti, Victor Zaslavsky, Elena Aga-Rossi, and Silvio Pons provided me with research opportunities and funds in Germany, Norway, Hungary, and Italy. Most recently, the Collegium Budapest, La Scuola di Alti Studi IMT di Lucca, and Luiss Guido Carli University in Rome provided me with magnificent environments and support for the final editing work.

My deepest gratitude is reserved for those who read the manuscript in its entirety or in parts. John Lewis Gaddis and William Taubman read several drafts of the manuscript, pushing me every time to make it clearer and shorter. Ralph Young, Bob Wintermute, and Uta Kresse-Raina were invaluable first readers. Jeffrey Brooks, William C. Wohlforth, David Farber, Richard Immerman, Petra Goedde, Viktor Zaslavsky, Howard Spodek, and David Zierler commented on different parts and chapters. And at the University of North Carolina Press, Chuck Grench and Paula Wald were patient and helpful in every way.

Writing and research demands solitude, yet also the unflagging support of loved ones. My wife, Elena, my children, Andrei and Misha, and my parents, Liudmila and Martin Zubok, made up my most important support group. My parents remained my greatest inspiration for this book. It took me a long time to write about the Soviet Cold War. They, however, had to live it from the beginning to the end. This book is dedicated to them.

(ABBREVIATIONS)

The following abbreviations are used throughout this book.

ABM	antiballistic missile
ADP	Azerbaijan Democratic Party
AK	Polish Home Army
CCP	Communist Party of China
CDU	Christian Democratic Union (Germany)
COMECON (CMEA)	Council for Mutual Economic Assistance
Cominform	Information Bureau of the Communist Parties
Comintern	Communist International
CPSU	Communist Party of the Soviet Union
CSU	Christian Social Union (Germany)
DRV	Democratic Republic of Vietnam (North Vietnam)
EDC	European Defense Community
FRG	Federal Republic of Germany
GDR	German Democratic Republic
GKO	State Defense Committee
GMD	Guomindang (China's nationalist government)
Gosplan	State Planning Committee
GRU	Main Intelligence Directorate at the General Staff (Soviet military intelligence)
ICBM	intercontinental ballistic missile
JAFC	Jewish Anti-Fascist Committee
KGB	Committee for State Security
Komsomol	All-Union Leninist Communist Union of Youth
MGB	Ministry of State Security (Stalin's secret police)
MPLA	Popular Movement for the Liberation of Angola
NDPD	National Democratic Party of Germany
NKGB	People's Commissariat for State Security (1941–46)
NKVD	People's Commissariat for Internal Affairs (1934–46)
PCI	Italian Communist Party
PRC	People's Republic of China
PUWP	Polish United Workers Party (Communist Party of Poland)

RVSN	Soviet Strategic Rocket Forces
SALT	Strategic Arms Limitations Treaty
SCC	Soviet Control Commission
SDI	Strategic Defense Initiative
SED	Socialist Unity Party of Germany
SMAG	Soviet Military Administration, Germany, 1945–49
SMERSH	"Death to the Spies" (Stalin's military intelligence in the Soviet Army, 1941–45)
SPD	Social Democratic Party of Germany
VOA	Voice of America
WTO	Warsaw Treaty Organization (Warsaw Pact)

(A FAILED EMPIRE)

(CHAPTER I)

THE SOVIET PEOPLE AND
STALIN BETWEEN WAR
AND PEACE, 1945

On the morning of June 24, 1945, rain was pouring down on Red Square, but tens of thousands of elite Soviet troops hardly noticed it. They stood at attention, ready to march through the square to celebrate their triumph over the Third Reich. At precisely ten o'clock, Marshal Georgy Zhukov emerged from the Kremlin's gates riding a white stallion and gave the signal for the Parade of Victory to begin. At the peak of the celebration, the medal-bedecked officers hurled two hundred captured German banners onto the pedestal of Lenin's Mausoleum. The pomp and circumstance of the parade was impressive but misleading. Despite its victory, the Soviet Union was an exhausted giant. "Stalin's empire was won with reservoirs of Soviet blood," concludes British historian Richard Overy.[1] Just how much blood is still debated by military historians and demographers. Contrary to common Western perceptions, Soviet human reserves were not limitless; by the end of World War II, the Soviet army was no less desperate for human material than was the German army. No wonder Soviet leadership and experts were precise in calculating the damage to Soviet property during the Nazi invasion but were afraid of revealing the real numbers of human casualties. In February 1946, Stalin said that the USSR had lost seven million. In 1961, Nikita Khrushchev "upgraded" the number to twenty million. Since 1990, after the official investigation, the count of human losses has risen to 26.6 million, including 8,668,400 uniformed personnel. Yet even this number is open to debate, with some Russian scholars claiming the tally to be incomplete.[2] In retrospect, the Soviet Union won a Pyrrhic victory over Nazi Germany.

Enormous combat and civilian losses resulted from the Nazi invasion and atrocities as well as from the total war methods practiced by the Soviet political and military leadership. An appalling indifference to human life marked Soviet conduct of the war from beginning to end. By contrast, the total American human losses in two theaters, European and Pacific, did not exceed 293,000.

The evidence made available after the collapse of the Soviet Union corroborates early American intelligence estimates of Soviet *economic* weakness.[3] The official estimate set the total damage at 679 billion rubles. This figure, according to this estimate, "surpasses the national wealth of England or Germany and constitutes one third of the overall national wealth of the United States." As with human losses, the estimates of material damage were equally huge. Later Soviet calculations assessed the cost of the war at 2.6 trillion rubles.[4]

New evidence reveals that the vast majority of Soviet functionaries and people did not want conflict with the West and preferred to focus on peaceful reconstruction. Yet, as we know, after the end of World War II, Soviet behavior in Eastern Europe was brutal and uncompromising. In the Middle East and the Far East, the Soviet Union pushed hard for bases, oil concessions, and spheres of influence. All this, along with ideological rhetoric, gradually brought Moscow into confrontation with the United States and Great Britain. How could such an exhausted and ruined country stand up to the West? What domestic and external factors accounted for the Soviet Union's international behavior? What were Stalin's goals and strategies?

TRIUMPH AND HANGOVER

The war against the Nazis had a liberating effect on the Soviet public.[5] During the 1930s, indiscriminate state terror had constantly blurred boundaries between good and evil—an individual could be a "Soviet man or woman" today and an "enemy of the people" tomorrow. Social paralysis, the result of the great terror of the 1930s, was gone in the crucible of war, and many people again began to think and act independently. In the trenches, people forged bonds of camaraderie and trusted each other again. As in European countries during World War I, the "front generation" or "generation of victors" emerged in the USSR during the Great Patriotic War. Those who belonged to this community satisfied the need for friendship, solidarity, and cooperation that was often lacking at home. For some, it remained the most important experience of their lives.[6]

The war had other profound effects as well. Official ineptitude, blunders, selfishness, and lies during the great Soviet retreat of 1941–42 undermined the authority of state and party institutions and many officials. The liberation of Eastern Europe allowed millions of people to break out of the xenophobic Soviet environment and see other lands for the first time. The war sacrifices validated idealism and romanticism among the best representatives of the young Soviet intelligentsia who volunteered to join the army. The spirit of a just war against Nazism and their experiences abroad pushed them to dream about a political and cultural liberalization. The alliance between the Soviet Union and Western democracies seemed to create a possibility for the introduction of civil freedoms and human rights.[7] Even established figures with few illusions shared this dream. In a conversation with journalist Ilya Ehrenburg, writer Alexei Tolstoy wondered: "What will be after the war? People are no longer the same." In the 1960s, Anastas Mikoyan, a member of Stalin's close circle, recalled that millions of Soviet people who returned home from the West "became different people, with a wider horizon and different demands." There was an omnipresent new sense that one deserved a better bargain from the regime.[8]

In 1945, some educated, high-minded officers in the Soviet army felt like the Decembrists. (The best young Russian officers had returned to Russia from the war against Napoleon imbued with political liberalism and later became the "Decembrists," the organizers of military insurrection against the autocracy.) One of them recalled: "It seemed to me that the Great Patriotic War would inevitably be followed by a vigorous social and literary revival—like after the war of 1812, and I was in a hurry to take part in this revival." The young war veterans expected the state to reward them for their suffering and sacrifices "with greater trust and increased rights of participation, not just free bus passes." Among them were future freethinkers, who would participate in the social and cultural Thaw after Stalin's death and would ultimately support the reforms of Mikhail Gorbachev.[9]

The war experience shaped the Soviet people's national identities like no event since the Russian Revolution. This especially affected ethnic Russians, whose national self-awareness had been rather weak in comparison to other ethnic groups of the USSR.[10] After the mid-1930s, Russians formed the bulk of the recruits into the party and state bureaucracies, and Russian history became the backbone of a new official doctrine of patriotism. Films, fiction, and history books presented the USSR as the successor to Imperial Russia. Princes and czars, the "gatherers" of the great empire, took the place of the "international proletariat" in the pantheon of heroes. But it was the German invasion that gave Russians a new feeling of national unity.[11] Nikolai Inozemtsev, an artillery intelligence sergeant and future director of the Institute for World Economy and

International Relations, wrote in his diary in July 1944: "Russians are the most talented, gifted nation in the world, with boundless capacities. Russia is the best country in the world, despite all our shortcomings and deviations." And on Victory Day, he wrote: "All our hearts are overflowing with pride and joy: 'We, Russians, can do anything!' Now, the whole world knows it. And this is the best guarantee of our security in the future."[12]

The war also showed the ugly and repressed sides of the Soviet army. Stalinism victimized the Soviet people, but it also drained their reservoirs of decency. Many recruits in the Soviet army had grown up as street rabble, as children of slums, who never acquired the habits of civilized urban life.[13] When millions of Soviet officers and soldiers crossed the boundaries of Hungary, Rumania, and the Third Reich, some of them lost their moral clarity in the frenzy of marauding, drinking, property destruction, murder of civilians, and rape. Ferocious and repeated waves of the troops' violence against civilians and property swept through the rest of Germany and Austria.[14] Soviet military journalist Grigory Pomerants was shocked at the end of the war by "the ugly things committed by heroes who had walked through the fire from Stalingrad to Berlin." If only the Russian people had had the same energy to demand civil rights![15]

New Russo-centric patriotism bred a sense of superiority and justified brutality. The Battle of Berlin became the cornerstone of the new Russian sense of greatness.[16] The new victory mythology repressed memories of the last-minute carnage (unnecessary from a military standpoint) and the brutality toward civilians. And Stalin's cult became a mass phenomenon, widely accepted by millions of Russians and non-Russians alike. A war veteran and writer, Viktor Nekrasov, recalled: "The victors are above judgment. We had forgiven Stalin all his misdeeds!"[17] For decades, millions of war veterans have celebrated Victory Day as a national holiday, and many of them drink to Stalin as their victorious war leader.

In real life, the positive and negative effects of war blurred and mingled. Trophy trinkets, clothing, watches, and other loot brought home from Europe had the same effect as American Lend-Lease products—they increased awareness among the Russian military and workers and members of their families that they did not live in the best possible world, contrary to state propaganda.[18] The same war veterans who looted and harassed European civilians openly began snubbing NKVD and SMERSH officials, the much-feared branches of secret police. Some of them challenged official propagandists in public and would not be silenced at party meetings. According to numerous reports, officers and soldiers clashed with local authorities and even distributed leaflets calling for the "overthrow of the power of injustice." SMERSH reported that some officers grumbled that "this socialist brothel should be blown up to hell." This mood was especially pronounced among Soviet troops stationed in Austria, East Germany, and Czechoslovakia.[19]

The rebellious mood never turned into a rebellion. After the extreme exertions of war had passed, the majority of veterans sank into a social stupor and tried to adapt themselves to everyday life. Pomerants recalls how "many demobilized soldiers and officers lost in the fall of 1946 the strength of their will and became like milksops." In postwar life, he concludes, "all of us with our decorations, medals and citations—became nothing." In the countryside, in small towns, and in urban slums, many became drunkards, loafers, and thieves. In Moscow, Leningrad, and other major cities, potential young leaders among veterans discovered that a party career was the only path for their social and political aspirations. Some took this career path. Many more found their escape route through intense education, but also in the attractions of young life—in romantic affairs and entertainment.[20]

Passivity resulted, to a great extent, from the shock and exhaustion many veterans felt after returning home. Soon after demobilization from the army, Alexander Yakovlev, a future party apparatchik and Gorbachev supporter, was standing at the train station of his hometown observing cars carrying Soviet POWs from German camps to Soviet camps in Siberia when he suddenly began to notice other harsh realities of Soviet life—starving children, the confiscation of grain from peasants, and the prison sentences for minor violations. "It became increasingly obvious that everybody lied," he recalled, referring to the public triumphalism after the war.[21] Another veteran, future philosopher Alexander Zinoviev, recalled: "The situation in the country turned out to be much worse than we imagined it based on rumors, living [with the occupying Soviet army abroad] in fabulous well-being. The war drained the country to the core."[22] The war took an especially heavy toll on the Russian, Ukrainian, and Belorussian countrysides: some regions lost more than half their "collective farmers," mostly males.[23]

In contrast to American GIs, who generally found prosperity and returned to family life at home, Soviet war veterans came home to countless tragedies of ruined lives, the suffering of crippled and maimed people, and the broken lives of millions of widows and orphaned children. There were almost two million officially recognized "invalids" with physical and mental handicaps. Even seemingly healthy veterans collapsed from inexplicable diseases, and hospitals were overwhelmed with young patients.[24]

The Soviet people yearned for peace and stability after the war. A sense of fatigue with war and military values settled into Soviet urban and peasant society. Gone was the jingoism and romantic patriotism that had inspired young, especially educated, men and women in the late 1930s.[25] At the same time, the culture of xenophobia and the Stalinist myth of hostile encirclement remained entrenched in the masses. Average citizens tended to believe the official propaganda that blamed the lack of immediate improvement and the unsatisfactory results of the war on the Western allies. Most importantly, the Soviet people lacked energy and institutions to continue with the "creeping de-Stalinization" begun during the Great Patriotic War. Many of them revered Stalin more than ever as a great leader.[26] Russian people in particular failed to transform their amazing national awakening during the war into a culture of individual self-esteem and autonomous civic action. For large groups of Russian society, the victory in World War II became forever linked to the notion of great power, collective glory, and ritualistic mourning for the dead.[27] As the Cold War began, these moods of the masses became useful for Stalin. They helped him to carry out his foreign policy and to stamp out potential discontent and dissent at home.

TEMPTATIONS OF "SOCIALIST IMPERIALISM"

The Soviet elites felt that the victory was the product of their collective efforts, not just of Stalin's leadership. On May 24, 1945, at a sumptuous Kremlin banquet to honor the commanders of the Red Army, this mood was almost palpable, and Stalin seemed to bow to it. Pavel Sudoplatov, NKVD operative and organizer of the guerrilla movement during the war, recalled: "He looked at us, young generals and admirals, as the generation he had raised, his children and his heirs." Would Stalin consent to govern the country together with the new ruling class (the nomenklatura) just as he had learned to rely on it during the war?[28]

At the same time, the victory and the unprecedented advance of Soviet power into the heart of Europe strengthened the bond between the elites and Stalin. Mikoyan recalled his feeling of joy at the comradely partnership that reemerged around Stalin during the war. He firmly believed that the murderous purges of the 1930s would not return. "Once again," he recalled, those who worked with Stalin had friendly feelings toward him and trusted in his judgment. The same feelings were shared by thousands of other military, political, and economic officials.[29] The Russian and Russified majority within the civilian and military bureaucracies revered Stalin not only as the war leader but also as a *national* leader. During the wartime, the term *derzhava* ("great power") entered the official lexicon. Films and novels glorified Russian princes and czars who had built a strong Russian state in the face of external and domestic enemies. At the same banquet that Sudoplatov described, Stalin raised a toast "to the health of the Russian people." Stalin praised Russians for their unmatched patience and loyalty to his regime. Displaying "clear mind, staunch character and patience," the Russian people made great sacrifices, thus becoming "the decisive force that ensured the historic victory."[30] Thus, instead of elevating all *Soviet* officials, Stalin put *Russians* first.

Russification campaigns took place in the new Soviet borderlands, especially in the Baltics and Ukraine. This meant more than a cultural pressure; in practice, it saw the forced deportation of hundreds of thousands of Latvians, Lithuanians, Estonians, and West Ukrainians to Siberia and Kazakhstan. Tens of thousands of migrants from Russia, White Russia, and the Russian-speaking East Ukraine took over their houses. The secret police and the restored Orthodox Church with the Patriarchate under state control moved to wrest the borderland Catholic churches, as well as the Ukrainian Uniate parishes of the Eastern rite, which submitted to papal authority, from the Vatican's control.[31]

Russians got promoted within the most crucial and sensitive segments of the state apparatus, replacing non-Russians, especially Jews. Stalin's apparatus discovered during the war, as Yuri Slezkine put it, that "Jews as a Soviet nationality were now an ethnic diaspora" with too many connections abroad. This also meant that the Soviet intelligentsia, in which Jews were the largest group, "was not really Russian—and thus not fully Soviet." Even before the Soviet troops discovered the Nazi extermination camps in Poland, the chief of Soviet propaganda, Alexander Scherbakov, on Stalin's order, launched a secret campaign to "purify" the party and the state from the Jews. Information on Jewish heroism in the war, as well as the horrible evidence of the Holocaust, remained suppressed. Many Soviet citizens began to look at Jews as those who were the first to flee from the enemy to the rear and the last to go to the front. Grassroots anti-Semitism spread like fire, now encouraged and abetted by officialdom. After the war, the planned purge of Jews in the state apparatus quickly spread to all Soviet institutions.[32]

The manipulation of traditional symbols and institutions and the rise of official anti-Semitism carried significant long-term risks for the Stalinist state. Russians praised the great leader, but Ukrainians and other nationalities felt slighted and even offended. Many officials and public figures, Jews and non-Jews, found the state anti-Semitism a huge blow to their faith in Communist "internationalism." Fissures and crevasses would open in the core of Soviet bureaucracies as a result of Stalin's manipulation of nationalist emotions, but that would only be discovered much later.[33]

Another common bond between the Kremlin leader and the Soviet elites stemmed from their great power chauvinism and expansionist mood. After the victory at Stalingrad, the Soviet Union assumed a leading role in the coalition of great powers, and this fact had an intoxicating effect on many members of the

Soviet nomenklatura. Even Old Bolsheviks like Ivan Maisky and Maxim Litvinov began to talk in the language of imperialist expansion, planning to create Soviet spheres of influence and to gain access to strategic sea routes. In January 1944, Maisky wrote to Stalin and Vyacheslav Molotov, commissar for foreign affairs, that the USSR must position itself in such a way after the war as to make it "unthinkable" for any combination of states in Europe and Asia to pose a challenge to Soviet security. Maisky suggested annexation of Southern Sakhalin and Kurile Islands from Japan. He also proposed that the USSR should have "a sufficient number of military, air, and naval bases" in Finland and Rumania, as well as strategic access routes to the Persian Gulf via Iran.[34] In November 1944, Litvinov sent a memo to Stalin and Molotov that the postwar Soviet sphere of influence in Europe (without specifying the nature of that "influence") should include Finland, Sweden, Poland, Hungary, Czechoslovakia, Rumania, "the Slav counties of the Balkan peninsula, and Turkey as well." In June and July 1945, Litvinov argued that the USSR should penetrate into such traditional zones of British influence as the zone of the Suez Canal, Syria, Libya, and Palestine.[35]

The former general secretary of the Comintern, now the head of the new party's department for international information, Georgy Dimitrov, regarded the Red Army as a more important tool of history than are revolutionary movements. In late July 1945, when Stalin and Molotov negotiated with Western leaders in Potsdam, Dimitrov and his deputy, Alexander Panyushkin, wrote to them: "The countries of the Middle East acquire increasing importance in the current international situation and urgently need our intense attention. We should actively study the situation in those countries and take certain measures *in the interests of our state.*"[36]

The spirit of "socialist imperialism" among Soviet officials overlapped with Stalin's intentions and ambitions. The Kremlin leader would take advantage of this spirit, as he would continue after the war to build up the Soviet Union as a military superpower.

Stalin's rhetoric that all Slavs must be unified against the resurrection of a future German threat found enormous appeal among the majority of Soviet officials. When the minister of tank industry, Vyacheslav Malyshev, heard Stalin in March 1945 talking about "new Slavophile-Leninists," he wrote enthusiastically in his diary of "a whole program for years ahead." Among Moscow officials, a new version of the prerevolutionary Pan Slavism was spreading fast. Russian general Alexander Gundorov, the head of the state-sponsored All-Slav Committee, planned to convene the first Congress of Slavs early in 1946, assuring the Politburo that there was already in existence the mass "new movement of the Slavs." Leonid Baranov, supervisor of the All-Slav Committee in the central party apparatus, defined the Russian people as the senior brothers of the Poles. Molotov, to the end of his days, saw the Russians as the only people with "some inner feeling" for doing things "large scale." Among many Russian officials, the distinction between the expansion of Soviet borders and influence for ideological and security reasons and the traditional Russian big-power chauvinism became increasingly blurred.[37]

For many military commanders and other high officials from the Soviet Union in occupied Europe, imperialism was a matter of self-interest. They cast aside the Bolshevik code of modesty and aversion to property and acted like Spanish conquistadores, accumulating war booty. Marshal Georgy Zhukov turned his homes in Russia into museums of rare china and furs, paintings, velvet, gold, and silk. Air Marshal Alexander Golovanov dismantled Joseph Goebbels's country villa and flew it to Russia. SMERSH general Ivan Serov plundered a treasure trove that allegedly included the crown of the king of Belgium.[38] Other Soviet marshals, generals, and secret police chiefs sent home planeloads of lingerie, cutlery, and furniture, but also gold, antiques, and paintings. In the first chaotic months, the Soviets, mostly commanders and officials, sent 100,000 railcars of various "construction materials" and "household goods" from Germany. Among them were 60,000 pianos, 459,000 radios, 188,000 carpets, almost a million "pieces of furniture," 264,000 wall clocks and standing clocks, 6,000 railcars with paper, 588 railcars with china and other tableware, 3.3 million pairs of shoes, 1.2 million coats, 1 million hats, and 7.1 million coats, dresses, shirts, and items of underwear. For the Soviets, Germany was a giant shopping mall where they did not pay for anything.[39]

Even for less rapacious officials, the enormity of Soviet war suffering and casualties justified postwar reparations from Germany and its satellites. Ivan Maisky, the head of the Soviet task force on war reparations, wrote in his diary while traveling through Russia and Ukraine to the Yalta Conference in February 1945: "The signs of war along the entire road: destroyed buildings left and right, emasculated rails, burnt villages, broken water pipes, brick rubble, exploded bridges." Maisky referred to the suffering of the Soviet people as an argument for higher reparations and the shipping of German industrial equipment to the Soviet Union.[40] One could also hear an argument that Soviet losses justified postwar imperialism and expansionism. In Leningrad, the secret police informers reported a philosophy professor saying: "I am not a chauvinist, but the issue of Polish territory, and the issue of our relations with neighbors concern me greatly after the casualties that we endured." Later this thesis would become a popular justification for Soviet domination in Eastern Europe and territorial demands on neighboring countries.[41]

Historian Yuri Slezkine compared Stalin's Soviet Union to a "communal apartment," with all major ("title") nationalities in possession of separate "rooms," but with common "shared facilities," including the army, security, and foreign policy.[42] Yet, just as the inhabitants of real Soviet communal flats harbored their own particularist interests behind expressed loyalty to the collectivist ethos, so did the leadership of the republics. In practice, they saw the victory in World War II as the moment to expand their borders at the expense of neighbors. Soviet officials from Ukraine, White Russia, Georgia, Armenia, and Azerbaijan also developed an imperialist itch mixed with nationalist aspirations. Ukrainian party officials were the most numerous and important group in the nomenklatura after the Russians. They rejoiced at the fact that in 1939, after the Nazi-Soviet pact, Western Ukraine became part of the USSR. In 1945, Stalin annexed the territories of Ruthenia and Bukovina from Hungary and Slovakia and attached them as well to Soviet Ukraine. Despite many terrible crimes perpetrated by the Communist regime against the Ukrainian people, Ukrainian Communist officials now worshipped Stalin as the gatherer of Ukrainian lands. Stalin deliberately cultivated this sentiment. Once, looking at the postwar Soviet map in the presence of Russian and non-Russian officials, Stalin cited with satisfaction that he "returned historic lands," once under foreign rule, to Ukraine and Belarus.[43]

Armenian, Azeri, and Georgian officials could not act as nationalist lobbies. But they could promote their agendas as part of building the great Soviet power. After Soviet armies reached the western borders of the USSR and accomplished the "reunification" of Ukraine and Belorussia, officials of Georgia, Armenia, and Azerbaijan began to think aloud about a chance to regain "ancestral lands" that belonged to Turkey and Iran and to reunite with their ethnic brethren living in those territories. Molotov recalled, during the 1970s, that in 1945 the leaders of Soviet Azerbaijan "wanted to double the territory of their Republic at the expense of Iran. We also made an attempt to claim a region to the south of Batum, because this Turkish territory was once populated by Georgians. The Azeris wanted to seize the Azeri part and the Georgians claimed a Georgian part. And we wanted to give Ararat back to the Armenians."[44] Archival evidence reveals a synergy between Stalin's strategic goals and the nationalist aspirations of Communist apparatchiks from the South Caucasus (see chapter 2).

The fact that the acquisition of new territories and spheres of influence evoked the demons of expansionism and nationalism among Soviet officials, Russian and non-Russian alike, provided Stalin's project of a postwar Pax Sovietica with the energy it required. As long as party and state elites coveted territories of neighboring countries and participated in the looting of Germany, it was easier for Stalin to control them. The imperial project absorbed forces that otherwise might have worked against the Stalinist regime.

THE SOVIETS AND THE UNITED STATES

Hitler's attack on the USSR on June 22, 1941, and the Japanese attack on the United States on December 7, 1941, brought the two nations together for the first time. The Soviets gained a powerful and resourceful ally. Franklin Delano Roosevelt and the New Dealers became Stalin's strategic partners in the Grand Alliance against the Axis powers, probably the most generous ones he would ever have. Even as the Nazis were advancing to the banks of the Volga, Roosevelt invited the Soviets to become co-organizers of the postwar security community. The American president told Molotov in Washington in negotiations in late May 1942 that "it would be necessary to create an international police force" in order to prevent war "in the next 25–30 years." After the war, Roosevelt continued, "the victors— the US, England, the USSR, must keep their armaments." Germany and its satellites, Japan, France, Italy, Rumania, Poland, and Czechoslovakia, "must be disarmed." Roosevelt's "four policemen," the United States, the United Kingdom, the USSR, and China, "will have to preserve peace by force." This unusual offer took Molotov by surprise, but after two days Stalin instructed him to "announce to Roosevelt without delay" that he was absolutely correct. In his summary of the Soviet-American talks of 1942, Stalin highlighted "an agreement with Roosevelt on the establishment after the war of an international military force to prevent aggression."[45]

In order to avoid publicity and criticism from anti-Soviet conservatives, Roosevelt, his confidant Harry Hopkins, and other New Dealers maintained formal and informal channels of communication with the Kremlin. Later, their unusual frankness led to claims that some New Dealers (perhaps even Hopkins) were, de facto, Soviet agents of influence.[46] This "transparency" of the U.S. administration and Roosevelt's marked friendliness to the Soviets at the Tehran Conference (November 28–December 1, 1943) and especially at the Yalta Conference (February 4–12, 1945) seemed to reveal his desire to secure a lasting partnership after the war.

Soviet officials, representatives of various bureaucratic elites, developed confusing, often contradictory attitudes toward the American ally. The United States had long evoked respect and admiration from Soviet technology-minded elites, who since the 1920s had vowed to turn Russia into "a new and more splendid America." Taylorism and Fordism (after Frederick Taylor and Henry Ford, the leading theorists and practitioners of organized production technologies) were household terms among Soviet industrial managers and engineers.[47] Stalin himself urged Soviet cadres in the mid-1920s to combine "Russian revolutionary scale" with the "American business approach." During the industrialization drive of 1928–36, hundreds of Red directors and engineers, including Politburo member Anastas Mikoyan, traveled to the United States to learn about mass production and management of modern industries, including machine building, metallurgy, meat processing, the dairy industry, and more. The Soviets imported American know-how wholesale, including entire technologies for ice cream, hot dogs, soft drinks, and large department stores (modeled after Macy's).[48]

The wartime contacts and especially Lend-Lease deliveries confirmed widespread perceptions of the United States as the country possessing exceptional economic-technological power.[49] In his circle, even Stalin acknowledged that if the Americans and the British "had not helped us with Lend-Lease, we would not have been able to cope with Germany, because we lost too much" in 1941–42.[50] Most of the clothing and other consumer goods intended for civilians got appropriated by bureaucrats. What little remained trickled down to grateful recipients. Wartime propaganda programs and Lend-Lease also provided entry into Soviet society for American cultural influences. Hollywood films, including *Casablanca*, became available to high officials and their families. At the U.S. Embassy, George Kennan, skeptical about the West's ability to influence Russia, admitted that the amount of goodwill that film screenings generated "cannot be overestimated."[51] Between 1941 and 1945, thousands of Soviet officials in the military, trade representatives, and intelligence operators crisscrossed the United States. The dynamism and scale of the American way of life evoked among the visitors a contradictory range of feelings: ideological hostility, fascination, bewilderment, and envy. Soviet visitors remembered their American trips for decades afterward and shared their impressions with children and relatives.[52]

At the same time, the cultural and ideological views of Soviet elites shaped their perceptions of America and Americans. Very few, even senior, Soviet officials understood how the U.S. government and society functioned. The Soviet ambassador to the United States, Alexander Troyanovsky, who had also served as ambassador in Tokyo, expressed his bewilderment that, "while Japan could be compared to the piano, the United States was an entire symphony orchestra."[53] The vast majority of Soviet officials grew up in a xenophobic and isolationist environment. They spoke Soviet "newspeak"—untranslatable into any other language.[54] Some Soviet functionaries felt that upper-class Americans treated them, at best, with condescension, from a position of material and cultural superiority. Marshal Fedor Golikov, the head of Soviet military intelligence (GRU), who led the military mission to the United States, was infuriated by Harry Hopkins, Roosevelt's assistant and one of the staunchest supporters of the U.S.-Soviet partnership. Golikov described him in his journal as "the Pharisee without constraints," "the big person's lackey," who decided that "we, the people of the Soviet state, must comport in his presence as beggars, must wait patiently and express gratitude for the crumbs from the lord's table." Much later, Molotov expressed similar feelings about FDR himself: "Roosevelt believed that Russians would come and bow down to America, would humbly beg, since [Russia] is a poor country, without industry, without bread—so they had no other option. But we looked at it differently. Our people were ready for sacrifice and struggle."[55]

Many Soviet bureaucrats and the military remained convinced, despite the aid shipped across the North Atlantic to the USSR, that the United States was deliberately delaying its own offensives in Europe until the Russians had killed most of the German army, and perhaps vice versa.[56] Soviet elites understood American assistance as payback for the enormous Soviet war contribution; for that reason they never bothered to express their gratitude and show reciprocity to their American allies, a cause of immense irritation to the Americans who dealt with them. In January 1945, Molotov surprised some Americans and outraged others when he presented an official request for American loans that sounded more like a demand than a request for a favor. This was, as it turned out, another case when Molotov refused "to beg for the crumbs from the lord's table." There was also the conviction in Soviet high circles that it would be in American interests to give loans to Russia as a medicine against the unavoidable postwar slump. Soviet intelligence operatives sought out American industrial and technological secrets, aided by a host of idealistic sympathizers. The Soviets acted like guests who, even as they were given lavish help and hospitality, unceremoniously helped themselves to the hosts' prize jewels.[57]

Roosevelt's policy of treating the USSR as an equal partner and great power spoiled Soviet officialdom. In late 1944, Stalin asked Roosevelt to agree to the restoration of the "former rights of Russia violated by the treacherous attack of Japan in 1904."[58] Roosevelt gave his blessing and did not even insist on a detailed understanding. Stalin remarked to Andrei Gromyko, Soviet ambassador to the United States, with satisfaction: "America has taken the correct stand. It is important from the viewpoint of our future relations with the United States."[59] Many in Moscow expected similar indulgence of Soviet plans in Eastern Europe. At the end of 1944, Soviet intelligence chiefs concluded that "neither the Americans, nor the British had a clear policy with regard to the postwar future of the [Eastern European] countries."[60]

Most Soviet officials believed that U.S.-Soviet cooperation, despite possible problems, would continue after the war. Gromyko concluded in July 1944 that, "in spite of all possible difficulties that are likely to emerge from time to time in our relations with the United States, there are certainly conditions for continuation of cooperation between our two countries in the postwar period."[61] Litvinov saw it as a major task of postwar Soviet foreign policy "to prevent the emergence of a bloc of Great Britain and the USA against the Soviet Union." He envisaged the possibility of "amicable agreement" between London and Moscow, as the United States retreated from Europe. And Molotov himself thought so at the time: "It was profitable to us to preserve our alliance with America. It was important."[62]

The data is very spotty on what thousands of Soviet elites and millions of citizens thought at that time. In 1945, however, Soviet newspapers and central authorities received many letters with a question: "Will the United States help us after the war, too?"[63]

The Yalta Conference became, with Roosevelt's assistance, a crowning victory of Stalin's statesmanship. Waves of optimism swept through Soviet bureaucracies from the top to the bottom. A memorandum on Yalta's results circulated by the Commissariat of Foreign Affairs among Soviet diplomats abroad read: "There was a palpable search for compromise on disputed issues. We assess the conference as a highly positive fact, particularly on Polish and Yugoslav issues, and on the issue of reparations." The Americans even refrained from competing with the Soviets in April 1945 for Berlin. Stalin privately praised the "chivalry" of General Dwight Eisenhower, the Allied commander in Europe, in that matter.[64]

In fact, Roosevelt died just at the time when his suspicions of Soviet intentions began to clash with his desire for postwar cooperation. FDR was outraged by the news about Soviet occupation methods in Eastern Europe and had an angry exchange with Stalin over the so-called Bern incident.[65] The president's sudden death on April 12, 1945, caught the Kremlin by complete surprise. Signing his condolences in the book of visitors at the American residence, Spaso House, in Moscow, Molotov "seemed deeply moved and disturbed." Even Stalin, concludes one of his biographers, felt upset by FDR's passing.[66] The great and familiar partner in war, and possibly in peace, was gone. The new president, Harry S. Truman, was an unknown quantity, and some words from the Missouri politician grated on Soviet ears. This concern explains Molotov's reaction to his first stormy encounter with Truman on April 23, 1945. Truman accused the Soviets of violating Yalta agreements on Poland and broke off the meeting without even waiting for Molotov's rebuttal. The shaken and distressed Molotov spent long hours at the Soviet embassy in Washington writing a cable to Stalin with a report of the meeting. Gromyko, who was present at the meeting, believed that Molotov "feared that Stalin might make him a scapegoat in this business." In the end, Molotov decided to let the episode pass unnoticed: his record of the conversation with Truman bore no trace of the president's pugnacity and Molotov's igno- minious exit.[67]

Soon Soviet intelligence officers in the United States began to report on the dangerous shift in attitudes toward the Soviet Union in Washington. They knew that many groups there, especially Catholic and labor organizations, not to men- tion the wide array of anti–New Deal organizations in both political parties, had remained viscerally anti-Communist and anti-Soviet during the Grand Alli- ance. These groups were eager to break any ties with the Soviet Union. Some military commanders (Major General Curtis Le May, General George Patton, and others) openly talked about "finishing the Reds" after defeating "the Krauts" and "the Japs."[68]

The first alarm rang sonorously in Moscow in late April 1945 when the Tru- man administration abruptly and without notice terminated Lend-Lease deliv- eries to the USSR. The resulting loss of supplies in the amount of 381 million U.S. dollars was a serious blow to the overstrained Soviet economy. The State Defense Committee (GKO), the state organ that replaced the Party Politburo during the war, decided to appropriate 113 million dollars from the gold reserves to make up for the missing parts and materials.[69] After protests from Moscow, the United States resumed Lend-Lease deliveries, citing a bureaucratic misunderstanding, but this did not allay Soviet suspicions. Soviet representatives in the United States and many officials in Moscow reacted with restrained indignation; they unani- mously regarded this episode as an attempt to apply political pressure on the USSR. Molotov's stern instructions to the Soviet ambassador did not conceal his anger. "Do not barge in with pitiful requests. If the U.S. wants to cut off the deliveries, it will be all the worse for them." Emotions in this instance fed unilateralist policies—the Kremlin's penchant to rely only on its own forces.[70]

In late May, the chief of the People's Commissariat for State Security (the NKGB, successor to the NKVD) intelligence station in New York cabled Moscow that "economic circles" that had had no influence on Roosevelt's foreign policy were undertaking "an organized effort to bring about a change in the policy of the [United States] toward the USSR." From American "friends," Communists, and sympathizers, the NKGB learned that Truman was maintaining friendly rela- tions with "extreme reactionaries" in the U.S. Senate, such as Senators Robert Taft, Burton K. Wheeler, Alben Barkley, and others. The cable reported that "the reactionaries are setting particular hopes on the possibility of getting direction of the [United States'] foreign policy wholly into their own hands, partly because [Truman] is notoriously untried and ill-informed on those matters." The message concluded: "As a result of [Truman's] succession to power a considerable change in the foreign policy of [the United States] should be expected, first and foremost in relation to the USSR."[71]

Soviet intelligence and diplomatic officials in Great Britain signaled Moscow about Winston Churchill's new belligerence in response to Soviet actions in Eastern Europe, especially Poland. The Soviet ambassador in London, Fedor Gusev, reported to Stalin: "Churchill spoke on Trieste and Poland with great irritation and open venom. We are dealing now with an unprincipled adventurer: he feels more at home in wartime than in peacetime." At the same time, the GRU intercepted Churchill's instruction to Field Marshal Bernard Montgomery to collect and store the captured German weapons for a possible rearming of German troops surrendering to the Western Allies. According to a GRU senior official, Mikhail Milstein, this report poisoned the mood in the Kremlin with new suspicions.[72]

By July 1945, the ominous clouds seemed to break. Truman sought to secure Soviet participation in a war against Japan and tried to make everyone believe that he continued Roosevelt's foreign policy with regard to the Soviet Union. Harry Hopkins made his last trip to Moscow as Truman's ambassador-at-large, spent hours with Stalin, and returned with what he assumed was a compromise on Poland and other thorny issues that had begun to divide the Grand Alliance. The alarm in the Kremlin and in diplomatic and intelligence circles receded. Yet the first days of the Potsdam Conference (July 17–August 2, 1945) were the last days of this complacency. The U.S.-Soviet partnership was about to end—the postwar tension between allies was escalating.

THE STALIN FACTOR

Soviet diplomat Anatoly Dobrynin once recalled with admiration that Stalin, on the train from Moscow to Baku (from where he would fly to the Tehran Conference of the Big Three) in 1943, had given orders to be left alone in his compartment. "He was not shown any documents and he sat there for three days as far as anyone knew just staring out of the window, thinking and concentrating."[73] What was he thinking about, looking at the ravaged country passing by? We most likely will never know. The evidence on Stalin's views in 1945 resembles bits and pieces of a jigsaw puzzle. Stalin preferred to discuss things orally with a few close lieutenants. He put his thoughts on paper only when he had no choice—for example, when he directed diplomatic talks from afar. As a result, even his lieutenants did not know or fully understand his intentions and plans. Stalin impressed, but also confused and misled, even the most experienced observers and analysts.

Stalin was a man of many identities. His experience growing up in the multi-ethnic, unstable, and vindictive Caucasus had given him an ability to wear many faces and act many roles.[74] Among Stalin's self-identities were the Georgian "Kinto" (an honorable bandit in the style of Robin Hood), revolutionary bank robber, Lenin's modest and devout pupil, "the man of steel" of the Bolshevik Party, great warlord, and "coryphaeus of science." Stalin even had a Russian identity by choice. He also considered himself to be a "realist" statesman in foreign affairs, and he managed to convince many observers of his "realism." Averell Harriman, U.S. ambassador in Moscow in 1943–45, recalled that he found Stalin "better informed than Roosevelt, more realistic than Churchill, in some ways the most effective of the war leaders." Much later, Henry Kissinger wrote that Stalin's ideas about the conduct of foreign policy were "strictly those of Old World *Realpolitik*," similar to what Russian statesmen had done for centuries.[75]

Was Stalin indeed a "realist"? A remarkable expression of Stalin's way of thinking on international relations is found in a cable sent from the Black Sea, where he was vacationing, to Moscow in September 1935. Hitler had been in power for two years in Germany, and Fascist Italy had defied the League of Nations by launching a ruthless and barbarous attack on Abyssinia in Africa. Commissar of Foreign Affairs Maxim Litvinov believed that Soviet security should be linked to the alliance with Western democracies, Great Britain and France, against the increasingly dangerous tandem of Fascist Italy and Nazi Germany. Litvinov, a cosmopolitan Old Bolshevik of Jewish descent, felt that the future Axis powers represented a mortal threat to the Soviet Union and European peace. During the worst years of Stalin's purges, Litvinov won many friends for the USSR in the League of Nations for standing against Fascist and Nazi aggression in defense of Europe's collective security.[76] Stalin, as some scholars have long suspected,[77] found Litvinov's activities useful, yet sharply disagreed with him on the reading of world trends. His letter to Molotov and Lazar Kaganovich, another Politburo member, reveals an opposing concept of security: "Two alliances are emerging: the bloc of Italy with France, and the bloc of England with Germany. The bigger the brawl between them, the better for the USSR. We can sell bread to both sides, so that they would continue to fight. It is not advantageous to us if one side defeats the other right now. It is to our advantage to see this brawl continue as much as possible, but without a quick victory of one side over the other."[78]

Stalin expected a prolonged conflict between the two imperialist blocs, a replay of World War I. The Munich agreement in 1938 between Great Britain and Germany confirmed Stalin's perceptions.[79] The Nazi-Soviet pact of 1939 was his attempt to continue the "brawl" between the two imperialist blocs in Europe, although the composition of these blocs turned out to be drastically different from what he had predicted. The Kremlin strategist would never admit that he disastrously miscalculated Hitler's intentions and that Litvinov's line proved correct.

Revolutionary Bolshevik ideology had shaped Stalin's early thinking about international affairs. In contrast to European Realpolitik statesmen, the Bolsheviks viewed the balance of power and the use of force through lenses of ideological radicalism. They used diplomatic games to preserve the Soviet Union as a base for a world revolution.[80] Bolsheviks were optimists, believing in the imminent collapse of the liberal capitalist order. They also believed they were armed with Marx's scientific theory, the knowledge of which made them superior to liberal capitalist statesmen and diplomats. Bolsheviks ridiculed Woodrow Wilson's attempts to offer a multilateral alternative to the traditional practice of power games and struggle for spheres of influence. For them, Wilsonianism was either hypocrisy or stupid idealism. In all its dealings with the liberal representatives of Western democracies, the Politburo enjoyed pulling the wool over their eyes.[81] During his power struggle against the opposition in 1925–27, Stalin formulated his own optimist-revolutionary position on the prospects for transforming China's Nationalist government, the Guomindang, into a Communist regime. Between 1927 and 1933, Stalin and his supporters imposed on the world Communist movement the doctrine of "the third period": it prophesied a new round of revolutions and wars that "must shatter the world much more than the wave of 1918–1919" and would result "in the proletariat's victory in a number of capitalist countries."[82]

Stalin's worldview was not, however, a mere replica of Bolshevik vision. It was an evolving amalgam, drawing on different sources. One source was Stalin's domestic political experience. After the years of the Kremlin's power struggle, the destruction of opponents, and state-building efforts, Stalin learned to be patient, to react flexibly to opportunities, and to avoid tying his name to any particular position. He, concludes James Goldgeier, "sought to preserve his options unless he felt certain of victory." Always an opportunist of power, he succeeded at home by allying with some of his rivals against others and then destroying them all. Presumably, he was inclined to the same scenario in foreign affairs.[83]

Stalin's dark, mistrusting mind and cruel, vindictive personality made a powerful imprint on his international vision. In contrast to many cosmopolitan-minded and optimist Bolsheviks, he was power-driven, xenophobic, and increasingly cynical.[84] For him, the world, like Communist Party politics, was a hostile and dangerous place. In Stalin's world, no one could be fully trusted. Any cooperation sooner or later could become a zero-sum game. Unilateralism and force was always a more reliable approach to foreign affairs than agreements and diplomacy. Molotov later said that he and Stalin had "relied on nobody—only on our own forces"[85] In October 1947, Stalin put his views in stark terms to a group of pro-Soviet British Labour Party MPs who came to see him at his Black Sea resort. Contemporary international life, he said, is governed not by "feelings of sympathy" but by "feelings of personal profit." If a country realizes it can seize and conquer another country, it will do so. If America or any other country realizes that England is completely dependent on it, that it has no other way out, then it would swallow England. "Nobody pities or respects the weak. Respect is reserved only for the strong."[86]

During the 1930s, the geopolitical legacy of czarist Russia, the historical predecessor of the USSR, became another crucial source of Stalin's foreign policy thinking.[87] A voracious reader of historical literature, Stalin came to believe he inherited the geopolitical problems faced by the czars. He especially liked to read on Russian diplomacy and international affairs on the eve and during World War I; he also paid close attention to the research of Evgeny Tarle, Arkady Yerusalimsky, and other Soviet historians who wrote on European Realpolitik, great power alliances, and territorial and colonial conquests. When the party theoretical journal wanted to print Friedrich Engels's article in which he described czarist Russia's foreign policy as expansionist and dangerous, Stalin sided with the czarist policies, not with the views of the cofounder of Marxism.[88] On the anniversary of the Bolshevik Revolution in 1937, Stalin said that the Russian czars "did do one good thing—they put together an enormous state stretching out to Kamchatka. We inherited this state." The theme of the Soviet Union as a successor to the great Russian empire became one of the mainstays of Stalin's foreign policy and domestic propaganda. Stalin even found time to criticize and edit drafts of school textbooks on Russian history, bringing them into line with his changed beliefs. Khrushchev recalled that, in 1945, "Stalin believed that he was in the same position as Alexander I after the defeat of Napoleon and that he could dictate the rules for all of Europe."[89]

Since the first months of their coming to power in Russia, Lenin and the Bolsheviks had had to balance their revolutionary ambitions and the state interests. This was the origin of the Soviet "revolutionary-imperial paradigm." Stalin offered a new, presumably more stable and effective interpretation of this paradigm. In the 1920s, the Bolsheviks had viewed the Soviet Union as a base for world revolution. Stalin began to view it as a "socialist empire." His worldview focused on the USSR's security and aggrandizement. At the same time, according to Stalin, these central goals demanded eventual changes of regime and socioeconomic order for the nations bordering on the Soviet Union.[90]

Stalin was convinced that international affairs were characterized by capitalist rivalry and the development of crisis, as well as the inevitable transition to global socialism. Two other convictions stemmed from this general belief. First, the Western powers, in Stalin's opinion, were likely to conspire against the Soviet Union in the short term. Second, Stalin was certain that the USSR, guided by his statesmanship, caution, and patience, would outfox and outlast any combination of capitalist great powers. During the worst years of the Nazi invasion, Stalin managed to stay on top of diplomacy within the Grand Alliance. As the Soviet Union rapidly moved from the position of backwardness and inferiority to a new place of strength and worldwide recognition, Stalin preferred to avoid committing to limits of Soviet ambitions and boundaries for Soviet security needs. He kept them open-ended, just as they had traditionally been when Russia expanded in czarist times. The Soviet-British "percentage agreement" of October 1944 is a classic example of the clash between Stalin's revolutionary-imperial paradigm and Churchill's Realpolitik. The British leader sought a power balance in Eastern Europe and offered Stalin a diplomatic arrangement on the division of influence in the Balkans. Stalin signed Churchill's "percentage agreement," but his future policies showed that he wanted to push the British completely out of Eastern Europe, relying on the power of the Red Army to set up friendly Communist regimes.[91]

In conversations with Yugoslav, Bulgarian, and other Communists, Stalin liked to don his "realist" mantle and teach his inexperienced junior partners a lesson or two. In January 1945, the Kremlin leader lectured a group of Yugoslav Communists: "In his time Lenin could not even dream of such a correlation of forces that we achieved in this war. Lenin kept in mind that all could come out against us and it would be good if some distant country, for instance America, would stay neutral. And now what we've got is that one group of bourgeoisie came out against us, and another group is with us."[92] A few days later, Stalin repeated the same thoughts in the presence of the Yugoslavs and the former Comintern leader Georgy Dimitrov. On this occasion, however, he added a prediction: "Today we are fighting in alliance with one faction against the other, and in the future we will fight against this capitalist faction as well."[93]

Stalin, posing as a prudent "realist" in dealing with his satellites, believed the Soviet army could help Communists seize power anywhere in Central Europe and the Balkans. When Vasil Kolarov, a Bulgarian Communist working with Dimitrov to create a pro-Soviet Bulgaria, proposed to annex a coastal portion of Greece to Bulgaria, the Soviets refused. "It was impossible," Molotov later commented. "I took advice from [Stalin], and was told that it should not be done, the time is not good. So we had to keep silent, although Kolarov pressed very hard."[94] Stalin once said about the Greek Communists: "They believed, mistakenly, that the Red Army would reach to the Aegean Sea. We cannot do it. We cannot send our troops to Greece. The Greeks made a stupid error."[95] As far as Greece was concerned, Stalin adhered to the "percentage agreement" with Churchill and ceded it to the British. The Kremlin leader thought it would be a "stupid error" to turn against the British in the Balkans before locking in Soviet wartime gains. There were priority goals, which required British cooperation or, at least, neutrality. He did not want a premature clash with one power from the allied "capitalist faction." This tactic worked well: Churchill reciprocated by refraining from public criticisms of Soviet violations of the Yalta principles in Rumania, Hungary, and Bulgaria for months afterward.

In spring 1945, the superiority of Stalin's statesmanship over that of his Western partners seemed beyond doubt. Churchillian Realpolitik ended in a fiasco, as the Soviet army, together with the Yugoslav, Bulgarian, and Albanian Communists, swept over the Balkans. Molotov recalled with satisfaction that the British woke up only after "half-of Europe broke away" from their sphere of influence: "They miscalculated. They were not Marxists like us."[96] It was the moment when Stalin's hubris must have been at its peak. Even before the Soviet people and elites celebrated the end of World War II, Stalin was already busy constructing a "socialist empire."

BUILDING THE EMPIRE

It has now been established beyond a doubt that Stalin was determined to keep Eastern Europe in the Soviet Union's grip at any cost. The Kremlin leader regarded Eastern Europe and the Balkans through strategic lenses as a potential Soviet security buffer against the West. European geography and history, including the recent history of the two world wars, dictated two major directions of Soviet expansion: one through Poland to the German heart of Europe, another through Rumania, Hungary, and Bulgaria to the Balkans and Austria.[97] At the same time, as his conversations with foreign Communists reveal, Stalin defined Soviet security in ideological terms. He also assumed that the Soviet sphere of influence must and would be secured in the countries of Eastern Europe by imposing on them new political and social orders, modeled after the Soviet Union.[98]

For Stalin, the two aspects of Soviet goals in Eastern Europe, security and regime-building, were two sides of the same coin. The real question, however, was how to achieve both goals. Some Soviet leaders, among them Nikita Khrushchev, hoped that *all* of Europe might turn to Communism after the war.[99] Stalin wanted the same, but he knew that the balance of power would not allow him to achieve this goal. He believed the French or Italian Communists had no chance to seize power while the Allied troops occupied Western Europe. Thus, the Kremlin "realist" was determined to operate within the Grand Alliance framework and to squeeze as much out of his temporary capitalist partners as possible.

Molotov recalled that at the Yalta Conference in February 1945 Stalin attributed enormous significance to the Declaration of Liberated Europe. Roosevelt's most immediate motivation for this document was to pacify potential domestic critics who were prepared to attack him for collaboration with Stalin. Roosevelt still believed that keeping Stalin as a member of the team was more important than breaking relations with him over Soviet repression in Eastern Europe. At the same time, the president hoped that getting Stalin's signature on this document might serve as a deterrent to more blatant Soviet aggression, especially in Poland.[100] Stalin, however, interpreted the Declaration as Roosevelt's recognition of the right of the Soviet Union to have a zone of influence in Eastern Europe. Earlier, the president had acknowledged Soviet strategic interests in the Far East. Molotov was concerned with the language of its American draft, but Stalin told him: "Do not worry. We will implement it in our way later. The essence is in correlation of forces."[101]

The Soviets and their Communist collaborators pursued two kinds of policies in Eastern Europe. First, there were visible social and political reforms: the dismantling of the old classes of owners (some of whom had already been compromised by their collaboration with Germans and fled their countries); the distribution of land among the peasants; the nationalizing of industries; and the creation of a multiparty parliamentary system or "people's democracy." Second, there was the ruthless suppression of armed nationalist opposition and the creation of structures that could later supplant the multiparty "people's democracy" and provide the basis for Communist regimes. Usually the latter meant putting Soviet agents in control of security agencies, the police, and the army; the infiltration of other ministries and political parties with Soviet fellow-travelers; and the compromising, framing, and eventually elimination of non-Communist political activists and journalists.[102]

Stalin provided general guidelines for these policies through personal meetings and correspondence with Eastern European Communists and via his lieutenants. He entrusted Andrei Zhdanov, Klement Voroshilov, and Andrei Vyshinsky with everyday implementation of these policies in Finland, Hungary, and Rumania, respectively. Reflecting the quasi-imperial aspect of their roles, they were alluded to in Moscow power circles as "proconsuls."[103] Inside the Eastern European countries, the Kremlin relied on Soviet military authorities, the secret police, and those Communist expatriates of Eastern European origin, many of them Jews, who had returned to their home countries from Moscow in the rearguard of the Soviet army.[104]

Chaos, war devastation, and nationalist passions in Eastern Europe helped Stalin and the Soviets achieve their goals there. In Hungary, Rumania, and Bulgaria, former reluctant allies of Nazi Germany, the arrival of the Soviet army opened acute social and ideological divisions. Every country was rife with virulent nationalism, accumulated ethnic rivalries, and historical grievances. Poland and Czechoslovakia burned with the desire to get rid of potentially subversive minorities, above all, Germans.[105] Stalin often invoked the specter of Germany as a "mortal enemy of the Slav world" in his conversations with the leaders of Poland, Czechoslovakia, Bulgaria, and Yugoslavia. He encouraged the Yugoslavs and Rumanians in the belief that he supported their territorial aspirations. He also supported Eastern European politics of ethnic cleansing. Until December 1945, Stalin toyed with the idea of using Pan-Slavic schemes and of organizing Eastern Europe and the Balkans into multiethnic confederations. Later, however, the Soviet leader abandoned this design for reasons that are still unclear. Perhaps he believed it would be easier to divide and rule smaller nation-states rather than multinational confederations.[106]

The Soviet army and the activities of the secret police remained a crucial factor in establishing initial Soviet control in Eastern Europe. In Poland, the Polish Home Army (AK) doggedly resisted Stalin's plans for Poland.[107] At the Yalta Conference and afterward the controversy over Poland's future produced the first sparks between the USSR and the Western Allies. Churchill complained that the power of the pro-Soviet government in Poland "rests on Soviet bayonets." He was absolutely correct. As soon as the Yalta Conference ended, SMERSH representative Ivan Serov reported to Stalin and Molotov from Poland that Polish Communists wanted to get rid of the leader of the Polish government-in-exile, Stanislaw Mikolajczyk. Stalin authorized the arrest of sixteen leaders of the Home Army but ordered Serov to not touch Mikolajczyk. Despite this precaution, Soviet heavy-handed methods backfired. Churchill and Anthony Eden protested against "abominable" Soviet actions. Stalin was especially displeased by the fact that Truman joined Churchill in the protest against the arrests of the AK leaders. In his public reply, Stalin cited the necessity of the arrests "to protect the rear behind the front-lines of the Red Army." The arrests continued. By the end of 1945, 20,000 people from the Polish underground, the remains of prewar Polish elites and public servants, were locked up in Soviet camps.[108]

Rumania also caused headaches in Moscow. Political elites of this country openly appealed to the British and the Americans for assistance. Prime Minister Nicolae Radescu and the leaders of the "historical" National Peasant Party and National Liberal Party did not conceal their fears of the Soviet Union. Rumanian Communists, repatriated to Bucharest from Moscow, organized the National Democratic Front. They instigated, with clandestine Soviet support, a coup against Radescu, bringing the country to the brink of civil war in late February 1945. Stalin sent Andrei Vyshinsky, one of his most odious henchmen and the infamous prosecutor at the trials of the 1930s, to Bucharest with an ultimatum to King Michael: Radescu must be replaced by Petru Grozu, a pro-Soviet politician. In support of this ultimatum, Stalin ordered two divisions to move into position near Bucharest. The Western powers did not interfere, but the American representatives, including State Department emissary Burton Berry and chief of the American Military Mission Courtlandt Van Rensselaer Schuyler, were aghast and began to share the Rumanian elites' fears of Soviet domination. Facing growing Western discontent, Stalin decided not to touch King Michael and the leaders of both "historical" parties.[109]

Further south, in the Balkans, Stalin built a Soviet sphere of influence in cooperation with Yugoslavia, a major ally. In 1944–45, Stalin believed that the idea of a confederation of Slavic peoples with the leading role taken by Yugoslav Communists would be a good tactical move toward building a socialist Central Europe and would distract the Western powers from Soviet plans to transform political and socioeconomic regimes there. The victorious leader of the Yugoslav Communist guerrillas, Josip Broz Tito, however, was too ambitious. Specifically, he and other Yugoslav Communists wanted Stalin to support their territorial claims against Italy, Austria, Hungary, and Rumania. They also sought Moscow's support for their project of a "greater Yugoslavia," which would include Albania and Bulgaria. For a while Stalin did not express annoyance, and in January 1945 he proposed to the Yugoslav Communists the creation of a dual state with Bulgarians, "like Austria-Hungary."[110]

In May 1945, Trieste, the city and surrounding area disputed between Yugoslavia and Italy since 1919, threatened to become another sore point in the relations between the Soviet Union and the Western allies. Stalin pushed the Yugoslavs to reduce their demands in order to settle the matter with the British and the Americans. Grudgingly, the Yugoslav leadership complied, but Tito could not contain his frustration. In a public speech, he said that the Yugoslavs did not want "to be small change" in "the politics of spheres of interests." This was a serious affront in Stalin's eyes. This must have been the moment when he began to look at Tito with suspicion.[111] Still, throughout the difficult haggling with the

Western powers over peace treaties with Germany's satellites during 1946, the Kremlin leadership defended Yugoslav's territorial claims in Trieste.[112] This behavior can be explained by the infatuation of Russian officials with Pan-Slavic ideas, as well as the vital position of Yugoslavia on the southern flank of the Soviet security perimeter.

In Eastern Europe and the Balkans, Stalin moved unilaterally and with complete ruthlessness. At the same time, he prudently measured his steps, advancing or retreating to avoid an early clash with the Western powers that might endanger the fulfillment of other important foreign policy goals. In particular, Stalin had to balance the tasks in Eastern Europe and the Balkans with the task of creating a pro-Soviet Germany (see chapter 3). Another goal was a future war with Japan.

The months after the Yalta Conference offered Stalin a grand opportunity to lock in war spoils in the Far East. In 1945, Stalin and Soviet diplomats regarded China as an American client and assumed that Soviet interests in the Pacific required expansion to prevent the replacement of Japanese domination there with American domination. Their goal was to make Manchuria part of the Soviet security belt in the Far East.[113] At the victory banquet with the military commanders on May 24, Stalin said that "good diplomacy" sometimes could "have more weight than 2–3 armies." Stalin demonstrated what it meant during his talks with the Chinese Guomindang government in Moscow in July and August 1945.[114] The Yalta agreements, acknowledged by Truman, gave the Kremlin leader a position of tremendous superiority with regard to the Guomindang. Stalin applied unrelenting pressure on the Nationalists, urging them to accept the Soviet Union as China's protector against Japan. He said to Chinese foreign minister T. V. Soong that Soviet demands in regard to Port Arthur, the Chinese Eastern Railway, Southern Sakhalin Island, and Outer Mongolia were "all guided by considerations of strengthening our strategic position against Japan."[115]

Stalin had some strengths to use inside China in bargaining with the Guomindang. Moscow was the only intermediary between the Nationalists and the Chinese Communist Party (CCP) that controlled the northern territories of China adjacent to Outer Mongolia. The Soviets also had another, less advertised asset: they secretly funded and armed a separatist Uigur movement in the areas of Xinjiang that bordered on the USSR. During the Moscow talks, Stalin offered to guarantee Chinese integrity in return for big concessions. "As to Communists in China," Stalin said to Dr. Soong, "we do not support and don't intend to support them. We consider that China has one government. We want to deal honestly with China and the allied nations."[116]

The Nationalist leadership resisted doggedly, particularly on the issue of Outer Mongolia. Yet Jiang Jieshi, the leader of China, and Dr. Soong did not have a choice. They knew that the Red Army was scheduled to invade Manchuria three months after the end of the war in Europe. They feared that the Soviets might then hand over Manchuria to the CCP. Hence, they agreed to sign the Sino-Soviet Treaty of Friendship and Alliance on August 14. At first, Stalin seemed to keep his promises: the CCP was forced to negotiate a truce with the Nationalist government. Chinese Communists asserted later that Stalin betrayed them and undermined their revolutionary strategy. At the time, however, Mao Ze-dong had to agree with Stalin's logic: the United States was supporting the Guomindang, and the Soviet intervention on the side of the CCP would have meant a quick end to the U.S.-Soviet partnership.[117]

In addition to the impending Soviet invasion of Manchuria, U.S.-Soviet cooperation at Yalta and Potsdam provided the Soviets with the grounds to claim special rights there. Truman could not publicly object to Soviet control over Outer Mongolia and only demanded observance of the Open Door policy. Harriman privately pushed Soong not to give in to Stalin's pressure, but even he had to admit that the Chinese "would never again have an opportunity to reach an agreement with Stalin on as favorable terms." As a result, Stalin wrested from the Guomindang concessions that, in some cases, exceeded the Yalta mandate.[118]

Stalin had equally ambitious plans regarding Japan. On the night of June 26–27, 1945, Stalin convened Politburo members and the high military command to discuss a war plan against Japan. Marshal Kirill Meretskov and Nikita Khrushchev wanted to land Soviet troops in northern Hokkaido. Molotov spoke against this idea, pointing out that such an operation would be a breach of the agreement made with Roosevelt at Yalta. Marshal Georgy Zhukov criticized it as a risky gamble from a military point of view. Stalin, however, supported the plan. He envisioned that this could give the Soviet Union a role in the occupation of Japan. Controlling Japan and its potential military resurgence was as important to Stalin as controlling Germany.[119]

On June 27, 1945, *Pravda* announced that Stalin had assumed the title of Generalissimo. It was the peak of the Kremlin *vozhd*'s (leader's) statesmanship. Three weeks later, the Potsdam Conference confirmed Yalta's framework of cooperation among the three great powers. It was an extremely favorable framework for Stalin's diplomacy and imperialist policies. At first, the British delegation, headed by Churchill and then, after his defeat at the polls, the new Labour prime minister Clement Attlee and foreign secretary Ernest Bevin, objected to Soviet positions across the board. In particular, they sharply criticized Soviet actions in Poland and resisted Soviet efforts to get some of the industrial reparations from the Ruhr. A number of Truman's advisers, among them the ambassador in Moscow, Averell Harriman, encouraged the president and his new secretary of state, James Byrnes, to support the British hard line. Truman, however, still needed Soviet assistance in the war against Japan and did not follow this advice. Truman and Byrnes also were receptive to Stalin's demand for a share of reparations from Western zones in Germany and agreed to create a central administration in Germany. In response to the critics, Truman proposed appointing an Allied commission to oversee elections in Rumania, Bulgaria, Hungary, Greece, and other countries. Yet, when Stalin objected, noting that the Americans did not invite the Soviet Union to oversee Italian elections, the president quickly dropped this issue. After Potsdam, Molotov informed Dimitrov that "the main decisions of the conference are beneficial to us." The Western powers, he said, confirmed that the Balkans would become the sphere of influence of the USSR.[120]

THUNDERBOLT

On August 6, 1945, the first atomic bomb destroyed Hiroshima; three days later, another bomb incinerated Nagasaki. Leading nuclear physicist Yuli Khariton recalled that in Moscow Soviet leaders viewed this "as atomic blackmail against the USSR, as a threat to unleash a new, even more terrible and devastating war."[121] Among Soviet elites, the sense of omnipotence gave way to a new uncertainty. Some Soviet officials told British journalist Alexander Werth that their hard-won victory over Germany was now "as good as wasted."[122]

On August 20, 1945, the Kremlin Generalissimo created a special committee to build atomic weapons and decided that this business must be undertaken "by the entire Party," meaning that the project became a new priority for the entire party-state nomenklatura, as in the previous cases of the collectivization and the industrialization in the 1930s. The project became the first postwar mobilization campaign, one that was highly secret and incredibly costly. Captains of wartime industry, including Dmitry Ustinov, Vyacheslav Malyshev, Boris Vannikov, and hundreds of others, returned to the feverish, sleepless lives they had experienced throughout the war with Germany. Many participants compared it to the Great Patriotic War; one witness recalled: "The works developed on a grandiose scale, mind-boggling things!" Two other grandiose rearmament projects, the first on missiles and the second on antiaircraft defense, soon followed.[123]

American historians still argue about a possible Soviet motivation in Truman's decision to use the atomic bomb.[124] Whether intended or not, the bomb had a powerful impact on the Soviets. All the previous alarm signals now matched a new and dangerous pattern. The United States still remained an ally, but could it become an enemy again? The abrupt dawn of the atomic age in the midst of Soviet triumph deepened the uncertainty that reigned in the Soviet Union. This uncertainty forced Soviet elites to rally around their leader. Stalin's unique power rested upon mythology and fear, but also on the elites, as well as the Soviet people, looking up to him to respond to external threats. After Hiroshima, Soviet elites united in an effort to conceal their renewed sense of weakness behind the facade of bravado.[125]

The elites also hoped that, under Stalin's leadership, the Soviet Union would not be denied the fruits of its great victory, including the new "socialist empire." And millions in Soviet society, traumatized by the recent bloodbath of World War II and shocked by the hardships of peace, fervently hoped there would not be another war but also trusted in the wisdom of the Kremlin *vozhd*.

(CHAPTER 2)

STALIN'S ROAD

TO THE COLD WAR,

1945–1948

It is the height of Anglo-American impudence.
No elementary feeling of respect toward their ally.
—Stalin to Molotov, September 1945

I think before ten years elapse they [the Western powers]
will whip our ass. Our prestige has been declining abominably!
Nobody will support the Soviet Union.
—Conversation between Soviet generals, December 1946

CBS correspondent Richard C. Hottelet sat in the apartment of the former commissar of foreign affairs of the Soviet Union, Maxim Litvinov, in Moscow on June 18, 1946. He could not believe his ears. Back in the safety of his office, the journalist recorded what he had heard from the Old Bolshevik. The Kremlin, Litvinov said, had chosen an outmoded concept of security for the Soviet Union—the more territory you get, the safer you become. This would lead to a confrontation with the Western powers, and the best one could hope for was "a prolonged armed truce."[1]

The Yalta and Potsdam decisions legitimized not only the Soviet sphere of influence in Central Europe but also its continued military presence in Germany and its territorial and political expansion in the Far East. In the fall of 1945, the framework of talks among the three great powers, despite the growing tension, still offered some hope for the Soviets, including the possibility of reparations from the Western zones of Germany. Following the first months of peace, however, Stalin began to take one action after another that tested the limits of Allied cooperation. Litvinov's fears and despair were justified: the Kremlin's behavior became a major contributor to the Cold War. But how was Stalin's choice of the "outmoded concept of security" made? What calculations, motives, and domestic forces were driving the Soviet Union toward cold war with the United States?

Hiroshima and Nagasaki, followed by Japan's unexpected early collapse, shattered Stalin's calculations that the war in the Pacific might last for months.[2] On August 19, 1945, Stalin still planned to land Soviet troops in Hokkaido. He sent a letter to Truman demanding Soviet occupation of the entire Kurile Islands. He also argued that Russian public opinion "would be seriously offended if the Russian troops would not have an occupation region in some part of the Japanese proper territory." Truman conceded on the Kuriles but flatly rejected Stalin's demand to participate in the occupation of Japan. On August 22, the Kremlin warlord had to cancel the landing on Hokkaido. The United States occupied Japan, and General Douglas McArthur began to rule it unilaterally, without ever bothering to ask for Soviet input.[3]

Suddenly all of the vague and unresolved diplomatic issues hidden in the U.S.-Soviet understanding on the Far East, as well as on Central Europe, came to the surface. On August 20–21, the American and British representatives in Rumania and Bulgaria informed the Rumanian king, the Bulgarian regent, and the Soviet Allied commissioners in Rumania and Bulgaria that they would not recognize the new governments in Bucharest and Sofia until they included pro-Western candidates. Local U.S. representatives were armed with instructions from U.S. secretary of state James Byrnes to encourage the opposition to fight against violations of the Declaration of Liberated Europe, "if necessary, with the assistance of the three allied [governments]." This new turn of events demonstrated that the Western powers in fact did not grant the Soviets a free hand in the Balkans, and this news galvanized local anti-Communist forces and seriously complicated Soviet plans all over Central Europe. From Latvia to Bulgaria, rumors spread that there would soon be a war between the United States and the USSR and that the Americans would drop the atomic bomb on Stalin and force him to retreat. Soon the foreign minister of Bulgaria announced, to Soviet dismay, that elections in that country would be postponed until it was possible to monitor them by an Allied Control Commission consisting of representatives of the three great powers. "Outrageous capitulation," wrote Georgy Dimitrov in his diary. Soviet sources in Sofia informed Moscow of "brutal pressure of Anglo-Americans."[4]

Heightening Soviet concerns, Byrnes and British secretary of state for foreign affairs Ernest Bevin now acted together, in the same manner Truman and Churchill had done earlier during the crisis over Poland. Stalin immediately instructed General Sergei Biryuzov, the Soviet military commander in Bulgaria: "There should be no concessions whatsoever. No changes in composition of the government."[5] In Stalin's eyes, developments in the Balkans, as well as in Japan, were part of a Western political offensive, a direct consequence of the changed power balance after Hiroshima. Many in Stalin's entourage, in the military, and in the scientific community felt very much the same way. This perception was remarkably similar to the conclusions, decades later, reached by Gar Alperovitz and other American historians who argued that American diplomacy after Hiroshima became "atomic diplomacy."[6]

On September 11, Byrnes, Bevin, and Molotov met at the London conference of foreign ministers. It became, as historian Vladimir Pechatnov concludes, "a reciprocal demonstration of toughness" between the United States and the Soviet Union. Stalin instructed Molotov to insist on the logic of Yalta, which, in his opinion, confirmed the principle of mutual noninterference of great powers into each other's spheres of influence. He cabled on September 12: "It might happen that the Allies could sign a peace treaty with Italy without us. So what? Then we have a precedent. We would get a possibility in our turn to reach a peace treaty with [the countries of Central Europe] without the Allies." He continued, that even if such behavior would deadlock the conference, "we should not be afraid of such an outcome either."[7]

In the first days of the conference, Byrnes suggested inviting France and China to the discussion of peace treaties with Germany's satellites. Molotov agreed to this without checking with Stalin; in his view, the Americans just wanted to enhance the role of the United Nations, whose other members, they insisted, should attend peace conferences on Finland, Hungary, and Rumania. But Stalin saw each initiative of Western statesmen as part of a larger design to undermine the concept of exclusive spheres of influence that had been agreed upon at Yalta and Potsdam. He was furious at Molotov and instructed his hapless deputy to retract his agreement on Chinese and French participation—a move that stalled the conference. Stalin wrote: "The Allies are pressing on you to break your will. But you must hold on to the end." Molotov agreed that he had "committed a grave oversight." From that moment, in Stalin's eyes, Molotov fell under suspicion of being the "appeaser" of the West.[8]

Whatever Byrnes's intentions were to play "atomic diplomacy," the secretary of state did not want to be seen as ruining popular hopes for postwar cooperation. On September 20, Byrnes attempted to save the conference by proposing to Molotov a treaty of demilitarization of Germany for twenty to twenty-five years. In his communication to Stalin, Molotov recommended accepting Byrnes's proposal, "if the Americans more or less move in our direction on the Balkan countries." But Stalin did not want to pull out Soviet troops from Germany in exchange for a piece of paper guaranteeing its demilitarization.[9] The Kremlin supreme leader instructed Molotov to reject Byrnes's idea. He explained to Molotov that Byrnes's proposal pursued four separate goals: "First, to divert our attention from the Far East, where Americans assume a role of tomorrow's friend of Japan, and to create thereby a perception that everything is fine there; second, to receive from the USSR a formal sanction for the US playing the same role in European affairs as the USSR, so that the US may hereafter, in league with England, take the future of Europe into their hands; third, to devalue the treaties of alliance that the USSR have already reached with European states; fourth, to pull out the rug from under any future treaties of alliance between the USSR and Rumania, Finland, etc."[10]

These words reveal Stalin's thinking to be a combination of insecurity and wide-ranging aspirations. In response to Byrnes's new proposal, Stalin instructed Molotov to propose the establishment of an Allied Control Commission on Japan, similar to that established for Germany. America's exclusive control over Japan was a threat to Stalin's vision of the postwar world, as much as was the U.S. atomic monopoly. Byrnes, supported by the British, refused to discuss the Soviet counterproposal. Stalin was furious: "It is the height of Anglo-American impudence," he cabled to Molotov. "No elementary feeling of respect towards their ally."[11]

Stalin still wanted to do business with the Americans and made attempts to avoid any show of disrespect for Truman.[12] At the same time, he decided to rebuff Byrnes, the suspected architect of "atomic diplomacy." On September 27, Stalin instructed Molotov to display "absolute adamancy" and forget about compromises with the United States. "A failure of the conference would mean the failure of Byrnes, and we must not grieve over that."[13] Molotov still hoped that after days of tough bargaining the Allies would offer a suitable compromise.[14] Stalin, however, was unyielding, and the London conference ended on October 2 in deadlock.

In the short term, Stalin's tactics of stonewalling the London conference produced its desired result. Byrnes was very upset by his failure to reach agreement with the Soviets and decided to back away from his earlier assertive policy. U.S. determination to oppose Soviet behavior in Central Europe declined substantially. Byrnes instructed Averell Harriman to break the deadlock at a personal meeting with Stalin. On October 24–25, Stalin played the gracious host to Harriman at his secret dacha on the Black Sea, in Gagri. During the meeting, Harriman noted that Stalin was "still very irked at our refusal to permit Soviet troops to land at Hokkaido." The Soviet leadership complained that General Douglas MacArthur was making decisions without bothering to transmit them to the Soviets. He said that the Soviet Union would not accept the role of "an American satellite in the Pacific." Perhaps, Stalin said, it would be better for the Soviet Union to step aside in Japan and let the Americans act as they wished. He, Stalin, was never in favor of isolationism, but "perhaps now the Soviet Union should adopt such a policy."[15]

Harriman found Stalin "inordinately suspicious of our every move," but he left the meeting thinking that Soviet security concerns in Central Europe could be satisfied without closing the region to American trade and economic and cultural influence.[16] He failed to see that for Stalin there was no room for Anglo-Saxons in Central Europe and the Balkans. On November 14, at the same dacha in Gagri, Stalin flatly told Wladyslaw Gomulka and other Polish Communists "to reject the open door policy" of the Americans. He warned the guests that the Anglo-Americans sought "to tear away our allies—Poland, Rumania, Yugoslavia and Bulgaria."[17]

Stalin's determination to close Central Europe to Western influence did not mean he abandoned diplomatic games. Suddenly, Byrnes became his preferred partner. The decisive factor was Byrnes's acquiescence to the Soviet demand to exclude France and China from the peace treaties negotiation format. On December 9, in his cable from the Black Sea to the Politburo foreign policy "Quartet" in the Kremlin (Molotov, Lavrenty Beria, Georgy Malenkov, and Mikoyan), Stalin wrote that "we won the struggle" and forced the United States and Britain to retreat in the Balkans. He berated Molotov again for giving in to pressure and intimidation from the United States. "It is obvious," he concluded, "that in dealing with such partners as the U.S. and Britain we cannot achieve anything serious if we begin to give in to intimidation and betray uncertainty. To get anything from this kind of partner, we must arm ourselves with the policy of tenacity and steadfastness."[18] The supreme leader demonstrated to his subordinates that they needed his guidance in postwar affairs as much as they had during the war.

When Stalin met with Byrnes in Moscow in December, he treated him as a guest of honor. But American concessions (the creation of the Allied Control Commission in Japan) fell short of his demands. Yet he still needed Byrnes's cooperation to achieve favorable results on German reparations, as well as on the peace treaties with Germany and its former satellites. Byrnes did not attempt to play the atomic card, did not act in tandem with the British, and did not press the Soviets on their separatist adventures in northern Iran. In general, both sides bargained in the give-and-take style Stalin felt was his strong suit, including mutual consolidation of spheres of influence and concessions.[19]

Byrnes also recognized the rigged elections in Bulgaria and Rumania, in return for small changes in the governments and public assurances that the Kremlin would respect political "freedoms" and the rights of the opposition.

Stalin immediately called the Bulgarian Communist leader, Georgy Dimitrov, in Sofia and told him to pick "a couple of representatives from the opposition" and give them "insignificant ministries." After that, according to Harriman, "the Russian attitude changed completely and thereafter, collaboration on many other world problems was easily secured."[20]

Stalin's diplomacy of linkage was successful in the Balkans. On January 7, 1946, Stalin shared his victorious mood with the Bulgarian Communist leaders. Stalin exclaimed: "Your opposition can go to the devil! They boycotted the elections. Now three great powers recognized these elections." The Western powers, he concluded, may be angry at the Bulgarian Communist government for arresting the opposition leaders, but "they will not dare" to blame the Soviet Union.[21] Stalin's tactics in the Balkans did not change after Churchill gave his famous speech at Fulton, Missouri, on March 5, 1946, warning the United States that the whole of Eastern Europe now was behind the "iron curtain" and under the increasing control of Moscow. Churchill's call for the U.S.-British alliance to balance Soviet power gave pause to some Eastern European Communist leaders, but Stalin, aware of their vacillations, kept pushing them. He criticized Dimitrov for his caution and ordered him to finish off the opposition immediately.[22]

Stalin was more careful with other European countries within Soviet reach. Finland, despite its proximity to Soviet borders, managed to escape the noose of Sovietization. At a meeting with a Finnish delegation in October 1945, Stalin called Soviet policy toward Finland "generosity by calculation." He said: "When we treat neighboring countries well, they will respond in kind." This "generosity" had strict limits: Stalin's lieutenant Andrei Zhdanov worked hard to squeeze every ounce of war reparations (in raw materials) out of Finland.[23] In the same calculated way, Stalin preferred to pretend that the Soviet Union continued to heed Anglo-American sensibilities on Poland. He repeatedly advised his Polish Communist clients "not to breach" the Yalta and Potsdam agreements. He told them to tolerate Stanislaw Mikolajczyk, even though he called him "a British puppet." Yet, when the Poles mentioned that Churchill's Fulton speech encouraged the opposition to expect "liberation" by the Western powers, Stalin confidently said that the United States and Great Britain were not ready to break up with the USSR. "They will try to intimidate us, but if we ignore it, then they gradually stop making noise."[24]

Stalin's struggle against American "atomic diplomacy" was not limited to Central Europe; it extended to the Far East as well. In October, the Kremlin took an uncompromising line toward the Guomindang and began to encourage the CCP forces in Manchuria. Chinese historians link this change to U.S. refusal to acknowledge a Soviet role in Japanese affairs at the London conference.[25] But it was part of Stalin's reaction to the "atomic diplomacy" practiced by Byrnes. When Stalin received reports in late September that U.S. marines were landing in Manchuria to aid the Guomindang, he was angered.[26] In his view, this portended a shift in the balance of forces and a threat to Soviet longer-term influence in Northeast Asia. The Kremlin again sought to exploit the presence of the Chinese Communists in Manchuria as a counterbalance to the Nationalist government.

In late November, Truman sent George Marshall, celebrated military leader, on a diplomatic mission to China to build up the Nationalists against the Soviets and the CCP. When Marshall arrived in China, however, Stalin had already shifted from the "policy of steadfastness" to tactics of compromise. Soviet representatives in Manchuria began to cooperate with Guomindang officials. As in Europe, in the Far East, Stalin wanted to signal to the Americans that he was prepared to return to the framework of Yalta. Stalin knew that Soviet troops had to leave Manchuria soon. But, meanwhile, the struggle for that crucial area continued. From December 1945 to January 1946, Jiang Jieshi, leader of the Republic of China, tried to revisit the understanding on Manchuria. This time, instead of the pro-American Dr. Soong, he sent his son, Jian Jingguo, to Moscow. Jian had grown up in the Soviet Union and was a former member of the Soviet Communist Party.[27]

Moscow met the envoy with skepticism. Solomon Lozovsky, deputy commissar for foreign affairs, wrote in his memo to the leadership that Jiang Jieshi was "trying to balance between the U.S. and the USSR." This ran counter to the Soviet objective—to keep the United States away from Manchuria. "We got rid of the Japanese neighbor on our borders and we cannot allow that Manchuria becomes an arena of economic and political influence of another great power." Vigorous measures, Lozovsky suggested, must be taken to prevent American economic penetration into northern China.[28] Stalin himself could not have put it better.

Truman helped the Soviets on December 15 by announcing that the United States would not intervene militarily in the Chinese civil war on the side of the Guomindang. This news weakened Jiang Jieshi's position on the eve of the Moscow talks. His son informed Stalin confidentially that the Guomindang Nationalist government, in exchange for Stalin's help in restoring its control over Manchuria and Xinjiang, was prepared to develop a "most intimate" alliance with the USSR. Jiang also promised to demilitarize the Soviet-Chinese border and to grant the USSR "the leading role in [the] Manchurian economy." However, Jiang Jieshi insisted on preserving the Open Door policy in northern China and let Stalin know that he was not prepared to be exclusively on the Soviet side.[29]

Stalin proposed an agreement on economic cooperation in China's Northeast that would exclude the Americans. His goal was complete control over Manchuria, and this could be most easily achieved by Soviet military occupation and, after their withdrawal, by the CCP forces as a counterbalance to the Guomindang Nationalist government and the Americans. Therefore, Stalin firmly refused Jiang Jieshi's plea to apply pressure on Mao Ze-dong; he only directed the Chinese Communists to assume a lower profile and focus on occupation of smaller cities and the countryside.[30]

The United States forcefully responded to what appeared to be a Sino-Soviet rapprochement. In February 1946, the Americans pushed Jiang Jieshi to abrogate the bilateral economic talks with Moscow. They also attempted to compromise the Sino-Soviet Treaty, by publishing the secret agreements on China reached by Roosevelt and Stalin. In response, Soviet representatives openly rejected the Open Door policy in the Chinese Northeast. Although Moscow announced withdrawal of its troops from Manchuria, the Kremlin finally allowed the CCP forces to occupy major cities in China's Northeast.[31]

What began so auspiciously for Moscow, however, led to major disruptions in the careful balance of the Yalta-Potsdam system. Although Stalin attempted to time the military withdrawal from Manchuria to pressure the Guomindang to make economic concessions to the Soviet Union and prevent the imposition of the Open Door policies there, he failed to achieve these aims.[32] And, despite Stalin's machinations, he was not able to turn Manchuria into an exclusive Soviet sphere of influence. In the end, he had to cede this area to the triumphant Chinese Communists, in exchange for Mao Ze-dong's promises of strategic alliance with the Soviet Union.

PROBING THE PERIPHERY

For several months, until August 1945, the Kremlin breathed in the heady atmosphere of limitless horizons and aspirations, and even Hiroshima could not immediately dash them. Stalin was building a security buffer in Central Europe and in the Far East, and he also began to pay special attention to Turkey and Iran.

For centuries, the rulers of Russia had coveted the Turkish Straits, linking the Black Sea and the Mediterranean. In 1915, at the peak of the Great War, in which Turkey sided with Germany and Austria-Hungary, Great Britain even promised to support Russia's aspirations to claim the straits and the littoral zone of Turkey as its sphere of influence. The victory of the Bolsheviks, however, made this secret agreement null and void. During the Soviet-German talks in Berlin in November 1940, Molotov, on Stalin's instructions, insisted that Bulgaria, the Turkish Straits, and the Black Sea area should be a Soviet sphere of influence.

Stalin returned to his demand with a vengeance during his talks with his Western partners in the Grand Alliance. He wanted to "revise" the Montreux Convention of 1936, which allowed Turkey to build military defenses on the straits and to close the passage to other countries' military ships moving through the straits during wartime.[33] Stalin wanted the Soviet navy to have access to the Mediterranean at any time. At the Tehran Conference in 1943, Churchill and Roosevelt agreed that some revision would be made, and during secret talks with Stalin in Moscow in October 1944 Churchill seemed to agree to Soviet demands.[34]

In 1944–45, Soviet diplomats, historians, and international law experts unanimously concurred that this was a unique moment to lay "the issue of the straits" to rest once and for all. Litvinov wrote to Stalin and Molotov in November 1944 that the British should be persuaded to cede to the Soviet Union "the responsibility" for the zone of the straits. Another expert in the Commissariat of Foreign Affairs suggested that the best way to guarantee Soviet security interests would be "a bilateral Soviet-Turkish agreement on a joint defense of the straits."[35] Reflecting the Kremlin's high expectations after the takeover of half of Europe, all these proposals rested on the assumption that Great Britain and the United States would recognize Soviet geopolitical predominance ("geographic proximity") in Turkey.[36]

The Soviet army swept through Bulgaria, and some in the military, spurred on by the victories, encouraged Stalin to invade Turkey.[37] The major problem for the Soviets, however, remained the fact that Turkey, unlike during World War I, preserved strict neutrality. Consequently, the Soviet army could not support Moscow's diplomacy with force. Nevertheless, the Kremlin ruler decided to act forcefully and unilaterally, without preliminary agreements with Western allies. On June 7, 1945, on Stalin's instructions, Molotov met with the Turkish ambassador in Moscow, Selim Sarper, and rejected Turkey's proposal to sign a new treaty of alliance with the Soviet Union. Instead, Moscow demanded from Turkey the abolishing of the Montreux Conventions and the establishing of joint protection for the straits in peacetime. The Soviets demanded the right to build military bases, jointly with Turkey, on the Turkish Straits. Molotov also shocked the Turks by insisting on the return of all "disputed" territories in the southern Caucasus that Soviet Russia had ceded to Turkey under the 1921 treaty.[38]

New evidence shows that, in his hubris, Stalin wanted to destroy Turkey's ability to act as an independent player between the British empire and the Soviet Union. The control over the straits was a geopolitical priority, since it would have turned the Soviet Union into a Mediterranean power. Territorial demands became an important second goal that, in Stalin's opinion, helped to achieve the first.

Stalin planned to use the "Armenian card" to annex the eastern Turkish provinces around Lake Van, Ardvin, and Kars. In 1915, over a million Armenians living in those provinces, then part of the Ottoman Empire, became the target of brutal massacres and forced deportations. In August 1920, according to the Treaty of Sevres, which divided the Ottoman Empire, these provinces were assigned to an "Armenian state." However, the Armenians lost the war against the Turkish army, led by Mustafa Kemal (Ataturk). Lenin and the Bolshevik government, including Stalin, became allied with Kemalist Turkey, and in the Soviet-Turkish Treaty of 1921, gave up the "Armenian" provinces. In the spring of 1945, Armenians worldwide pinned their hopes on the Kremlin's policies. Armenian organizations, including the wealthiest ones in the United States, appealed to Stalin to organize mass repatriation of Armenians into Soviet Armenia—with the hope that the USSR would give them the lands "reclaimed" from Turkey. In May, Stalin authorized the officials of Soviet Armenia to explore the possibility of a massive Armenian repatriation. This, in his calculations, could help to undermine possible Western support of Turkey and provide a "humanitarian" cover to Soviet demands.[39]

The Turkish government responded that it would be ready to reach a bilateral agreement but rejected Soviet territorial claims and the demand for "joint" defense of the straits. However, as Molotov recalled later, Stalin ordered him to keep pushing.[40] On the eve of the Yalta Conference, Stalin told the Bulgarian Communist leader, Vasil Kolarov, that "there is no place for Turkey on the Balkans."[41] At the same time, the Kremlin leader probably expected that the Americans, still interested in getting the USSR to join the war in the Pacific, would remain neutral on the Turkish issue. At Potsdam, the British and the Americans confirmed their general agreement to make changes in the control of the straits. Truman, however, introduced a proposal that advocated free and unrestricted navigation of international inland waterways and opposed any fortifications on the Turkish Straits. Despite this proposal, internal Soviet assessments of Potsdam were optimistic. On August 30, the eve of the London meeting of foreign ministers, Stalin said to the Bulgarian Communists that the problem with the Turkish bases on the Dardanelles "will be solved at the conference." If not, he added, the Soviet Union would then raise the question of an outlet on the Mediterranean.[42]

In London, Molotov presented the Allies with a proposal to give the Soviet Union a mandate over Tripolitania (Libya), a former Italian colony. This was not just a tactical device but an expression of the Soviet postwar expansionist mood. Stalin-Molotov secret correspondence reveals that the Soviet leadership was banking on a vague promise that Roosevelt's secretary of state, Edward

Stettinius, had given them during the San Francisco conference in April 1945. When Stalin learned that the Americans sided with the British in opposing the establishment of a Soviet naval base there, he instructed Molotov to demand at least bases for the merchant fleet. In the end, U.S.-British resistance denied the Soviets the much-coveted presence in the Mediterranean.[43]

Turkey also put up strong resistance to Soviet demands. Had Stalin proposed a bilateral security alliance and special rights in the straits without bases in June 1945 to the Turkish government, Turkey probably would have agreed.[44] However, the Soviet ultimatum created a nationalist backlash—the Turkish leadership refused to keep the straits shut for all naval powers except the USSR. After Stalin's death, Khrushchev made these views public at a Central Committee plenum: "Turks are no fools. The Dardanelles is not only Turkish business. It is the spot where interests of many states intersect."[45] The ultimatum to Turkey revealed the limits of Stalin's power—his Napoleonic hubris prevailed over caution. Stalin, however, was not ready to give up. True to his political style, he continued the "war of nerves" against Turkey, adding pressure and then feigning retreat.

In late 1945 and early 1946, the Kremlin preferred, as historian Jamil Hasanli concludes, to implement Soviet objectives in Turkey through Georgian and Armenian officials.[46] Stalin tapped into nationalist aspirations in those Soviet republics. In fact, these aspirations led, unexpectedly, to considerable tension between Armenian and Georgian Communists. Armenia's sudden prominence in Stalin's plans vexed the officials of Georgia. They nurtured their own "national project," according to which the disputed Turkish provinces allegedly constituted Georgian ancestral lands. Khrushchev claimed in 1955 that Lavrenty Beria, Stalin's secret police henchman and leader of the Soviet atomic project, together with Georgian officials, persuaded Stalin to try to annex the southeastern part of the Black Sea coast from Turkey. In his memoirs about his father, Beria's son confirmed this.[47] In May and June 1945, Georgian diplomats and scholars obtained authorization in Moscow to do research on Georgia's "rights" to claim the Turkish lands around Trabzon, populated by the Lazi, an ethnic group that supposedly was part of the ancient Georgian people. Davy Sturua, whose father was the chairman of Georgia's Supreme Soviet, recalled that many Georgians eagerly anticipated the "liberation" of that land. Had Stalin seized those lands, Sturua concluded, "he would have become God in Georgia." By September 1945, the leaders of Georgia and Armenia submitted their conflicting claims to the same Turkish provinces to the Kremlin: their language and arguments had nothing to do with Communist "internationalism" but instead with nationalism.[48]

On December 2, 1945, the Soviet press published a government decree authorizing repatriation of Armenians from abroad to Soviet Armenia. On December 20, Soviet newspapers published an article by two authoritative Georgian academicians, "On Our Lawful Demands to Turkey." The article (based on their earlier memos written to Molotov and Beria) appealed to "world public opinion" to help Georgia get back the "ancestral lands" that the Turks had conquered centuries ago. At that time, rumors circulated in South Caucasus that the Soviet Union was getting ready for a war with Turkey. There were indications of Soviet military preparations in Bulgaria and Georgia.[49]

In early December 1945, rumors of war with the Soviet Union provoked large anti-Soviet nationalist demonstrations in Istanbul. Reporting on these events to Moscow, Soviet ambassador S. A. Vinogradov proposed to present them to Washington and London as evidence of a "fascist threat." He also suggested that they could be a good pretext for severing diplomatic relations with Turkey and for "taking measures to ensure our security," a euphemism for military preparations. To the ambassador's shock, on December 7 Stalin rejected Vinogradov's proposals. "Weapon-rattling may have a nature of provocation," he wrote in a cable, referring to the ambassador's idea of using military exercises for blackmailing Turkey. Stalin then urged Vinogradov to "not lose one's head and avoid making thoughtless proposals that may lead to political aggravation for our state."[50]

The Kremlin *vozhd* still hoped to neutralize the growing resistance of Western powers to Soviet demands to Turkey. The "Armenian card" and the letter of Georgian academics were timed to influence the discussions at the conference of foreign ministers of the great powers in Moscow on December 16–26, 1945. There, the Kremlin ruler wanted to charm Byrnes, not scare him away. Besides, Stalin's sense of priority and urgency led him to redirect his energies from Turkey to Iran, where chances for the success of Soviet expansion seemed to be very high at that time.

Stalin's policies toward Iran were another attempt to combine important strategic objectives with the mobilization of regional and domestic nationalism. During World War II, Iran began to gravitate into the German orbit. In 1941, after Hitler's attack on the Soviet Union, Soviet troops and British troops occupied the country, dividing their occupation zones roughly along the old demarcation line between British and Russian imperial interests from the beginning of the century. According to the agreements of Yalta and Potsdam, these troops would be withdrawn from Iran within six months of the end of the war. In the meantime, the Politburo, however, decided to gain access to Iranian oil and, when the

Tehran government resisted, decided to use the population of southern Azerbaijan (part of northern Iran) as a means of pressure on Iran and the West. The head of the Soviet Azerbaijan Republic, Mir Jafar Bagirov, repeatedly appealed to Stalin to use the favorable situation of Soviet occupation of northern Iran for "reunification" of Soviet and Iranian Azerbaijan. Historian Fernande Scheid concludes that Stalin decided to use Azeri nationalism, while attempting to play "a rather old-fashioned game of power politics, taking as much as he could without jeopardizing the relationship with his allies."[51]

Oil was the Kremlin's most important consideration. The dramatic dash of Hitler's mechanized armies toward the oil refineries of Grozny and Baku in 1942 helped to focus Soviet attention on the broader issue of the "struggle for oil." Former Soviet oil minister Nikolai Baibakov recalled that in 1944 Stalin suddenly asked at him if the Western allies would "crush us if they get a chance." If Western powers were able to deny the USSR access to oil reserves, Stalin explained, then all Soviet war arsenals would become worthless. Baibakov left Stalin's office reflecting that the USSR needed "much, very much oil."[52]

Throughout the war and the Soviet occupation of Iran, the Soviets tried to legalize their rights to drill oil in northern Iran. The anti-Communist Iranian government and the majority in the Majlis (parliament), supported by the British interests, successfully rebuffed these attempts. On August 16, 1944, Beria reported to Stalin and Molotov that "the British, and possibly Americans, secretly work against a transfer of oil fields in Northern Iran to the Soviet Union." The report emphasized that "the U.S. actively began to seek oil contracts for American companies in Iranian Baluchistan" and concluded that "successes of U.S. oil policy in the Middle East began to impinge on British interests and led to aggravation of Anglo-American contradictions." Beria recommended pushing for a Soviet-Iranian agreement on oil concessions in northern Iran and making "a decision on Soviet participation in Anglo-American oil talks." The last suggestion implied that the Soviet Union could join the oil club of three great powers in Iran.[53]

Stalin ignored the last point but implemented the first. The development of oil fields in Iran became his priority, along with the development of Soviet oil reserves beyond the Urals, as part of the Soviet Union's postwar economic plans. In September 1944, Molotov's deputy and Stalin's protégé, Sergei Kavtaradze, went to Tehran to demand oil concessions. Despite great pressure, Prime Minister Muhammad Sa'id refused to negotiate until after the end of the war and the complete withdrawal of foreign troops from Iranian territory. In June 1945, Soviet policy toward Iran entered a new, more aggressive phase. After consultation with the "troika" of Molotov, Kavtaradze, and Bagirov, Stalin ordered exploration of oil fields in northern Iran (at Bender-Shah and Shahi) with the aim of starting to drill in late September.[54]

Aside from the importance of oil, Stalin's strategic motives in Iran were to keep the Western powers, particularly the United States, away from Soviet borders. George Kennan, American charge d'affaires in Moscow, recognized this motive, as well as the British consul in Mashhad, who wrote in his memoirs that it was, "above all, the efforts of Standard and Shell to secure oil-prospecting rights that changed the Russians in Persia from hot-war allies into cold-war rivals."[55] Stalin's security criteria were the same for northern Iran as they were for Xinjiang and Manchuria: Soviet control over strategic communications and a total ban on a Western business presence and even on the presence of foreign nationals.

There were other parallels between Soviet behavior in Manchuria and Iran. The Soviet army remained Stalin's biggest asset as long as it occupied northern Iran. He also had allies inside Iran that he used to manipulate the Iranian government. The People's Party of Iran (Tudeh), a Marxist-Leninist organization from the Comintern days, enjoyed some support among leftist Iranian intellectuals and nationalists. However, events of 1944–45 proved that the Tudeh was a very limited asset. Stalin decided to use the Azeri nationalist card to create a separatist movement in northern Iran. Then the Soviets could blackmail the Iranian government, just as they had done with the Guomindang using the Chinese Communists.[56]

On July 6, 1945, Stalin sanctioned "measures to organize a separatist movement in Southern Azerbaijan" and other provinces of northern Iran. The decision aimed "to create inside the Iranian state a national autonomous Azerbaijani region with broad jurisdiction," to instigate separatist movements in Gilan, Mazenderan, Gorgan, and Khorasan, and "to encourage" Iranian Kurds to assert their autonomy. The Soviet Union would provide armaments, printing presses, and money to the separatists. Defense Minister Nikolai Bulganin and the Azerbaijan leader Bagirov were in charge of these policies. The day-to-day practical implementation of the plan fell to Bagirov and the group of Soviet advisers in Tabriz and Tehran, most of them ethnic Azeris.[57] Stalin told Bagirov that it was time to reunify Azerbaijan and northern Iran. In the months that followed, Bagirov and the entire Azeri party machine enthusiastically implemented Stalin's instructions.[58]

Even British and American officials recognized that there was enough local fuel for nationalist insurrection in northern Iran—the Soviets only had to light a match.[59] The only problem that Stalin had was the shortage of time after the abrupt end of the war with Japan. Louise L'Estrange Fawcett correctly observed:

"It can be no coincidence that the ADP's [Azerbaijan Democratic Party's] reaction coincided almost exactly with the end of the war with Japan, which marked the beginning of the six-month period" after which Moscow, London, and Washington had agreed to withdraw their troops from Iran. In September, the clock began to tick toward the deadline for withdrawal.[60]

From late September until December, the new autonomist movement, supported by Bagirov and the NKVD, created new power structures in Azerbaijan and almost totally dismantled Tehran's administration there. Soviet occupational authorities engineered a forceful merge of Tudeh's northern branches with the new pro-Soviet ADP. The leadership of the Tudeh, mostly veteran revolutionaries of the early 1920s, wanted to turn Iran into a leader of the anticolonial struggle in the Middle East and South Asia. But these dreams were brushed aside by the Soviets since they did not fit with Stalin's plans. The Soviet embassy in Tehran instructed the Tudeh to refrain from revolutionary activities in major Iranian cities. Meanwhile, the creation of the Azeri autonomist movement evoked an enthusiastic response among the Azeri population. The nationalist card seemed to have brought an immediate political victory for Moscow.[61]

In December 1945, on the eve of Stalin's meeting with Byrnes and Bevin in Moscow, the Soviets launched two secessionist regimes: in Iranian Azerbaijan and in the Republic of Kurdistan. Throughout the Iranian crisis, all sides, including the USSR, Great Britain, and the United States, had oil and influence in Iran as primary considerations. For the moment, however, Stalin seemed to be holding all the cards, but he preferred to avoid a direct showdown with the West. He may have expected that the British and the Americans would eventually prefer to resolve the future of Iran at a trilateral conference (as Russia and Great Britain had done in 1907).[62] Indeed, Byrnes refused to join the British in their protest against the Soviet instigation of Iranian separatism. The secretary of state was eager to reach a general agreement with Stalin.[63]

Stalin's methods reveal a recognizable pattern. Each time, the Soviet leader sided with expansionist-minded subordinates and effectively mobilized jingoist sentiments in the Soviet bureaucracy. The Soviets acted unilaterally, under the camouflage of secrecy and denial. They exploited the presence of the indigenous revolutionary and nationalist movements but preferred to create movements under their control in order to further their goals. Although Stalin pretended to stay within the framework of great power diplomacy, he constantly tested its limits. This pattern allowed Stalin to achieve impressive tactical victories in Central Europe and the Far East. The Kremlin ruler, however, did not realize that every such victory wasted Soviet postwar political capital in the United States. Ultimately, it exhausted the potential for Stalin's diplomacy.

The Iranian government began to realize it would have to negotiate a deal directly with Moscow. On February 19, 1946, the new Iranian prime minister, Ahmad Qavam al-Saltana, came to Moscow to meet Stalin. The talks lasted for three weeks. During the war, Qavam had leaned toward the Soviet side, and this factor may have influenced Soviet tactics. Stalin and Molotov acted as a "good cop–bad cop" team: on the one hand, they dangled before Qavam a promise to act as mediators between Tehran and the separatist regimes; on the other hand, they pressed the prime minister to grant oil concessions to the Soviet Union. Qavam pointed out the Majlis's explicit ban on any oil concessions while foreign troops remained in Iranian territory. Stalin encouraged Qavam to change the Iranian constitution and rule without the Majlis. Soviet troops, he promised, would "secure" Qavam's rule. To emphasize the last point, Soviet tank formations began a movement toward Tehran. The Iranian leader ignored this poisoned offer; however, he promised Stalin he would obtain an oil concession for the Soviet Union after the Majlis elections.[64]

Soon it became clear that Qavam had outfoxed Stalin. Jamil Hasanli concludes that the Iranian prime minister "correctly assessed U.S. capabilities in the postwar world" and shifted his orientation from the Soviet Union to the United States. While the talks dragged on in Moscow, the international deadline for withdrawal of foreign troops from Iran passed on March 2, 1946. The Soviet Union found itself in an open breach of this agreement. The Iranian government and the Majlis, encouraged by American diplomats, decided to bring this case to the United Nations, a brilliant move that changed the whole game in Iran. Suddenly, American public opinion became galvanized by "the Iranian crisis": now at stake was not only the future of Iran's oil but also the ability of the new United Nations to defend its members against the encroachments of the big powers.[65]

The Soviet-Iranian conflict occurred at the time of an anti-Soviet shift in U.S. foreign policy and military circles: by March these groups began to see every Kremlin move as part of an aggressive Communist pattern. Truman decided to send the battleship USS *Missouri* to the Turkish Straits to support Turkey in the face of the Soviet ultimatum. On February 28, Byrnes publicly proclaimed a new policy of "patience with firmness" toward the Soviet Union. George Kennan sent his "long telegram" from Moscow a day after Stalin's first meeting with Qavam. He explained that the United States could not turn the Soviet Union into a reliable international partner and suggested a containment of Soviet expansionism. On the next day after Churchill's speech in Fulton, Missouri, the United States delivered a note of protest, saying that it could not "remain indifferent" to the delay of

Soviet military withdrawal from Iran. The Iranian prime minister left Moscow on the day *Pravda* published Stalin's angry reply to Churchill. The support of Iran in the spring of 1946, one historian concluded, "marked the transition from a passive to an active policy" for the postwar United States.[66]

The hearing of the Iranian affair at the United Nations was scheduled for March 25. As Molotov began to prepare for this event, he discovered that the Soviet Union faced diplomatic isolation. "We began to probe [on Iran]," he recollected, "but nobody supported us."[67] Stalin failed to predict the far-reaching impact of the Iranian crisis. He regarded the fuss about Iran as just another test of nerves, an ongoing rivalry among a few statesmen. The sudden intensity of American involvement puzzled him. One day before the UN hearing, the Kremlin ruler ordered the immediate withdrawal of troops and instructed the Soviet ambassador in Tehran to strike a deal with Qavam. This pattern of behavior, pressing until the last moment before the collision and then pulling away, reflected Stalin's understanding of how international affairs worked. The damage, however, was done: Stalin's pressure on Iran, combined with his belligerence toward Turkey, put the Soviet Union on a collision course not only with the Truman administration but also with broad segments of American public opinion.

In response to cries of betrayal from the dispirited leader of the ADP, Jafar Pishevari, Stalin sent him an amazingly hypocritical letter. He asserted that bigger "revolutionary" reasons, which Pishevari was unable to see, necessitated the Soviet pullout. If Soviet troops had stayed in Iran, Stalin wrote, this would have "undercut the basis of our liberationist policies in Europe and Asia." The Soviet withdrawal, he continued, would delegitimize the Anglo-American military presence in other countries and facilitate a movement of liberation there and "would render our policy of liberation more justified and efficient."[68]

Soviet diplomatic defeat at first was not apparent. Stalin felt vindicated for a brief time in April 1946 when Qavam agreed to grant oil concessions to the Soviets, contingent upon the approval of the newly elected Majlis. Only in September did Stalin admit that the Iranian parliament was not about to ratify Qavam's concession. As usual, he blamed his underlings for "an oversight" but did not punish anybody.[69] In October, the Iranian prime minister engineered a rightist crackdown on the separatists. Kurdish and Azeri regimes in northern Iran, left without Soviet military support, were doomed. When Iranian troops entered the northern provinces, Stalin abandoned the rebels to their fate. Responding to frantic appeals from Baku, he opened the Soviet border for ADP elites and some refugees, but did nothing else. Despite the collapse, Bagirov and many others in Soviet Azerbaijan continued to hope that "in a case of military conflict" between the Soviet Union and Iran, there would be a chance to annex

Iranian territories and "reunify" Azerbaijan.[70] However, the Kremlin leadership had never wanted to provoke a war over Azerbaijan.

Almost simultaneously, Stalin suffered another regional defeat. On August 7, 1946, the Soviets sent a note to the Turks, restating their "proposal" of the "joint" control of the straits. There was not a word about territorial demands in the note, and Soviet diplomats hinted that if an agreement on the straits was reached, these demands would be dropped. The Turks, now backed by Washington and London, responded with a firm refusal. Again, Stalin's new move in his war of nerves against Turkey backfired by producing a genuine "war scare" among U.S. politicians and the military. Prompted by foggy intelligence signals and exaggerated estimates about Soviet military concentration near Turkey's borders, some in these circles began to contemplate, for the first time, an atomic strike against the Soviet Union, including the plants of the Urals and the Caucasus oil industry. This time, as some evidence suggests, Stalin may have realized just how close he was to the brink and called the campaign off. Publicly, however, he dismissed the American atomic monopoly with his usual bravado.[71]

Once again, Stalin was not ready to clash with the United States over Turkey—to the great chagrin of Georgian officials. Around that time, Akaki Mgeladze, the senior Georgian official, expressed his frustration in a private conversation with Marshal Fedor Tolbukhin, commander of the Trans-Caucasus military district. Ukrainians, Mgeladze complained, had "regained" all their lands but Georgians were still waiting. Tolbukhin expressed his complete sympathy for the aspirations of the Georgian people.[72]

The behavior of the United States was another crucial factor that confused Stalin's calculations. From February 1946 on, the United States adopted a new strategy of actively defending Western Europe, as well as Turkey and Iran, seeing these regions and countries as potential victims of "Communist expansion." Since the fall of 1945, the United States, not the Soviet Union, had acted as the defining factor in global international relations. And by 1946, the Truman administration decided to contain the Soviet Union, dramatically changing the outlines of international relations. The Americans were already moving toward confrontation, not cooperation, with the Soviet Union. The possibilities of success for Stalin's great power games began to diminish.

The Soviet Union still enjoyed enormous authority and had many millions of friends in the West.[73] Yet the most influential friends were gone. Roosevelt's death and the subsequent departure of Harry Hopkins, Henry Morgenthau, Harold Ickes, and the other New Dealers forever ended the Soviet Union's "special relations" with the United States. The last ally Stalin had in the U.S. government was Secretary of Commerce Henry Wallace, who took a bold stand for continuing the wartime cooperation with Moscow. In fact, there was communication between Wallace and the Kremlin dictator. In late October 1945, Wallace used the NKGB's station chief in Washington to communicate the following message to Stalin: "Truman was a petty politician who reached his current post by accident. He often has 'good' intentions but too easily falls under the influence of people around him." Wallace described himself as "fighting for Truman's soul" with a very powerful group that included Byrnes. That group, he alleged, was extremely anti-Soviet; they "advance an idea of a dominating Anglo-Saxon bloc consisting mainly of the U.S. and England" confronting the "extremely hostile Slavic world" led by the Soviet Union. Wallace offered to play the role of Soviet "agent of influence" in the United States. He pleaded with Stalin to help him and his supporters.[74]

The NKGB transmitted this extraordinary appeal to Stalin. His reaction is unknown. In any case, Stalin was not about to alter his international behavior to help Wallace and American leftists. Nevertheless, he expected to use Wallace and his friends in his struggle for American public opinion against Byrnes and other adversaries.

We also do not know how Stalin reacted to the analytical and intelligence feedback regarding American attitudes toward the Soviet Union. In fall 1945, Igor Gouzenko, Soviet cipher clerk in Ottawa, and Elizabeth Bentley, an American citizen running a ring of Soviet spies in the United States, defected and told Canadian intelligence and the FBI about Soviet intelligence activities in North America. These defections produced a snowball effect in the following months. They led not only to a rapid heightening in the anti-Soviet mood in Canada and the United States but also to the blackout in Soviet intelligence efforts in these countries. The NKGB and GRU hierarchies delayed informing Stalin, Molotov, and Beria about their intelligence failures until the end of November. Meanwhile, as historian Allen Weinstein and journalist Alexander Vassiliev discovered, Bentley's defection "managed virtually overnight to freeze all active NKGB intelligence activity in the United States." Fearful for their remaining intelligence assets, the NKGB froze all contacts with an extremely valuable British agent in Washington, "Homer" (Donald Maclean). The GRU probably did the same with its networks.[75] Thus, American policy-making circles suddenly became more opaque to Stalin, just at the moment when the rapid switch to the policy of containment occurred.

Despite the effect of the Gouzenko affair, Stalin knew about the rapid toughening of the U.S. stance toward the Soviet Union. Soviet intelligence, according to Russian historian Vladimir Pechatnov, eventually picked up a copy of Kennan's "long telegram" in Washington. Stalin and Molotov also understood the geostrategic implications of a U.S.-British alliance: a combination of American economic potential and atomic power and the British empire's military bases around the globe led to a dangerous encirclement of the Soviet Union. Yet this knowledge ultimately did little to alter Stalin's decisions. Pechatnov wonders if Stalin was aware "of the connection between his own actions and a growing resistance to them." The answer is, probably not.[76]

Stalin assumed that the other powers would remain selfish, scheming, and quarrelsome, in accordance with the Leninist concept of imperialism. When Stalin assessed his Western opponents, he did it based on his notion of their "imperialist" nature and logic. When the Labour government in London did not show consistency in this regard, Stalin heaped scorn on them. Ernest Bevin and Clement Attlee, he said in November 1945, "are great fools; they have the power in a great country and they don't know what to do with it. They are empirically oriented."[77] Stalin's contempt for Bevin contrasted with his attitude, ranging from respect to cold fury, toward Churchill.

Ideological influences, as John Lewis Gaddis has noted, explained Stalin's expansionism and his belief that the Soviet Union could get away with it. In particular, Stalin's expectation of an inevitable postwar economic crisis and his belief in "imperialist contradictions" among capitalist states made him dismiss the possibility of Western cooperation.[78] Also, Stalin's expansionism was linked to his domestic politics of mobilization, which included Russo-centric propaganda and his appeal to other forms of nationalism. Nationalist sentiments and aspirations among Soviet elites and the broader public gave domestic support for the Kremlin's policies of "socialist imperialism" in 1945–46.

It is not possible to determine whether Stalin expected that his toughness in the Balkans and his probing in Turkey and Iran would provoke a rupture with the Western allies. It is clear, though, that Stalin's actions helped pave the way for the Cold War. His tactics in the Middle East helped to bring about a postwar cooperation between Great Britain and the United States and made U.S. administrations react harshly to "Soviet expansionism." Stalin's assumptions played a trick on him. Stalin was brutally effective inasmuch as his territorial and political goals could be supported by the force of the Soviet army. However, as a diplomatic and public relations practice, this stance was disastrous, just as Litvinov had feared. Without adequate feedback about his own failures, he persevered in the course that helped to turn the tension between the USSR and the United States into a full-scale confrontation. And, later, his black-and-white worldview, faith in brute force, and Marxist-Leninist ideological baggage left him without any alternative to the Cold War and the unilateral mobilization of Soviet economic and military power.

The new American global power and the determination of the Truman administration to use it was an independent factor. The United States, many historians agree, began to act as a global power not only in response to the Soviet challenge but also according to its own blueprint for the world. The post-Wilsonian program to build a "free and democratic" Europe and contain Communism elsewhere was a new revolutionary factor that was fundamentally changing foreign affairs. And there were powerful forces in American political circles and society that had always believed, as W. R. Smyser concludes, that "only [the United States] could have interest and forces all around the world." In the minds of these thinkers, for the postwar peace the Soviet Union could have a regional role but could not play the role of a truly great power.[79] At the same time, one wonders if these forces would have had their way and if the United States would have moved to center stage in world politics so rapidly without the "help" of the Soviet threat and Stalin's actions.

Stalin's extrapolation of the lessons of European international relations during the previous century kept his mind closed to the motives behind American global interventionism. Stalin could foresee the end of American isolationism, but he failed to give credence to the huge impulse behind the ideas of the "American century," which, couched in multilateral language, drove the United States to stay in Europe. Until the fall of 1945, Stalin received many benefits from his partnership with Washington. His experience dealing with Americans led him to believe he could squeeze out other marginal gains without encountering U.S. resistance, so long as the Soviet actions targeted the British spheres of influence. Much to Stalin's surprise, the Truman administration decided that there was no alternative to containment of Soviet expansionism in every part of the world, including Central Europe. This decision set the stage for decades of Cold War.

Stalin did avoid one huge mistake. He never openly posed as an aggressor and carefully preserved the veneer of international legitimacy on his expansionism. The Soviet leader left to the West the role of breaking the agreements of Yalta and Potsdam and starting a confrontation. Later, Molotov could claim: "What does the 'cold war' mean? We were simply on the offensive. They became angry at us, of course, but we had to consolidate what we conquered."[80] The majority of Soviet citizens shared this perception. For decades to come, they would continue to believe that not Stalin but the United States had unleashed the Cold War.

Stalin feared that the effect of Hiroshima, combined with the overall sense of laxity and fatigue after the war, could cause Soviet elites to seek an accommodation with the United States, perhaps even an acceptance of U.S. superiority. Molotov's "softness" during the London conference made him a target of Stalin's anger and suspicion.[81] Back in Moscow in early October 1945, Molotov had to admit his errors before his own subordinates at the Commissariat of Foreign Affairs. He described the conference as a battlefield where "certain American and British quarters" launched the first "diplomatic attack on the foreign policy gains of the Soviet Union."[82]

This was just the beginning of Molotov's troubles. In early October, Stalin left for a vacation on the Black Sea—his first in many years. The war had greatly aged the Kremlin leader, and foreign journalists began to speculate about Stalin's ill health and possible retirement. They even named Molotov and Zhukov as his successors. Reading press dispatches, Stalin began to suspect that his closest lieutenants (Beria, Malenkov, Molotov, and Mikoyan) might no longer need his leadership and would not be averse to accommodating the United States and Great Britain behind his back. Stalin was incensed when he read that Molotov, speaking at a reception for foreign journalists, hinted at the forthcoming relaxation of state censorship on world media. In a coded telegram, Stalin lashed out at Molotov's "liberalism and ad-libbing." He blamed his lieutenant for attempting to carry out a policy of "concessions to Anglo-Americans," to "give foreigners an impression that he had his own policy distinct from the policy of the Government and Stalin, the impression that with him, Molotov, [the West] could do business." By one stroke of a pen he excluded Molotov from the narrow circle of leadership and proposed to Beria, Malenkov, and Mikoyan the removal of Molotov from his positions as first deputy to Stalin and foreign minister. The attempt of other lieutenants to defend Molotov infuriated Stalin even more. After some time and Molotov's pleas for mercy, Stalin agreed to put his old friend Vyacheslav on probation and authorized him to continue negotiations with Byrnes.[83]

While Stalin was planting the mine under Molotov, he cracked his whip over all his lieutenants. He wrote to them: "There are now many in seats of authority who wax ecstatic like children when hearing praises of the Churchills, the Trumans, and the Byrnses and, conversely, losing their heart after unfavorable references from these misters. As I see it, these are dangerous attitudes, since they spawn in our ranks servility before foreign figures. Against this servility before foreigners we must fight tooth and nail."[84] This cable contained the gist of the ideological campaign of xenophobic isolationism that would erupt in a few months. This campaign would force all Stalin's subordinates to reconfirm their loyalty and zeal on the new front, uprooting the mood of "kowtowing before the West" allegedly present in the Soviet state apparatus and society.

Had Stalin died at that moment, his colleagues might have chosen a more accommodating course toward the United States. They lacked his unique talent for doom scenarios; they also shared the nomenklatura's preference that life after the war should be less demanding. As their actions after 1953 would demonstrate, they did not and could not ignore, as Stalin did, the country's exhaustion and misery. Still, Stalin's subordinates were prisoners of the revolutionary-imperial paradigm. Xenophobic and isolationist, they were torn between the desire for peaceful reconstruction and the temptations of "socialist imperialism." They wanted cooperation with Western powers, but on Soviet terms, with preservation of Soviet economic autarky and freedom of action.

In the fall of 1945, the Soviet leadership and officials debated if the Soviet Union should join the postwar international economic and financial institutions (the International Monetary Fund and the World Bank) created at Bretton Woods. Some high officials dealing with state budgets, finances, industries, and trade argued, for pragmatic and economic grounds, for Soviet participation. The commissar of finances, Arseny Zverev, insisted that a Soviet presence in these institutions, even in an observer's capacity, would help in future trade and loan negotiations with the West. This position received support from Mikoyan and Lozovsky. They considered American loans and technology as necessary to Soviet economic recovery. Other officials, including Nikolai Voznesensky, the head of Gosplan, the State Planning Committee, argued that foreign debts would undermine Soviet economic independence. In a memorandum to Molotov in October 1945, Ivan Maisky cautioned that Americans used their loans to the British to open their empire for U.S. economic and financial penetration. Particularly worrisome, he wrote, was American insistence that money would be disbursed under their control and that Great Britain should dismantle its state mechanisms for trade monopoly.[85]

By February 1946, according to Vladimir Pechatnov, isolationist attitudes prevailed inside the Soviet bureaucracy. Some officials appealed "to Stalin's reluctance both to make the Soviet economy more transparent and to deposit part of the Soviet gold reserve" with the International Monetary Fund. Stalin decided not to join the Bretton Woods system. In March, the official correspondence of the finance ministry already stressed the new stance—that the Western powers might interpret a Soviet presence in the international institutions as a sign of Soviet weakness and readiness for unilateral concessions "under US pressure." Molotov, when asked in the 1970s, said that the Americans "were trying to draw us into their company, but in the subordinate role. We would have got into the position of dependence, and still would not have obtained anything from them."[86]

The Generalissimo used the occasion of the first postwar "elections" for the Supreme Soviet to set new guidelines for the Communist Party and state cadres on February 9, 1946, in the Bolshoi Theater. Stalin's speech, infused with ideological language, announced an unabashedly unilateralist postwar course. For many observers, it meant a final break with the spirit of the Grand Alliance; there was not a single friendly word in the speech to the Western powers. The speech commanded the officials in the audience to convert the Soviet Union into a superpower in one decade, "to surpass in the near future the achievements of science beyond the borders of our country" (a hint at the future atomic-missile race), and to "increase the level of our industry, for instance, threefold in comparison with the pre-war level." This, the speech concluded, would be the only condition that would ensure Soviet security "against any eventualities." Stalin wrote the speech himself, edited it several times, and even prescribed the audience's reaction by inserting the words "furious applause," "applause and standing ovation," and so on, in the speech draft after the key paragraphs.[87] The speech was broadcast on the radio and printed in tens of millions of copies. Shrewd listeners and readers immediately recognized it as a death knell to hopes of a better life, as well as postwar cooperation with Western allies. Stalin ordered the nomenklatura to make another big leap forward.[88]

The new course, in effect, transformed the postwar period into a time of mobilization and preparation for future lethal "eventualities." The official statistics show the drop in military expenditures, from 128.7 billion rubles in 1945 to 73.7 billion rubles in 1946. They remained at this level, which was higher than the prewar level, in 1947 as well. This figure did not include the costs of the atomic project, which came from the "special" funds of the state. The plans for 1946 also included forty new naval bases. The consumer-oriented sectors of the economy, above all agriculture, remained in a disastrous condition, as the official estimate from Finance Minister Zverev to Stalin in October 1946 indicated:[89]

	1940	1942	1944	1945
Bread (in millions of tons)	24.0	12.1	10.0	11.0
Meat (in thousands of tons)	1,417	672	516	624
Butter (in thousands of tons)	228	111	106	117
Sugar (in thousands of tons)	2,181	114	245	465
Clothing items (in millions)	183.0	54.0	47.0	50.0
Shoes, pairs (in millions)	211.0	52.7	67.4	66.1

The living standards of the Soviet people, the victors, plummeted to a level below that of the vanquished Germans. During the war, the state had requisitioned a large part of people's incomes through the enforced purchase of war bonds, semivoluntary donations, and indirect taxes. Inflation did additional damage.[90] The prewar living standard, already very low, looked by 1946 like an unreachable dream.

Churchill's iron curtain speech supplied Stalin with another excellent opportunity for preparing Soviet citizens for the life of destitution and hunger ahead. In his reply in *Pravda* on March 14, 1946, personally drafted and carefully edited, Stalin called the former British ally "a warmonger," compared him to Hitler, and contrasted Soviet "internationalism" with Churchill's search for "racist" Anglo-Saxon world domination. The harshness of the response was calculated: in this way, Stalin indicated his uncompromising attitude toward any Western attempt to challenge the Soviet sphere of influence in Central Europe. The common public wish from now on would not be cooperation with the Western powers but the prevention of war with them. This fear was exactly what Stalin needed to promote his mobilization campaign.[91]

Stalin put Andrei Zhdanov in charge of the mobilization campaign (known as *Zhdanovshchina*). Zhdanov had not excelled in his wartime role as Leningrad's party chief, yet his background made him good enough for the propaganda job. He came from a well-educated family—his father, like Lenin's father, was an inspector of public schools, and his mother belonged to the nobility and had graduated from the Moscow Conservatory. He was cultured and a good speaker. In April 1946, Zhdanov transmitted "the order of comrade Stalin" to the central party apparatus and propagandists: to refute decisively the assumption that "people should take some time to recover after the war, etc."[92]

Another target of Stalin's campaign was war commanders. The Kremlin leader suspected the conquerors of Europe of Bonapartist tendencies. Stalin wanted to whip them into shape as the mass demobilization continued. By September 1946, the strength of the Soviet army had dropped, according to American intelligence estimates, from a peak of 12.5 million to 4.5 million.[93] Meanwhile, the military elite was resting on its laurels, and its combat spirit evaporated in the orgy of drinking, womanizing, and expropriations. In March 1946, a first tentative purge was carried out of the top echelon of "the generation of victors." A number of military leaders, state managers, and engineers were framed in the "affair of the aircraft industry." General Alexei Shakhurin, commissar of the aircraft-building industry, and marshal of aviation Alexander Novikov, commander in chief of the Soviet air force, were abruptly fired and then arrested on trumped-up charges of arming the Red Army with "flawed" aircraft.[94]

At the same time, Stalin's military counterintelligence "discovered" that Marshal Georgy Zhukov had brought carloads of goods and treasures from Germany for his household and personal use. Now the Soviet national hero, who led the Victory Parade on a white stallion, went into semiexile as commander of the Odessa military district.[95] At the same time, Georgy Malenkov, Stalin's loyal lieutenant, who had been in charge of the aircraft industry during the war, lost his positions in the Party Secretariat and the Organizational Bureau (he, however, was quickly pardoned by Stalin). What the dictator wanted was to demonstrate that war accomplishments did not protect against purges. Adding insult to injury for the veterans and for millions of others, in late 1946, Stalin cancelled the public celebration and the national holiday on Victory Day; instead, people got a day off on New Year's Day.

Some downgraded veterans woke up to the horrid realities of Stalin's rule. It was at this time that the NKGB began to monitor all Soviet military leaders, and some of these conversations have now reached historians. These records include private conversations between army general Vasily Gordov and his former chief of staff, General Fedor Rybalchenko, on New Year's Eve in 1946. Gordov, a ruthless army commander at Stalingrad, Berlin, and Prague, was one of Zhukov's sympathizers and lost his high position. Anger and alcohol loosened the tongues of both generals. They agreed that people in the West lived incomparably better than Soviet people, and that life in the countryside was downright miserable. Rybalchenko said that "people are angry about their life and complain openly, on trains and everywhere. Famine is unbelievable, but newspapers just lie. Only the government lives well, while people are starving." Gordov wondered aloud if there was a way to work and live abroad ("in Finland or in Scandinavian countries"). The generals regretted the absence of Western assistance and feared that Stalin's policy of confrontation with the Anglo-American bloc would end up in war and Soviet defeat. Rybalchenko concluded: "I think before ten years elapse they will whip our ass. Everybody says there would be war. Our prestige has been declining abominably! Nobody will support the Soviet Union."[96]

The discontented military was fully aware of Stalin's role in instigating new purges. When Rybalchenko proposed that Gordov should beg Stalin for forgiveness, the latter only scoffed at this proposal. He exclaimed with pride, characteristic of the postwar elite: "Why should I go and debase myself?" Three days later, alone with his wife, Gordov confessed that his trip to the countryside (before his "elections" as a deputy of the Supreme Soviet) made him "completely reborn." "I am convinced that if today we disband collective farms, tomorrow there will be order, market, everything in abundance. People should be left alone; they have the right to live better lives. They won these rights in the battle!" Stalin, concluded Gordov, "ruined Russia."[97]

Such criticism of Stalin among Soviet elites was still rare.[98] But discontent was growing by the end of 1946, when a severe drought struck the most fertile lands in Ukraine, Crimea, Moldova, the Volga region, and the central region of Russia, the Far East, Siberia, and Kazakhstan. This natural calamity, combined with the lack of manpower and resources after the war, created the danger of mass famine.[99] But it was Stalin and his policies that, instead of averting famine, caused this man-made catastrophe, similar to the famine of 1932–33.

As in the 1930s, Stalin refused to admit that a disaster was taking place and preferred to denounce "wreckers" and "speculators," who were allegedly responsible for the bread shortage. The Kremlin leader had huge "strategic" grain reserves that he had ruthlessly accumulated for war needs. Now he refused to release this grain for consumption. Stalin also had 1,500 tons of gold in state coffers to buy food abroad. Molotov and Mikoyan later recalled that Stalin banned the sale of gold. He even rejected food assistance from the UN Relief and Rehabilitation Administration to Russia (while allowing some assistance to Ukraine and White Russia). At the same time he pledged to send Soviet food to Poland and Czechoslovakia, as well as to French and Italian Communists.[100]

Stalin returned to the prewar policy of impoverishing the Soviet people, especially the peasantry and agricultural workers, in order to provide money for industrial rebuilding and rearmament. Between 1946 and 1948, taxes on peasants increased by 30 percent, and by 1950 they had jumped by 150 percent. The state also refused to pay back the war bonds, billions of rubles that had been "borrowed," in fact confiscated, from the Soviet people. Instead, new reconstruction bonds were imposed on the struggling citizenry.[101]

Stalin certainly knew how many people resented the authorities and him personally. But he also knew that only the elite presented a real danger. Mikoyan recalled: Stalin "knew that the main feature of the Russian *muzhik* was his patience and endurance."[102] The purges that aimed at undermining the elites' pride and autonomy gradually turned into a new round of terror against them. In 1945 and 1946, there was a decline in the number of indictments by the NKVD's Special Commission, from 26,600 to 8,000, but by 1949 the level had jumped to 38,500.[103] In January 1947, General Gordov, his wife, and General Rybalchenko were arrested and imprisoned, along with other military figures and their family members.[104] The purges were still limited, and they proceeded very quietly, without public denunciations. But within a couple of years, when the Cold War polarized the world and Stalin's position became unshakeable, the Kremlin dictator began to spill the elites' blood on a growing scale.

STALIN "CONSOLIDATES" SOVIET SOCIETY

Norman Naimark observes that "war provides cover for rulers to carry out projects of ethnic cleansing" and "provides the opportunity to deal with a troublesome minority by suspending civil law." For Stalin, the growing confrontation with the West provided a chance to restore full control over the elites. It also gave him a justification for the Russification of Soviet elites and bureaucracy and the consolidation of Soviet society with the help of strong nationalist themes and a rigid ethnic hierarchy.[105]

The campaign against "cosmopolitanism," an official cover for anti-Semitic policies, was a major part of this consolidation. Stalin's suspicion of Jews began to grow with the onset of the Cold War. He began to imagine a conspiracy of Soviet Jewish elites, Jewish organizations in the United States, and Jews in his immediate entourage. Since the 1920s, many Politburo members, including Molotov, Voroshilov, Mikhail Kalinin, and Andrei Andreev, had married Jewish women, and now this began to feed Stalin's suspicions.[106] In 1946, Zhdanov passed Stalin's order down through the ranks: accelerate the removal of "cosmopolitan" cadres, primarily ethnic Jews, from the Soviet bureaucracy, including from the key positions of Soviet propaganda, ideology, and culture. The first blow, reflecting the new priorities, was against the Soviet Information Bureau (Sovinformburo), the voice, known throughout the world, of Kremlin wartime propaganda. Zhdanov bluntly told the official who had trouble understanding precisely who the cosmopolitan enemy was in his agency to "get rid of the synagogue there." Soviet Jews had served the Soviet regime, filling the ranks of the professional and cultural elite for two decades. Now it was time to purge them.[107]

In spring 1948, prominent Zionists appealed to Moscow to send "fifty thousand" Soviet Jews as "volunteers" to Palestine to help them against the Arabs, promising, in return, sympathy to Soviet interests. Soviet officials and experts on the Middle East reacted with great skepticism; the prevalent view was that the class nature of Zionism would definitely put Zionists on the side of the United States, not the USSR. Surprisingly, despite his growing anti-Semitism, Stalin overruled the skeptics and authorized massive military assistance to the Zionists through Czechoslovakia. In May 1948, even before the war in Palestine ended, the Soviet Union recognized the state of Israel de jure, even before the United States had done so. Molotov asserted in the 1970s that "everybody, except Stalin and myself," had been against this decision. He explained that to avoid recognizing Israel would have allowed the enemies of the USSR to depict it as opposed to Jewish national self-determination.[108] But more probably, Stalin concluded that supporting the Zionist movement could be his only tool to weaken British influence in the Middle East. Also, he must have hoped to exacerbate the British-American tensions over Zionism and even to gain access to the Mediterranean.[109]

However, Israel, as most experts predicted, quickly began to lean on the United States. Also, the phenomenal show of support for Israel among world Jewry, including Soviet Jews, startled the Kremlin leader. Even Voroshilov's wife, Ekaterina (Golda Gorbman), said to his relatives on the day Israel was proclaimed: "Now we have our own country, too." The Jewish Anti-Fascist Committee (JAFC) had already become in Stalin's eyes the hotbed of Jewish nationalism connected to Zionist circles in the United States and Israel. Stalin knew that many Soviet Jews saw the head of the JAFC, the famous actor Solomon Mikhoels, as their informal national leader. At the end of the war, they appealed to Molotov, his wife, Polina Zhemchuzhina, Voroshilov, and Kaganovich to help set up a Jewish republic in Crimea. Even before the recognition of Israel, the dictator began to take measures to eliminate what he imagined as a potential Zionist conspiracy inside the Soviet Union. In January 1948, the MGB (the successor to the NKGB), at Stalin's order, killed Mikhoels, staging it as a road accident. By the end of 1948, other leaders of the JAFC were arrested and interrogated. Among many other things, they were accused of an alleged plot to turn Crimea into a Zionist-American beachhead inside the Soviet Union. In January 1949, Molotov's deputy, Lozovsky, the former head of the Sovinformburo and the political supervisor of the JAFC, was arrested. Molotov's wife was also arrested. Molotov recalled that "his knees began to shake," when Stalin read at the Politburo the materials collected against Polina Zhemchuzhina. The same fate befell the wives of Soviet "President" Mikhail Kalinin and of Alexander Poskrebyshev, Stalin's personal secretary.[110] These, as it turned out, were only the first steps toward a colossal campaign against a "Zionist conspiracy" that culminated shortly before Stalin's death with the arrests of the "Kremlin doctors affair" and the announcement that these doctors allegedly prepared, on the instructions of an American Zionist center, the assassination of Soviet political and military leaders. Soviet Jews, including many in the Soviet bureaucracy and cultural elites, expected imminent arrest and deportation to Siberia.[111]

The central role of Crimea in the JAFC case indicated Stalin's continuing obsession with the southern flank of the Soviet Union and unsuccessful pressures on Turkey and Iran. In 1947–48, Turkey became a recipient of American financial and military assistance and a key American regional ally. Iran was moving in the same direction. Meanwhile, Stalin's unfulfilled promises to the peoples of South Caucasus began to backfire as well. The Communists of Georgia, Armenia, and Azerbaijan, all Stalin's appointees, acted like quarrelling housewives in a communal kitchen. After the dream of returning "ancestral lands" in Turkey did not materialize, the leaders of Georgia and Armenia began to scheme against Azerbaijan. Armenia's party secretary, Grigory Arutynov, complained that he had no room to settle and resources to feed the repatriates (although, instead of the projected 400,000 Armenians, only 90,000 arrived in Soviet Armenia). He proposed to resettle Azeri peasants, living on Armenian territory, in Azerbaijan. He also suggested transferring Nagorny Karabagh, a hilly area historically disputed between the Azeris and the Armenians, from the Soviet Republic of Azerbaijan to the Soviet Republic of Armenia. Bagirov responded with counterarguments and counterclaims. Georgians and Armenians hinted to Moscow about the growth of "Armenian nationalism" in the region.[112]

In December 1947, Stalin accepted Arutynov's proposal to resettle Azeri peasants outside of Armenia. However, he did not support the redrawing of the republic's borders. And at some point, he decided to resume the "ethnic cleansing" of South Caucasus from suspicious and potentially disloyal elements. In September 1948, a fire on the steamer *Pobeda* (Victory), which was bringing Armenian repatriates, triggered Stalin's suspicions. From his Black Sea dacha he cabled to Malenkov: "There are American agents among the repatriates. They prepared a terrorist act on the steamer 'Pobeda.'" On the next day Malenkov cabled back: "You are right, of course. We will take all necessary measures." The Politburo immediately passed the order to stop repatriation.[113] In April and May 1949, the Politburo decreed that all "Armenian nationalists" (including some repatriates from all over the world), as well as all "former Turkish citizens" from Armenia, Georgia, and Azerbaijan, be deported to Kazakhstan and Siberia. Greeks were also deported. The deportations from South Caucasus in 1944–49 involved 157,000 people.[114] This "cleansing" did not end the nationalist tensions. Still, Stalin managed to bring the regional politics, destabilized by his foreign policy adventures, back under control.

Simultaneously, Stalin delivered a lethal blow to the "Leningraders," meaning those party and state officials from the Russian Federation, especially Leningrad, who had been ethnic Russians and had become popular among the Russian public during the war. These officials hoped that Stalin would continue to rely on them for postwar reconstruction. This group included Nikolai Voznesensky, the Gosplan head; chairman of the Council of Ministers of the Russian Federation and member of the Party Orgburo Mikhail Rodionov; Central Committee secretary and Orgburo member Alexei Kuznetsov; and first secretary of Leningrad's

Communist Party organization Petr Popkov. They were protégés of Andrei Zhda-nov and had been in charge of Leningrad's heroic defense during the 900 days of the German siege. Beria and Malenkov, threatened by this group's ascendancy, did everything to compromise the Leningraders in Stalin's eyes and finally suc-ceeded. The Kremlin launched an investigation into the "Leningrad affair," as well as the "Gosplan affair" against Voznesensky. In February and March 1949, Stalin dismissed Voznesensky, Rodionov, Kuznetsov, and Popkov from their po-sitions. After several months, the MGB arrested them, along with another 65 high officials and 145 family members and relatives. The "investigation" used appall-ing methods of torture. Stalin made the Politburo members, including Malenkov and Minister of Defense Nikolai Bulganin, attend interrogations personally. On October 1, 1950, 23 high officials, including Voznesensky, Rodionov, Kuznetsov, and Popkov, were executed. About the same time, the arrested generals, includ-ing Gordov, Rybalchenko, and Grigory Kulik, were also shot.[115]

Within a few short years, Stalin had successfully stolen the glory of victory and the fruits of peace from the Soviet people, victors in World War II. Of course, he could not have done this without the support of millions of willing collaborators, including military and civilian elites. Many war veterans slipped from heroic roles back into the position of "cogs" in the state machinery. They welcomed and supported the transformation of the USSR into a world empire and superpower. Reawakened chauvinism and nationalism and ideological belief in the aggressive hostility of "Western imperialism" toward the Soviet Union—all these factors contributed to the powerful amalgam that made millions of Soviet citizens sub-scribe in good conscience to Stalin's postwar plans.[116] Many veterans came to regard the Soviet empire and its security buffer of Central Europe as the necessary substitute for bread, happiness, and a comfortable life after victory. They also compensated for the permanent lack of domestic security by projecting their fears outside, by resurrecting the cult of Soviet military power, displaying overt hostility toward the West, and embracing a new anti-Americanism. This became the core of the Soviet collective identity for decades to come.[117]

While appealing to the impulses of Russian chauvinism, state propaganda and the media excoriated Jewish "cosmopolitans." During the purge of Jews from Moscow State University, Anatoly Chernyaev listened to his friend, a war veteran, explaining to him: "For several years the party has been fighting against Jewish domination. It is cleansing itself from the Jews." At this same time, another brave young veteran spoke up against anti-Semitism. He immediately lost his party membership and disappeared from the university.[118] The anti-Semitic purge gave those who supported anti-Semitic policies a false sense of solidarity and power akin to what many Germans had felt under Hitler. Another witness described such types: "The war had given them a taste of power. They were incapable of critical thinking. They studied to be masters of life."[119]

At one of the anti-cosmopolitan meetings at Moscow State University, Professor Sergei Dmitriev asked his colleague what the reason for this campaign could be. The answer was: "War. People must be prepared for a new war. And it is approaching."[120] The intensifying Cold War certainly helped Stalin to justify his anti-Semitic campaign, as well as the deportations of Armenians and Greeks, as well as of Ukrainians, Latvians, and Lithuanians. It helped him consolidate the Russian core of his "socialist empire." The winds of a new war also helped Stalin to stamp out any potential discontent and dissent among the elites. The majority of state officials and military officers in the Soviet Union were convinced that the West was on the offensive and had to be contained.

This perception grew when the United States tested two atomic bombs at the Bikini atoll in the Pacific in July 1946. The tests took place just two weeks after the Americans presented their plan of "international control" of atomic energy and on the eve of the Paris Peace Conference (July 29 to October 15, 1946), convened to negotiate the peace treaties with Germany and its satellites. Two Soviet observers witnessed the tests and reported to the Kremlin leadership on its results. One of them, Major General Semen Alexandrov, a geologist and the chief engineer of the uranium explorations for the Soviet atomic project, brought the film on the tests to Moscow and showed it in the Kremlin, as well as to his friends and colleagues.[121]

Few in the Soviet political class had any doubt that the American atomic monopoly had become the tool of U.S. postwar diplomacy and that it threatened Soviet security. Even the most intelligent and sophisticated party members could not escape the forcefulness of Stalin's zero-sum vision of the new postwar situation. Writer Konstantin Simonov experienced the Soviet war saga from the tragic defeats of the summers of 1941 and 1942 to the triumph in Berlin and identified himself with the "generation of victors." In early 1946, the Politburo sent him and a small group of other journalists and writers to the United States on a propaganda mission. The contrast between American affluence and Soviet ruin was almost unbearable for him. He was also disturbed by the first waves of anti-Soviet backlash that lapped on American shores. Upon his return home, Simonov wrote a play, The Russian Question, in which U.S. imperialists, politicians, and newspaper magnates seek a preemptive war against the Soviet Union. The play's main character, a progressive American journalist, seeks to denounce this cabal. He travels to the Soviet Union and sees with his own eyes that Russians do not want another war. The play was a crude caricature of American politics and media, but without a doubt Simonov passionately believed in what he wrote. How could the Soviet Union threaten anyone, when it had suffered so many losses? Yet, at the same time, he was also convinced that without postwar mobilization and reconstruction the Soviet Union would be pushed around and perhaps be crushed by the awesome American power. Stalin liked Simonov's play. *The Russian Question* was serialized in journals, read on radio, and staged on countless stages of the Soviet Union and seen by millions. Ten years later, Simonov still subscribed to the idea that in 1946 the Soviet Union had a stark choice—to grow strong quickly or perish.[122]

Stalin's goal was a "socialist empire," invincible and protected on all its flanks. But this project suffered from inherent flaws. Successful empires throughout human history, among them Roman, Chinese, and British, used other factors in addition to naked force to establish control over huge disparate territories. They recruited indigenous elites, often tolerated ethnic, cultural, and religious diversity, and promoted free trade and communications.[123] Stalin's socialist empire used powerful ideology, nationalism, and social engineering to refashion society and elites. It introduced the uniformity of state industrialization and party systems. At the same time, it took away civil freedoms, wealth, cooperation, and human dignity and offered instead an illusion of social justice.

The socialist empire exploited the patience, illusions, and suffering of millions of Russians and non-Russians, the people populating its core. It also exploited the faith of millions of true believers in Communism in Europe and Asia, where Marxism-Leninism played the role of a secular religion. This pyramid of faith and illusions was crowned by the cult of Stalin himself, the infallible leader. The leader, however, was mortal: inevitably, Stalin's death would produce a crisis of legitimacy and a succession struggle among his heirs.

Most important, the Soviet Union faced a confident and dynamic rival in the West. The United States, with its financial, economic, and military power, helped to rebuild the countries of Western Europe and Japan as free market economies and mass consumption societies. The struggle against the West left Stalin no opportunity to prevail. This became most painfully clear in Germany, where the Soviets confronted major problems when they tried to turn their zone of occupation into the linchpin of their empire in Central Europe.

(CHAPTER 3)

STALEMATE IN GERMANY,

1945-1953

> All we need is a bourgeois Germany if it is peaceful.
> —Beria, May 1953

> How could a sober-thinking Marxist, one who stands on the
> positions close to socialism or Soviet power, believe in a bourgeois,
> peaceful Germany . . . that would be under the control of four powers?
> —Molotov, July 1953

Germany's division was one of the most striking outcomes of the clash between the Soviet Union and the Western democracies. But only recently has critical reassessment of Western involvement emerged.[1] And the full extent of Stalin's role cannot be documented even today. The details of many smaller-scale decisions and their implementation remain clouded: Stalin's cipher cables and many records of conversations are still classified in the Russian archives. Nevertheless, the available documents reveal that many developments in East Germany had Stalin's unique imprint and some of them would never have taken place without his explicit authorization. The top Soviet political commissar in East Germany, Vladimir Semenov, recalled in the 1960s the "subtle diplomatic moves" that Stalin made in pursuing Soviet policy on the German Question.[2]

An examination of East German and Soviet archives has convinced some scholars that Stalin would have preferred to build a united non-Communist Germany, not to create a separate East German satellite.[3] Some experts believe that the Soviets had never intended the Sovietization of East Germany but rather stumbled into it in the chaotic process of improvisation.[4] My conclusions in this chapter are just the opposite. Evidence shows that Stalin and Soviet elites never entertained the idea of a neutral Germany. At a minimum, the Soviets wanted to neutralize the part of Germany under Western control and build their own socialist Germany in their zone of occupation. From the ideological angle, building socialism in the Eastern Zone brought together the Bolshevik internationalist dreams of the 1920s and the acquisition of the empire during the 1940s.

From the economic standpoint, the zone became the source of an enormous flow of reparations, of self-enrichment for Soviet elites, of high technologies for industrialists and scientists, and of almost the entire supply of weapons-grade uranium for Soviet nuclear arms. The division of Germany was also an excellent pretext for constructing a socialist empire in Central Europe. World War II left Soviet elites and the citizenry feeling entitled to have a decisive say in Germany's future. This sentiment, justified by the enormous war casualties, lasted for decades.

Last, but not least, Stalin never wanted to withdraw Soviet troops from East Germany. As the confrontation deepened, East Germany became a true hub—militarily and geostrategically—of Soviet power in Europe. Hundreds of thousands of Soviet troops ended up being deployed there, ready to rush, at a moment's notice, all the way to the English Channel.

As it turned out, East Germany became the most troubled link of the Soviet empire. As an "expert on nationalities," Stalin was careful not to reinvigorate the forces of German nationalism; he felt it was vital to blame the split of the German nation on the Western powers. Thus, the Soviets concealed the gradual integration of East Germany into the Soviet empire, leaving the border between East and West Germany open. These circumstances turned Germany into a place of relatively open competition between free market and Communist systems. In the early occupation years, Soviet authorities seemed to be successful in consolidating "their Germany." By the end of Stalin's life, however, it became clear that the struggle for the pivotal country of Europe was just beginning and that the Soviets could not win it.

ESTABLISHING THE OCCUPATION REGIME

The Soviet authorities planned for occupation, documents suggest, beginning in 1943, well before the first Soviet soldier entered East Prussia. Yet, understandably, those plans were quite vague. Ivan Maisky wrote in his private journal: "Our goal is to prevent the emergence of a new German aggression." This could be achieved, if not by "proletarian revolution" and the "creation in Germany of a strong Soviet regime," then only by the "substantial and durable weakening of Germany that would render it physically incapable of any aggression."[5] Twenty years later, Marshal Rodion Malinovsky and Marshal Sergei Biryuzov stated that they believed that it was Stalin's intention to destroy the German economy in 1945: "He did not believe that we would stay in Germany, and he was afraid that it all would turn once more against us."[6]

Stalin, always suspicious of Western intentions, wanted to prevent a last-minute alliance between Germany and the Western powers. At the Yalta conference, he even did not want to reveal the Soviet Union's extremely strong interest in reparations.[7] According to Maisky, Stalin "did not want to scare the Allies with our demands and make them interested in new opportunities." He also played down Soviet plans to use German POWs as forced labor to rebuild Soviet cities and the economy.[8] In reality, Soviet interest in economic exploitation of Germany was enormous. On May 11, 1945, Stalin instructed Malenkov, Molotov, Gosplan head Nikolai Voznesensky, Maisky, and other officials that the transfer of Germany's military-industrial potential to the Soviet Union must be carried out with maximum speed to ensure economic recovery of the industrialized areas, "particularly [the coal mines of] Donbass." During the discussion, Molotov stressed that the Soviets must strip West Berlin of all its industrial assets before its transfer to the Western powers. "Berlin cost us too much."[9]

At the end of the war, the Kremlin's plans for the future of Germany centered above all on the issues of borders and occupation.[10] Stalin and his lieutenants redrew the map of Germany and erased Prussia, "the hornet's nest of German militarism," from the map. The eastern part of Prussia with the city of Königsberg became part of the Soviet Union. The western part and the city of Danzig went to the reconstituted Poland. Stalin also decided to transfer to Poland the German lands of Silesia and Pomerania, in compensation for the eastern Polish lands that the Soviet Union had annexed in 1939 and retained at the end of the war. The Soviets encouraged the Poles and the Czechs to expel ethnic Germans. The Western allies did not object. Overall, by the end of 1945, 3.6 million German refugees had moved from Eastern Europe to the Soviet zone of occupation; hundreds of thousands fled to the Western zones. It was an awesome geopolitical coup that changed the map of Central Europe.[11]

Despite the initial cooperative stance of the Western powers, Stalin braced for a struggle for Germany. In late March 1945, he told a group of visiting Czechoslovak officials that the Western allies would "conspire" with the Germans. They would try to rescue them from punishment for their crimes, would treat them "more leniently."[12] In May 1945, Stalin said that "the battle for Germany's soul" would be "protracted and difficult."[13] And at a June 4, 1945, meeting with German Communists, Stalin advised them that the British and the Americans planned to dismember Germany, but that he, Stalin, was against it. Still, he said, "there will be two Germanys in spite of all the unity of the allies." To occupy a strong position in German politics, Stalin urged German Communists to merge with Social Democrats and become the party of "German unity" that could reach out to Western zones. The Socialist Unity Party of Germany (the SED) was established in the Soviet zone in February 1946.[14]

Not indigenous Communists but instead the Soviet Military Administration in

Germany (SMAG) became the crucial agency for pursuing Soviet objectives in Germany. In early 1946, SMAG had already emerged as a sprawling bureaucracy in the growing competition with Western occupational authorities. The SMAG apparatus amounted to 4,000 officers, who had privileges appropriate to "imperial administration" in a colony: a double salary in Soviet rubles and German marks; a better living standard than the highest bureaucrats in the Soviet Union; a position from which to lord it over the former "master race" of Europe; and exposure to various influences from Western zones. The Kremlin leader had the two rival secret police agencies, the MVD and the MGB, help SMAG and provide Stalin with a check on its activities.[15]

Marshal Georgy Zhukov, the first head of SMAG, quickly lost his job: his immense popularity, combined with a headstrong character, bothered Stalin. His successor, Marshal Vasily Sokolovsky, was the most sophisticated, cultured, and at the same time modest and unassuming person in the Soviet military command.[16] Stalin also instituted the position of political commissar in Germany. In February 1946, this job went to Vladimir Semenov, a thirty-four-year-old doctor of philosophy and a middle-ranking diplomat; nothing in his past life prepared him for the enormity of his task. His first reaction was to study archival documents on the history of Napoleon's occupation of the German states in the early nineteenth century. Unfortunately for the young appointee, history gave him no insights for future activities.[17]

The uncertainty of the political situation in Germany and in relationship to the Western powers made Stalin deliberately cautious and vague in his instructions to SMAG and Semenov. While Stalin had no doubt there would be a struggle for Germany, he was uncertain about the degree of American involvement. In October 1944, in conversation with Stalin, Churchill said that the "Americans probably have no intention to participate in a long-term occupation [of Germany]."[18] But numerous events since fall 1945 signaled the American intention to stay in Germany. The new assertiveness of the United States after Hiroshima indicated to Moscow that the Americans wanted to challenge Soviet control over Central Europe and the Balkans. From that moment on, the issue for Stalin was not so much the presence of American military power in Germany but rather the maintenance of the Soviet military presence in Central Europe, above all in the Eastern Zone.

In September 1945, Stalin rejected the proposal by U.S. secretary of state James Byrnes to sign a treaty that would demilitarize Germany for twenty to twenty-five years. During his talks with Byrnes in Moscow in December 1945, Stalin, pleased with the American decision to preserve the Yalta-Potsdam formula of cooperation, decided to agree "in principle" to discuss the idea of German demilitarization. It was a tactical move. Stalin's strong opposition to Byrnes's idea remained in force. Moreover, it came to be shared by the majority in Soviet high echelons. And it became obvious in February 1946, when Byrnes presented to the Soviets a draft agreement on demilitarization of Germany. Stalin and Soviet officials debated this proposal for months. In May 1946, thirty-eight officials, including Politburo members, military, and diplomats, presented their conclusions to Stalin.[19] Zhukov wrote: "Americans would like to finish the occupation of Germany as soon as possible and to remove the armed forces of the USSR, and then to demand a withdrawal of our troops from Poland, and then from the Balkans." They also wanted to disrupt the Soviets in the dismantling of German industries and extraction of reparations and "to preserve in Germany the military potential as a necessary base for carrying out their aggressive aims in the future."[20] Deputy Foreign Minister Solomon Lozovsky was even more categorical in his memorandum. Acceptance of the American project, he wrote, would lead to a liquidation of the occupational zones, withdrawal of Soviet troops, and economic and political reunification of Germany under American domination. This, in turn, would lead "in a few years to a German-Anglo-American war against the USSR." A summary prepared by the Ministry of Foreign Affairs concluded that in presenting the proposal on German demilitarization, the U.S. government pursued the following goals: bringing an end to German occupation; terminating Soviet reparations from Germany; dismantling the Yalta-Potsdam formula and reducing Soviet control over Germany and Soviet influence in European affairs; accelerating restoration of Germany's economic power; and turning Germany against the Soviet Union. These conclusions became a standard formula in diplomatic correspondence evaluating American foreign policy.[21]

Nowhere in Soviet documents on Germany can one see any trace of a fundamental rethinking of Soviet security considerations in view of American atomic capabilities. Yet, undoubtedly, the shadow of Hiroshima's atomic mushroom was present in Soviet thinking on the German Question. Molotov, in a conversation with Byrnes on May 5, 1946, wondered why the United States "leaves no corner in the world without attention" and "builds its air bases everywhere," including Iceland, Greece, Italy, Turkey, and China.[22] From those bases, as Stalin, Molotov, and the Soviet military saw it, American bombers with atomic weapons could easily strike any spot in the Soviet Union. Later, in the early 1950s, this factor would drive a huge increase in the Soviet military presence in Central Europe in order to counteract a possible U.S. nuclear attack.

Stalin and Soviet high officials agreed that an early military withdrawal from Germany would deny the Soviet Union the right to keep its troops in Central Europe and the Balkans. Then the devastated Germany and other countries of

Central Europe would automatically become dependent on American economic and financial assistance and with political strings attached. The best option remaining for the Soviets was the continuation of the joint occupational regime for an indefinite period. Zhukov, Sokolovsky, and Semenov intended "to use the American initiative in any way to tie their hands (and British hands as well) on the German Question in the future."[23] Then, at least, they could hope that the inevitable postwar economic crisis would come and the United States would give up its plans for European hegemony and retreat into isolationism.

The Americans, meanwhile, switched to the "containment" mode and cooled to the idea of cooperating with the Soviets in Germany. Byrnes reached an agreement with Bevin to merge American and British zones into Bizonia. In his speech in Stuttgart on September 6, the secretary of state, accompanied by Republican senator Arthur H. Vandenberg and Democratic senator Tom Connally, said: "We are not withdrawing. We are staying here." In sum, Byrnes proposed that the United States, not the Soviets, should be a major sponsor of Germany's sovereignty and democratic future. In addition to assurance of German sovereignty over the Ruhr and the Rhineland, Byrnes hinted that the United States did not regard the new German border with Poland (the Oder-Neisse line) as irrevocable.[24]

Byrnes's speech reinforced the Soviet official consensus that the U.S. administration wanted to get rid of the Soviet presence in Germany and deny the Soviet Union a sphere of influence in Central Europe. Still, there was room for "softer" and "harder" interpretations. On the "hard-line" flank, Molotov's deputy, Sergei Kavtaradze, wrote that the United States was potentially "the most aggressive state" in the world and wanted to convert Germany into the base of their "dictatorial position in Europe." According to this assessment, the speech was part of the strategic plan aimed at the Soviet Union. Other Foreign Ministry officials wrote that Byrnes wanted to mobilize German "reactionary" nationalism against the Soviet Union, yet they did not characterize American actions as an aggressive plan. Some of them continued to argue that political and diplomatic compromise on the German Question was possible.[25] The official discourse, however, did not provide any clues to the nature of this compromise.

Only Stalin's guidance could ease this problem. The Kremlin potentate discussed German affairs with Molotov, Vyshinsky, Vladimir Dekanozov, Zhukov, Sokolovsky, and other officials. In his instructions to the German Communist leaders Walter Ulbricht and Wilhelm Pieck in February 1946, Stalin used the same language the Bolsheviks had used to chart their political strategies during the Russian revolutions: the "program-minimum" was to preserve a German unity; the "program-maximum" stipulated construction of socialism in Germany along the "democratic road."[26] If one takes this jargon seriously, it meant that Stalin was prepared to temporize with the Sovietization of the Soviet zone in the hope that Communist influence could spread throughout the rest of Germany. Stalin's two-stage scenario would have made sense, if there had indeed been a postwar economic crisis and the United States had pulled out its troops from West Germany. This, however, did not happen in 1946 or later.

Semenov recalled in his journal that Stalin had met with him and German Communists at least "once in 2–3 months." He also claimed he received instructions directly from Stalin to focus exclusively on major strategic questions and construct, bit by bit, a new Germany in the Soviet zone. According to him, there are records of "over a hundred" conversations with Stalin on the issues of political strategy in postwar Germany. But the journal of Stalin's visitors shows only eight meetings between the Kremlin ruler and East Germans in the Kremlin, and archival explorations have failed to produce the rest.[27] Since 1946, Stalin's health problems increasingly caused him to delegate German affairs to his lieutenants and the bureaucracy.

The vagueness or even absence of Stalin's instructions is difficult to interpret. It can be explained by the continuing uncertainty of the German Question, but also by other factors. As he often did earlier in his career, the Kremlin leader encouraged political feuds among his subordinates and played a mediating role in bureaucratic conflicts. He tolerated and even encouraged different, sometimes conflicting, versions of Soviet policy toward Germany. As a result, Soviet bureaucratic politics complicated SMAG's activities. Soviet officials in Germany were subordinate to various structures in Moscow, including the Ministry of Defense and the Ministry of Foreign Affairs; at the same time, some of them enjoyed direct contacts with Stalin and his lieutenants, as well as with the heads of various departments in the party's Central Committee. SMAG officials had different domains, according to their functions and tasks, with intersecting, but sometimes conflicting, responsibilities. Their working relations with different groups of Germans and their patronage ties to different bosses in Moscow, as well as the intensified political infighting in Stalin's entourage, added to the picture of confusion.[28]

The evidence does not point to Semenov having an exclusive role in Soviet policy making in Germany.[29] There were other architects of Soviet policies in the zone. One of them was the head of SMAG's division of political information and propaganda, Colonel Sergei Tyulpanov, a military intellectual with expertise in international economics and propaganda. Tyulpanov seemed to have had powerful patrons in Moscow, including Stalin's influential lieutenants Lev Mekhlis and Alexei Kuznetsov. The latter was one of the Leningraders, the party officials who had worked under Andrei Zhdanov. As a result, until 1948, Tyulpanov worked independently from Semenov and his SMAG superiors, managing media and censorship, cinema, and political parties and trade unions, as well as science and culture, in the zone. He even survived the repeated sharp criticism from a number of high Soviet officials, who blamed him for the failures of the SED and Communist propaganda in West Germany.[30]

Soviet interests in Germany were so diverse and contradictory that Sokolovsky, Tyulpanov, and other SMAG officials continually had to walk the tightrope. On the one hand, they sought to organize East Germany in the only way they knew, that is, in the Soviet way. On the other hand, they and their patrons in the party leadership understood that abusing civilians, as well as dismantling industrial assets in the Soviet zone, would only complicate the struggle for Germany.[31] In partial compensation for the dismantling, East Germans got more food to eat. At the height of the severe postwar famine in the USSR, Stalin did not extract agricultural reparations from Germans, although it would have saved many Russians and Ukrainians from starvation.[32] In October 1945, Stalin decided to curb industrial looting in the Eastern Zone. In November, he told visiting Polish Communists that the Soviets were planning to leave some industries in Germany and would only extract their final production. The Soviets organized 31 stock companies (SAGs) that operated on the basis of 119 German plants and factories originally scheduled for removal. "By the end of 1946," writes Norman Naimark, "the Soviets owned close to 30 percent of all production in eastern Germany." A stock company of highest strategic value was the Wismut uranium project in Lower Saxony that produced the fuel for the first Soviet atomic bombs.[33]

The contradictions among different priorities, the dismantling, the construction of a new Germany in the zone, and the struggle for the whole of Germany, remained unresolved. The transfer of industrial assets to the Soviet Union continued, dictated by the needs of Soviet industries as well as by the gigantic armament projects. The Western counterparts declined all requests for resources and equipment from Western zones, which led to more dismantling in the Soviet zone.[34] Meanwhile, the intensification of the Cold War and the consolidation of the Western zones under U.S. and British guidance allowed Stalin, SMAG, and the East German Communists to move ahead with the task of transformation and consolidation of East Germany. This task became the priority for the Soviets.

INTEGRATING EAST GERMANY INTO THE SOVIET BLOC

Unilateral measures to transform the Soviet zone of Germany began from the first day of Soviet occupation. Beginning in 1945, the Soviets and the German Communists carried out radical land reform, compartmentalization of large estates, and distribution of wealth among the small and middle farmers. Semenov recalled that Stalin devoted much attention to the planning and execution of land reforms. The Bolsheviks believed they retained power and prevailed in the civil war largely because they sanctioned confiscation of landlords' land and property by peasants. The same could help German Communists. German *Bauern*, the peasant farmers, did not mind getting the land from the *Junkers*, the landowners' class, as long as it was done legally. Land reforms in East Germany as well as elsewhere in Central Europe were a definite political success for the Soviets and their Communist appointees.[35]

At his meeting with Ulbricht and Pieck in February 1946, Stalin approved the concept of "a special German road to socialism." He hoped that the establishment of the SED would "create a good precedent for Western zones."[36] Yet the "Socialist Unity Party" remained, in the eyes of many Germans, especially women, linked to the Soviet dismantling, violence, and rape that had taken place in the zone. The party suffered a humiliating defeat in the first postwar municipal elections in the zone, particularly in Greater Berlin, in October 1946, when 49 percent voted for the parties of the center and the right. From that moment on, the Soviets simply left nothing to chance, and specialists of SMAG helped the SED to falsify future election results. The new party became the essential vehicle for establishing a political regime following the Soviet model in the Eastern Zone. When Stalin met with the SED delegation at the end of January 1947, he instructed the East German Communists to create secret police and paramilitary forces in the zone "without clamor." In June 1946, the Soviets created a coordinating body for security organs called the German Directorate for the Interior.[37]

One more card that Stalin intended to play in Germany was that of German nationalism. Several decades of experience had taught Stalin that nationalism could be a more potent force than revolutionary romanticism and Communist internationalism. Molotov recalled: "He saw how Hitler managed to organize German people. Hitler led his people, and we felt it by the way Germans fought during the war."[38] In January 1947, Stalin asked the SED delegates: "Are there many Nazi elements in Germany? What kind of force do they represent? In particular in the Western zones?" The SED leaders admitted their ignorance on this subject. Then Stalin advised them to supplant the policy of elimination of Nazi collaborators "by a different one—aimed to attract them, in order to avoid pushing all former Nazis to the enemy camp." The former Nazi activists should be allowed, he continued, to organize their own party that would "operate in the same bloc with the SED." Wilhelm Pieck expressed doubts as to whether SMAG would permit the formation of such a party. Stalin laughed and said he would facilitate it as much as he could.[39]

Semenov took the minutes of the meeting, and he recalled Stalin saying: "There were overall ten million members in the Nazi Party, and they all had families, friends and acquaintances. This is a big number. For how long should we ignore their concerns?" The Kremlin leader suggested a title for their new party: National Democratic Party of Germany. He asked Semenov if SMAG could find in some prison a former regional Nazi leader and put him at the helm of this party. When Semenov said that perhaps all of them had been executed, Stalin expressed regrets. He then suggested that the former Nazis should be allowed to have their own newspaper, "perhaps even with the title *Völkische Beobachter*," the notorious official daily of the Third Reich.[40]

These new tactics from Stalin's arsenal conflicted notably with his earlier manipulation of the "German threat" in the Slavic countries of Central Europe, but also with the core beliefs of Communist elites and with anti-German feelings of Russians. The proposal to cooperate with ex-Nazis dismayed both German Communists and SMAG officials, who waited a year to implement it. Only in May 1948, after the appropriate propagandist preparation, did SMAG disband the commissions on de-Nazification. In June, the first congress of the National Democratic Party of Germany (NDPD) opened in Berlin, with Semenov attending it in secret, his face covered with a newspaper. This was, Semenov recalls, "just the first link in the chain of important actions" in creating the new pro-Soviet and anti-Western balance in German politics. The complete rehabilitation of the former Nazis, as well as the officers of the Wehrmacht, coincided with the formation of the GDR in 1949.[41]

Stalin must have expected that the idea of a centralized, reunified, and neutral Germany would be so irresistible for German nationalists that they would overcome their enmity toward the Soviets and the Communists. And he certainly wanted to turn German nationalism against the West, at the same time as Byrnes and the Americans began to exploit German national sentiments against the USSR. On Stalin's instructions, Soviet diplomacy and propaganda relentlessly pushed the idea of a centralized German state and contrasted the Soviet stand with Western proposals of federalization and decentralization. The Western powers "really want to have four Germanys but they hide it in every way," said Stalin in January 1947, and reaffirmed the Soviet line: "A central government must be created, and it can sign the peace treaty." As a Russian scholar observes, Stalin was reluctant "to shoulder the responsibility for Germany's division. He wanted that role to be played by the Western powers." Therefore, he deliberately "stayed one step behind the Western powers' actions."[42] Indeed, every Soviet step toward creating units of military and secret police inside the zone was taken after the Western powers took their own decisive steps toward the separation of West Germany: Bizonia, the Marshall Plan, and the formation of West Germany.

Until 1947, Stalin played a crucial role in restraining East German Communists and some SMAG enthusiasts who wanted a rapid "construction of socialism" in the zone. He may have been waiting for drastic changes in Europe's economic and political environment that could have come with economic crisis, U.S. elections, or other developments. Meanwhile, the German Question began to generate fuel for a great power confrontation. The Truman administration continued to shift from the policy of withdrawal from Germany to the policy of long-term economic reconstruction of Western zones. After the failure of the second conference of foreign ministers in Moscow (March–April 1947) to reach an agreement on Germany, the U.S. secretary of state, George Marshall, came to the conclusion that "the patient was dying while doctors deliberate," and the Truman administration launched the Marshall Plan to jump-start European economic recovery.[43]

At first the Kremlin had no clue what motivated the new U.S. initiative. Perhaps, Soviet economists suggested, the United States anticipated a major economic crisis and wanted to give away another "Lend-Lease" to create new markets for their goods. There was a revived hope among Soviet economic managers that this time the USSR might obtain American loans that had not materialized in 1945–46. At first, the Soviets did not link the Marshall Plan to the German Question: Molotov was only instructed to block attempts to reduce German reparations in exchange for American loans. After consultations with the Yugoslav Communist leaders, Stalin and Molotov decided that the delegations of other Central European countries should go to Paris, where a conference on economic assistance to Europe was to take place. The Czechoslovak, Polish, and Rumanian governments announced that they would participate in the conference, when Stalin changed his mind.[44]

On June 29, 1948, Molotov reported to Stalin from Paris, where he had consulted with the British and French leaders: The Americans "are eager to use this opportunity to break into the internal economies of European countries and especially to redirect the flow of European trade in their own interest." By early July, the new intelligence from Paris and London, especially the secret U.S.-British talks behind the backs of the Soviets, revealed to the Kremlin that the Truman administration had in mind a far-reaching plan of economic and political integration of Europe: the Marshall Plan aimed at containing Soviet influence and reviving the European, and above all the German, economy, according to American blueprints. On July 7, 1947, Molotov sent a new directive to the Central European governments, "advising" them to cancel their participation in the Paris conference, because "under the guise of the plan of European recovery," the organizers of the Marshall Plan "in reality want to create a Western bloc that would include Western Germany."[45] When the Czechoslovak government refused to comply, citing their economic dependence on Western markets and loans, Stalin summoned them to Moscow and presented them with an ultimatum: even their attending the Paris conference would be regarded by the Soviets as a hostile act. The browbeaten Czechoslovak delegation had to pledge obedience. In return, Stalin promised he would order the Soviet industrial ministries to purchase Czechoslovak goods and pledged to provide immediate assistance in the amount of 200,000 tons of wheat, barley, and oats.[46]

The Soviet flip-flop on the Marshall Plan demonstrated a pattern in Stalin's reaction to the growing American involvement in Europe: from suspicion and temporizing to a fierce counterattack. Stalin's reading of the Marshall Plan left no room for German neutrality. A report from the Soviet ambassador in Washington, reflecting the new thinking in the Kremlin, depicted the U.S. plans as building a bloc encircling the USSR, "passing in the West across West Germany" and beyond. Reports from London and other Western capitals repeated the same story.[47] Stalin's instructions to foreign Communists pushed them to shift from parliamentary activities to political violence and preparations for war. In the fall of 1947, the Kremlin sought to destabilize Western Europe through strikes and demonstrations organized by French and Italian Communist parties and trade unions. The chewing out of the Czechs indicated that Stalin finally realized that his wait-and-see scenario for Germany and Central Europe had to be discarded. Communist parties in Central Europe were told to march to the Kremlin's drum and join the Information Bureau of the Communist Parties (Cominform), headquartered in Belgrade, Yugoslavia. Still, Stalin's instructions to the Central European Communists were to combine resolution with prudence. He hoped to present the acceleration of "Sovietization" as a gradual and natural process with Moscow's hand as hidden as possible.[48]

Stalin had been considering strengthening his control over European Communist parties since 1946, but the establishment of the Cominform was accelerated by the Marshall Plan. It reflected Stalin's conviction that, from now on, the Soviets could manage Central Europe only with iron ideological and party discipline. The Communist parties had to renounce "national roads to socialism;" they quickly became Stalinized and rigidly subordinate to Kremlin policies. The imposition of Stalinist controls led to the "purge" of Tito's Yugoslavia. This event bore a strong imprint of Stalin's personality. Stalin's outburst of hatred toward Tito and the Yugoslav Communist leadership was a surprise, even to his subordinates. It was, however, typical of Stalin's behavior in Soviet politics during his consolidation of power, when he alternated between affection and hatred toward his political friends and supporters. Stalin's treatment of Central European Communist leaders was not markedly different from the way he treated his closest lieutenants, Molotov and Zhdanov—it was a mixture of deceiving charm, unprovoked sadism, suspicion, and contempt. In the case of the Yugoslavs, Stalin's treatment backfired and produced a rebellion of the most valued Soviet partner in Central Europe.[49]

Thus, the consolidation of Central Europe à la Stalin produced an internal, as well as an external, enemy. The ferocious campaign against "Titoism" performed the same function in 1948–49 as the bogus campaign against "Trotskyism" had done in 1935–38. It helped to consolidate Stalin's absolute control and preclude even remote possibilities of opposition and resistance to his will. At the same time, Stalin was obsessed with the idea of assassinating Tito, just as he had been with Trotsky's assassination.[50]

The rapid consolidation of the Soviet bloc in Central Europe brought about great changes in Soviet policies in Germany. They shifted decisively toward the creation of a Sovietized East Germany at the expense of the campaign for German unity. Stalin did not allow the SED to become a member of the Cominform. Yet, the SED leaders, including former Social Democrats, expressed unequivocal loyalty to the Soviet Union and denounced the Marshall Plan. In the fall of 1947, Stalin pushed the East German Communist leadership to organize military formations under the auspices of the German Directorate of the Interior, the police apparatus in the Soviet zone. In November 1947, a Department of Intelligence and Information was set up inside the Directorate of the Interior, with the goal of detecting and uprooting by extralegal methods any opposition to the East German regime. In July 1948, as the Berlin crisis deepened, the Soviet leader sanctioned a plan to equip and train 10,000 East German soldiers, as an "alert police" living in barracks.[51] All these measures were formulated and implemented in deep secrecy. Stalin fully understood that they constituted a flagrant violation of Yalta and Potsdam decisions, and this policy stood in stark contrast to Soviet propaganda and diplomacy that promoted the option of a reunified, neutral, and demilitarized Germany.

In September 1948, the SED denounced a special German road to socialism, the concept it had adhered to since its creation in 1946, as "rotten and dangerous," a path to nationalist "deviations." In the atmosphere of anti-Yugoslav hysteria, East German Communists preferred to be on the safe side, trying to join the ranks of loyal Stalinists even without an invitation from the Kremlin to do so.[52]

From December 1947 to February 1948, Western leaders, after separate meetings in London without the Soviet Union, began to organize a West German federal state. This state would receive American assistance through the Marshall Plan, and the Ruhr production plans would be revised to ensure a quick economic revival of Western zones. Stalin might still hope that a capitalist economic crisis would occur to ruin Western plans, but he could no longer postpone his reaction to the emergence of West Germany. His response was to act at the point of maximum Soviet superiority over the West, in Berlin. In March 1948, answering complaints of SED officials about the Western presence in Berlin, Stalin remarked: "Maybe we shall succeed in kicking them out."[53] He decided to blockade West Berlin in an attempt in remove the Allies from the city or, even better, to force them to renegotiate their London agreements.

In addition to the London agreements, the introduction of the new currency in West Germany and West Berlin became a trigger for Soviet action. Introduction of a new currency would sharply increase the costs of the Soviet occupation of Germany (15 billion rubles in 1947). Until then, SMAG could print the old occupational marks that remained in circulation in Western zones. Financial separation of the Soviet zone from West Germany threatened to end this bonanza.[54]

By making West Berlin a hostage to Western separatist plans, Stalin hoped he had a reasonable chance of success in killing two birds with one stone. If the Western powers chose to negotiate, this would complicate their plans to create a West German state. These talks would also give SMAG more time to carry out their own preparations in the zone. If Western authorities refused to bargain, they risked losing their base in Berlin. The Soviet leader felt confident in his ability to adjust his use of force around West Berlin to avoid provoking war and to make the Western powers look responsible for the crisis. Significantly, he ordered a delay in printing new banknotes for the Soviet zone until the Western powers introduced their D-mark in Berlin.[55]

The Berlin blockade was another of Stalin's probes, in which caution joined with a brutal determination to push whenever the balance of forces was right. Other European developments provide a revealing context for the Soviet move against West Berlin. In February 1948, the Kremlin succeeded with this tactic, when the Communists seized power in Czechoslovakia and the liberal-democratic government surrendered without a fight. At the same time, Stalin came to the conclusion that the United States and Great Britain would never let Communist forces win in Greece. At the meeting with Yugoslav and Bulgarian leaders on February 10, Stalin said that "if there are no conditions for victory" in Greece, "one must not be afraid to admit it." He suggested that the "guerrilla movement," supported in 1947 by the Kremlin and the Yugoslavs, should be "terminated." It was Yugoslavia's disagreement with Stalin's calculation that precipitated, along with other factors, the Stalin-Tito split.[56]

While the Berlin crisis was brewing, the imminent victory of the Italian Communist Party (PCI) in April 1948 threatened the balance of power in Europe. Historian Victor Zaslavsky has found ample evidence that the militants of PCI were prepared, if necessary, to seize power by means of military insurrection. The PCI leader, Palmiro Togliatti, schooled in Stalinist "realism," however, had grave doubts about the outcome of such an adventure. On March 23, Togliatti used secret channels to send a letter to Stalin, asking for advice. He warned the Kremlin leader that PCI's military confrontation with the opposing political camp could "lead to a big war." Togliatti informed Stalin that, in the case of a civil war in Italy, the United States, Great Britain, and France would support the anti-Communist side; then PCI would need the assistance of the Yugoslav army and the forces of other Eastern European countries in order to maintain its control over northern Italy. Togliatti's letter evoked an immediate response from Stalin. He instructed PCI not to use "armed insurrection for any reasons" to seize power in Italy.[57] Stalin, true to his cautious calculation of the balance of forces, decided that Italy, located within the British-American sphere of influence, was a long shot. West Berlin, however, was inside the Soviet zone of occupation, and the German issue was crucial enough to justify a calculated risk.

In May 1948, as historian Vladimir Pechatnov discovered, Stalin planned a devious "peace offensive" against the Truman administration. His goal was to undermine U.S. policies in Europe, presenting them as the only cause of the emerging division of Europe and Germany. He used the secret channel to Henry Wallace (who ran for president against Truman) to convey to him, and via him to the American public, that the Soviets "are not waging any Cold War. The United States is waging it." Stalin wanted to create an impression that it would be possible to overcome the U.S.-Soviet contradictions through negotiations. The Soviet leader continued to hint at this illusory prospect in an "open letter" addressed to Wallace and supporting his peace proposals.[58]

Unexpectedly, the Soviet blockade of West Berlin became a propaganda fiasco and a strategic failure. The mild winter, Anglo-American ingenuity in organizing the airlift, and the stoicism of the people of West Berlin defeated Soviet purposes. The West taught Stalin a costly lesson by mounting harsh economic sanctions against the Soviet zone and making the Soviets pay for the damage. Finally, the Western currency reform in West Germany and West Berlin was a great success, thanks in great part to the Soviet boycott.[59] The psychological and political effects of the Berlin blockade were fatal to Soviet influence in West Berlin and West Germany. It helped to forge a new friendship and anti-Communist alliance between the West Germans and the Allies, particularly the Americans. The American and British presence in West Germany and West Berlin gained a popular legitimacy that it had lacked before. The Berlin crisis facilitated the formation of the North Atlantic Treaty Organization (NATO) by the United States, Canada, and ten West European nations, announced on April 9, 1949. NATO permanently and formally legitimized the U.S. military presence in Western Europe and West Germany. On May 11, 1949, after brief talks, the Soviet Union lifted the blockade and signed an agreement with the three Western powers. This agreement recognized de facto permanent Western political rights in Berlin and agreed, in a separate protocol, to the division of the city into West and East. On May 23, 1949, just days after the blockade was lifted, the Western zones became the Federal Republic of Germany (FRG).

Several of Stalin's basic assumptions about Germany, based on the interwar experience, turned out to be false. First, the tactics of an alliance with pan-German nationalists did not produce its expected benefits. Stalin failed to realize that the collapse of the Nazi regime in the spring of 1945 left most Germans wary of any form of nationalism. As political developments in West Germany after 1948 demonstrated, the most potent factors there were not nationalism, but a desire for economic normalization, traditional regionalism, and alienation from East German lands, going back to the reaction against Prussia's domination in the First Reich. These factors were seen in the support Konrad Adenauer received in the upper and middle classes of the Rhineland, the support that allowed him to become the first chancellor of the Federal Republic of Germany.[60]

Instead of nationalist tensions in West Germany, there was an unexpected symbiosis between U.S. troops in West Germany and German civilians, especially women. Many German women liked American GIs, who became providers of scarce food and basic goods. While, in popular opinion, the Soviets were "takers," looters, and dismantlers, the Americans were "givers." During the Berlin blockade, German opinion shifted even more drastically in favor of the United States and against the Soviets.[61]

Secondly, the 1940s did not end in a crisis for world capitalism. Stalin banked a great deal on this assumption. He envisioned intense rivalries among Western European countries and the United States, reflecting the Leninist view of the inherent contradictions of the market-based economy.[62] In reality, the postwar economic recession that began in 1948 was not nearly as serious as expected. Soviet dreams that a new Great Slump would make the United States isolationist and more conciliatory toward Moscow's wishes did not come true.

Once again, Stalin refused to admit his miscalculation. In March 1948, he told SED officials that the unification of Germany would be "a protracted process" and would take "several years." This delay, he continued, would benefit the SED, because the Communists would be able to intensify their propaganda work and "prepare the masses for Germany's reunification." Once the people's minds "are prepared," then "the Americans will have to capitulate."[63] In December 1948, at another meeting with the East German Communists, Stalin exuded a fake optimism. The SED leaders admitted that they and their allies had ruined their political reputation in West Germany; everybody regarded them as "Soviet agents." In reply, the Kremlin master disingenuously reproached Ulbricht and his comrades for renouncing a special German road to socialism: why did they try to fight "naked" like the ancient Germans who had fought against the Roman legions? "One must use a disguise," he said. Stalin suggested that "several good communists" in West Germany should leave the party and infiltrate the SPD, in order to subvert Social Democrats from within, just as the Polish and Hungarian Communists had done to their opposition parties.[64]

The SED leaders took advantage of the Soviet fiasco and the proclamation of the West German state to request more autonomy from Soviet occupation authorities. Under the pressure of events, Stalin allowed the SED to prepare for the establishment of a formal state, the German Democratic Republic. The GDR was officially born on October 7, 1949. In 1949, Stalin set up the Council for Mutual Economic Assistance (the COMECON or CMEA), the Soviet response to the Marshall Plan and the Western economic bloc. Its primary task was to develop "basic types of production that would allow us [the Soviet bloc] to get rid of essential equipment and raw materials imported from capitalist countries." Soon the GDR was allowed to join it.[65]

Some evidence indicates that the Kremlin master felt humiliated by his retreat in Germany. As the Berlin blockade was nearing its ignoble finale, Stalin resumed his attacks on Molotov and arrested his wife. Molotov's near-fall, as historians Gorlizky and Khlevniuk believe, "was in part the price Molotov paid for the failure of Soviet policy in Germany." In March 1949, Molotov lost his post as foreign minister. A year later, Stalin still fumed at "the dishonest, perfidious, and arrogant behavior of the United States in Europe, the Balkans, the Middle East, and especially its decision to form NATO." His way of getting back at the arrogant Americans was to support Kim Il Sung's plan to annex South Korea.[66]

THE KOREAN WAR AND EAST GERMANY

The outbreak of war in Korea in June 1950 radically militarized the Cold War and reduced the room for peace talks and settlements in Europe virtually to nothing. According to Molotov, the war was "pressed on us by the Koreans themselves.

Stalin said it was impossible to avoid the national question of a united Korea."[67] Still, the decision to go to war was Stalin's; once made, it killed any possibility for the peaceful reunification of Germany.

The new alliance between Stalin and Mao Ze-dong paved the road for the Korean War and was a major factor in shifting Stalin's strategies from Europe and Germany to the Far East. Until 1949, the Kremlin provided minimal assistance to Asian Communists and revolutionaries, including Mao Ze-dong in China and Ho Chi Minh in Vietnam.[68] The victory of the Chinese Communists forced Stalin to reconsider his priorities. The triumph of the CCP in the most-populous country of the world contrasted with the stalemate in Germany and the failures of Communists in France and Italy. In July 1949, at the meeting with the CCP delegation in the Kremlin, Stalin admitted his past mistakes in doubting the victory of the Communists in China. Still, in December 1949 he was reluctant to do the same, when Mao Ze-dong came to Moscow to participate in the celebration of the Soviet leader's birthday. Only when Mao refused to leave the USSR without a definitive Sino-Soviet arrangement did Stalin agree to the new Sino-Soviet alliance and a new set of agreements. Mikoyan and Molotov helped to change the leader's mind. During the Stalin-Mao talks that followed, the Kremlin master vowed to close the curtain on the "Yalta system," the Realpolitik arrangements among the great powers that had given the USSR international legitimacy and diplomatic advantages in Europe and Asia. "To hell with Yalta!" the Kremlin leader told Mao, agreeing that the Chinese should take the lead in promoting the revolutionary process in Asia.[69] Tough bargaining and mutual acrimony, however, characterized the negotiations to the end. Unexpectedly, the Chinese requested that all Soviet possessions in Manchuria, including the railroad and the Port Arthur base, would be returned to China. This angered Stalin, but eventually he decided that the alliance with China was more important than Soviet interests in Manchuria. The new Sino-Soviet Treaty, signed on February 14, 1950, became the greatest success of Soviet foreign policy for many years. At the same time, it laid the ground for a future Sino-Soviet rivalry, as Mao felt humiliated by Stalin's condescension and refusal to treat China as an equal partner.[70]

For the first time since the 1920s, Stalin had to treat foreign Communists not simply as the tools for Soviet foreign policy goals but as independent forces or even partners. This led to the substantial, if not altogether genuine, reappearance of the revolutionary "romantic" element in Stalinist international discourse and policies. In Indochina, the Chinese and the Soviets agreed to provide aid to the Viet Minh army. In Korea, Stalin abandoned his previous restraint in regard to the Korean Communists, who begged for Soviet assistance to liberate the Korean peninsula from the pro-American regime of Syngman Rhee. In January 1950,

Stalin authorized the North Korean leader, Kim Il Sung, to prepare for a war of national reunification and pledged full military assistance. Historian Evgeny Bajanov accurately summarized new evidence on this decision. Stalin changed his mind on a Korean war because of (1) the victory of the Communists in China; (2) the Soviet acquisition of the atom bomb (first tested in August 1949); (3) the establishment of NATO and general worsening of Soviet relations with the West; and (4) a perceived weakening of Washington's positions and of its will to get involved militarily in Asia. At the same time, when Kim Il Sung and another North Korean leader, Pak Hong-young, visited Moscow between March 30 and April 25 to plan a war, Stalin told them that the USSR would not intervene directly, especially if the Americans sent troops to save South Korea.[71]

The outbreak of the Korean War led to a new war scare in Western Europe; many expected Soviet tanks to dash into West Germany at any time. U.S. policy makers, however, assumed that a war in Europe was improbable. They concluded that the USSR would continue to probe for Western weaknesses in Europe, as well as in Asia. To discourage these probes, the Americans quadrupled their military budget, feverishly built up the stockpiles of atomic bombs, and pushed a reluctant France and other NATO members to sanction the creation of West German armed forces.[72] Soviet observers and intelligence had no trouble monitoring the changing geopolitical landscape in Western Europe: namely, the integration of French and German coal and steel industries, the preparations for the recognition of the Federal Republic of Germany's sovereignty, and the plans to set up a "European army" with West German divisions as its core.[73] American assessments of Soviet intentions were generally correct. Cautious probes remained Stalin's signature policies, despite his verbal emulation of Mao's revolutionary romanticism.

U.S. intervention prevented North Korean plans for a quick "revolutionary" victory. Still, as Soviet archival evidence shows, Stalin had learned from the past and was prepared for a nasty surprise. On August 27, 1950, in a cable to the Czechoslovak Communist president, Klement Gottwald, the Soviet leader explained his view on the war in Asia. The Soviet Union, he argued, deliberately abstained from the crucial vote at the United Nations that proclaimed North Korea an aggressor state. This was a calculated move to get the Americans "entangled in the military intervention in Korea" in which the United States would "squander its military prestige and moral authority." If North Korea began to lose the war, then China would come to North Korea's assistance. And "America, as any other state, cannot cope with China having at its disposal large armed forces." A long and protracted war between China and the United States would be, in Stalin's opinion, a good thing. It would give the Soviet Union more time to grow in strength. Also, it would "distract the United States from Europe to the Far East." And "the third world war will be postponed for the indefinite term, and this would give the time necessary to consolidate socialism in Europe."[74]

Over the next two years, the Soviet leader enacted this scenario. He successfully persuaded Mao and the Chinese Communists to fight against the United States in Korea. He told them that the United States would not dare to escalate the war. He even boasted that the USSR was not afraid of confronting the Americans, because "together we will be stronger than the USA and England, while the other European capitalist states (with the exception of Germany which is unable to provide any assistance to the United States now) do not present a serious military threat."[75]

In reality, the cautious schemer was determined to avoid a premature clash with the United States in Asia and Europe. Stalin was very impressed by U.S. airpower, as were hundreds of Soviet military pilots who fought against the Americans in the skies over Korea. The Soviet aircraft industry and the development of radar and air defenses received an enormous boost in 1951–53 but continued to lag behind the United States.[76] The Soviet atomic arsenal consisted only of a very few bombs, and there was no means to deliver them to the United States. As Marshal Sergei Akhromeyev told diplomat Anatoly Dobrynin twenty-three years later, Stalin still had to rely on a Soviet non-nuclear response to an American nuclear attack. In practice, it meant that the Soviet military had to maintain an armored force in East Germany capable of delivering a lightning blow to NATO armies and occupying Western Europe all the way to the English Channel. According to Akhromeyev, Stalin believed that an armored threat would counter the American nuclear threat. In addition to this, Stalin directed all Central European satellites in January 1951 "to create a modern and powerful military force" within two to three years.[77] This auxiliary force would add to the credibility of the Soviet land superiority.

These Soviet military plans turned Germany into the major theater of a possible future war and enormously increased the strategic importance of the GDR. Along with the collapse of the Yalta international order and the revolutionary radicalism of Stalin and Mao in the Far East, this development heralded the need for change in Soviet policies for Germany. At first the GDR was left out of this crash campaign of military mobilization and production. Stalin still wanted to use the possibility of peaceful German reunification for various political goals: to aggravate discord in the NATO, delay and derail the process of West German rearmament, and cover up the military preparations in the East. Soviet propagandists exploited to the utmost the fact that several Nazi-era generals were involved in the efforts to create a West German army. In September 1951, Stalin and the

Politburo instructed the SED leadership to confront the Western powers with the proposal of "all-German elections aiming to create a unified, democratic, peaceful Germany."[78] It was a propaganda probe. The Kremlin never intended to hold such elections, since the Communists would have certainly lost them.

The East German leadership implemented this campaign with its habitual heavy-handedness. As both Norman Naimark and Hope Harrison argue, the GDR leaders were not mere pawns and transmitters of Moscow's will. Their unspoken goal was to build up the GDR as a "socialist" country, that is, to carry out the same purges and transformations that had been proceeding in other countries of Central Europe. The role of the provisional government, pending the negotiations with the West, had no appeal for them. And the plans of the European Defense Community (EDC) that involved West German armed forces gave Ulbricht and his colleagues new arguments to demand the full integration of the GDR into the Communist political-military bloc. In particular, in early 1952, they sought to exploit the forthcoming signing of the agreement by Western powers enhancing West Germany's sovereignty ("General Treaty") and the agreement on EDC as the moment for Moscow to act.[79]

The Soviet occupational authorities in East Germany (in October 1949, SMAG was renamed the Soviet Control Commission [SCC]), General Vasily Chuikov and Vladimir Semenov, believed it was vital to respond to Western developments by building up the GDR's legitimacy and by making its leadership appear to be independent of the USSR. Foreign Minister Andrei Vyshinsky, who replaced Molotov, however, did not want any drastic actions. He even expressed doubts about the authenticity of a copy of the "General Treaty" obtained by the East Germans. The ministry's memoranda to the Politburo continued to treat the GDR as a part of the "defeated state" and objected to recognizing it as an actor rather than the subject of the peace settlement in Germany. The last point indicated, remarkably, that even during the Korean War there were people in the Soviet leadership who continued to regard the Yalta international framework as validating the Soviet presence in Germany. There was no great desire in Moscow's diplomatic and military communities to recognize the sovereignty of the GDR.[80]

Stalin continued to deny, perhaps even to himself, that the Soviet Union had lost the strategic initiative on the German Question. Prodded by the SCC reports, he decided to stage one more dramatic act in his campaign for German reunification. On March 10, 1952, he sent a note to the three Western powers proposing new peace treaty terms. The future Germany would be created through free elections and become neutral, but with its own armed forces. Unfortunately, there are no sources into Stalin's thinking at that time. His previous policies, however, leave little doubt that this was an attempt to give a second life to the sputtering Soviet propaganda of German unity, undermine the Western alliance, and sow discord among West Germans. The detailed analysis of Soviet plans for Austria, which had long become a hostage of the German Question and Soviet military plans, also shows that Kremlin diplomacy at that time was just a camouflage for war preparations. But the new initiative failed to derail the plans for the European army. Western governments and the Federal Republic of Germany quickly rejected this note as a propaganda move.[81]

Days after that rejection, on April 7, 1952, Stalin revealed his real plans to the East German Communist leaders. The GDR, he responded, could now join the other "peoples' democracies" in making preparations for war. East German youth, subjected to antiwar propaganda, had now to be taught to get ready "to defend" their country against the West. "As soon as you've got any kind of army," he said to the East Germans, Western powers "will talk differently with you. You will get recognition and affection, since everybody likes force." Stalin proposed creating a comprehensive East German army: thirty divisions of infantry and marines, an air force, and a submarine fleet, with hundreds of tanks and thousands of artillery pieces. This army would be deployed along Western frontiers. Behind these forces, Stalin planned to deploy the Soviet army.[82]

During his second meeting with the leaders of the GDR, Stalin did more than reverse his previous policy. He revealed what he had never stopped thinking about since the beginning of the occupation. "The Americans," he said, "need their army in Western Germany to hold Western Europe in their hands. They say that they have their army in defense against us. But the real goal of this army is to control Europe." Stalin sounded gloomy and resigned. "The Americans will draw Western Germany into the Atlantic Pact. They will create West German troops. Adenauer is in the Americans' pocket. All ex-fascists and generals also are there." Finally, the Kremlin *vozhd* admitted stalemate in Germany. He told the East German Communists what they wanted to hear: "You must organize your own state. The line of demarcation between the Western and Eastern Germany should be regarded as a border, and not as a simple but as a dangerous border." In other words, Stalin began to treat the GDR not as a provisional arrangement but as a permanent strategic asset. Still, Stalin did not take the last step, closing the sector border with West Berlin. Burnt by his Berlin blockade fiasco, he only "recommended" that the movement of people across this border should be restricted. Western agents, he said, move too freely around the German Democratic Republic. They may go to extremes and assassinate Ulbricht and the SCC head, General Vasily Chuikov."[83]

Stalin's increasing age reduced his capacity to work, but his agile mind could still function with ferocious energy. For years he had planned to turn East

Germany into the frontline of a future war with the West. At the same time, true to his vision of German nationalism, he still pushed for appealing to the Social Democrats and nationalist segments of the West German population, in an attempt to undercut the support for the American military presence in the Federal Republic. "The propaganda campaign for German unity should continue at all times. You are now holding this weapon and should never lose your grip on it. We will also continue submitting proposals on the aspects of German unity in order to expose the Americans."[84]

Stalin's decisions of April 1952, historian Ruud van Dijk concludes, "resolved the basic contradiction of his German policy" between the realities in the zone and the proclaimed policies on Germany.[85] Simultaneously, they created other problems. In the following months, Ulbricht per agreement with Stalin shifted from a moderate method of Sovietization of the GDR to full-scale proclamation of "the dictatorship of the proletariat" and the crash course on the construction of socialism. On July 9, 1952, the Kremlin passed the Politburo decision that formally sanctioned the course for the "construction of socialism" in the GDR. Later, Molotov claimed that Ulbricht mistakenly interpreted this as the authorization for an *accelerated* course of the construction of socialism. Stalin, however, never objected to Ulbricht's actions. In any case, the SED leader felt he acted with Moscow's authorization, and he acted with zeal. All-out militarization of the GDR involved confiscations and arrests of saboteurs and denunciations of Western "warmongers" and "internal enemies." The regime crushed the private sector in commerce and production and embarked on a collectivization campaign in the countryside.

Even a much healthier economy, one not devastated by the war and Soviet looting, could not have fulfilled the astronomical production plans coming from Moscow. The results of the Stalin-Ulbricht new policy were disastrous: skyrocketing inflation, an agricultural crisis, and grossly distorted economic development. Making matters worse, Stalin did nothing to reduce the burden of East German reparations and other payments. By 1953, the GDR had paid more than 4 billion U.S. dollars in reparations but still owed the Soviet Union and Poland 2.7 billion dollars, or annual budget expenses of more than 211 million dollars. Also, the GDR continued to pay about 229 million dollars annually to cover Soviet occupational expenses in the GDR. Finally, Stalin, with the same unsentimental economy he displayed in dealing with the Chinese and Korean Communists (who paid in U.S. dollars for Soviet war matériel they used to combat the Americans in Korea), sold to the East German Communist state sixty-six plants and factories that the Soviets had earlier confiscated. The Soviets valued them in the amount of 180 million dollars, to be paid by cash or shipments of goods.[86]

In fact, the people of the GDR were much better off than the Soviet people. Inside the USSR, the costs of war preparations caused living standards to stagnate at an abysmally low level.[87] But East German citizens did not know how "lucky" they were in comparison to their Soviet comrades. They compared their standards with the lives of their West German counterparts. Before the crash militarization course, living standards in East Germany had been similar to those in West Germany. After the "economic miracle" took off in the Federal Republic in 1950 and 1951, the living conditions of West Germans began to advance rapidly, leaving the citizens of the GDR far behind. The United States gave generous economic and financial assistance to West Germany through the Marshall Plan and other programs. Most importantly, the U.S. consumer market was available to German goods. A combination of better economic opportunities in the West and the growing oppression and hardship in the East began to impel many young, professionally trained and educated people to leave the GDR. From January 1951 to April 1953, almost half a million people left the GDR for West Berlin and West Germany. Among them were professional workers, farmers, military conscripts, and even many members of the SED and the Union of Free German Youth. Among those who remained, the level of discontent grew. Walter Ulbricht became the object of popular resentment, even hatred.[88]

Stalin's policies in Germany in 1952 made sense for only one contingency— total war mobilization. Stalin's actions at the end of his life, as well as documented activities of his regime, suggest that the dictator believed in the inevitability of war. In the spring of 1952, simultaneous with the shift of German policy, the Kremlin leader ordered the creation of 100 air divisions of 10,000 midrange jet-propelled bombers. This number was almost double the amount that Soviet Air Force commanders believed was necessary for war needs. There were large-scale military preparations in the Siberian Far East and the Far North, including a study of the capacities for a large-scale invasion of Alaska. One wonders what would have happened had Stalin lived longer and tried to implement these fantastic plans.[89]

Stalin was losing his grip on German affairs. He simply had too many irons in the fire. Aside from military preparations, he was busy with a new round of murderous political intrigues, among them a purge of the secret services, investigations of "the Kremlin doctors' affair," orchestration of a public anti-Semitic campaign, and a plot that led to the purge of the state security bureaucracy and perhaps to elimination of Beria. Stalin also devoted time to his theoretical writings on the "economic problems of socialism" and on linguistics.[90] Meanwhile, the GDR leadership continued its march toward a political and economic crisis.

Stalin's death on March 5, 1953, brought the crisis of German policies to the surface. It also made possible a revision of many of Stalin's misguided and bankrupt policies.[91] Stalin's successors in the Politburo (renamed the Presidium in October 1952), in particular Molotov, Malenkov, and Beria, immediately proposed a new peace initiative to reduce the danger of war. Together with the Chinese leadership, they opened armistice talks with the United States on Korea. They also abrogated the policy of pressure on Turkey and allowed Russian women who had married foreigners to leave the Soviet Union. There were other international issues that the troika began to discuss, among them the neutrality option for Austria, the improvement of relations with Iran, and the future of the GDR. Taken together, these changes went far beyond mere propaganda.[92]

The new Soviet "peace initiative" was the result of the insecurity of the Kremlin leaders. Khrushchev recalled: "In the days leading up to Stalin's death we believed that America would invade the Soviet Union and we would go to war."[93] The gigantic U.S. military buildup, including the first thermonuclear test in November 1952, focused the Kremlin's attention on the threat of imminent clash with the United States. Stalin's successors wanted to avoid this clash and gain breathing space to build up Soviet defenses.

Another major impulse for changing the Kremlin's foreign policy came from the GDR, where the new policies produced a social and economic crisis. In March 1953, the SED leadership asked for Soviet permission to close sector borders with the West, in order to stop the flight to the West. Simultaneously, it appealed to Moscow for substantial economic assistance.[94] Later, at the Party Plenum in July, Molotov summarized the reasons for the crisis in East Germany as follows: "They took the crash course of industrialization and had excessively ambitious plan of construction. Besides, they pay the costs of occupation for our army, they pay reparations."[95] Bad signals also continued to come from West Germany. On April 18, the Committee of Information at the Soviet Foreign Ministry reported that the Adenauer government "significantly increased *revanchist* propaganda and scared the West German population with the threat from the East." Experts signaled to the Presidium that there were no specific policies designed to thwart the ratification of the Bonn and Paris treaties by the Bundestag and the Bundesrat, the two houses of the West German parliament.[96]

The Kremlin leadership waited almost three months to act on Germany. The delay may have stemmed from the fact that the new rulers faced other urgent problems. The war in Korea continued to cause the death of thousands of North Koreans and Chinese and presented a continuing danger for the escalation of hostilities. Nobody could guarantee that the widespread discontent among the Soviet people would not lead to protests and riots after Stalin's death. According to the new head of the Soviet government, Georgy Malenkov, the main task of the new leadership was "to avoid confusion in the ranks of our party, in the working class, in the country."[97]

Molotov, once again the foreign minister, took the lead in evaluating the German Question. He recalled Vladimir Semenov from the GDR to Moscow to participate in the Foreign Ministry's review of German policies. Semenov, Yakov Malik, Grigory Pushkin, and Mikhail Gribanov drafted one set of proposals after another. Speaking in July 1953, Molotov said that "the facts, we have learned recently, made it absolutely obvious that the political and economic situation in the German Democratic Republic became unfavorable." The Foreign Ministry archives, however, reveal that he and his experts quibbled over peripheral issues.[98] Semenov, the most knowledgeable of the experts, dared to suggest that the Soviets should end the occupation status of the GDR and sign "a treaty on friendship, cooperation and mutual assistance" with Ulbricht.[99] None of the experts dared to mention Ulbricht's policies of the "accelerated construction of socialism" in East Germany.

There is no record of internal discussions, but by all indications Molotov never wavered from his view that German peace talks were a zero-sum game between East and West. He agreed with Semenov, who suggested creating "more favorable conditions for the socialist construction" in the GDR by reducing reparations and other economic obligations to the USSR.[100] On May 5, Molotov proposed to the Presidium that the GDR should stop reparation payments after 1954. At the same time, Molotov was categorically against closing the sector border in Berlin, as the GDR leadership had suggested.[101]

On the surface, Molotov, Malenkov, and Beria, the leading troika in charge of foreign affairs, had few disagreements. In reality, beneath this veneer of unity, rivalry was brewing inside the Kremlin. After Stalin's death, Beria assumed the leadership of the Ministry of the Interior, the result of the merger of the two agencies of secret police and intelligence. He organized a brain trust among lieutenants that helped him to come up with a startling number of initiatives on many issues of domestic and foreign policy. From the start, Beria distanced himself from Stalin's bloody legacy and began exposing his crimes to incredulous members of the Central Committee. Inside the Presidium, he sought support from Malenkov and Khrushchev, hoping to outmaneuver them both. By contrast, he regarded Molotov, the man with the greatest authority among the party elite, as a threat and wanted to undercut his prestige and policies.[102]

The evidence on Beria's views on Germany at that time is vague. In his diary, written more than ten years later, Semenov concludes that both Beria and Stalin treated the GDR as a tool in the struggle for Germany. Beria only "wanted to accelerate this struggle in the summer of 1953."[103] Anatoly Sudoplatov, a senior officer of Soviet intelligence, recalls that on the eve of May Day in 1953, Beria ordered him to test the feasibility of unifying Germany. He told Sudoplatov that "the best way to strengthen our world position would be to create a neutral, unified Germany run by a coalition government. Germany would be the balancing factor between American and Soviet interests in Western Europe." According to this scheme, the GDR would become an autonomous province in the newly unified Germany. "As immediate steps, Beria intended, without informing Molotov's Foreign Ministry, to use his intelligence contacts for unofficial approaches to prominent politicians in Western Europe."[104] It is not clear whether Beria also had in mind to establish a back channel with the United States.

On May 6, Beria sent a report to Malenkov, Molotov, Khrushchev, Bulganin, Kaganovich, and Voroshilov concerning the catastrophic flight of refugees from the GDR: 220,000 had left since 1952, including over 3,000 members of the SED and the Union of Free German Youth. In contrast to other reports, this one blamed the exodus on the GDR leadership's policies. Beria proposed asking the Soviet Control Commission in the GDR to present recommendations on how to reduce the exodus "in order to make the necessary recommendations to our German friends."[105]

At this point, Ulbricht committed a huge error that undercut his support in Moscow. On May 5, he declared that the GDR had "entered a new stage of a dictatorship of the proletariat." This socialist rhetoric from East Berlin came at the time when Winston Churchill proposed in the House of Commons holding a conference with the new Soviet leadership. In the eyes of Beria, Malenkov, Molotov, and some other members of the Kremlin ruling group, the new opportunities to split NATO unity stood in open conflict with Ulbricht's course.[106] This galvanized Presidium discussions on the GDR. On May 14, the Presidium, at Molotov's suggestion, instructed Ulbricht to refrain from this provocative rhetoric.[107] Simultaneously, Molotov and the Foreign Ministry experts acknowledged the facts presented in Beria's report.[108] In his internal memo, Semenov agreed that the collectivization of East German agriculture and the practices of mass arrests and repression of large groups should be stopped. He even proposed a partial amnesty. At the same time, the main Soviet interest, in his opinion, was to strengthen, not undermine the GDR Communist leadership.[109] At the Presidium meeting on May 20, Molotov joined in the criticism of the GDR leadership. It appears that he swallowed his doubts and did not want to cause a split in the collective leadership.[110] Ulbricht's days seemed to be numbered. Scholars now agree that May–June 1953 was the only time when the Soviet leadership considered a radical change in German policy.

Suddenly, a debate within the collective leadership erupted. At its center was the question: What kind of Germany did the Soviet Union need? On May 27, at the Presidium meeting, Molotov recommended that the SED should "not carry out an accelerated construction of socialism." No minutes of the meeting are available, but after Beria's arrest, Molotov told the Party Plenum that Beria interrupted with a remark: "Why do we need this socialism in Germany, what kind of socialism is there? All we need is a bourgeois Germany if it is peaceful." According to Molotov, other members of the leadership were astonished: they did not believe that bourgeois Germany, the same country that had unleashed two world wars, could be peaceful. Molotov concluded: "How could a sober-thinking Marxist, one who stands on the positions close to socialism or Soviet power, believe in some kind of a bourgeois Germany that would allegedly be peaceful and under the control of four powers?"[111] Khrushchev and Bulganin sided with Molotov.

In his memoirs, Mikoyan recalled that Beria and Malenkov seemed to be in agreement on this issue. "They aimed to gain the leading role in the Presidium, and suddenly there was such a defeat!" Beria allegedly telephoned Bulganin after the meeting and told him he would lose his post of defense minister if he aligned himself with Khrushchev. Beria admitted in his letter from prison that he treated Khrushchev and Bulganin with "unacceptable rudeness and insolence" at the meeting on May 27.[112]

A careful reconstruction of the patchy evidence and the logic of events indicates that on May 27 not only Beria and Malenkov, but also Molotov, Khrushchev, and the rest of the Kremlin leadership, voted for the radical changes in the GDR. Later, when the collective leadership got rid of Beria, they decided that the "treason" on the German Question must be added to the list of his crimes.[113]

The outcome of the discussions within the collective leadership was the state decree of June 2, "On Measures to Improve the Health of the Political Situation in the GDR." This document differed in content and tone from all the Foreign Ministry drafts, went much further than the SCC recommendations of May 18, and incorporated almost verbatim most of Beria's memo.[114] It stated that the main reason for the crisis in the GDR was "the mistaken course of the construction of socialism in East Germany without real internal and external conditions." The document implicitly recognized Stalin's responsibility for this policy and proposed a sweeping New Course that called for the end of collectivization, a slowdown of "the extraordinary intense pace of development of heavy industry," and a "sharp increase of the production of mass consumption goods." It also stipulated a cut in "administrative and special expenses," stabilization of the

GDR currency, a stop to the arrests and the release of arrested people, and the end of persecution of churches and the restoration of confiscated church property.[115]

The New Course reversed Stalin's policies that aimed at converting East Germany into a bulwark for an imminent war with the West. The future of the GDR was now linked to "the peaceful settlement of fundamental international problems." The Kremlin leadership instructed the GDR leadership "to put the tasks of the political struggle for restoration of national unity of Germany and for conclusion of a peace treaty in the center of attention of the broad masses of German people, both in the GDR and in West Germany."[116]

On June 2–4, an SED delegation secretly arrived in Moscow to receive instructions on the policy change. Ulbricht, sensing he was in danger, attempted to propose cosmetic reforms. At that moment, however, the news about the riots in Bulgaria and the unrest in Czechoslovakia reached the Presidium; this seemed to tilt the Kremlin leadership even more in favor of an immediate reversal of Stalin's policies for the European satellites.[117] According to Otto Grotewohl's notes, Beria said that "we all made the mistake [in 1952]; there are no accusations." Another East German witness, however, recorded Beria's contempt and anger with regard to Ulbricht. Malenkov also was on record saying: "If we don't correct the situation now, a catastrophe will happen." The Kremlin leaders radically scaled down Stalin's plans for the GDR's armament. "No airplanes; no tanks," jotted Grotewohl in his notes of the meeting.[118]

Worst of all, Moscow ordered the SED leadership to introduce the New Course immediately. The GDR leaders cabled home from Moscow the instruction to remove the literature on the "construction of socialism" in East Germany from libraries and bookstores. The Presidium appointed Vladimir Semenov to be high commissioner in East Germany and sent him back on the same plane with the SED delegation to implement the Kremlin orders. The new instructions put the GDR leadership in an impossible political situation. After a year of total mobilization and extreme Stalinist propaganda, they had to beat a retreat immediately, with no time to save face. Molotov even recommended that the press publish "frank criticism" of the SED policies since July 1952.[119] It is astounding how blind the Soviet leaders were to the provocative nature of these measures.

After the arrest of Beria, Khrushchev blamed him for the attempt "to sell out" the GDR. Later, he also claimed that Malenkov was in cahoots with Beria. In his defense, Malenkov made a significant remark clarifying his position: "During the discussion of the German question I believed that in the existing international situation, when we began the big political campaign, for the sake of the issue of reunification of Germany, we must not put forward the task of construction of

socialism in the democratic Germany."[120] The broader historical context highlights the radical potential of the New Course. The first months after Stalin's
death were a time of high uncertainty, but also of new opportunities. On June 3,
British prime minister Winston Churchill hinted to Soviet ambassador Yakov
Malik that he was prepared to begin confidential talks with the new Soviet leadership like the ones he had had with Stalin. He informed Malik that he was about to
meet with Eisenhower to sell him on the idea of an immediate summit of great
powers to improve the international situation. Churchill said that he believed that
he would "succeed to improve international relations and create the atmosphere
of greater confidence for at least the next 3–5 years."[121]

Beria and Malenkov seemed to be trying to explore possibilities for relaxation
of the Cold War. Beria, in particular, was inclined to use secret police channels to
achieve foreign policy goals. He sought to establish a secret back channel to the
Yugoslav leader Marshal Tito, who was still vilified by Soviet propaganda as the
leader of the "fascist clique." In a desperate note from prison, Beria reminded
Malenkov that he "prepared the mission on Yugoslavia" with his consent and
advice. The note also mentioned another "mission" in France, implying a request
for Pierre Cot, a Soviet agent of influence, to approach the French prime minister,
Pierre Mendes-France, with the proposal to start secret talks on the German
Question. At that time, France's public opinion and elites were split over the
issues of the "European army" and rearmament of West Germany.[122]

Meanwhile, the crisis in the GDR exploded and changed the whole situation.
On June 16, workers in East Berlin demonstrated against the GDR regime. Mass
rallies quickly became a political uprising all over the GDR; crowds from West
Berlin crossed into East Berlin and joined the protesters. The regime lost control
of the situation. The use of Soviet troops on June 17 quickly dispersed the crowd
and restored order in the capital; gradually the situation in the GDR stabilized. It
was the first serious disruption to shake the Soviet bloc after Stalin's death.[123]

At first, it was not clear how these events affected the Soviet leadership and its
consensus on the New Course in the GDR. In his memoirs, Sudoplatov claimed
that even after the revolt in the GDR, Beria "did not give up on the idea of German
reunification." The demonstration of Soviet power "might only increase the
chances of the USSR to reach a compromise with Western powers." He sent
his agents to West Germany to establish confidential contacts with politicians
there.[124] Simultaneously, Marshal Sokolovsky, his deputy high commissioner
Semenov, and Pavel Yudin sent a detailed report on the uprising to the Soviet leadership with withering criticism of Ulbricht. The SCC leadership recommended relieving him of the responsibilities of deputy prime minister of the GDR

and "allow[ing] him to concentrate his attention" on party work. The position of general secretary had to be abolished, and the party secretariat had to be reduced in size.[125]

This last proposal accidentally touched on the very essence of the power struggle in the Kremlin that was about to come to a head. In late May 1953, Nikita Khrushchev, then the head of the Central Committee's Secretariat, decided that Beria was too dangerous. He began to suspect that the secret police chief was preparing to stab a knife in his back and undermine the Party Secretariat, Khrushchev's power base. There were also signals that Beria was acting behind the back of Khrushchev in domestic party politics. Khrushchev realized he had to act against Beria. This realization might have dawned on him after the Presidium discussion of the GDR on May 27. Eventually, even Malenkov revealed his misgivings about Beria and joined the plot against him.[126]

The arrest of Beria on June 26 during the meeting of the Presidium of the Council of Ministers profoundly changed the power balance inside the Kremlin. Khrushchev claimed to be the heroic organizer of Beria's removal. Soviet elites, including the military, acclaimed him as a savior from the years of terror. At the July Party Plenum, convened to denounce Beria, Khrushchev triumphantly proclaimed the primacy of the party apparatus over the state bureaucracies, above all over the secret police. Malenkov, who remained the head of the state, solemnly declared that he never intended to be the number one and that there would be always a "collective leadership."[127]

Soviet officials in Germany continued to send reports criticizing Ulbricht and his apparatus for lack of political courage and initiative during the uprising.[128] This criticism, however, no longer received a sympathetic hearing and support within the Soviet leadership. Khrushchev respected Ulbricht and believed he was a good comrade. More importantly, Khrushchev and Molotov publicly denounced the idea of a "unified and neutral Germany" as Beria's conspiracy. Khrushchev declared that Beria "revealed himself on the German question as an *agent-provocateur*, not a Communist, when he proposed to renounce the construction of socialism, to make concessions to the West. Then we asked him: "What does it mean? It means that 18 million Germans would pass under the custody of Americans. And how could there be a neutral democratic bourgeois Germany between Americans and us? If a treaty is not guaranteed by force, then it is worth nothing, and everybody will laugh at us and our naiveté." The majority of the Soviet party and state elites who attended the Plenum applauded Khrushchev. Most of them had lived through the war and shared Khrushchev's strong feelings that reunifying Germany on a "bourgeois" foundation would undo the victory of 1945. Others considered East Germany as the jewel of the Soviet bloc because of its role in the Soviet military-industrial complex. On behalf of the Soviet atomic project, its leader, Avraami Zaveniagin, told the Plenum that "much uranium is extracted in the GDR, perhaps no less than Americans have at their disposal." He spoke about Soviet dependence on uranium from the Wismut project in lower Saxony.[129]

The new winds immediately affected Soviet policies in the GDR. Molotov's influence on Soviet foreign policy was on the rise, and Beria's initiatives, not only in Germany but also in Yugoslavia and Austria, were automatically disavowed and repealed.[130] The Politburo firmly rejected the proposal by SCC authorities to re-place Ulbricht and remove the Party Secretariat from state affairs as "untimely." In Molotov's opinion, "Semenov drifted to the right." Sensing the change, Ul-bricht immediately cracked down on his domestic rivals. SED Politburo members Rudolf Herrnstadt and Wilhelm Zeissner had earned the highest praise from the Soviet Control Commission during the uprising, and, in the opinion of Hope Harrison, "if the Beria episode had not intervened, [they] may have succeeded in their efforts to remove Ulbricht from power." In this new climate, however, the Soviet leadership supported Ulbricht's decision to oust them, because they, espe-cially Zeissner, were Beria's protégés.[131]

American behavior during the revolt in East Germany contributed to the shift in Kremlin policies. On the one hand, the United States made maximum propa-ganda use of the revolt, supplied food to East Berliners, and began to push for "free elections" as a precondition for German reunification. On the other hand, the United States and the other Western powers did not come to the rescue of the East Germans with military power. Even if the West had indeed prepared "the Day X" in the GDR, as some Soviet analysts were quick to assert, Western leaders did not dare to go all the way in supporting the rebellion.[132]

The entire "peaceful initiative" that justified the New Course in the GDR came to a halt after Beria's arrest and the revolt in East Germany. Indeed, it was impossible to reduce military forces in Europe without a negotiated solution of the German Question, the conundrum that Soviet leaders would not be able to resolve for the next thirty-five years. The rise of Khrushchev, the survival of Ulbricht, and the demise of the New Course destroyed any opportunity for a turnabout in Soviet policies on East Germany. Millions of Germans had to live through several more decades of the Cold War, waiting for another miracle to allow them to be sovereign, free, and reunited.

(CHAPTER 4)
KREMLIN POLITICS AND
"PEACEFUL COEXISTENCE,"
1953-1957

Around the end of 1955, Molotov instructed one of his staff
members to find among Lenin's writings some reference to the
idea that naïveté in foreign policy was tantamount to a crime.
Obviously, the idea was to use such a quotation
against Khrushchev.
—Recollections of Oleg Troyanovsky, Soviet diplomat

The position of Molotov is erroneous, profoundly mistaken,
and does not correspond to the interests of our state.
—Gromyko, on Molotov's diplomacy at the July 1955
Party Plenum

After Stalin's death, a "new" Soviet foreign policy emerged that sought to reopen the diplomatic space that Moscow had enjoyed before the start of the Cold War. In February 1956, at the Twentieth Party Congress, the Soviet leadership renounced expectations of imminent war. The Stalinist thesis of the inevitability of a period of wars and revolutions gave way to a new thesis: long-term "peaceful coexistence" and nonmilitary competition between the capitalist and Communist systems.

However, détente in East-West relations did not occur. And, in fact, the Cold War got a second wind. Mutual fears and mistrust remained high between the two opposing blocs. Some Soviet memoirists give the opinion that the lack of a flexible and positive Western response to the new Soviet foreign policy was a missed opportunity to reduce Cold War tensions.[1] Indeed, President Dwight D. Eisenhower, Secretary of State John Foster Dulles, and the majority of American Kremlin-watchers regarded the changes in the Kremlin and the new Soviet diplomatic flexibility not as an opportunity but as a threat. American policy makers were concerned that the rhetoric of "peaceful coexistence" could disrupt their plans to build up a European center of power, which, together with Great Britain, would bear the burden of "containing" the Soviet bloc. Domestic politics and the culture of anti-Communism contributed to the reluctance of the Eisenhower administration to negotiate with the Soviet Union.[2]

A closer look at the Soviet side reveals that it was also not ready for negotiations and compromises. New documents reveal that many of the Kremlin rulers, despite the shift to peaceful coexistence, retained some basic elements of the revolutionary-imperial paradigm and continuity with Stalin's foreign policy. The new Kremlin rulers were eager to reassert the Soviet position as a global revolutionary leader and began to build alliances with revolutionary-nationalist leaders and groups in the Middle East, South and Southeast Asia, Africa, and Latin America. The new documents also demonstrate that the relationships among Stalin's successors in 1953–57 had a significant impact on the Kremlin's decision making regarding Soviet policies within the bloc as well as toward the United States and its allies. Soviet politics after Stalin's death favored revolutionary-imperial discourse—it was politically suicidal to be seen as soft on Western imperialism. The members of the collective leadership competed among themselves to win support among the party and state elites, offering strategies of strengthening and expanding Soviet power and international influence.[3]

WHO WILL TALK TO THE WEST?

The Kremlin oligarchs who assumed power after Stalin's death in March 1953 and proclaimed the collective leadership were the ultimate survivors.[4] They had learned to wage a permanent struggle for their positions between the suspicious tyrant and the army of lesser-rank party and state officials, the political nomenklatura that looked up to them with both reverence and envy. Throughout his regime, Stalin ensured that no oligarch felt secure at any time. At the Party Plenum in October 1952, Stalin denounced Molotov and Mikoyan as traitors and possibly Western spies. Simultaneously, he dramatically expanded the Politburo (it now became the Presidium), including in it a large group of younger party officials, probably a threat that Stalin could at any time replace his old lieutenants with younger bureaucrats.[5]

The oligarchs also learned to respond to Stalin's machinations and rule in his absence. After the murderous "Leningrad affair," the oligarchic pact of mutual tolerance deepened.[6] Even before Stalin died, the oligarchs cut all the nooses he had put around their necks. Molotov and Mikoyan regained their power over foreign policy and trade; the "Mingrelian affair," a corruption investigation in Georgia directed against Beria, was cancelled; and the younger nomenklatura members were excluded from the Presidium. At the decisive moment of power transfer, their common interest in survival overrode individual rivalries and policy disagreements. Some oligarchs genuinely feared that any disunity would lead to the loss of control and the caving in to external pressures.[7]

Oligarchic rule, due to its consensual nature, rarely favors innovation and change. Yet, as we saw in the previous chapter, the collective leadership moved with alacrity to adopt new domestic and foreign policies. The oligarchs lacked legitimacy and needed to demonstrate their initiative and determination at home and abroad. Next to the towering images and statues of Stalin, the collective leadership did not look terribly impressive. Moscow professor Sergei Dmitriev wrote in his diary of his impressions at seeing the collective leadership on a home TV set in November 1955: "The entire Presidium consists of boring and grey personalities. When one sees them, it comes to mind that the revolution had occurred long, long ago, all revolutionary cadres were exterminated, and bureaucratic nonentities triumphed. There is nothing live, spontaneous, and humane in what they say, not a word, not a single memorable gesture. Everybody looks featureless, faceless, and erased. One only misses the inscription at the entrance to Dante's Inferno."[8]

Stalin's successors could not rule by terror and had to win the support of party officials, the military, the secret police, and other state bureaucracies. In the party and bureaucracy, everybody knew that collective leadership was a transitional phase of Kremlin politics; one of the oligarchs would eventually have to become the winner in the coming succession struggle. An editor of the leading literary journal expressed this mood in his diary: "Collective leadership—and what about the conductor?"[9]

After Beria's arrest, Khrushchev quickly moved into the position of conductor. Malenkov, however, remained the chairman of the Council of Ministers, a position of high visibility. Many in the country continued to regard him as Stalin's successor. Speaking to the Supreme Soviet on August 8, 1953, Malenkov announced several sensational policies to radically improve the living standards of Soviet people within "the next two or three years." For the first time since 1928, the state pledged to increase investments in agriculture and the consumer-related economy at the expense of the military-industrial complex and the machine-building sector. Malenkov also announced the reduction by half of stifling agricultural taxes, as well as the increase in the size of peasant household and private plots. These measures almost doubled the disposable income of the peasantry within one year. Serious problems with food continued to plague the USSR, but at least peasants stopped cutting down their orchards and killing their cows to avoid exorbitant property taxes. Instead, they again began to sell meat and milk in marketplaces. Malenkov became their favorite leader since Lenin, as *muzhiks* across Russia drank to his health the glasses filled to the brim with village moonshine.[10]

In his speech, Malenkov also made the dramatic announcement that the USSR had its own hydrogen bomb. Soviet nuclear physicists, including one of the inventors of the bomb, Andrei Sakharov, listened to Malenkov's speech at the testing ground in Kazakhstan with mixed feelings of pride and anxiety. In fact, the bomb would be successfully tested a week later. The announcement had the desired effect on the public; Malenkov appeared as the leader of a nuclear super-power, both in the eyes of foreign leaders and in those of the domestic audience.[11] Khrushchev interpreted this speech as an attempt at personal popularity at his expense. He especially could never forget or forgive Malenkov for usurping his role as a major spokesman for the peasants and for agricultural affairs. In September 1953, Khrushchev took back this role at the Party Plenum convened to approve new agricultural policies. Five months later, he convened another plenum and presented there the plan for cultivating virgin lands in Kazakhstan, a grand program promising a quick end to the chronic food crisis. This turned out to be a costly ecological disaster, but, as William Taubman wrote, "in the meantime he was displaying the leadership that Malenkov lacked."[12]

In September 1953, Khrushchev became the Communist Party's first secretary. Poorly educated, crude, and volatile, and at the same time earthly, accessible, quick-witted, and enormously energetic, Khrushchev appealed to the peasant-stock Soviet officials as "one of their own." While Malenkov criticized the party control over economic and cultural matters and sought to broaden his base among industrial managers and scientific and cultural elites, Khrushchev quickly established full command over the party structures and the secret police, now called the Committee for State Security (KGB). His crony Ivan Serov, former emissary of Stalin's secret police in Poland and East Germany, became the first KGB chairman. Khrushchev used these sinews of power to push Malenkov out of the limelight, cut his access to information, and even blackmail him by disclosing his role in implementation of the nefarious "Leningrad affair." Even Malenkov's personal chancery became part of the central party apparatus controlled by Khrushchev. Khrushchev chaired the Presidium and dominated in public appearances of the collective leadership.[13]

The succession struggle in the era of the Cold War involved the question of international leadership. The Soviet political class and a wide segment of Soviet citizens regarded statesmanship as an almost supernatural quality. Who among the collective leadership would try to wear Stalin's mantle of world statesman and talk to the leaders of other great powers? Who would combine perceptiveness, wisdom, and an understanding of long-term world trends to defend Soviet interests in the international arena? The winner in the Kremlin games would not only gain absolute control over the enormous party and state bureaucracy; he would lead the Communist world and "progressive humanity" in a fierce struggle with the capitalist world.

An early summit, as proposed by Winston Churchill in May 1953, might have undermined Molotov's seniority in foreign affairs and put Malenkov as the head of state into the international limelight. By the end of 1954, however, Malenkov's window of opportunity was closing fast. Khrushchev began to argue before the other Presidium members that Malenkov would not be tough enough to succeed in future negotiations with the West. This argument justified Malenkov's removal on January 22, 1955, from the post of chairman of the Council of Ministers. The Party Plenum approved this decision nine days later.[14]

At the plenum, Khrushchev and Molotov for the first time revealed to the party elite that Malenkov had supported Beria on "selling" the GDR in May 1953. Khrushchev told the plenum that in the spring of 1953 he "used to say to other comrades, in particular to comrade Molotov: now Churchill is so terribly eager to have a meeting and I, honestly, fear that if he comes to meet face to face with Malenkov, then Malenkov may get cold feet and surrender." The bottom line was clear: the premier lacked backbone and therefore could not represent the Soviet Union at a summit with capitalist leaders. In his memoirs, Khrushchev is blunt: "We had to replace Malenkov. The talks in Geneva required another kind of person."[15] It turned out that only Khrushchev himself was that kind of person.

Khrushchev, professing to be loyal to the collective leadership principle, refused to combine the positions of first secretary and chairman of the Council of Ministers. Instead, he proposed his friend, Minister of Defense Nikolai Bulganin, for the latter position.[16] This choice demonstrated the hypocrisy of Khrushchev's earlier criticism of Malenkov: the new head of government cut a notoriously weak figure. Stalin considered him a harmless enough personality to entrust him with the armed forces (the *vozhd* preferred to give such crucial power to a weak character, fearing a potential Bonaparte). With a partner like this, Khrushchev's leadership would not be challenged. At the same time, in February 1955, Khrushchev acquired another crucial position as the head of the Supreme Defense Council, a permanent body in charge of defense matters and the armed forces. Among the council's members were the new minister of defense, Marshal Georgy Zhukov, a staunch ally of Khrushchev, and Vyacheslav Malyshev, the head of the Ministry for the Medium Machine-Building, a name invented for camouflage and meaning the nuclear complex. In effect, Khrushchev became the commander in chief of the Soviet Union.[17] From this point on, this power position would be inherited by subsequent general secretaries of the party, from Leonid Brezhnev to Mikhail Gorbachev.

His new power base allowed Khrushchev to interfere in foreign affairs and security policies, fields he was unfamiliar with. Earlier he had opposed some elements of the "peace offensive" because they bore the imprimatur of his rivals. Now he began to return to some of Beria's and Malenkov's foreign policy initiatives that he had earlier branded as treasonous. This opened the way for the most productive, reformist, and moderate phase in Soviet foreign policy in years. Yet, for a while, the Kremlin oligarchs continued to function as the collective leadership. Anastas Mikoyan, without leadership ambitions of his own, played a useful role as a trusted and loyal mentor of the first secretary on foreign affairs. Also, as historian Elena Zubkova observes, "Malenkov, a man of compromise, counterbalanced the impulsive and brusque Khrushchev." Presidium newcomers Zhukov, Matvei Saburov, and Mikhail Pervukhin actively participated in the decision-making process on foreign affairs.[18]

Molotov, however, remained the staunchest conservative critic of the foreign policy initiatives now pushed by Khrushchev. Since the fall of 1954, Molotov and Khrushchev had stood on opposite sides on almost every single issue, from the virgin lands to control over defense issues.[19] The struggle for supremacy between the two began in earnest during the talks on Austrian neutrality during February–April 1955. The Austrian government feared sharing the fate of the divided Germany and approached the Kremlin with an offer to negotiate a separate agreement on the end of Soviet occupation.[20] Molotov argued against it. "We cannot afford to withdraw Soviet troops from Austria," echoed a secret memorandum from senior diplomats in November 1953, "since it would actually mean placing Austria in the hands of the Americans and weakening our positions in Central and South Central Europe." Khrushchev, by contrast, argued that Austrian neutrality would weaken NATO, and the Presidium majority agreed with him. After the Soviet-Austrian agreement was reached, the triumphant first secretary took advantage of an informal moment at a reception to shake his finger at Molotov's deputies from the Foreign Ministry. From now on, he said, they had to take the cues not from their boss but from "the Party leadership."[21]

The visit of the Soviet official delegation to Yugoslavia (May 26–June 2, 1955) dealt a final blow to Molotov's role in foreign affairs. Khrushchev, Bulganin, and Georgy Zhukov, now minister of defense, wanted to repair the Soviet-Yugoslav split and were ready to apologize for Stalin's anti-Tito campaign in 1948–1953. They believed that a rapprochement with Yugoslavia would bring this country back into the Soviet sphere and enhance Moscow's geopolitical positions in Southern Europe and the Balkans. In Molotov's view, however, the Tito regime would never be a responsible partner of the USSR. Armed with quotations from Lenin's works, Molotov claimed that anyone praising the Yugoslav leadership "could not be a Leninist." Molotov doggedly fought against this trip and was not even included in the delegation.[22] The crux of the matter became who, Molotov or Khrushchev, would define what a "Leninist" meant in foreign policy. The gaping rift in the Presidium forced Khrushchev to turn to the plenum of the Central Committee for support against the obstinate foreign minister.

The Party Plenum took place on July 4–12, 1955, on the eve of the Geneva conference with the leaders of the United States, Great Britain, and France—the first summit of the great powers in ten years. The plenum turned out to be a remarkably frank discussion of Soviet foreign policy and its underlying motives. For the first time, Presidium oligarchs shared with the broader party and state elites the intimate details of Kremlin politics. Khrushchev knew that in the eyes of these elites Molotov was the man who had worked with Lenin and Stalin. He and his supporters, therefore, chose to attack Molotov's professional and Bolshevik authority.

Khrushchev cited in great detail the Presidium debates on the Austrian question. Molotov, he said, absurdly claimed that there could be another *Anschluss* of Austria by West Germany. He insisted that the Soviet Union must reserve the right to reintroduce its troops into Austria.[23] The Yugoslav Question touched on the ideological core of the Soviet view of the Cold War. The Kremlin's decision to recognize Yugoslavia as "truly socialist" meant that Stalin's policies were wrong and that Moscow's absolute authority to lead the Communist camp could be questioned. Molotov viewed this as the beginning of a dangerous slippery slope for world Communism and Soviet supremacy. His main thesis was that the Yugoslav version of "nationally oriented socialism" could spread to other Communist parties. Molotov warned that this could lead to the loss of Moscow's control over Poland and other countries of Eastern Europe.[24]

Molotov's resistance to the rapprochement with Yugoslavia, Khrushchev and his allies asserted, proved that the foreign minister had become dogmatic and did not understand Soviet security interests. Bulganin told the assembly that Yugoslavia returning to the Soviet bloc would give the Soviet army and navy excellent positions on the Adriatic Sea. Soviet forces then would be able to threaten "the vital lines of communications of the Anglo-American military forces," including the Suez Canal. Khrushchev reinforced these arguments."[25]

Before this plenum, the Soviet leaders blamed the Soviet-Yugoslav split of 1948 on "the Beria-Abakumov gang" (Viktor Abakumov was the head of SMERSH and MGB).[26] But during the plenum, Khrushchev suddenly remarked that the responsibility for the Soviet-Yugoslav split fell "on Stalin and Molotov." A remarkably frank exchange followed:

MOLOTOV: That's new. We signed the letter [to the Yugoslavs] on behalf of the Central Committee.

KHRUSHCHEV: Without asking the Central Committee.

MOLOTOV: This is not true.

KHRUSHCHEV: This is exactly true.

MOLOTOV: Now you can say whatever comes into your head.

KHRUSHCHEV: I am a member of the Presidium, but no one asked for my opinion.[27]

The split with Yugoslavia, Khrushchev told the delegates, was only one in the series of costly errors that Stalin and Molotov had made after 1945. In a startling assertion, the first secretary suggested that these errors may have helped to trigger the Cold War. "We started the Korean war and even now still have to sort things out." "Who needed that war?" asked Khrushchev rhetorically. Khrushchev's impromptu barb was so provocative that it was edited out of the printed version of the plenum transcripts.[28]

At the plenum, Molotov was deposed as an authority in foreign affairs, although he remained the foreign minister until June 1956. From now on the mantle of senior statesman passed to Khrushchev. For a while, Khrushchev still felt uncertain about this new role and sought to share responsibility with others. The delegation to the Geneva summit of four great powers in July 1955 consisted of Bulganin as the formal head, Khrushchev, Molotov, and Zhukov. Publicly they behaved as a group of equals. Eisenhower and other Western politicians, however, quickly figured out that Khrushchev was the real boss. From now on they knew whom the West should talk to in the Kremlin.

"NEW FOREIGN POLICY"

The Kremlin oligarchs observed the world through the lenses inherited from Stalin. Like Stalin, they felt inferior and insecure in relation to the United States. From their vantage point, the Americans were busy encircling the USSR with military bases and installing pro-American regimes (the coup of August 1953 in Iran that removed Dr. Mohammad Mossadeq from power was just one example). They also knew that John Foster Dulles hoped that the unrelenting pressure on the USSR after Stalin's death would "lead to disintegration" of Soviet domination over the countries of Central Europe.[29] Troyanovsky recalled that "Khrushchev constantly feared that the United States would compel the Soviet Union and its allies to retreat in some region of the world."[30]

At the same time, the new leaders drew different conclusions from their observations. Khrushchev, Molotov, Malenkov, and other oligarchs recognized what Stalin, in his hubris, could not. From the Berlin blockade to the Korean War, Soviet policies created fears of a Soviet blitzkrieg among Western Europeans and thus laid the foundation for NATO. Now the Soviet leaders wanted to dismantle this foundation, reduce anti-Soviet fears among the middle classes of Western Europe, and encourage pacifist elements within NATO member countries.

The failure of Molotov's diplomacy during 1954 triggered a rethinking of Soviet international behavior in the Kremlin. After a majority of Communists and Gaullists in the French Assembly wrecked the plans for the "European Army" (European Defense Community), NATO members agreed on November 23, 1954, in Paris to accept West Germany as a new member. This move firmly anchored West Germany in the Western alliance. The need for a new foreign policy in Europe became evident to the Kremlin leadership.[31] The incomplete record of the Kremlin discussions, recorded by Vladimir Malin, head of the Central Committee General Department, indicates that the new foreign policy began as the ad hoc effort of the collective leadership to correct the mistakes of Stalin's course. Later, however, it developed its own momentum and conceptual foundations. Andrei Alexandrov-Agentov, a veteran diplomat, recalled that Khrushchev, Mikoyan, and Malenkov were "the initiators of revision of Stalinist traditions in foreign policy and creation of an approach to new world problems that was innovative to a certain degree."[32]

According to Alexandrov-Agentov, a new approach "consisted of three main elements: to prop up to the maximum and tie to the Soviet Union the 'people's democracies' of Eastern and Central Europe; to create, wherever possible, a neutral buffer between the two opposing military political blocs; and to gradually establish economic and other more or less normal forms of peaceful cooperation with the NATO countries."[33] Khrushchev, as many Western leaders feared, aimed at undermining NATO and ultimately forcing the United States to withdraw from Europe. Later, in February 1960, at the Presidium, Khrushchev would admit that this was his "dearest dream."[34] In pursuit of the first objective of the "new foreign policy," the Kremlin created the Warsaw Treaty Organization in May 1955. Just as NATO provided legitimacy for the presence of American troops in Western Europe, the new organization gave the Soviet Union an additional reason to station Soviet troops in Eastern Europe.[35] As events in Hungary soon demonstrated, the new bloc was a useful framework for justifying Soviet military invasion of an "allied" country in order to "save" a Communist regime within its boundaries. The Soviets appeared to be acting not only in their own interests but also in the interests of the entire alliance. Most immediately, in the light of the forthcoming pullout of Soviet troops from Austria, the treaty validated the deployment of Soviet troops in Hungary and Rumania.

The concept of neutrality emerged from the Presidium discussions on the Austrian state treaty in March–April 1955, the first successful gamble in the Kremlin's new foreign policy.[36] Reconciliation with Yugoslavia, while pursuing the goal of returning this country to the Soviet camp, also had the immediate purpose of the "preventing of further expansion of the zone of NATO in Europe."[37] Specifically, this meant encouraging the neutral status of Sweden and Finland and ruining U.S. plans to create a so-called Balkan pact, involving Yugoslavia, Greece, and Turkey. From these specific cases, the Kremlin moved to the idea of promoting neutrality at large, offering Western Europe a substitute for U.S. protection and the idea of a pan-European system of security and cooperation.

The aims of the new foreign policy grew out of the revolutionary-imperial paradigm, but they were significantly more flexible than Stalin's policy. Aside from a new tolerance for neutrality, there was a new stake in economic cooperation and trade. Stalin was obsessed with keeping the Soviet Union closed to Western influences and preferred autarky and isolation to economic and trade ties with Western countries.[38] The collective leadership, above all Mikoyan, who was responsible for foreign trade, believed that Stalin had been mistaken. They returned to the idea drawn from the arsenal of Bolshevik diplomacy in the 1920s, when Soviet leaders had regarded trade deals with various capitalist countries as the way to both obtain vital investments and technologies and acquire the support of big business in improving political relations. Many in the Presidium expected that crowds of capitalists would stand in line at the doors of Soviet embassies in Washington, Paris, London, Bonn, and Tokyo.[39]

Other favorite tools of the new foreign policy were "public diplomacy" and the propaganda of disarmament. Public diplomacy involved authorized trips of Soviet artists, scientists, writers, musicians, and journalists to Western countries, with the aim of dispelling anti-Communist notions about the Soviet Union as a totalitarian society. When Khrushchev and other Soviet leaders began to go abroad, starting with the trip to Yugoslavia in May 1955, they traveled, in an apt phrase of David Caute, "like Renaissance princes, accompanied by a retinue of performers —ballerinas, singers, and pianists were taken along." The Presidium decided to invite world youth to a festival in Moscow, to see how friendly, peaceful, and open Soviet society was.[40] The collective leadership also went much further than Stalin's propagandist measures on disarmament and, in comparison with Stalin, expected much more from their new initiatives. In May 1955, to the surprise of many, the Soviet Union agreed to lower the levels of conventional forces in Europe and to establish a system of inspection at military checkpoints (railroads, airports, and so on) to reduce fears of a surprise conventional attack.[41] In the short term, these initiatives pushed the United States to revise its own position and start negotiating with the Soviets. In the longer term, the Presidium set the far-reaching goal of changing the image of the Soviet threat in the West.

The transformation of Soviet foreign policy in 1955 was part of the de-Stalinization process. But it would be simplistic to portray its origins as simply the struggle between friends and foes of Stalin's legacy. Changes in foreign and domestic policies stemmed, above all, from the new external and domestic situation after Stalin's death.[42] On the eve of the Twentieth Party Congress, the Presidium sought to put all the elements of a new foreign policy together. Instead of Stalin's doctrine on the inevitability of war, the members decided to promote a new worldview in which the capitalist world would coexist with and peacefully compete against the Soviet Union and its allies. Their main thesis was that the new foreign policy would help persuade the Western "petty bourgeoisie" and other "vacillating elements" of the Soviet Union's peaceful intentions. Malenkov, a coauthor of this policy, spoke with satisfaction that "the system of peace forces has been strengthened." The head of the Party Control Committee, Nikolai Shvernik, summed it up: "During one year we did a great job. We persuaded the masses that we do not want war."[43]

Party elites and powerful bureaucracies applauded the new foreign policy. Still, the collective leadership could not count on their automatic support. As the July 1955 plenum showed, the issues of foreign policy once again became, just as in the political struggles of the 1920s, linked to the broader issues of ideological legitimacy. Khrushchev, Molotov, Malenkov, and other potentates had to explain and defend their foreign policy choices at meetings with the party elites.

The theme of a "great Russian state" retained a major appeal to ethnic Russians among the party and state functionaries. In contrast, the architects of the new foreign policy began to reemphasize the internationalist themes of "unity of working people" and "fraternal solidarity," popular in the days of Comintern and eclipsed during Stalin's reign. Khrushchev's beliefs, and also his temperament, had a lot to do with the weakening of Russo-centric chauvinism and the reintroduction of ideological romanticism into Soviet foreign policy. Unlike Stalin's mind, Khrushchev's mind was not pessimistic and evil; he was not obsessed with worst-case scenarios. Khrushchev believed that the Russian Revolution was about bringing happiness and equality to the working masses, not about recreating the Russo-centric empire under a new guise. Stalin evoked the images of Russian czars, great statesmen, and warriors as his peers. In contrast, Khrushchev often compared himself to the Jewish boy Pinya, from his favorite story, an underdog who escaped all pitfalls to become a leader.[44]

Khrushchev was not educated enough to be ideologically dogmatic, like Molotov. It is doubtful that he ever read Lenin's works on imperialism that had so shaped the perceptions of his opponent. The arguments he used in foreign policy discussions lacked structure and logic: Khrushchev's speechwriters usually had to completely rewrite his speeches, removing earthy and erratic pronouncements. At the same time, Khrushchev was a genuine and passionate believer in the global victory of Communism. He expected that the combination of Soviet state power and revolutionary means would help to bury world capitalism. As a revolutionary romantic, he rejected Stalin's cautious Eurasian imperialism. For him the entire world was ripe for Communism.

Stalin's diplomacy cynically exploited the Communist faith and those who shared it for his goal of expanding his power and empire. Stalin paid lip service to "proletarian solidarity" and "Communist brotherhood." Khrushchev, by contrast, believed in social justice and a Communist paradise on earth, the solidarity of workers and peasants around the world, and the obligation of the USSR to support the struggle of colonized peoples for independence. He took seriously the moral and ideological capital the Soviet Union had gained in the struggle against Nazism. And he was dismayed by Stalin's naked imperialist policies since 1945, especially with regard to Turkey, Iran, and China. Although Khrushchev firmly believed that the Soviet Union was entitled to maintain a military presence in Central Europe, he felt that Stalin's crude pressure on Poland, Hungary, and other countries in the region had hurt the Communist cause there and compromised local Communist parties.[45]

Khrushchev offered simple solutions to complex foreign policy issues and expressed them in the language of the Bolshevized worker, the salt of the party, who rose to its highest position. This initially increased his appeal to many in the nomenklatura who were the children of peasants and workers and became *khoziaistvenniki* (economic managers) in the enormous state apparatus. These simple solutions, however, would create many problems for the Soviet Union, when the new and bombastic leader appeared on the international stage. When this happened, Khrushchev would find it increasingly difficult to sell his global and romantic version of the revolutionary-imperial paradigm to the skeptical and cautious party and state elites.

THE GENEVA TEST

Khrushchev had always returned to Eisenhower's speech of April 1953 in which the U.S. president addressed Stalin's successors with an appeal to part with Stalin's ways. The Presidium portrayed the speech as an ultimatum, but Khrushchev remembered "four conditions" set forth by President Eisenhower—truce in Korea, settlement on Austria, return of German and Japanese POWs from

Soviet camps, and steps to curb the arms race.[46] By the summer of 1955, from the viewpoint of the Soviet leadership, they had met Eisenhower's terms in Korea and Austria and had introduced much more far-reaching disarmament initiatives than had Washington.

Significantly, the settlement of the German Question was not among the American conditions. The Western powers did not expect any agreement on German reunification; they moved, however, to exploit the theme of German reunification more effectively. Since early 1954, the British had advanced the Eden Plan. Its essence was that free elections should determine the government in the unified Germany.[47] The Kremlin politicians rejected the Eden Plan, although this hurt their propaganda purposes in Germany and NATO countries. Since Beria's arrest, the idea of German reunification, especially according to Western blueprints, had become unthinkable in Moscow. The Soviet leaders, briefed by intelligence analysts, knew that the U.S. administration was not ready for serious negotiations.[48] They hoped, however, to split NATO ranks, by reaching out to Great Britain and France. The French government in particular, distracted by the colonial war in Algeria, became seriously interested in improving relations with the Soviet Union.[49]

The major goal of Khrushchev and his comrades at the summit in Geneva was to find out if the Eisenhower administration had on its mind a war against the Soviet Union. For Presidium members, the surprise Nazi attack on June 22, 1941, was the largest trauma of their lives. They could not afford again to misread the enemy's intentions. Another goal was to demonstrate to the U.S. leadership that they would not be intimidated by nuclear blackmail and other kinds of pressure. At Khrushchev's suggestion, Marshal Georgy Zhukov joined the delegation on the assumption that he and Eisenhower, the two military leaders who liked and respected each other (Eisenhower even invited Zhukov to the United States in 1945, but Stalin said no), would be able to have a frank talk. In Geneva, Khrushchev and Zhukov did their best to make one major point to Eisenhower: Western views of the failure of the post-Stalin leadership were false; the new leadership sat firmly in the saddle and had more unity and support than ever before.[50]

The Eisenhower administration had conflicting priorities. As historian Richard Immerman concludes, John Foster Dulles's "agenda for the summit was not to settle outstanding problems of war and peace, but to lay the foundation for future progress toward the retraction or rollback of Soviet power." The secretary of state explained his big idea, which was "to get the Russians out of the satellite states. . . . Now for the first time this is in the realm of possibility." Eisenhower, as new evidence reveals, held a different priority: to attempt to control nuclear armaments.[51] The Eisenhower administration faced the need to reconsider its long-term policy of resistance to any top-level contacts with any Communist leaders. As John Foster Dulles noted ruefully after the Geneva summit, "We never wanted to go to Geneva, but the pressure of people of the world forced us to do so."[52]

The Kremlin delegation arrived in Geneva in July 1955 in a state of excitement and uneasiness. Khrushchev and his comrades were in fear of being "ambushed" by unexpected Western initiatives. According to Georgy Kornienko, a veteran of the Committee of Information, an analytical division at the Foreign Ministry, a group of the committee experts flew to Geneva with the Soviet delegation and throughout the meeting worked closely with all branches of Soviet intelligence services, supplying the Soviet delegation with fresh intercepts of communications from the other side and helping in their interpretation.[53]

Still, a dramatic unveiling of Eisenhower's "Open Skies," a proposal to allow plane reconnaissance overflights to reduce mutual fear of nuclear war, took the Soviet delegation by surprise. President Eisenhower, concerned with the runaway dynamics of the nuclear arms race, regarded this proposal as a chance "to open a tiny gate in the disarmament fence." In 1955, however, neither the American nor the Soviet leadership was ready to implement this idea. Bulganin, as the Americans noted, reacted with interest, but Khrushchev quickly dismissed Open Skies as a "blatant espionage ploy."[54]

The troika of Khrushchev, Bulganin, and Zhukov left the conference without any agreements, yet with big sighs of relief. They came away with the conviction that they could manage relations with capitalist great powers as well as Stalin had, perhaps even better. Western leaders at the summit did not manage to intimidate or disorient them. It was also key that Eisenhower talked to them without condescension, almost as if they were equal partners. American sources prove the correctness of the latter assessment.[55] Khrushchev concluded that Eisenhower was a relaxed, benign, and not particularly impressive fellow who delegated foreign affairs to his secretary of state, John Foster Dulles. Other Soviet observers shared this perception.[56] The Eisenhower-Zhukov informal talks confirmed the Soviet leaders' impression that the U.S. president was afraid of nuclear war.[57]

The "spirit of Geneva" after the summit brought hopes for European détente. But the commitment of the Kremlin oligarchy to the revolutionary-imperial paradigm provided no basis for agreement between the USSR and the United States. While demonstrating to the world their readiness for the confidence-building measures to promote disarmament, the Kremlin and the military top brass never intended to carry out these promises. Before advancing these disarmament initiatives, the Presidium confidentially informed the Chinese Communist leadership that there was no danger that Western controllers would inundate the Soviet secret installations, because the "Anglo-American bloc will not agree to eliminate atomic weapons and to ban the production of these weapons." By November 1955, the "spirit of Geneva" was already fading. Molotov, still Soviet foreign minister, rejected any proposals to broaden Soviet contacts with the outside world as "interference in internal affairs.[58]

The failure of the Geneva summit to reach agreement on German unity meant that the division of Germany would remain a source of instability and insecurity in Europe. Even before the summit, West German chancellor Konrad Adenauer, reacting to public pressure after West Germany joined NATO and the Austrian State Treaty was signed, proposed coming to Moscow after the Geneva talks for separate negotiations. In September 1955, Adenauer, along with a large delegation, came to Moscow and conducted strenuous and emotional talks with the Kremlin leadership. The talks resulted in the establishment of West German–Soviet diplomatic relations and the release of the last German POWs. Immediately afterward, the Soviet leadership invited the GDR's prime minister, Otto Grotewohl, to Moscow to sign a bilateral treaty that boosted even further the sovereignty of the East German regime.[59]

This looked like a smart diplomatic move. But the Soviet leadership was driving itself into a corner from which it could not emerge without losing face. Soviet insistence on permanent division of Germany gave Ulbricht, who was emerging as an unchallenged leader of the GDR, an ever-greater leverage on Soviet policy.[60] Also, the Kremlin put itself in danger of appearing as an opponent of German reunification. Understanding this danger, Molotov proposed in November 1955 that the Soviet line on German talks should accept the basics of the Eden Plan. In return for Soviet agreement to hold universal and free elections in all of Germany, Molotov told the Presidium that the Western powers would have to repeal West Germany's membership in NATO and establish the All-German Council for implementation of reunification. They would also have to agree, together with the Soviet Union, to withdraw all foreign troops from both German states within three months. Molotov argued that the Western powers would never agree to such a proposal, because it involved a great challenge to NATO's unity. At the same time, he argued, this would restore Soviet face among Germans.[61]

Molotov's argument made sense, but Khrushchev killed his proposal. In Khrushchev's opinion, the Eisenhower administration might call the Soviet bluff and "could agree to withdrawal of troops." Also, the Western powers could interpret the shift of the Soviet position as a victory for their "position of strength." And, most important, the GDR Communists would say: "You are betraying us." Khrushchev, supported by the rest of the Presidium, confidently predicted that the Soviets could achieve two goals simultaneously: preservation of the socialist East

Germany and the destabilization of NATO. This episode demonstrated once again that the GDR, once an instrument of Soviet goals in Europe, had become a major Soviet asset and not available for bargaining.[62]

The summit in Geneva, Khrushchev recalled later, "convinced us once again that there was not any sort of prewar situation in existence at that time, and our enemies were afraid of us in the same way as we were afraid of them." The Kremlin rulers concluded that Soviet diplomacy had shaken the American leadership out of its comfortable position of superiority and forced the Americans to come to the negotiating table. This conclusion emboldened Khrushchev and his colleagues, contrary to their initial desires to pursue a cautious defensive course and to take the offensive outside the major theaters of the Cold War. By the fall of 1955, this would result in a major Soviet gamble in the Arab Middle East.

SUPPORTING RADICAL ALLIES

Stalin had failed to formulate any coherent policy in the Middle East. In January 1953, at the peak of the "Kremlin doctors' affair," Stalin broke diplomatic relations with Israel; at that time, he probably planned to use the bogus issue of a "Zionist conspiracy" as a pretext for a gigantic purge.[63] From 1949 to 1954, the official Soviet position was that the Arab countries of the Middle East, as well as Turkey and Iran, were ruled by reactionary regimes and were the pawns in the British-American struggle for the Middle East. Some Soviet experts and diplomats wanted the Kremlin to support Arab opposition to American attempts to create an anti-Soviet bloc in the region but did not dare to speak against the official line. After Stalin's death, the official estimation of the Arab nationalist regimes did not change; diplomatic correspondence and secret memoranda for the Presidium called Egypt's leader, General Muhammad Naguib, and his successor, General Gamal Abdel Nasser, "enemies," and even "fascists," despite their nonaligned positions in the Cold War. According to the Committee of Information's analysis in March 1954, Nasser used the threat of possible rapprochement with the Soviet Union as a means to blackmail the British into concessions on the control of the Suez Canal.[64] Similar views led Moscow to rebuff the approaches from the prime minister of Iran, Mohammad Mossadeq, in 1952 and 1953, which probably cost the Soviet Union a chance of improving relations with that country.[65]

The struggle against Molotov and the search for spectacular achievements led Khrushchev and his supporters to rediscover the potential of Arab nationalism in the Middle East. In July 1955, immediately after the devastating criticism of Molotov at the Party Plenum, the Presidium sent Khrushchev's new favorite

Central Committee secretary, Dmitry Shepilov, on a reconnaissance mission to the Middle East. Shepilov met Nasser and invited him to Moscow; he also began to establish friendly relations with leaders of other Arab states who refused to join the Western blocs. Shepilov came back to Moscow from the Middle East convinced that the region had great potential for another "peace offensive" against the Western powers. Andrei Sakharov and other nuclear designers happened to be invited to the Presidium on the day that it discussed Shepilov's report. An official explained that the leaders were discussing a decisive change of principles of Soviet policy on the Middle East: "From now on we will support the Arab nationalists. The longer-term target is the destruction of the established relations of the Arabs with Europe and the United States, creation of the 'oil crisis'—this will generate problems for Europe and will make it more dependent on us."[66] In the midst of the strategic stalemate in Europe and the Far East, this region provided a new outlet for the Kremlin's renewed optimism and ideological romanticism.

The consequences of this policy turn were immediate. The languishing Egyptian-Czechoslovak talks on the sale of arms rapidly came to a successful conclusion, and a flood of Soviet-designed Czechoslovak weaponry streamed into Egypt and Syria. Moscow supplied Egypt with half a million tons of oil and agreed to provide atomic energy technology. To no avail, concerned Western and Israeli officials tried to remonstrate against new Soviet policies publicly and privately.[67] The struggle between Moscow and the West for the Arab Middle East was beginning: in the next two decades, it would generate an unprecedented arms race in the region and produce three wars. In the immediate future, Moscow would be triumphant and destroy Western plans of containment on the southern flank of the Soviet Union. At the same time, as in the case of the GDR, heavy Soviet investment in its Arab clients would turn Egypt and Syria into major assets, similar to East Germany, that the Kremlin could not afford to lose. The Middle Eastern venture began as a geopolitical gamble, but it ended as a contributing factor to the Soviet imperial overstretch of the 1970s.

As the Soviets were making a breakthrough in the Middle East, they were seeking to strengthen their alliance with China. Sino-Soviet relations remained a crucial aspect of Soviet foreign policy. The Sino-Soviet Alliance of February 1950 made Soviet foreign policy resemble that of Imperial Russia's eagle, looking both westward and eastward. After Stalin's death, the Kremlin no longer could or wanted to treat Chinese leaders as junior partners. The Presidium leaders competed among themselves in reaching out to Beijing. Their first success was to procure an invitation for a People's Republic of China (PRC) delegation to the

Geneva conference on Indochina in May–July 1954. At the conference, Zhou Enlai shared the table with representatives of the United States, France, Great Britain, and the Soviet Union. Molotov treated the Chinese with pointed respect; he and other Soviet leaders considered it a major aim of Kremlin diplomacy to return China to the club of great powers.[68] In September and October 1954, Khrushchev became the first leader of the Communist Party of the Soviet Union (CPSU) to travel to the PRC. It was a mutually advantageous encounter: Khrushchev acquired the ammunition to wrest the mantle of statesman from Malenkov and Molotov; the Chinese leaders obtained much-needed political and economic support from Moscow at a time when Beijing was coming into confrontation with Taiwan's Nationalists over the offshore islands.[69]

Khrushchev believed that he did everything necessary to put the Sino-Soviet relations on a steady course. He finally fulfilled Stalin's promise to return all Soviet assets in Manchuria to China (that is, joint companies, the Soviet base in Port Arthur, and the railroad). He rejected bureaucratic objections to the generous terms of Soviet assistance to the PRC. Historian Odd Arne Westad called Soviet assistance to China in 1954–59 the "Soviet Union's Marshall Plan." The assistance equaled 7 percent of Soviet national income for that period. Thousands of Soviet experts worked in China, helping the Chinese to modernize their industry, create a basis for modern science and technology, and build educational and health systems. By August 1956, the Soviets were sending to China most of the new industrial equipment they were producing, at the expense of their own economic plans. A romantic view of Sino-Soviet relations as being "truly fraternal" and based on common, rather than national, interests spread among Soviet elites. The Presidium even decided to help the Chinese create their own atomic program. Subsequently, Soviet nuclear labs received instructions to help the Chinese build a uranium bomb and even provide them with a functional prototype.[70]

The Kremlin reacted with uneasiness to Beijing's intentions to "liberate" Taiwan during the Taiwan crisis (August 1954–April 1955). The Kremlin potentates had learned the lessons of the Korean War. Another war in the Far East would have derailed Soviet plans in Europe and, more ominously, drawn the Soviet Union into a conflict with the United States at a time when American strategic nuclear forces could reach and destroy any target in the Soviet Union— and Soviet forces still had nothing with which to retaliate.[71] Nevertheless, the desire to strengthen the Sino-Soviet Alliance was so strong in the Kremlin that Soviet leaders offered political, economic, and military support to the PRC during the Taiwan crisis. At the Geneva summit, the Soviet delegation appealed to Eisenhower to move toward a peace settlement with the PRC.[72]

On the surface, Sino-Soviet relations flourished. Underneath, however, they already contained the seeds of an eventual split. The Chinese supported the idea of the Warsaw Pact but were meaningfully silent on other elements of Soviet diplomacy, especially the reconciliation with Tito.[73] In the eyes of the Chinese leadership, the Kremlin still played the role of the senior partner, and they wanted "equal relations." Historian Chen Jian believes that Beijing's pursuit of an elusive "equality" in reality reflected a Chinese mentality of superiority.[74] It meant that whatever the new Soviet leadership did, nothing could satisfy the Chinese allies. Mao Ze-dong, in particular, was inclined to challenge Soviet supremacy in the Communist world and to advocate confronting "American imperialism" as the truly revolutionary alternative to détente diplomacy.[75] At the same time, at the end of April 1955, Zhou Enlai took part in the Bandung conference of Asian countries in Indonesia, at which the PRC reaffirmed its allegiance to the declaration on *Pancha Shila*, the five principles of peaceful coexistence borrowed from Buddhist moral code (India's prime minister, Jawaharlal Nehru, began to refer to them in 1952, and they became the basis of the Indian-Chinese talks in June 1954). In retrospect, the new Chinese policy was a rival's response to the new Soviet foreign policy.

THE YEAR OF CRISES

Khrushchev's attack on Stalin in a secret speech at the Twentieth Congress of the CPSU on February 25, 1956, opened the last and most dramatic stage of the succession struggle. New archival access has allowed historians to study the internal politics surrounding this extraordinary event.[76] Egged on by the first secretary, the Presidium commission for rehabilitation of Stalin's victims prepared the memoranda on Stalin's repressions. The facts collected by the commission contained in the archives give a graphic picture of the murder of the Bolshevik Old Guard on Stalin's orders; no wonder that even determined Stalinists in the Presidium and the Secretariat were shocked to the core, including Pyotr Pospelov, the head of the commission.[77] Still, Molotov, Kaganovich, and Voroshilov spoke against presenting these findings to the Congress. Khrushchev disarmed his opponents by threatening to appeal to the Congress delegates. And he resorted to the device that had helped him in the past against Malenkov and Molotov: he convened the plenum and obtained from the unsuspecting delegates a formal authorization for the special report on Stalin.[78] The commission memorandum did not satisfy Khrushchev, and as the Congress was already in progress, he continued to work on his Stalin speech. When Khrushchev finally read the speech, he improvised; and his improvisations, according to the accounts of witnesses, were more emotional and categorical than the prepared text. Khrushchev could not abide half-measures: once he decided to destroy Stalin's cult, he began to hack it to pieces. When he saw resistance, he bulldozed it.[79]

For a while, it seemed that the politics of de-Stalinization and the new foreign policy reinforced each other. A good example is the rapid rise of Dmitry Shepilov, who in June 1956 replaced Molotov as foreign minister. Shepilov quickly rose from the position of editor of *Pravda* to the post of Central Committee secretary. He helped Khrushchev to edit his secret speech. Shepilov had what Khrushchev lacked: education, erudition, a good pen, and knowledge of Marxist literature. The first secretary expected him to represent abroad the new face of Soviet diplomacy in the spirit of dialogue, compromise, and a relaxation of tensions.

Until that moment, the struggle between Khrushchev and Molotov complicated the day-to-day functions of Soviet foreign policy. Even after the July 1955 plenum, Foreign Ministry officials remained caught between the hammer of Molotov and the anvil of Khrushchev. Their ideas and proposals served as the weapons in the clash between the foreign minister and the first secretary, and as a result these proposals ended up being sacrificed, mutilated, and delayed.[80] This disastrous mingling of politics and personal rivalry with the process of foreign policy decision making seemed to have disappeared after Molotov's removal. According to Shepilov's own recollection, Khrushchev treated him with respect and afforded him complete trust.[81]

Shepilov's arrival at the Foreign Ministry made Soviet foreign policy more responsive to the advice of experts and created a chance to reform the ministry's ossified structure. Stalin and Molotov had cut off the diplomatic bureaucracy from the real business of foreign policy making. Diplomats and Foreign Ministry officials lived in fear of "contamination" from suspicious contacts with foreigners. Soviet journalists and writers who visited the Soviet UN Mission in New York in 1955 reported that Soviet diplomats reminded them of "hermit crabs": they avoided any contacts with the representatives of the country on which they were supposed to report. Shepilov, adept at a more interactive, democratic style of leadership, encouraged change.[82]

But the change was short-lived. Khrushchev did not want a strong, independent-minded foreign minister. This became clear during the Middle Eastern crisis provoked by the decision of Egypt's leader, Nasser, to nationalize the Suez Canal. In early August 1956, the Presidium sent Shepilov to an international conference in London to discuss this issue. Initially, Khrushchev advocated caution in a speech at the Presidium. Instead of an aggressive, tough stand against Great Britain and France, the owners of the canal, the first secretary advocated a "soft, objective and deeply analytical" approach. Supported by Zhukov, Malenkov,

Bulganin, and others, Khrushchev suggested that the Soviet Union should assure the Western powers about its intentions: there were no plans "to swallow Egypt and to capture the Suez canal." The Soviet Union, Khrushchev suggested, should indicate its interest "only in the unimpeded movement of ships [in the canal]."[83]

At the conference, Shepilov carried out the moderate instructions and did much to promote a joint U.S.-Soviet mediation in the crisis and avoid excessive friction between the Soviet Union, on the one hand, and Britain and France on the other. This, however, became more difficult later, when the Western powers rejected Soviet initiatives. Khrushchev spontaneously shifted from moderation to a hard line. The first secretary must have been tempted by the chance to teach London and Paris a bitter lesson and demonstrate his solidarity with Nasser.[84] Shepilov ignored Presidium instructions to denounce the Western countries for "blatant pillage and high-way robbery." Khrushchev was outraged by his protégé's show of independence. Speaking at the Presidium on August 27, 1956, Khrushchev characterized Shepilov's initiative as "dangerous."[85] When war broke out between Egypt and Great Britain, France, and Israel in late October, Khrushchev's pugnacity and ideological temptations would prevail over moderation. He would use nuclear brinkmanship for the first time to dramatize a Soviet political presence in the Middle East.[86]

Beginning in late summer 1956, Poland had become a hotbed of unrest in the Soviet bloc. The collective leadership, despite the recent reconciliation with Tito's Yugoslavia, viewed the slogan, "Polish road to socialism," as the beginning of the end for the Warsaw Pact. In their internal discussions, the Presidium members used the same language as *Pravda* used: "The [Western] imperialists" seek "to separate us," using the language of national roads, "and defeat one by one." With the aim of propping up the loyal Polish Communists, the Presidium agreed to remove Soviet KGB advisers from Polish security organs and provide economic assistance to the Polish state.[87] But the experience in the GDR in 1953 was fresh on its mind.

The Kremlin's concern turned into panic on October 19, 1956, when it learned that the Polish Communists were convening a plenum, without any consultation with Moscow, to replace Edward Ochab as their leader with Wladyslaw Gomulka, who had been expelled from the Polish United Workers Party (PUWP) (the Communist Party of Poland) and imprisoned from 1951 to 1954 for "nationalist deviations." At the same time, the Polish leadership demanded that Soviet advisers in the Polish army also leave, as well as Marshal Konstantin Rokossovsky, a Soviet citizen of Polish descent who had been appointed by Stalin as Poland's minister of defense. Khrushchev and other Kremlin potentates immediately flew to Warsaw and attempted to bully Gomulka and his Polish colleagues with tough words and raw power, using the presence of Soviet troops on Polish soil. The Kremlin delegation returned home on October 20 in an agitated mood. On that day, the Presidium concluded that "the remaining solution is to terminate what is going on in Poland." The notes of Vladimir Malin at this point become especially cryptic, but it is probable that the Kremlin rulers decided to take preliminary steps to use Soviet troops and replace the Polish leadership. After Rokossovsky was removed from the PUWP Politburo, however, the collective leadership temporized. Suddenly, Khrushchev suggested "tolerance" and admitted that "military intervention, under the circumstances, must be cancelled." The Presidium unanimously agreed.[88]

The main reason for this surprising change must have been Gomulka's speech at the plenum after the Kremlin delegation left Poland. He pledged to build "socialism" and fulfill obligations to the Warsaw Treaty Organization. Another factor in the Kremlin's change of heart was the reaction of the Chinese. The Poles appealed to other Communist Party leaders, above all to the Chinese leaders, begging them to intercede and prevent an impending Soviet invasion. Later, after the fact, Mao Ze-dong asserted that "the CCP categorically rejected the Soviet proposal [for intervention] and attempted to put forward the Chinese position directly by immediately sending a delegation to Moscow with Liu Shaoqi at its head." At an urgent meeting of the CCP Politburo, Mao Ze-dong blamed the crisis in Poland on the tendency toward "big-power chauvinism" in Moscow. Immediately after the meeting, he asked Soviet ambassador Pavel Yudin to convey China's opposition to military intervention to Khrushchev.[89]

On October 23, Budapest and the rest of Hungary rose up against the Communist regime. In view of the apparent danger, the collective leadership closed its ranks and acted by consensus. Still, the old political and personal rifts were not completely gone. Advocates of de-Stalinization and the new foreign policy had good reasons to oppose direct Soviet military intervention in Hungary because it undermined Soviet efforts to sell its new peaceful image to the West beginning in 1955. Molotov, Kaganovich, and Voroshilov clearly blamed these policies and Khrushchev personally for what was happening. Since the Presidium continued to act by consensus, the rifts within it could not lead to open splits. Khrushchev's supporters and even Khrushchev himself shifted their positions depending on the direction and framework of the debates. Like the discussions on the German Question in the spring and summer of 1953, the decision-making process on Hungary was in turmoil, reflecting the complexity of the situation as well as the personal and political calculations of the Kremlin politicians. On October 26, both supporters and secret enemies of Khrushchev in the Presidium approved the introduction of Soviet troops into Budapest. On October 30, the Presidium, however, switched to the policy of negotiations and authorized a declaration on new principles guiding Soviet relations "with other socialist countries."[90]

Foreign observers had long considered this declaration a perfidious trick on the part of Moscow, but historians have recently learned that this declaration resulted from the complex debates at the Presidium that ended with the decision to forgo the use of military force in Hungary. The failure of the first indecisive use of Soviet troops to extinguish the uprising in Budapest and the number of casualties tipped the scales. From Budapest, Mikoyan, the Presidium special emissary, defended the policy of negotiations and compromise with consistency and courage. Mikhail Suslov, another emissary, was obliged to do the same. Zhukov and Malenkov supported the withdrawal of troops.[91]

An unexpected factor in the Presidium discussion was pressure from a Chinese delegation headed by Liu Shaoqi. The Chinese had come to Moscow on October 23 to discuss the Polish question. Instead, the Chinese became kibitzers on the Kremlin's discussions about the Hungarian revolution. At first, Mao Zedong, ignoring the realities in the streets of Budapest, instructed the delegation in Moscow to oppose Soviet interference in Hungarian, as well as Polish, affairs. Amazingly, the Chinese suggested that the Soviet leadership should subscribe to the Bandung conference's principles of "peaceful coexistence" concerning relationships among Warsaw Pact countries. Apparently, Mao felt it was the opportune moment to teach the Soviets a lesson about their imperialist arrogance and enhance the CCP's central role in the Communist movement by mediating between the Soviets and their Eastern European satellites. Swayed by arguments from his own supporters and the arguments of the Chinese Communists, Khrushchev proposed the policy of negotiations and the declaration based on the Chinese proposal.[92]

The proposal to leave Hungary alone split the Presidium. Bulganin, Molotov, Voroshilov, and Kaganovich defended the Soviet right to interfere in the affairs of "fraternal parties." This, of course, meant that Soviet military force could be used to restore Communist regimes. Then Foreign Minister Shepilov delivered an eloquent speech in favor of withdrawal. He said that the course of events revealed "the crisis in our relations with the countries of people's democracy. Anti-Soviet elements are widespread" in Central Europe, and, therefore, the declaration should be only the first step toward "elimination of the elements of diktat" between the Soviet Union and other members of the Warsaw Pact. Zhukov, Ekaterina Furtseva, and Matvei Saburov spoke one after another in favor of withdrawal.[93]

The noninterventionist momentum was reversed on the following day, October 31, when the Presidium voted with the same unanimity to order Marshal Ivan Konev to prepare for decisive military intervention in Hungary. Matvei Saburov reminded the Presidium that the day before they had agreed that military intervention in Hungary would "vindicate NATO." Molotov dryly countered that "yesterday's decision was only a compromise," and the rest of the Presidium members spoke unanimously, overturning what they had said only twenty-four hours earlier.[94]

Some scholars have attributed this startling flip-flop to external events, above all, the reports of the gruesome lynching of Communists in Hungary, Gomulka's fears that the collapse of Communism in Hungary would cause Poland to be next, and the Franco-British-Israeli aggression against Egypt. There was also a large "spillover" effect inside the Soviet Union itself: unrest in the Baltics and Western Ukraine and student hunger strikes and demonstrations in Moscow, Leningrad, and other cities. Trust in the leadership had fallen among intellectuals and other social groups.[95] All these developments and factors, however, had existed on the previous day. The Franco-British declaration of war in Egypt was hardly a cause for Khrushchev's shift. On October 28, for example, the Soviet leader said about the Suez crisis: "The English and French are stirring up trouble in Egypt. We should not get caught in the same company." In other words, he did not want for the Soviet Union to be seen as an aggressive power, preparing an invasion of another country. On October 31, however, Khrushchev gave a different twist to the same situation: "If we depart from Hungary, it will give a great boost to the Americans, English, and French—the imperialists. To Egypt they will then add Hungary."[96] The decisive news that tipped the scales was the declaration by the Hungarian leader Imre Nagy that his government had decided to remove Hungary from the Warsaw Pact.

Khrushchev was in a terrible bind. He did not want to undermine his own foreign policy and the new image of the Soviet Union. At the same time, he had long feared that the Soviet Union might retreat from Central Europe and that then his rivals in the collective leadership might gain the upper hand. He was probably correct, since the majority of the party apparatus and the upper echelons of the military believed that the radical de-Stalinization was Khrushchev's great political error.[97] On October 31, Khrushchev stole the thunder from his hard-line critics who would have been at his throat had he "lost" Hungary. At the same time, reacting to Molotov's criticism of his unilateralist actions, Khrushchev decided that military intervention could take place only if the leaders of the other "people's democracies," the Chinese Communists and Tito's Yugoslavia, gave their consent to it. After a few days of trips and consultations, the military option received unanimous support. On the morning of November 4, 1956, Marshal Konev's armies invaded Hungary.[98]

Mikoyan wrote in his memoirs that the Soviet intervention in Hungary "buried" the hopes for détente. Inside the Soviet Union, the process of liberalization was replaced by a wave of arrests and expulsions of students, workers, and intellectuals. The first secretary came out of the crisis looking almost like a lame duck. During the Presidium discussions on Hungary in early November, Khrushchev was unusually silent. When he attempted, as he often did, to pick on Molotov, the latter dressed him down: "You should stop bossing us."[99] The Chinese leadership also began to speak to the Soviets with much greater authority than before. According to the Chinese version of events, the intervention of the PRC saved Poland from Soviet invasion but then gave resolve to a vacillating Khrushchev in his determination to restore "socialism" in Hungary.[100] After the Soviet invasion of Hungary, Zhou Enlai made a tour of Central Europe and then came to Moscow on January 18, 1957. Zhou lectured Khrushchev on three mistakes: the lack of an all-round analysis, the lack of self-criticism, and the lack of consultation with the fraternal countries. He left with the opinion that the Kremlin leadership was lacking in sophistication and political maturity.[101]

Khrushchev, from his position of weakness, needed Mao's friendship and tolerated the new Chinese role. At the meeting with Zhou Enlai, he caved in to Chinese criticism. At a reception in the Chinese embassy, he invited all Communists "to learn from Stalin how to fight." Later Molotov recalled with sarcasm: "When comrade Zhou Enlai came, we began to rhapsodize that everyone should be such a Communist as Stalin was; but when Zhou Enlai left, we stopped saying it."[102]

Molotov, who believed that "Titoists" would never be reliable friends and allies, must have had a bittersweet feeling when Soviet-Yugoslav relations soured again after the rapprochement of 1955. Although Tito supported the Soviet decision to intervene in Hungary and the removal of the Hungarian leader Imre Nagy from political life, he felt embarrassed, when—almost by accident—Nagy and his comrades ended up hiding in the Yugoslav embassy in Budapest. Tito, valuing Yugoslavia's independent international reputation, refused to hand over Nagy to the Soviets. A shrill altercation between Tito and the Kremlin leaders ensued. Then, in his speech at Pula on November 11, 1956, Tito spoke about "systemic causes" of Stalinism, blaming the Hungarian tragedy in part on the conservative forces in the CPSU. He also said that Communist parties could now be categorized as either Stalinist or non-Stalinist. This speech enraged Khrushchev, who would refer to it for years as "treasonous and despicable." The Presidium voted to allow the public ideological polemics with Tito to appear in the pages of *Pravda*. The situation did not improve, when the KGB managed to lure Nagy and his associates out of the Yugoslav embassy, arrest them, and place them under custody in Rumania. Later, the Rumanians transferred them to the Hungarian quisling government of Janos Kadar. Nagy and some of his associates were executed after a secret trial, with the approval of the Kremlin and European Communist leaders. Privately, Tito must have breathed a sigh of relief. In public, however, the Yugoslav government protested the execution.[103]

Khrushchev's flip-flops undermined his authority as a statesman among Stalinists and anti-Stalinists alike. There was a stream of letters from party members to the Central Committee full of dismay and even contempt for Khrushchev's leadership. Some demanded rehabilitating Stalin as a great statesman and warned that the enemy would catch the Soviet Union "demobilized" and relaxed if Khrushchev continued to get his way. Others wondered if there were "two Khrushchevs" in the party's Central Committee: one denounced Stalin and the other urged the Soviet people to learn from him.[104]

DEMISE OF THE COLLECTIVE LEADERSHIP

Khrushchev's weakness encouraged his rivals in the Presidium to join forces against him. In June 1957, Molotov and Kaganovich decided this was a good moment to oust Khrushchev and ambushed him at a meeting of the Presidium. Khrushchev was one of the few people who did not see the danger to his authority. "He created enemies as if on purpose," reflected Mikoyan later, "but did not realize it himself." Malenkov, Bulganin, Voroshilov, Saburov, and Pervukhin, former allies of Khrushchev whom he also managed to alienate, joined the plot against him. Even Dmitry Shepilov decided that Khrushchev had to go.[105]

But a lack of political unity among the plotters was a problem: Molotov and Shepilov criticized Khrushchev from very different angles and for different reasons. The plotters also forgot that Khrushchev had all the muscle of state power in his hands. Most members of the Secretariat, all Khrushchev protégés, supported him against the Presidium potentates. The defense minister, Marshal Zhukov, and the chairman of the KGB, Ivan Serov, proved to be crucial allies throughout the crisis. With the help of the Secretariat members, Zhukov, and Serov, Khrushchev convened an emergency Central Committee plenum that restored his supremacy and denounced the plotters as an "anti-party group." The materials of the June 1957 plenum, although obviously slanted in favor of the victorious Khrushchev and against the "anti-party group" of his opponents, offer remarkable insight into the intertwining nature of Soviet politics and foreign policy.[106]

The opposition blamed Khrushchev for destroying the collective leadership and creating a new monopoly on decision making in foreign policy and on other issues. Molotov denounced Khrushchev's new doctrine that an agreement between the two nuclear powers, the Soviet Union and the United States, could be a solid foundation for an international détente. He stated his belief that, as long as imperialism existed, another world war could only be postponed but not prevented. Molotov also claimed that Khrushchev's doctrine ignored the role of "all other socialist countries, besides the USSR," especially the PRC. In addition to these doctrinal matters, Molotov felt revulsion at the homespun, uncouth, and casual style of Khrushchev and his personalized diplomacy.[107]

Mikoyan provided the strongest counter to the opposition. He recalled the recent series of crises in Poland, Hungary, and Suez and concluded that both the unity of Soviet leadership and Khrushchev's bold initiatives had contributed to their successful resolutions. Mikoyan also blamed Molotov, Malenkov, and Kaganovich for a narrow, purely budgetary, approach to trade and economic relations with the Communist countries of Central Europe, as well as with neutral Austria and Finland. Khrushchev, he said, on the contrary, regarded subsidies to these countries as a vital necessity, dictated by Soviet security interests. "We believe we must create an economic base for our influence on Austria, to strengthen its neutral status, so that West Germany would not be [the economic and trade] monopolist in Austria." And as to the Soviet bloc, "If we leave East Germany and Czechoslovakia without [purchase] orders, then the entire socialist camp will begin to collapse."[108]

Many plenum delegates sympathized with Molotov's conservative views more than with Khrushchev's crisis-mongering and subsidies. The party and state elites were not pro-détente—many of them were more hard-line, militaristic, and rigid than the "enlightened" majority in the Presidium. While rejecting Molotov's dogmatism and denouncing Stalin's foreign policy errors, the majority at the plenums used strong ideological language in their discussions of international affairs and military security. Yet it was not foreign policy that determined their stance. Rather, some of the delegates feared that, if Molotov and Kaganovich won, "blood would flow again." Also, the removal of the old oligarchic group meant promotion for Khrushchev's appointees. One of the speakers complained that Molotov "still considers us as wearing short pants."[109] Leonid Brezhnev was in the group that replaced the purged oligarchs in the political leadership. As the future showed, the new Presidium after 1957 was full of mediocrity that was inferior to the old oligarchy in energy, talents, knowledge, and horizons.[110] They had, however, one advantage from Khrushchev's viewpoint: he believed they were completely dependent on him.

In October, Khrushchev crowned his ascendancy by firing his greatest ally, but also at times critic and independent figure, Defense Minister Marshal Georgy Zhukov. As before, he convened a special plenum on October 28–29, 1957, to legitimize his action. The plenum transcript does not shed much light on the murky details of this affair but does indicate that there were some reasons (at least in the immediate post-Stalinist atmosphere of power struggles) for Khrushchev to suspect that Zhukov, together with GRU head Sergei Shtemenko, had plotted against him. But it is even more likely that Khrushchev heard from the KGB what he wanted to hear about Zhukov. Shortly before this happened, Zhukov, together with Andrei Gromyko, proposed to the Presidium that Moscow should accept the American Open Skies idea. He was convinced that the United States would back down, giving Soviet propaganda extra points. Khrushchev was skeptical, and at the October plenum he used this episode to criticize Zhukov both for his softness on Eisenhower's idea and for warmongering, claiming that Zhukov wanted to use the aerial reconnaissance to prepare for the first strike.[111] It was not the last time that political infighting in the Kremlin killed a potentially promising diplomatic opening.

These trumped-up charges aside, the plenum discussions give some valuable insights into the thinking and discussions at the highest level of the Soviet political-military leadership. Khrushchev sought to demonstrate to the delegates, especially to the military, that he, not Zhukov, knew better how to combine diplomatic peace offensives with the growth of military strength.[112] Whatever doubts the Soviet military had at the time about the whole affair, it unanimously supported the party leader and denounced Zhukov.

This was the last plenum under Khrushchev in which substantive foreign policy discussions became material for the power struggle at the top. The collective leadership and periodic rounds of Kremlin infighting were now history. Khrushchev, increasingly surrounded by yes-men, quickly found himself the decision maker in a vacuum. After removal of the "antiparty group" and Zhukov, the policy discussions at the Presidium quickly became ritualistic and sterile. An autodidact with extraordinary shrewdness and instincts, Khrushchev did not feel much need for outside expertise and advice. Whatever analytical branches still existed in the KGB, the Foreign Ministry, and the Central Committee withered away under Khrushchev's rule.[113]

Khrushchev's choice for Shepilov's successor was indicative of his intentions. Dour and uncharismatic Andrei Gromyko could not and did not shine on the international stage. Khrushchev decided to be his own foreign minister—as he was his own chief of intelligence, minister of agriculture, and many other roles. The young and suave diplomat Oleg Troyanovsky, who became foreign policy assistant to Khrushchev in April of 1958, recalls that he immediately felt the coming of a major change in Soviet foreign policy.[114] The Soviet leader, triumphant in domestic politics, decided that he was ready for a foreign policy breakthrough. He was eager to demonstrate to the political elites and the military that he could outdo Stalin in expanding Soviet power and influence.

(CHAPTER 5)
THE NUCLEAR EDUCATION
OF KHRUSHCHEV,
1953–1963

Let this device [nuclear bomb] hang over capitalists
like the sword of Damocles.
—Khrushchev to Soviet nuclear designers, July 1961

On October 4, 1957, a Soviet intercontinental ballistic missile (ICBM) launched a satellite, the orbit of which took it on a path over North America.[1] Sputnik was an innocuous and peaceful satellite, but American analysts also recognized that the same missile could carry a multimegaton nuclear charge. Almost immediately, these same experts warned of a "missile gap" that might eventually give the USSR the ability to destroy American strategic forces in a surprise attack. For Americans, this brought back memories of Pearl Harbor, which increased their sense of sudden loss of security. Across the United States, middle-class families saved money to build fallout shelters. Children took part in frightening "duck-and-cover" drills, learning how their desks would save them from a nuclear blast. A friend of mine who grew up in New York in the 1950s recalls looking at the Manhattan skyline during a drill to see if the Empire State Building was still there.[2]

In reality, now it was the Soviets' turn to have nuclear fears. The strategic military balance hugely favored the United States. Soviet strategic defense, writes Steven Zaloga, was "horribly expensive, technically unsound, and bound for premature obsolescence." And the Soviets had no nuclear strategic forces to retaliate in case of an American first strike. At the same time, the United States relied on the "first use" strategy for atomic weapons. Americans planned to use nuclear weapons against the Soviet Union to prevent the Soviets from overrunning Western Europe. The Pentagon built bases for strategic bombers and missiles not only on American territory but also on the territories of allies, namely Great Britain, West Germany, Italy, and Turkey.[3]

Until recently, very little was known about Soviet reactions to the thermonuclear revolution and the nuclear arms race with the United States. Some scholars suggested that the nuclear factor forced Moscow to behave more responsibly and moderately in the Cold War.[4] In reality, the opposite happened. The American containment strategy and strategic superiority left the Soviets feeling they had no choices between resistance and unconditional surrender.[5] Facing this choice, the mercurial Soviet leader Nikita Khrushchev chose to resist. He decided to trump American nuclear superiority with Soviet nuclear brinkmanship, using nuclear missiles as the last argument during international crises. His choice resulted in the most dangerous Soviet ventures during the entire Cold War.

THE BOMB AND THE DOGMA

Stalin died just at the start of the thermonuclear revolution. By 1953, Soviet military programs had already produced several types of atomic weapons, medium-range missiles, antimissile defense systems, cruise missiles, and nuclear submarines. But it turned out to be just the first phase in the upswing of the Soviet nuclear strategic forces. Viktor Adamsky, a veteran of the Soviet nuclear project, recalls that "the years of 1953–1962 were the most productive in the development of thermonuclear weapons."[6]

While Stalin was alive, the atomic program was rarely, if ever, discussed at the Politburo, and information on American and Soviet tests never spread outside a limited circle of officials, including Lavrenty Beria, Minister of Defense Bulganin, and the top military echelons.[7] Then came the news of the impending big test of the fission-boosted bomb designed by Andrei Sakharov and Vitali Ginzburg in the secret laboratory, "Arzamas-16." In July 1953, a deputy head of the nuclear project, Avraami Zaveniagin, reported to the Party Plenum delegates: "The Americans, at Truman's order, began to work on the hydrogen bomb. Our people and our country are no slouch. The hydrogen bomb is tens of times more powerful than a plain atomic bomb, and its explosion, now under preparation, will mean the liquidation of the second monopoly of the Americans. It will be an event of paramount importance in world politics."[8]

The first Soviet hydrogen test on August 12, 1953, gave the Soviet leaders an enormous boost of optimism. For a while, the Kremlin leaders believed, mistakenly, that the Soviet Union had become the leader in the nuclear race. Khrushchev recalls his enthusiasm: "No one else, neither the Americans nor the British, had such a bomb. I was overwhelmed by the idea. We did everything in our power to assure the rapid realization of Sakharov's plans." Andrei Sakharov immediately became a darling of the Kremlin. According to a plan, approved on November 20, 1953, by the Presidium of the Council of Ministers, Sakharov's bomb, upgraded to a one-to-two-megaton yield, would be attached to a huge intercontinental missile. This missile would be designed by another colossal complex that Stalin had created. The chief designer of the intercontinental missile, Sergei Korolev, pledged to conduct its final tests by the end of 1957.[9]

Thermonuclear power immediately became the object of Kremlin politics. After the arrest of Beria, the "atomic czar" under Stalin, other members of the collective leadership claimed he wanted to use the successful test in his bid for power. True or not, it was obvious the nuclear program was too important to remain the exclusive fiefdom of any single politician. Immediately after Beria's arrest, the Special Atomic Committee and the First Chief Directorate, the main structures in charge of nuclear programs, were merged into the Ministry of Medium Machine-Building Industry. Vyacheslav Malyshev, the head of tank production during World War II, became the atomic minister. Although he was close to Malenkov, he was not a member of the Presidium.[10] This did not end the political bickering around the Bomb.

Meanwhile, the United States dispelled Moscow's claims of superiority in thermonuclear developments. In January and February 1954, Secretary of State Dulles turned up his rhetoric of "massive retaliation" to full volume. And on March 1, the United States started a new series of nuclear tests with the explosion of a fifteen-megaton hydrogen bomb, with an explosive strength three times more than scientists had predicted. After the huge fallout cloud, covering 7,000 square miles over the Pacific, irradiated a Japanese fishing trawler, a global outcry arose to ban further testing of this kind. At a press conference on March 10, Eisenhower and Lewis Strauss, head of the Atomic Energy Commission, admitted that a super bomb could destroy a whole metropolitan area and a thermonuclear war could endanger civilization. Three months earlier, on December 8, 1953, President Eisenhower had made his "Atoms for Peace" proposal to the United Nations, an effort intended to dispel the image of the United States as a state preparing for thermonuclear war. The proposal suggested joint efforts in the exploration of peaceful nuclear energy to help underdeveloped parts of the world. In the light of subsequent American tests, however, this proposal began to look disingenuous, a fig leaf covering the demonstration of nuclear superiority.[11]

Soviet nuclear designers realized that the Americans had made a breakthrough to construction of multimegaton weapons. The Sakharov bomb could not yield such power. As a result, Igor Kurchatov and other nuclear physicists lost interest in the Sakharov design and soon zeroed in on the principle of radiation compression, the idea that Edward Teller and Stanislaus Ulam had discovered in January 1951 in the United States.[12] About the same time, the atomic minister, Malyshev, asked Kurchatov to draft a response to Eisenhower's "Atoms for Peace." Soviet scientists used this opportunity to bring the startling facts about the thermonuclear revolution to the attention of Kremlin leaders. The resulting essay, "The Danger of Atomic War and President Eisenhower's Proposal," reached the desks of Malenkov, Khrushchev, and Molotov on April 1, 1954.[13] "Modern atomic practice, based on the utilization of thermonuclear reaction," the physicists wrote, "allows for increasing the explosive energy contained in a bomb practically to an unlimited extent. Defense against such a weapon is practically impossible, so it is clear that the use of atomic weapons on a mass scale will lead to the devastation of the warring countries. One cannot help admitting that a huge threat, which could obliterate all life on Earth, hangs over mankind." The authors suggested exposing the duplicity of Eisenhower's proposal and publicizing the dangers of thermonuclear war.[14]

It is probable that these ideas had reached Georgy Malenkov earlier and that he had decided again to preempt other members of the collective leadership with an authoritative pronouncement. On March 12, 1954, the chairman of the Council of Ministers said in a public speech that the continuation of the Cold War between the USSR and the United States would lead to hostilities, "which with modern weapons mean the end of world civilization." This was a startling departure from the Soviet political discourse on nuclear weapons. For instance, Mikoyan's speech on the same day contained the traditional refrain that "hydrogen weapons in the hands of the Soviet Union are a means for deterring aggressors and for waging peace."[15]

Malenkov's speech reflected the growing nuclear fears in the Kremlin. On February 4, 1954, the Party Secretariat sanctioned upgrading underground bunkers and bomb shelters for the military and the government in case of nuclear war. Molotov and Khrushchev, however, used Malenkov's departure from the party line to charge him with ideological heresy. They claimed that his pessimistic conclusion would demoralize Soviet people and allies around the world, because it disputed the inevitability of the triumph of Communism over capitalism. They also attacked the speech from the position of "realism": any concern about nuclear weapons, they argued, could be interpreted by the enemy as a sign of weakness. In his next public speech, Malenkov admitted that a nuclear war would actually lead to the "collapse of the whole capitalist system."[16]

According to Molotov, another war would bring a "final victory" over "the aggressive forces of imperialism." Minister of Defense Nikolai Bulganin and most high-ranking Soviet military figures agreed. They still refused to acknowledge the revolutionary implications of thermonuclear weapons. In September 1954, the Presidium authorized the military exercise at Totskoye near the Urals. A Hiroshima-type atomic bomb was detonated there for the purpose of training troops. Bulganin and a group of marshals and generals attended the exercise and were optimistic: after taking certain precautions, the Soviet army would be able to wage atomic warfare.[17]

Khrushchev, despite his public stand, was initially greatly troubled by demonstrations of thermonuclear power. After the August 1953 Soviet test, his son recalled, Khrushchev watched a secret film on the nuclear explosion and came home depressed and could not calm down for days. The film showed houses shattered and people knocked off their feet at a distance of dozens of miles from ground zero. A witness of the test recalled that the impact of this explosion "apparently transcended some kind of psychological barrier. The effect of the first atomic bomb explosion had not inspired such flesh-creeping terror, *although it had been incomparably more terrible than anything seen in the still recent war.*" Khrushchev, who had been exposed to the horrors of war in 1941–44, must have felt a similar shudder. He confirmed his shock later in conversation with an Egyptian journalist: "When I was appointed First Secretary of the Central Committee and learned all the facts about nuclear power I could not sleep for several days."[18]

After the initial shock, Khrushchev realized that if the fear of thermonuclear power was mutual, it would prevent a future war between the Soviet Union and the United States. He suspected that the Eisenhower administration, despite its preparations and rhetoric, would not use such terrible weapons, especially if Americans feared possible retaliation. A natural optimist, Khrushchev transformed his anxiety into the determination to overcome American superiority. Once he consolidated his hold on power, he introduced dramatic changes in the structure of the Soviet armed forces. By early 1955, he discontinued Stalin's program of construction of a large navy, arguing that it could not withstand a strike by the new weaponry, conventional or atomic. He came to believe, as Eisenhower had earlier, that missiles would dominate future warfare.[19]

The fear of nuclear war did not change Khrushchev's belief in the revolutionary-imperial paradigm. True, he no longer thought, as Stalin and Molotov had, that a future war would make the world communist. But he felt that the mutual balance of fear disadvantaged the United States more than the Soviet Union. It would mean that "American imperialism," despite its economic, financial, technological, and military superiority, would not dare to challenge Communist control over Central Europe. Moreover, the Soviet Union and its allies would get more chances, under the cloak of nuclear fears, to promote the causes of decolonization, the anti-imperialist struggle, and Communism far beyond Soviet borders. The Soviet leadership, in Khrushchev's opinion, also had another advantage over the U.S. government; it was relatively free from "domestic deterrence," that is, public fears of nuclear war that could conflict with the global goals. The Soviet propaganda machine had developed a habit of suppressing the slightest signs of pacifism and used enormous resources to combat erosion of the ideological militancy in the society. With the exception of Malenkov's speech, the Kremlin leaders studiously avoided scaring the Soviet people with the consequences of a nuclear war. There were no "duck-and-cover" exercises in Soviet schools in the 1950s (although Soviet kids had plenty of paramilitary training), and the press and radio kept readers on a very slim diet of information about nuclear tests, American or Soviet. The physicists' remarkable letter of April 1954 was never published.[20]

However, the Soviet public did know about atomic bombs and did read about the destruction of Hiroshima. Not only soldiers on duty but also many civilians looked anxiously at planes in the skies, fearing them to be an *Enola Gay*. There was an obvious gap between the realities of the nuclear age and the party ideological dogma that predated them. This gap provoked questions and doubts. In the summer of 1954, a member of the Party Secretariat, Pyotr Pospelov, reported to Khrushchev the "mistakes" made by the world chess champion Mikhail Botvinnik in his letter to the party leadership. How, Botvinnik had asked, was one supposed to match the danger of nuclear annihilation with the official ideological thesis that wars were begun by imperialist "warmongers" in search of profits? Should the Soviet Union reach accommodation with these imperialists? Would this accommodation be a betrayal of "socialist" ideals? These questions aimed right at the heart of Soviet ideology and Cold War propaganda.[21]

On November 22, 1955, Soviet nuclear designers successfully tested a 1.6-megaton bomb. Unlike the one tested in August 1953, this bomb was a genuine "super," using the radiation compression principle and nuclear fusion. Igor Kurchatov and his designers knew they now could, just like the Americans, build multimegaton, ever-more-powerful, weapons. After the test, Andrei Sakharov suggested to Marshal Mitrofan Nedelin, the military commander of the test, that it would be a catastrophe if thermonuclear weapons were ever used. Sakharov was not alone in his doubts. Even Kurchatov, the scientific director of the Soviet nuclear project, would develop pacifist ideas, to the great displeasure of Khrushchev.[22]

Ideological optimism and militarist bravado suppressed fears of nuclear war in the top military circles. One exception was Marshal Georgy Zhukov, who replaced Bulganin as minister of defense. He agreed with President Eisenhower in July 1955 that with the appearance of atomic and hydrogen weapons many notions that were valid in the past had changed. Zhukov noted that "he personally saw how lethal this weapon is." The president and the marshal also agreed that only gradual trust-building and arms control measures could save the two sides from the current situation and overcome mutual fears.[23]

KHRUSHCHEV'S NEW LOOK

In February 1956, Khrushchev and his colleagues in the collective leadership were ready to bring ideological dogma to the nuclear age. At the Twentieth Party Congress, Khrushchev renounced Stalin's doctrine of the inevitability of world war and laid out the principles of "peaceful coexistence" between capitalism and socialism. But Khrushchev revised Stalin's interpretation of Marxism-Leninism only halfway. On the one hand, he said that imperialism does breed wars and repeated that capitalism would find its grave in another world war, should it unleash one. On the other hand, he added, "the situation has changed radically, because today there are mighty social and political forces possessing formidable means to prevent the imperialists from unleashing war." Influential circles in the West, Khrushchev concluded, had begun to realize that there could be no victor in an atomic war.[24]

Khrushchev argued that the Soviet view of Western imperialism remained the same, but that Soviet thermonuclear power could force the imperialists to be reasonable. After the test of the super bomb in November 1955, the Soviet leader could rely on the fresh demonstration of power. On February 20, 1956, the successful launch of the first medium-range ballistic missile with a nuclear warhead occurred. Khrushchev felt awed at the enormous destructive potential of the nuclear missile strike. But again, as in 1953, he conquered his emotions and began to search for the ways to use the newly acquired power. His conclusion for the public was: "Let these bombs get on the nerves of those who would like to unleash war."[25]

Khrushchev's most immediate goal was to create the appearance of a nuclear stalemate so as to undermine NATO and the other anti-Communist alliances engineered or sponsored by Eisenhower and John Foster Dulles in 1954 and 1955, specifically the Central Treaty Organization (CENTO or the Baghdad Pact) and the Southeast Asia Treaty Organization (SEATO). American missiles were deployed in Turkey, a member of CENTO. Khrushchev wanted to get rid of these missiles. He also wanted the United States to acknowledge the USSR as an equal power. In Khrushchev's opinion, the Americans would do so only if presented with a stark choice between war and peace. "There are only two ways," the first secretary said at the Twentieth Congress. "Either peaceful coexistence or the most destructive war in history. There is no third way."[26] To drive this point home to the Americans, Khrushchev needed to convince them that he was prepared to use the new terrible weapons. Thus, the implementation of his new vision led logically not to a moderate version of nuclear deterrence but to nuclear brinkmanship and dangerous bluff.

In a sense, Khrushchev emulated the policies and rhetoric of President Eisenhower and Secretary Dulles, who privately abhorred the prospect of nuclear Armageddon yet directed all their energies to maintaining American nuclear superiority in order to achieve specific foreign policy goals. Dulles, as a recent study has concluded, sought to "make nuclear weapons useful as something other than a Sword of Damocles suspended over the entire world." During the Geneva summit of 1955, Khrushchev realized that both Eisenhower and Dulles had deep misgivings about nuclear weapons. Khrushchev understood that their game (mistakenly, he believed that Dulles, not Eisenhower, was the chief strategist) was to intimidate the Soviet Union without becoming too provocative. And he decided to respond in kind. He felt that, "as a war veteran," Eisenhower would not allow confrontation between the Soviet Union and the United States to get out of hand. With such counterparts in Washington, Khrushchev believed there was a margin of safety in brinkmanship.[27]

Because the Soviet Union still lacked both ICBMs and reliable strategic bombers to deliver a strike against the United States, the first target of Soviet nuclear threats became Western European members of NATO. The first apparent success from the point of view of the Soviets was in November 1956, during the Suez crisis of Anglo-Franco-Israeli aggression against Egypt. At Khrushchev's suggestion, the Kremlin threatened the aggressors with a nuclear strike, while seeking to neutralize the United States by offering to send a joint Soviet-American "peacekeeping" mission to the Middle East. In reality, it was American pressure on London and Paris that ended the war, but Khrushchev firmly believed that Soviet threats did the trick and that "Dulles was the one whose nerves snapped." In June 1957, Mikoyan told the delegates of the Party Plenum that "everybody acknowledged that with this we decided the fate of Egypt."[28]

The outcome of the Egyptian affair emboldened Khrushchev to believe that nuclear power overshadowed all other factors in international relations. Thereafter, he began to regard the nuclear buildup not only as a means of deterrence but, according to the nineteenth-century Prussian war theoretician Carl von Clausewitz, as the continuation of state policies by other means.[29] In May 1957, Khrushchev said in an interview that the Cold War confrontation apparently boiled down to the relations between the two countries, the Soviet Union and the United States.[30]

In August 1957, the long-awaited technological breakthrough in missile technology occurred. The Soviet aerospace firm headed by Sergei Korolev successfully tested the R-7 missile ("Semyorka") as the world's first ICBM. On September 7, Khrushchev observed one of the missile's tests. He allowed Korolev to proceed with his pioneering plans of space exploration, and on October 4, Sputnik stunned the Americans and the rest of the world. In the longer term, the Sputnik effect galvanized the United States into launching another costly round in the arms race in order to restore public confidence in American superiority. Khrushchev, however, achieved what he wanted: now Americans feared nuclear war even more than the Soviets did. In February 1960, he said to the Presidium that the intercontinental missiles made an agreement with the United States possible, because "main-street Americans have begun to shake from fear for the first time in their lives."[31]

In the following years, the Soviet military-industrial complex focused even more on producing ever larger and more numerous nuclear weapons and missiles. Still, for many years, the Soviet Union had only a hypothetical strategic capacity against the United States. The R-7 was an inefficient and horribly costly weapon. A 300-ton behemoth, it operated on liquid oxygen fuel, which made every launch a nightmare. Each launch site cost half a billion rubles. In 1959, Soviet missile designers began to develop two other missiles, the R-9 and the R-16, but neither was good for serial deployment—they operated on liquid fuel and were extremely vulnerable to air attack. The deployment of the first generation of reliable intercontinental missiles began only in April 1962. Meanwhile, Korolev's behemoth had to be transported by railroad to the launching pad in Plesetsk in northern Russia. By the end of 1959, only four of these behemoths and two launching pads for them had become operational. In case of a U.S. first strike, the Soviets would have time for one launch only, and, according to Sergei Khrushchev, they targeted four U.S. "hostage cities" for retaliation: New York, Washington, Chicago, and Los Angeles.[32]

More prudent leadership in these circumstances would have waited years before bragging about new strategic capabilities, but not Khrushchev. On December 15, 1959, the Kremlin announced the creation of the Strategic Rocket Forces (RVSN), a new branch of the Soviet armed forces. Economic factors contributed to Khrushchev's impatience. He repeatedly promised to win the economic competition with the United States and sharply raise Soviet living standards. The global appeal of the Soviet planned economy, especially in India, Indonesia, Egypt, and other countries of the decolonizing world, was then enormous. Yet the romantic vision of the planned economy produced ever-diminishing practical results. Just at the time the RVSN was created, the Soviet economy began to slow down. The rapid rise of living standards since 1953 stopped. Khrushchev boasted that Soviet consumerism would outpace that of the Americans, but the facts belied his boasts. The nonmilitary sectors of the economy languished; the agricultural program of "virgin lands," after initial success, turned into a major disappointment; and Khrushchev's hasty measures to curb private peasant households created shortages of meat, milk, and butter. Massive assistance to China, growing generosity to Egypt, and rapidly rising subsidies to Poland and Hungary after 1956 put new strains on the Soviet economy and budget. To "correct deep disproportions in the people's economy," the Soviet government had to scrap the last three years of the five-year plan and announce a new "seven-year" plan. The promise to produce both guns and butter turned out to be more difficult than Khrushchev had expected.[33]

Meanwhile, the requirements of the new armament and research and development programs grew precipitously and far surpassed the allocated resources. From 1958 to 1961, military production in the USSR more than doubled, increasing from 2.9 to 5.6 percent of the Soviet national income. Strategic missiles turned out to be more expensive than Khrushchev had thought. Construction of launching pads and silos, including a new colossal complex at Tyuratam, Kazakhstan, as well as giant plants for the mass production of strategic arms, required enormous capital investments. Nuclear and missile projects necessitated the building of "secret cities" that had to attract the best workforce and maintain high living standards for it. One "secret city," Snezhinsk near Chelyabinsk, in the Urals, hosted the second Soviet nuclear laboratory. By 1960, its population had reached 20,000 people. Another "secret city" near Krasnoiarsk in Siberia began to produce weapons-grade plutonium in 1958. The reactors and twenty-two workshops were located in a huge artificial cavern at a depth of 200 to 250 meters beneath the earth; the complex had its own subway system and high-quality urban infrastructure that serviced and housed many thousands of scientists, engineers, and workers.[34]

Facing the growing discrepancy between promises and performance, Khrushchev was impatient to test his New Look. He hoped to achieve breakthroughs in the German Question and use the Soviet nuclear-missile programs as a "great economizer" in defense spending.

TESTING THE NEW LOOK IN BERLIN

In November 1958, Khrushchev presented the United States, Great Britain, and France with an ultimatum: either convert West Berlin into a "free city" within six months, or he would act unilaterally and give control over Western access to Berlin to the government of the GDR. At first, the impulsive Soviet leader was prepared to declare the Potsdam agreements—the basis for the presence of the Western powers in Berlin—to be defunct, because of Western violations. However, he realized that this radical step could hurt Soviet diplomacy in the longer term. So Khrushchev focused just on the idea of the "free city"—and on a separate peace treaty agreement that Moscow could reach with the GDR. As it turned out, the deadline was repeatedly postponed over the course of about four years.[35] Since the United States and other Western powers refused to accede to the ultimatum, Khrushchev's move created the East-West standoff that became known as the second Berlin crisis. Initially his approach seemed to bring about the expected results. NATO became visibly fractured under the renewed Soviet pressure. British prime minister Harold Macmillan hastily visited Khrushchev in February 1959 in an open attempt to mediate between him and Eisenhower. A long-delayed conference of foreign ministers on the German Question took place in Geneva from May to August. Finally, in July, Eisenhower extended an invitation to the Soviet leader to visit the United States. The results of the Khrushchev-Eisenhower talks at Camp David, from Khrushchev's viewpoint, were promising: Eisenhower acknowledged that the situation, with Berlin a divided city in the middle of East Germany, was "abnormal." He seemed to be agreeing to resume the quest for a diplomatic resolution of the German Question within the framework of a four-power summit, scheduled for the spring of 1960.[36]

There are divergent views on the origins of this confrontation. Hope Harrison concludes: "Khrushchev's concern about the GDR, combined with his desire to gain prestige by successful negotiations with the West, were the most consistent influences on him during the crisis." Other scholars believe that the Soviet leader reacted to the growing integration of West Germany into NATO and to American plans for "nuclear sharing," the result of the NATO "first strike" nuclear doctrine, which presented a security threat to the Soviet Union. There is evidence that the Kremlin was concerned with the prospect of West Germany gaining access to nuclear weapons.[37]

Khrushchev had multiple motives in the Berlin crisis. First, he was committed to ensuring the existence of the socialist GDR, a commitment he had repeatedly and publicly proclaimed during his criticism of Beria and Malenkov. Second, he was determined to demonstrate the effectiveness of his New Look in making Western powers abandon the containment strategy and begin to negotiate with the Soviet Union. Finally, as his rhetoric suggests, he hoped that a victory in Berlin would trigger the unraveling of Western imperialism globally and would help promote the revolutionary process in the countries of Asia and Africa.

Khrushchev laughed at the fears of his son, Sergei. "No one would undertake war over Berlin. On the other hand, it was time to fix the existing post-war balance of forces." Khrushchev hoped, according to his son, that he could scare the Western powers into making them "sit at the negotiating table."[38] The Soviet leader felt that the Soviet Union's nuclear power gave him an opportunity to succeed where Stalin had failed ten years earlier, namely in moving the relationship with the United States onto equal terms. He wanted to bring back to life the Yalta-Potsdam formula of great power diplomacy destroyed by Hiroshima and America's containment strategy.

Nuclear missiles were at the core of this gamble. The Soviet leader wanted to present the Western governments and citizenry with a stark choice: accept responsibility for the consequences of thermonuclear war or dismantle the anti-Soviet ramparts. It is sometimes overlooked that the flip side of Khrushchev's diplomacy of crisis-mongering and nuclear brinkmanship in 1958–61 was his campaign for disarmament. The Soviet leader wanted to offset the impression of Soviet bellicosity. In April 1957, Khrushchev told the Presidium that the Soviet Union should step up a propaganda campaign to ban nuclear weapons. Otherwise, he said, "we would lose the support of broad masses" in the West.[39] In November 1958, the Soviet Union declared a unilateral moratorium on nuclear testing (a few days after the United States and Great Britain had done the same). In February 1960, Khrushchev proposed to the Presidium that the Americans be offered the destruction of the Soviet ICBMs and nuclear weapons, on the condition that they would eliminate their military bases on the Soviet periphery and their strategic bombers. "Then NATO, SEATO, and CENTO"—all U.S.-forged alliances in Eurasia—"would fall into precipice." Mistakenly, he assumed that this proposal would be irresistible to the frightened American and West European publics.[40]

In September 1959, Khrushchev arrived in the United States at the invitation of President Eisenhower. Speaking for the first time at the UN General Assembly, he unveiled, for propaganda purposes, a plan of "general and complete disarmament." On the one hand, Khrushchev must have felt that his gamble worked. He toured America from coast to coast, clearly enjoying the fact that the most powerful capitalist country had to swallow its arrogance and entertain "the number one communist." His son-in-law Alexei Adzhubei and a host of Soviet journalists launched a mini-cult of Khrushchev in the Soviet Union, presenting him as an indefatigable peace fighter. It was an additional bonus of the New Look, but perhaps it was the one Khrushchev coveted most. On the other hand, his meeting "face to face with America" revealed Khrushchev's lack of preparedness for the diplomatic game. Khrushchev was both impressed and upset by American power and opulence; deep inside, he was insecure and looked for a pretext to give a rebuff. And he could not elicit from Eisenhower any specific concessions on West Berlin.[41]

Khrushchev was especially eager to demonstrate to his domestic constituency that his approach could bring immediate economic benefits. After his much-heralded trip to the United States and in anticipation of another summit in Paris in 1960, where he expected to extract Western concessions on Germany, the chairman decided to make the economic implications of his views public. In December 1959, in a secret memo to Presidium members, Khrushchev proposed a stunningly radical plan of reduction of armed forces. The Soviet Union, he argued, no longer needed a mass army, because nuclear-missile forces would provide a sufficient deterrent to potential aggressors. The reform would give the USSR "major political, moral, and economic advantages." On January 12, 1960, in his speech to the Supreme Soviet, Khrushchev announced the reduction of the armed forces by 1.2 million men in three years. A quarter of a million officers were forced to retire, many without adequate material compensation, retraining, pension, or housing.[42] This military reform was, in Khrushchev's mind, a logical follow-up to the creation of the RVSN just a month earlier.

Nobody dared to criticize Khrushchev's hasty steps, but privately some senior military officers were appalled. Doubts about the emphasis on nuclear missiles and expansionist schemes, not supported by real power, had started soon after the Suez crisis. Later Khrushchev's critics would contend: "We were one breath away from the big war. Our country had not yet recovered from the war with Hitler; people did not want war, did not expect it. Fortunately, all turned out well, and comrade Khrushchev immediately presented it as the product of his genius."[43] The military brass could not publicly oppose Khrushchev's military reforms, but they grumbled about "Nikita's folly" and resisted it by all possible means. Chief of General Staff Marshal Vasily Sokolovsky resigned in protest over Khrushchev's 1960 cuts. Some of the most intelligent generals took advantage of "theoretical discussion" in the classified journal Military Thought to question Khrushchev's excessive reliance on nuclear weapons. In 1960 and 1962, General Petr Kurochkin, Colonel-General Amazasp Babadzhanyan, and other authors agreed with Maxwell Taylor in The Uncertain Trumpet and Henry Kissinger in Nuclear Weapons and Foreign Policy (both books were translated and published in the Soviet Union) that an exclusive emphasis on nuclear retaliation left no choice between surrender and suicide.[44]

Khrushchev failed to persuade his marshals and generals, but he forced them to accept his New Look. Defense Minister Rodion Malinovsky created a task force at the Academy of the General Staff to prepare a classified book on military strategy in the nuclear age and ordered a reluctant Marshal Sokolovsky to bring the project to fruition. The book elaborated on the thesis that the next war would be a nuclear war and described the immense importance of the opening phase of the war (the first strike). It also established that the main reason for Soviet possession of nuclear weapons was to deter an American strike, not to wage a nuclear war. A nuclear war would be too devastating and thus must be avoided. The manuscript had to be redrafted several times, until Khrushchev liked the final product and approved its unclassified publication in 1962 under the title *Military Strategy*. In the opinion of the Soviet leader, it was a "sobering" reminder to American "hot heads."[45]

Khrushchev confronted another unexpected critic of his approaches, the leadership of the PRC. In November 1957, at the world conference of Communist parties, Mao hailed the new nuclear missile might of the Soviet Union as a reason for Communist forces to be more aggressive against Western imperialism. At the same time, he asked Khrushchev to share nuclear and missile technology with the PRC. From 1957 to 1959, the Chinese received the technology for the medium-range R-12 missile and cruise missiles and the complete know-how for the construction of atomic weapons. The Soviets even pledged to give the Chinese a working sample of the atomic bomb. Yet Mao could never forgive Khrushchev for his "secret speech" denouncing Stalin without consulting the Chinese. He believed that de-Stalinization was a grave error, perhaps even a challenge to his own authority. And Khrushchev's vision of nuclear bipolarity became anathema for Mao, because it relegated China to a secondary position in the pecking order of great powers.[46]

Mao's hidden animosity became public when the Soviet military asked Beijing to build joint bases for the Soviet navy and submarine fleet in the Pacific. Mao angrily rejected the proposal. On July 31, 1958, Khrushchev, in deep secrecy, flew to Beijing with the aim of soothing the PRC leader. Instead, he was subjected to a barrage of insults and humiliating treatment by the host. He was also shocked to discover a chasm opening between his vision of the nuclear age and Mao's ambitions. Mao did to Khrushchev what Stalin had done to the Americans after Hiroshima: he defied the nuclear factor altogether by describing it as "a paper tiger." "I tried to explain to him," recalled Khrushchev, "that one or two missiles could turn all the divisions in China to dust. But he wouldn't even listen to my arguments and obviously regarded me as a coward." Khrushchev did not disclose his concerns to his colleagues at the Presidium, but the prolonged Sino-Soviet honeymoon was over.[47]

The Chinese continued to startle the Soviets. On August 23, 1958, the People's Liberation Army of the PRC, without warning either Moscow or Washington, started shelling Quemoy, one of the offshore islands and still held by the Guomindang. Mao commented in his private circle: "The islands are two batons that keep Khrushchev and Eisenhower dancing." By staging this provocation, the Chinese leader drew both the U.S. and the Soviet leadership into a game of nuclear brinkmanship—but this time against their will and in accordance with his own scenario. In their official correspondence with the Kremlin, the Chinese leaders suggested that in the event that the United States used tactical nuclear weapons against the PRC, the Soviet Union should not declare war on America, the Sino-Soviet Treaty of 1950 notwithstanding. Perplexed by this suggestion, Khrushchev and the rest of the Presidium wrote to Beijing that such a scenario would be "a crime before the world working class" and would give the enemy "hope that they will be able to separate us."[48]

Khrushchev would not mind helping China with the islands, as long as Chinese actions coordinated with Moscow's strategy. Yet Mao's nuclear bravado struck him as either irresponsible dogmatism or "Asiatic cunning." Khrushchev soured on the idea of sharing nuclear power with the Communist ally in the East. On June 20, 1959, the Presidium quietly cancelled Sino-Soviet atomic cooperation. An atomic device with complete documentation, ready to be shipped to China, was destroyed. Mao's challenge to Khrushchev's authority profoundly troubled the Soviet leader. According to Troyanovsky, China was always on Khrushchev's mind.[49] At the same time, as the Chinese shelling of the islands failed to produce any results, Khrushchev expected that his nuclear bluff would be productive in Germany and West Berlin.

BRINKMANSHIP FALTERS

Just at the time when Khrushchev proposed the unilateral cuts of Soviet troops, his New Look began to falter. The first big glitch occurred, again, in China, where the Soviet leader appeared in October 1959, immediately after his triumphant trip to the United States. Evidently, the Soviet leader believed he was arriving in Beijing in triumph. He had obtained from President Eisenhower a commitment for a conference of great powers in Paris on Germany and Berlin. Mao Ze-dong, however, openly mocked what seemed to look like the second edition of the Yalta-Potsdam "system." The Chinese leaders, celebrating the anniversary of their revolutionary victory, decided to teach the Soviet leader a lesson and blamed him for accommodating the United States at their expense. To Mao's evident satisfaction, Khrushchev quickly lost his temper, and the meeting degenerated into an angry exchange. In vain, Andrei Gromyko and Mikhail Suslov, present at the meeting, tried to get the talks back on a positive track.

Khrushchev returned from China in a terrible mood, cursing Mao.[50] At the next Party Plenum, he instructed Suslov to report on the bad behavior of the Chinese comrades, but many of his colleagues in the Presidium and the state apparatus blamed deterioration of the Sino-Soviet relations on his rude and clumsy behavior.

Mao's criticism increased Khrushchev's self-doubts. The Soviet leader was taking an enormous risk. His arms reductions antagonized the military and created an uncertain future for the giant military-industrial complex, which involved, to varying degrees, 80 percent of the industrial enterprises of the Soviet Union. His old critics, Molotov, Kaganovich, and Voroshilov, were still party members who eagerly awaited the collapse of his schemes. Expectations for Khrushchev's upcoming trip to Paris and President Eisenhower's state visit to the Soviet Union were very high in official circles, and especially among the Soviet public. In case of failure, the political authority of the chairman and even his grip on the party elite would suffer irreparable harm. The Soviet leader, never a skillful negotiator, abruptly retreated from his euphoria and began to doubt. What if the Western leaders left him with empty hands?[51]

Soviet air-defense missiles shot down an American U-2 spy plane on its reconnaissance flight over Soviet missile bases on May 1, 1960, and Khrushchev seized this episode to show his toughness not only to the West, but also to the Chinese and his own military. When Eisenhower unexpectedly claimed responsibility for the flight, Khrushchev felt betrayed and angry. In Paris, he demanded a personal apology from the U.S. president, irrevocably ruining his relationship with the American leader. By the end of 1960, all plans for détente with the United States were in tatters. The Soviet leader had destroyed the fruits of many months of pressure and negotiations. Many Soviet diplomats regretted it. Defense Minister Malinovsky and the military, however, were satisfied because Khrushchev's New Look now appeared to be doomed.[52]

This episode revealed Khrushchev's lack of diplomatic skills. Khrushchev wanted some kind of accommodation with the United States, yet ideologically and psychologically he was ill-prepared to negotiate with Eisenhower and other Western leaders. The collapse of the Paris summit left Khrushchev with only one part of his foreign policy standing, the aggressive pressure on the West. The Soviet leaders decided to wait for the results of the U.S. presidential elections to find out who his next bargaining partner would be.

The fiasco also demonstrated the tenacity of Khrushchev's ideological worldview. He could not stand it when Mao and his own colleagues at home began to suspect him of being "soft" on Western imperialism. Even before the U-2 incident, in January 1960, Khrushchev assured the delegates of the Communist parties in Moscow that his policy of deterrence of war and peaceful coexistence meant more, not less, support for the "wars of national liberation" in the third world. After the collapse of great power diplomacy in Paris, he unleashed all his revolutionary instincts. His long-held conviction that Soviet nuclear power would accelerate the revolutionary process globally now translated into feverish activity to promote decolonization. He personally led the Soviet campaign of support of national-liberation movements in Africa, from Algeria to the Congo. A Soviet expert on the third world, Georgy Mirsky, recalled that at a time "when the revolutionary process in the Western countries was frozen," Khrushchev's leadership expected "to use post-colonialist momentum, break into the 'soft underbelly of imperialism' and win sympathies of the millions of people who woke up to the new life."[53]

This peculiar revival of "revolutionary" diplomacy, almost in the Comintern style, culminated in Khrushchev's memorable visit to New York to attend the UN General Assembly in September and October 1960. Confined by the U.S. government to Manhattan "for security reasons," the Soviet leader spent almost a month crisscrossing the island. He was a whirlwind of energy. He proposed to radically reform the United Nations, castigated Western colonialism from the UN podium using his shoe to make a point, dashed to Harlem to meet Cuban revolutionary leader Fidel Castro, and denounced American imperialism to anyone who would listen. In his message to Presidium members, he wrote that he enjoyed "cursing capitalists and imperialists" and yet counted every hour he was forced to stay in this "wretched capitalist country" and in New York, this "lair of the Golden Devil." His behavior in New York, especially the episode with the shoe, scandalized his own delegation.[54]

The victory of John F. Kennedy heartened Khrushchev, because his bête noir, Richard Nixon, lost. Yet he also became convinced that Kennedy was a lightweight, a spoiled rich young man, unready for serious confrontation. By all indications, Kennedy was not "another Franklin Roosevelt," that is, the kind of partner the Soviets had missed since 1945. Khrushchev felt he could intimidate the new president by his brinkmanship tactics. His confidence grew after the first successful space flight of Yuri Gagarin in April 1961. By contrast, Kennedy's reputation plummeted after the failed invasion of Cuba at Bay of Pigs by CIA-trained guerrillas.[55] It was a moment Khrushchev could not miss, an opportunity for nuclear pressure on the White House.

On May 26, 1961, Khrushchev told the Presidium that the Soviet Union should sign a separate treaty with the GDR. Western powers would have to choose between retreat and nuclear war. He confessed that he could not guarantee what the Americans would do in response. The Bay of Pigs invasion, he said, was proof that the U.S. government was not in the firm hands of one leader but rather "under influence of various groups and ad hoc situations." Yet Khrushchev concluded that the gamble was worth taking. "I would say the chance is more than ninety five percent there would not be a war." The Presidium members, by then all obedient associates of Khrushchev, did not object. Brezhnev, Suslov, and Gromyko supported Khrushchev's position. Cautious Mikoyan said that the United States "might start hostilities without using atomic weapons" but assessed this risk as minimal.[56] Encouraged by this fake unanimity, the first secretary behaved at the summit with Kennedy, in Vienna, Austria, on June 3–4, 1961, with shocking boorishness. Soviet diplomat Georgy Kornienko was stunned to learn that Khrushchev had said to Kennedy that it was better to let the war start now, before the emergence of new, even more terrible means of warfare. This remark was so provocative that both U.S. and Soviet official transcripts omitted it.[57]

Many scholars of the Berlin crisis have taken for granted that Khrushchev was deterred from unilateral action on West Berlin by Kennedy's tough countermeasures. As evidence, they cite Kennedy's July 25, 1961, speech, in which the U.S. president took steps to mobilize armed forces and announced that the Western allies would use all military options to defend their rights in West Berlin. They also cite the speech by Deputy Secretary of Defense Roswell Gilpatric on October 21, 1961, in which he disclosed that the United States had a large numerical superiority in nuclear missiles over the Soviet Union. "We have a second-strike capability," said Gilpatric, "which is at least as extensive as what the Soviets can deliver by striking first. Therefore, we are confident that the Soviets will not provoke a major nuclear conflict."[58]

Indeed, Khrushchev never acted on his threat to sign a unilateral peace treaty with the GDR, despite his desire to boost the East German regime and sovereignty. At the same time, Khrushchev's understanding of American behavior was different from what the White House sought to project. Soviet intelligence repeatedly informed the Kremlin leader about the Pentagon's plans for a preemptive nuclear attack on the Soviet Union, using American strategic superiority. Apparently this only strengthened his instincts for brinkmanship. Not the perception of Kennedy's resolve but rather Kennedy's domestic weakness impressed the Soviet leader. In August 1961, at the secret meeting of the Warsaw Pact leaders in Moscow, Khrushchev repeated his lamentations that Kennedy, unlike Eisenhower and Dulles, could not be a predictable partner in the brinkmanship game. If Kennedy pulls back from the brink, like Dulles had done many times, "he will be called a coward" at home.[59]

If so, what could be gained by provoking Kennedy? Khrushchev's inconsistency began to worry even his friends and allies. A number of leaders of the

Warsaw Pact, including Walter Ulbricht of the GDR and Georgy Georgiu-Dej in Rumania, already highly critical of the Soviet leader's de-Stalinization, began to have doubts about his foreign policy. The discontent among the Soviet military continued. Oleg Penkovsky, a high-ranking Soviet GRU official who began to spy for British and American intelligence in 1960, reported to the CIA that some in the Soviet military grumbled that "if Stalin were alive, he would have done everything quietly, but this fool is blurting out his threats and intentions and is forcing our possible enemies to increase their military strength."[60]

There were other signs that the strategy of nuclear bluffing was reaching its limits. The balance of fear had to be maintained by demonstrating the horrible potential of ever-more-powerful nuclear weapons. But the construction of protected silos and the testing of reliable ballistic missiles was far from complete, despite hectic and costly measures. In October 1960, a new R-16 missile accidentally ignited on a launching pad in Tyuratam, Kazakhstan, killing Marshal Nedelin, the head of the RVSN, and seventy-three other top designers, engineers, and officers. In the absence of a credible deterrent, any stopgap measure attracted the Kremlin's attention. The Soviet General Staff and the KGB competed in suggesting measures to discourage the United States from contemplating the use of force.[61] On July 10, 1961, Khrushchev informed the managers and scientists of the atomic complex about a decision to renounce the moratorium on nuclear tests that had been observed since November 1958. He enthusiastically supported the idea of nuclear designers Andrei Sakharov and Yakov Zeldovich to test a new 100-megaton device. Khrushchev said, according to Sakharov: "Let this device hang over capitalists like the sword of Damocles."[62]

The failure of the U.S.-Soviet summit generated fears of permanent closure of intra-German borders. A growing number of refugees rushed from East Germany to the West. The rapid deterioration of the situation in the GDR allowed Ulbricht the opportunity to present the Soviet leader with his own ultimatum. Either the Soviet leader must sign a separate treaty with the GDR and end the uncertainty or he would "lose" the GDR. Khrushchev faced a prolonged confrontation with the United States—he could see that Kennedy was not about to give up West Berlin. And signing a separate treaty with the GDR could lead to Western countermeasures. Khrushchev was not afraid of a nuclear outbreak. But he did fear economic sanctions against the GDR. The Kremlin leader knew that in this case the East German economy, heavily dependent on West German supplies, would crash—and the USSR would have to rescue its satellite at a tremendous cost. The estimates ran as high as 400 tons of gold and at least two billion rubles as credits. For Khrushchev, it was unacceptable. Searching for another option, he decided to build the wall around West Berlin. On August 13, 1961, Berlin became a divided city, and preparations for erecting the permanent structure began. The Berlin Wall provided, in Khrushchev's eyes, a substitute for a provocative unilateral treaty with the Ulbricht regime. The Soviet leader believed that West Berlin would wither away economically. He also assumed that West Germany, without its bulwark in the East, would gradually shift from confrontation to negotiation and economic partnership with the Soviet bloc.[63] At the same time, the Kremlin leader continued to maintain his nuclear pressure. In a response to Gilpatric's speech, the Soviet Union detonated the monstrous 100-megaton bomb at half strength on October 30 above the Arctic Circle at Novaya Zemlia. A jubilant Khrushchev told the Party Congress: "When the enemies of peace threaten us with force, they must be and will be countered with force."[64]

A few days earlier, on September 25, a spat between the Americans and the East German border guards at Checkpoint Charlie in Berlin grew into a demonstration of U.S. military force. Khrushchev immediately ordered Soviet tanks to advance to the checkpoint. There they stood, their engines running, faced by American tanks.

Most important, despite the obvious crudity of Soviet behavior in Berlin and the violation of the test moratorium, Khrushchev demonstrated that he, not Ulbricht, was in control in East Germany. During the confrontation at Checkpoint Charlie, the Soviet leader remained perfectly calm. On October 26, GRU colonel Georgy Bolshakov, a special liaison of the Kremlin with the Kennedys, reported that the U.S. president wanted to resume talks on the German Question and find a compromise on West Berlin. Khrushchev withdrew the tanks from Checkpoint Charlie, and soon the Americans reciprocated. Kennedy's behavior confirmed, in Khrushchev's mind, that the Americans would not start a war over West Berlin.[65] The Soviet leader's belief in nuclear pressure remained unshakable. As 1962 began, Khrushchev told the Presidium members: "We must increase pressure and let our adversary feel that our strength is growing." He assured his colleagues that he would know when to stop. "The game is still worth playing."[66]

A great problem with Khrushchev's nuclear brinkmanship was the lack of clear strategic goals. His allegiance to the revolutionary-imperial paradigm left Soviet foreign policy straddled, as it had been during the 1920s, between support of the radicals and revolutionaries in Africa, Asia, and Latin America and the search for geopolitical accommodation with the West. Khrushchev wanted Western "imperialism" to retreat on all fronts, including West Berlin, but it was an utterly unrealistic expectation. Khrushchev's nuclear threats could not substitute for Soviet lack of capabilities. The chairman's increasing impulsiveness aggravated this situation. He made decisions on the basis of his own judgment only, virtually without analytical input from his colleagues, the Foreign Ministry, the KGB, or the Ministry of Defense.[67] And he continued to feel a mixture of scorn and impatience about Kennedy. He told the Presidium that Eisenhower and Kennedy might consist of "the same shit" as far as the German Question was concerned. Sakharov recalled Khrushchev saying: "In 1960 we helped to elect Kennedy with our policy. But we do not give a damn about Kennedy, if he is tied hand and foot."[68] It seemed that brinkmanship spared Khrushchev the need to look for more complicated and nuanced approaches in foreign affairs. Meanwhile, the developments in the Caribbean led Khrushchev to take his most dangerous step. On May 21, 1962, he decided to send nuclear missiles to Cuba.

THE CUBAN HURRICANE

The Cuban missile crisis of October–November 1962 was the ultimate exercise in nuclear brinkmanship, the one case in which it might well have caused a world war.[69] There has also been an ongoing discussion about the motives that pushed Khrushchev to send missiles thousands of miles away from the Soviet Union. Scholars have connected Khrushchev's gamble in Cuba to his desire to break Western resistance in West Berlin.[70] Others have asserted that the missiles in Cuba were to help the Soviet leader regain his balance.[71] Recent studies trace the crisis back to the Soviet leader's impulsive personality and his increasingly desperate search for a panacea, a dramatic gesture to rescue his failing foreign and domestic policies. William Taubman concludes that the Cuban missiles were Khrushchev's "cure-all that cured nothing."[72] Only recently have scholars come to recognize how important it was for Khrushchev to protect Cuba against possible and credible American aggression. Belief in the ultimate victory of Communism and the desire to accelerate this victory were always factors in Khrushchev's motivation and behavior. His nuclear brinkmanship was not only a strategy to gain geopolitical advantages for the Soviet Union but also an instrument to constrain Western imperialism, facilitate decolonization, and, ultimately, promote the global spread of Communism.[73]

The issue of Cuba's security was linked to the growing problem of Khrushchev's authority in the Communist world and at home. The Cuban Revolution had become a big factor in Soviet domestic politics, as growing segments of Soviet leadership, elites, and general public, especially the educated youth, sympathized with Castro and his "bearded friends" (barbudos).[74] The more the domestic expectations about the "anti-imperialist" revolutions in the third world grew, the more Khrushchev felt a personal responsibility to promote their fruition. Troyanovsky wrote in his memoirs "that Khrushchev constantly feared that the United States would compel the Soviet Union and its allies to retreat in some region of the world. Not without reason he believed that he would be held responsible for that." This feeling grew stronger as Khrushchev heard the increasingly strident accusations from Beijing that he was appeasing the imperialists. Historians Aleksandr Fursenko and Timothy Naftali demonstrate the crucial role of this factor in Khrushchev's decision to deploy the missiles in Cuba.[75]

Khrushchev was not alone in believing that sooner or later the United States would invade Cuba, most likely during the Kennedy administration. Many intelligence estimates, both Soviet and Cuban, pointed in this direction.[76] Declassified American sources on MONGOOSE, the covert actions against Castro's Cuba, demonstrate that Khrushchev's fears were not completely off the mark: powerful elements in the Kennedy administration indeed wanted "to develop new and imaginative approaches to the possibility of getting rid of the Castro regime."[77]

At the same time, the temptation to improve the Soviet position in the strategic balance of the superpowers was also great. Troyanovsky believes that Khrushchev wanted to redress, "at least partially," the nuclear imbalance between the Soviet Union and the United States. In 1962, the United States began deploying Minuteman and Titan missiles that were far superior in quality and quantity to what the Soviets had in their arsenal. The strategic disparity was rapidly increasing, undermining the credibility of Khrushchev's policy of nuclear pressure.[78] "In addition to protecting Cuba," Khrushchev argued before the Presidium, "our missiles would equalize what the West likes to call 'the balance of power.' " The Americans had surrounded the Soviet Union with their missile and air bases. Now "they would learn just what it feels like to have enemy missiles pointing at you."[79] Cuba, of course, was deep inside what the United States perceived as its exclusive sphere of influence. The American military had absolute predominance in the Caribbean. This meant that the delivery and deployment of missiles and the huge amount of supporting equipment and troops would have to be carried out right under the nose of the Americans. Khrushchev proposed to the Presidium that the Soviet Union deliver nuclear missiles in secrecy and announce their arrival afterward. Whatever doubts the members of the Presidium and the Secretariat had, they did not reveal them and voted unanimously for Khrushchev's plan. The military called it "Anadyr," after a river in Siberia, to mislead Western intelligence.[80]

The Kennedy administration overlooked a key element in Soviet motivation, the provocative nature of U.S. actions aimed at Cuba. The consensus in Washington was that the Soviets would never deploy their nuclear missiles outside of the USSR. The Americans knew nothing of an important precedent: in the spring of 1959, at the height of the Berlin crisis, Soviet medium-range missiles and their nuclear warheads arrived in the GDR. The Soviets pulled them out in August, when Khrushchev's trip to the United States was in preparation.[81] This episode seems to confirm that Khrushchev wanted to create a nuclear-missile force but not to provoke a war, and to back up his position in talks, in case that would be necessary.

In July 1962, when the Cuban delegation, with Raul Castro at its head, arrived in Moscow to sign a secret Soviet-Cuban agreement on missile deployment and other issues of Cuba's defense, Khrushchev exuded confidence. But the Cubans found Khrushchev overconfident and bombastic. If the Yankees find out about the missiles before the agreement is made public, he told them, there would be nothing to worry about. "I am going to grab Kennedy by his balls. If the problem arises I will send you a message—and that will be signal for you to invite the Baltic Fleet to visit Cuba."[82] The Soviet military, despite its earlier quiet criticism of Khrushchev's arrogance and recklessness, acted in the same manner. Marshal Sergei Biryuzov, the commander of the RVSN, who traveled to Cuba to do reconnaissance, concluded that it would be easy to conceal Soviet missiles among Cuban palm trees. As it turned out, the top brass simply misled their commander in chief, because they wanted a base close to their primary enemy.[83] From the beginning, "Anadyr" proposed to deploy on Cuba "a Group of Soviet Forces comprising all branches of the Armed Forces," including the dispatch of a squadron of surface ships from the Baltic Fleet and a squadron of submarines. Had the operation succeeded, the Soviet Union would have had 51,000 troops, missile bases, and a naval base on the island.[84] The combination of Khrushchev's nuclear policies and the agenda of the military turned "Anadyr" into a juggernaut that could no longer be stopped.

As risky as it was, "Anadyr" paled next to other macabre schemes bandied about by the military. In 1960–62, the leaders of the Soviet space program, encouraged by the propaganda bonanza after Gagarin's flight, began to lobby for the construction of military space stations, presumably capable of launching nuclear missiles against any part of U.S. territory. General Nikolai Kamanin, deputy for space to the commander of the Soviet air force, was frustrated that the high military command and Khrushchev did not see the potential in the militarization of space. He wrote in his diary on September 13, 1962: "Malinovsky, [Andrei] Grechko, and [head of the General Staff Matvei] Zakharov have been missing opportunities for us to become the first in creating a space force—I would even say, an absolute military force which could facilitate the domination of Communism on Earth."[85]

In May 1959, a military research group headed by engineer Major A. Iroshnikov sent a proposal to Khrushchev to create twenty to twenty-five artificial islands around the United States that could be used as Soviet bases "for launching atomic rockets of intermediary range." The project's authors expected that "the construction of our islands in the immediate proximity to the vital U.S. centers" could force the U.S. government "to agree, in the process of further negotiations, to liquidate its air-fields and missile pads in the countries bordering on the USSR." This scheme reached the desk of Marshal Sokolovsky, who found the whole project technically feasible but "ill-advised."[86] The test of the super bomb in October 1961 generated other wild-eyed projects. Andrei Sakharov, future recipient of a Nobel Peace Prize, suggested that a similar device might be launched in a large torpedo from a submarine. Later, in 1962, academician Mikhail Lavrentiev wrote a memorandum to Khrushchev proposing the use of a 100-megaton device to generate an artificial and huge wave, similar to an earthquake-generated tsunami, along the North American coastline. In case of a war with the United States, Lavrentiev concluded, this could inflict irreparable damage on the enemy. After a series of tests, Soviet scientists found that the continental shelf would protect New York City and other U.S. cities from such a super surf. The extraordinary project was dropped.[87]

On October 22, 1962, Kennedy, prompted by the U-2 aerial reconnaissance pictures of Soviet missiles in Cuba, publicly denounced the Soviet deployment in Cuba. From the start, the Soviet leader miscalculated what the initial American reaction to Soviet deployments in Cuba would be. The Soviets must have hoped that if the Americans discovered the Soviet missiles, they would try first to approach the Kremlin through a secret channel and perhaps offer a trade between them and the Jupiter missiles in Turkey. Various signals fed this illusion, until Kennedy went public with his announcement of Soviet "perfidy." Suddenly the crisis was a public event, and this, as both sides knew, severely increased pressures on the leadership. Kennedy, at least, had a week of secret deliberations in his narrow circle before the crisis became public. Khrushchev learned about Kennedy's announcement only a day before.[88]

Just hours before Kennedy's speech, Khrushchev convened an emergency Presidium meeting to discuss possible Soviet responses to American actions. He called the new situation "tragic." The longer-range Soviet missiles and their nuclear warheads still had not arrived in Cuba. And the Kremlin had missed the chance of publicizing the Soviet-Cuban defense treaty and thus lacked international legal grounds for the deployment of its missiles. The Americans could try to invade Cuba or launch an air strike against the island. "If we do not use nuclear weapons," Khrushchev said, "then they would capture Cuba." "In fact, we do not want to unleash a war," Khrushchev explained. "We wanted to intimidate, to contain the U.S. with regard to Cuba." And now "they can attack us, and we shall respond," he concluded. "This may end in a big war." Khrushchev, as the Presidium debates reveal, did not want to preclude the *possibility* of using nuclear weapons—the essence of his brinkmanship policy. The military supported him; Marshals Malinovsky, Andrei Grechko, and others disliked the idea of disarming unilaterally. They believed their U.S. counterparts would not hesitate to use nuclear weapons first. Defense Minister Malinovsky read to the Presidium members the draft instruction to General Issa Pliyev, the commander of Soviet forces in Cuba: "If there is a [U.S.] landing, [use] the tactical atomic weapons." The strategic nuclear missiles could not be used without an order from Moscow. In the discussion that followed, Anastas Mikoyan objected: "Doesn't using these [tactical] missiles mean the start of a thermonuclear war?" Khrushchev vacillated. Still, after the prolonged debates, he agreed to changes in the instructions to Pliyev. No nuclear weapons were to be used, even in the event of attack on Cuba.[89] As a result, the Soviet strategic missiles in Cuba were never ready for war. Their nuclear warheads were kept miles away in special storage sites and stayed there throughout the crisis.[90] At Malinovsky's insistence, Khrushchev ordered the commanders of four Soviet submarines, each armed with a nuclear-tipped torpedo, to approach the Cuban shore, in order to increase the Soviet nuclear deterrent. The military claimed, again incorrectly, that this maneuver could be done without the Americans detecting it. The commanders and political commissars of four Soviet submarines, which sought to make their way through U.S. antisubmarine defenses, did not have a clear idea of what to do with their nuclear weapons if fired upon by the U.S. Navy or U.S. aircraft. Some of their leaders were under the impression that they could use them. Fortunately, they did not do so when the U.S. Navy destroyers detected the submarines and forced them to the surface.[91]

By October 23, Khrushchev had recovered from the initial shock and had learned that President Kennedy and his brother, Attorney General Robert Kennedy, were also hesitant and fearful. At the Presidium on October 25, he said: "No doubt, Americans got scared." He acknowledged that strategic missiles must leave Cuba before the situation reached "the boiling point," but this moment had not yet come.[92]

On October 27, in the absence of clear intelligence on Kennedy's intentions, Khrushchev decided to offer terms to Kennedy. In his message to the president, he said that the Soviet Union would remove its missiles from Cuba if the United States removed "its analogous weapons from Turkey." Following that, the United States and the Soviet Union, he continued, "would pledge to the UN Security Council to respect the integrity of the frontiers and the sovereignty" of both Turkey and Cuba. Khrushchev backed away from nuclear brinkmanship, to the great relief of many in the Soviet foreign policy establishment. As Viktor Israelyan, a senior official in the Foreign Ministry, recalls in his recent memoirs, Khrushchev's message evoked a great sigh of relief, and also "in broad public in Moscow." Israelyan and his colleagues also greeted Khrushchev's negotiating terms as providing equal, decent, and mutually acceptable terms of compromise.[93]

At a second meeting during the night of October 27, Robert Kennedy and Anatoly Dobrynin agreed that the Soviets would withdraw the missiles from Cuba in return for two U.S. concessions, a public pledge not to invade Cuba and a secret one to take the missiles out of Turkey. Kennedy explained that any publicity on the missile deal would create an uproar at home and among NATO allies and as a result would undercut his brother's political standing.[94] The deal looked like an acceptable and fair option for the Soviets. But simultaneous events dashed Soviet hopes for a dignified exit from the crisis. Signals from Soviet and Cuban intelligence, the embassy in the United States, and the Soviet military in Cuba added to the perception that the situation was rapidly getting out of control. In a cable written on the night of October 26–27, Fidel Castro advised the Soviet leader to launch a preemptive nuclear attack in case an American invasion or strike on Soviet missiles was imminent. At a conference in Havana in 1992, Castro explained his cable as an attempt to prevent "a repetition of the events of the Second World War," when the Nazis had caught the Soviets by surprise. Khrushchev, however, was aghast. Castro had failed to understand the logic of his nuclear brinkmanship.[95]

Finally, it dawned upon Khrushchev how dangerous the game he had started was. The chairman's views on nuclear war were straightforward: once it started, it could not be limited. In July, Khrushchev had angrily dismissed the new American doctrine of targeting military installations instead of cities. "What is their aim?" he wondered at the Presidium. He answered: "To get the population used to the idea that nuclear war will happen." Armed with such a doctrine, the American military could now convince Kennedy to start such a war. He sent an urgent telegram to the commander of the Soviet forces in Cuba, General Pliyev, confirming "categorically" the ban on using nuclear weapons from planes and on tactical weapons, as well as on strategic missiles.[96] On the same day, a Soviet operator of a surface-to-air missile shot down a U-2 plane over Cuba, killing its pilot. Khrushchev learned about this on Sunday, October 28, and was under the impression that Castro had ordered the operation. About this time, the GRU informed the Presidium that Kennedy was about to give another televised address. It turned out to be a repetition of the "quarantine speech," but Khrushchev mistook it for an announcement of war. He immediately accepted American terms: at 6:00 A.M., Moscow time, only two hours before Kennedy's speech, Soviet radio announced to the world the unilateral withdrawal of "all Soviet offensive arms" from Cuba. The announcement made no mention of the with-drawal of American missiles from Turkey.[97]

Later, Khrushchev's bravado returned; he maintained that the Soviet retreat from Cuba was not the defeat Castro and the Chinese Communists perceived it to be. And he attempted to keep tactical missiles, cruise missiles, and bombers in Cuba after sending their atomic payloads back to the Soviet Union.[98] On October 30, he gave his own version of what had happened to the Czechoslovak Communist Party delegation that happened to be in Moscow. "We knew that the Americans wanted to attack Cuba," Khrushchev asserted. "Both we and the Americans talked about Berlin—both sides with the same aim, namely to draw attention away from Cuba; the Americans in order to attack it; we, in order to make the USA uneasy and postpone the attack." The Soviet leader then said that the Americans had been about to start a giant maneuver codenamed ORTSAC (Castro spelled backward) at sea with 20,000 marines, a ploy to invade Cuba. "We believe that shortly before the start of the maneuvers, their intelligence discovered our missiles were in Cuba, and the Americans became furious." Castro's telegram suggesting a preemptive Soviet nuclear strike prompted Khrushchev to articulate his views about nuclear warfare. "It is clear that today with a first strike one cannot knock the opponent out of the fight. There can always be a counter-strike, which can be devastating. There are, after all, missiles in the earth, which intelligence does not know about. There are missiles on submarines, which cannot be knocked out of the fight right away, and so on. What would we gain if we ourselves started a war? After all, millions of people would die, in our country too. Only a person who has no idea what nuclear war means, or who has been so blinded, like Castro, by revolutionary passion, can talk like that." The Soviet leader hastened to add that it was not he who lost the game of brinkmanship. "From our intelligence reports we knew that the Americans were afraid of war. Through certain persons they made it clear they would be grateful if we helped them get out of this conflict." Khrushchev concluded with this face-saving thesis: The missiles in Cuba were "essentially of little military importance" to the USSR and had "served their main purpose."[99]

BACKING AWAY FROM THE BRINK

In his memoirs, Mikoyan observed that the crisis began as a pure gamble but ended "surprisingly well."[100] What did he mean? Kennedy and Khrushchev both claimed victory. Yet both were chastened by their experiences in the crisis. They had a glimpse into the nuclear abyss and discovered that even carefully calculated schemes of nuclear brinkmanship could lead to a catastrophe. They also realized how many things could go wrong during such a crisis.[101] Troyanovsky observed Khrushchev closely throughout the events of October, and in his opinion they "had a tremendous educational value for both sides and both leaders." The crisis "made them realize, not in theory, but in practical terms, that nuclear annihilation was a real possibility and, consequently, that brinkmanship had to be ruled out." Above all, Khrushchev dramatically revised his opinion of the U.S. president. From now on, he began to regard Kennedy as a valued negotiating partner, not a pushover target of nuclear brinkmanship.[102] This was the start of the mutual move toward U.S.-Soviet détente that would blossom, despite many obstacles, ten years later.

The outcome of the Cuban missile crisis killed Khrushchev's New Look, although he never admitted it. Public repercussions of the crisis inside the Soviet Union were minimal, and many Soviet citizens, inured to constant news about "provocations of American militarism against the island of liberty" in the Caribbean, did not lose sleep over the crisis until its worst phase was over. Political elites, however, took the Cuban crisis with utmost seriousness. Moscow party functionaries decided to send their families to the countryside. When provincial officials learned more details, they were shocked. A Ukrainian party leader, Petro Shelest, wrote in his diary in November 1962: "We stood on the brink of war. In a word, we created the situation of untenable military tension, and then tried to extricate ourselves out of it." Shelest and many of his colleagues felt that "crazy Nikita" got them into a big mess.[103]

The Cuban missile crisis also put an end to Khrushchev's brinkmanship and ultimatums regarding West Berlin. In July 1962, the Soviet leader seemed to be planning to put more pressure on the Western powers there. If the Cuban gamble had succeeded, Khrushchev would have gained an enormous psychological and political edge over Kennedy. Yet, from October 22 on, Khrushchev dismissed all suggestions from his subordinates to respond to the American actions against Cuba with a blockade of West Berlin.[104]

Unfortunately for Khrushchev, he could not reveal his secret agreement with Kennedy on withdrawal of American missiles from Turkey. The American media celebrated Kennedy's victory, but Khrushchev's reputation at home suffered disastrously. Many senior military and diplomats were convinced that Khrushchev had lost his nerve and hastily accepted the American ultimatum without any concessions. Negotiations between the Soviet deputy foreign minister, Nikolai Kuznetsov, the American ambassador to the United Nations, Adlai Stevenson, and Kennedy's personal representative, John McCloy, added to this impression. The Americans skillfully exploited Khrushchev's plight and rejected any Soviet attempts to save face. Also, they used Khrushchev's vague pledge about the withdrawal of "offensive weapons" (the Kremlin doggedly refused to mention the presence of Soviet missiles in Cuba in his public speeches) and forced the Soviets to remove all their weapons systems, including the Ilyushin bombers Moscow had promised to hand over to the Cubans.[105] Many in Moscow's halls of power believed Khrushchev should not have deployed missiles to Cuba in the first place, but once he had done so, he should have held his ground. The outcome of the crisis, with the Soviet weapons leaving Cuba under close U.S. supervision, left a bad taste for the military high command.[106]

To the Cuban leadership and to Khrushchev's enemies in Beijing, the end of the crisis looked like abject capitulation. Khrushchev forgot to consult with Castro before the public announcement of Soviet withdrawal. He also did not disclose to Castro the nature of his secret deal with Kennedy, justifiably fearing that the touchy Cuban leader would treat it as an insult to Cuban sovereignty and would divulge this secret to the world. Castro, in turn, felt personally betrayed and believed that Khrushchev had betrayed the Communist cause as well. When Khrushchev accidentally blurted out the news about the missiles trade-off with Kennedy during Castro's visit to Moscow in the spring of 1963, the Cuban leader was livid with fury and humiliation.[107]

The crisis cast a long shadow; never again would Soviet leaders risk a head-to-head clash "between the two systems" in the manner practiced by Khrushchev. After the harsh Cuban lesson, the Kremlin leaders began to take more seriously the idea of arms control. The military and the leaders of the huge military-industrial complex, especially the head of the nuclear ministry, Efim Slavsky, and the head of the military-industrial commission, Dmitry Ustinov, continued to oppose any limitations on military development. But an influential scientific lobby prepared the ground for this change. Many Soviet nuclear scientists were sympathetic to the worldwide antinuclear campaign. Since the late 1950s and until his death in February 1960, Igor Kurchatov had lobbied hard for a moratorium on nuclear testing.[108] In early 1963, when both Khrushchev and the Kennedy administration began to move toward agreement on a partial test ban, a major impulse came from nuclear scientists. Viktor Adamsky, a member of Sakharov's theoretical group in the nuclear design bureau, Arzamas-16, wrote a proposal to Khrushchev urging him to accept the terms that had earlier been offered by the Americans but rejected by the Soviets. Sakharov approved the letter and on the next day flew to Moscow to show it to the atomic minister, Efim Slavsky. The latter agreed to transmit the letter to Khrushchev. The scientists succeeded in pressing the right buttons to please Khrushchev. A few days later, Slavsky informed Sakharov that Khrushchev had accepted the proposal.[109]

At that time, the Soviets could not overcome their mistrust of intrusive inspections and the presence of NATO inspectors on Soviet territory. Even Khrushchev, who would speak eloquently in his memoirs about the "malaise" of Stalinist xenophobia, remained adamant on this point. He told his Presidium colleagues that even two or three inspections, his initial negotiating position in talks with the United States, would mean "letting spies" into the Soviet Union. Even if the Western powers agree, "we do not need it." By 1963, the Soviet atomic program no longer required large-scale atmospheric tests to build a strategic arsenal and achieve strategic parity with the Americans. Most important, the partial test ban did not require on-site inspections. When the issue of inspection was dropped, the last obstacle to the agreement fell. On August 5, 1963, the American-British-Soviet negotiations ended in the signing in the Kremlin of the Limited Test-Ban Treaty. Khrushchev's son recalls that the Soviet leader was "extraordinarily glad, even happy," with this achievement.[110]

Meanwhile, Khrushchev openly attacked Chinese "revolutionary" rhetoric on war and peace.[111] In his speech to the Supreme Soviet in December 1962, he ridiculed the Chinese notion of imperialism as "a paper tiger." "This paper tiger, he said, has atomic teeth and this cannot be regarded frivolously." In July 1963, the Soviet leadership was determined "to cross the swords publicly with the Chinese"; their main goal at the meeting of the Warsaw Pact that month was to rally the support of allies against Beijing. As the U.S. embassy correctly concluded at that time, the "outbreak of virtually undeclared war" between Moscow and Beijing in the spring of 1963 "explained Soviet acceptance of a partial test ban agreement which it could have had at any time during the past year."[112]

These perceptions led to a bizarre episode in Soviet-U.S. relations. Against the background exchanges and consultations with Khrushchev on the test ban, the Kennedy administration implicitly and sometimes explicitly proposed combining efforts to thwart the Chinese nuclear program. On July 15, Kennedy instructed his negotiator, Averell Harriman, "to elicit K's view of means of limiting or preventing Chinese nuclear development and his willingness either to take Soviet action or to accept U.S. action aimed in this direction." This was a scarcely concealed probe on the idea of a preventive strike on Chinese nuclear facilities. Harriman and other U.S. representatives met with Khrushchev several times in the period between July 15 and July 27 and discussed this matter, but to their disappointment, "Khrushchev and Gromyko have shown no interest and in fact brushed subject off on several occasions."[113] As it happened, the American proposal came at the worst possible moment, when both the meeting of the Warsaw Treaty Organization and the secret Sino-Soviet ideological discussions were taking place in Moscow. For ideological reasons, Khrushchev could not risk a secret alliance with Washington.[114]

In hindsight, Khrushchev stands out as a rare case of a nuclear optimist. His nuclear brinkmanship was exceptionally crude and aggressive, reckless and ideology-driven. The architect of the New Look played hardball. But he relied more on his instincts than on strategic calculations. And he was not a master of diplomatic compromise. His improvisations, lack of tact, rudeness, and spontaneity let him down, after several strokes of luck. His ideological beliefs, coupled with his emotional vacillations between insecurity and overconfidence, made him a failure as a negotiator. Also, the Soviet leader was never able to come to a systematic or consistent conclusion regarding nuclear strategy. There remained a huge gap in Soviet political and military thinking between the emphasis on nuclear weapons as a means of prevention of war and the official military doctrine with its pursuit of "victory" at any cost in a future war. At their internal meetings after the Cuban missile crisis, the head of General Staff, Zakharov, the minister of defense, Malinovsky, and the head of RVSN, Biryuzov, admitted that the outcome of a war between the superpowers would be decided by a massive wave of nuclear strikes. At the same time, they clearly wanted to quash Khrushchev's schemes of sharp cuts of conventional arms. On February 7, 1963, Malinovsky, at an internal military conference, said that all branches and types of Soviet armed forces should be preserved and developed, since there could emerge "local non-nuclear wars," for instance in South Vietnam, and since even "in thermonuclear war" it would be necessary "to eliminate the remnants of the enemy's forces and keep the captured territories under control." Not surprisingly, after the downfall of Khrushchev in October 1964, his successors began to pursue numerical parity with NATO, a choice that required enormous expenditures and, eventually, would lead to overextension of the Soviet economy.[115]

Khrushchev's threats to the West and the military doctrine of victory in nuclear war that he imposed on the Soviet military left a dark shadow on Soviet-U.S. relations. Khrushchev's missile rattling left a profound impression in the U.S. political leadership and strategic analytical communities. It took twelve years of careful diplomacy and an extraordinarily costly military buildup for Khrushchev's successors to reach the same stage of negotiating with Western powers that he had squandered in May 1960. But even the years of détente could not repair the damage Khrushchev had done. His attempt to browbeat Kennedy in Vienna haunted several U.S. presidents. Similarly, for a long time, Americans continued to be allergic to any Soviet activities around Cuba, which resulted in the mini-crises of 1970 and 1979. The neoconservative pundits in the mid-1970s used the publications of Khrushchev's era, including Military Strategy, to argue that the Soviets indeed intended to fight and win nuclear war.

Soviet Cold War cartoon of 1949. What appears to be Harry Truman and Winston Churchill promoting NATO is actually macabre Pentagon warmongers in disguise. (Courtesy of the Archive of the President of the Russian Federation, Moscow)

Josef Stalin and his future apostate Nikita Khrushchev at Lenin's mausoleum, sometime in 1949–50. (Courtesy of the Archive of the President of the Russian Federation, Moscow)

Khrushchev heading for work at the Kremlin, flanked by Georgy Malenkov and Anastas Mikoyan, 1954. (Courtesy of the Archive of the President of the Russian Federation, Moscow)

Armed and dangerous. Khrushchev liked nuclear brinkmanship, but he also liked shooting ducks. (Courtesy of the Archive of the President of the Russian Federation, Moscow)

Heroes of a superpower. First cosmonaut Yuri Gagarin, at left, at a reception with Commander in Chief Khrushchev in April 1961. *Left to right:* Defense Minister Marshal Rodion Malinovsky (hidden behind Gagarin), Marshal Andrei Grechko, Khrushchev, Chief of General Staff Marshal Matvei Zakharov, Commander of the Strategic Rocket Forces Kirill Moskalenko, Marshal Vasily Sokolovsky (?), and commander of Moscow's anti-air defense Pavel Batitsky. (Courtesy of the Archive of the President of the Russian Federation, Moscow)

Voyage of peace? Khrushchev advertised himself as "the fighter for peace," but instead he made his reputation by exercising ham-fisted tactics of brinkmanship. (Courtesy of the Archive of the President of the Russian Federation, Moscow)

Leonid Brezhnev takes part in the Victory Parade on Red Square, June 24, 1945. Later he attended Stalin's banquet. Twenty years later, a the general secretary of the Communist Party o the Soviet Union, he continued to admire the warlord Stalin. (Courtesy of the Archive of the President of the Russian Federation, Moscow)

Brezhnev once said, "Charm can take you a long way in politics." He used it well, as long as his health allowed it. (Courtesy of the Archive of the President of the Russian Federation, Moscow)

Protesters denouncing the "Chinese aggressors" who had once been Soviet "friends forever," 1969. This generation of Soviet people hailed and then denounced Stalin and Khrushchev. (Courtesy of the Archive of the President of the Russian Federation, Moscow)

"Détente" means "relaxation." Brezhnev and West German state secretary Egon Bahr after a relaxing hunting trip in Zavidovo, Russia, 1971. (Courtesy of the Archive of the President of the Russian Federation, Moscow)

The Old Guard's exit. Mikhail Gorbachev and the Politburo "elders" at the Moscow train station around 1981. In the front row, left to right, are Gorbachev, Andrei Gromyko, Nikolai Tikhonov, Leonid Brezhnev, Mikhail Suslov, Konstantin Chernenko, Yuri Andropov, Boris Ponomarev, and Brezhnev's son-in-law Yuri Churbanov. Behind Brezhnev are Dmitry Ustinov and Viktor Grishin. (Courtesy of the Archive of the President of the Russian Federation, Moscow)

Somber Gorbachev at the end of 1991. After six years of lofty promises of reforms, he presided over the dissolution of the Soviet "empire." (Courtesy of the Archive of the President of the Russian Federation, Moscow)

(CHAPTER 6)

THE SOVIET HOME FRONT

FIRST CRACKS, 1953-1968

The Soviet way of life can breed its own enemies.
It generates and educates its adversaries.
—Historian Sergei Dmitriev, in his diary, October 1958

As the drama of the Cuban missile crisis unfolded, the intelligentsia of Moscow and Leningrad hardly noticed it. In early November 1962, the members of the intelligentsia, as well as millions of other Soviet readers, were frantically looking for copies of a thick literary journal that had just published Alexander Solzhenitsyn's *One Day in the Life of Ivan Denisovich*, about the fate of a Russian peasant in Stalin's concentration camp.[1] During the second decade of the Cold War, momentous changes began to take place on the Soviet home front, in society and culture, in public opinion and collective identities.

The Cold War was not just another great power confrontation. It was also a clash between opposite social and economic projects, a theater of cultural and ideological warfare. As such, David Caute concludes, it was shaped "by the shared and bitterly contested heritage of the European Enlightenment; and, not least, by the astonishing global ascendancy of printing presses, of film, radio, and television, not overlooking the proliferation of theaters and concert halls open to the broad public, particularly in the USSR."[2]

Recent studies have concluded that global confrontation and this competition of ideologies profoundly affected American society just as the modernization of American culture and society began to influence U.S. foreign policy and international behavior.[3] And a similar interaction occurred on the Soviet side. The "new" foreign policy and Khrushchev's denunciation of Stalin at the Party Congress in February 1956 took place at the time of rapid modernization of Soviet society. Restricted to small groups of elites and militarized industries under Stalin, this modernization became a much broader phenomenon after his death. The demands of competition with the United States forced the Soviet leadership not only to promote science and technology but also to expand higher education and to give more freedom and power to the scientific and engineering elites. From 1928 to 1960, the number of college students grew twelve-fold and reached 2.4 million. The number of college-educated professionals increased from 233,000 to 3.5 million.[4] The post-Stalin rulers wanted to prove that the Soviet model could produce a happy society of creative and highly educated people. Khrushchev and other members of the Presidium agreed to sharply reduce work hours and taxes; they increased investments in public housing, education, mass culture, and the health system. They also set out to create modern urban infrastructures and consumer-oriented industries, neglected or dismantled during the Stalin years. According to Russian historian Elena Zubkova, "Government policy, it seemed, did in fact turn its face to the people."[5] By the early 1960s, government social policies and economic growth boosted optimism among the Soviet population, especially among professionals and students, the growing educated "middle class."[6]

The cultural Thaw and de-Stalinization unleashed by Khrushchev were also far-reaching, although by no means inevitable, factors in Soviet modernization. The gray uniformity of Stalinist culture also started to lessen. Soviet citizens, as their fear of political repression subsided, began to speak in increasingly diverse voices. Passive resistance to unpopular state practices grew, and "oases" of thinking, relatively free from state propaganda, began to spread.[7] These developments attracted the close attention of Western scholars.[8] Recently, Jeremi Suri has argued that de-Stalinization during the 1960s led to the dissident movement, which, in turn, together with the movements in Central Europe, began to challenge the fundamentals of the Soviet regime. This led the Kremlin leadership to a more conservative, détente-oriented diplomacy.[9] Suri's view exaggerates the impact of the dissident movement and downplays other important motives behind the Soviet policy of détente. It is, nevertheless, a promising first attempt to connect histories that too long have remained disconnected.

In this chapter, I argue that the Thaw and Khrushchev's de-Stalinization project did not have an immediate visible effect on Soviet foreign policy. It was, however, intimately related to the outcome of the Cold War. It produced far-reaching divisions within the educated strata of Soviet society and marked the end of the total isolation of Soviet society from the West. The destruction of Stalin's cult wounded the Soviet ideological consensus. It is beyond the scope of this book to analyze changes that occurred in specific branches of the Soviet bureaucracy (the military, secret police, party elites), as well as among workers, various nationalities, war veterans, and so on. The focus here is on the elite groups and networks that emerged in the late 1950s and moved to the center of political and cultural life thirty years later, during the final stage of the Cold War drama. These elites were "enlightened" party apparatchiks, intellectuals, artists, and writers of Moscow and other major urban centers who called themselves *shestidesyatniki*, or "men and women of the Sixties," and who were determined to reform and liberalize their country. Their collective efforts would provide the essential background for the dramatic shift in Soviet international behavior under Mikhail Gorbachev from 1985 to 1989.

THE THAW

Stalin's regime shaped Soviet intellectual life and mass culture for decades. Many elements of Stalinist propaganda and mass culture outlived terror and even Communism itself and continue to affect people even in today's Russia. Beginning in the 1930s, Stalin's goal was to instill in intellectuals, cultural elites, and the masses the ideas of service to great power interests, vigilance toward internal enemies, and readiness to go to war against external foes. Stalin's preparations for a showdown with the United States in turn determined the direction and focus of Soviet propaganda and cultural policies. In the spirit of the revolutionary-imperial paradigm, the official propaganda promoted Russian great power chauvinism and the idea of the central role of the Soviet Union in world affairs.[10]

Recent historical research reveals that Stalin acted as the supreme editor of Soviet culture, that is, the narratives of the official discourse defining collective identities, values, and beliefs.[11] In no other regime in modern history, aside from Nazi Germany, did the promotion of culture (*kultura*) preoccupy the political leadership so much and involve such considerable expenditure. A number of cultural institutions, among them the Bolshoi Theater and leading museums in Moscow and Leningrad, benefited from state munificence. Stalin cultivated and nurtured the creative elites, especially writers, whom he called "engineers of human souls." After 1934, the members of the Soviet Writers' Union, de facto members of the state propaganda machinery, became a privileged class. Established writers got millions of copies of their books published, and privileged artists and sculptors grew rich from state orders. A Russian cultural historian, Maria Zezina, observed that by the time of Stalin's death "a vast majority of creative intelligentsia was sincerely devoted to Soviet power and did not dream of any opposition to it."[12]

At the same time, countless writers, musicians, artists, and other cultural figures fell victim to purges and spent decades in the Gulag. The decline of the arts was especially striking, as the brilliance, diversity, and avant-garde experiments of the 1920s gave way to triumphant conformism, kitsch, and mediocrity. The cultural avant-garde was banned as "formalistic" and "anti-national." All had to conform to the doctrine of "socialist realism," officially imposed in 1946. This doctrine promoted creation of a false world in accordance with Stalin's ideological prescription—the world of the Big Lie, in sharp contrast with Soviet realities. The doctrine of "social realism" was not just a part of the ruling ideology. It was embedded in all mechanisms of cultural production, including the hierarchy of "creative unions" and collective self-censorship.[13] The cultural establishment was divided into unspoken factions, in a vicious fight for resources and privileges. All this resulted in a rapid decline not only of the quantity but ultimately of the quality of the Soviet Union's "cultural output."

Stalin's meddling in the realm of science brought even more contradictory results. On the one hand, in nuclear, missile, and armament programs, he promoted the young cadres, entrusted them with crucial tasks, and showered them with considerable perks and privileges. Igor Kurchatov, appointed the scientific director of the atomic project, wrote down after his conversation with the leader: "Comrade Stalin loves Russia and Russian science." After 1945, Soviet scientists and university professors became a privileged caste; their salaries were far above average. At the same time, the Kremlin ruler's direct and often obsessive interference promoted Trofim Lysenko's pseudoscientific monopoly in biology and resulted in the ban on genetics and cybernetics.[14]

Anti-Semitism became a part of state policies that greatly affected all intellectual and cultural spheres of life. The anti-Semitic campaign reached its climax in January 1953 after Stalin unleashed "the Kremlin doctors' affair." Soviet propaganda news claimed that there was a conspiracy between prominent Soviet physicians ("the Kremlin doctors") and Zionist organizations in the United States, with the goal of murdering members of the Soviet political and military leadership. At any moment, Stalin might order the deportation of Soviet Jews to the Far East. The anti-Semitism had an enormous divisive and corroding influence on Soviet elites and the educated society. In particular, it gave rise to anti-Stalinist and eventually anti-Soviet sentiment in educated circles—doctors, professors, educators, writers, journalists, professionals, and the creative intelligentsia in general—where persons of Jewish descent had been strongly represented since the 1920s.[15]

Hopes for liberalization and a better life that had been building among intellectuals and cultural elites since the war of 1941–45 grew in educated circles of Soviet society. Sharp observers realized that Stalinist policies in cultural, intellectual, and scientific spheres, as well as everywhere else, had reached an impasse.[16] After Stalin's death, the framework and basic mechanisms of state control over education, culture, and science continued essentially unchanged. Yet the anti-Semitic witch hunt, and the mass hysteria and preparations for pogroms, ended after Stalin's death. The harsh propaganda of militarism and Russian nationalism ebbed; the new Soviet leaders called for restoration of "socialist legality." Gradually, the shocking shifts of 1953, including rehabilitations of the first groups of political prisoners from the Gulag and the sharp reduction of the power of the secret police and its network of secret informers, made room for the cultural Thaw.

The new leader, Nikita Khrushchev, was not a new Great Teacher guiding people's minds and capturing their imaginations. Nikita was strikingly under-educated and erratic. He neither wanted to nor could direct Soviet culture. He was obviously tipsy at his first meeting with Soviet writers in the spring of 1957. Possessing no means to charm his guests, he tried to remonstrate and intimidate them. The result was disastrous. In contrast to Stalin, Khrushchev was a joke; his behavior left intellectuals amused, appalled, and humiliated at once. A popular saying, a pun on Khrushchev's denunciation of "the personality cult" of Stalin, went: "There was a cult, but at least there was also a personality."[17]

In the fall of 1953, Novy Mir published several literary essays by Vladimir Pomerantsev that contained a simple thesis: a writer should write with candor about what he or she thinks and sees. This was a first dig at socialist realism and the mendacity of Stalinist culture. Pomerantsev had spent several years outside the Soviet Union, working for the Soviet Military Administration in Germany. This may have spared him from the paralysis of fear and self-censorship that entrapped many of his colleagues.[18] During 1954 and 1955, university dormitories in Moscow, Leningrad, and other cities were abuzz with debates about "candor" in literature and life that quickly became debates about the gap between ideological promise and Soviet reality. Those debates involved future Soviet dissidents, visiting students from Central Europe, and those who later made successful careers in the League of Communist Youth (Komsomol) and the party. Among them were two dorm roommates: a Czech student, Zdenek Mlynar, who would become a leading figure in the "Prague Spring" in 1968, and Mikhail Gorbachev, who would become the last general secretary of the Communist Party of the USSR three decades later.

A creative minority of theater directors, film directors, editors of magazines, lawyers, historians, and philosophers began to test the limits of state censorship, venturing over the boundaries of party discipline in search of innovation and originality.[19] Writer Ilya Ehrenburg, Stalin's emissary to Western pro-Soviet intellectuals, wrote a novel, The Thaw, that gave the name to the new era. Alexander Tvardovsky and Konstantin Simonov began to transform the journal Novy Mir into an outlet for talented and unorthodox literary works. Film directors Mikhail Kalatozov, Mikhail Romm, and other stars of the Soviet "factories of dreams" came out with films extolling humanistic values and virtues. These people, aided by more sympathetic officials in charge of cultural affairs, formed the milieu in which a new generation of talented men and women grew up and reached for greater freedom.[20]

The cultural Thaw evolved into a much more radical phenomenon after Khrushchev's secret speech. Khrushchev had neither the vision nor the intellectual ability to foresee the consequences of this speech. The text of his secret speech was leaked to the West. The U.S. State Department published the report, and soon CIA-funded Radio Liberty and Radio Free Europe began to broadcast it, to the dismay of Communists in the East and the West.[21] Inside the Soviet Union, Khrushchev sent the secret speech to local party organizations with the instruction to read it to all rank-and-file party members and even broader audiences of "working collectives," the total number probably being twenty to twenty-five million people. The report put the entire ideological and propaganda apparatus into a state of paralysis. At universities, working sites, and even in the streets, people spoke their minds—officials, the KGB, and secret informers were speechless.[22]

Millions of people in the Soviet Union wanted to know more than the speech revealed. Sergei Dmitriev wrote in his diary: "There is no serious interpretation of the facts in the speech. Its implications for foreign policy can hardly be understood. And what is its domestic meaning? At schools students began to tear Stalin's portraits off the walls and trample them under their feet. They ask: who created the cult of personality? If there was only one personality, what did the rest of the party do? Every party committee in every region, district, and area had their 'vozhd' and heroes."[23]

Some Soviet students, according to an American observer, felt that "their faith had been shattered, and henceforth they could believe in nothing" that the Soviet regime told them to believe in.[24] At the end of May 1956, students at Moscow State University boycotted the university canteen, which was notorious for its bad food. It was a semi-intentional reenactment of the revolt on the battleship *Potemkin* during the revolution of 1905—the episode was widely known to the Soviet people from Sergei Eisenstein's celebrated film. Instead of a crackdown, baffled authorities negotiated with the students. Only later were some of them expelled and sent to live in the provinces.[25]

During the fall semester, students at many universities in Moscow, Leningrad, and elsewhere produced posters, bulletins, and journals unauthorized by the authorities. The autumn revolutions in Poland and then in Hungary had a considerable impact not only on the neighboring regions of Western Ukraine and the Baltic but also on students in Moscow, Leningrad, and other major cities. After the Soviet army suppressed the Hungarian revolution in November 1956, students at the Moscow and Leningrad universities gathered for meetings of solidarity with Hungary.[26] Some hotheads itched for action. In the Archangel region, a young man distributed a leaflet comparing Soviet power to the Nazi regime. The leaflet read: "Stalin's Party is a criminal and anti-national [organization]. It degenerated and turned into a closed group consisting of degenerates, cowards, and traitors." Future dissident Vladimir Bukovsky, then in high school, dreamed of getting weapons and storming the Kremlin.[27]

As their predecessors had done a century earlier in czarist Russia, radicalized students turned to literature for guidance. The focus of their attention was the new novel *Not by Bread Alone*, by Vladimir Dudintsev, published in *Novy Mir*. The novel described a conflict between an honest innovator and the bureaucrats who tormented him and blocked his creative activity. Meetings between writers and students encouraged radicalism. Konstantin Simonov, the editor of *Novy Mir*, spoke publicly about the need to repeal the 1946 party resolutions on party censorship of literature and art. Widely respected writer Konstantin Paustovsky spoke about a new class of conservative and obtuse careerists in science, culture, and other fields. He expressed the conviction that the Soviet people "would get rid of this group." These words electrified students and they spread around Russia in handwritten copies. Others took Dudintsev's book as a judgment on the whole Communist ruling elite. One anonymous letter to the Ukrainian Writers Union read: "Dudintsev is thousand times correct. There is a whole group in power, the product of the terrible past." The author of the letter called himself "a representative of a quite numerous strata of medium Soviet intelligentsia." "We opened our eyes," the letter concluded. "We learned to tell truth from lie. There can be no return to the past. The edifice of lies that people like you helped to erect is falling apart. And it will collapse."[28]

Breaking with the Stalinist Big Lie did not automatically mean a break with Communist ideology and the revolutionary legacy. In the prevailing mentality, a profound hunger for personal freedom warred with a sincere belief in the validity of socialist collectivism.[29] Other sources also demonstrate that 1956 was only the beginning of a great "emancipation of mind" from the ideas of a Communist utopia.[30] There were many who regarded de-Stalinization as a path to restore the values and norms of the first postrevolutionary years and of "the true Leninism." At the end of a three-day meeting of the Moscow Writers' Union, after the discussion of the secret speech, the audience spontaneously sang "The International." A future dissident, Raisa Orlova, was overwhelmed: "Finally, the true and pure revolutionary ideal has returned, something you can give yourself to without reservations."[31] Marat Cheshkov, then a member of a clandestine group of Moscow intellectuals, recalled: "For me, and also for the majority of the politically engaged youth, Marxism-Leninism remained the unshakable foundation." He also admitted he "could not conceive, firstly, a society without the socialist order, secondly, without a politically centralized organization, i.e., the Party."[32]

Anti-Stalinist socialist radicalism was centered in Moscow and Leningrad, at universities and in educated circles. The provinces, where the intelligentsia was inconsequential and dispersed, remained quiet and conformist. After coming to Moscow State University from the provincial Rostov University, Alexander Bovin, a future "enlightened" adviser of Leonid Brezhnev, was surprised to find that he was far too moderate for his classmates. "I was not ready for such a high-pitch democratic and anti-Stalinist mood." Bovin disagreed with "unabashed" criticism of the party and the entire Soviet system; he also defended Soviet policies in Poland and Hungary. Other students interrupted and booed him down.[33] Coincidentally, these skirmishes took place at the department of philosophy from which another student, Mikhail Gorbachev's wife, Raisa Maximovna, had graduated just one year earlier. Bovin would later become an "enlightened" apparatchik, advocating cautious liberalization from above.

The bulk of the party and state bureaucracy, the military, and the secret police was forced to support Khrushchev's course of de-Stalinization, but privately these people resented its radicalism and ideological implications. Dmitry Ustinov, the man in charge of the military-industrial complex and secretary of the Central Committee after March 1965, would continue to fume twenty years after Khrushchev's fall that "no one enemy brought us so much harm as Khrushchev did in his policy towards the past of our party and our state, and towards Stalin."[34] Thousands from the military, diplomatic, and economic managers circles felt that their lives and achievements, especially during the Great Patriotic War, were compromised by the criticism of Stalin. Others felt that Khrushchev and the political oligarchs just wanted to turn Stalin into a scapegoat. General Petr Grigorenko was offended by Khrushchev "dancing the cancan on the tomb of the great man."[35]

At first, the confusion in the state bureaucracies and the KGB allowed for spontaneous de-Stalinization from below. The officials in charge of censorship, propaganda, and media were confused. On the one hand, the new radicalism of students and intellectuals frightened them. One the other hand, few of them wanted to resort to repressions only a few months after the denunciation of Stalin, without a clear signal from above.[36] In November 1956, the Soviet invasion of Hungary restored the conservative majority's self-confidence. The invasion came as a cold shower for radical anti-Stalinists, especially students, who realized, as one of them recalled, "that in this country we were completely alone. The masses were possessed by absolute chauvinism. 99% of the population shared entirely the imperial aspirations of the authorities."[37] Many intellectuals, even those who advocated de-Stalinization, rallied hastily under the Soviet banners. They were eager to demonstrate that they never had had any doubts about the Soviet cause in the Cold War. Almost seventy Soviet writers signed the "open letter" to Western colleagues justifying the military action. Among them were the leaders of the cultural Thaw: Ehrenburg, Tvardovsky, and Paustovsky.[38]

In December 1956, Khrushchev and the Politburo concluded that the unrest among intellectuals and students endangered political control over the society.[39] Hundreds, perhaps thousands, were expelled from research institutions and universities. The KGB made arrests around the country to suppress dissent. The authorities restored the quotas limiting the number of children of intellectuals among university students; they also took measures to increase the numbers of "children of workers and peasants" in the student body.[40]

The events of 1956 revealed Soviet leaders' fear of the subversive potential of intellectuals and cultural elites. A special three-day meeting at central party head-quarters with a group of writers resembled the Spanish Inquisition. Dmitry Shepilov, the most educated member of the new leadership, told writers that the 1946 policies in the cultural sphere would remain in force as long as the Cold War continued. When Konstantin Simonov, the editor of Novy Mir, asked the party bosses for permission to write a little bit of "truth about the realities" in the country, Shepilov rejected this request. Now, he said, as before, the United States sought to undermine Soviet society with ideological and cultural means. There-fore, literature must stay completely at the service of the party and serve its national security policies.[41]

This Cold War rationale would slow down the liberalization of Soviet cultural and educational policies for decades to come. Soviet cultural elites feared being branded as anti-Soviet and consequently as unpatriotic. The reaction reached a climax in the so-called Pasternak affair. In spring 1956, poet Boris Pasternak finished his novel Doctor Zhivago, which depicted the tragic fate of the Russian intelligentsia after the revolution. He submitted the manuscript to Novy Mir. At the same time, he broke the Soviet taboo and sent the manuscript to Italy, to the Communist maverick publisher Giacomo Feltrinelli. Novy Mir rejected the manu-script, and in November 1957, Doctor Zhivago appeared in print in the West and became a world literary sensation. In October 1958, Pasternak received the Nobel Prize for literature. Khrushchev unleashed a huge campaign to denounce Paster-nak, which became a test of the loyalty of the entire Soviet cultural establishment. As in December 1956, the authorities cited the bipolar logic of the Cold War: those who are not completely with us are against us. Stalinism seemed to be back, as the entire state apparatus wielded its power to crush one individual. In a frenzy of ostentatious patriotism, mixed with fear of losing state favors, the vast majority of Soviet writers voted to expel Pasternak as a traitor from the Writers' Union and even demanded his expulsion from the Soviet Union. Pasternak was forced to renounce the Nobel Prize, and his health gave out under the strain. He died of cancer on May 30, 1960.[42]

The swift restoration of "order" in 1956 and the Pasternak affair were sobering reminders to those who expected quick change. Still, the momentum of grassroots de-Stalinization continued. The control of state ideological and cultural institutions over the younger generation and cultural elites continued to erode.

THE ENEMY IMAGE BLURS

After Stalin's death, the Soviet Union slowly began to open up to the outside world. In 1955, Soviet authorities authorized foreign tourism, banned under Stalin. They also eased a nearly total ban on foreign travel for Soviet citizens. In 1957, 2,700 Americans visited the Soviet Union, and over 700,000 Soviet citizens traveled abroad. But only 789 of these visited the United States.[43] The closed nature of Soviet society and the state control of the flow of information generated enormous curiosity in Soviet society about the outside world and especially about America and Americans. The few American tourists and educational and cultural exchange visitors became the objects of immense curiosity. During the summer of 1957, a young Yale graduate (and future CIA analyst and diplomatic historian), Raymond Garthoff, traveled around the Soviet Union and met with hundreds of students. Outside Leningrad, he and his colleague found themselves surrounded by 150 students at an agricultural college. Students were so excited and grateful for the opportunity that they escorted the two Americans in a ceremonial march to the train station.[44]

Many Soviet citizens, avid readers, found their windows to the West in translated literature. After Stalin's death, a great number of works of American writers in translation, among them Ernest Hemingway, John Steinbeck, and J. D. Salinger, were published in hundreds of thousands of copies; they were available in thousands of public libraries around the Soviet Union. American films became another window into the New World for the curious public. After World War II, state authorities authorized a controlled release of trophy German and American films captured in Europe. These were mostly musicals, light-hearted comedies, and soap operas. The response of the Soviet public, from children to the old, to these releases was wildly enthusiastic. Music from American films, especially swing by Glenn Miller's orchestra, successfully competed with the Russian classics repertoire. The *Tarzan* series with Johnny Weismuller and *His Butler's Sister* with Deanna Durbin became as much a part of the generational experience as American canned food from Lend-Lease, ration cards, and fatherless childhood.[45]

During the Thaw, the trickle of Western films became bigger. State film distributors in Moscow and the provinces liked American blockbusters for monetary reasons and won bureaucratic fights against party propagandists concerned by the enormous popularity of Hollywood productions among viewers in the cities and the countryside. Many of the best-known American dramatic films (by Elia Kazan, Cecil B. DeMille, and others) did not reach broad Soviet audiences because of their cultural and religious content. Still, millions saw *The Magnificent Seven* with Yul Brynner, *Some Like It Hot* with Marilyn Monroe and Jack Lemmon, and others. Their impact on Soviet audiences cannot be overestimated. As the Nobel Peace Prize–winning Russian poet Joseph Brodsky, who lived then in Leningrad, recalled, these films "held us in greater sway and thrall than all the subsequent output of the neorealists or the *nouvelle vague*. The Tarzan series alone, I daresay, did more for de-Stalinization than all Khrushchev's speeches at the 20th party congress and after."[46] Writer Vasily Aksenov remembers: "There was a time when my peers and I conversed mostly with citations from those films. For us it was a window onto the outside world from the Stalinist stinking lair."[47]

The ferment that eroded the anti-American propaganda images worked above all on educated and privileged Soviet youth. Under the impact of de-Stalinization and the cultural Thaw, many educated youngsters sought to distance themselves from the Soviet past. They mistrusted and ignored Soviet propaganda and tried to dress and behave differently, in Western fashion. The state media ostracized them, calling them "loafers," "parasites," and *stilyagi* ("style-apers"). Garthoff recalled that the youths he met and talked with in 1957 fell into several categories. Some of them were "naive," especially those recently graduated from secondary school. They had not yet discovered contradictions between what they were taught and reality; they still believed in the propaganda about the United States. The older youths could be divided into the "believers," the precocious cynics, and the "golden youth" who found their escape from the dullness of Soviet cultural life in unabashed Westernism and Americanism.[48] For those of the "golden youth" who were skeptical or disillusioned, everything American became a powerful antidote to state propaganda. Young artists, writers, poets, and musicians exhibited the same attitudes. Joseph Brodsky observed that he and his friends tried to be "more American than the Americans themselves."[49]

American radio broadcasts and music exercised huge "soft" power upon many young Soviets. American jazz and swing were repeatedly banned in the

Soviet Union before World War II and again when the Cold War started. Many young people developed the habit of listening to the Voice of America's radio programs, almost exclusively because of the VOA's music programs. The number of shortwave radios in Soviet homes grew from half a million in 1949 to twenty million in 1958. At the end of his life, Stalin ordered the production of shortwave radios to be stopped by 1954. Instead, Soviet industry began to produce four million such radios annually, primarily for commercial reasons.[50] Particularly popular was the VOA's *Time for Jazz*. Its disc jockey, Willis Conover, owner of a fabulous deep baritone, became a secret hero of many Moscow and Leningrad youngsters. They sang, without understanding many of the words, the songs of Benny Goodman and Glenn Miller and listened to Ella Fitzgerald, Louis Armstrong, Duke Ellington, and the improvisations of Charlie Parker. Later came Elvis Presley. According to all accounts, the VOA's audience numbered millions. Records of American music stars were not available in stores, and getting a foreign-made vinyl disk was considered a miracle. By the late 1950s, tape recorders began to change this and broaden the exposure of Soviet youth to Western music.[51]

Ironically, Khrushchev and his erratic policies helped more than anything else to punch holes in the iron curtain. Despite the comeback of the hard-liners at the end of 1956, Khrushchev wanted to continue de-Stalinization. Paradoxically, the Cold War served as a justification both for asserting the "moral and political unity" of the Soviet people and for introducing the modest reforms aimed at projecting a benevolent image of the Soviet Union in the West. After the crackdown in Hungary, Khrushchev, Mikoyan, and Shepilov advocated the return to a "peace offensive." This resulted in an event with far-reaching domestic consequences, the World Youth Festival, held in Moscow in July and August of 1957. For a quarter of a century, the Soviet Union had remained virtually closed to foreigners, and there was almost no tourist infrastructure in place. The festival's organizers tackled many daunting tasks, such as what to do with the squalid look of most urban areas; the inadequacy and small number of hotels; the absence of nightlife, advertising, attractive quality clothing, carnival costumes and paraphernalia; and the lack of fast-food places and restaurants and opportunities for shopping. All this exposed the relative backwardness of Soviet society and economy in comparison with the capitalist West.[52]

Khrushchev let the leadership of the Komsomol run the show, with instructions "to smother foreign guests in our embrace." As a result, the festival became the first "socialist carnival" in the streets and squares of Moscow since 1918. Even the Kremlin flung its doors open for the young crowds.[53] Soviet authorities were unprepared for the scale of the event and failed to maintain centralized control over it. The festival turned into a giant grassroots happening that paralyzed all attempts at spin control, as well as crowd control. Three million Moscovites provided enthusiastic hospitality to over 30,000 young foreigners. The curiosity and enthusiasm of the hosts was immeasurable. Many corners of the capital turned into impromptu discussion clubs—a completely new experience for Soviet citizens.[54]

The festival did in peacetime what the last stage of World War II had done before. In 1945, the war brought Ivan into Europe. In 1957, the Soviet regime itself brought the world to Moscow. The appearance of young Americans, Europeans, Africans, Latins, and Asians in the streets of the Soviet capital shattered propagandist clichés. In the Soviet media, a memoirist recalls, "Americans were depicted in two ways—either as poor unemployed, gaunt, unshaven people in dregs or as a big-bellied bourgeois in tuxedo and tall hat, with a fat cigar in the mouth. And there was a third category—hopeless Negroes, all of them victims of Ku-Klux-Klan."[55] As Russians saw freethinking and stylishly dressed youth, their xenophobia and fear of secret police informers evaporated virtually overnight. Many witnesses of the festival would concur later that it was a historical landmark as important as Khrushchev's secret speech. Jazzman Alexei Kozlov believes that "the festival of 1957 was the beginning of the collapse of the Soviet system. After the festival the process of fragmentation of Stalinist society became irreversible. The festival bred a whole generation of dissidents and intellectuals who lived a double life. At the same time, a new generation of party-Komsomol functionaries was born, double-dealers who understood everything perfectly well but outwardly professed to be loyal to the system."[56] Vladimir Bukovsky recalls that after the festival "all this talk about 'putrefying capitalism' became ridiculous." Film critic Maya Turovskaya believes that at the festival Soviet citizens could touch the world for the first time after three decades: "The generation of the Sixties might have been different without the festival."[57]

Nikita Khrushchev genuinely thought that the Soviet Union could catch up with and surpass the United States in the fields of science, technology, consumer goods, and overall living standards. In 1957 he came up with a slogan, "Catch up and surpass America," the cornerstone of his promise to build Communist society over the next twenty years. Khrushchev, buoyed by the fast-growing economy and the huge success of Sputnik, was not afraid of showing American achievements to Soviet citizens. When the first American national exhibition opened in Moscow in Sokolniki Park in July 1959, several million Muscovites poured in to gaze at American artifacts and to taste Pepsi-Cola. Khrushchev laid out his intentions to the GDR leader, Walter Ulbricht: "The Americans believe that the Soviet people, looking at their achievements, will turn away from the

Soviet government. But the Americans do not understand our people. We want to turn the exhibit against the Americans. We will tell our people: look, this is what the richest country of capitalism has achieved in one hundred years. Socialism will give us the opportunity to achieve this significantly faster."[58]

Whatever Khrushchev's intentions may have been, the long-term effects of his bragging did not help Soviet anti-American propaganda. His promises to reach the American level of prosperity (that is, the material symbols of this prosperity) impressed millions of Soviets. Zdenek Mlynar rightly observed: "Stalin never allowed the comparison of socialism with capitalist realities because he insisted that here we build an absolutely new world, comparable to nothing." Khrushchev came up with a new slogan and fundamentally changed the perception of the world for the average Soviet person. Over the course of the next years, people became accustomed to comparing their lives to American living standards and developed a complex of inferiority. One generation after another recognized that, in reality, American living standards remained much higher than in the Soviet Union. And, Mlynar continues, those who looked for explanation could easily come to the conclusion that the main obstacle that prevented them from achieving an American-style life was the existing economic and political system.[59]

As the Khrushchev era evolved, two mutually confusing messages coexisted in Soviet propaganda about the United States. One was the modified version of the traditional Stalinist enemy image in which the United States remained the big "other" that opposed the Soviet Union; American capitalism and the American way of life were presented as antithetical to Soviet "socialism" and way of life. Another message was a rather positive picture of American society as an umbrella for both foes and friends, and of U.S. technological achievements as a blueprint for Soviet technical progress. Khrushchev allowed Americans to demonstrate their achievements at the Sokolniki Park exhibition, but the Soviet press was full of stories on hunger, crime, unemployment, and the persecution of blacks in the United States.[60]

The dualistic image of the United States left many questions unanswered. Very few in the Soviet Union could speak with authority about American society and culture. In 1957, the official weekly of the Soviet Writers' Union, Literaturnaia Gazeta (Literary Gazette), published a series of articles by Alexander Kazem-Bek, a Russian nationalist who had lived in the United States and then voluntarily returned to the Soviet Union. The articles denounced the United States as "a country without culture," as opposed to the Soviet Union and Europe. Immediately, Ilya Ehrenburg, an opponent of cultural xenophobia, published a rejoinder. He wrote that America was a country of many "progressive" writers and artists.[61] This polemic gave a rare glimpse into the growing tension between the xenophobic and "cosmopolitan" groups inside the state bureaucracy and cultural establishment.[62]

Later, during the 1960s, the spread of American material and cultural symbols became pandemic. Music and clothing styles, the idolization of mass culture stars, and beatnik-like behavior took root, first of all, among the children of the Soviet nomenklatura. Inside this nonconformist youth milieu, American radio broadcasting and cultural exhibitions became extremely effective tools in fighting official anti-Americanism. John F. Kennedy, Ernest Hemingway, and Marilyn Monroe replaced the hackneyed icons of traditional Soviet heroes. The number of fans of cultural Americanism is impossible to establish; but it became especially high during the 1970s and the 1980s, when the Soviet Union entered a period of ideological vacuum and economic stagnation.[63]

THE OPTIMISTIC SIXTIES

The Thaw and a growing openness to Western influences affected millions. This impact, however, should not be exaggerated. After the crackdown on student dissent in December 1956, the party and state invested enormous resources in ideological control over the population, especially the youth. For every freethinking publication and Western film, there were thousands of newspaper and journal articles, books, and movies that promoted Soviet patriotism and orthodoxy. The rapid expansion of high school education during the post-Stalin decade did not automatically generate liberal values; for a while it served as a major vehicle for indoctrination and conformist mentality. Although cleansed of images and glorification of Stalin, school textbooks of history and literature continued to impose on young minds a single integrated narrative of Soviet history, culture, and ideology, constructed within a strict and censored framework. New cohorts of students graduated still believing that they lived in the best, happiest, and mightiest of all countries. By the end of the 1950s, Soviet society continued to maintain not only a strong Cold War consensus but also a huge store of Communist romantic illusions. In early 1959, Khrushchev decided to exploit these illusions by proclaiming at the Party Congress that the USSR had completed the "full and final construction of socialism." During the next two years, he and a group of speechwriters brought out a bombastic, sky-is-the-limit, program of catching up with the United States and "finishing the construction of Communist society" in the Soviet Union within two decades. In July 1961, in a speech to the Central Committee, Khrushchev promised that the next generation of Soviet people would live in the prosperity of a Communist paradise. The Soviet Union, the leader boasted, would "rise to such a great height that, by comparison, the main capitalist countries will remain far below and way behind." After national "discussion" in which 4.6 million people took part, the Twenty-second Party Congress unanimously adopted the program in October 1961.[64]

Among the flagships of official romanticism and idealism were the mass-circulation newspapers *Izvestia*, headed by Khrushchev's son-in-law Alexei Adzhubei, and *Komsomolskaia Pravda*, the Komsomol newspaper. As Adzhubei later recalled, "We used to finish our meetings with indispensable slogans about the victory of Communism. We had no feeling of failure, deadlock or stagnation. I would like to stress: there was still the reserve of energy, many remained optimistic."[65] In 1960, a group of young journalists organized the first Soviet institute for the study of public opinion. The topic of the first poll was, "Will humanity prevent a world war?"[66]

Cinema was another powerful medium in which aged filmmakers of the 1920s and 1930s and their young pupils sought to re-create the spirit of revolutionary optimism and socialist romanticism. With sanction from above, they attempted to return the revolutionary heroes and Bolsheviks to the front stage from which they had virtually disappeared under Stalin. The new films (for example, *Communist*, with Gennady Gubanov) sought to put a human touch on the iron party men.[67]

Under Khrushchev, younger cadres rose in the party and state bureaucracy, people who combined war experience with a good education. It became fashionable among party leaders to hire intellectuals as "consultants." This gave birth to the phenomenon of "enlightened" apparatchiks, usually working in Moscow in the central bureaucratic structures. Among them were future "new thinkers" of the Gorbachev era: Georgy Arbatov, Anatoly Chernyaev, Fedor Burlatsky, Nikolai Inozemtsev, Georgy Shakhnazarov, and many others. Gorbachev himself was a beneficiary of this upward trend; as a young, educated, and energetic party member, he was quickly promoted through the ranks of the nomenklatura in the southern region of Stavropol. The late 1950s and early 1960s were relatively good times for young Communist intellectuals. One of them recalled: "Under Khrushchev a merry, joyful, and even easy-going life began for our circles. We were young. We scored first successes, defended first dissertations, and published first articles and books." All this created a "general optimistic tone of life." Social, cultural, and ideological differences did not corrode the atmosphere of this camaraderie.[68] These young people supported Khrushchev, despite his antics and lack of education, viewing him as a vehicle of change, the force that could sweep away old discredited cadres. This, they believed, would clear the way for their careers.

The new recruits were distinguished by their skill at critical thinking and their reformist intentions. The younger apparatchiks and intellectuals believed they could contribute to the regime's liberalization by supporting Khrushchev's de-Stalinization. They were proud to call themselves the "children of the Twentieth Party Congress" and, together with the older established figures from the Soviet cultural and educational establishment, worked hard to revive the mass patriotism and enthusiasm that they believed had existed three decades earlier and been wasted by Stalin.

The "enlightened" apparatchiks skillfully walked the fine line between their openness to humanistic values, on the one hand, and careerism, conformity, and patriotism on the other. Unfortunately, the Cold War left little room for a middle ground. In a pinch, most of them supported the Soviet cause and empire: Realpolitik invariably triumphed over their humanistic yearnings and reformist idealism. In 1956, most of them were not ready to support the anti-Communist revolutions in Poland and Hungary. During the festival, in August 1957, Adzhubei, an informal leader of the new recruits, reproved Polish journalist Eligiusz Liasota, an editor of the liberal Polish literary magazine, Po Prostu: "Listen, you can do in Poland what you want, but keep in mind that it rubs off on us here as well. You come and spread this plague, [you want to] subvert us. We will not allow this to happen."[69] The "children of the Twentieth Party Congress" wanted to reform the Soviet regime, not destroy it.

The biggest obstacle in their eyes was the rigid bureaucratic apparatus that held the country in steel bands and blocked innovation and change. Still, the reform-minded Communists hoped this apparatus could be repopulated with "enlightened" cadres and transformed from within. One of them recalled later: "I reckoned on the development of party structures and state structures, on their differentiation, since the task of management of society and economy became more and more complex. Therefore, there would be a greater autonomy from the party apparatus."[70] The unofficial motto in some patriotic educated families of the time was: join the party and "purify" it from within.[71]

For a few years after the secret speech, there were still reasons for Soviet patriotism and belief in the potential of reformed Communism. The Soviet Union still demonstrated impressive economic growth, restoring and expanding its industrial power. In the countries of Asia, Africa, and Latin America, the appeal of the Soviet way of modernization reached its peak. Soviet leadership in the space race confirmed the vitality and global appeal of the Soviet economic model. On April 12, 1961, Yuri Gagarin, a lieutenant-major in the Soviet Air Force, orbited Earth and became the first man in space. There was a wave of immense pride and hope among millions of Soviet citizens and spontaneous patriotic demonstrations in Moscow and Leningrad. Many of the "enlightened" apparatchiks understood the utopianism in Khrushchev's promises of the rapid arrival of prosperity and the collectivist paradise. Yet, as Chernyaev, a future assistant of Gorbachev, recalled, they wanted to believe in it.[72] The vision of a new Communist frontier, the heated atmosphere of the race with the United States, and the intensified mythmaking activities of official propaganda created a unique mood in the educated loyal circles of Soviet society. The early 1960s marked the peak of Soviet patriotism, the time when "Soviet civilization" reached the age of maturity.[73]

In sympathetic workplaces, in private apartments, in kitchens, people played guitars, drank, fell in love. But in their free time, they also read countless books, both those legally published and those illegally typed by samizdat (publish-it-yourself) enthusiasts. They debated with utmost seriousness on how to improve and change the system without repudiating the Communist legacy. Among the themes of that time were the "end of ideology," the rise of technocratic elites, the convergence of capitalist and socialist systems, and the role of cybernetics in managing public affairs. Mikhail and Raisa Gorbachev, residing after their graduation from Moscow State University in 1955 in Stavropol, far from Moscow, managed to be part of this new intellectual subculture. Raisa began to do sociological studies in the countryside. The couple spent hours discussing philosophical and political ideas. The Gorbachevs read and debated the ideas of Western New Left philosophers Jean-Paul Sartre, Martin Heidegger, and Herbert Marcuse.[74]

Many future "new thinkers" gained similar access through their positions at academic institutes and as consultants of the Central Committee of the Communist Party. Also, they met foreigners on a daily basis and went on foreign trips. In 1958, Alexander Yakovlev, a young war veteran and party official and future architect of glasnost under Gorbachev, went to the United States on the first exchange program and spent a year of studies at Columbia University. Some of the party intellectuals lived and worked in Prague, as journalists and editors on the journal The Problems of Peace and Socialism. It was a unique place in which Soviet functionaries in charge of international propaganda and experts on international affairs and world economy lived side by side and freely with Western leftists. According to Chernyaev's recollection, in the early 1960s Prague was a "cosmopolitan paradise compared to Moscow." The Prague group included Georgy Arbatov, Gennady Gerasimov, Oleg Bogomolov, Vadim Zagladin, Georgy Shakhnazarov, and others, who would form the core of the perestroika brain trust after Gorbachev had come to power.[75]

In the collective thinking of Soviet progressives and young people in the early 1960s, the cult of science became a substitute for religion. As astute observers note, the atheism of that period "was not the result of government despotism. It relied on the ideology of Soviet intelligentsia. Soviet intelligentsia looked towards the future, then towards the past, but never—at the present." The optimistic spirit of the time was rooted in a strong belief in human reason, in the collective ability to overcome any difficulties if armed with scientific knowledge and freed from bureaucratic constraints.[76]

The scientific community was the primary forum for the optimistic leftist intellectual culture in the Soviet Union. Boosted by the growth of the military-industrial complex and competition with the United States, scientists seemed to be one of the most influential elite groups in the Soviet Union, a prototype of a civil society. The military-industrial complex offered scientists hundreds of thousands of new jobs. By 1962, the complex consisted of 966 plants, research and development labs, design bureaus, and institutes, with the total number of the employed reaching 3.7 million people. Many young scientists found jobs in academic research centers in Siberia and the Far East and in a few dozen secret cities and special academic cities, model urban projects built by the atomic ministry, the Academy of Science, and other institutions related to the military-industrial-academic nexus. Those who lived there had stable employment, relatively high salaries, and wonderful social benefits, from free kindergartens to free housing. The closed ghetto of secret cities was a surreally free place inside the Soviet Union. A journalist who managed to visit one of the secret cities in 1963 met with scientists who could talk freely on political and cultural topics without any fear. Scientists discussed the introduction of a "democracy" of scientists and intellectuals that would be a third way between Stalinist Communism and Western capitalism. Some of them believed the Soviet system could be changed "scientifically" by an alliance of scientists and "enlightened" party apparatchiks.[77]

Within the scientific community, the yearning for greater freedom from the dominant ideology and nonscientific bureaucracies coexisted with the fierce competition for and total dependence on state funding and resources. Soviet science historian Nikolai Krementsov describes "the merging of the scientific community and the party-state control apparatus on the level of both institutions and individuals." Scientists, as their advice to Khrushchev regarding the 1963 partial test-ban treaty demonstrated, learned to push the right buttons and manipulate the regime's ideological and military-industrial aspirations.[78]

Initially, most members of these reform-minded communities supported Khrushchev's efforts to expand Soviet global influence, and especially his course of assistance to the national liberation and anticolonial movements in Asia, Africa, and Latin America. Tens of thousands of Soviet specialists, engineers, scientists, and technicians worked in China in the late 1950s, providing "fraternal assistance" in the rapid modernization of that country. Witnesses recall how sincere and enthusiastic their attitudes were. Soviet physicist Evgeny Negin recalled that by 1959 "the relations between the Soviet Union and China could be best described in the words of the song 'Moscow-Beijing,' that became popular even in Stalin's time: 'Russians and Chinese are brothers forever.' It seemed that the friendship sanctified by the same ideological choice, would be unbreakable. It seemed much more solid than the ties based on sober pragmatic interests."[79]

The Sino-Soviet split came as a shock for Soviet public opinion in the early 1960s, and it contributed to a more critical view of Khrushchev's foreign policy. Still, general support of internationalist activism continued for a while. There were, of course, many other "friends," that is, possibilities for proletarian solidarity. Radical Arab regimes in Egypt, Syria, Iraq, and Algeria and the faraway and exotic India, Burma, and Indonesia—all provided new objects of fascination. There was also postcolonial Africa: Ghana, Ethiopia, Guinea, Mali, Congo. The euphoria within the Soviet political leadership about the prospects for promoting Soviet-style socialism in these countries was linked to stratagems of the Cold War: the struggle for the third world would reach its peak during the 1970s. At the same time, it initially resonated with optimistic and romantic currents in the Soviet educated elites.[80]

The 1959 revolution in Cuba fuelled new hopes in Moscow that Communism still represented the wave of the future. The victory of Fidel Castro, Che Guevara, and other *barbudos* captured the imaginations of many Soviet citizens, including members of the nomenklatura who traveled to Cuba to explore a new "socialist frontier."[81] The young poet, Yevgeny Yevtushenko, an unofficial literary mouthpiece of Communist reformers, rushed to Cuba to glorify "the Island of Liberty," as described in his ebullient stanzas. Everyone sang the new song: "Cuba, My Love!" Ernest Hemingway, whose novels *Farewell to Arms* and *For Whom the Bell Tolls* had earlier been banned in the Soviet Union, now became a part of the Cuban cult. When Anastas Mikoyan, second in the Soviet leadership, flew to Cuba in February 1960, he spent the whole trip reading Hemingway's novels in the expectation of seeing the great writer, who at that time lived on the island.[82]

For the young men and women of the sixties, the Cuban Revolution revalidated the Bolshevik Revolution of October 1917. It also offered the illusory hope that a genuine revolution could occur without leading to blood and tyranny. Cuba reconnected Soviet foreign policy, tainted by Stalin's cynical imperialism, with messianic revolutionary horizons. "The Island of Liberty" was well within the U.S. sphere of influence but still managed to break loose of the superpower's gravitational pull. Latin America no longer seemed to be out of reach. "One should look beyond Cuba," predicted Komsomol boss Pavlov at the meeting with propagandists in January 1961. "At any time other Latin American countries may follow after Cuba. Americans are literally sitting on the powder keg in Latin

America. Venezuela may blow up at any moment. There are mass strikes in Chile. The same applies to Brazil and Guatemala."[83] The craze about Cuba did not subside even after the Cuban missile crisis; when Castro traveled around the Soviet Union at Khrushchev's invitation in the spring of 1963, he was welcomed by enthusiastic and cheering crowds of Soviet people wherever he went.

EROSION OF SOVIET IDENTITY

Revolutionary romanticism competed with Western influences for the souls of Soviet intellectuals. But the usual result of peeking out from behind the iron curtain was culture shock at the first glimpse of a free, diverse, and thriving life without ideological uniformity, fear of secret police, and regimented existence. Film director Andrei Konchalovsky, from the highly privileged family of the author of the Soviet national anthem, vividly described his impressions during his first trip abroad to Venice's film festival in 1962. Spectacular glimpses of historic Venice, Rome, and Paris, long impossible for educated Russians, left Konchalovsky flabbergasted. Venice, with its splendid Grand Canal, palaces, merry crowds, myriad lights, and Parisian hotels in which white-aproned chambermaids dusted off the glittering brass doorknobs, deepened the dismay that arose from the contrast between all this and the bleak Soviet existence. Many years later, Konchalovsky recalled: "All my ideological vacillations and antipatriotic steps that followed can be traced back to this episode."[84] Konchalovsky would later emigrate to the West and work in Hollywood.

Gradually, trips abroad ceased to be the search for a "socialist frontier" and became a coveted prize for party and state functionaries as well as members of the cultural establishment. There was even a trickle of official "youth tourism": during 1961, 8,000 Komsomol functionaries traveled to the United States, Great Britain, Switzerland, West Germany, and other countries.[85] Many of them found that abroad the consumerist paradise Khrushchev promised in the future already existed in the West. In the mid-1960s, Mikhail Gorbachev, then a party official in Stavropol, made his first foreign trip to East Germany. In 1971, after he was promoted to first secretary of the Stavropol area and became a member of the national-level nomenklatura, Gorbachev went to Italy, rented a car, and saw Rome, Palermo, Florence, and Turino. Raisa Gorbachev continued her sociological studies abroad, filling many little pads with notes. At one point, her observations boiled down to one question for her husband: "Misha, why do we live worse than they do?"[86]

Another longer-term effect of the cultural changes was the decline of militarism and jingoism. Khrushchev's enthusiasm about nuclear weapons pushed him in 1959 to propose a drastic departure from the practice of universal conscription and long military service, one of the pillars of Stalinist society.[87] An ever-larger number of young men, particularly students, received permanent deferrals that freed them from military service altogether. In 1960 and 1961, the Soviet army diminished by one-third, and hundreds of thousands of teenagers were able to get deferrals from the draft and hundreds of thousands of junior officers entered civilian life, either reluctantly or with enthusiasm. In January 1961, the Soviet version of ROTC was abolished at colleges, universities, and high schools.[88] (These returned in 1965, after Khrushchev was ousted from power.)

The post-Stalin peace offensives and new limitations on militarism and military propaganda in the Soviet Union made the revival of antimilitarism and even pacifism possible in Soviet society. The civil war between the Red and the Whites, as well as World War II, remained major subjects in Soviet films, literature, memoirs, and drama. But the depiction of these wars became less pompous and increasingly realistic. Soviet writers who had seen the war as young officers, soldiers, or journalists began to produce the first honest accounts of their experiences and to make the first attempts at analysis. Among the most realistic war novels were Viktor Nekrasov's In the Trenches of Stalingrad and Konstantin Simonov's The Living and the Dead and the stories of Bulat Okudzhava, Oleg Bykov, Alex Adamovich, Yuri Bondarev, and others. Simonov's novel blamed Stalin and his purges of the military for the horrible defeats and losses in the first years of the Great Patriotic War. The orthodox Literaturnaia Gazeta criticized the "deheroicizing" of the war, and top Kremlin propagandist Yuri Zhukov wrote in Izvestia that "quite a few works" had portrayed war in "a depressing manner, as one continuous human slaughter."[89]

The educated public, especially in Moscow, Leningrad, and other big cities became familiar with the "lost generation" literature that had appeared in France and Great Britain and particularly in Germany after the Great War of 1914–1918. Antiwar Western writers, among them Erich Maria Remarque, became hugely popular among Soviet youth. The cinema played the leading role in changing mass perceptions about war and militarism. The films of war veteran Grigory Chukhrai, The Forty-first, Ballad of a Soldier, and Clear Skies, as well as Cranes Are Flying, by the older filmmaker Mikhail Kalatozov, presented war as a background for individual dramas, where patriotism, heroism, and duty, but also treachery, cowardice, and careerism, were not rigid categories but matters of choice and chance. In contrast to the militaristic pastiche of Stalin's time, Andrei Tarkovsky's film My Name Is Ivan focused on the story of a ruined childhood. The message of these films was patriotic yet antimilitaristic. They reminded millions of Russians of their most painful and heroic collective experience, but also of their shattered postwar hopes for a better life.[90]

There were no protests "to ban the Bomb" inside Soviet society, and there was remarkably little public response to the Berlin crisis and the Cuban missile crisis. Still, some educated individuals developed feelings and reactions similar to American beatniks Allen Ginsberg and Jack Kerouac, whose dissent against the dominant culture grew from their fear of nuclear war. The writer Alex Adamovich and the bard Bulat Okudzhava not only deplored the slaughter of their generation in World War II but also encouraged changes in public mentality to avoid the next, infinitely more horrible catastrophe. Andrei Sinyavsky in 1961 published "The Icicle," a short story with the theme of nuclear testing and fallout. In the fall of 1962, poet Andrei Voznesensky said in an interview abroad: "I admire the beatniks: They are poets of the atomic age." One writer, a regular contributor to Novy Mir, wrote in his diary: "Any preparation for war is revolting. I am not afraid for myself, but for my son and millions like him. If this conviction is called pacifism, then I am a pacifist." Later Adamovich recalled that for him and some idealists of the sixties, "our pacifism was linked to our desire to achieve a broader goal." This goal was the transformation of Stalinist society and mentality.[91]

Soviet nuclear designers, most privileged of all scientists, with excellent connections in the political leadership and bureaucracies, attempted to influence Soviet security policies. After the 1955 thermonuclear test, Sakharov suggested to Marshal Mitrofan Nedelin, the military commander of the test, that it would be a catastrophe if thermonuclear weapons were ever used. Nedelin answered the scientist with a lewd joke that meant, mind your business and give us nuclear weapons and we alone will decide how to use them. Sakharov was flabbergasted. As he recalled, "The ideas and emotions kindled at that moment have not diminished to this day, and they completely altered my thinking." There was a rift opening between the scientists who worked to create the Soviet military sword and the military-party bureaucrats who held this sword in their arms. "Beginning in the late fifties," recalled Sakharov, "one got an increasingly clearer picture of the collective might of the military industrial complex and of its vigorous, unprincipled leaders, blind to everything except their 'job.'" A growing awareness about the nuclear disarmament movement outside the Soviet Union made Soviet nuclear scientists increasingly critical of the government's policies, especially the direct and indirect use of force in the international arena.[92]

Demographic changes also contributed to the diminishing impact of militarism. Seventy million Soviet citizens were born between 1945 and 1966, in the period of peace. Their number in big cities was disproportionately large because of continuing rapid urbanization. These cohorts, in contrast to the youth of the 1930s and 1940s, were not imbued with the spirit of sacrifice. Increasing numbers of them were non-Russians who looked askance at the Russo-centric themes of Soviet patriotism.[93] The youth of the early 1960s had heard from their fathers and older brothers about the terrible price of victory. Vladimir Visotsky, the Soviet Bob Dylan, liked to talk to war veterans, and he articulated their memories with extreme poignancy: the Great Patriotic War was the people's greatest tragedy. "Battalions keep marching and marching westwards. And women back home keep wailing in funeral grief."[94] Those who served in the army found there not only camaraderie but also hazing, crude noncommissioned officers, and old-style drilling practices that were a travesty of training, especially against the backdrop of the nuclear age. The young writer Vladimir Voinovich gave a satirical twist to the growing antimilitarist mood in The Life and Extraordinary Adventures of Private Ivan Chonkin, a masterly parody on the flood of "patriotic" literature about the Great Patriotic War. He published the novel abroad in 1969, which later contributed to his expulsion from the Writers' Union.[95]

Educated young people began to take any opportunity to avoid military service. As with the student movement in 1956, it would be wrong, however, to exaggerate the scale and tempo of changes. They affected above all a privileged minority from Moscow, Leningrad, and other cities. And as long as the Cold War continued, the new antimilitary trends did not come to the surface.

The Khrushchev era also saw the emergence of powerful national identities that belied the official concept of "Friendship of the Peoples." Some of them, such as the nationalist movements in the Baltics, Ukraine, and the Caucasus, had originated long before the Thaw. Some emerged during the 1920s as a result of the Bolshevik nationality policies.[96] Others, including those in the Russian core of the Soviet Union, attested to the new strains that resulted from the Stalinist legacy. The Jewish Question and the issue of anti-Semitism were pivotal, because of the strong representation of people of Jewish descent in Soviet educated society. After 1953, the more overt anti-Semitic campaigns stopped, but the regime never tried to redress the wrongs committed during the "anti-cosmopolitan" campaigns. No attempt was made to rehabilitate people of Jewish descent and Jewish cultural figures purged in 1948–52; nor did the regime reopen those institutions of Jewish education and culture that had been closed at that time. Institutional anti-Semitism continued in many hidden and informal ways. People of "Jewish nationality" were permanently marked on secret bureaucratic forms as untrustworthy and not fit to serve in key state organizations and at the top of the party and state hierarchy (the military-industrial complex, nuclear energy, and Academy of Science were notable exceptions). The fact that after 1955 the Soviet Union supported the Arab states against Israel negatively affected Soviet Jews. They were treated as a diaspora whose loyalty potentially was to another state.[97] They had to jump over additional bureaucratic hurdles, compared to Russians, to obtain authorization for travel outside the Soviet Union. Khrushchev and his entourage frowned at Jewish cultural identity and Jewish membership in cultural and scientific elites. And in Ukraine, where grassroots anti-Semitism had old roots, officials promoted anti-Semitic publication under the aegis of "anti-Zionist propaganda."[98]

Many members of the cultural elites with "Jewish nationality" on their passports still thought of Stalinism as a tragic deviation from the positive socialist experiment. Poet and writer David Samoilov wrote in his journal in April 1956 that Stalinism was "the child of Russian misery"; it called to service the people from lower classes and "replaced the real, simple human ideal with anti-human ideas of chauvinism, enmity, suspicion, and anti-humanism."[99] The assimilation of urbane sophisticated Jews into Soviet society went so far that few of them retained their ethnic, or indeed their religious, identities.

Younger educated Jews, however, felt increasingly alienated from this Soviet identity. Their high level of education and sophistication made them distinct from Russians, Ukrainians, and other ethnic groups. They also felt the oppressive nature of the regime, because they discovered they did not have the brilliant career opportunities their parents had had in the 1920s and 1930s. Mikhail Agursky, son of Soviet Communists who became an ardent Zionist, recalled his feelings back in the 1960s: "Could one really expect that a nation that had given the Soviet state political leaders, diplomats, generals, and top economic managers would agree to become an estate whose boldest dream would be a position as head of a lab?"[100]

Many writers, poets, intellectuals, musicians, artists, and actors from Jewish backgrounds suffered from the attacks on "cosmopolitanism" and therefore had considerably fewer illusions about the Soviet regime and the realities around them. This brought them into the vanguard of the movement for cultural and political liberalization. At that time, being a Jew meant to be an advocate for internationalism, dialogue, and greater tolerance. In 1961, Yevgeny Yevtushenko wrote a poem, "Babi Yar," that broke the taboo of silence in the Soviet Union over the Holocaust. Composer Dmitry Shostakovich immediately used the poem's words for his new symphony, the Thirteenth. In December 1962, film director Mikhail Romm criticized Stalin's Russo-centric propaganda and called for the end of self-isolation from Western culture.[101] Ehrenburg and Romm had abandoned their Jewish roots in the search for socialist internationalist ideals, and Yevtushenko and Shostakovich were ethnic Russians who abhorred ethnic nationalism. All of them proclaimed themselves "Jews" in opposition to the remnants of Stalinist regime—xenophobia, chauvinism, and anti-Semitism.[102]

For some Jews, Israel became their main temptation and dream of an alternative existence. In the war of October 1956, Israel was the target of blistering criticism in the Soviet press. Jews with strong Soviet identities denounced Israeli aggression against Egypt.[103] But a few months later, the appearance of the Israeli delegation at the Moscow Youth Festival created a sensation. The delegates were young veterans of the recent war, whose demeanor, dignity, and fearlessness, and above all the pride of being Jewish, was new and astonishing.[104] Official reports about the Festival were full of alarm: "Zionists continue to distribute the literature they brought among Moscow Jews," "the workers of Moscow cinema studio for two days have been filming only the Zionist part of the Israeli delegation," and so on. A crowd of young men who could not get tickets to the Israeli delegation's music performance crushed the cast iron fence in front of the Moscow Soviet Theater and stormed into the performance hall. These episodes reflected the renewal of curiosity and sympathy for Israel among Soviet Jews. For the first time, some of them became interested in their religious and cultural identity. Despite very intense anti-Zionist propaganda, an increasing number of Jews began to apply for emigration to their rediscovered Middle East "homeland."[105]

On the opposite side from this "Jewish" movement emerged another movement that emphasized traditional Russian nationalism and rejected the legacy of the revolution. "By the Khrushchev era," concludes Itzhak Brudny, "many Russian nationalist intellectuals held research or teaching positions in elite Soviet universities and research institutes, or were staff members of or regular contributors to important newspapers, magazines, and literary journals." These people protested against the destruction of historical Russian monuments and churches; they deplored the progressive degradation of the Russian countryside, the repository of traditional Russian cultural norms and values. Anti-Semitism became a big component of the ideology of the new Russian nationalism; in fact, with the growing openness, Russian nationalists imported the main anti-Semitic arguments from white émigrés living in the West, above all the thesis of the revolution as a "Jewish-Bolshevik conspiracy" against Russian people.[106]

The rise of educated Russian elites led to growing friction and factional struggles in Soviet culture, education, and even science. These pernicious crosscurrents in culture received another powerful impulse from the Middle East. The triumph of Israel over the Arab armies in the Six-Day War in 1967 filled Soviet Jews with pride and set them against the "Russians" and the rest of Soviet society. These developments led some younger Jews to shed their Soviet identity and think about emigration from the Soviet Union.[107]

Khrushchev's behavior toward the end of his career accelerated the demise of the de-Stalinization project. Khrushchev was trying to straddle the gap between his hatred of Stalin and his preference for Stalinist methods of administration and mobilization. He was never consistent, and he often undermined himself with rambling speeches and reckless behavior. Historian Sergei Dmitriev recorded in his journal in March 1961: "Everybody is sick and tired of Khrushchev. His foreign voyages and empty and erratic verbiage have finally reached the state of idiocy. In the public and political atmosphere one increasingly notices the signs of absolute inertia, intellectual vacuum, and a lack of purpose. There are no thoughts, no movement."[108]

Khrushchev's inconsistency in cultural policies made him more enemies than friends among the bureaucracies and influential cultural elites. In November 1962, on his order, *Novy Mir* published Solzhenitsyn's novel *One Day in the Life of Ivan Denisovich*. For a brief moment, elated, reform-minded intellectuals believed that all the walls had fallen and the ultimate truth about Stalinism could now be freely discussed. Yet just one month later, on December 1, Khrushchev, prodded by the retrograde figures in the Soviet cultural and propagandist establishment, appeared at an exhibition of young modernist artists and sculptors and denounced them as "degenerates" and "pederasts." He claimed that their art was as good as "dog-shit." In his uncouth raving, Khrushchev reflected personal and generational preferences for realist classical art. But, without fully realizing it, the Soviet leader had jumped into the *Kulturkampf* on the side of the "Russian" faction against the anti-Stalinist cultural vanguard. At two meetings with the Soviet intelligentsia in December 1962 and March 1963, Khrushchev was even more rambling, rude, and intolerant than at the previous meetings in 1957. In blunt words, he told the young writers and poets that their modernist, Westernizing, and liberal bent put them on the wrong side of the Cold War divide. Khrushchev warned them that if they still want to be "the artillery of the party," they must cease the "friendly fire" against their own camp. Most young artists and intellectuals no longer wanted to be the party's "artillerists" but believed that their art had helped to promote "the line of the 20th party congress," that is, de-Stalinization. They counted on Khrushchev's support against "Stalinists." Yevgeny Yevtushenko, Andrei Voznesensky, Vasily Aksenov, the sculptor Ernst Neizvestny, and other innovative writers and poets became the targets of vicious organized attacks. They finally realized that the entire, crude, ruthless force of the state opposed them.[109] This realization marked the origins of sustained cultural and political dissent in the Soviet Union.

Both Stalinists and anti-Stalinists approved of Khrushchev's removal in October 1964. People who supported the Thaw and de-Stalinization believed that Khrushchev was a spent force and any future leadership would be better than his. Soon, however, they realized how wrong they were. The new guard in the Kremlin quickly terminated de-Stalinization from above. The majority of party leaders and ideologists did not like what they saw in the educated strata of society: growing individualism, creeping Westernism, popularity of American music and mass culture, growing pacifism, and pluralistic attitudes. Where the party ideologists failed, the KGB began to step in: a special division of Soviet secret police had the task of "guiding" Soviet cultural and intellectual elites and "shielding" them from "harmful influences." A KGB report at the end of 1965 tried to minimize the damage the previous decade had done to the regime: "One cannot say that specific anti-Soviet and politically damaging manifestations testify to the growth of general discontent in the country or to serious intentions to create anti-Soviet underground. This is out of question."[110]

The new leadership and the KGB, however, provoked more antiregime manifestations in the same year. In May 1965, Leonid Brezhnev publicly praised Stalin as a war leader. And in September, the secret police arrested the writers Andrei Sinyavsky and Yuli Daniel for "the crime" of publishing their novels abroad under pseudonyms. Suddenly, hundreds of leading Soviet intellectuals, writers, artists, and scientists began to send petitions to the party leadership with appeals to free the arrested writers and to stop the backslide to neo-Stalinism. A new movement was born, which demanded public trials and constitutional rights. "Dissidents," as the members of this movement came to be called, began to appeal to the world via the foreign media.[111]

The Soviet invasion of Czechoslovakia in August 1968 substantiated the fears of the Soviet anti-Stalinist intelligentsia that the post-Khrushchev leadership might take the country in a neo-Stalinist direction. The crushing of the Prague Spring and its "socialism with a human face" dashed the hopes of many educated Soviet patriots that the existing system could be reformed. This produced a remarkable rise of antigovernment sentiment, even among some who were established in the Soviet elites. The history of this sentiment and the dissident movement is beyond the scope of this book. It must only be emphasized that, although the number of open dissidents was insignificant, their sympathizers and supporters among the educated elites numbered in the hundreds of thousands. It is also noteworthy that quite a few dissidents were former enthusiastic Communist reformists who began to feel betrayed, angry, and alienated from the regime. They also felt alienated from the vast masses of their fellow citizens, who were less educated and not capable of understanding their motives for turning against the regime. The growing sense of alienation and isolation from the state, as well as from the passive majority, led many dissidents to emigrate to the West. Many "enlightened" apparatchiks, however, continued their careers, while waiting for another change of fortune.

The analysis of the period from 1956 to 1968 suggests that the Soviet Union still possessed considerable internal energy and even, as we have seen, was capable of bouts of ideological vigor and optimistic idealism. The Khrushchev decade produced a new cohort of social, cultural, and political leaders, the "men and women of the sixties," who aspired to lead the Soviet Union down the path toward "socialism with a human face." Their patriotic energy and identity were based on Communist ideology and the selective idealized perceptions of the revolution and the leftist culture of the 1920s. By the end of Khrushchev's rule, however, the utopian energies that nourished Soviet patriotism had been exhausted. Soviet identity, rejuvenated by these energies, also began to fragment and erode under powerful external and internal influences. Among the new trends in the educated strata were a passionate cultural Americanism, an antimilitarist and antigovernment intellectualism, as well as a growing conservative Russian nationalism. Last but not least, the "enlightened" apparatchiks lost their prospects for rapid career rise and became increasingly attracted by Western consumerism.

Ultimately, the Kremlin leadership and Soviet bureaucracy mismanaged the process of relative liberalization after Stalin's death. They ended up alienating the cultural, intellectual, and scientific elites that had been the most optimistic and patriotic at the beginning of the "great" decade. Some actions, from the crackdown on artistic creativity to the invasion of Czechoslovakia, inflicted deep wounds on the patriotic Soviet home front and sowed seeds of dissent among some members of Soviet elites. The self-inflicted wounds did not look fatal at first. But they did not heal.

Under Leonid Brezhnev, the Soviet leadership abandoned reformist projects. It was content to live with the fossilized ideology and sought to repress cultural dissent and force its participants into exile and immigration. Unwilling and unable to carry out domestic reforms, Brezhnev instead launched détente with the Western powers. Détente and the international legitimacy it granted to him and the Soviet leadership became a substitute for the missing dynamism of the Soviet experiment. At the same time, Soviet participation in the détente process led to further erosion of the Stalinist legacy of xenophobia and to the reintegration of the Soviet Union into the wider world.

(CHAPTER 7)
BREZHNEV AND THE
ROAD TO DÉTENTE,
1965–1972

We must conduct negotiations in a big way, not a small-minded
way. And the arrangement we achieve should encourage
tranquility in the world.
—Brezhnev to Kissinger, April 21, 1972

On May 29, 1972, Richard Nixon and Leonid Brezhnev met in the richly adorned and ancient St. Catherine Hall of a historic Kremlin palace to sign an array of bilateral documents, among them the Strategic Arms Limitations Agreement, the Antiballistic Missile Treaty, and "The Basic Principles of U.S.-Soviet Relations." This solemn occasion was the peak of Brezhnev's political career. It was also the highest point of international prestige of the Soviet Union since the beginning of the Cold War.

The origins and meaning of détente have always been subjects of controversy. Beginning in the mid-1970s, neoconservative critics of the Nixon, Ford, and Carter administrations attacked détente as immoral appeasement of Soviet power. They also believed that the Soviet Union used détente as a devious camouflage for its secret plans of global aggression and military superiority. Supporters of détente defended it as the only prudent choice in a world of nuclear terror and as the only means to move toward the reunification of a Europe divided by the Cold War. In recent years, following the collapse of the Soviet Union, both sides have claimed they were right. The critics have argued that the rearmament and global attack on Soviet interests under Reagan helped overcome the legacy of détente and assured Western victory. Proponents assert that détente contributed to ending the super-power confrontation, since it inadvertently led to the "imperial overstretch" of the Soviet Union and was thus an important element in the causal chain leading to Soviet decline and collapse.[1]

The preponderance of détente studies has been on the Western side. The Soviet side of the story is sketchy and incomplete.[2] Earlier studies of détente greatly advanced our understanding of the nature of Soviet politics and policy making under Brezhnev. Yet they also suffered from a paucity of sources and the poor correlation between Western explanations and Soviet realities.[3] This chapter is an attempt to elucidate the motives of Soviet behavior, specifically, the contribution of Leonid Brezhnev and his immediate foreign policy entourage to the policies of détente in the period from 1968 to 1972. I will consider several questions: What were the main arguments and motives in Kremlin politics as far as détente was concerned? What did the Brezhnev leadership make out of such important developments as the U.S. defeat in the Vietnam War and the rapprochement between the United States and the People's Republic of China? Was there any Soviet strategy to exploit what seemed to be a U.S. decline?

One must begin with factors that provide an essential background for the analysis of the Soviet road to détente. Among them are the collective thinking of the post-Khrushchev leadership, Kremlin politics, the return to ideological orthodoxy after 1964, and the continuing split between the conservative apparatchiks and the supporters of the new, de-Stalinized foreign policy. Most important of all, however, in my view, were Brezhnev's personal views and attitudes, his rise to the leadership position, and his international outlook. Under his leadership, after a brief renaissance of a hard line, the Kremlin began to search for accommodation with the United States and for détente in Europe.

DRIFT AFTER NIKITA

The ouster of Nikita Khrushchev in October 1964 left the guiding of foreign policy in the hands of the collective leadership of the Politburo, the second group of the party oligarchs that emerged after Stalin's death. Most Politburo members were highly critical of Khrushchev for his bluffing and gambling over the Suez crisis in 1956, the Berlin crisis in 1958–61, and most particularly the crisis over Cuba in 1962. Politburo member Dmitry Polyansky prepared a special report on Khrushchev's mistakes. Its sections on foreign policy contained the following paragraph: "Comrade Khrushchev declares carelessly that Stalin failed to penetrate into Latin America, and that he [Khrushchev] managed to do it. But only a gambler may assert that under modern conditions our state can grant real military assistance to any country of that continent. Missiles will not do in this case: they will burn to the ground the country that requires assistance—nothing else. And if we, in defending a Latin American country, were to have delivered a first nuclear strike against the United States, then not only we would have been a target for a counterstrike,—everybody would have recoiled from us." The memo concluded that Soviet behavior during the Cuban missile crisis raised the international standing of the United States and damaged the prestige of the Soviet

Union and its armed forces. The report also curtly mentioned that "Soviet-Cuban relations seriously deteriorated."[4]

Polyansky's report borrowed many points from Molotov's 1955 objections to the new foreign policy. Polyansky rejected Khrushchev's thesis that "if the USSR and the US reach agreement, there would be no war in the world." This thesis, he continued, was wrong for several reasons. First, accommodation with the United States was a fallacy, because Americans "strive for world hegemony." Second, it was erroneous to consider Great Britain, France, and West Germany as only "obedient servants of the Americans," rather than capitalist countries with their own interests. According to Polyansky, the task of Soviet foreign policy was to take advantage of "the discord and contradictions among the countries of the imperialist camp, thus demonstrating that the US is not a hegemonic power of this camp and has no right to pretend to play this role."[5]

Alexander Shelepin, a young upstart at the Presidium, threw many of the report's criticisms in Khrushchev's face at the Politburo on October 13, 1964. It appears that Politburo members were ready to denounce Khrushchev's foreign policy at the plenary meeting of the Central Committee in the event that Khrushchev appealed to the plenum delegates as he had done in June 1957. But the Soviet leader surrendered without a fight, and the plenum ratified Khrushchev's ouster without discussing his foreign policy record.[6] As it turned out, the new leadership had no consensus on foreign affairs. Although they concurred that Khrushchev's brinkmanship was disastrous, they could not agree on what kind of foreign policy would be desirable for Soviet interests.

The new rulers felt even less confident in foreign affairs than Stalin's lieutenants had ten years earlier. First Party Secretary Leonid Brezhnev, Chairman of the Council of Ministers Alexei Kosygin, and Chairman of the Supreme Soviet Nikolai Podgorny had very little experience in international affairs or the issues of international security.[7] Foreign Minister Andrei Gromyko, Minister of Defense Rodion Malinovsky, and chairman of the KGB Vladimir Semichastny were not even Presidium members and played subordinate political roles. Mikoyan, who stayed in the leadership until November 1965, recalled that "the level of discussion at the Presidium markedly declined." Sometimes "cranky ideas came up, and Brezhnev with some others simply failed to understand their consequences."[8]

The role of leading Soviet statesman fell by default to Kosygin, whose background lay exclusively in domestic economy.[9] During the first three years after Khrushchev's ouster, he gained some international prestige and prominence. From August 1965 to January 1966, he successfully acted as international mediator between India and Pakistan, who were on the brink of a full-scale war. After 1966, Kosygin became the chief spokesman on the issues of arms control. He carried out his duties stoically but without enthusiasm—he apparently never developed a taste for international affairs. Kosygin's views and beliefs were typical of the cohort of "red directors," the managers of huge industrial enterprises who had risen to prominence during the 1930s and 1940s. He worshiped industrial and military power but also believed in the ultimate superiority of the Soviet system and in the moral mission of the Soviet Union to lead all Communist and progressive forces against Western imperialism. The Sino-Soviet split deeply chagrined Kosygin, and for a while he refused to accept its irrevocability. In a close circle, he said: "We are communists and they are communists. It is hard to believe we will not be able to reach an agreement if we meet face to face."[10]

International media and foreign commentators also focused at the time on Alexander Shelepin, who, after Khrushchev's fall, became an active spokesman on foreign policy issues. A graduate of the Moscow Institute of Philosophy and Literature, Shelepin was, in contrast to most of Politburo members, a well-educated person. At the same time, he admired Stalin's leadership and had the reputation of being a realist. His career in the Youth Communist League under Stalin and as chairman of the KGB under Khrushchev gave him a narrow but visible power base among younger, ambitious, and elitist apparatchiks. There were rumors about a "Shelepin faction" among apparatchiks. In reality, Shelepin had more enemies than friends in elite circles.[11]

Shelepin, Polyansky, and their followers in the top party echelon, as their criticism of Khrushchev's record demonstrated, longed to return Soviet foreign and security policies to a more Russo-centric and militarist version of the revolutionary-imperial paradigm. At first, nobody in the post-Khrushchev leadership was prepared to challenge this. Although some of them had helped Khrushchev to criticize and defeat Molotov's orthodoxy in 1955, their real views were much more conservative, and hostility to the West, as well as militant unilateralism in foreign policy, became part of their group identity.[12]

The Stalinist worldview, the revolutionary-imperial paradigm, continued to hold the post-Khrushchev cohort of political leaders in its grip. Ustinov, Brezhnev, Podgorny, and many others in the new collective leadership belonged to the generation whose members had made spectacular careers under Stalin. The majority of them admired Stalin's leadership in the Great Patriotic War, fully identified with the 1945 victory, and supported mobilization and rearmament during the early Cold War. They remained personally committed to Stalin's legacy of forging a Soviet military superpower in the confrontation with the United States. Khrushchev's de-Stalinization struck at the core of their collective identity. It left their past leaderless, desacralized, and utterly compromised.

Stalin, who knew his cadres better than anyone else, was concerned about the ability of the next generations of Soviet nomenklatura to provide ideological leadership. In his words, the political class that replaced and destroyed the Old Bolsheviks was too busy "with practical work and construction" and studied Marxism "through brochures." And the generation of party and state officials that followed was, in Stalin's estimation, even less prepared. The majority of them were raised on pamphlets, newspaper articles, and quotations. "If things continue this way," Stalin concluded, "people might degenerate. This will mean the death [of Communism]." Stalin believed that future party leaders should combine theoretical vision with practical political talent.[13]

Indeed, there was nobody in the Kremlin who could be a political leader with a vision. Mikhail Suslov, the last survivor among the theoretically minded party apparatchiks, turned out to be the least imaginative and politically talented. The post-Khrushchev oligarchy, as Robert English writes, embodied "the last hostages" of orthodox thinking. Their collective thinking did not stem from profound ideological faith or revolutionary passion but was rather the product of their lack of education and tolerance for diversity and their Stalinist formative experiences.[14]

In the domestic sphere, there was an attempt to roll back the Thaw in the cultural and ideological spheres. Even semantic changes pointed in the direction of Stalinist orthodoxy: Brezhnev changed his title to general secretary, as it had been under Stalin; the top party structure (called the Presidium of the Central Committee from 1952 to 1964) once again became the Politburo. Russocentrism, Russification policies in Soviet republics, and deafening militaristic propaganda, characteristic of late Stalinism, also resurfaced. In Moscow, Leningrad, Kiev, and other major cities, the members of the intelligentsia of Jewish descent lived in fear of another anti-Semitic campaign.[15]

The sociocultural profile and collective mentality of the new cohort could have tremendous consequences for Soviet international behavior and the future of the Soviet Union itself. On the one hand, the majority of the post-Khrushchev leadership shared the ideological (revolutionary) component of the international paradigm. In domestic politics, many of them supported the abrogation of de-Stalinization, the greater suppression of cultural diversity, and the freezing of liberal trends in literature and art. On the other hand, they were not the masters but rather the prisoners of ideology, afraid to abandon the orthodox tenets and unable to reform them.

The new oligarchs ridiculed Khrushchev's ill-fated and misguided interventions into the field of Marxism-Leninism, especially his "editing" of the Party Program. Yet many of them also suffered from a curious complex of ideological inferiority. In other words, they feared that their own lack of education and theoretical sophistication might somehow lead them astray in the matters of "high policy." Brezhnev and other Politburo members delegated the intricate business of defining "ideological correctness" to Mikhail Suslov, who had been trained in orthodox party history and the textbook version of Marxism-Leninism. Memos on international affairs initially had to pass through the filters of the central party apparatus, which was dominated by Suslov and propagandists with provincial, parochial backgrounds. Some of these people (for example, the head of the Science Department, Sergei Trapeznikov; the head of the Propaganda Department, V. I. Stepakov; and Brezhnev's deputy, V. A. Golikov) were Brezhnev's old friends and specialists on collectivized agriculture. They espoused Russocentric and Stalinist views in domestic policies and admired the Chinese, the followers of leftist dogma, in foreign affairs. During preparation of Brezhnev's report for the coming Party Congress in March 1966, these orthodox advisers suggested deleting the sentences on the "principle of peaceful coexistence" and "prevention of a world war," on "great diversity" in the methods of building socialism in different countries, and on "non-interference in internal affairs of other communist parties." They held the 1952 propaganda view of the United States and wanted the party report "to show the beastly colonial nature, aggressiveness, war-mongering" of the United States, as well as the "growing fascist trend" in "American imperialism." Golikov declared in internal discussions: "We must not forget that world war is coming." Rumors also circulated about a phrase Shelepin allegedly had used: "People must know the truth: a war with America is inevitable."[16]

Not surprisingly, the new collective leadership agreed that the first priority of Soviet foreign policy must be reconciliation with "fraternal" Communist China rather than détente with the capitalist West. It ignored the fact that China was sliding toward revolutionary chaos, soon to be known as the Great Proletarian Cultural Revolution. Some Soviet diplomats in Beijing tried to report this to Moscow, but these reports met with incredulity and ignorance. The ambassador in Beijing, Stepan Chervonenko, the former party secretary in Ukraine, knew the mood in the Soviet leadership better and changed the report's spin to more positive tones. Sergei Lapin, who replaced Chervonenko in 1965, was a cynical apparatchik and did not even bother to provide adequate analysis. In January 1965, the Politburo rejected the proposal from the Foreign Ministry and the Central Committee's Department for Socialist Countries to take immediate steps to improve relations with the United States. Shelepin attacked the heads of these institutions, Andrei Gromyko and Yuri Andropov, for their lack of "class position" and "class consciousness."[17]

The escalation of the war in Vietnam in 1965 led to the first significant foreign policy discussions in the post-Khrushchev Kremlin. Previously, the Soviet leadership had not ascribed any geopolitical importance to Vietnam and Indochina. They sought, in vain, to dissuade Hanoi from starting the war against the South. They feared, historian Ilya Gaiduk concludes, that this war would be "an impediment to the process of détente with the United States and its allies."[18] The direct U.S. intervention, however, forced the Politburo's hand. Now the ideological call for "fraternal duty" prevailed. The supporters of a pro-China foreign policy began to argue that Soviet assistance to Vietnamese Communists would create a means for reconciliation between the USSR and the PRC by dint of their joint assistance to the North Vietnamese. The Soviet Union began to increase supplies of arms and other kinds of assistance to North Vietnam.[19]

In February 1965, Kosygin, accompanied by Andropov and a number of other Soviet officials and consultants, went to the Far East in an attempt to build a new foreign policy strategy. His official destination was Hanoi, but he made two stops in Beijing. He met with Zhou Enlai and, on the way back, with Mao Ze-dong. Kosygin's talks in Beijing were disheartening: the Chinese were rigid and ideologically aggressive, attacked Soviet "revisionism," and refused to coordinate any policies with the Soviets, even on the matter of assistance to North Vietnam. The talks in Hanoi were also sobering for the Soviet leadership. Andropov's consultant Alexander Bovin, who was on this trip, observed how Kosygin failed to dissuade the North Vietnamese leaders from all-out war with the United States. The Vietnamese and the Soviets, despite their common Marxist-Leninist ideology, came from different worlds. The Hanoi leaders were revolutionaries, veterans of underground and anticolonial fighting. The Soviet officials were state administrators, who had matured and grown into their positions in the corridors of bureaucratic power. After many years of feeling like pawns in Soviet and Chinese power games, Hanoi's Communist leaders were determined to score a complete victory, disregarding human costs and the advice from Moscow.[20]

Still, American intervention in Vietnam stoked the ideological instincts of the collective leadership and the Soviet military and led to a serious deterioration of Soviet-American relations.[21] The party organized mass propaganda campaigns, demonstrations, and meetings of "solidarity with people of Vietnam" around the Soviet Union. The Politburo reacted with deliberate coolness to the initial approaches of the Johnson administration to start talks on limitations in the strategic arms race.[22] Furthermore, Kosygin was infuriated when the United States bombed Hanoi and the port of Haiphong in February 1965 during his official visit to North Vietnam.[23] There were still quite a few in the Soviet foreign policy elites who believed that North Vietnam was not worth a quarrel with the United States.

These figures were forced to keep a low profile, however, as the chorus of indignation against the American bombing campaign grew.[24]

In May 1965, as the American bombing campaign in North Vietnam intensified, news of American intervention in the Dominican Republic aroused emotions in the Politburo. Defense Minister Malinovsky portrayed developments in Vietnam and Central America as an escalation of the global confrontation and brooded that "the Dominican events will be followed by actions against Cuba." In response, he proposed Soviet "active countermeasures," among them military demonstrations in Berlin and on the border with West Germany and the redeployment of airborne troops and other units from Soviet territory to the GDR and Hungary. As Mikoyan remembered, the defense minister "emphasized that we should be ready to strike on West Berlin."[25]

In the middle of 1966, Bovin recalls, in response to new American escalation in Vietnam, the Soviet military and some Politburo members began to talk again about cutting Americans down to size and intimidating them with demonstrations of Soviet force. Yet, even the most ardent advocates of a showdown had to admit that the Soviet Union had no means by which to affect the policies of Washington and Hanoi in Vietnam. Besides, the memories of the Berlin and Cuban missile crises were still too fresh. Mikoyan, Kosygin, Brezhnev, Podgorny, and Suslov advocated for restraint.[26]

1967 brought new shocks that challenged the Kremlin leaders' emotions. The Communist camp in Southeast Asia lay in ruins. In Indonesia, the Soviets had lost all influence after President Sukarno was replaced and the subsequent murder of an estimated 300,000 Communists and their sympathizers by the military under the leadership of General Suharto. And in the June 1967 Six Days War, Israel destroyed the armies of Egypt, Syria, and Jordan. Soviet influence seemed to be crumbling from Jakarta to Cairo. The rout of the Arab states stunned the Soviet leadership and elites. The Politburo could do nothing to help Sukarno, but the Middle East was an entirely different matter. Israel's victory had strong domestic repercussions for the Soviet Union: Growing pro-Zionist sympathies among Soviet Jews spiked in the largest manifestation of their solidarity with Israel since the proclamation of its statehood in 1948. In Moscow and Leningrad synagogues, KGB agents heard people praising Israeli defense minister Moshe Dayan and demanding weapons to go to fight for Israel.[27] The international implications, however, remained the most painful. The Politburo regarded the alliance with radical Arab regimes as the biggest geopolitical achievement of Soviet foreign policy since the end of World War II. Soviet officials preached ideological solidarity with the Arabs and gave Egypt and Syria extensive military, intelligence, and psychological support. At the same time, the Kremlin feared that another war between the Arabs and the Israelis could lead to escalation of the Soviet-American tension and a greater American involvement in Middle Eastern affairs on the side of Israel.[28]

During the Arab-Israeli Six Days War and its aftermath, the Politburo was in session almost around the clock. A participant wrote in his diary about the black mood of those days: "After militant boastful declarations of Nasser we did not expect that the Arab army would be defeated in a second."[29] The Politburo had to devise a new policy in the region. However, at a specially convened Party Plenum, anti-Zionist emotions and ideological schemes prevailed over reality. The Soviet leadership decided to break diplomatic relations with Israel for the second time since 1953 until Israel reached a settlement with the Arabs and returned their lands in exchange for security guarantees (according to UN Resolution no. 242). A few experts realized that this effectively froze Soviet diplomacy in the region, but the majority, including Gromyko and Suslov, stuck with the new line. Simultaneously, the Soviets continued to invest in Egypt and Syria, throwing good money after bad (Egypt alone owed the Soviet Union about fifteen billion rubles), in a desperate attempt to maintain a Soviet presence in the Middle East. As a result, Soviet Middle East diplomacy became a hostage of Arab radicalism and demands. Again, as in Vietnam, the new collective leadership demonstrated that, in contrast to Stalin, it was the prisoner, not the architect, of the revolutionary-imperial paradigm. Moscow restored relations with Israel only in 1991, shortly before the collapse of the USSR.[30]

At the peak of the Six Days War, the Politburo sent Kosygin to the United States for urgent talks with President Lyndon Johnson. The meeting in Glassboro, New Jersey, could have reopened the possibility for calm and pragmatic summits undermined by Nikita Khrushchev in 1960–61. President Johnson, increasingly desperate to end the war in Indochina, was ready for far-reaching negotiations. He wanted the Soviets to be a mediator in a Vietnam settlement and proposed to start talks on mutual cuts of strategic arsenals and military budgets. Johnson and Secretary of Defense Robert McNamara especially wanted to negotiate a ban on antiballistic missile defense (ABMs). Kosygin, however, was unprepared for serious talks and irritated over American support for Israel. Dobrynin, who observed him at the summit, called him a "reluctant" negotiator. To make matters worse, Kosygin totally misunderstood the intentions of Johnson and McNamara with regard to ABMs. In a rare display of anger, he declared: "Defense is moral, aggression is immoral." According to Dobrynin's summary, "Moscow at that time sought first of all to achieve nuclear parity in strategic offensive weapons."[31] It would take several years and the emergence of Brezhnev as a political leader and "peacemaker" before the post-Khrushchev cohort would be ready for negotiations with the United States.

BREZHNEV'S SERMON

Brezhnev participated in the Politburo foreign policy discussions throughout all these crises but avoided taking a clear stand on controversial issues. The new leader of the Communist Party of the Soviet Union knew he was neither in Stalin's nor Khrushchev's league in terms of experience, knowledge, energy, and character. Like a host of apparatchiks whom World War II and Stalin's purges of the Old Bolsheviks had catapulted to privilege and authority, Brezhnev had enormous practical acumen but very limited education and social horizons. Along with many young Communists of the 1930s, he acquired the habit of keeping a diary to raise his intellectual level. The diary's content, however, reveals a total lack of intellectual and spiritual interests. To every historian's despair, Brezhnev recorded mostly routine and banal events of his private life.[32]

Russian historian Dmitry Volkogonov portrayed Brezhnev as the blandest and most one-dimensional of all Soviet leaders. To Brezhnev he attributed "the psychology of a middle-rank party bureaucrat—vainglorious, cautious, conservative personality."[33] Indeed, those who knew Brezhnev from his military service spoke dismissively of his leadership qualities. One of Brezhnev's war buddies observed: "Leonid will never grow above his head."[34]

Catapulted into political leadership by Khrushchev's downfall, Brezhnev was in constant need of psychological support. He complained to his foreign policy assistant, Andrei Alexandrov-Agentov, that he had never dealt with foreign policy and knew nothing about it. He humbly admitted that his horizon remained that of a regional party secretary. "Here I am, sitting in the Kremlin and looking at the world only via the papers that reach my desk."[35] Brezhnev's assistant Georgy Arbatov would recall that Brezhnev was very weak in matters of Marxist-Leninist theory and felt this keenly. "He thought that to do something 'un-Marxist' now was impermissible—the entire party, the whole world, was watching him."[36] One could expect that with such a background Brezhnev would have joined the chorus of hard-liners and found a safe niche on the dogmatic and rigid flank of Soviet policy making. Initially, his behavior conformed to this expectation. It was a great surprise, therefore, when Brezhnev later became the main defender of détente in the Soviet leadership. As it turned out, other aspects of his personal views and character facilitated this surprising transformation.

Isaiah Berlin, in his book about Russian thinkers, distinguishes between the "foxes," who know many truths, and the "hedgehogs": who know only one but the most important truth. Brezhnev was not a thinker, but in foreign policy he had one strong belief, like the hedgehog in Berlin's classification. His belief was disarmingly simple: war must be avoided at all costs. During his meetings with foreign leaders, Brezhnev told them time and again about a conversation he had had with his father, a steelworker, at the beginning of World War II. When Hitler was overrunning Czechoslovakia and France, his father asked him: What is the world's highest mountain? "Everest," Brezhnev answered. Then his father asked him about the height of the Eiffel Tower. "About 300 meters," Brezhnev answered. Then Brezhnev's father suggested that a tower of this height should be erected on the top of Everest. Hitler and his cronies should be hanged there on a scaffold for the whole world to see. Brezhnev considered it a fantasy at the time, but then the war began. After it was over, the Nuremberg Trial condemned the captured Nazi leaders and hanged some of them. Brezhnev's father turned out to be prophetic. This story left an indelible impression on Brezhnev, his international worldview, and his policies—indeed, on his whole work and life. Brezhnev's interpreter, Viktor Sukhodrev, heard this story so many times that he began to call it "the Sermon on the Mount." When Brezhnev met with Richard Nixon for the first time, the Soviet party leader suggested they should conclude an agreement, a bizarre version of a peace pact, directed against any third country that would act aggressively. The Americans interpreted it as a crude attempt at a pact between the superpowers designed to destroy American alliances. They did not know that it was not a devious Politburo scheme but rather a personal dream of the general secretary.[37]

World War II was a major life-shaping experience for Brezhnev, who was then in his late thirties. As a division-rank political commissar, he experienced grueling combat firsthand; from 1942 to 1945 he marched with the troops from the Caucasus to the Carpathian Mountains. He firmly believed, however, that no price was too high for victory. In June 1945, he took part in the Victory Parade on Red Square and attended Stalin's banquet for the victors. For many years, he continued to admire Stalin as a warlord. By 1964, he was already a member of the Central Committee Secretariat, and in this capacity he supervised the Soviet space program and numerous projects of the military-industrial complex, including the production of nuclear weapons and the construction of missile pads and silos.[38] Brezhnev's hagiographic memoirs, which were written by professional ghostwriters, give only a glimpse of these crucial pages of his life.

Similar experiences converted many in the nomenklatura, among them Brezhnev's close friends Dmitry Ustinov and Andrei Grechko, into ardent advocates of military strength and preparedness. Brezhnev believed in military preparedness, but he also was genuinely concerned about the prospect of war and wanted to negotiate peace among the great powers. He was not unlike Ronald Reagan in thinking that the military buildup was important not for its own sake but as a prelude to international agreements. This belief that strength and peace do not contradict each other would cause many problems during the 1970s, when the continuous Soviet strategic buildup would allow American neoconservative critics and Pentagon experts to claim that the Kremlin was seeking military superiority. In the end, their public campaign about a growing "Soviet military threat" would undermine Soviet-American détente. At the beginning of the decade, however, Brezhnev's belief helped him see the need to cooperate with the United States.

Brezhnev deeply loathed brinkmanship and the crisis-mongering that had characterized Khrushchev's foreign policy since 1956. Twenty years after the Cuban missile crisis, he still could not contain his anger at Khrushchev for unleashing it: "We almost slipped into a nuclear war! And what effort did it cost us to pull ourselves out of this, to make the world believe that we really want peace!"[39] He reserved similarly harsh criticism for the Berlin crisis, saying to advisers in November 1971: "Instead of diplomatic achievements we built—bluntly speaking—the Chinese wall in Berlin, and hoped to resolve the problem in this way."[40] Overcoming Khrushchev's legacy of brinkmanship and building a firm foundation for world peace would become the mainspring of Brezhnev's foreign policy activism in the early 1970s.

Other facets of Brezhnev's leadership facilitated his conversion into a détente statesman. Henry Kissinger wrote in his memoirs that Brezhnev was "brutal" (in contrast to the "refined" Mao Ze-dong and Zhou Enlai). In reality, Brezhnev displayed more amiability than evil, more vanity than premeditated cruelty. During the pivotal moment of the post-Stalin power struggle in June 1957, Molotov rudely dressed Brezhnev down and the future Soviet leader fainted. Even when Brezhnev contemplated a removal of Khrushchev in 1964, his biggest fear was the danger of direct confrontation with the formidable Nikita.[41] As a person and politician, he abhorred confrontation and extremism. In his youth, his relatives knew him as "handsome and charming, a careful dresser and ladies' man." During his whole career under Stalin and Khrushchev, Brezhnev learned how to please people. Among friends, he was "modest, gregarious, with simple habits, a great conversationalist without any arrogance of power." Brezhnev once confessed: "Charm can take you a long way in politics." One sophisticated schoolteacher, who saw him during a performance at the Bolshoi Theater in 1963, wrote in her diary: "Brezhnev is downright handsome: blue eyes, black eyebrows, dimpled cheeks. Now I realize why I always felt sympathy for him."[42] It was as natural for Brezhnev to smile cordially as for Khrushchev to threaten with his fist.

By nature, Brezhnev was a centrist politician and an enemy of radical political moves in any direction. The general secretary did not object when, after 1964, his conservative allies and cronies began to roll back the Thaw in the areas of culture, propaganda, and ideology. At the same time, Brezhnev did not want to antagonize the large group of Soviet scientific, artistic, and cultural elites who feared a neo-Stalinist coup. He also was skeptical of an ideological rapprochement with the Chinese. He knew that the "Soviet Chinese," that is, the most ardent advocates of ideological reactions, grouped around Alexander Shelepin and almost openly talked about him, Brezhnev, as a transitional figure and a small-time politician vulnerable to booze and women.[43]

Militant attitudes reigned among the majority of Brezhnev's colleagues. To begin acting as a peacemaker in this milieu was extremely difficult and dangerous for one's career. Against all expectations, Brezhnev succeeded in this endeavor. For all his intellectual mediocrity, he was capable of good political instincts and tact. Advisers recall that in questions of power "Brezhnev was a great realist" and could bring along the conservative majority whenever he wanted.[44] After 1964, he focused on the most important task: cadres and networking. With several allies at the Politburo, including Mikhail Suslov and Andrei Kirilenko, he tirelessly phoned regional party secretaries, inquiring about their problems and needs and even asking for advice. In 1967, he gradually began to remove his rivals from positions of authority, beginning with Shelepin. By 1968, Brezhnev became the uncontested head of the party apparatus: the keys of political power were now in his hands.[45]

About the same time, Brezhnev began to show a greater interest in foreign policy and became impatient with Kosygin's international prominence. He was smart enough to realize he could not compete with Kosygin in the area of domestic economy. By contrast, foreign policy opened big opportunities for personal diplomacy and there Brezhnev's modest talents could be displayed most advantageously. The post of general secretary gave him a formidable advantage: by tradition, the occupant of this post was also the commander in chief and the head of the Defense Council. Thus, Brezhnev was formally responsible for security and military policies. And he had the power of appointments, the crucial tool in Soviet politics.[46]

Later, some Western observers connected Brezhnev's removal of hard-liners with the victory of pro-détente forces in the Politburo. In reality, there were no doves in Brezhnev's entourage. The majority of the Politburo remained ideologically orthodox even during détente. When the Politburo commission on arms control was established early in 1968, it was packed with Brezhnev's hard-line friends, among them Ustinov (as chairman) and Grechko.[47] Dmitry Ustinov was

Stalin's whiz kid, a brilliant autodidactic technocrat who had organized the evacuation of Soviet industries under the nose of the advancing Nazis in 1941 and who later was a mover and shaker in the Soviet missile project. For two decades, he was a tireless leader of the Soviet military-industrial complex. He feared that the United States might at the first opportunity strike at the Soviet Union and was determined to master enough force to deter the Americans. Andrei Grechko began his military career when, at the age of sixteen, he joined the Red Cavalry during the civil war that broke out after the Bolsheviks seized power in Russia in 1917. He had been Brezhnev's military superior during the Great Patriotic War and since 1967 the Soviet minister of defense. He firmly believed in Soviet victory in a future world war and felt nothing but contempt for the United States and NATO.[48] Both Ustinov and Grechko argued for an unrelenting arms race and feared that any arms limitations would threaten Soviet security.[49] They were worthy counterparts of American hawks.

Between 1965 and 1968, Brezhnev allowed Ustinov to shake up and centralize the enormous military-industrial complex that had previously been troubled by competition among various ministries and design bureaus. The general secretary also threw his full support behind the construction and deployment of the strategic triad of intercontinental ballistic missiles (ICBMs) in hardened silos, nuclear submarines with ballistic missiles, and strategic bombers. The scale of the ICBM program was particularly impressive: American satellite intelligence recorded with concern that in 1965 and 1966 the Soviets doubled their arsenal, catching up with the U.S. strategic forces. From then on, the Soviet ICBM force grew by about 300 new silo launchers a year. This was a colossal armament program that, according to an expert, "was the largest single weapons efforts in Soviet history and the most expensive, significantly outstripping the nuclear program of the late 1940s." By 1968, the strategic missile force was consuming about 18 percent of the Soviet defense budget. Brezhnev could not say no to any military production and deployment proposal.[50]

What ultimately distinguished the general secretary from his orthodox friends was not greater ideological tolerance and a less conservative outlook. It was his dream to become a peacemaker. It was also, as his speechwriter Anatoly Chernyaev correctly noted, the burden of great power that dictated state interests that did not fit into ideological orthodoxy. As Brezhnev became involved in foreign affairs, their logic taught him to rely not on the conservative and ignorant majority but on a few "enlightened" foreign policy experts working in the central party apparatus.[51]

These people included Evgeny Samoteikin, Georgy Arbatov, Alexander Bovin, Nikolai Inozemtsev, Vadim Zagladin, Nikolai Shishlin, Rafail Fedorov, Anatoly

Blatov, and Anatoly Chernyaev. They specialized in foreign affairs, came from universities and academic research institutes, and were much more open-minded and sophisticated thinkers than the average nomenklatura members. They were shaped by the cultural Thaw, de-Stalinization, and other liberalizing influences of the period from 1956 to 1964. They considered themselves Soviet patriots but also pragmatic freethinkers, and began to see the ossified ideology as a big obstacle to state interests. Many of them had been recruited by Andropov and his rival Boris Ponomarev to join the Central Committee apparatus. Andropov supported these people, telling them to think and write without regard to ideology. "I will know myself what to report to the Politburo." There was a constant bureaucratic struggle between them and Stalinists like Trapeznikov and Fedor Golikov. From 1965 to 1968, the "enlightened" apparatchiks formed the nucleus of Brezhnev's speechwriting team and therefore became part of his inner circle of advisers.[52]

Brezhnev's group of speechwriters also included his assistant Andrei Alexandrov-Agentov, a trained philologist and diplomat and an expert on Iceland and Scandinavia. Earlier, he had worked as assistant to Alexandra Kollontai and then to Gromyko. Alexandrov-Agentov was a devotee of Marxist-Leninist theory and a true believer in the international Communist movement, but he was not a rigid ideologue in international affairs. As Chernyaev observed, he "believed that realpolitik worked for our communist future."[53]

Brezhnev's early mentor in foreign policy was Foreign Minister Andrei Gromyko, in many respects a profoundly conservative figure but also a highly professional diplomat. Gromyko was obsequious and always implemented "with religious fervor" the instructions of the leader whom he served at the moment.[54] At the same time, he despised ideological intrusions into foreign policy and greatly admired Stalin's diplomacy during the Grand Alliance years. Gromyko's main goal was to obtain from the Western powers recognition of the new borders of the USSR and Soviet satellites in Central Europe, including the borders of the GDR. His next goal was to reach, after tough bargaining, a political accommodation with the United States. In January 1967, in a policy memorandum of the Ministry of Foreign Affairs to the Politburo, Gromyko argued: "We must resolutely continue to dissociate ourselves politically and ideologically from adventurous schemes of the Chinese leaders who have pinned their hopes on the inevitability of an armed conflict between the socialist countries headed by the Soviet Union and the United States within 8 to 10 years. The opinion that a war with the United States is inevitable would reflect precisely the position of the Chinese. On the whole, international tension does not suit the state interests of the Soviet Union and its friends. In conditions of détente it is easier to consolidate and broaden the positions of the Soviet Union in the world."[55]

This memo highlighted promising developments in capitalist countries, especially the turn toward détente in the Western capitals. Despite the war in Vietnam, Gromyko and other Soviet diplomats, among them the ambassador in Washington, Anatoly Dobrynin, and the head of the U.S. desk in the Ministry of Foreign Affairs, Georgy Kornienko, favored negotiations with Lyndon Johnson.[56] Gradually, Brezhnev himself came to realize that the policy of détente and negotiations with the capitalist great powers would be the shortest road to successful statesmanship and international recognition. This happened, however, only after several momentous developments in Europe and Asia and after a change of leadership in the United States.

IMPULSES FOR DÉTENTE

The single most important event at the end of the 1960s affecting Brezhnev's outlook on international affairs was the Czechoslovak crisis of 1968. The rapid flourishing of the Prague Spring presented a dire threat to Brezhnev's career. As leader of the CPSU, he bore direct responsibility for the preservation of the Soviet military sphere of influence in Central Europe. The Czechoslovak strategic location, advanced armament industries, and uranium mines made it an indispensable part of the Warsaw Pact.[57] The Soviet leadership feared "falling dominos" in Central Europe no less than the Johnson administration feared them in Southeast Asia. And Soviet fears were even more justified, considering the revolutions in Poland and Hungary in 1956, the stubborn neutrality of Yugoslavia, the gradual distancing of Rumania from the Warsaw Pact after 1962, and the constant instability in the GDR.[58] Worst of all, many in the Soviet leadership could possibly blame Brezhnev personally for such a catastrophe. After all, Alexander Dubcek, the head of the Czechoslovak Communist Party since January 1968, was Brezhnev's protégé. The Soviet leader had withheld his support for Antonin Novotny, the old-time Stalinist leader of Czechoslovakia, and had endorsed the Czechoslovak Action Program for reforms. Ukrainian first secretary Petro Shelest believed that Brezhnev's "rotten liberalism" made the Prague Spring possible. As the crisis unfolded, both Polish leader Gomulka and GDR leader Ulbricht pushed for invasion and openly criticized Brezhnev for emotionalism, naïveté, and vacillations.[59]

Brezhnev's character made him a reluctant interventionist. One witness recalled that even in the summer of 1968 there was uncertainty and diversity of opinion in the party headquarters in Moscow. People were shouting at the top of their lungs: "Do not send tanks to Czechoslovakia!" and "It is time to send tanks and finish this mess!" But all archival evidence demonstrates that throughout the

Czechoslovak crisis Brezhnev hoped to avoid "extreme measures," that is, military invasion. Instead, he preferred to increase political pressure on Dubcek and the Czechoslovak leadership.[60] Brezhnev feared that a Soviet invasion could trigger a NATO response, leading to a European war. The burden of decision was almost too much for the general secretary. During the months of the crisis, people often saw him shaken, pale, and lost, with trembling hands. In a revealing private remark, he admitted: "I may look soft, but I can strike so hard that afterwards I feel sick for three days." According to some reports, during 1968, Brezhnev began to take tranquilizers in order to alleviate unbearable pressure on his psyche. This would later grow into a fatal habit.[61]

On July 26–27, the Politburo, presided over by Brezhnev, decided to set a provisional date for the invasion of Czechoslovakia. The Soviets continued, however, to negotiate with Dubcek and the Czechoslovak leadership. Brezhnev, among others, tried to bully "Sasha" Dubcek into drastic measures to reverse liberalization and reforms. Once all their attempts failed, the Kremlin leaders finally made the decision on August 21, and the forces of the Soviet Union and other countries of the Warsaw Pact (except for Rumania) occupied Czechoslovakia.[62]

Two men were particularly helpful and supportive of Brezhnev during the crisis. Foreign Minister Andrei Gromyko helped assuage Brezhnev's fears of possible confrontation with the West over Czechoslovakia. He told the Politburo that "the international relations now are such that the extreme measures [that is, invasion of Czechoslovakia] cannot produce aggravation of the international situation. There will be no big war. . . . If we preserve Czechoslovakia—it will make us stronger."[63] Yuri Andropov, Brezhnev's appointee to chair the KGB, used the resources of his agency to steel Brezhnev's resolve. In his reports to the Politburo, Andropov pointed out that there was no alternative to a full-scale invasion. Under his guidance, the KGB falsely depicted peaceful events in Czechoslovakia as preparations for an armed uprising à la Hungary in 1956. Since Andropov had been ambassador in Budapest during the Hungarian revolution of 1956, his recommendations carried special weight.[64]

The crisis gave Brezhnev a crash course on crisis management and international relations. His morale soared when the much-feared reaction in the United States and West Germany to the Soviet invasion did not materialize. The signals from Western leaders that favored business as usual after the invasion of Czechoslovakia indicated a political victory for the Soviet Union. It boosted the Kremlin's self-confidence, battered earlier by the erosion of the socialist camp. In September 1968, Gromyko reported to the Politburo: "The determination that the Soviet Union demonstrated with regard to the Czechoslovak events made the leaders of the United States consider more soberly their potential in that region and see once again the determination of our country's leadership in defending the vital interests of the Soviet Union."[65] In his speeches to senior diplomatic cadres, the foreign minister sounded even more upbeat: "Look, comrades, how radically the correlation of forces in the world changed in recent years. Not so long ago we in the Politburo had to think carefully, time and again, before taking any foreign policy step—What would the U.S. do? What would France do? This period is over. When we believe now that something must be done in the interests of the Soviet Union, we do it without hesitation, and then we study their reaction. Whatever noise they can make, the new correlation of forces is such that they no longer dare to move against us."[66] About the same time, Alexander Bovin, one of the speechwriters for Brezhnev, found the general secretary supremely confident and relaxed. "From the crucible of Czechoslovakia emerged a different Brezhnev."[67]

But the longer-term costs of Brezhnev's 1968 success were high. After the initial shock, the Czechs boycotted Soviet attempts to stifle liberal reforms; it took years of forced "normalization" to freeze Czechoslovak society. The Prague Spring created a widespread "spill-over" in the Western non-Russian areas of the Soviet Union, arguably even more destabilizing than during the Polish and Hungarian revolutions of 1956.[68] The invasion killed any remaining socialist illusions on the part of the anti-Stalinist members of the educated classes in Moscow, Leningrad, and other cultural centers of Russia. A handful of them dared to protest openly, but many were in moral and intellectual agony. The fault line between the supporters of de-Stalinization and the Soviet system created in 1956 became an unbridgeable chasm. It was "the biggest political error during the postwar time," wrote Bovin in his diary. Those who had worked in Prague for the international Communist journal, The Problems of World and Socialism, concluded that the invasion was a crime. Chernyaev wanted to resign from the Central Committee International Department. He stayed, however, and played the role of conformist. Many future reformers, including Mikhail Gorbachev and Alexander Yakovlev, did the same.[69]

This fallout notwithstanding, the general secretary passed the test and proved to his colleagues that he could protect Soviet security interests under pressure. For all his later willingness to conduct peaceful dialogue with the Western powers, Brezhnev would have found it much harder to do if he had not earned his credentials as the executioner of Czechoslovakia. In 1972, he told the Party Plenum: "Without [the invasion of] Czechoslovakia—there would have been no Brandt in Germany, no Nixon in Moscow, no détente."[70]

Sino-Soviet conflict commanded Brezhnev's attention several months later. A new and dangerous military confrontation loomed in the Far East.[71] In the political and military leadership, the hope for reconciliation with China quickly gave way to fears of China's irrational aggressiveness, the new version of the old Russian chauvinistic myth about "yellow peril." A joke circulated in Moscow: A Soviet commander in the Far East calls the Kremlin in panic, asking: "What should I do? Five million Chinese have just crossed the border and surrendered!" This joke did not raise spirits among those responsible for Soviet security in the Far East. Indeed, would they give the order to fire on the crowds of unarmed Chinese civilians if they started flooding over the Soviet borders? Soviet marshals and generals, trained for waging and winning a nuclear war, had no scenarios for this event.[72]

Apparently, Brezhnev shared racism-colored fears of China. He neither trusted the Maoist leadership nor wanted to negotiate with them, leaving this unpleasant business to Kosygin. But China's nuclear capabilities bothered him. Later, in May 1973, Brezhnev, according to Kissinger, considered the possibility of a preemptive strike on China. Almost ten years earlier, when John F. Kennedy sounded out Khrushchev about a possible surgical strike against the Chinese nuclear arsenal, the Soviet leadership ignored those signals.[73] Echoes of this proposal probably came to Brezhnev's attention. Later he would try several times to offer U.S. leadership the idea of a joint front against possible violators of peace in Beijing.[74]

The idea fit Brezhnev's "Sermon on the Mount" philosophy. Its main goal, however, was practical: to deter the Chinese from future provocations on Soviet borders. During talks between Kosygin and Zhou Enlai in a Beijing airport in 1969, Zhou began the conversation with "a rumor" about a Soviet preemptive nuclear strike. A Soviet diplomat, present at the meeting, interpreted it as a sign that the Chinese leadership was "very scared by this possibility." Zhou Enlai clearly hinted to the Soviet side that China neither planned nor was able to launch a war against the USSR. After the talks, Moscow organized additional intimidating signals and Beijing authorities offered a secret nonaggression pact with the Soviet Union. Russian scholars conclude that Moscow's tactics of deterring Beijing through nuclear intimidation were effective.[75] At the same time, Soviet intimidation produced the classic "security dilemma" effect: Mao began to seek rapprochement with the United States against the northern enemy, putting aside ideological constraints.

A third momentous development that opened the door for Brezhnev's involvement in détente policies was the rapprochement with the new leadership in West Germany. Some Western European countries, especially France, had sought to improve relations with Moscow ever since Stalin's death. But the key to European détente lay in West Germany. As long as Konrad Adenauer remained chancellor, the Bonn government refused to recognize the GDR in any form. The Berlin Wall dramatically raised the price the German people were paying for such a policy. A top Soviet expert recalled later that "much of what happened in Europe—and the origins of the Helsinki process—had roots in the second division of spheres of influence in Europe that took place on August 13, 1961." The failure of the Western powers to prevent the division of Berlin had a profound impact on the mayor of West Berlin, Willy Brandt, and his adviser, Egon Bahr. Brandt, by then the leader of the Social Democratic Party (SPD), became vice chancellor in 1966 and was elected chancellor in September 1969, campaigning on the platform of Ostpolitik, a new foreign policy that promised to reopen the borders between the two parts of Germany.[76]

Alexandrov-Agentov believed that Brezhnev was fortunate to deal with Brandt, "a man of crystal integrity, sincerely peace-loving and with firm antifascist convictions who not only hated Nazism, but fought against it during the war."[77] In order to respond to Ostpolitik, Brezhnev had to overcome many hurdles: his memories of World War II, the propagandist image of West Germany as a nest of neo-Nazism and revanchism, and the old ideological enmity between Communists and Social Democrats.[78] Brezhnev abhorred the idea of destabilizing the GDR, in his eyes the country "paid for by the sacrifice of Soviet people, with the blood of Soviet soldiers." He also had to manage a difficult relationship with the GDR leader, Ulbricht, who treated any Moscow-Bonn contacts with deep suspicion and had the means to spy on them and spoil them. Still fresh in the collective memory in the Kremlin was the "Adzhubei episode" of 1964, when Khrushchev's son-in-law, allegedly after consuming too much alcohol, offered an informal deal to the West German leadership at Ulbricht's expense. Mindful of all this, Gromyko and the Soviet Foreign Ministry deliberately played it safe with regard to the GDR and ignored promising changes in Bonn.[79]

The new head of the KGB, Yuri Andropov, helped Brezhnev begin the Soviet–West German dialogue. Like Gromyko, Andropov considered Stalin's wartime diplomacy a brilliant example of Realpolitik. Andropov's vision of détente was classic "peace through strength." He is on record as saying: "Nobody wants to talk to the weak."[80] At the same time, Andropov had long ago decided that economic, technological, and cultural cooperation with West Germany and the Germans should be an anchor of future Soviet foreign policy aimed at ending U.S. domination in Western Europe. He was also reportedly hopeful that in the future closer relations with and technology transfers from West Germany could help the modernization of the Soviet Union. Early in 1968, Andropov, with Brezhnev's quiet approval, sent journalist Valery Lednev and KGB officer Vyacheslav Kevorkov to Egon Bahr with the task of setting up a back channel exchange. The secret nature of this channel helped to break through the wall of mutual suspicions and pretenses. It also permitted Brezhnev to conduct a pragmatic dialogue with Bonn without looking over his shoulder at Ulbricht. After the Czechoslovak crisis, the back channel was ready for activation.[81]

Brezhnev waited for the other side to make the first formal move. His own ideological and political doubts still bothered him. Only in October 1969, after Brandt won elections and became chancellor, did Brezhnev ask Andropov and Gromyko to seek an agreement with West Germany.[82] The sluggish dynamics of Soviet–West German relations began to accelerate, as Egon Bahr began to shuttle between Bonn and Moscow. He spent half a year in 1970 in the corridors of Soviet power and even learned some important rules of the Soviet bureaucratic "kitchen." Brezhnev grew to like him. On August 12, 1970, a nonaggression pact between West Germany and the Soviet Union was concluded in Moscow. Another treaty, with Poland, acknowledging the post-1945 geopolitical reality, was signed in December 1970. In May 1971, Walter Ulbricht, a major opponent of the Moscow-Bonn dialogue and a personal critic of Brezhnev, resigned under joint pressure from the Kremlin and from the group of younger GDR officials headed by Erich Honecker. This opened the road to mutual recognition and a treaty between the two German states a year and a half later.[83]

Another obstacle was the difficult problem of West Berlin. This problem obviously could not be solved on a bilateral basis, since it involved the GDR and four Western occupying powers. By 1971, fortunately, U.S. president Richard Nixon, through his national security adviser, Henry Kissinger, indicated a strong interest in rapprochement with the Kremlin. The Americans were eager to "embed" Brandt's Ostpolitik in the framework of their own strategy toward the Soviet Union. As a quid pro quo for Soviet assistance in helping the Americans to withdraw from Vietnam, Nixon and Kissinger promised the Politburo to facilitate a settlement on West Berlin. Formally, the talks on West Berlin proceeded within the four-powers framework on the level of foreign ministers. In reality, in the best traditions of secret diplomacy, a web of back channels emerged among the White House, the Kremlin, and Brandt. In September 1971, the Western powers formally acknowledged that West Berlin was not part of the Federal Republic of Germany.[84]

Thus, Brezhnev achieved what Khrushchev had failed to achieve, despite great pressure, ten years earlier. The dramatic struggle around Berlin and the GDR that had caused the two most severe international crises in Europe since World War II finally become history. On September 16–18, 1971, Brezhnev entertained Brandt near Yalta, at the state dacha built in Oreanda, where Czar Nicholas I had had a palace. This "second Yalta" meeting, held in the immediate vicinity of Livadia, where the "Big Three" had met in 1945, was a relaxed event that fit Brezhnev's style and character. He was impeccably dressed, treated Brandt to sumptuous feasts, drove him on a speed hydrofoil ride, swam with him in his giant swimming pool, and led Russian-style chaotic conversations about politics and life. In his clumsy, gregarious way, Brezhnev wrecked the entire schedule of the meeting, to the initial irritation of his German guest. "The light and joyous spirit of mutual affection and trust hovered over everything," Alexandrov-Agentov rhapsodized in his memoirs. "One could see that Brezhnev liked Brandt very much, and the latter seemed also satisfied with his host. Later they would rather easily find common language even on quite complex and sensitive issues." The Crimean meeting was a psychological breakthrough for Brezhnev. He achieved something that Khrushchev most likely had wanted to do but never could: a leader of a major capitalist country, above all Germany, became Brezhnev's "friend."[85]

The opening to West Germany created the duo of Gromyko and Andropov. Both became Brezhnev's most reliable political allies on the matter of détente. The pragmatic, opportunistic nature of this duo was apparent: eventually Gromyko and Andropov benefited from it greatly and ended their careers in the highest positions. Characteristically, like Brezhnev, they constantly asserted their hard-line ideological credentials. Andropov continued to apply "the lessons of Hungary" to foreign policy. Even in a facetious verse he wrote to his advisers, he insisted that the "socialist achievements" must be defended, "if necessary, by the axe." And Gromyko, at a conference of high Foreign Ministry officials, said that West Germany had made concessions to the Soviet Union on practically all the issues. And "we gave them nothing."[86]

Triumphalism aside, Gromyko's tough remarks reflected the pressure of domestic politics on the decision makers. Portraying the rapprochement with West Germany as a foreign policy success meant bolstering the political authority of those who had advocated it, and above all, Brezhnev's personal authority. This was not easy, since Brezhnev was not Stalin and the Soviet Union was no longer a totalitarian monolith. Molotov in retirement remarked that "agreement on the borders of the two Germanys is a big deal," but praised Brandt, not Brezhnev, for it. Other Stalinists, present everywhere in the party apparatus, continued to believe that geopolitical deals should not come at the expense of the ideological goals of Soviet foreign policy. There was also a broad array of increasingly influential cultural and intellectual figures whom Walter Laqueur considered "Russian fascists": anti-Western proponents of transformation of the Soviet Union into a Great Russia.[87] In 1976, long after the policy of détente was hailed as a great success by party propagandists, Brezhnev remarked: "I genuinely want peace and will never back down. Some people, however, dislike this policy. And they are not [out in the streets], but inside the Kremlin. They are not some propagandists from regional committees. They are people like me. Only they think differently!"[88] These concerns about potential opposition continued to dominate Brezhnev's détente policies on all levels.

Initially, "those who thought differently" tried to pull Brezhnev over to their side. Eventually, however, Stalinists and Russian nationalists lost the battle for Brezhnev's soul. Brezhnev grew to depend on his small circle of foreign policy speechwriters and assistants, and these people began to influence, "with word and pen," the shape of not only foreign, but also domestic, public pronouncements of the general secretary. By contrast, Brezhnev increasingly distanced himself from the most extreme views of his ignorant, crudely anti-American cronies who did not approve of détente for dogmatic ideological reasons. From time to time, Brezhnev showed written examples of "anonymous" criticism of hard-liners to his liberal assistants, as if telling them: "There are wolves ready to devour you, but I will not give you away to them."[89]

Some of Brezhnev's speechwriters (Arbatov, Chernyaev, Shakhnazarov) later supported Mikhail Gorbachev and contributed to glasnost and the "new thinking" that transformed Soviet foreign policy and the Soviet Union itself. Their impact was considerable: they couched Brezhnev's speeches and reports in much less militant and ideological language than the majority of the nomenklatura and many of Brezhnev's old friends and cronies expected and preferred. Yet, in retrospect, their role was strictly limited. Their attempts to liberate Soviet policies of détente from the dead weight of ideology and to open Brezhnev's mind to new international realities brought few results. The general secretary remained staunchly antireformist in domestic politics and dependent on ideological orthodoxy. The main impulses for détente initially came from outside and were successful to the extent that they matched Brezhnev's deeply held convictions and ambitions.

The general secretary wanted to convert the growing military power of the Soviet Union into the coin of international diplomacy and prestige. With the help of Andropov, Gromyko, and his "enlightened" assistants and speechwriters, Brezhnev began to formulate his grand international vision, a program of constructing peace in Europe and openings toward the West. The centerpiece of this program was the idea of an all-European conference on security and cooperation. The Soviet leader announced this at the next Party Congress, which was scheduled for the spring of 1970 but was held in March–April 1971. A scholar of détente concluded that at the Congress "Leonid Brezhnev established his leadership of the Politburo in foreign affairs." He also "openly identified himself with the Soviet response to Brandt's *Ostpolitik*."[90] The unanimous support and the ovation that Brezhnev received from the Congress delegates for his Peace Program and the opening toward West Germany was not merely a ritualistic act but a crucial political event. From now on, Brezhnev was in a better position to silence the critics of his foreign policy. To make this point clear at the Congress, Gromyko spoke against the anonymous figures inside the party and the country who interpret "any agreement with capitalist states as some kind of conspiracy."[91]

In October 1971, Brezhnev lectured his speechwriters: "We have been constantly fighting for détente and we have already achieved much. Today in our talks with the largest states of the West we aim at agreement, not at confrontation. And we will do everything to make the [Conference on European Security and Cooperation] proclaim a declaration on the principles of peaceful coexistence in Europe. This will postpone war perhaps by twenty-five years, probably even by a century. To this end we focus all our thoughts and activities of our Foreign Ministry and public organizations of our country, as well as those of our allies."[92] But "the fight for détente" was to grow ever more complicated. And the reason was not so much domestic constraints as developments in the outside world. The Brezhnev leadership had to overcome the biggest obstacle of all: the war in Vietnam and the persistence of the U.S.-Soviet confrontation.

BIRTH PANGS OF U.S.-SOVIET DÉTENTE

For years, Brezhnev and his friends in the Soviet military command and the military-industrial complex had regarded the United States as the main adversary. The ideas of arms control and negotiated compromise with the United States did not mesh well with their mind-set, which was permeated by anti-Americanism. Making matters worse was the Khrushchev-era military doctrine, which aimed at *winning* a nuclear war. The Ministry of Defense insisted, in addition to strategic parity, on getting some kind of a force, equivalent to the American, British, and French medium-range and short-range nuclear missiles, deployed in Western Europe and in the seas around the Soviet Union.[93] Ultimately, the Soviet military command (much in the same way as its U.S. counterpart) wanted to retain complete freedom in the continuing arms race. The Soviet military continued to be suspicious of a few diplomats who began to understand that victory in a nuclear war was impossible and that the goal should be negotiated parity based on mutual trust. Minister of Defense Grechko claimed at a Politburo meeting that the head of the Strategic Arms Limitation Treaty (SALT) delegation, Vladimir Semenov, "was giving in to American pressure." At first, Brezhnev also was not particularly supportive of the diplomats. When he instructed the SALT delegation before the talks began in Helsinki in October 1969, he told them sternly to keep their mouths shut about military secrets. The KGB, he warned them, was just around the corner.[94]

The establishment of the back channel between Washington and Moscow in February 1969 did not produce results for months. Every Soviet message to the White House had to go through the cumbersome procedure of Politburo collective approval. Nixon's intentions were the subject of guesses and strong suspicions in Moscow. For years, Soviet leaders knew him only as a devout anti-Communist and expected the worst from his presidency.[95] Sharp differences in priorities did not help Soviet-American relations either. The Politburo believed that the bilateral arms control negotiations were a top priority. Nixon, however, was obsessed with Vietnam and tied all arms control issues to his demand that the Kremlin should apply pressure on Hanoi to end the Vietnam War.[96] Nobody in the Kremlin was ready to do this. When Nixon proposed a summit meeting, Foreign Minster Gromyko, sensing the prevailing mood of the leadership, spoke at the Politburo meeting against any hurry to meet with the U.S. president. He insisted on linking the summit to a successful signing of the agreements on West Berlin. The Politburo agreed, and Nixon's offer was left unanswered for months.[97]

Not until 1971 did Brezhnev show strong personal interest in the back channel communications. By the summer of that year, however, he was willing to meet with Nixon and even visit the United States. Several factors intervened to bring about this change. The first development was Brezhnev's growing self-confidence after the Party Congress in March–April 1971 and as a result of the successful meetings with Bahr and Brandt. Another factor was the sudden announcement of Nixon's trip to China. The Sino-Soviet border clashes finally convinced Washington policy makers that joint support of North Vietnam by the two Communist giants was fiction. Nixon and his national security adviser, Henry Kissinger, launched their "triangular diplomacy," parallel and coordinated rapprochement with Beijing and Moscow. From that moment, Gromyko's procrastination tactics no longer looked prudent.[98]

The final push soon came, on August 5, 1971, when Brezhnev received his first personal letter from Nixon. Until then, the official Soviet addressee of the back channel correspondence was Kosygin. The president appealed to Brezhnev to become his partner in discussing "big issues." The general secretary immediately responded with a suggestion to hold a Soviet-American summit in Moscow in May–June 1972. Dobrynin received instructions from Moscow that from now on Brezhnev would personally supervise preparations for the summit.[99]

As in the case of *Ostpolitik*, the general secretary decided to invest his political capital in the relationship with Nixon only when he saw reasonable prospects for a breakthrough. Still, the final miles leading to the Moscow summit were strewn with rocks. The first crisis broke out when Brandt faced a no-confidence vote in the Bundestag that threatened to disrupt the ratification of the Soviet–West German Treaty. It would have been a tremendous embarrassment for Soviet diplomacy and Brezhnev—the results of the Soviet-German rapprochement would have been suspended or, even worse, reversed. Brezhnev appealed to the White House to intervene in West German politics to help Brandt. At some point, the KGB even contemplated bribing some deputies of the Bundestag.[100] On April 26, 1972, Brandt won the vote of confidence by a two-vote margin. On May 17, the Bundestag ratified the Moscow Treaty. This gave Brezhnev the high ground, politically and psychologically, for negotiations with Nixon in Moscow.

Another development that tested the emerging Soviet-American dialogue at the highest levels followed in South Asia. In November 1971, a war broke out between Pakistan and India. Just three months earlier, the Soviet Union had signed the Treaty on Peace, Friendship, and Cooperation with India. The Soviet leadership committed itself to deliver a large supply of armaments. Brezhnev's assistant later recalled that this was primarily a geopolitical move to offset Nixon's rapprochement with China. But what happened next stunned the leadership of both superpowers. Emboldened by the treaty and arms supplies, Indian president Indira Gandhi authorized the Indian army to make incursions into Bangladesh, then Eastern Pakistan, to assist Bengali separatists. Then the Pakistanis attacked Indian airfields. Although the Pakistan army quickly lost the war in the east, the war could still spread into Kashmir, the main contested region between the two states.[101]

Nixon and Kissinger responded to the Indian-Pakistani war almost hysterically; they saw it as a Soviet plot to undermine the entire edifice of American triangular diplomacy, specifically American attempts to build up China (and its ally Pakistan) as a counterweight to the Soviet Union. They demanded Brezhnev's guarantees that India would not attack Western Pakistan. Nixon seemed to be ready to link the future summit in Moscow to Soviet behavior on this issue. He also sent the U.S. Navy to the Bay of Bengal. The Soviets, including Dobrynin, could not see why the White House supported Pakistan, whom they believed had started the war, against India. Brezhnev, puzzled at first, was soon enraged. In his narrow circle, he even suggested giving India the secret of the atomic bomb. His advisers did their best to kill this idea. Several years later, when Alexandrov-Agentov reminded Brezhnev of this episode, he still reacted angrily and spoke spitefully about American behavior.[102]

But the biggest obstacle to the summit remained the Vietnam War. In the spring of 1972 Hanoi launched a new offensive in South Vietnam, without even bothering to consult with Moscow. In April, the U.S. Air Force resumed the bombing campaign against the North and accidentally hit four Soviet merchant ships, killing several sailors. In early May, Nixon ordered even more brutal bombing attacks on Hanoi and the mining of Haiphong harbor.[103] Kosygin, Podgorny, Shelest, and other Politburo members believed that the summit with Nixon should be cancelled because of the bombing and the deaths of the Soviet personnel.[104] Brezhnev wavered. He was, recalls his assistant, "shocked and furious at Washington's provocative actions." Nixon's motives to preserve his prestige in the eyes of the American public concerned Brezhnev very little. "He only felt that the Soviet-American meeting, the business that required so much of his energy and time, was now an object of a gamble, and that [Nixon] was trying to push him into the corner."[105]

But Brezhnev's personal interest in the summit prevailed over emotions, and he pleaded with colleagues for moderation. As it was clearly impossible to force Hanoi to stop its military actions halfway, Brezhnev and Gromyko tried to mediate between Kissinger and the Hanoi representatives. They also quickly agreed that Kissinger should secretly come to Moscow for troubleshooting discussions. Nixon's national security adviser was in Moscow on April 21 and 22. Instead of pressing the Soviet leader on Vietnam (as Nixon wanted him to do), Kissinger did his best to strike a cordial relationship with Brezhnev. In the matters of substance, Kissinger was in a mood for compromise: he gave way to Brezhnev and Gromyko on the text of "The Basic Principles of Relations between the USSR and the USA." As Brezhnev's foreign policy assistant summarized, "This document was tantamount to recognition of the most important principles that the Soviet side stood and struggled for during many years." The most important for the general secretary was acknowledgment of "equality" as a basis for Soviet-American détente.[106]

Brezhnev's conversations with Kissinger, now declassified, reveal the general secretary at his prime as a negotiator: a confident, energetic, and jovial man in a stylish dark blue suit with gold watch chain, not giving an inch in substance and style to his partner, the former Harvard professor. At the time, Brezhnev was in good physical shape. He used his charm, mastered the topics of conversation quickly, did not read from the script, and easily answered Kissinger's arguments. The general secretary tried his best humor on his guest, and the American responded in kind.[107] He also wondered when the United States was going to leave Vietnam. "De Gaulle fought seven years in Algeria," he reminded Kissinger. "It was simply a waste of time and effort. You face the same prospect." He also told Nixon's skeptical adviser: "I certainly support President Nixon's idea of ending the war. That is the end-goal of all of us. Certainly the Soviet Union has no axe to grind. We seek no advantage to us whatsoever." At the same time, Brezhnev clearly wanted to move from Vietnam on to other issues of "general détente." He told Kissinger that "the current discussions represent the start of a major future process, the start of building mutual trust." There should be "other goodwill measures to solidify good relations between the USSR and the U.S.," in the spirit of "the noble mission that rests on their shoulders."[108]

Brezhnev's personal diplomacy began under exceptionally favorable conditions. Never since the times of the Grand Alliance had an American president tried so hard to win Soviet trust and allow the Kremlin leadership so much access to the White House. Nixon and Kissinger, each for their own reasons, kept the State Department, the rest of the administration, and indeed the entire U.S. political establishment in the dark about their strategies. Kissinger chose Dobrynin and later Brezhnev as his confidants to complain about the "Byzantine bureaucracy" of Washington and Nixon's "idiosyncratic style." Several times Dobrynin was Kissinger's exclusive guest in the top-secret Situation Room in the West Wing of the White House. Brezhnev, as his assistant recalled, was "mightily amused" by Kissinger's repeated pleas to keep some aspects of their talks as their personal secret. At the same time, he could not help being flattered by such an exclusive relationship.[109]

But Kissinger's mission, successful as it was, could not dispel the storm gathering in Moscow on account of Vietnam. The Politburo remained divided, and some of its members urged rescinding Nixon's invitation to Moscow and reaffirming the Soviet Union's prestige in the Communist camp by acting as a staunch ally of Hanoi. The leading skeptic was Nikolai Podgorny, chairman of the Supreme Soviet and therefore technically "head of state." His background and cultural level was very similar to Brezhnev's, but he lacked his friend's charm and flexibility. Podgorny had been watching Brezhnev's foreign policy activism with jealousy and since 1971 had tried to poke his nose into diplomatic affairs. Gromyko, with Brezhnev's blessing, firmly rebuffed these encroachments. But in April and May 1972, Podgorny sensed his opportunity to speak up on foreign affairs. His potential ally was the Ukrainian party leader, Petro Shelest, a staunch believer in "class-based" foreign policy and a closet critic of Brezhnev's leadership qualities. Shelest wrote in his diary: "Our successes in foreign affairs wholly depend on our domestic strength, on our people's faith in us, on our fulfillment of our plans and commitments." Détente, in his opinion, was a slippery slope. Worst of all, Brezhnev's allies and friends wavered: Minister of Defense Grechko spoke against inviting Nixon to Moscow, and Mikhail Suslov, the supreme judge of the ideological purity of state policies, was suspiciously silent on the forthcoming summit.[110] Alexandrov-Agentov recalls that there was "a real danger" that emotional arguments about solidarity with Vietnam "might resonate among the considerable part of the Central Committee and among the public."[111]

Faithful to his consensus-building style, Brezhnev waited for others in the Politburo to defend the idea of a summit. To everybody's surprise, Kosygin spoke in favor of it. He and Gromyko argued that a cancellation of the summit could derail ratification of the Moscow treaty with West Germany still pending at the time in Bonn, and it could put an indefinite hold on the agreements with Kissinger on SALT and ABMs that created the framework of strategic parity between the United States and the USSR. The winning argument was that the North Vietnamese should not be allowed to exercise a veto over Soviet relations with the United States.[112] For the moment, state interests prevailed over ideological passions.

This was the time at which the Soviets sharply increased the purchase of Western technology and began several projects aimed at the modernization of the chemical and automobile industries. They were building two giant vehicle manufacturing plants—one for cars (Tolyatti) and another for trucks (the Kama River plant).[113] Kosygin's support for détente reflected the widespread expectation among the captains of Soviet industries that European détente and a U.S.-Soviet summit would reopen access to Western economic, financial, and technological resources. Chernyaev's diary record of the Politburo meeting on April 6 provides a colorful illustration of this. Deputy of Kosygin and longtime Minister of Oil Nikolai Baibakov and Minister of External Trade Nikolai Patolichev presented a draft agreement on the economic and trade agreements with the United States. Podgorny sharply objected to cooperation with the Americans on constructing gas and oil pipelines from Tyumen and Yakutia, two permafrost areas to the east of the Urals. Couldn't the Soviets develop Siberia without foreign capital and technical assistance? Brezhnev invited Baibakov to speak. He "calmly took the microphone, barely hiding an ironic expression on his face." Using facts and figures, he demonstrated the profitability and benefits of the agreements. "If we reject the agreement," Baibakov continued, "we will not be able to access the oil reserves of [Yakutia] for at least thirty more years. Technically we can lay a gas pipeline. But we lack metal for pipes, machinery, and equipment." Eventually, the Politburo voted for the drafts.[114]

The full clout of the general secretary had to be brought to bear to overcome the resistance of the military. By mid-April, the obstructionist stand of the Ministry of Defense forced the top SALT negotiator, Vladimir Semenov, to turn to Brezhnev for assistance. At a meeting of the Defense Council in May 1972, Brezhnev abandoned his customary caution and spoke in full voice. According to a witness, he asked Grechko: "If we make no concessions, the nuclear arms race will go further. Can you give me, the Commander-in-Chief of Armed Forces, a firm guarantee that in such a situation we will get superiority over the United States and the correlation of forces will become more advantageous to us?" When Grechko mumbled indicating a negative response, Brezhnev concluded: "Then what is wrong? Why should we continue to exhaust our economy, increase military expenses?" With great reluctance, the military dropped their objections to the arms agreements. During the Moscow summit, the head of the Military-Industrial Commission, Leonid Smirnov, played a constructive role in finding compromise settlements with the American delegation. Grechko had to go along with them, but his resistance to the negotiated compromises with the Americans continued.[115]

Brezhnev also decided to convene a secret plenary session of the Central Committee and appeal for support for his decision to meet with Nixon. The days before and during the plenum, less than a week before Nixon's arrival, were perhaps the most nerve-wracking time for Brezhnev since the Czechoslovak crisis. The uncertainty about ratification of the Moscow Treaty in Bonn added to the tension. Alexandrov-Agentov recalled "the atmosphere of condensed anxiety" at Brezhnev's dacha, where Gromyko, Ponomarev, and a team of speechwriters worked. "Leonid Ilyich was in those days like a walking bundle of nerves, popping in and out of the room, smoking one cigarette after another."[116] One is struck by Brezhnev's personal emotional investment and his feelings of insecurity and vulnerability, despite the power of his office. This was, of course, vintage Brezhnev. Kissinger, during his first secret talks with Brezhnev, observed "an uneasy, quite touching, meld of defensiveness and vulnerability somewhat out of keeping with the assertive personal style. At this point the personalities of Nixon and Brezhnev intersected."[117]

Fortune again smiled on Brezhnev. At the plenum, Kosygin, Gromyko, Suslov, and Andropov spoke strongly for détente with the United States. This event marked a big victory for Brezhnev.[118] Now he could safely assume the mantle of a statesman without fearing for his back at home. When Nixon arrived at the Kremlin for talks on May 22, Brezhnev suddenly whisked him into his office (once Stalin's quarters) for a private conversation. Podgorny and Kosygin, as well as Kissinger, were left outside, furious. Soviet interpreter Viktor Sukhodrev, the only living witness of this meeting, believes it was a pivotal moment in Brezhnev's personal commitment to Soviet-American détente. During the talk, Brezhnev raised the question of whether the United States and the Soviet Union could reach an agreement on the nonuse of nuclear weapons against each other. The antinuclear agreement could, in his view, form a sound basis for lasting peace in the world. This proposal revealed the limits of Brezhnev's strategic vision and sophistication. Brezhnev reduced the essence of the Cold War to a mutual fear of a nuclear war between the United States and the Soviet Union. He also believed that an agreement between leaders would be sufficient to dispel this fear. But Brezhnev's proposal also showed the strength of his belief in détente. As Brezhnev's entourage claims, this idea did not come from Gromyko's briefings but sprang from the heart of the general secretary.[119]

The crucial part of the meeting was Brezhnev's suggestion to establish a personal relationship and engage in a special personal correspondence with the U.S. president. Nixon eagerly responded, reminding Brezhnev of the special relationship between Roosevelt and Stalin during the war. For Brezhnev, this was a move behind the Politburo's back. As is always true in human affairs, but particularly in Brezhnev's case, perceptions were more important than substance. Two years later, Averell Harriman recorded the general secretary saying: "Perhaps most Americans did not realize the importance of those first few minutes of conversation with President Nixon in 1972, which had had a decisive effect. The President had said, 'I know you are loyal to your system and we are loyal to ours. So let's put this question aside and build a good relationship despite this difference in systems.' Brezhnev said he had given the President his hand in friendship and had agreed there would be no interference in one another's internal affairs and the two countries would subscribe to peaceful coexistence. A whole series of political and economic agreements had been reached on this basis."[120]

According to Sukhodrev, Brezhnev made the same remark in his narrow circle over and over again. He was impressed that the U.S. president was prepared to leave all strategic interests and details aside and just talk about how to improve Soviet-American relations.[121] The perception of friendship with the U.S. president elevated Brezhnev way above his colleagues and rivals, to the historic place that only Stalin had reached before. Détente became Brezhnev's personal project and he intended to keep it going.

DÉTENTE WITHOUT BREZHNEV?

This close look at the origins of détente proves that the rapid decline of Cold War tensions in the period from 1970 to 1972 was not inevitable nor preordained. True, the shadow of the nuclear arms race and the rapid proliferation of nuclear missiles and warheads in the United States and the Soviet Union greatly contributed to the perception of a dangerous stalemate and helped to rationalize détente in terms of state interests, by presenting arms control as the optimal policy for both sides. This rationalization has since been enshrined in mountains of books, particularly those written during the 1970s and 1980s, since the outcome of the global bilateral confrontation was still not certain. But to imply that the psychological and economic costs of the nuclear arms race, and the danger of nuclear war, were enough to compel statesmen to seek accommodation in the late 1960s and early 1970s would be the same as suggesting that the prospect of accidental death could be a sufficient reason to cancel Formula One or NASCAR races. In other words, it would mean ascribing too much rationality and wisdom to great powers and their leaders.

True, Soviet political leadership felt intense pressure to reenergize the economy and produce both guns and butter. Détente could be an easy way out of this double bind. There was a desperate need for hard currency and Western technologies.[122] Upon a closer look, however, these economic concerns, strategic calculations, and attention to the nuclear balance carried much less weight in the Kremlin policy debates and contributed less to the Soviet change of heart in favor of détente than one might expect. The majority of Politburo members, as well as the party secretaries and the military—men like Kosygin, Suslov, Podgorny, Shelest, Ustinov, and Grechko—all had deep reservations for different reasons about dancing the "détente waltz" with the Americans. Andropov in the KGB and Gromyko in the Foreign Ministry initially lacked the clout and political will to go too far out on the limb in favor of negotiations with the West. It was Brezhnev's personal and increasingly emotional involvement and his talents as a domestic consensus builder that proved to be the most important factor in securing the policy of détente in the period from 1968 to 1972.

The orthodox views and collective experiences of the majority of the members of Soviet elites and the Politburo prevented them from seeing world realities and acting on them in the way neorealist scholars have assumed they did. At the same time, despite their orthodox zeal, the majority in the Politburo did not live up to the dark expectations and warnings of American neoconservatives. Although some documents prepared by the Foreign Ministry and the KGB did portray détente as the best possibility for the accumulation of Soviet power and spread of Soviet influence in the world, the debates in the Politburo never produced any devious plan of Soviet aggression and domination, as neoconservatives feared. This Politburo, despite its periodic bouts of ideological emotions and jingoism, was not prepared for global and open conflict with the United States. The majority lacked the global vision and the clarity of purpose for what the Soviet Union should do with its growing military power. They did not even see how to benefit from the fact that the United States was bogged down in Southeast Asia. After China, the Soviet leadership "lost" Indonesia and was rapidly losing influence in Egypt and the Middle East. Nothing was gained from their assistance to North

Vietnam. Between 1964 and 1971, the Soviet leadership subjugated its primary security interests, including direct negotiations with the United States, to the vaguely constructed cause of "proletarian solidarity" with Communist Vietnam and to the support of radical Arab regimes. The Soviet leaders also closed their eyes to the fact that the North Vietnamese and Egyptian leaderships remained impervious to Soviet political influence and, in effect, fought their own wars without taking Soviet interests into account.

Soviet behavior in the years leading up to détente can only be explained if one takes into account the dynamics of the Soviet post-totalitarian politics in which consensus concealed "the fight of bulldogs under the carpet" and in which the leader was more broker and negotiator than dictator. The new evidence reveals complex and very important "two-level" games between Soviet foreign policy and domestic politics, and between global strategy and local commitments to various satellites (for example, the GDR and North Vietnam). It is obvious that this change required serious efforts at persuasion, propaganda, and political coercion; from 1964 until 1972, the pro-détente consensus in the Soviet political leadership was extremely fragile and still could have fallen apart. Consolidating this consensus and investing political capital into détente at crucial moments was the main contribution of Leonid Brezhnev to international history.

Kissinger disparaged Brezhnev in his memoirs. "He sought to obscure his lack of assurance by boisterousness, and his sense of latent inadequacy by occasional bullying." In Kissinger's opinion, Brezhnev's ethnic Russian background contributed to his insecurity: He "represented a nation that had survived not by civilizing its conquerors but by outlasting them, a people suspended between Europe and Asia and not wholly of either, with a culture that had destroyed its traditions without yet entirely replacing them."[123]

Indeed, Brezhnev felt insecure in the international arena. But, by contrast to the irascible Nikita Khrushchev, whose lack of assurance translated into bouts of revolutionary diplomacy and crisis-mongering, Brezhnev transformed his insecurity into a quest for international recognition. Détente for Brezhnev also became an important substitute for domestic reforms, the substitute that obscured the already-present drift and decline in economy, technology, and science and, above all, in the ideological sphere. The general secretary suffered from comparison with Stalin and Lenin, and even with Khrushchev. He lacked the will, vision, and intellect to become an efficient and charismatic leader in the Soviet Communist regime. By 1972, Brezhnev had been in office for eight years. The length of his term was approaching that of Khrushchev. He needed a clear and visible success, and these dynamics became obvious during the presummit crisis in April and May 1972.

The initial effect of the Moscow summit on the Soviet people and the elites was powerful. In pursuing détente with Germany and the United States, Brezhnev found the heretofore missing source for his domestic legitimacy. Although there were no studies on Soviet public opinion done at the time, fragmentary evidence, including personal diaries, indicates that Brezhnev's popularity and support for his peacemaking increased among millions of average Soviet citizens, including less-educated people with war memories and those who had strong anti-American feelings.[124] The April plenum of 1973, at which Brezhnev received overwhelming support for his policy of rapprochement with the United States and West Germany, was a high point of his political career. Anti-American propaganda, pervasive in Soviet news, suddenly ceased. A trickle of positive publications on life and culture in the United States, once extremely rare in other than a few elitist journals, now grew into the media torrent that reached the general public, the first such occasion since Kennedy's assassination. The jamming by the state of the Voice of America stopped, and Soviet youth gained access to American pop culture and the Beatles' songs on short-frequency wavelengths. Chernyaev even called Nixon's visit a foreign policy equivalent of Khrushchev's 1956 secret speech. He wrote: "These May days of 1972 will be counted as the start of an era of convergence [of capitalism and Communism]—in its truly revolutionary sense of the word, the one that would save humanity."[125]

Very soon this hyperbolic assessment had to be toned down. The nature of the Soviet political and economic system, of Soviet politics and the character of the leadership, made it impossible for détente to turn into an exit from the Cold War. The consensus he presided over was not as belligerent and xenophobic as the one that had existed under his predecessors. Still, it was clearly based on the formula of "peace through strength," and it left all the props of Soviet ideological orthodoxy intact, so as to make détente palatable for hard-liners. Last, but not least, Brezhnev presided over the most expensive and far-reaching armaments programs in Soviet history. In doing so, he stayed in the good graces of his conservative friends, Ustinov, Grechko, and the rest of the military and military-industrial establishment.[126]

Brezhnev harbored sincere hopes that his personal friendships with Brandt and Nixon would help reduce Cold War tensions. A hard-nosed realist in party politics, he lapsed into romanticism in international relations. This was not a revolutionary kind of romanticism. Brezhnev did not believe as much in the promotion of revolutions and anticolonial movements around the world as in serving Soviet interests by establishing friendships with other state leaders. He mistakenly believed that these friendships and economic cooperation between the Soviet Union and other great powers could overcome fundamental political, economic, and ideological differences between East and West.

Without Brezhnev and his "Sermon on the Mount," the détente of the period from 1970 to 1972 either might not have happened at all or might have been much less of an event than it was. Brezhnev's emotional makeup and his experience in World War II enhanced his sensitivity toward the dangers of war between NATO and the Warsaw Pact countries and a nuclear showdown between the Soviet Union and the United States. One need only imagine an unsmiling Kosygin, a gloomy Gromyko, or a hawkish Shelepin taking Brezhnev's place at the summits with Western leaders and the difference becomes clear. Brezhnev's penchant to please, his vainglorious and gregarious nature, his love for foreign cars and other trinkets can be seen as weaknesses of character—but they worked well for détente. In a sense, this was the first Soviet leader who consciously and with pleasure donned the mantle of a peacemaker and a commonsense statesman, and not of a blustering revolutionary or of a domineering emperor. He was also the first in the Kremlin who used the broadly televised images of his proximity to world capitalist leaders as a public relations ploy inside the Soviet Union. Egon Bahr correctly noted in his memoirs that "Brezhnev was necessary for transition to Gorbachev; what the latter accomplished, the former introduced. He was an asset for world peace."[127]

(CHAPTER 8)
DÉTENTE'S DECLINE
AND SOVIET OVERREACH,
1973-1979

What should the Soviet Union fear?
Only its own impotence, relaxation, laxity.
—Molotov, May 1972

History turned a new page on Christmas Eve of 1979, as columns of Soviet motorized troops crossed the bridges hastily built over the Amu Darya River near the city of Termez and began to pull into the dark gorges between the snowy peaks of Afghanistan. Soviet citizens learned the news from foreign short-wave broadcasts. Around the same time, the elite commando forces "Alfa" and "Berkut" stormed the palace of the general secretary of the People's Democratic Party of Afghanistan, Hafizullah Amin, killing him, his family, and his guards. The KGB set up a puppet government headed by Babrak Karmal, an exiled Afghan Communist. A few days later, the Soviet news agency TASS announced that the invasion was caused by "extremely complicated conditions which put in danger the conquests of the Afghan revolution and the security interests of our country." The news was a surprise even to most of the Soviet foreign policy elite. Experts on the region were not informed about the invasion in advance. Leading scholars from the Institute of Oriental Studies of the Soviet Academy of Science instantly realized that the Kremlin's old men had committed a fatal policy error. Afghanistan was a historically unconquerable territory, populated by fiercely xenophobic Muslim mountaineers. Yet only one private citizen, father of the Soviet nuclear bomb and dissident academician Andrei Sakharov, voiced an open protest against the invasion. The Politburo immediately expelled him from Moscow to Gorky, beyond the reach of foreign correspondents.[1]

Around the world, the impact of the sudden Soviet invasion was much greater than the shock of the similar invasion of Czechoslovakia in 1968. The latter did not stop the détente process in Europe and gave only a brief setback to the U.S.-Soviet talks on strategic arms. Not so in 1979. Western European reaction was mixed, but American retaliation was immediate and harsh. President Jimmy

Carter and his national security adviser, Zbigniew Brzezinski, concluded that the invasion of Afghanistan could only be the beginning of a strategic thrust toward the Persian Gulf, the largest oil pool in the world. This meant a clear and imminent danger to the most vital interests of the United States. In a series of punitive sanctions, the White House froze and suspended most détente agreements, talks, trade, and cultural relations with the Soviets. Carter even imposed an embargo on profitable grain sales to the USSR and appealed to the world to boycott the Olympic Games scheduled to take place in Moscow that summer.

Fifteen years later, new evidence from the Kremlin's archives revealed that the Soviet leadership had no aggressive plans to reach the Persian Gulf. Scholars have concluded that the Soviet leaders reacted above all to the developments in Afghanistan and the region around it. Selig S. Harrison summarized: "Afghan political developments propelled Brezhnev and his advisers on their course much faster than they had anticipated or programmed, in ways they were unable to control, and with undesired results they did not envisage."[2]

In retrospect, the invasion of Afghanistan, despite its initial military success, presents itself as one of the first signs of Soviet imperial overstretch. As if to prove this point, a revolution erupted in Poland in the summer of 1980. The rise of the anti-Communist national movement "Solidarity" was a greater threat to Soviet geopolitical positions in Central Europe than was the Prague Spring. The Kremlin leaders, however, decided not to send troops, allowing the Polish revolution to continue until December 1981.[3] The fear of American reaction played only a marginal role in this decision. Vojtech Mastny writes, "Moscow's conduct in the Polish crisis was not significantly influenced by any specific Western policies."[4]

If the Soviet invasion of Afghanistan was a disastrous miscalculation and not an offensive scheme, should it invite a reappraisal of the entire preceding period? As many books on the Cold War in the 1970s informed us, this was the time of rapid decline of "high" détente between the Soviet Union and the West. An intense arms race, qualitative as well as quantitative, continued; proxy wars raged between the superpowers in Africa, above all in Angola (1975–76) and Ethiopia (1977–78). Zbigniew Brzezinski believed that "détente was buried in the sands of Ogaden," because of Soviet interference in the African Horn war between Ethiopia and Somalia. Most Soviet foreign policy veterans also insist that détente was a spent force before the end of 1979. However, they blame this on misunderstandings between the Carter administration and the Kremlin rulers.[5]

A closer look at the domestic scene in America and the Soviet Union helps explain the decline of détente. In the United States, by 1975, it had become a tainted term, a target of criticism from many politicians in both political parties.

Less understood and explored are Soviet attitudes toward the deterioration of relations with Washington. This chapter explores Brezhnev's diminishing ability to shape Soviet foreign policy and maintain positive momentum in Soviet-American relations. As his personal interest and health deteriorated, other factors of a bureaucratic and ideological nature doomed Soviet foreign and security policies to drift, stagnate, and dangerously overreach.

DÉTENTE AND HUMAN RIGHTS

As the year 1972 drew to a close, prospects for Soviet-American "partnership" looked better than at any other time since 1945. The U.S. Senate ratified the ABM treaty and approved a provisional agreement on SALT. In October, a package of Soviet-American economic and trade agreements was signed, clearing the way for nondiscriminatory trade status for Soviet exports to the United States and official credit support for U.S. exports to the Soviet Union. Nixon publicly promised to provide long-term credits to Moscow. The back channel was bursting with activity as Americans shared with Moscow exhaustive information on the concluding stages of the Paris talks on peace in Vietnam.[6] In November, both of Brezhnev's major partners in the West, Nixon and Brandt, were reelected—one by a landslide, the other by a secure margin.

On November 20, Brezhnev appeared at the Party Secretariat after a long period of illness. "Everything goes well," he said to the applauding apparatchiks. "After all, the victorious forces turned out to be the forces of peace, not of war." Brezhnev looked forward to the preliminary meeting in Helsinki to discuss preparations for a conference on European security. As a result of Soviet–West German rapprochement, concluded Brezhnev, "we inspire and organize European affairs. We should keep this in mind and never let this slip out of our hands."[7] Also in November, at Soviet insistence, delegates from Eastern and Western Europe, along with the Soviet Union, the United States, and Canada, agreed to develop the Organization for Security and Cooperation in Europe. This organization, in Brezhnev's opinion, would become the ultimate political structure on the continent, replacing NATO and the Warsaw bloc.

During the first half of 1973, the general secretary reaped the harvest of successful Soviet diplomacy. In May, he became the first Soviet leader to visit West Germany, the country that Soviet propaganda had vilified for decades as the nest of neo-Nazism. Brezhnev was thrilled by everything he saw, including his residence, Palais Giemnich, in the vicinity of Bonn, and his new BMW sports car, a gift from Brandt. The good personal relations between the two leaders translated into fruitful negotiations between politicians and industrialists: the Soviet Union increased the supplies of oil, gas, and cotton in exchange for German equipment, technologies, and much-coveted consumer goods.[8]

In June 1973, Brezhnev went to the United States, and there again he did not conceal his excitement and pleasure. He toured Washington and spent time at Camp David and in Nixon's house in San Clemente, California. He also drove American cars at high speeds with a terrified Nixon at his side, hugged Hollywood celebrity Chuck Connors, and played like a child with a toy six-shooter and a cowboy belt he got from the president. But, in fact, the results of the visit were very modest. There was still no breakthrough on trade and economic cooperation. Yet Brezhnev beamed with satisfaction when, on June 22, the anniversary of the Nazi invasion of the Soviet Union, he and Nixon signed a bilateral Agreement on the Prevention of Nuclear War.[9]

For the general secretary, the nonnuclear pledge agreement was an important step toward fulfilling his father's wish. Nixon and Kissinger saw it differently. They would later claim it was a move aimed at driving a wedge between the United States and NATO. In his memoirs, Kissinger insisted that he was the first to perceive Brezhnev's proposal as "a dangerous Soviet maneuver to lure us into renouncing the use of nuclear weapons, on which the free world's defense after all depended." Kissinger even wrote that it was a devious Soviet move to justify a preemptive attack on China. In reality, at the time of its signing, Kissinger and Nixon considered this agreement as a purely symbolic one. Its "decoupling" effect for NATO allies did not concern them too much, and they did not even consult the West Europeans. And the Chinese ability to initiate a nuclear war bothered the Americans at that time as much as that of the Soviets.[10]

This gap between Brezhnev's intentions and how his American partners perceived them (or at least wanted to portray them) indicated the limits of trust between Washington and Moscow. Indeed, both sides viewed détente as managed competition, as a continuation of the Cold War by less dangerous means. Raymond Garthoff, participant and scholar of détente, observed that both sides wanted to obtain, whenever possible, a unilateral advantage over the other side. As Brezhnev rejoiced over the strengthening of the Soviet political position in Europe, Nixon busily journeyed around the Soviet periphery: to Iran, seeking to establish the Shah as American proconsul in the Persian Gulf, and to Poland, reviving anti-Soviet hopes in the midst of the Warsaw Pact.[11]

It was not so much strategy, but rather domestic politics, ideology, and bureaucratic interests that ensured that American politicians and Soviet rulers continued to stand on the familiar ground of "negotiating from strength." After the signing of the SALT agreement, Nixon urged an increase in strategic arms. Brezhnev, when he was in West Germany, refused even to discuss the forthcoming deployment of brand-new Soviet intermediate range missiles, the "Pioneer," later known in the West as SS-20's. Brezhnev's assistant Alexandrov-Agentov believes that Brezhnev "followed the lead of our military leadership, above all Ustinov, supported by Gromyko." The military was very proud of the new mobile and high-precision missiles, regarding them as a long-awaited response to the NATO bases surrounding the USSR.[12]

The only hope for Soviet-American détente in this situation was if both Brezhnev and Nixon regarded détente as a joint project worthy of their investments of time and political capital. Nixon and Kissinger indeed had a personal stake in détente and zealously pushed aside all others in the U.S. government and Congress who might have taken credit for it. Still, for them détente was one of many irons in the fire. Nixon's paramount goals before November 1972 were negotiating an end to the Vietnam War and winning reelection. Kissinger played an even more complex game that included China and the Middle East. And from the very start, the potential for an anti-détente backlash in the United States was much higher than in any other country of the West. Initially, Nixon could control the conservative right, but the Watergate scandal would soon erode this control and would ensure that Nixon's numerous liberal enemies could attack détente along with the rest of the president's record.[13]

Brezhnev's agenda was noticeably different. Anatoly Chernyaev, the "enlightened" apparatchik in the Central Committee International Department, noted in his diary that "the main life project of Brezhnev is the idea of peace. With this he wants to stay in people's memory."[14] Wherever he could afford it, Brezhnev made the extra effort to help his new "friends," Brandt and Nixon, and to rescue détente from the attacks of domestic opposition. The general secretary even contemplated some kind of an alliance among the three leaders. In September 1972, he nudged Kissinger to do something to help Brandt's reelection. "Both you and we are interested in seeing [him win]." Kissinger evasively responded that if the coalition in West Germany won, of the Christian Democrats and the Christian Social Union (CDU-CSU), the Nixon administration would "use our influence with them not to change policy."[15]

The issue of Jewish immigration tested Brezhnev's willingness to help Nixon and Kissinger in their domestic games. Since 1971, the Soviet Union, acting under growing pressure, had established modest quotas for Jewish emigration. After the Moscow summit and back channel negotiations with Kissinger, the Soviet leadership agreed to raise the quota of those who could apply "for permanent residence in Israel." In the period from 1945 to 1968, only 8,300 Jews were allowed to leave the Soviet Union. From 1969 to 1972, Jewish emigration rose from 2,673 to 29,821 per year and continued to grow exponentially.[16] Brezhnev had to spend considerable political capital to allow this emigration, since, ideologically, it was tantamount to betrayal of the Soviet "motherland." Besides, many apparatchiks shared anti-Semitic prejudices and resented letting the Jews emigrate so easily. In August 1972, Soviet authorities issued a special decree that required Jewish emigrants "to compensate" the state for the cost of their education as a prerequisite for obtaining permission to leave. This scheme of "Jews for cash" soon caused the political fallout that was disastrous for Soviet détente goals.

The American Jewish community used this practice as a casus belli against Soviet, and indirectly against American, anti-Semitism. The American media launched a furious campaign against the "exit tax" for Soviet Jews, and a powerful Jewish-liberal-conservative opposition to the package of trade and financial agreements with the Soviet Union emerged in the U.S. Congress. Henry M. Jackson, Democratic senator from the state of Washington, a politician with presidential ambitions, made the ratification of the U.S.-Soviet trade bill conditional on "freedom for Soviet Jews." Charles Vanik of Ohio seconded this amendment in the House of Representatives. The Jackson-Vanik amendment signified a radical shift in the U.S. Congress and took from the hands of Nixon and Kissinger the most visible "carrots" they could offer to Brezhnev: nondiscriminatory trade status for the Soviet Union and state credit support for U.S. exports to the USSR.[17] This campaign revealed how superficial and fragile U.S. domestic support for agreements with the Soviet Union was. It was also a striking illustration of the power of interest groups and ideological factors in American foreign policy.[18]

Initially, Brezhnev kept his distance from the growing turmoil; he was not anti-Semitic, but at the same time he had no desire to get burned by such a hot issue.[19] Repeated pleas from the White House to do something made him change his mind. After obtaining the support of the chief party ideologist, Mikhail Suslov, he quietly asked the KGB and the Ministry of Interior to waive the exit tax for most emigrating Jews, especially the middle-aged and elderly. Amazingly, Brezhnev's informal instruction was ignored by the bureaucracies, and in the spring of 1973 some immigrants still were required to pay the exit tax. During the first two months after the introduction of the exit tax, fewer than four hundred Jews paid 1.5 million rubles for the right to leave the Soviet Union.[20]

New signals from Washington followed, and on March 20 the general secretary brought up the issue before the Politburo. The transcript of the meeting depicts Brezhnev's caginess. The general secretary had to reckon with the sensitivity and explosive power of the Jewish Question. He shared with his colleagues his thoughts about the possibility of lifting the ban, imposed by Stalin, on Jewish cultural life in the Soviet Union. He quickly added, however, that he was mentioning it only "as food for thought." As a result, the exit tax was repealed, but "informally," in order to not signal any concession to the pro-Jewish lobby in the United States. Brezhnev also agreed with Suslov, Andropov, Kosygin, and Grechko that people with education and skills, specialists from secret and military labs, or top-level scientists and professionals should not be given an exit visa to Israel—"because I do not want to seek a quarrel with the Arabs," he admitted. The entire system of state-imposed discrimination against Jews stayed intact.[21]

Years later, Anatoly Dobrynin wrote that the position of Brezhnev and Gromyko on Jewish immigration was "irrational."[22] This opinion ignores a dilemma that the Jackson-Vanik amendment placed before Soviet architects of détente. Trade and financial agreements with the United States had high symbolic and material value for them. At the same time, the new American conditions were totally unacceptable, because they contradicted the principle of parity and equality, the major Soviet goal in détente. They asked themselves, Why should the United States dictate political terms to another superpower with regard to economic agreements that were beneficial for them as well? What would the Arab allies in the Middle East say to the unlimited emigration of Soviet Jews to Israel? Even deeper lay the problem of domestic politics and ideology: authorized mass emigration would severely damage both the propaganda of the Soviet "socialist paradise" that nobody leaves and the process of assimilation of Jews into "the family of Soviet peoples." Why should only Jewish immigration be allowed? What would other ethnic groups in the Soviet Union say? The growing number of Russian nationalists among members of the cultural elites and bureaucracy suspected the Soviet leaders of being too lenient on the Jews. Nationalists singled out Brezhnev, claiming that his wife was a "Jewess" (Victoria Brezhnev came from a Karaite family, and the Karaites traditionally practiced Judaism). Brezhnev could not have been ignorant of these rumors, which were politically damaging to his authority.[23]

Still, Brezhnev was prepared to help Nixon deal with pro-Jewish opposition and obtain ratification of economic and financial agreements in the U.S. Congress. By March 1973, the general secretary was communicating constantly with Andropov, Gromyko, Grechko, Minister of Interior Nikolai Shchelokov, and other officials, looking for a solution on Jewish immigration that would satisfy the Americans but would not look like a concession under external pressure. At the Politburo, Brezhnev emotionally criticized the unnamed saboteurs of his détente in the ranks of Soviet bureaucracy. He appealed to his colleagues: "Either we earn money on this business or we will continue our intended policy towards the United States. Jackson pre-empted us. If things turn out his way, then our work and our efforts will be worth nothing!" The result of all this furious activity was a system of quotas on the immigration of professionals and the authorization to inform Nixon and U.S. senators via the back channel that the exit tax would be applied only in extraordinary circumstances.[24]

But limited concessions did not placate Jackson and his allies. The opposition expanded their claims to demand freedom of immigration in general. The neoconservatives, cold warriors who at that time surrounded Jackson and would later migrate to Ronald Reagan's flank of the Republican Party, rejected any compromise with the Soviet regime.[25] The failure of Nixon to deal with the Jewish-liberal-conservative opposition was a very serious blow to U.S.-Soviet relations. It precluded chances, however remote, for expansion of economic and trade relations, which could have broadened political support for détente in American society. And it encouraged an opposition to deliver more blows to détente. This opposition was broad and in many ways similar to the movement against recognition of the Soviet regime before 1933. Ideological reasons, which caused the rejection of atheistic Bolshevism in 1933, and the prominence of human rights issue now, overrode security and economic interests.

This development signaled the end of a Nixon-Kissinger Realpolitik policy toward the Soviet regime. And it launched a new transnational alliance between dissident intellectuals in the Soviet Union and American media, Zionists, and human rights organizations. The frustrated advocates of de-Stalinization, Jews, anti-Soviet nationalists, and liberal democrats in Moscow began to appeal to American journalists to apply pressure on the Brezhnev leadership. They saw the American enemies of détente, especially Senator Jackson, as their natural allies. Alexander Solzhenitsyn, along with American neoconservatives, believed that détente was a sinister Soviet plot and that there could be no compromise with the Kremlin.[26]

Suddenly, Brezhnev's détente was in trouble from within. Ideological conservatives in the Soviet apparatus could now argue that rapprochement with the West was dangerous for the regime, since it allowed the United States a Trojan horse inside Soviet society. Persecution by the KGB, arrests, and mental hospitals did not solve the problem of the dissidents but only added fuel to the fire. Jewish activists began to harass and later even bomb Soviet offices abroad. From time to time, Brezhnev called Andropov and told him to "be more careful."[27] The KGB chief was also surprisingly sensitive to international public opinion. He feared that, like Beria and KGB heads before him, he would never be able to have a statesman's career. As his confidant recalled, "Andropov's desire to leave the post of the head of state security untarnished was so great that it very soon turned into a complex."[28]

Andropov's solution was resourceful: he advocated further Jewish emigration and favored forcing most vocal dissidents to go abroad as well. The KGB began to present dissidents, Jews and non-Jews, with a stark choice: long imprisonment or emigration via a "Jewish channel." During the 1970s, many figures of the liberal-democratic movement of the 1960s, writers, artists, and intellectuals, chose to leave the USSR. Some, like Vladimir Bukovsky and Alexander Ginzburg, were sent abroad from their prison cells. Cellist Mstislav Rostropovich and his wife, opera singer Galina Vishnevskaya, were stripped of their citizenship when they were on artistic tour abroad. This solution, for all its cynicism, was bloodless, and Brezhnev liked it. It allowed the Soviet leader to balance between his hard-line friends at home and his "friends" in the West.

The icon of 1960s de-Stalinization, writer Alexander Solzhenitsyn, remained the largest thorn in the regime's side. The writer publicly defied Soviet authorities. In September 1968, just a month after the Soviet intervention in Czechoslovakia, the publication of Solzhenitsyn's *Cancer Ward* and *The First Circle* in Europe and America earned him world fame. In 1970, he was awarded the Nobel Prize for literature. In contrast to Boris Pasternak, who had renounced the prize under immense pressure in 1958, Solzhenitsyn seemed to relish the state-organized campaign against him.[29]

The Politburo discussed several times what to do with Solzhenitsyn; his case became a flash point for clashing attitudes in the leadership regarding domestic dissent and détente with the West. Andropov recommended that the Politburo allow Solzhenitsyn to go to Stockholm to receive the prize and then use the opportunity to strip him of his citizenship. But Brezhnev's friend and Andropov's rival, Minister of Interior Shchelokov, objected. He proposed "to fight for Solzhenitsyn, not toss him out." On the eve of Nixon's visit to Moscow, the Politburo discussed Solzhenitsyn again. Andropov and Kosygin suggested he should be expelled, but again, nothing was done.[30] The Politburo procrastination demonstrated that de-Stalinization and cultural thaw had left a deep mark even on ideological conservatives. International uproar around the "Pasternak affair" in 1958 and the more recent trial and imprisonment of writers Andrei Sinyavsky and Yuli Daniel in 1965 made the Politburo extremely reluctant to make martyrs of any figures from the Soviet cultural elites.

In the summer of 1973, Solzhenitsyn's case came to the Politburo again after the KGB confiscated Solzhenitsyn's mammoth manuscript about Stalinist terror and camps, *The Gulag Archipelago*. This discovery led to a denouement that perhaps neither Solzhenitsyn nor Brezhnev expected. In September and October 1973, Brezhnev vetoed Andropov's proposal to expel the writer from the Soviet Union. He feared that negative fallout would have been a disservice to Brandt and Nixon and a complicating factor for his trips abroad. He postponed the issue again by appointing a special commission on Solzhenitsyn. But the writer, driven by missionary zeal as well as a desire to protect himself and his family, launched a preemptive public relations campaign in the West. He publicized "A Letter to the Soviet Leaders," in which he urged them to replace the Marxist-Leninist ideology with the Russian Orthodox faith. On the first day of 1974, the Western media announced the publication of the Russian version of The Gulag Archipelago.[31]

Seven days later, Brezhnev raised the issue of Solzhenitsyn's case after discussing Soviet diplomatic efforts at the Conference on European Security and Cooperation in Helsinki. Andropov returned to his old proposal to cut the Gordian knot by expelling the writer from the USSR. Gromyko supported Andropov but suggested another delay, until the conclusion of the conference in Helsinki. At this moment, Nikolai Podgorny demanded the immediate arrest of the Nobel laureate. "In China they publicly execute people; in Chile the fascist regime shoots and tortures people; the British in Ireland use sanctions against working people, and we are dealing with a blatant enemy and just prefer to walk around. If we expel Solzhenitsyn, we reveal our weakness." Kosygin seconded this proposal and suggested that Solzhenitsyn should be put on public trial and then sent to the mines in eastern Siberia. "Foreign correspondents will not go there—it is too cold down there." Both, in essence, blamed Brezhnev for his softness and implied that Brezhnev's foreign trips and his toying with détente began to hurt other state interests. Even Brezhnev's old supporter, Andrei Kirilenko, said sarcastically: "Every time when we speak about Solzhenitsyn as the enemy of Soviet regime, this just happens to coincide with some important [international] events and we postpone the decision." In the end, Brezhnev, in a deft move, agreed that Solzhenitsyn should eventually be put on trial but did not make any decision about his arrest.[32]

At this point, Andropov concluded that the Politburo wanted to ruin his career by saddling him with Solzhenitsyn's case.[33] Through the secret channel to Egon Bahr, the KGB chairman quickly arranged an agreement with the West German government to provide an asylum to the unsuspecting dissident writer. In a personal memo to Brezhnev, Andropov warned that it had become impossible, "despite our desire not to harm our international relations, to delay the solution of the Solzhenitsyn problem any longer, because it could have extremely unpleasant consequences for us inside the country." The KGB chief concluded that failure to act might embolden numerous anti-Soviet opposition groups, and, in the event that the authorities would have to put the writer on trial, it would cause even "greater damage." Brezhnev had to give his consent, and Solzhenitsyn was on the plane to Frankfurt am Main.[34]

Unfortunately for Brezhnev and Andropov, the issue of human rights and vocal dissidents did not go away with the celebrated writer. True, many dissidents vanished without a trace in the West or spent their energy in factional strife and struggle for positions and grants. But some stayed. Nathan Shcharansky organized the Zionist movement inside the Soviet Union and demanded full religious and cultural rights for Jews. A sizable group of Jews could not emigrate because of their security clearances and continued to provide grist for the anti-Soviet campaigns among American Jews. Andrei Sakharov and a number of other human rights activists refused to emigrate and continued their public activities.

The human rights issue surfaced again in the Politburo discussion of the draft of the Helsinki Final Act, the document to be signed soon at the Conference on European Security and Cooperation in Helsinki in July 1975. The head of the Soviet delegation, Deputy Foreign Minister Anatoly Kovalev, one of the "enlightened" diplomats, persuaded Gromyko to make concessions to Western Europeans who wanted to include in the draft Final Act a so-called third basket: provisions on the free movement of people, family reunification and visits, and informational, cultural, and educational openness. In return, Western countries agreed to accept the territorial and political status quo in Eastern Europe as it emerged after World War II. When the draft Final Act reached the Politburo, ideological conservatives there expressed outrage and dismay. Would the Soviet Union be open to subversion and interference from the outside? Kovalev prepared for the storm, but to his surprise Gromyko brought up a historical argument. He compared the Helsinki agreements to the Congress of Vienna of 1815 and Brezhnev to Czar Alexander. Gromyko cited his "understanding" with Kissinger that neither side should interfere with the other's domestic affairs, the Final Act notwithstanding. He concluded that the Soviets got what they wanted, and as far as human rights were concerned, "we remain the masters in our own house."[35] The conservatives withdrew their objections: after all, Stalin had also signed the Yalta Declaration of Liberated Europe, in exchange for other Western concessions.

On August 1, 1975, Brezhnev and Nixon's successor, Gerald Ford, along with thirty-three leaders of other European countries and Canada affixed their signatures to the historic Helsinki Final Act. In the short term, the act did not lead to any liberalization inside the Soviet Union. Soviet propaganda touted this event as Brezhnev's greatest victory, and the general secretary presented it as such before the Party Congress. Personally, he regarded it as the culmination of his statesmanship. In the long run, however, the commitments to human rights embedded in the act proved to be a time bomb under the Soviet regime. Gromyko, who dismissed dissidents as having negligible power, was correct: they never played a significant role in undermining the regime. But his reading of global ideological and political trends was profoundly flawed. The triumph of czarist diplomacy at the Congress of Vienna was short-lived. Russia later became the bogeyman of liberal Europe, which prepared Russian defeat in the Crimean War in 1853–55. In 1975, the Kremlin once again celebrated geopolitical victory without anticipating its dire consequences.

TROUBLED PARTNERSHIP

The Brezhnev-Nixon partnership was challenged by the sudden outbreak of the Yom Kippur War on October 6, 1973. The Soviet role in this war has long been the subject of great controversy. Today this story can be analyzed with much more clarity, thanks to the recollections of ex-Soviet veterans, above all the senior Soviet diplomat Viktor Israelyan. A key player in this outbreak was Egyptian president Anwar Sadat, who prepared the surprise attack against Israel in an effort to restore Arab pride and lost territories. He kept the Politburo and Soviet representatives in Egypt in the dark—although, of course, the KGB and the military must have known about the preparations. As with the North Vietnamese earlier, the Kremlin leaders could not control or restrain their foreign clients.[36]

After Nixon went to Moscow, the Egyptian leader, upset that the Soviet-American rapprochement might mean joint support of the status quo in the Middle East, began to contemplate a double game. He announced the eviction of 17,000 Soviet military advisers and experts from Egypt. Nixon immediately sent a personal word to Brezhnev via the back channel that he did not know anything about Sadat's decision and had had no secret contact with him. In reality, the United States quickly responded to the secret signals from Sadat.[37]

Brezhnev was concerned by Egyptian and Syrian preparations. He would have preferred to work with the United States to prevent another war in the Middle East. During his trip to Washington in the summer of 1973, he warned Nixon that Moscow could hardly control its Arab friends. Nixon and Kissinger did not take Brezhnev's warnings seriously and did not pursue the subject. Kissinger's goal was to undermine Soviet influence in the Middle East, and therefore he refused to accept Moscow's role as an architect of peace there. Besides, preoccupied with the American exit from Vietnam, the Americans did not see the gathering clouds in this other region.[38] Facing American reluctance to act together, the Soviet leadership did not see any reason to alert Israel about the impending Arab attack.[39]

Soviet political and military leaders wanted to help Anwar Sadat defeat Israel and to regain Egyptian territories. At the same time, they were certain from the start of the war that the Arabs would lose it. This forecast proved correct, and they moved to prevent a complete collapse of their Arab allies. During the roller coaster of the Yom Kippur War, Brezhnev had to wear two hats: one as Politburo leader and another as the détente statesman. He accomplished this with surprising skill. He deftly neutralized the hard-liners who wanted drastic actions. For instance, he sent Kosygin, who demanded action, on a secret mission to Cairo; there the Soviet premier wasted his time and energy trying to get Sadat to follow Soviet advice. And he cut out Podgorny, whose belligerence was rivaled only by his ignorance.[40] The Kremlin leader consistently asserted his priority to be that of working together with the U.S. administration in the spirit of détente, the Basic Principles, and the agreement to prevent nuclear war. Kissinger admitted in a narrow circle of his advisers that the Soviets "have tried to be fairly reasonable all across the board. Even in the Middle East where our political strategy put them in an awful bind, they haven't really tried to screw us."[41]

One reason for this behavior was Brezhnev's desire to continue his special relationship with Nixon. During the crisis, the two men exchanged handwritten amiable notes for the first time, and Brezhnev happily boasted to the Politburo: "Nixon feels a deep respect for all Soviet leaders and for me personally." By that time, however, Nixon was engulfed by the Watergate scandal, and Kissinger, already confirmed as the secretary of state, ran U.S. foreign policy on his behalf. Kissinger and his staff did not miss the chance to exploit Egypt's defeat to undermine Soviet influence in that country. During the last stage of the war, Kissinger ignored Soviet offers of cooperation to gain time for victorious Israeli advances into Egyptian territory.[42] Brezhnev and his colleagues began to grumble about "the growing role of Zionism in the United States." On October 19, Andropov warned Brezhnev that "the threat of impeachment for Nixon now has become more real than several months ago. It cannot be excluded that under present conditions the Jewish lobby in the Congress will put serious constraints on Nixon's actions and his willingness to carry out the agreement reached during your visit to the United States."[43]

The Soviets had to do something to save Sadat and Egypt from a complete rout. After a long and heated discussion, the Politburo crafted an ambiguous message to Nixon, recycling the famous 1956 offer to Eisenhower to dispatch joint U.S.-Soviet forces to the Middle East to stop the war. Only at the last minute did Brezhnev agree to give some "teeth" to the message: in case the United States did not want to use joint force to stop the war, the Soviet Union "should be faced with the urgent necessity to consider taking appropriate steps unilaterally." Two paratrooper divisions in the Caucasus were brought to a state of readiness and Soviet warships in the Mediterranean were instructed to move toward Egypt in a demonstration of force. At bottom, the Soviet gesture was a mild bluff, and it was carefully designed not to frighten the Americans.[44]

Kissinger, however, panicked. Without informing the Soviets via the back channel, he put American strategic forces on DEFCON-3, the condition just short of full nuclear alert. When the Politburo reconvened the next morning to discuss a possible reaction, many blamed this move on Kissinger's machinations. Grechko, Andropov, Ustinov, Kirilenko, and some others suggested Soviet mobilization.[45] Brezhnev, mindful of Khrushchev's brinkmanship, proposed to ignore the alert. Perhaps, he reasoned, Nixon's nerves were frazzled by the domestic campaign against him. "Let him cool down and explain the reason for the nuclear alert first." It was perhaps one of the finest moments of Brezhnev's statesmanship. In fact, Nixon was in a drunken stupor, and Kissinger was managing the Middle East crisis as a one-man show, ignoring the president. When Nixon woke up on October 25, he rescinded the alert and sent a personal conciliatory response to Brezhnev. Finally, joint U.S.-Soviet diplomacy found traction, Israeli armed forces stopped their advance, and the crisis began to wind down.[46]

The American unilateralism in the Middle East did not produce the decline of Soviet-American détente.[47] On the contrary, the Yom Kippur War left Brezhnev even more convinced that peace between Israel and the Arabs could only be built by joint Soviet-American actions. In a letter to Nixon on October 28, Brezhnev hinted at the machinations of some forces that sought to ruin "personal mutual trust between us." He no longer concealed his suspicions with regard to Kissinger.[48] And he was so irritated by Sadat's manipulative behavior that he began to think about establishing diplomatic relations with Israel. He told Gromyko that the Arabs could go to hell, if they wanted to make the Soviet people "fight for them." Chernyaev, a witness to this emotional outbreak, wrote: "This is realpolitik. But the society knew nothing about it." Soviet propaganda made the Soviet people believe that Israel was an aggressor again. As in 1967, newspapers stirred up anti-Zionist emotions, and party organizations arranged rallies of solidarity with the "progressive" Arab regimes.[49]

Brezhnev's attempts to act as a closet pragmatic in the Middle East proved to be fruitless. After 1974, the United States seized the initiative in the Israeli-Egyptian settlement and in the next four years worked out the Camp David accords. The Soviets had already pumped tens of billions of rubles into Egypt and bitterly resented Sadat's betrayal. The "loss of Egypt" had a lasting psychological impact on subsequent Politburo decision making with regard to African crises.

And in 1979 these memories would play a crucial role in fomenting Soviet suspicions that Hafizullah Amin could "do a Sadat" to them again in Afghanistan.[50]

Watergate and Nixon's resignation in August 1974 caused another lasting trauma to Brezhnev. During the last months of Nixon's presidency, his correspondence with the Soviet leader assumed an increasingly surreal nature. The isolated president began to view partnership with the general secretary as a peaceful island in the storm-tossed sea of the Watergate scandal. Nixon signaled via the back channel that the two leaders had common enemies, among them Jewish groups in the United States. He even talked, to the dismay of his staff, about "a Brezhnev-Nixon doctrine" as a solid foundation for world peace. Remarkably, Brezhnev never attempted to exploit Watergate for his own political purposes, as some of Nixon's advisers feared would happen. In fact, he was the last foreign leader continuing to support Nixon without reservations. Just as Stalin and Molotov in 1945 could not understand Churchill's electoral defeat, Brezhnev and his advisers could not fathom how the bugging of a suite in the Watergate Building could cause the resignation of such a formidable statesman after his landslide reelection. In their eyes, the only plausible explanation was that the enemies of détente chose a good pretext to get rid of its chief American architect.[51]

The blow was all the more painful since just three months earlier, in May, Brezhnev had lost another détente partner. West German chancellor Willy Brandt resigned in the wake of a sex scandal and the revelation that one of his closest aides, Guenther Guillaume, was a GDR spy. GDR leader Erich Honecker and chief of the East German secret police (the Stasi) Erich Mielke had kept Guillaume in Brandt's entourage, despite Soviet disapproval. East German leaders clearly had their own interests in spying on Brandt and compromising him. They detested the Soviet–West German back channel and the friendship between Brandt and Brezhnev that jeopardized the traditional leverage of the GDR on the Kremlin. Brezhnev was disappointed with his sudden resignation. He was also resentful of Honecker.[52]

Among the original architects of détente, only the Soviet leader remained in power, although his health was rapidly deteriorating. Earlier in his life, Brezhnev had had two heart attacks. During the 1960s, he was still in good physical shape, but toward the end of this decade he developed a gradual brain atherosclerosis that produced periods of asthenia after moments of strain. After the Czechoslovak crisis, Brezhnev had developed the habit of taking one or two pills of an opiate-based sedative. Sometimes he overdosed and ended up in a comatose state, followed by a period of general sluggishness.[53]

Brezhnev's foreign partners began to notice irregularities in Brezhnev's schedule and sudden disappearances. During Kissinger's trip to Moscow in April 1972, Brezhnev took the appalled American statesman on a crazy car race to shake off his grogginess after a bad overdose.[54] During the Yom Kippur War, when Brezhnev had to work day and night, his nerves began to give out again. Almost every afternoon, Sadat called on the Soviet ambassador in Egypt to tell Brezhnev of the catastrophic situation, demanding immediate assistance. Brezhnev had no time to rest. Andropov, aware of the leader's physical problems, demonstrated his concern in a bizarre way. He portrayed Kissinger and Sadat as acting in cahoots, trying to ruin Brezhnev's health by creating "an excessive strain."[55] He knew that Brezhnev was becoming a drug addict and ordered his personal guards and a nurse to secretly supply him with sedative pills. At first Andropov pretended to intercede, but in the end he averted his eyes. He might even have begun to help Brezhnev get the pills.[56]

The pills, of course, only aggravated the Soviet leader's progressive malaise. Brezhnev's attention span shortened and his grasp of details began to slip. Even his character changed, and he became more suspicious and peevish and less open to understanding and compromise. The top Kremlin physician, Evgeny Chazov, concluded that Brezhnev's addiction "contributed to the collapse of the national leadership." Chernyaev, from his vantage point in the party's International Department, deplored the transformation of "the great country built on the foundations of the great revolution" into a mediocre state without dynamic leadership and inspiring ideology, with a chronic shortage of basic consumer goods.[57]

Meanwhile, the arms race and technological developments on both the Soviet and American sides continued apace and in various aspects began to get ahead of the sluggish tempo of the arms control talks. U.S. deployment of multiple individual reentry vehicles (MIRVs), that is, many independently guided warheads on a single missile, spawned a quantum leap in strategic nuclear arsenals. The Americans also developed a high-precision cruise missile. Meanwhile, the Soviet military-industrial complex was also engaged in a feverish qualitative and quantitative race. It produced its own MIRVs, the "Pioneer" (SS-20) rockets, and a new medium-size Tu-22M bomber (called "Backfire" by the Americans). The Soviets developed new "Typhoon" class nuclear submarines and built a powerful navy. During the decade after 1972, the Soviets produced 4,125 land-based and sea-launched ICBMs, while the United States produced 929. What worried American strategic planners above all was a huge new ICBM that could carry ten warheads and be fitted into the available silos, thus replacing old, less powerful and reliable rockets. The Americans called it the SS-18. Its real name, "Satan," suggested that

Soviet rocket designers, despite their atheistic upbringing, found inspiration in infernal imagery. The Soviets began to deploy these missiles in 1975 and stopped only when their number in silos reached 308.[58]

Why did the Soviet side build these hellish missiles and in such great numbers? According to some authoritative sources, the Kremlin leadership continued to suffer from the Cuban missile syndrome, that is, the ignominious withdrawal after the 1962 crisis.[59] There were also factors of geography that, in the opinion of the Soviet general staff, favored the United States. The Soviet military believed they confronted not only U.S. forces on NATO bases near Soviet borders, but also the nuclear forces of Great Britain and France. They also had to deploy some missiles and conventional forces against China. Finally, the Soviet military-industrial elite still felt that their strategic stockpile was inferior to the American one in *qualitative* terms. This made them even more determined to make up the discrepancy with *numbers*. In 1994, Viktor Starodubov, former assistant to Dmitry Ustinov, explained with disarming logic that the Soviets built so many "heavy" missiles because "they were one of few things we could build well."[60] In retrospect, the Soviet buildup of the 1970s did not give the Kremlin strategic superiority, as neoconservative analysts warned. The Soviet Union did not have the capability to launch a surprise disarming strike against the United States; the Americans remained ahead of the Soviet Union in many ways, although without the huge advantages that Washington had enjoyed earlier.[61]

At Politburo meetings, Brezhnev never confronted Ustinov, Grechko, and the head of the Military-Industrial Commission, Leonid Smirnov, on the issue of the missile buildup. He was a believer in negotiations from the position of strength and did not see why the Soviet buildup of the 1970s could be viewed as threatening in Washington and other Western capitals. It is worth repeating that Brezhnev wanted to negotiate without blackmail, as Khrushchev had done. He continued to believe that arms control mechanisms and agreements, including SALT, could become a foundation for lasting cooperation between the Soviet Union and the United States. His aim was to convene a conference on security and cooperation in Europe by the time of the next Communist Party Congress.[62] This would enable Brezhnev to validate the peace program he had proclaimed at the previous Party Congress in 1971 and boost his peacemaker image among the party cadres and the Soviet people.

Brezhnev sought to engage Nixon's successor, Gerald Ford, in order to work together to overcome the hurdles on the road to a comprehensive strategic arms treaty. After elaborate back channel consultations, Ford and Brezhnev agreed to meet at Vladivostok, the Soviet outpost in the Far East, in late November 1974. The Soviet guiding principle for the strategic talks was equal levels of security with NATO. This, above all, meant counting the NATO "forward-based" nuclear forces, that is, American missiles, bombers, and submarines based around the Soviet Union, as well as the nuclear forces of Great Britain and France. These countries refused to add their systems to the equation, but Kosygin, Podgorny, several other Politburo hard-liners, and the entire military leadership insisted on this principle. Though Brezhnev felt exasperated by Western intransigence, he also believed his colleagues did not fully share his commitment to negotiate.[63]

In a one-on-one conversation with Brezhnev in October 1974, Kissinger suggested the idea of comprehensive and roughly equal levels for the strategic forces of both sides. The secretary of state, mindful of the waning support for détente in his country, asked Brezhnev to keep this idea secret. Otherwise, he warned, Senator Jackson "would get tipped off." The general secretary immediately agreed to use it as the basis for negotiations with Ford. His only condition was that any further American amendments would not be "in the nature of fundamental new proposals or anything new in principle."[64]

When Brezhnev and Ford met in Vladivostok on November 23 and 24, 1974, the general secretary was antsy and uncertain. Reenacting his first meeting with Nixon in Moscow, the Soviet leader invited Ford and Kissinger to his compartment on a special train to build a human relationship. To break the ice, he offered them tea with cognac. Brezhnev recalled the personal agreement he had had with Nixon "on one thing—not to interfere in each other's internal affairs." When Ford wondered how they should continue to negotiate, in a smaller or larger group, the general secretary interjected vividly: "This depends on the two of us. It is clear that the world is looking at us, and that the world public opinion is most interested in how to ensure that there will be no nuclear war." In the next few minutes, Brezhnev laid out his own view on the nuclear arms race: "We have not achieved any real limitation, and in fact we have been spurring the arms race further and further. This is wrong. Tomorrow science can present us with inventions we cannot even imagine today, and I just don't know how much farther we can go in building up so-called security. Who knows, maybe the day after tomorrow the arms race will reach even outer space. The people don't know all this, otherwise they would really have given us hell. We are spending billions on all these things, billions that would be much better spent for the benefit of the people."[65]

In 1985 and 1986, similar views in Moscow came to be known as "new thinking." Incidentally, Georgy Kornienko and Sergei Akhromeyev, two members of the arms control panel of experts that prepared the Soviet negotiating positions for Vladivostok, later became coauthors of Gorbachev's first comprehensive proposal on nuclear disarmament. At the moment, however, Ford's response was evasive and formulaic, revealing his lack of vision. He became president without national elections, and his pardon of Nixon made him more enemies than friends. Besides, Kissinger warned him that the only thing on Brezhnev's mind was the idea of joint Soviet-American actions in the event that China behaved aggressively. Later Kissinger expressed regret that he and Ford "did not explore" Brezhnev's insight further.[66]

After the first talk on the train, Brezhnev suffered a seizure, and, although his physicians managed to control it, they recommended that he delay the talks. He refused. The talks were arduous and extremely intense. The American position hardened because of slipping domestic support for détente and growing skepticism about SALT in Congress and also due to the hard-line stand of Secretary of Defense James Schlesinger and the Joint Chiefs of Staff. In the end, Kissinger's earlier idea remained the last-resort option. If the Soviets agreed to exclude the NATO forward-based systems from the agreement, then the Americans would agree to waive limitations on the "Satan" missiles and the number of their warheads. Unfortunately, this was not part of the approved Politburo position.[67]

From Vladivostok, Brezhnev called his Moscow colleagues, who, eight time zones away, were still in bed. Andropov, Ustinov, and Kosygin took Brezhnev's side. But Minister of Defense Grechko, backed by Podgorny, refused to make concessions. Brezhnev yelled at Grechko, his wartime friend, so loudly that his assistants could hear it through the office walls. When no arguments helped, he suggested that he would break off the negotiations and come to Moscow for an emergency Politburo meeting. The deeply shaken Grechko gave up. The road to the SALT agreement seemed open after two years of deadlock. To return Brezhnev's favor, Ford softened the American stance and indicated to European allies that he would remove last objections to the creation of the Organization of Security and Cooperation in Europe—a coveted goal of the general secretary.[68]

Both leaders made hard choices, and it seemed that an affinity was about to blossom. But Ford and Kissinger came home to vocal ideological opposition to the Vladivostok agreements. Soviet "heavy" missiles allowed critics in the United States to attack détente by arguing that the Soviet leaders were preparing for nuclear war, putting themselves in a position "to strike first if it appears imminent."[69] The Democratic majority in Congress elected in the wake of Watergate wanted to assert its supremacy over the White House. Senators and representatives reproached Ford and Kissinger for secret diplomacy and indifference to human rights. Ford's refusal to invite Solzhenitsyn to the White House caused a public uproar. In December 1974, the two-year-long debate about the U.S.-Soviet trade bill ended in victory for Jackson and his supporters. This was a slap in the face for the Soviets; now Soviet-American trade was subject to worse terms in the

Trade Act than before it had been passed. The Soviets could no longer get American credits for building oil and gas pipelines and had to turn to the Western Europeans. Moscow abrogated the trade agreements signed in 1972.[70] This humiliating setback ruined the détente expectations among Soviet captains of industry and economic managers.

After the Vladivostok talks, Brezhnev collapsed in his train compartment. He recovered after a few weeks but now could read only with difficulty, and only texts in an enlarged font typed with a special typewriter. During his trip to Poland at the very end of the year, he grabbed a baton from the orchestra's conductor during the ceremonial farewell and began to wave it to the music of the "International." At the Helsinki summit, Brezhnev was in a semi-coma and barely managed to affix his signature to the Final Act. He did not appear at the Politburo for weeks, even months.[71] In October 1975, Chernyaev noted in his diary that "Brezhnev exhausted himself in the struggle for peace."[72]

Brezhnev never again showed such passion and commitment to talks with the Americans as he did in Vladivostok. However, the fall of détente must not be related only to his loss of energy and initiative. From 1972 to 1975, the general secretary's increasing malaise did not prevent him from being a forceful and energetic negotiator. Perhaps active statesmanship remained the last thing to stand between Brezhnev and his addiction. In the close circle of his advisers and speechwriters in December 1975, preparing for the next Party Congress, Brezhnev complained: "Even after Helsinki, Ford and Kissinger and all kinds of senators demand to arm America even more. They want to make it the strongest power. I am against an arms race, but when the Americans declare they would build up, then the Ministry of Defense reports to me that in this case they cannot guarantee security. And what should I, as chairman of the Defense Council, do? Should I give them 140 billions or 156 billions? And I do give them money, again and again—money that disappears into the funnel."[73]

Brezhnev had not wanted to meet Ford without a guarantee that they would sign the SALT Treaty. Alexandrov-Agentov recalled that Brezhnev's guiding principle was to invest his political capital only when he saw "a promise of success." And Ambassador Dobrynin and KGB analysts wrote from Washington that the Kremlin should wait until the next presidential election to continue negotiations.[74] Not only Brezhnev, but Andropov, Gromyko, and all other advisers, failed to recognize that American politics entered a new phase after Watergate. The Kremlin leaders perceived Nixon "as some kind of American General Secretary." They could not understand why Ford could not reassert his power over Congress and why he kowtowed to various lobbies and public groups. Moreover, the Soviet leadership did not see that the unique combination of political and personal factors that had led to détente up to 1974 was gone.

The success of détente from 1969 to 1973 reflected long-term trends in Western politics during the 1960s, including great social and cultural turmoil and the growth of American isolationism and European antimilitarism. Fragmentation of the home front and the domestic impact of the Berlin Wall and the Vietnam War made a new generation of statesmen in West Germany and the United States willing to negotiate with the Soviets from the position of equality. In contrast, the leaders in the Kremlin imagined détente in a completely different way. They believed that it was the reward for years of the costly military-strategic buildup that had changed the global correlation of forces in favor of the Soviets. This understandable misperception was a fatal flaw. Soon it became amply demonstrated once again on the fields of proxy battles between the superpowers in Africa.

SCRAMBLE FOR AFRICA

For all its fateful consequences, the escalation of Soviet intervention in Africa was a bizarre sideshow to the Kremlin's international agenda. Africa remained mainly on the periphery of Soviet foreign policy. Soviet experts later claimed that Soviet leaders had no specific doctrine or long-term plans for Africa.[75] Yuri Andropov once confided that the Soviets "were dragged into Africa" against their best interests.[76] How did it happen?

The Politburo "discovered" Africa at the same time it began its support for the radical Arab nationalists. From the beginning, the Soviets acted on the ideological premise that decolonization of the continent would be a major blow to world capitalism and a great victory for Communism. Ivan Maisky wrote to Khrushchev and Bulganin in December 1955 that "the next act of the struggle for global domination of socialism will unfold through the liberation of colonial and semi-colonial people from imperialist exploitation." He added: "At the same time, the loss of colonies and semi-colonies by the imperialist powers must accelerate the victory of socialism in Europe, and eventually in the USA."[77]

Khrushchev himself dreamed of transforming selected African countries into "windows of socialism" and bulwarks of the expanding socialist camp. Crucial for him and other true believers in the party was that many in Africa looked with hope and even enthusiasm at the Soviet model of industrialization and social modernization. African anticolonial leaders of the late 1950s saw the Soviet Union not as a totalitarian state but as a beacon of progress, an alternative to the much-hated former colonial powers and their capitalist ways.[78]

This ideological impulse was reinforced by Moscow's resentment at the Western penchant for considering Africa as its exclusive sphere of influence. Stalin's failure to obtain naval bases in Libya was not forgotten. A veteran Soviet diplomat had the feeling that the United States behaved "as if there was an extension of the Monroe Doctrine from America to Africa."[79] The extreme political volatility in postcolonial Africa after decolonization created a permanent possibility for the carving and recarving of spheres of influence between the two hostile Cold War blocs. Generally speaking, it was a recycling of the same sort of situation that had propelled European powers into carving up all of Africa in the second half of the nineteenth century. Karen Brutents, the expert on Africa in the Central Committee International Department, and Leonid Shebarshin, a top intelligence officer, compared the Soviet Union and the United States to boxers for whom the exchange of blows became the main motive and goal. The Congo crisis, involving Eisenhower and Khrushchev, as well as the UN secretary general, Dag Hammarskjold, and the Congolese leader, Patrice Lumumba, was at the center of Soviet domestic and world news for months.[80]

The results of this first Soviet offensive in Africa were sobering. After making considerable investments, the Soviets lost the battle over the Congo and were kicked out of Ghana and Guinea. The end of the experiment to turn Guinea into "a window of socialism" was especially painful and cooled Soviet faith in the possibility of Africa's transformation for a decade.[81] The Polyansky report of 1964 criticized Khrushchev's course of supporting African "progressive regimes." It concluded: "We often lack any practical knowledge of those countries, yet provide them across-the-board financial, technical-economic, military and other assistance." Soviet generosity in Africa in many cases "led to deplorable results: the leaders of those countries ate what we gave them, and then turned away from us. Capitalists laugh at us and they have reason to do so." At the same time, the Kremlin leaders never disavowed the ideological justification for Soviet involvement in Africa. They just believed that Khrushchev had been carried away and forgot to be selective "from the point of view of class criteria."[82]

Lessons were again forgotten during the 1970s. One may suspect that the rivalry between Moscow and Beijing for hegemony over "progressive forces" and national liberation movements around the world facilitated the Soviet return to Africanism. But by 1970, the KGB and the Central Committee International Department reported with confidence to the Politburo that the Chinese "offensive" in Africa was defeated. Brezhnev told Kissinger in April 1972 that a Soviet diplomat in Algeria once found a Chinese restaurant in the middle of the desert. "Anyone who came into the restaurant for a meal left with a bundle of free Chinese propaganda. This was the period when they tried to split the world

Communist movement. Well, when they lost in their attempt at hegemony over the movement and lost their foothold, they closed up this restaurant in Algeria."[83] Yet it was in the fall of 1970, after Moscow's struggle against China's "dumplings diplomacy" had ended, that Andropov's KGB proposed and obtained Politburo support for a more active African policy.[84]

The factors that brought the Soviets back to Africa were the revolutionary-imperial paradigm that still dominated Kremlin thinking, the political and ideological vacuum on the continent, and the active solicitation of Soviet involvement by African leaders themselves. As the KGB reported, after years of trying to secure aid from the United States and Western European powers, African nationalists concluded that "the Soviet Union was the only major power which could assist them in reaching their political and social goals."[85] Kremlin leaders could not miss another "historic opportunity" to influence the processes of decolonization and modernization on the African continent.

This time, however, Soviet intervention in Africa was not simply an ideology-driven crusade. Sub-Saharan Africa and the Horn of Africa became the site for the Soviet military to demonstrate their new power-projection abilities. The scramble for Africa between the Soviets and the United States, as it turned out, was a manifestation of a major reason for Soviet behavior in the 1970s: to act as a global power equal to others.[86] Since 1964, the Soviet Union had begun building a strategic navy and a sizable fleet of transport aircraft. During the Yom Kippur War these capacities came to the world's attention. The Soviet naval command, especially Admiral Sergei Gorshkov, itched to compete with the U.S. Navy and demanded bases in Africa. In 1974, they obtained one in Somalia.[87] As the future would soon reveal, this acquisition was not worth the trouble.

The picture of Soviet expansion in Africa would be incomplete without new socioeconomic factors. After the four-fold rise of oil prices after the Yom Kippur War, the Soviet Union became the main beneficiary of windfall profits that resulted from that development. Soviet production of crude oil had grown from 8 million barrels per day in 1973 to 11 million barrels per day by 1980, making the Soviet Union the leader on the world oil market. During the 1970s, Soviet annual hard currency revenues from selling oil and natural gas increased by 2250 percent and reached $20 billion. The rapid growth of this financial surplus enabled the Kremlin to pay the price for imperial expansion in Africa.[88]

The same years marked the emergence of Brezhnev's "little deal," an unwritten social compact between the regime, the Soviet elites, and the people. This was an elaborate system of perks, privileges, a "shadow economy," and various special ways of earning enough for a comfortable, even well-to-do existence. Numerous signs of affluence appeared in Soviet society. Soviet expansion in Africa opened little-advertised but plentiful new possibilities for the "little deal." It created tens of thousands of highly paid positions for the Soviet military and many members of the Soviet nomenklatura. Embassies in African countries became favorite places of semi-exile for the members of the high party elite who had lost Brezhnev's favor. Sociologist Georgy Derluguian, who served as an interpreter for the Soviet embassy in Moputu, Mozambique, in the early 1980s, received a salary in special "foreign currency checks"; purchasing value of this salary was fifteen to twenty times higher than an average Soviet salary at the time. After a few years of "doing internationalist duty" in Africa, Soviet citizens could buy apartments in Moscow, cars, country houses (dachas), and Western-made consumer goods through the special chain of state stores, the Beryozka, where only foreign currencies, not rubles, were accepted. As a result, concludes Derluguian, these motives made Soviet ministries and agencies lobby for "international assistance" to various African regimes with an allegedly "socialist orientation." "As in many empires, elemental bureaucratic intrigues and the desire to create new lucrative positions stood behind the expansion of spheres of influence."[89]

The sparring between the superpowers in Africa helped to camouflage this profit seeking. The U.S.-Soviet scramble for Africa began to intensify at the same time as détente reached its peak. Intelligence services eyed each other in the remotest corners of the African continent. A senior American diplomat traveled on an inspection mission around Africa in 1974 and found that "the United States wanted to have a full presence everywhere, as befitting the leader of the Western world, and also in particular to keep an eye on Soviet representatives. The Soviet Union, for prestige and penetration, also then had resident embassies almost everywhere in Africa."[90] Pride and the logic of bilateral rivalry, not strategic or economic interests, put the two sides on a collision course.

Two events accelerated this course: the "carnation revolution" in Portugal in April 1974 and the fall of South Vietnam in April 1975. Chernyaev, in the International Department, enthusiastically compared the coup in Portugal to the end of the Romanov dynasty in Russia. "A huge event," he wrote in his journal. Another official in the same department suggested that Soviet involvement in Angola and the Horn of Africa and later the invasion of Afghanistan were the result of "a wrong conclusion from the American defeat in Vietnam."[91] Ford and Kissinger, under fire from domestic critics of détente, also became convinced that after the Vietnam fiasco some dominoes might start to fall. Kissinger, in particular, was concerned by the role of the Communists in Portugal and believed that the United States had to prevent the Soviets from filling the vacuum in Angola, Portugal's former colony. On the eve of the Helsinki Conference, Ford signed a secret order to begin CIA covert operations in Angola, "to restore the balance" in this country in favor of the Americans.[92]

Soviet involvement in Angola in 1975, like the previous large-scale Soviet offensive in Africa, lacked any clear strategic plan or goal. This time, however, it also suffered from a dangerous drift in the decision-making process. Brezhnev had very little interest in African events and delegated daily affairs there to the apparatus in general and nobody in particular. In the absence of a dynamic leader, foreign and security policy was in the hands of the troika of Foreign Minister Gromyko, the KGB's Andropov, and Minister of Defense Grechko (after his death in April 1976 this post went to Ustinov). Yet the troika did not act as a cohesive team but rather as an uneasy alliance of aging functionaries, involved in mutual logrolling and back scratching. They all owed their positions to Brezhnev; at the same time (as Khrushchev's fall demonstrated), together they represented a political threat to the general secretary. Even the hint of a partnership among them beyond the official boundaries could make them suspect in the eyes of Brezhnev and mean the end to their careers. For that reason, the troika took great care to see each other only in formal settings, at Politburo meetings. They were also extremely reluctant to challenge each other's bureaucratic territory. As a result, Gromyko had the first say in diplomatic affairs. Grechko and Ustinov had a virtual monopoly in military matters. Andropov was knowledgeable in both fields, due to his intelligence information. However, he felt extremely insecure and preferred to go along with the other two in the areas of their interests.[93] All members of the troika had an interest in perpetuating the status quo, which was the increasingly fictitious leadership of Leonid Brezhnev. The general secretary, even in his weakened condition, remained the only authority that validated the troika's domination over other Politburo members, who could at any moment attempt to take over the policy-making process.

For these functional and personal reasons, the Soviet leadership was incapable of bold schemes and initiatives. It took other dynamic and ideologically motivated players to drag the Soviet leaders into the African gambit, including Angola's Agostino Neto and Ethiopia's Mengistu Haile Mariam, but especially Fidel Castro and his revolutionary colleagues in Cuba.[94] Contrary to U.S. belief, the Cuban leaders were not mere puppets or surrogates of Moscow. Since the 1960s, Fidel and Raul Castro, Che Guevara (until his death in 1967), and other Cuban revolutionaries had supported revolutionary guerrilla operations in Algeria, Zaire, Congo (Brazzaville), and Guinea-Bissau. The flight of the United States from Vietnam in 1975 was, Cubans believed, a chance for another round of anti-imperialist struggles in sub-Saharan Africa.[95]

Until the early 1970s, Cuban-Soviet relations remained very strained, as the shadow of Soviet "betrayal" in 1962 hung over Havana.[96] The KGB and the Central Committee International Department tried to restore close ties to the Cubans—Andropov and Boris Ponomarev, who headed these organizations, were the heirs of the Comintern internationalist revolutionary traditions. In 1965, Andropov told one of his advisers that the future competition with the United States would take place not in Europe but in Africa and in Latin America. After the Soviet Union gained bases there, it would be able to enjoy an equal status with the Americans.[97] Grechko and the military strongly supported this logic. Angola was an attractive target. Since 1970, the KGB had advocated assistance and training for the Popular Movement for the Liberation of Angola (MPLA), whose leader, Agostino Neto, was an old friend of the Castro brothers. From late 1974 on, Angola became the site of rapidly expanding Soviet-Cuban cooperation.[98]

The full story of the escalation of the Soviet presence in Angola is still buried in the archives. According to one version, Gromyko, Grechko, and Andropov recommended that the Politburo send modest nonmilitary assistance to the MPLA but cautioned against direct involvement in the Angolan civil war. A few days later, however, the International Department transmitted the Angolan request for arms to the Politburo. After briefly hesitating, the same troika reversed its position and supported the request. In early December 1974, immediately after the Vladivostok summit, the pipeline for military assistance was opened.[99] This reversal may have been the result of lobbying by Soviet and Cuban friends of Neto, as well as bureaucratic logrolling in the absence of Brezhnev's direct involvement. The same pattern of reversed decisions repeated itself on a bigger scale in 1979 with regard to Afghanistan.

The American decision to support the enemies of the MPLA narrowed the Kremlin's choices. Gromyko's first deputy, Georgy Kornienko, believed that the escalation of Soviet involvement in Angola was due only to American subversive policies. In the fall of 1975, the troika, supported by Suslov, argued that it was their "moral internationalist duty" to assist Angola. At one moment, as Brezhnev worked with his speechwriters at his dacha, Georgy Arbatov, one of the "enlightened" advisers, warned him that intervention in Angola would seriously affect détente. Alexandrov-Agentov angrily objected. He recalled the Soviet aid to the Republicans during the Spanish civil war in 1935. He also reminded Brezhnev how belligerently the United States had behaved when its client Pakistan was threatened in 1971. The general secretary, whose energy for and interest in détente was ebbing by that time, avoided taking sides in the debate. Later, however, he went along with the prevailing interventionist mood. In October 1975, Dobrynin informed Brezhnev about the growing negative fallout from the Angolan events in the United States, but this only irritated the general secretary. He was convinced that the Americans failed to recognize Soviet "honest intentions." The Soviet Union, he said, did not seek any military bases in Angola but merely wanted to assist local internationalists.[100]

This situation provided more leverage to the Cubans. Two weeks after the signing of the Final Act in Helsinki, Castro sent Brezhnev a plan for transporting Cuban regular military units to Angola. At that time, Brezhnev flatly refused to expand Soviet military assistance in Angola or to transport Cubans there. Yet, by November, puzzlingly, the first Cuban combat troops were fighting on the side of MPLA. Kornienko later asserted that the Cubans outfoxed the Soviet military representatives in Cuba, making them believe that they had authorization from the Kremlin to fly them across the ocean. Gromyko, Grechko, and Andropov were surprised; they agreed that Cuban involvement could lead to a sharp American reaction, complications for détente, and even tension around Cuba itself. Meanwhile, the Cubans had already begun "Operation Carlota" to save the MPLA. What makes this story even more puzzling is the total absence of evidence coming from the Cuban archives in Havana.[101]

Two years earlier, Brezhnev had done nothing to assist the collapsing socialist government of Salvador Allende in Chile and rejected his plea for loans. In the same year, the Soviets began to lose their influence in Egypt. In August 1975, the great expectations for Communist victory in Portugal were dashed.[102] In preparations for his report to the Party Congress, Brezhnev faced three visible international setbacks. Putting Angola on this list would be one too many. The Kremlin masters felt obliged "to save Angola" and support the Cubans, as Soviet prestige was now at stake. Kornienko recalls that "the reflex of internationalist duty was at work, especially since this episode occurred after the armed intervention into Angola on the part of the South-African Republic had taken place. This intervention was de facto supported by the United States, if not organized by them." Besides, abandoning Cuban troops fighting in Angola against enemy troops funded by American money and manned in part by foreign mercenaries would have meant sacrificing a small Caribbean ally for the second time—the first being the Soviet retreat during the Cuban missile crisis.[103]

In early 1976, Gerald Ford dropped the word "détente" from his lexicon. Kissinger, deeply concerned about the proxy use of Cuban troops by the Soviets, declared that the U.S.-Soviet partnership could not "survive any more Angolas." Meanwhile, with Soviet massive military assistance, Cuban troops cleared most of Angola of South African mercenaries and the CIA-backed National Front for the Liberation of Angola. African states began to recognize the MPLA-led Angolan regime. Nothing succeeds like success. Soviet and Cuban advisers began to train South African blacks, the militants of the African National Congress. Soviet influence grew in Zimbabwe and Mozambique. The Cuban victory allowed the Soviets to overcome the strain in Soviet-Cuban relations.[104] And this victory was a wonderful gift for Brezhnev and the Party Congress. It helped the Soviet leadership to win support in the nonaligned movement and from those groups in the world that supported the anticolonial and antiapartheid movements.[105]

WOES WITH CARTER

Despite the fracas over Angola, Brezhnev and others in the Politburo expected Ford to win the election and resume the détente partnership. Once again, the volatility of American politics dashed Kremlin expectations. In November 1976, the former governor of Georgia, Jimmy Carter, a little-known peanut farmer, defeated Ford. Carter had a curious combination of good intentions, strong ideas, vagueness in priorities, and micromanaging style. He had an urge to go beyond the "old agenda" of the Cold War and was committed to the idea of nuclear disarmament. The new president promised a "new foreign policy" that would be less secretive and opaque and more aware of human rights.

Publicly, Carter declared that it was time to overcome "the inordinate fear of communism." Privately, however, a major concern in the White House was whether the Soviet Union would test Carter in the manner Khrushchev had tested Kennedy in 1961. Brezhnev quickly assured Carter that there would be no testing this time.[106] The Kremlin had its own fears about Carter. Some Soviet experts believed that the new and inexperienced president could become a prisoner of anti-détente forces. Carter's secretary of state, Cyrus Vance, was known as a measured pro-détente figure. By contrast, the new national security adviser, Zbigniew Brzezinski, raised immediate concerns. Son of a Polish diplomat and a leading scholar of Soviet totalitarianism, he had gained notoriety in Moscow as an architect of strategies to weaken Soviet influence in Central Europe and as a mastermind behind the Trilateral Commission that sought harmony among the three centers of capitalism, the United States, Western Europe, and Japan.[107]

Carter's campaign for human rights immediately marred his relations with the Kremlin. Helsinki Watch groups, formed by activists of the democratic and nationalist movements after August 1975, were active in Moscow, but also in the Ukraine, Lithuania, Georgia, and Armenia; they monitored Soviet violations of the Final Act and reported it to the foreign media. A veteran of the Moscow group recalls that "our most optimistic predictions now seemed within reach: it appeared likely that the new U.S. foreign policy would include insistence that the Soviets live up to the promises made in Helsinki. The alliance of Western politicians and Soviet dissidents was starting to emerge." In retaliation, in January and February 1977, the KGB cracked down on the Helsinki Watch groups and arrested their activists, including Yuri Orlov, Alexander Ginzburg, and Anatoly Scharansky. On February 18, Dobrynin was instructed to convey to Vance that the new American policy fundamentally violated the Basic Principles that Brezhnev and Nixon had agreed to in 1972. Ten days later, Carter invited dissident Vladimir Bukovsky to the White House.[108]

For Brezhnev, the continuation of partnership and progress in arms control was more important than squabbles on human rights. On the eve of Carter's inauguration, the Soviet leader sought to send him a positive signal. Speaking in Tula, on January 18, 1977, Brezhnev, for the first time, presented the Soviet security doctrine in clear defensive terms. The Soviet Union, he said, does not seek superiority for delivering a first strike, and the goal of Soviet military policy was to build a defensive potential sufficient for deterring any potential aggressor. Brezhnev expected that his speech would neutralize a "Soviet military threat" campaign in the American media and help Carter. One of his speechwriters, however, realized that this gesture was not enough. "The noise about the Soviet threat is based on facts," wrote Chernyaev in his diary. "Periodic statements that we threaten nobody will not do the job. If we do not undertake a real change in our military policy, the arms race aimed at our economic exhaustion will continue."[109]

The Soviets longed for policy continuity and confidential relations with the White House, something they had grown accustomed to in the era of Nixon and Kissinger. Carter, however, showed the Soviets that the terms of partnership had to be changed. In vain, Dobrynin sought to reactivate the back channel to Carter via Brzezinski. The new president was determined to deal with the Soviets without secret diplomacy. He wanted to conduct foreign policy through Vance and the State Department. Also, he adopted the arms control proposal developed by Senator Jackson's neoconservative analysts, among them Richard Perle and Paul Nitze. This proposal envisaged "deep cuts" in some strategic systems, above all, the elimination of half of the Satan rockets.[110] This, of course, meant that the much-criticized Vladivostok framework for SALT would be discarded. It also meant that the Soviet side would lose half of its best and biggest missiles in silos, while the Americans would only make a pledge not to deploy future comparable systems. It also deferred the issue of limitations on American cruise missiles and Soviet Backfires, something that the Soviets believed was close to settlement.[111]

Brezhnev was enraged. He felt that he had paid with his own health for the Vladivostok agreement. A new proposal would have meant another round of domestic and international bargaining, something that the ailing general secretary could not afford to do. He instructed Gromyko, Ustinov, and Andropov to draft a "tough letter" to Carter urging him to reach a fast agreement on the basis of his agreements with Ford at Vladivostok. In the letter, Brezhnev emphasized that this would open the road for their personal meeting, a matter of great importance for the Soviet leader. Carter, surprised by the stern tone of Brezhnev's message, nevertheless stuck to his guns. He announced that Vance would go to the Soviet Union with a big delegation and new proposals, one with "deep cuts" and another based on the Vladivostok framework, but without limits on cruise missiles and Soviet Backfire bombers. Both proposals were unacceptable to the Soviet military. Before Vance arrived in Moscow, the general secretary met with the troika at his dacha; in all probability all present decided it was time "to teach the Americans a lesson."[112]

Soviet rejection of the American proposals was inevitable, but its harshness came as a nasty surprise. At the first meeting on March 28, 1977, Brezhnev was peevish and irritated. He and Gromyko did not disguise their contempt for Carter's policies and some of their remarks were offensive to Carter personally. They interrupted Vance and did not even allow him to read the fallback proposal, which could have opened the road to a compromise. The U.S. delegation returned home empty-handed. Rubbing salt into their wounds, Gromyko denounced the American proposals at a specially convened press conference. As Vance later put it, "We got a wet rug in the face, and were told to go home."[113]

Brezhnev's health was definitely a factor in the Moscow fiasco, but the new gap between political priorities of the two sides was much more important. Particularly crucial was the fact that the Soviets wanted to achieve a numerical parity, and this was intolerable to the American side, which previously had had a clear superiority. Even ten years later, when Ronald Reagan and Mikhail Gorbachev signed a treaty eliminating intermediate range missiles, they failed to agree on a comprehensive framework for the remaining strategic armaments.[114]

The clash on human rights also was another symptom of the widening gap between the Kremlin and the White House. After the years of dealing with the pragmatic Kissinger, the Soviet leaders were convinced that Carter just wanted to take cheap propaganda shots at their expense. The Soviet leaders, products of Stalinist political culture, simply could not conceive why the president paid so much attention to the fate of individual dissidents. Gromyko even forbade his aides from putting information on this matter on his desk. In a conversation with Vance, he wondered: How can the explosion of propaganda hostile to the USSR be explained? Why would the White House not stress the constructive aspects of Soviet foreign policy the way Moscow was doing?[115] Andropov had long insisted that the human rights campaigns were nothing but "attempts of the adversary to activate the hostile elements in the USSR by means of providing them financial and other material assistance."[116] Nobody realized at the time that the failure of the Moscow talks meant the end of the top-level Soviet-American partnership, a major engine of détente. In February 1977, Brezhnev, on Gromyko's advice, wrote to Carter that he would meet him only when the SALT agreement was ready for signing. As a result, the next Soviet-American summit did not take place until June 1979, in Vienna, when Brezhnev was already on the verge of physical and mental disintegration.[117]

It is easy now to look at the years after 1977 as the period of the inexorable worsening of Soviet-American relations. Scholars have analyzed major areas and developments that, in their various opinions, contributed to this outcome: continuing Soviet interventionism in Africa; a slow and ultimately fruitless arms control process; and a growing anti-Soviet mood in American domestic politics. Yet all those problems and difficulties had existed before, and still détente had blossomed. And even greater obstacles would not prevent Reagan and Gorbachev from becoming negotiating partners later in the 1980s. One comes to the conclusion that détente would have continued, despite all these problems, had Brezhnev still been willing to make a determined effort to maintain a political partnership with the American leadership. This conclusion does not mean to diminish the complexity of international relations and the decision-making processes in the Soviet regime and the American democracy. It highlights, however, the crucial role of top personalities and their political will at a critical juncture of international history when new opportunities and dangers were arising.

Jimmy Carter's lack of clear assumptions about the Soviet Union played as much a part in the undoing of détente as Brezhnev's beliefs had in conceiving it. Under the influence of Brzezinski and neoconservative critics, the U.S. president began to suspect that the Soviet Union was a reckless, unpredictable power, confusing the aging and reactive Kremlin leadership with the activist rambunctious leadership of Nikita Khrushchev. In May 1978, Carter wrote to Brzezinski that "the combination of increasing Soviet military power and political short-sightedness fed by big power ambitions might tempt the Soviet Union both to exploit local turbulence, especially in the Third World, and to intimidate our friends, in order to seek political advantage, and eventually even political preponderance. This is why I do take seriously Soviet action in Africa, and this is why I am concerned about the Soviet military buildup in Europe. I also see some Soviet designs pointed toward the Indian Ocean through South Asia, and perhaps toward the encirclement of China." In order to contain the Soviets in Africa, Brzezinski and Secretary of Defense Harold Brown came up with a Realpolitik move, a rapprochement with Beijing in order to use "the China card" against the Soviets. Vance opposed such a policy as dangerous for Soviet-American relations, but

Carter sided with Brzezinski and Brown. He sent Brzezinski to Beijing with broad authority to normalize relations with the Chinese Communists. This, Raymond Garthoff observed, set in motion developments that had much broader and deeper consequences than Soviet behavior warranted at the time. About the same time, Dobrynin told Averell Harriman, who attempted to defend the policies of the administration, that nothing would help any longer "to change the emotional atmosphere that existed in Moscow today."[118] The action-reaction cycle, so pronounced in Soviet-American relations before Nixon's trip to Moscow in May 1972, was back in force.

The Politburo, for its part, completely failed to understand the depth of Carter's motivation to develop arms control and reduce tensions. Instead, Brezhnev and his associates thought that the president was a pawn in the hands of his advisers. Gromyko remarked privately to Vance that "Brzezinski has already surpassed himself" in making statements that "are aimed at nearly bringing us back to the period of the Cold War." In June 1978, Brezhnev complained at the Politburo that Carter "is not simply falling under the usual influence of the most shameless anti-Soviet types and leaders of the military-industrial complex of the USA. He intends to struggle for reelection for the new term as president under the banner of anti-Soviet policy and return to the Cold War." Two months later another harsh assessment came to Moscow in the form of a quarterly "political letter" from the Soviet embassy in Washington. It concluded that Carter was reevaluating Soviet-American relations. "The initiative for this affair came from Brzezinski and several presidential advisers on domestic affairs; they convinced Carter that he would succeed in stopping the process of worsening his position in the country if he would openly initiate a harsher course vis-à-vis the Soviet Union." The report quoted the leader of the U.S. Communist Party, Gus Hall, who referred to Brzezinski as the "Rasputin of the Carter regime."[119]

The Vienna summit in June 1979 demonstrated that under different circumstances Brezhnev and Carter might have become good partners. The president was considerate and patient—he visibly tried to find some kind of emotional bond with the Soviet leader. After signing the SALT agreements, the president suddenly reached out to Brezhnev and embraced him. He passed discreetly to Brezhnev the draft of proposals for the next round of arms control talks that proposed reductions of strategic systems. He even refrained from the customary reference to human rights. Brezhnev, despite his asthenia, was moved and later remarked to his associates that Carter was "quite a nice guy, after all." During the farewell, Carter turned to Soviet interpreter Viktor Sukhodrev and said with his famous smile: "Come back to the United States and bring your President with you."[120] Six months later, the Soviets invaded Afghanistan.

Politburo members, particularly the troika of Gromyko, Andropov, and Ustinov, continued to misunderstand détente as primarily and even exclusively the result of a "new correlation of forces" and Soviet military strength. For a while, these misperceptions did not look fateful. But Afghanistan changed everything. The military coup in distant Kabul in April 1978 brought sectarian leftists to power. They immediately proclaimed the "April revolution" and appealed to the Soviet Union for assistance. The Soviets had nothing to do with this development and were poorly prepared to deal with it. According to the most recent evidence, even the KGB learned about the leftist coup ex post facto. As Raymond Garthoff observed, Richard Nixon and his regional ally, the Shah of Iran, may have thrown the first pebble that led to the avalanche of events in Afghanistan. In 1976 and 1977, the Shah persuaded President Mohammed Daoud of Afghanistan to move away from his alignment with the Soviet Union and crack down on Afghan leftists.[121] Ironically, the Shah's regime collapsed soon after the situation in Afghanistan began to unravel. The regional balance was destroyed, with disastrous consequences for many years ahead.

From the Kremlin's viewpoint, the proximity of Afghanistan to Soviet borders and Central Asia made "revolution" there different from otherwise similar cases in Africa. The growing instability on the southern frontiers only increased a temptation to turn Afghanistan into a stable satellite firmly under Soviet tutelage. The shadowy Cold War mentality prevailed in the KGB. As a former senior KGB officer recalls, he viewed Afghanistan as a Soviet sphere of interest and believed that the Soviet Union "had to do whatever possible to prevent the Americans and the CIA from installing an anti-Soviet regime there." After the 1978 coup, Soviet-Afghan contacts quickly mushroomed via the channels of the Defense Ministry, the KGB, the Foreign Ministry, and a host of other agencies and ministries dealing with, among others, economy, trade, construction, and education. Party delegations and many advisers from Moscow and the Central Asian Soviet republics flocked to Kabul. No doubt the same motives, as during the scramble for Africa, were driving the Soviet political leadership and bureaucracies. Incidentally, the Soviet representatives and advisers in Afghanistan enjoyed the same high salaries in foreign currency as their colleagues had in Angola, Ethiopia, Mozambique, South Yemen, and other countries of the third world, where they performed "internationalist duty" to "assist the regimes with socialist orientation."[122]

Very quickly, the Soviet advisers and visitors fell into the trap of fractious revolutionary politics. The leaders of the Khalq faction, Prime Minister Nur Mohammad Taraki and his entrepreneurial deputy, Hafizullah Amin, began to purge the rival Parcham group. The Afghan leaders believed in revolutionary terror and drew inspiration from the Stalinist purges. In September 1978, Boris Ponomarev, of the International Committee, undertook a secret mission to Afghanistan, to warn Taraki that the Soviet Union would turn away from him if he continued to destroy his fellow revolutionaries. These warnings, as well as Soviet appeals for unity, fell on deaf ears. The Afghani revolutionaries correctly believed that the Soviet Union simply could not afford to let them down. Shortly before Ponomarev's mission, the head of the KGB's intelligence directorate, Vladimir Kryuchkov, visited Kabul and signed an agreement on sharing intelligence and cooperation. The main purpose of the agreement was "to fight the growing CIA presence in Kabul and throughout Afghanistan."[123] On December 5, 1978, Brezhnev and Taraki met in Moscow and signed the Treaty of Friendship, Good Neighborliness, and Cooperation. Taraki returned to Kabul convinced that Brezhnev personally supported him. Indeed, Brezhnev liked the deceptively debonair leader of Afghanistan.[124]

In March 1979, a cruel wake-up call reached Moscow. The city and area of Herat had rebelled against the Khalq regime, and an insurgent mob had brutally killed Kabul's officials, Soviet advisers, and their families. Taraki and Amin made desperate calls to Moscow pleading for Soviet military intervention "to save the revolution." It was the first strong sign that another force, militant Afghan nationalism and Islamic fundamentalism, had come on the scene. The Politburo, once again, was caught by surprise and was not adequately equipped to analyze this new development. The Kremlin discussions reveal with startling clarity the perils of the fictitious Brezhnev leadership in a crisis situation. At the start of the discussion, the foreign policy troika advocated Soviet military intervention to save the Kabul regime. They agreed that "losing Afghanistan" as part of the Soviet sphere of influence would be unacceptable, geopolitically and ideologically. Brezhnev was absent, resting at his dacha. The interventionist tide gained momentum fast.[125]

The next day, everything changed: all support for intervention literally evaporated overnight. Ustinov was the first to spell out the truth: the Kabul leadership wanted Soviet troops to fight Islamic fundamentalism, a danger they had themselves created by their radical reforms. Andropov argued that "we can uphold the revolution in Afghanistan only with the aid of our bayonets, and that is completely impermissible for us." Gromyko came up with another argument: "All that we have done in recent years with such effort in terms of détente of international relations, arms reductions, and much more—all that would be overthrown. China, of course, will receive a nice gift. All the nonaligned countries will be against us." The foreign minister also reminded the Politburo that military intervention would lead to cancellation of the summit with Carter in Vienna and also the visit of French president Giscard d'Estaing, scheduled for the end of March.[126]

Why this shift? New information, particularly a telephone conversation between Kosygin and Taraki, clarified the realities in Afghanistan. An even more decisive factor, however, must have been Brezhnev's personal intervention and the position of his foreign policy assistant, Alexandrov-Agentov.[127] As Gromyko spelled out, Brezhnev maintained a stake in détente. His interest in signing the SALT agreement with the United States and avoiding anything that might complicate his meetings with other Western leaders carried the decisive weight. He also, by nature, regarded any military intervention as a weapon of last resort. Brezhnev appeared in person at the Politburo, which was in session continuously for three days, against intervention. After a Soviet military plane brought Taraki to Moscow, he was informed that Soviet forces would not be deployed in Afghanistan. The Soviets pledged additional assistance to the Afghan army and put pressure on Pakistan and Iran to limit the penetration of Islamic radical forces into Afghanistan. After listening to Taraki's brief reply, Brezhnev stood up and left, as if to say that the matter was closed.[128]

The decision against intervention, however, did not seem final. The initial interventionist stand of the troika spelled trouble for the future. The illusory project of leading Afghanistan "along the path of socialist reform" was not renounced. In fact, Gromyko, Andropov, Ustinov, and Ponomarev reaffirmed it in their memorandum to the Politburo soon after Taraki left Moscow. As a result, Soviet material investments in the Kabul regime increased, and the number of Soviet advisers, mostly of the military and the KGB, reached an estimated 4,000 people.[129]

All this proved fateful when the next power struggle in Afghanistan took place between Taraki and Amin. Indeed, the outcome could have been predicted. Hafizullah Amin was a much more shrewd and efficient leader, with personal attributes and style that strongly resembled those of Iraqi leader Saddam Hussein. Amin's role model was Joseph Stalin; he relied on brutal force in building the regime and was prepared to take big risks in pursuing his ambitious goals. His energy in building the Afghan army and putting down the revolt in Herat won him the sympathies of Soviet military advisers. Brezhnev, however, was on Taraki's side. In early September 1979, the Afghan prime minister stopped in Moscow on the way home after a meeting of nonaligned countries in Havana. Brezhnev and Andropov told him that Amin was planning a coup against him and had just removed his people from the key positions in the security services. There is reason to believe that after that conversation the KGB, together with the Soviet embassy in Kabul, attempted to remove Amin but that the plot backfired. Whatever happened, Amin arrested Taraki and on October 9 ordered him strangled in his prison cell. After that, Amin expelled the Soviet ambassador.[130] The assassination of Brezhnev's favorite suddenly involved the general secretary personally and emotionally in the affairs of the Afghan revolution. Brezhnev allegedly told Andropov and Ustinov: "What kind of scum is this Amin—to strangle the man with whom he participated in the revolution? Who is now at the helm of the Afghan revolution? What will people say in other countries? Can one trust Brezhnev's words?" The momentum for Soviet military intervention and the removal of Amin began to grow from that point on. Very soon after Taraki's murder, Brezhnev's foreign policy assistant, Alexandrov-Agentov, reportedly told one official of the International Department that it was necessary to send troops to Afghanistan.[131]

The quick escalation of the revolution in Iran after January 1979, proclamation of the Islamic Republic in Iran on March 31 of the same year, and rapidly growing Iranian support of fundamentalist rebels in southwest Afghanistan probably contributed to the reassessment of the nonintervention decision. The Kremlin leaders could not know that the Iranian revolution would introduce a new era of radical Islam that would outlive the Cold War and the Soviet Union. They suspected and, initially, grossly exaggerated an American involvement with the growing fundamentalist movement in Afghanistan. Ustinov, Andropov, and Alexandrov-Agentov in particular began to think about Afghanistan exclusively in the light of Soviet-American zero-sum competition.[132] The introduction of U.S. forces into the Persian Gulf after the capture of the American embassy by Islamic radicals on November 4, 1979, alarmed the General Staff. General Valentin Varennikov recalled that at that time "we were concerned that if the United States were forced from Iran, they would move their bases to Pakistan and seize Afghanistan." Minister of Defense Ustinov reportedly wondered: If Americans do all these preparations under our noses, why should we hunker down, play cautious, and lose Afghanistan?[133] Under these circumstances, the KGB reports from Kabul that Amin was playing a double game and meeting secretly with Americans were particularly disturbing. Sadat's betrayal a few years earlier prepared a fertile ground for suspicions to grow.

The Soviet decision to eliminate Amin and "save" Afghanistan is a remarkable case of "group think" at the very top of Soviet leadership, above all among the policy-making troika. At some point in October and November, Andropov supported Ustinov's position and the two began to plot an invasion. Then Gromyko and Alexandrov-Agentov gave their consent. The principals kept the preparations in deep secret from the rest of the Politburo and from their own staff analysts.

From the viewpoint of the troika, the most important task was to get Brezhnev on board. In early December 1979, Andropov presented arguments to him in favor of the invasion. He wrote: "Now there is no guarantee that Amin, in order to secure his personal power would not go over to the West." The letter proposed staging a coup against Amin and bringing the exiled faction of Afghan revolutionaries to power in Kabul.[134]

Recent research has shown that Andropov's basic contention about Amin's imminent treason stemmed from amazingly tenuous evidence. The KGB chief seems to have played the same role he had played in 1968 during the Czechoslovak crisis: he used information and misinformation to steel Brezhnev's resolve for intervention. On December 8, Andropov and Ustinov told Brezhnev about the possibility of deployment of U.S. short-range missiles in Afghanistan that might target Soviet military installations in Kazakhstan and Siberia. Ustinov suggested taking advantage of Amin's repeated requests for Soviet troops and sending several divisions into Afghanistan, to ensure a smooth takeover. The original intention was to withdraw these troops immediately after a new regime had been established.[135]

Even at this point, concerns about serious consequences for détente could have overruled, once again, the arguments for intervention. But this time neither Brezhnev nor Gromyko objected. In the fall of 1979, détente seemed to be sinking to its nadir. The little dose of goodwill generated by the Brezhnev-Carter summit had evaporated. At the prodding of several Democratic senators, the White House raised a false alarm about the presence of a Soviet brigade in Cuba, a completely trumped-up charge. This contributed to Moscow's suspicion that somebody in Washington had decided to challenge the Soviet Union across the board.[136]

The "last straw" that tipped the scales in favor of intervention was NATO's decision to deploy a new generation of strategic nuclear weapons in Western Europe—Pershing missiles and cruise missiles. The decision officially made at a special meeting of NATO foreign and defense ministers in Brussels on December 12 was forecast by Soviet analysts a few days ahead. It gave validity to the arguments of Ustinov and Andropov, who, at their meeting with Brezhnev on December 8, emphasized that the Afghanistan problem became part of a worsening strategic situation and that American short-range missiles could also be deployed in Afghanistan.[137]

The top Soviet military brass was the last group that tried to voice objections to the planned intervention. The General Staff's chief, Marshal Nikolai Ogarkov, expressed his and his colleagues' reservations to Brezhnev and the troika in an informal exchange on the eve of a Politburo meeting on Afghanistan on December 10. He cited the perils of Soviet troops mired in unfamiliar and difficult conditions and reminded the political leaders that the fears of hostile American activities in the region were imaginary. Instead of discussing Ogarkov's concerns, Ustinov, whose relations with the marshal were strained, told him to shut up and obey the leadership. Minutes later, at the Politburo session, Ogarkov tried again to warn of serious fallout from the invasion. "We would align the entire Islamic East against us and suffer political damage around the world." Andropov cut him off: "Focus on military affairs! Leave policy-making to us, the party, and Leonid Ilyich!" On that day, the Politburo did not come to a decision. Two days later, on December 12, Andropov, Ustinov, and Gromyko learned that NATO had decided to deploy Pershing missiles and cruise missiles in Europe. This time the Politburo approved the Ustinov-Andropov plan to "save" Afghanistan through the combination of a coup and military intervention. Brezhnev, very feeble but visibly emotional, affixed his signature to the decision to intervene.[138]

The crude incompetence of the Soviet invasion blew away Moscow's official cover that the Kabul government had actually requested the Soviet Union to defend them. The clumsiness of the KGB contributed to the problem. At first, Soviet agents attempted to poison Amin, but when the poison failed to work, commandos stormed Amin's palace, causing a bloodbath. Fierce American and international reaction to this bloody coup caused the entire edifice of superpower détente to crumble. There is evidence that Brezhnev took the dismantling of détente by Washington personally and dimly understood that the intervention in Afghanistan was a gross error. His foreign policy adviser recalled that the general secretary once complained to Andropov and Ustinov: "You got me into this mess!"[139]

Brezhnev's career as a statesman was at its end—a very bleak one. Chernyaev wrote in his diary: "I do not believe that ever before in Russian history, even under Stalin, was there a period when such important actions were taken without a hint of discussion, advice and deliberation. We entered a very dangerous period when the ruling circle cannot fully appreciate what it is doing and why."[140] Chernyaev and other "enlightened" functionaries waited for a miracle that could help the Soviet Union weather this dangerous stretch.

(CHAPTER 9)

THE OLD GUARD'S EXIT,
1980-1987

The quota of interventions abroad has been exhausted.
—Andropov, fall 1980

The superpower confrontation of the early 1980s had a feeling of déjà vu. The rampant arms race, covert battles between secret services around the world, and fierce psychological warfare gave the situation a resemblance to the last years of Stalin's rule. The Reagan administration sought to roll back the Soviet empire, just as the Truman and Eisenhower administrations had done in the early 1950s. Some in the West forecast a dangerous decade and predicted that "the Soviet Union would risk nuclear war if her leaders believed the integrity of the empire to be at stake."[1]

This chapter focuses on the behavior of the Kremlin in the face of growing confrontation. The last years of Brezhnev's rule and the next two years of inter-regnum under the leadership of Yuri Andropov and Konstantin Chernenko were times of deterioration of the political and economic foundations of Soviet power. Western analysts, including those in the CIA, suspected that the Soviet economy was in bad shape and that the Soviet hold on Central Europe was shaky. But they did not imagine how bad the situation really was. The Solidarity movement in Poland in 1980 and 1981 and the growing dependency of other countries of the Warsaw Pact on the economic and financial power of Western capitalist countries gravely undermined the empire built by Stalin. The Kremlin rulers lacked the political will and resourcefulness to stop the erosion of Soviet power. At no point from 1981 to 1985 did the Kremlin leaders contemplate anything resembling preparations for an ultimate showdown with the West.[2]

POLAND: A CORNERSTONE CRACKS

In August 1980, labor strikes in Gdansk escalated into a crisis of the Communist regime in Poland. The phenomenal success of Solidarity, especially the impressive coordination and efficiency of this seemingly chaotic democratic movement, led the Kremlin rulers and some advisers to suspect a "hidden hand," perhaps a well-trained "underground" funded from abroad and leading the revolution. Even worse from the Soviet perspective was the enormous international outpouring of support for these "anti-socialist forces." The KGB reported on the ties between Solidarity, the Polish Catholic Church, the Vatican, and Polish émigré organizations in the United States. Zbigniew Brzezinski and Pope John Paul II were named as the most dangerous instigators of Polish events.[3]

The Polish revolution spilled over, politically and psychologically, into the borderlands of the Soviet Union itself. In 1981, the KGB reported about mass strikes at some plants and factories in the Baltic republics, especially in Latvia, that were influenced by the Polish workers' movement.[4] In the spring of 1981, the KGB's Yuri Andropov informed the Politburo that "the Polish events are influencing the situation in the western provinces of our country, particularly in Belorussia." Soviet authorities slammed down a new iron curtain on the borders with Poland, closing tourism, student programs, and cultural exchange with this "fraternal" country. Subscription to Polish periodicals was suspended and Polish radio was jammed.[5]

Many people in the Soviet Union and around the world nervously waited for the next Kremlin reaction to the Solidarity movement. Some foreign policy experts in the Central Committee in Moscow and members of the National Security Council in Washington feared a familiar prospect: a Soviet invasion as in Czechoslovakia in 1968. Leonid Brezhnev, however, was not ready for such a step. Even in his dotage, the increasingly detached and irritated general secretary did not want to give his consent to another military operation, least of all against the Poles.[6]

Brezhnev's determination to avoid intervention in Poland was known only in a very narrow circle. By that time, the general secretary had virtually disappeared from the Kremlin, becoming a recluse in his state dacha. In his absence, the troika of Andropov, Ustinov, and Gromyko monopolized security affairs. Mikhail Suslov also played a visible role—he became the head of the special Politburo commission on the Polish crisis. Of those people, Minister of Defense Dmitry Ustinov had the greatest reason to push for military intervention: Poland had to be secured as a crucial link between the Group of Soviet Forces in Germany and the Soviet Union. The Warsaw Pact made no sense without Poland; indeed, its headquarters was near the Polish city of Legnice. There were several instances when Ustinov's subordinates, chiefly Marshal Viktor Kulikov, commander in chief of the united forces of the Warsaw Pact, advocated "saving" Poland at any cost.[7]

KGB chairman Yuri Andropov was a pivotal figure in the Politburo's decision-making circle. He had been the ardent advocate of Soviet invasions of Hungary, Czechoslovakia, and Afghanistan. In the fall of 1980, however, Andropov said to a trusted subordinate: "The quota of interventions abroad has been exhausted."[8] Andropov had already begun to position himself as Brezhnev's heir apparent and realized that another military intervention would be a disastrous career move. The invasion of Poland would have killed European détente, still on the ropes after the Afghan intervention. It might even have meant the collapse of the entire Helsinki process, the biggest achievement of Soviet statesmanship of the 1970s.

Even Suslov concluded it would be preferable to admit a few social democrats into Poland's Communist government than to use Soviet troops.[9] This, however, did not mean that the Kremlin gave up on Poland. The Politburo began to lean toward "the Pilsudski scenario," meaning a nationalist-militarist dictatorship reminiscent of the regime established by Jozef Pilsudski in the 1920s. Among the candidates for "Communist Pilsudski" were the Polish first secretary, Stanyslaw Kania, and the head of the Polish armed forces, General Wojciech Jaruzelski. In December 1980, Brezhnev told Kania from a prepared script: "If we see that you are being overthrown," he said, "then we would go in." The whole meeting served the purpose of intimidating Kania with the prospect of Soviet invasion to make him take drastic steps against the Solidarity movement.[10] But the Polish party leader lacked the resolve and character needed to carry out the proposed coup. Leonid Zamyatin, a highly placed Soviet propaganda official, came back from Warsaw with the impression that the Polish party leader had become a nervous wreck and had taken refuge in drink.[11] Thus the way to force the Polish leadership into action was to make him and his entire entourage believe that a Soviet invasion was imminent. To facilitate this, a large-scale military exercise of the Warsaw Pact armies inside Poland and near its borders was organized to coincide with the meeting. This was a carbon copy of the Soviet actions in Czechoslovakia before the Kremlin had decided to invade.[12]

Twelve years earlier, the object of pressure had been Alexander Dubcek. Now it was Kania. In March 1981, Kania and Jaruzelski came to Moscow again, and Ustinov dressed down the Polish party leader like a schoolboy. "Comrade Kania," he shouted, "our patience is lost! We have people in Poland on whom we can rely. We give you two weeks' ultimatum to restore order in Poland!"[13] Soon after the Polish delegation left Moscow, Warsaw Pact forces and the KGB began a full-scale campaign of intimidation of Poland, including large-scale military exercises that lasted three weeks. Ustinov's threat, however, was empty: the Kremlin leaders were not planning an invasion.[14]

During the summer of 1981 the Soviets did their best to find and organize "healthy forces" inside the Polish Communist Party that could be an additional source of pressure on Kania and Jaruzelski. What they found disheartened them: hard-line Communists in Poland were a vanishing breed, replaced by educated and reform-minded people, among them journalist Myaczyslaw Rakowski, whom many in the Kremlin viewed as a dangerous "rightist revisionist." The Communist leaders of the GDR, Hungary, and Czechoslovakia, and especially Rumania's leader, Nicolae Ceaucescu, were even more fearful of these developments. At their meetings with Brezhnev at his summer resort in the Crimea, they began to demand military intervention. Brezhnev, however, adamantly refused.[15]

Brezhnev still believed he could resuscitate détente in Europe and abhorred the prospect of invasion of Poland. In addition, he and other Soviet leaders were deterred by the economic dimensions of the Polish crisis. Fighting with the Poles would be disastrous enough, but equally calamitous would be the economic costs of invasion and occupation. Chernyaev commented in his journal in August 1981: "Brezhnev's approach is the only wise approach. We simply cannot afford to keep Poland as our economic dependent."[16] Indeed, the Kremlin did not have the surplus resources to pay for its rapidly expanding commitments. By the 1980s, the Soviet Union assisted or maintained sixty-nine Soviet satellites and clients around the world. Beginning in the second half of the 1960s, over a quarter of the Soviet GDP was spent every year on financing the military buildup. The regime routinely filled holes in the budget by borrowing from people's savings, selling vodka, and secretly amassing a budget deficit. Another crucial source of revenue was the export of oil and gas: from 1971 to 1980, the Soviet Union increased its oil and gas production sevenfold and eightfold, respectively, a rate matched by the ever-increasing Soviet deliveries of heavily subsidized oil and gas to Warsaw Pact countries.[17] After 1974, when world prices of oil quadrupled, Moscow was forced to double the price of Soviet oil delivered to its Warsaw Pact allies, compensating them through ten-year, low-interest loans. Soviet economic interests demanded reduction of such generous aid to Central European regimes, but the interests of the "socialist empire" and bloc commitments dictated instead further increases in this aid.[18]

The economic sanctions placed on the USSR by President Carter after the invasion of Afghanistan exacerbated economic tensions inside the Soviet bloc. No longer could the Soviet leaders force their client Central European regimes to share the economic burdens of the renewed Cold War. At a meeting in Moscow in February 1980, the party secretaries of these countries informed their Kremlin comrades that they could not afford any reduction of economic and trade relations with the West. The economic dependency of Warsaw Pact member states on NATO countries, previously the problem of only the GDR, had now become the case for Czechoslovakia, Hungary, Rumania, and Bulgaria as well.[19] Essentially, the Communist allies told Moscow that plugging the holes in the "socialist community" would be exclusively a Soviet expense.

The Polish crisis painfully revealed the precarious position of the Soviet Union as the only economic and financial donor to the Eastern bloc. During the year after August 1980, the Soviets pumped four billion dollars into Poland, without any noticeable results. The Polish economy kept declining and anti-Soviet sentiment in Poland kept rising. Meanwhile, food shortages in the USSR continued and even worsened. Soviet agriculture, despite gargantuan state investments, sputtered, and the centralized system of food distribution suffered bottlenecks. Heavily subsidized bread, butter, oil, and meat disappeared from stores into the flourishing "black market" and sold at inflated prices. There were growing food lines, even in privileged Moscow. In this situation, the Kremlin had to suffer the ultimate embarrassment of allowing large-scale Western assistance to save the Poles from starvation. In November 1980, Brezhnev informed the leaders of the GDR, Czechoslovakia, Hungary, and Bulgaria that the Soviet Union would have to cut supplies of oil to these countries, "with a view of selling this oil on the capitalist market and transferring the gained hard currency" to help the Polish regime.[20] It became obvious that in the event of military invasion of Poland by Warsaw Pact forces, the USSR would have to pick up the tab of the occupation costs. And nobody could predict the impact of Western economic sanctions on the COMECON members.

On October 18, Prime Minister General Wojciech Jaruzelski took over the party leadership from Kania. Jaruzelski represented Moscow's last hope. Contrary to many hostile depictions in the West and inside Poland, Jaruzelski was not the obedient tool in Soviet hands. Deported to Siberia by the NKVD after the partition of Poland in 1939, he became an officer in the Soviet-sponsored Polish Army during World War II. Jaruzelski spoke Russian fluently and grew up believing in the primary importance of Poland's security. He also convinced himself that only the Soviet Union could guarantee Polish territorial integrity. For months, Jaruzelski resisted Soviet pressure to impose martial law. By November 1981, however, he had to give in: Poland teetered on the economic brink, with the imminent prospect of a harsh winter without enough fuel and food. Simultaneously, the moderate leaders of Solidarity began to lose ground to more radical and impatient forces demanding an end to the Communist Party regime in Poland. Jaruzelski began secret preparations for a coup. Still, he held the Kremlin in suspense. After a last-minute meeting with Jaruzelski, Nikolai Baibakov reported to the Politburo that the general had been transformed into a neurotic, "uncertain of his capacity to do anything." Jaruzelski repeatedly warned Moscow that the Polish Catholic Church might join forces with Solidarity and "declare a holy war against the Polish authorities." The general ended up by asking for emergency economic assistance and the provision of Soviet troops as the backup force for the Polish army and police.[21] Jaruzelski was trying to turn the tables on his blackmailers in the Kremlin.

At an emergency Politburo meeting, Andropov took the floor. The KGB chief warned that Jaruzelski wanted to "blame everything" on the Soviet Union. Andropov firmly concluded that the Soviet Union could not afford a military intervention under any circumstances, even if the Solidarity movement came to power. "We must be concerned above all with our own country and the strengthening of the Soviet Union," the speaker concluded. "That is our paramount guideline." Andropov knew that food shortages threatened to engulf even Moscow and Leningrad and was concerned about domestic stability. The revolt of Polish workers made Andropov wonder if Soviet workers would stay patient forever.[22]

The KGB chairman came close not only to rejecting the so-called Brezhnev Doctrine but also to revising the expansive version of the revolutionary-imperial paradigm that the Kremlin had been practicing. Matthew Ouimet correctly concluded that the Polish Solidarity crisis "left the Brezhnev Doctrine of Limited Sovereignty very much like the man after whom it had been named. Both had become mannequins propped up by a fading imperial power desperate to preserve its role in world affairs. . . . Though still unaware of their accomplishment, the Polish people had forced the Soviet colossus into an imperial retreat from which it would never recover."[23]

Jaruzelski's imposition of martial law on December 13, 1981, removed the immediate challenge to the Warsaw Pact. But the Polish crisis was not at an end; it was symptomatic of the growing structural crisis of the entire bloc. The costs of keeping control of Poland remained high. Despite Soviet protestations, Jaruzelski received 1.5 billion dollars' worth of economic aid in 1981. Vast amounts of grain, butter, and meat went to Poland and immediately vanished there, like a drop in a bottomless pit. Polish industries also received vitally needed raw materials, including iron ore, nonferrous metals, tires, and, most important of all, Soviet oil.[24]

The Polish crisis was the most severe in the series of grave crises that began to buffet the Kremlin in the early 1980s. For the first time since the blooming of European détente and the Soviet invasion of Czechoslovakia, Soviet leaders clearly realized the limits of Soviet power, even in the areas adjacent to Soviet borders. Despite its approaching senility, the Kremlin Old Guard was poised on the brink of a fundamental reappraisal of Soviet security interests and foreign policy. However, these men did not take a final step in this direction. They looked backward, not forward, in the search for solutions.

The secret debates on Poland in the Kremlin overlapped with another painful discussion: how to deal with the provocative and bellicose behavior of the Reagan administration toward the Soviet Union. Reagan knew very well from Colonel Ryszard Kuklinski, an American spy in the Warsaw Pact military command, about the Soviet pressure on Poland. He took the imposition of martial law as a personal insult.[25] The president was determined to punish the Soviet Union to the maximum and to maximize Soviet economic problems. After December 1981, Reagan pushed Western European countries to impose an embargo on the construction of the transcontinental oil pipeline, the "Urengoi–Western Europe," a project pivotal for increasing Soviet oil revenues in the future. In the end, West Germany and France failed to support the U.S. sanctions, and, as a Russian scholar commented, "Reagan lost the first round against the USSR." The construction of the pipeline, however, was delayed by a few critical years. Simultaneously, CIA director William Casey and Secretary of Defense Caspar Weinberger sanctioned a number of highly provocative secret operations, including military exercises in the vicinity of Soviet borders and Soviet naval bases, to apply pressure on the Kremlin. The administration lobbied Saudi Arabia and the OPEC countries for a sharp reduction of world oil prices. These revelations of the administration's hard-liners, despite their tendency for exaggeration, reveal that the American pressure on the Soviets was at a level not seen since the 1950s.[26]

For Andropov, the actions of the Reagan administration began to form an ominous pattern. In a mirror image of U.S. fears at that time, the KGB chief began to warn that "the administration in Washington is attempting to push the whole development of international relations on to a dangerous path intensifying the danger of war."[27] In May 1981, Andropov invited Brezhnev to a closed session of KGB officers and, in his presence, told the surprised audience that the United States was making preparations for a surprise nuclear attack on the USSR. He declared that, from now on, a new strategic early warning system was to be created, on the basis of cooperation between the KGB and the GRU (Soviet military intelligence). The new intelligence operation was named RYAN—after the first letters of the Russian words *raketno-yadernoye napadeniie* (nuclear-missile attack). The skeptical intelligence professionals wrongly presumed this preposterous idea came from Ustinov and the military. Since the 1970s, the military no longer had assumed that an American attack might take place unexpectedly at any moment. Marshal Sergei Akhromeyev recalled later that he regarded the situation as "difficult, but not crisis-ridden." In fact, the RYAN idea was Andropov's own. Vigilant to the point of being somewhat neurotic, the KGB chief had old visions of "Barbarossa" and the early Cold War reawakened.[28]

Andropov hoped to shake up the Soviet bureaucracy and society, which were stagnant. Brezhnev, however, was against any radical departures. The general secretary repeated the détente mantra, expecting that sooner or later the Americans would reciprocate. Many in the Politburo hoped that Reagan would return to "realist" grounds of cooperating with the Soviet Union. Hoping to mollify Western public opinion with symbolic gestures, Brezhnev gave a speech in June 1982 renouncing the first use of nuclear weapons. Soon after, Ustinov publicly declared that the Soviet Union "does not count on achieving victory in a nuclear war."[29] This meant a de facto abandonment of the offensive military doctrine of the 1960s.

On November 10, 1982, Leonid Brezhnev died in his sleep. Almost immediately, the Politburo announced that sixty-eight-year-old Yuri Andropov was the new Soviet leader. For the first time, the Kremlin leadership managed to avoid the intrigues and power struggles that had crippled it during previous successions. Cold War tensions must have contributed to this outcome, but there was also the fact that the KGB leader enjoyed the full support of Ustinov and Gromyko. Tragically for Andropov, by that time he was already in the final phase of terminal kidney disease.

Andropov viewed Reagan with unrelenting suspicion. When Reagan sent a handwritten letter to Brezhnev proposing to talk about nuclear disarmament, Andropov and other members of the ruling troika in the Kremlin dismissed this as a phony gesture. Meanwhile U.S.-Soviet relations plunged to another low. On March 8, 1983, the U.S. president spoke of the Soviet Union as "an evil empire," breaking with the rhetoric of the previous administrations, which, at least publicly, had avoided challenging the legitimacy of the Soviet regime. On March 23, 1983, Reagan dropped another bombshell, announcing the Strategic Defense Initiative (SDI), with the goal of making all nuclear weapons "impotent and obsolete." For the Soviet military and the Kremlin leaders, it sounded like a threat to neutralize all Soviet ballistic missiles and make the USSR vulnerable to an American first strike. Adding to Reagan's "evil empire" speech and SDI initiative, U.S. military and intelligence activities around the world deepened Andropov's insecurity. In April and May 1983, the American Pacific Fleet, during a massive exercise, probed for gaps in Soviet ocean surveillance and early warning systems. The Americans also practiced simulated assaults on Soviet strategic submarines with nuclear missiles on board. The Kremlin responded with its own intense series of global military exercises, including, for the first time, a general rehearsal for mobilization and interaction with strategic nuclear forces. Against this backdrop, Operation RYAN continued unabated during 1983; all KGB agents abroad received "permanent operational assignments to uncover NATO preparations for a nuclear missile attack on the USSR."[30]

In hindsight, some veterans of the Reagan administration viewed this as the source and origin of subsequent changes in Soviet behavior. The CIA's Robert Gates assumes that "SDI did have a significant impact on the Soviet political and military leadership" by presenting it with the prospect of "an incredibly expensive new arms race in an area in which the USSR could hardly hope to compete effectively." Gates believes that "the idea of SDI" convinced "even some of the conservative members of the Soviet leadership that major internal changes were needed in the USSR."[31] In reality, Soviet reaction was far more ambiguous. There was no feeling of impending doom in political and military circles. A panel of scientists and experts on arms control negotiations, headed by physicist Evgeny Velikhov, concluded that Reagan's SDI initiative probably did not require immediate countermeasures. But this conclusion did not end the debate. The Soviet military realized that, in the longer run, SDI could boost the development of new military technologies. Ustinov took an energetic interest in the SDI problem. Together with the president of the Academy of Science, Anatoly Alexandrov, he started planning a long-term effort in response to Reagan's initiative. Some people inside the military-industrial complex, including academician Gersh Budker and missile designer Vladimir Chelomei, came up with proposals for Soviet versions of SDI.[32]

The Reagan administration sold SDI to the Congress by arguing that in two years this initiative would force the Soviets to start talks on nuclear disarmament on U.S. terms. At first, however, quite the opposite happened. Only days into office, Andropov launched a campaign against corruption, for the restoration of discipline, and for patriotic vigilance.[33] Also, ominously, he made "a final warning" to those inside the Soviet Union who "consciously or unconsciously served as a mouthpiece for foreign interests by spreading all kinds of gossip and rumors." As often had occurred in the past, the policy of toughness and vigilance evoked a broad positive response among elites and the public. Mikhail Gorbachev, who later expressed his disapproval of Andropov's hard line, supported it wholeheartedly in 1983. The military, KGB officers, and many in the diplomatic corps applauded Andropov's campaign. Years later, a sizable group of Russians, perhaps even a majority, continued to look back at Andropov with respect and nostalgia.[34]

Andropov's deep mistrust of Reagan became entrenched, fortified by emotions—contempt, animosity, and a tinge of fear. Anatoly Dobrynin heard him saying: "Reagan is unpredictable. You should expect anything from him." On July 11, 1983, the U.S. president sent a handwritten personal message to Andropov. He assured the general secretary that the government and the people of the United States were dedicated to "the course of peace" and "the elimination of the nuclear threat." Reagan concluded: "Historically our predecessors have made better progress when communicating has been private and candid. If you wish to engage in such communication you will find me ready." In a narrow circle, the general secretary interpreted this offer as "duplicity and desire to disorient the Soviet leadership." Andropov responded with a polite and formal letter that ignored Reagan's offer.[35]

The more the pressure from Washington, the tougher the Politburo's stand. The war of nerves reached its climax in the KAL-007 affair in September 1983. When a Korean Airlines' Boeing-747 strayed over the Kurile Islands, an important part of the Soviet defense perimeter, on September 1, the nervous air-defense command mistook it for an American spy plane and ordered Soviet jet fighters to destroy it. Misled by Ustinov and the military, who promised him that the "Americans would never find out about it," Andropov, already hospitalized with kidney failure, decided to publicly deny the tragic accident. Reagan and Secretary of State George Shultz felt genuinely appalled at the loss of life and the Kremlin's prevarications. Yet many others in the CIA, the Pentagon, and the media were determined to score a propaganda victory over the "evil empire." Soviet denials of the truth provided them with a golden opportunity to unmask the Soviets before the entire world as callous murderers of innocent civilians.[36]

The worldwide hate campaign against the Soviet Union orchestrated by the Reagan administration was the last straw for Andropov, at that time a bitter and dying man. On September 29, Pravda published his "farewell address" on Soviet-American relations. Andropov informed the Soviet people that the Reagan administration was set upon a dangerous course "to ensure a dominating position in the world for the United States of America." He denounced the Korean airliner incident as a "sophisticated provocation organized by U.S. special services" and blamed Reagan personally for using propaganda methods "inadmissible in state-to-state relations." Then came the punch line: "If anybody ever had any illusions about the possibility of an evolution to the better in the policy of the present American administration, these illusions are completely dispelled now."[37]

The last months of 1983 seemed to have corroborated Andropov's grim verdict. In late September, Soviet satellite surveillance systems repeatedly reported that a massive U.S. ICBM launch had taken place. The alarms turned out to be false, but the tension grew.[38] In late October, U.S. marines invaded Grenada in the Caribbean Sea and deposed the Marxist government of Maurice Bishop. In

November, NATO forces conducted the Able Archer exercises; to Soviet intelligence sources, this looked almost indistinguishable from preparations for an imminent attack. Also, despite the enormous antiwar demonstrations and the deep divide in Western public opinion, the first Pershing missiles began to arrive on American bases in West Germany. On December 1, the Kremlin sent repeated warnings to the allied governments of the Warsaw Treaty Organization. The Soviet leadership informed them about a decision to deploy atomic submarines with nuclear missiles along U.S. coasts in response to "the increased nuclear threat to the Soviet Union." Without such measures, read the text, "the adventurers from Washington might easily be tempted to make a first nuclear strike with the goal of prevailing in a limited nuclear war. The disruption of the military balance in their favor could prompt the ruling circles in the USA to undertake a sudden attack on the socialist countries." The American invasion of Grenada was cited as proof that "American imperialism can risk unleashing a full-scale war for the sake of its venal class interests."[39]

The Kremlin's discourse on international relations seemed to hark back to the mid-1960s. Andropov's anger and frustration, as well as his terminal illness, colored this new alarmist rhetoric. Another Soviet message to Warsaw Pact leaders stated that Washington "has declared a 'crusade' against socialism as a social system. Those who have now ordered to deploy new nuclear weapons on our threshold link their practical policies to this reckless undertaking."[40] Reflecting the new foreign policy course, Soviet negotiators walked out of the Geneva arms control talks on November 23, 1983. Only at the last minute did Foreign Ministry diplomats and General Staff experts manage to convince the Politburo to leave the door open for a Soviet return to the negotiating table.[41] On December 16, Andropov told a Soviet arms control negotiator who came to visit him in a hospital that the Soviet Union and the United States were on a collision course for the first time since the Cuban missile crisis. He complained that the Reagan administration was doing everything to bleed the Soviets in Afghanistan and was not interested in Soviet withdrawal there. "If we begin to make concessions," the dying leader darkly mused, "defeat would be inevitable."[42]

Meanwhile, alerted to the tension he provoked by intelligence signals and the Western peace movement, Reagan decided it was now time to talk with the Soviets. Convinced that the Kremlin might share his interest in avoiding nuclear war, he made a conciliatory speech in January 1984 meant to be "an initiative to end the Cold War." Secretary of State George Schulz, Robert McFarlane, Jack Matlock, and other Reagan advisers disagreed with the CIA's Casey and the Pentagon's Weinberger, who wanted to use the war in Afghanistan to undermine the Soviet system. The Reagan advisers group thought that American policy should not challenge the legitimacy of the Soviet system, nor should it pursue military superiority and pressure the Soviet system into collapse. They worked out a four-part framework for future talks, including the renunciation of the use of force in international disputes, respect for human rights, open exchange of information and ideas, and reduction of armaments.[43] The embittered Moscow leadership, however, continued to believe that the administration was the hostage of the "bleeders" who wanted to beat the Soviet Union into the ground. They refused to notice the change in the White House. In September 1984, the same month he agreed to meet with Reagan for the first time since the Korean airliner incident, Gromyko told his assistants: "Reagan and his team have taken up as their aim to destroy the socialist camp. Fascism is on the march in America."[44]

Apparently, the Soviet foreign minister believed that Soviet-American relations had sunk to the lows of the early 1950s. Still, he was convinced that state interests required a dialogue with the American leader. Dobrynin concluded that "the impact of Reagan's hard-line policy on the internal debates in the Kremlin and on the evolution of the Soviet leadership was exactly the opposite from the one intended by Washington. It strengthened those in the Politburo, the Central Committee, and the security apparatus who had been pressing for a mirror-image of Reagan's own policy."[45] The author, then a junior researcher at the Institute of U.S. and Canada Studies in Moscow, could observe that Andropov's tough response to Reagan produced grave concern among experts. At the same time, American rhetoric in the anti-Soviet crusade irritated and angered even those who normally advocated improvement of U.S.-Soviet relations. Among the public, many began to wonder: "Will there be a war? When will it come?"[46]

Andropov's influence on Soviet international behavior was a bizarre mixture of grim realism and worst-case mentality, aggravated by his long association with the KGB. Until his health collapsed, he had enough will and vision to make his mark on foreign policy. His death on February 9, 1984, however, cut all his undertakings short. His successor, another septuagenarian, Konstantin Chernenko, was a walking mummy, who suffered from severe asthma and lived on tranquilizers. During Chernenko's brief tenure, Ustinov and Gromyko retained a virtual monopoly in military and foreign affairs. Nostalgia for Stalinist times began to surface in Kremlin deliberations. The Politburo even found time to readmit Vyacheslav Molotov to the Communist Party. Ustinov sharply criticized Khrushchev's policy of de-Stalinization, blaming Soviet international problems on it, and proposed to change the name of Volgograd back to Stalingrad. Some Kremlin elders looked nostalgically back to the 1940s when the Soviet Union were still a fortress country and the Soviet people had endured endless sacrifices and hardships.[47]

The General Staff was not unanimous on an adequate response to Reagan. Some believed it would require an increase in the military budget of 14 percent. Direct military expenses, that is, the cost of the armed forces and armaments, already amounted to 61 billion rubles and accounted for 8 percent of the GNP and 16.5 percent of the state budget. Total defense-related expenses, including indirect costs, as Brezhnev admitted in 1976, were two-and-one-half-times higher, around 40 percent of the budget. This figure was higher than in 1940, when the Soviet Union was preparing for World War II. Simple calculation shows that, in a time of a stagnant GNP, any drastic rise in defense expenditures would have necessitated drastic cuts in living standards and an end to Brezhnev's "live and let live" deal with the Soviet people.[48]

Soviet evidence does not indicate any debates in the Politburo on increasing military expenditures. The head of the Soviet General Staff, Marshal Nikolai Ogarkov, attempted to start a debate at the Defense Council. He criticized the stagnation in the military-industrial complex, which was controlled by Ustinov. In his opinion, there was too much inefficiency and too many costly mammoth projects and a suicidal penchant to pursue the United States in the arms race. Instead of debate, Ustinov dismissed Ogarkov, for a long time a thorn in his side. The Kremlin leaders also ignored the proposals borrowed from the 1940s, including a shift to a six-day working schedule and creation of a special "defense fund" to raise money for rearmament programs.[49] New realities discouraged the return to the old methods of mobilization. The society had irrevocably changed since the 1940s. The huge human resources Stalin had mobilized and squandered, those millions of the collectivized peasantry, young workers, and enthusiastic party cadres, were no longer available. There was little idealism among the elite educated youth; frustrated consumerism, cynicism, and pleasure-seeking took its place. Andropov's police measures to enforce discipline and a work ethic among blue-collar workers and the white-collar class quickly degenerated into a farce. Even the Politburo leaders were not the same as forty years earlier: most of them, because of their old age, began to think more about their health, reduction of their workload, and retirement perks than about the preservation of Soviet power. Konstantin Chernenko, Vladimir Scherbitsky, Dinmuhammad Kunaev, Nikolai Tikhonov, and other "elders" quietly resisted younger cadres brought to the Politburo and the Secretariat by Andropov, among them Mikhail Gorbachev, Yegor Ligachev, and Nikolai Ryzhkov.[50]

The Politburo elders fiddled, but the Grim Reaper did not wait. Ustinov died on December 20, 1984, and on March 10, 1985, it was Chernenko's turn. While Chernenko's funeral was in preparation, there was a flurry of behind-the-scenes bargaining. As a result, the last survivor of the ruling troika, Andrei Gromyko, cast his decisive vote for Mikhail Gorbachev, the youngest Politburo member. In return for his support, Gromyko soon became the head of the Supreme Soviet of the Soviet Union, an elevated position of a largely ceremonial nature.[51] Enormous power finally fell from the loosened grip of Stalinist appointees into the hands of a new, relatively inexperienced leader. Unfortunately for Gorbachev, huge problems and complicated responsibilities almost overwhelmed the assets he inherited.

A NEW FACE IN THE KREMLIN

Since 1985, many Western observers and Gorbachev's closest assistants have compared Gorbachev to Nikita Khrushchev. Despite a huge difference in generational experience, education, and style, both of them, indeed, had many things in common: a peasant social background; a sincere, even feverish, reformist urge; unflagging optimism and ebullient self-confidence; moral revulsion against the Soviet past; and a belief in the common sense of the Soviet people. Both reformers believed in the Communist system and in the major tenets of Marxism-Leninism. Both men also had great psychological potential for innovation and were willing to take responsibility for plunging into the unknown.[52] William Taubman, the author of a celebrated biography of Nikita Khrushchev, notes that Gorbachev regarded Brezhnev's domestic legacy as a conservative reaction against Khrushchev's de-Stalinization. Gorbachev took it as his mission to pick up where Khrushchev had failed.[53]

Gorbachev's personality, however, was the opposite of that of the fiery Nikita. Gorbachev was a consensus builder, not a fighter. Khrushchev was impatient; he attacked a problem like a tank attacking enemy defenses. By contrast, Gorbachev procrastinated and wove cobwebs of bureaucratic politics (see chapter 10). Khrushchev repeatedly put his life and career at risk during Stalin's purges, the war, and the plot against Beria. Gorbachev never had a close brush with death and received the supreme power almost on a silver plate. Behind him was a "junior team" of candidate members of the Politburo recruited by Andropov, among them Ligachev, Ryzhkov, and the KGB's Viktor Chebrikov. The military also welcomed his candidacy. Gorbachev's potential rivals, chairman of the Council of Ministers Nikolai Tikhonov, Leningrad party secretary Grigory Romanov, and Moscow party secretary Viktor Grishin, soon resigned without protest. There was no attempt to form a provisional collective leadership to supervise the young and untried general secretary.[54]

This remarkably easy victory testified to the strength of Andropov's network.

The peripheral and lower-rank party elites, not to mention the public, applauded Gorbachev with genuine enthusiasm. After years of senile administration, they welcomed a young, energetic leader. But despite such broad support, Gorbachev remained apprehensive and cautious. In his acceptance remarks at the Politburo, he declared that "there is no need to change policy." The existing course was the "true, correct, and genuinely Leninist" one. Only later, at the Party Plenum in April and during a televised trip to Leningrad in May 1985, did he say what many wanted to hear. The Soviet Union was in need of "perestroika."[55] A synonym for the taboo word "reform," "perestroika" (restructuring) meant, at first, only the changes in economic management. Later it would become the code word for Gorbachev's rule, yet its meaning eluded definition and systematization. Gorbachev's domestic caution betrayed a lack of specific cures for the ailing Soviet economy and society. Just as Franklin Delano Roosevelt did with his New Deal, Gorbachev wanted to improve the existing system; yet he had no idea how to achieve this. He knew, however, that the goal was to save socialism from stagnation and imminent crisis. In his memoirs, Gorbachev writes almost apologetically about his first steps: "One could not, naturally, liberate one's consciousness at once from previous blinkers and chains." It took Gorbachev two years to "free his mind" and prepare himself for the necessary radical reforms.

Gorbachev's domestic policies during his first two years in power rarely diverged from the blueprints designed during Andropov's brief reign. The new general secretary believed that removing Brezhnev's corrupt cronies and inefficient bureaucrats would make the Soviet system run well. The Kremlin's special investigators and the KGB moved against the powerful corrupt networks in the central Soviet bureaucracies, as well as in the regional nomenklaturas of East Ukraine, South Russia, Kazakhstan, and Central Asia. Ligachev, with Gorbachev's approval, removed and reshuffled hundreds of regional party secretaries. Gorbachev also did not want to depart from the centralized planned economy. Years later, he explained that he had first wanted to use the existing state and party mechanisms for industrial modernization and only after that was accomplished, in the early 1990s, "prepare the conditions for a radical economic reform." The program of conservative modernization consisted of two parts. First, it stipulated almost doubling investment in heavy industry, largely through deficit financing. Under the wishful slogan of "acceleration," the Politburo planned to increase industrial production by over 20 percent in fifteen years. In a bizarre relapse into Khrushchev's "harebrained schemes" of the late 1950s, the Kremlin leaders even discussed how to catch up with the United States in industrial production.[56] Second, it envisioned administrative measures to fight corruption and laxity and to improve work discipline. The hallmark of the course was the national anti-alcoholism campaign. Gorbachev, along with other Andropov recruits, had an illusion that a sharp reduction in alcohol retail sales would save Russians from compulsive drinking, their worst social problem. In reality, these initiatives achieved none of the goals they set and produced a huge financial black hole that would come to haunt the Soviet Union and Gorbachev in the next two to three years.[57]

In contrast to his domestic policies, Gorbachev's foreign policy became an arena for early innovations. Despite the international tensions from 1981 to 1983, the Politburo and the majority in Soviet bureaucracies did not want another uncontrolled confrontation with the West. They hoped it would be possible to return to détente. It also began to dawn on some officials and experts in the General Staff, the Ministry of Foreign Affairs, the KGB, and the Military-Industrial Commission that Soviet behavior had inadvertently contributed to the demise of détente. The decisions to deploy the SS-20 medium-range missiles in Central Europe and to invade Afghanistan fell under increasing scrutiny. There was strong bureaucratic momentum to resume the abrogated talks with the United States and NATO. Even before Chernenko's death in January 1985, Andrei Gromyko met with Secretary of State George Schulz and agreed on the framework for U.S.-Soviet arms talks. In April 1985, the Politburo halted deployment of SS-20 missiles.[58]

For personal and political reasons, Gorbachev was eager to achieve an early success in foreign affairs. In his memoirs, he recalls that very early on he had decided on "the need for serious changes in foreign policy." He explains the main reason: "Reforms in economic life and political system" were impossible without an "advantageous international environment."[59] The general secretary delegated domestic policies to Yegor Ligachev and Nikolai Ryzhkov and quickly moved to assert his supremacy in foreign affairs. His first step was to diminish Gromyko's role in this sphere. Rather than turning to Gromyko's deputies, Kornienko and Dobrynin, Gorbachev asked Georgia's party secretary, Eduard Shevardnadze, to serve as foreign minister. Shevardnadze knew nothing about foreign affairs but had enjoyed Gorbachev's trust since the 1970s. By 1987, Gorbachev and Shevardnadze, helped by a handful of loyal assistants, were monopolizing the making of foreign policy.[60]

It was in foreign policy discussions that Gorbachev first mentioned the need for "*novoe myshlenie*" (new thinking). Like "perestroika," it was a euphemism with an extremely broad interpretative range. Most of Gorbachev's colleagues and the party elites, who had become cynical during the decades of vacuous ideological campaigns, assumed it was mere rhetoric, at best an attractive propaganda slogan.[61] They were wrong. The general secretary regarded foreign policy not just as a tool to win breathing space for domestic reforms but as a vehicle for change. He wanted to open the Soviet Union to the outside world and thus overcome Stalin's legacy of xenophobia and isolation. The old ideological dogmas had to be questioned and, if need be, dismantled. Soon the "new thinking" became a synonym for a fundamental ideological reassessment.

At first, Gorbachev's "new thinking" was the product of voracious reading, including books by Western socialist politicians and thinkers, which had been translated and published in limited editions for the party leadership. He also enjoyed frank discussions with trusted subordinates at private gatherings. His inner circle for such discussions included his wife, Raisa, Alexander Yakovlev, Valery Boldin, Yevgeni Primakov, and Eduard Shevardnadze. Raisa was the crucial participant of this private circle. By contrast to other Politburo spouses, who accepted the roles of housewives and had no ambitions, Raisa was a self-styled "woman of the sixties." A graduate of Moscow State University of 1955 vintage like Gorbachev, she was trained as a sociologist, had a perfectionist's passion for detail and systematization, and actively participated in cultural and intellectual events. When Gorbachev joined the Party Secretariat in 1978 and the couple moved from Stavropol to Moscow, Raisa "immediately plunged into the world of academic discussions, symposia, and conferences." She also plugged into the network of the graduates of Moscow State University and the Institute of Philosophy she had known since the period from 1950 to 1955. Every night, often after the Politburo sessions and other important meetings, Gorbachev took his wife out for a walk, on which they discussed the day's events and often came up with new ideas. "He was unable to make decisions without her advice," a senior Soviet official later told Jack Matlock.[62]

Yakovlev was another key participant in the inner group and its most intellectually ambitious member. He had had an early career as a party ideologist, was an exchange student at Columbia University in 1958, and later became the acting head of the Central Committee Department of Ideology and Propaganda. He organized, among others, virulent anti-American campaigns in the media. At the same time, he resisted the growing neo-Stalinist and conservative nationalist trend among the apparatchiks. As the result of a bureaucratic intrigue in 1971, Yakovlev was demoted and sent to Canada as ambassador. There, in external "exile," he secretly refashioned himself as a reform-minded social democrat. At the end of 1985, he proposed to Gorbachev far-reaching political reforms, aiming at the abolishment of the one-party system. Ultimately, as he recalled, the arguments revolved around the need to reject the Leninist-Stalinist precept of a class-divided world, to grasp "the fact that we live in an interdependent, contra-dictory, but ultimately integral world." The general secretary was not yet ready for radical steps, but he listened to Yakovlev attentively.[63]

Gorbachev acquired an immediate and ardent following among the small group of "enlightened" apparatchiks, those who had started their careers in the 1950s and early 1960s and who called themselves "the children of the Twentieth Party Congress." This vibrant group consisted of people who had worked in Andropov's and Brezhnev's close circle as speechwriters, the directors of aca-demic think tanks, and the international relations experts from the International Department of the Central Committee.[64] Some had worked as Brezhnev's speech-writers and "enlightened" advisers. But these well-informed people had grown disillusioned and cynical during the late Brezhnev years. They were sick of stag-nation and corruption and still hoped to resume the policies of de-Stalinization and the cultural Thaw abrogated in the late 1960s. They also had been among the earliest and most consistent supporters of détente with the West. The head of the Institute of U.S. and Canada Studies, Georgy Arbatov, immediately sent Gor-bachev a list of innovative proposals aimed at breaking Soviet international isola-tion: immediate withdrawal from Afghanistan; unilateral reductions of Soviet forces in Europe and on the border with China; and even a return to Japan of the Kurile Islands annexed in 1945.[65]

Gorbachev, skeptical of the academician's quick fixes, dispatched the memos to the archive. At the same time, in January 1986, he invited another "enlight-ened" apparatchik and talented speechwriter, Anatoly Chernyaev, to become a personal foreign policy assistant. Chernyaev shared all the ideas proposed by Arbatov and also was in favor of free emigration and the release of political prisoners. In October 1985, the general secretary granted the intellectual elites the long-lost privilege of meeting with foreigners without asking for permission. It was a momentous break with the xenophobic regime that had been in place since it was established by Stalin in the 1930s.[66] The general secretary already began to position himself as an "enlightened" ruler surrounded by intellectuals and freethinkers.

The rejection of the Stalinist bipolar worldview became the heart of Gor-bachev's "new thinking." The logical conclusion from this would be the renun-ciation of global power games and recognition that the security of the Soviet Union was inseparable from, and in part compatible with, the security interests of other countries, including the United States. Gorbachev felt that curbing the nuclear arms race was especially urgent. He felt uneasy about military power, especially nuclear arms. The roots of this attitude went back to his formative experience. Gorbachev's birthplace, the land of the Kuban Cossacks, had suffered terribly from revolutionary violence, fratricidal civil war, and Stalin's collectivization. Then the Nazi invasion came. Gorbachev belonged, in his own words, to the generation of war children. "The war touched us with its flame and made an impact on our characters and our entire worldview."[67] As a graduate of Moscow State University's Law Department, he was exempted from military service and exposed to views that clashed with official militarist propaganda.

In contrast to Stalin, Khrushchev, and Brezhnev, who supervised the military-industrial complex and understood the nuts and bolts of Soviet military power, Gorbachev came into contact with nuclear issues only when he became the general secretary of the CPSU.[68] According to the tradition established by Stalin and Khrushchev, the leader of the party was also the head of the Defense Council. Oleg Baklanov, who was the head of the Soviet atomic and missile complexes, later recalled that as late as 1987 Gorbachev demonstrated a lack of interest in or knowledge of missile technology.[69] In an interview with a Russian nuclear physicist, Gorbachev admitted a moral revulsion when he realized his personal responsibility for the accumulation and possible use of nuclear weapons. He also admitted that he was familiar with the report on "nuclear winter," which predicted that the fallout from a massive use of nuclear weapons would destroy life on the planet. When Gorbachev participated in a secret strategic game simulating the Soviet response to a nuclear attack, he was asked to give a command for the retaliation strike. He allegedly refused to press the nuclear button, "even for training purposes."[70]

Gorbachev and the "new thinkers" faced the enormous reality of the U.S.-Soviet confrontation, both inside the Soviet apparatus and across the ocean. Secretary of Defense Caspar Weinberger, CIA director William Casey, and White House staff were determined to win in a crusade against Soviet Communism.[71] Reagan was impatient to meet with the new Soviet leader and, with the help of Shultz and McFarlane's National Security Council staff, prepared himself for negotiations. Unfortunately, Gorbachev and his immediate entourage knew nothing of Reagan's good intentions.[72]

Reagan's rhetoric on the third world irritated "new thinkers." Washington insisted on unilateral Soviet military withdrawal from Afghanistan, Angola, Ethiopia, and other troubled areas, while blocking any discussion of American interference in Central America. The Soviets also assumed, quite correctly, that senior members of the Reagan administration wanted to "bleed" Soviet troops in Afghanistan rather than facilitate their withdrawal. Therefore, Gorbachev was determined to avoid any international actions that could be interpreted as Soviet retreat or concession. Despite the numerous letters from soldiers' mothers and the appeals of his intellectual advisers, the Soviet leader decided against immediate withdrawal of Soviet troops from Afghanistan. He jotted down on his working pad in the spring of 1985: "The conflict should be resolved in stages." He also wrote: "One thing is crucial: complete surrender of positions is unacceptable." In 1985 and 1986, the Soviet armed forces greatly intensified military operations against the Islamic fundamentalists; the inept Karmal was replaced with a stronger figure, the head of the Afghan security services, Muhammad Najibullah. The delay of Soviet withdrawal from Afghanistan, along with the misguided anti-alcoholism campaign and the absence of economic reforms, caused problems for Gorbachev's administration later on.[73]

The arena in which Gorbachev moved with the greatest speed was arms control. By the summer of 1985 he was corresponding with Ronald Reagan on how to reduce the threat of nuclear war and curb the nuclear arms race. Gorbachev dropped the condition, imposed since 1977, that any meeting between the superpower leaders must be linked to the signing of significant agreements. Most of Reagan's advisers were against the idea of a summit with the young and energetic Soviet leader, but the president had waited since 1983 for a personal and frank exchange of opinions, and he agreed to meet Gorbachev in Geneva in November 1985. In preparation for this first summit, the leaders restored the diplomatic back channel between Washington and Moscow and conducted a high-volume correspondence through it. Rejecting Reagan's broader framework for talks on Afghanistan and human rights, Gorbachev suggested focusing on the reduction of nuclear weapons. He warned Reagan that the Soviet Union would not tolerate the SDI program. Although the SDI did not present an immediate danger to Soviet security interests, it could eventually open a new, dangerous, and costly round of the U.S.-Soviet arms race. "The program of 'star wars [SDI],'" he opined, "already seriously undermines stability. We urgently advise you to wind down this sharply destabilizing and dangerous program." On the eve of the Geneva summit, Gorbachev wrote to Reagan that "aversion of nuclear war, removal of military threat is our mutual and dominant interest." He pushed the American president to agree to the "non-militarization of space." In support of Gorbachev's rhetoric, in August 1985 the Soviet Union announced unilaterally a moratorium on nuclear tests.[74]

Gorbachev's foreign policy agenda still looked strikingly similar to Brezhnev's agenda from the early 1970s. The pre-summit instructions approved by the Politburo also reflected it; they reiterated the détente clichés, while reaffirming Soviet geopolitical ambitions in the third world. The experts who drafted the pre-summit instructions for the Politburo correctly predicted that there would be no agreement on the third world conflicts. Also, they warned, "Reagan certainly would not agree to ban SDI."[75]

Soviet diplomats and the military carefully watched Gorbachev's performance in Geneva and were satisfied. The Soviet leader used his charm but was a tough negotiator. As expected, the leaders agreed on only one thing—"a nuclear war could not be won and must never be fought." It was a common opinion in Moscow that one could hardly achieve more with the current U.S. administration. Before the Politburo and party elites, Gorbachev criticized Reagan's "crude primitivism, caveman views and intellectual impotence." He continued to believe that the American president was a pawn of the military-industrial complex and pledged to strengthen Soviet defenses. Privately, however, the general secretary was shocked to find that Reagan genuinely believed in what he said. And he was "almost embarrassed" by his failure to convince Reagan to abandon SDI. The Soviet leader tried to guess Reagan's motives and failed to understand them. He recalls musing after the summit: Was this military program a fantasy, a means of pressing the USSR into diplomatic concessions? Or was it an "awkward attempt to lull us into complacency," while preparing the first strike?[76]

In the aftermath of Geneva, the Soviet leader feverishly searched for new ideas and approaches that could help break the vicious circle of the U.S.-Soviet rivalry. Unlike Brezhnev, who under similar circumstances waited for American initiatives, Gorbachev decided to go on a "peace offensive" and engage the U.S. president on the issue of nuclear disarmament. On New Year's Eve 1985, he met with Soviet arms negotiators and demanded fresh ideas and approaches. On the basis of their ideas and proposals, Gorbachev announced a plan of general and complete nuclear disarmament by the year 2000. Dismissed by the Reagan administration as a propaganda ploy, this plan reflected the profound allegiance of Gorbachev to the idea of nuclear disarmament. The sweeping and quasi-utopian nature of the initiative revealed again Gorbachev's optimistic nature and belief in big ideas. Anatoly Chernyaev recalls that Gorbachev and his entourage came to believe that "one can remove a war threat by focusing only on the issue of disarmament."[77]

Gorbachev used these conversations to prepare for the Party Congress to be held in February and March 1986, a ceremonial, but nevertheless vital moment in domestic politics. He retreated to a Black Sea resort where, together with Yakovlev and Boldin, he studied the proposals from academic think tanks and discussed the draft of the political report to the Party Congress. His predecessors could never square the circle between their desire for détente and their bipolar ideological vision of the world. Gorbachev replaced the formula of the "two camps," socialist and imperialist, with the idea of the world's integrity and interdependence. This theoretical innovation, he recalled later, "had a huge impact on our own policy and the policy of the rest of the world." The draft stated that "the policy of total, military confrontation has no future," and that the "arms race, as well as a nuclear war, cannot be won," and that "the task of building security appears as a political task, and it can be resolved only by political means."[78] This episode reveals Gorbachev's strong inclination toward new and broad theoretical concepts, rather than the nuts and bolts of foreign policy.

When Gorbachev presented his draft for his colleagues' discussion, many of them insisted on adding to it the old ideological postulates. A veteran head of the Central Committee's International Department, Boris Ponomarev, privately grumbled: "What is this 'new thinking' about? Let the Americans change their thinking instead. What are you trying to do to our foreign policy? Are you against force, which is the only language that imperialism understands?"[79] The final version of Gorbachev's report was a compromise between new ideas and the old language of "proletarian internationalism." Still, as Robert English concludes, the report removed the ideological tenet that peaceful coexistence is another form of class struggle, and that nuclear war, if it occurs, would lead to socialism's triumph. Stalin's doctrine of "two camps," an integral part of the Soviet revolutionary-imperial paradigm since 1947, was no more.[80]

The intellectual component of the Soviet national security establishment, particularly consultants and the leaders of think tanks, regarded the disarmament initiative and Gorbachev's Congress report as a turning point. Raymond Garthoff, a long-time observer of the Soviets, happened to be in Moscow at the time and was surprised when his old contacts admitted that U.S. security interests were legitimate and could be, in principle, reconciled with Soviet interests.[81] Immediately after the Party Congress, the general secretary warned his inner circle of advisers not to regard Soviet initiatives merely as a means to score propaganda points. "We really seek détente and disarmament. Dishonest game is no longer possible today. It is impossible to cheat anybody anyway." In the same conversation, Gorbachev stressed that the "new thinking" made it imperative for the Soviet Union to recognize U.S. national interests and seek a compromise with the other superpower and its allies.[82]

Washington, however, did not trust Soviet words. The Reagan administration wanted to see signs of real change in Soviet behavior in Afghanistan and on human rights, the most important criteria for the president's assessment of Soviet intentions. The Americans ignored the Soviet nuclear moratorium and announced a big series of nuclear tests. The CIA continued to escalate the war against the Soviet Union in Afghanistan and waged intelligence warfare against the KGB. In March 1986, two American warships carried out a highly provocative maneuver in Soviet territorial waters six miles off the coast of the Crimea, where

Gorbachev was vacationing at the time. Operations of the same nature were carried out off the coast of Libya, an ally of the USSR, leading to a confrontation and U.S. air strikes on this country.[83] Above all, many in Reagan's entourage regarded SDI as a stone that could kill three or more birds: it could provide a moral basis for the costly military buildup, boost the domestic economy, and scare the Soviets into retreat on all fronts.[84]

Gorbachev reacted harshly. He ordered his speechwriters to "give the US a substantial kick in the shin." Before the Politburo he was rude: "We cannot cook anything with this gang." For a moment he even mentioned again freezing high-level contacts with the U.S. administration.[85] A closer study of Soviet internal discussions, however, reveals that Gorbachev's harsh rhetoric was just that: rhetoric. He rejected the tit-for-tat approach and continued to insist on rapprochement with the United States and the rest of the world. "We are in a diplomatic offensive, because we have been proposing realistic approaches to the world, and acknowledge US interests, but not their hegemonic demands." A month earlier, he had said to his advisers that even if the Americans and the Western Europeans continued to waltz around the issue of disarmament, the Soviet Union should move ahead and continue "the Geneva process" in its own interests.[86] Thus, concepts of "new thinking" motivated Gorbachev to build détente, independently or even *against* the wishes of the American side. It is also noteworthy that Gorbachev saw his new multilateralist worldview as "realistic."

The Soviet leader, however, could not get SDI off his mind.[87] Gorbachev spent considerable time inspecting research and development laboratories and discussing possible "countermeasures" to SDI with leading scientists. At Gorbachev's request, new head of the Council of Ministers Nikolai Ryzhkov reviewed the three-year-old conclusions of the expert commission chaired by Evgeny Velikhov in order to find an "asymmetrical response" to SDI. Soviet experts concluded that such a response would cost ten times less than a full-scale program.[88] Did the general secretary recognize the contradiction between his new vision of security and his obsession with Reagan's "star wars"? Sometimes he came close to that. In late March 1986, Gorbachev began to think aloud in his narrow circle of advisers about "the dangerous program" of SDI: "Maybe we should just stop being afraid of the SDI! [The Reagan administration] indeed expects that the USSR is afraid of SDI in the moral, economic, political, and military sense. That is why they are putting pressure on us—to exhaust us. But for us this is a problem not of fear, but of responsibility, because the consequences would be unpredictable."[89]

Gorbachev needed more help in overcoming his inner contradictory assumptions. Two dramatic events provided this help.

On April 26, 1986, at 1:30 A.M., a huge explosion destroyed the fourth block of the Chernobyl nuclear reactor. The explosion caused the second-worst manmade nuclear catastrophe, after the bombing of Hiroshima and Nagasaki. This sudden disaster in Ukraine created a radically new perspective on security affairs for Gorbachev and the entire Soviet leadership. At first, a majority of the Soviet leadership and the Soviet military-industrial complex instinctively chose to down-play and cover up the incident, in essence bluffing in the face of the whole world, as it had following the KAL-007 tragedy. Just as then, the bluff was called, and the international uproar over the nuclear fallout, resulting from the accident, pene-trated through radio broadcasting to Soviet society. Panic spread in waves, and from Ukraine it soon reached Moscow. Soviet authorities, after days of delay, evacuated 100,000 people from the irradiated area. A decade later, it became known that the radiation spread after the Chernobyl accident killed 8,000 men and women. It affected the health and well-being of 435,000 people, and the list is not yet finished.[90]

The Chernobyl catastrophe consumed the Politburo's energies for three months. It shattered ossified bureaucratic structures and the old militarized mentality to the core.[91] Gorbachev was humiliated by the international scandal and indignant at the rigidity of bureaucratic structures, and he chose to scapegoat the military-industrial complex. The most secret and impenetrable part of the Soviet system, its nuclear program, became the object of blistering criticism, its heroic and romantic image tarnished beyond repair. Military scientists and the military command were shaken, too. It was the first time that the Soviet armed forces participated in a rescue and decontamination operation on such a large scale. To the head of the General Staff, Marshal Sergei Akhromeyev, Chernobyl was remi-niscent of the Great Patriotic War. But, instead of lessons of vigilance and military buildup, the catastrophe revealed that the military doctrine of "victory" in nuclear war was a hollow hulk. And it dawned on the military command what a disaster it would be to have even limited nuclear warfare in a Europe studded with atomic reactors. Akhromeyev recalled that after Chernobyl "a nuclear danger for our people ceased to be abstraction. It became a palpable reality."[92]

Chernobyl's effect on the Soviet political leadership was greater than any other single event since the Cuban missile crisis. "We learned what nuclear war can be," Gorbachev said to the Politburo. Certainly, the catastrophe was much more responsible for the drastic changes in Soviet official mentality than the previous years of American pressure and military buildup. The catastrophe demanded the end of xenophobia and obsessive secrecy and a reappraisal of security policies in the nuclear age. Within a year after this accident, Soviet foreign policy, positions on nuclear arms control, the approach to negotiations with the United States, and military doctrine would drastically change. Chernobyl also forced the Politburo to introduce glasnost, the practice of public discussion of contentious issues that the country had not known since the 1920s. Several weeks after the disaster, Gorbachev said to his colleagues: "Our work is now transparent to the whole people, to the whole world. *There are no interests* that could force us to hide the truth."[93]

Gorbachev suggested to his Politburo colleagues that the Soviet Union should come up with better and bolder disarmament initiatives to stop the arms race. In late May 1986, the general secretary made an unprecedented appearance in the Foreign Ministry and addressed a large group of diplomats. The Reagan administration, Gorbachev told them, was trying to box in the Soviet Union in an exhausting arms race. "Soviet foreign policy," he concluded, "must alleviate the burden" of military expenditures, must "do anything in its capabilities to loosen the vise of defense expenditures." Diplomats were told to get rid of the mentality of bureaucrats without individual voice and initiative, the mentality that had prevailed during the tenures of Molotov and Gromyko. Gorbachev criticized the old Soviet diplomacy for "senseless stubbornness." Instead of digging Cold War trenches and waiting for a more conciliatory leadership in Washington, Soviet diplomacy had to engage the Reagan administration, envelop it with peace initiatives, and influence it via its own Western European allies.[94]

The first tangible result of the post-Chernobyl foreign policy was a breakthrough on conventional arms control and verification in Stockholm. These talks had lasted for years, as the Soviet side refused to accept on-site inspections proposed by the Americans. The General Staff was horrified at the prospect of NATO inspections, which might reveal the many Potemkin villages in the armed forces. At the Politburo, Akhromeyev challenged the top Soviet negotiator in Stockholm, casting doubt on his "Soviet patriotism." After Chernobyl, however, secrecy no longer won the day. Instead, at Politburo instructions, Akhromeyev himself had to go to Stockholm to announce Soviet acceptance of on-site inspections. The marshal, deeply shaken by Chernobyl, obeyed and after a few weeks the treaty was signed.[95]

By that time, the general secretary had undertaken a private study of international relations that included the works of the Palme Commission and Western social democrats on disarmament and "common security." He also read the Russell-Einstein Manifesto of 1955 and the works of the Pugwash Movement of scientists against nuclear war.[96] Armed with new ideas, Gorbachev next appealed to the socialist-leaning U.S. allies, arguing for a new security philosophy. President of France François Mitterrand, Prime Minister of Spain Felipe Gonzalez, and Prime Minister of Canada Pierre Elliot Trudeau expressed sympathies with the "new thinking" and were very critical of the U.S. leadership. At a meeting with the French president in July 1986, the Soviet leader attacked Reagan and "the forces and groupings that brought him to power" for promoting SDI and failing to understand the new security needs of humanity. Mitterrand admitted that "the military-industrial complex might be applying strong pressure on the US administration." At the same time, he added, "one should keep in mind that Reagan, for all the influence of his own milieu, is not without common sense and intuition." He appealed to Gorbachev not to view the political situation in the United States as something set in stone: "The situation may change." He also catered to Gorbachev's genuine security concerns, posing as a middleman between the Soviet Union and the Americans.[97]

British conservative prime minister Margaret Thatcher played the role of an informal ambassador between Gorbachev and Reagan. There was a remarkable personal affinity between Thatcher and Gorbachev, despite the ideological chasm that separated them. From the start, Thatcher fully grasped the double-sided idea of reform and disarmament promoted by Gorbachev but categorically rejected the idea of a nuclear-free world as a dangerous romantic utopia. In retrospect, Thatcher was right, as the process of disarmament followed her vision more closely. But, as Chernyaev commented, "if Gorbachev had not been so pushy, and so implacable in his desire to prove to all that nuclear weapons are an absolute evil and one cannot build world politics on it, then the process [of détente] would never have begun at all."[98]

Another informal middleman between the Kremlin and the White House was retired U.S. president Richard Nixon. Nixon still enjoyed a good standing among Soviet leaders as the architect of détente in the 1970s. In July 1986, he told Gorbachev: "You are right—there are people in the [Reagan] administration that do not want agreements with the Soviet Union. It seems to them that if they can isolate the Soviet Union diplomatically, apply economic pressure on it, achieve military superiority then the Soviet order would collapse. Of course, this is not going to happen. During many years Reagan, as you know, was considered a part of the grouping that shared these views. However, today he is not one of them. I learned from conversations with him that the meeting with you had a slow, but undeniable impact on the evolution of his thoughts."[99]

These conversations made Gorbachev more impatient to put his "new thinking" to work. Another impulse came from bad economic and financial news. Perestroika was not going well; slogans of domestic reforms contrasted sharply with a sluggish economy and continued social stagnation. One month after the accident, the cost of Chernobyl had already come to three billion rubles. The unforeseen expenses affected Politburo discussions of the financial burden that the continuation of the strategic arms race with the West would entail. Perhaps for the first time since the debates during the Polish crisis, it became poignantly clear that the Soviet Union was seriously overcommitted financially. In July 1986, Gorbachev admitted that the Soviet budget had lost nine billion rubles, due to the rapid drop in oil prices. The Soviets also expected a trade deficit. And the anti-alcohol campaign had reduced state revenues by 15 billion rubles.[100] In domestic affairs, the general secretary, with the help of Ligachev in the Party Secretariat, radically repopulated the bureaucratic and party cadres, hoping to rejuvenate the Soviet party-administrative system.[101] But Gorbachev was not yet ready for drastic measures, such as fixing prices and fighting hidden inflation. And he did not know how to transform the socialist economy. He hoped to alleviate the economic situation by reducing international tensions, thus obtaining the "peace dividends"—lower military expenditures and Western credits.

U.S.-Soviet relations were exacerbated by what amounted to a virtual espionage war, and this war caused real casualties. In Moscow, the KGB obtained from the CIA's Aldrich Ames complete information on American spies in the Soviet Union. In 1986, with Gorbachev's consent, they were arrested; some of them were tried and sentenced to death. At the same time in the United States, long-time Soviet moles in the FBI and the National Security Agency were found out and arrested. The nasty warfare continued to escalate in late August, when the FBI arrested a KGB agent, Gennady Zakharov, working under cover at the UN Secretariat. In retaliation, the KGB framed and arrested U.S. News and World Report correspondent Nicholas Daniloff.[102] A new wave of anti-Soviet feelings in the American mass media, vigorously promoted by the Reagan administration, seemed to return U.S.-Soviet relations to the 1983 low.

Gorbachev was impatient for a dramatic breakthrough. In early September, in the midst of the Zakharov-Daniloff controversy, he wrote a letter to Reagan, proposing that, instead of waiting for the next regular summit in Washington, they have a quick one-on-one meeting, "let us say in Iceland or in London." In an attempt to separate Reagan from his right-wing entourage, Gorbachev suggested "a strictly confidential, private and frank discussion (possibly with only our foreign ministers present)." The purpose of the meeting would be "to draft agreements on two or three very specific questions," to ensure they would be ready for signing at the next summit.[103]

Later, Margaret Thatcher and Reagan's advisers claimed that Gorbachev had lured Reagan into a trap. Indeed, Gorbachev was prepared not only to discuss "two or three very specific questions" but also to present a revolutionary agreement on nuclear arms reductions. But the Soviet leader was not trying to ambush Reagan. As part of summit preparations, he instructed the General Staff to abandon the offensive strategy of reaching the English Channel in several days and to work out a new military doctrine based on "strategic sufficiency" and defensive posture.[104] He also told the military that he would like to accept Reagan's proposal on elimination of all Soviet and U.S. medium-range missiles in Europe ("zero option"). Finally, he suggested that the Soviet negotiating package include acceptance of 50 percent cuts on the "heavy" ICBMs, the backbone of the Soviet strategic arsenal.[105] As a result of all this, the meeting in Reykjavik, Iceland, turned out to be the most dramatic diplomatic event in the concluding years of the Cold War.

Soviet proposals were based on the ideas of "strategic sufficiency," which had long circulated in Moscow's academic institutes and among arms control negotiators. These ideas held that it was not vital to maintain a numeric parity in strategic armaments. Of course, nobody except Gorbachev dared to propose these ideas openly, fearing cries of treason from the Ministry of Defense and the General Staff. Even Gorbachev had to explain his "new thinking" as a pragmatic necessity. He argued at the Politburo in early October 1986 that the USSR could not afford to react to the Reagan challenge in traditional tit-for-tat fashion: "We will be pulled into an arms race that is beyond our capabilities, and we will lose it, because we are at the limit of our capabilities. Moreover, we can expect that Japan and the FRG could very soon add their economic potential to the American one. If the new round begins, the pressure on our economy will be unbelievable."[106]

SDI again proved to be a stumbling bloc for Gorbachev's "new thinking." British political scientist Archie Brown believes that for Gorbachev at that moment SDI was not so much a security concern as an excuse to argue "for the kind of policy innovation which would break the deadlock and end the vicious spiral of arms race."[107] The evidence speaks to the contrary: Reagan's program was indeed a real concern for the Soviet leader. He still could not understand if Reagan's intentions were aggressive or not. As with the Geneva summit, Politburo instructions for the Reykjavik meeting were a compromise between Gorbachev's new ideological approaches and his traditional security fears. While the military leadership would have done the same, it was Gorbachev who firmly linked any agreement on cuts of strategic armaments to a single condition: Reagan had to bury the idea of SDI and affirm American adherence to the 1972 ABM treaty. Speaking to a small group of "new thinkers" during the preparations for Reykjavik, Gorbachev argued that it was necessary to dislodge Reagan from his position on SDI. "If it fails, then we will be able to say: This is what we were ready for!"[108]

The Reykjavik summit began with an amiable one-on-one conversation between the two leaders.[109] The president began by laying out the U.S. four-point
agenda, linking the progress in disarmament to changes in Soviet behavior in the
third world and observance of human rights at home. Gorbachev assured Reagan
that he would support "ultimate liquidation of nuclear weapons" on the principles of "equal security." He also said he would go "as far on the matter of
verification as would be necessary" to remove U.S. doubts. At the same time, the
Soviet leader clearly linked a date for a Washington summit to the reaching of an
agreement on arms reductions—an echo of the similar Soviet linkage during the
Carter administration.[110]

What went on between the two leaders seemed almost surreal to other participants, veterans of the decades of standoff. Reagan and Gorbachev seemed to have
resolved more disarmament issues than all their predecessors had done. In the
view of American experts, Gorbachev made more concessions than they had
received from the Soviet Union in twenty-five years. Secretary of State George
Schultz reacted to this curtly: "Fine, let him keep making them. His proposals are
the result of five years of pressure from us."[111] Other more ideologically driven
members of the administration were alarmed. Reagan saw an opportunity to
accomplish what he viewed as his mission—to prevent the nuclear Armageddon.
Without bothering to consult the Pentagon or American allies, he laid out on the
table, first, the idea of complete elimination of nuclear ballistic missiles by the
year 1996, and then the elimination of all nuclear weapons. Gorbachev agreed,
but insisted on excluding any plans to test components of missile defense in
space. Reagan, however, was convinced by his friend Caspar Weinberger that
Congress would "kill" SDI if it was limited to laboratories. He asked Gorbachev
for "a personal favor" to allow testing in space. A concession on SDI, he told the
general secretary, would have a "huge influence on our future relations." Gorbachev, however, stuck to his guns: complete renunciation of SDI, including the
interim period of laboratory testing, or nothing.[112] The summit collapsed, and
the visibly shaken general secretary and the U.S. president had to face the consequences of their failure at home. As is clear today, ten or more years of laboratory
testing would not have "killed" or "created" the antimissile shield, as Reagan
and Gorbachev feared. Gorbachev was not ready for elimination of all Soviet
nuclear weapons, not to mention Soviet ballistic missiles.[113]

Gorbachev left for Moscow complaining that the Americans "did not abandon the quest for superiority" and just came to Reykjavik came to pocket his
concessions—essentially true as far as most of the U.S. delegation was concerned. To the Politburo, Gorbachev said that Reagan "is unable to handle his
gang" and "appears to be a liar."[114] Just a few years later, however, the Soviet

leader described the Reykjavik effect as an epiphany, similar to the shock of Chernobyl. It may be that, again, traditional fears battled in the soul of the general secretary with concepts of "new thinking." Inwardly, he was surprised to discover that Reagan's belief in nuclear disarmament seemed to be genuine. Other Soviet participants in the summit felt the same. Anatoly Dobrynin recalled later that "Reagan's vision of nuclear apocalypse and his deeply rooted but almost hidden conviction that nuclear weapons should ultimately be abolished, would prove more powerful than his visceral anti-Communism."[115] The image of Reagan as enemy in the Soviet foreign policy establishment shaped by the earlier confrontation began to change, but this happened slowly, in fits and starts.

"NEW THINKING" AND THE LOOMING CRISIS

The failure of the Reykjavik summit did not diminish Gorbachev's appetite for "new thinking" in global affairs. On the contrary, he soon went to Kyrgyzstan to discuss the nuclear threat and political responses to it on a beautiful mountain lake with the world's intellectual elite: writers, sociologists, economists, ecologists, futurologists. Excited by the quality of the audience, Gorbachev spoke publicly for the first time about the priority of "human interests over class interests." Gorbachev's theoretical innovations evoked puzzlement from Ligachev and party propagandists. "A bomb exploded in the camp of orthodox thinkers!" rejoiced Gorbachev in his memoirs. By spring 1987, Gorbachev's ideological transformation made him feel alienated from his most loyal and effective supporters, Ligachev and Ryzhkov. They could no longer see eye to eye with him ideologically.[116] The post-Reykjavik months highlighted the first stage of disagreement between Gorbachev and his Politburo colleagues, who had viewed his "new thinking" as mere rhetorical cover for a pragmatic policy of temporary retreat and retrenchment of Soviet power. From changing people in key command positions to achieve economic "acceleration," Gorbachev began to shift to changing the guiding ideology of the Soviet Union.

The anti-Soviet "crusaders" in the Reagan administration meanwhile continued to complicate Gorbachev's reformist plans. On December 1, the administration announced that the United States would not observe the limitations on its strategic forces imposed by SALT-2. The provocative behavior of the U.S. leadership, for the second time after the second summit, presented the Politburo with a choice: to give up on Reagan and wait for future opportunities or continue the peace offensive with more vigor and strength. At the Politburo, Gromyko could not help uttering a skeptical remark about Gorbachev's fixation on disarmament: "If we destroy nuclear weapons that we had been building for twenty five years, what would then happen? Will we depend on good faith of the Americans? Where is a guarantee that they will not surpass us in the space race? No, further concessions will not get us American agreement. The United States will not agree to an equal agreement."[117]

In addition to Gromyko, Ligachev and KGB chairman Viktor Chebrikov also voiced concern about the Reagan administration's "crusade" against the Soviet Union. Gorbachev, however, was already determined to pursue his new policies no matter what. He said that playing the tit-for-tat game with the Reagan administration would be "a nice present to these types who disrupt treaties and spit on public opinion. They would say: the Soviets had just waited for such a moment." The Politburo decided to exert pressure on the Reagan administration through moderate members of the U.S. Congress, U.S. allies, and the American public.[118]

Just about this time, the Soviet top brass were told to relinquish their longtime goals of achieving superiority over the enemy and agree to deep unilateral cuts in the Soviet strategic stockpile. Soon after Reykjavik, Sergei Akhromeyev presented the draft of the new military doctrine at the Academy of the General Staff, the elite senior military school. The document stated the impossibility of victory in a future war (since it would be nuclear) and proposed that the Soviet military should no longer strive for parity with the Americans. The document threw the military audience into a state of profound shock. There were muffled cries of treason.[119] These cries reached Gorbachev's ears, and a sharp exchange took place at the meeting on December 1 between Gorbachev and Marshal Akhromeyev, who had just resigned from the General Staff only to be appointed a military assistant to the general secretary.

GORBACHEV: We have not made any real concessions. However, our generals try to scare us, they are afraid to be left with nothing to do. I know there is a lot of hissing in their midst—what kind of leadership is this that is disarming the country?

VITALY VOROTNIKOV (POLITBURO MEMBER): People do think so!

GORBACHEV: Ogarkov is very upset. He demands more and more. At a time when 25 million people here live below the officially proclaimed minimal living standard.

AKHROMEYEV: Generals are good people. Yes, they are good party members. However, if a general believes he cares about the country more than the Politburo does, we should sort it out with him.

GORBACHEV: If we fail to struggle for peace, people will not support us. And if we let down our defense, people will not support us either. They are robust chauvinists.[120]

Gorbachev used his rhetorical skills to overcome the resistance from the military and obtain what he wanted. On New Year's Eve, acting as commander in chief and head of the Defense Council, he approved the new military doctrine. This was a momentous change—but it also marked the end of the initial enthusiasm that the military had felt about Gorbachev and his reformist course.

Gorbachev's "new thinking" continued to evolve, even in the absence of any signs of détente with the United States, in marked contrast to Brezhnev's détente politics. But a surprising consensus, at least in appearance, prevailed in the Politburo. Nobody among the conservatives or the military was willing to challenge the general secretary. Even the General Staff, for all its dismay at the new disarmament proposals and military doctrine, never dared to oppose Gorbachev's policies at the Politburo. Also, contrary to the impression that Gorbachev's memoirs may convey, the direction of his evolution was still unclear to conservative modernizers and "new thinkers" in the party, as well as to state elites. The general secretary was bafflingly inconsistent in his rhetoric and, in particular, in his actions. He seemed to thrive on ambiguity and enjoyed the role of moderator, listening with equal attention to the opposite opinions, mediating in discussions, papering over rifts, and nipping confrontation in the bud. The most formidable of the conservative strongholds, the KGB, still believed in early 1987 that Gorbachev was implementing Andropov's program of controlled conservative modernization and imperial retrenchment. It did not occur to the KGB leadership that Gorbachev intended to dismantle the entire regime of police repression that had survived de-Stalinization and become entrenched during the Brezhnev-Andropov years. Vladimir Kryuchkov, head of the KGB branch for foreign intelligence, recalled that he had never doubted Gorbachev's devotion to the Soviet system and "socialism" and was horrified later by the extent of his "betrayal."[121]

Gorbachev was careful not to challenge the basics of official ideology openly. On the contrary, his ideological vigor and frequent public pledges "to live up to the potential of socialism" confused the sophisticated Moscow elites who had long regarded Communist ideology to be a cadaver. His misguided economic gambits and the anti-alcohol campaign indicated to many outside and inside the Soviet Union that he just wanted to give new vigor to the old system. Yakovlev complained privately that the Soviet leader remained a captive of ideological, class-based mythology. "During the first three years of perestroika," Chernyaev admits, the Soviet leader "thought about improvement of the society in Marxist-Leninist categories. Gorbachev was convinced that had Lenin lived ten years longer, there would have been a fine socialism in the USSR." The general secretary worshipped the founder of Bolshevism; he kept Lenin's works on his desk and reread them in the search for clues and inspiration.[122]

Thus the time of open ideological and political divides over Gorbachev's course still lay ahead. On some foreign policy issues, the dividing line was not so much ideological principles as the strategies of Soviet retrenchment. This revealed itself most strikingly in Politburo discussions of the hopeless situation in Afghanistan. Assisted by CIA funds, the Pakistani regime of General Zia-ul Haq armed and trained Islamic fundamentalists who waged unrelenting war against the Soviet troops and the pro-Soviet Afghan regime. The Soviets could not defeat the unconventional fundamentalist formations operating from Pakistani territory.[123] Gorbachev, along with the rest of the Politburo, was still against the immediate withdrawal of troops. He argued that the Soviets should set up a friendly moderate Islamic regime in Afghanistan and thus avoid a situation in which the United States or the fundamentalist forces would control this country. By 1987, it became clear that this was a chimerical idea, primarily due to the alliance between the United States, Pakistan, and the fundamentalist Muslim forces. Minister of Defense Sergei Sokolov, Marshal Akhromeyev, and the commander of Soviet troops in Afghanistan, General Valentin Varennikov, advocated immediate withdrawal of Soviet troops. Deputy Foreign Minister Georgy Kornienko supported them. Ironically, even Gromyko, the last living original proponent of the invasion of Afghanistan, stood up for immediate withdrawal.[124]

The two ranking members of the Politburo commission on Afghanistan, Shevardnadze and the KGB's Kryuchkov, however, insisted on continuing efforts to "save" Afghanistan, fearing a bloodbath in Kabul and damage to Soviet security interests in case of a fundamentalist victory. Back in 1986, the KGB had promoted Najibullah as a better alternative to Babrak Karmal and now stuck with its candidate. At that time, the leading advocate of the "new thinking," Yakovlev, had also supported the Afghanization of the war. Gorbachev, as the records and memoirs reveal, supported their position and ignored the warnings of Akhromeyev and Kornienko. Later, Gorbachev and Yakovlev both claimed that it was the relentless policy of the United States that prolonged the war in Afghanistan.[125]

Gorbachev's position on Afghanistan was not an isolated episode. In general, he continued to support and maintain all traditional Soviet clients and friends in the third world, including the anti-Israeli nationalistic Arab regimes, Vietnam, Mengistu Haile Mariam's regime in Ethiopia, Castro's Cuba, and the Sandinistas in Nicaragua.[126] The dynamics and motivation behind this costly policy demands explanation. Did Gorbachev want to reform the Soviet Union while sustaining its great power role and alliances around the world? Did he, as well as Shevardnadze, still adhere, through inertia, to the legacy of the revolutionary-imperial paradigm in the third world?

Conservative modernizers in the Politburo, like hard-liners in the Reagan administration, assumed that it was so. But the general secretary was most likely procrastinating, not quite ready to begin a unilateral dismantling of the Soviet empire. It also appears that the third world issues never really interested Gorbachev, whose "new thinking" ideology made him focus on the integration of the Soviet Union into the "first world"—cooperation with the most advanced capitalist powers. In 1987, Gorbachev was already beginning to articulate his beliefs in the global interdependence between Soviet socialism and democratic capitalism. Just like Khrushchev in 1955–57, the Soviet leader began to combine peace offensives and de-Stalinization, negotiations with the West and liberalization at home. But Khrushchev had resumed domestic repression after the Hungarian and Polish uprisings. Gorbachev wanted to go further than his reformist predecessor and never turn back. He used the preparations for Reykjavik to demand reassessment of Soviet policies on human rights, immigration, and persecution of domestic political and religious dissidents. After the failure of the Reykjavik summit, Gorbachev argued that it was vital to win back the sympathies of Western European leaders, the educated elite, and the general public. Without pressure from Western Europeans, it would be impossible to bring the Reagan administration around to a more conciliatory position. In particular, Gorbachev suggested at the Politburo that Andrei Sakharov, the most famous dissident in the Soviet Union, should be allowed to return to Moscow from his exile in Nizhniy Novgorod. In January 1987, the Soviets stopped jamming the BBC, the Voice of America, and West Germany's Deutsche Welle.[127]

By this time, the majority of Soviet officials, even in the KGB, grudgingly recognized that the persecutions of dissidents and religious groups presented a major obstacle for negotiations with the United States. They remembered how upset Reagan had been in 1983 by the Soviet refusal to allow a group of Pentecostal Christians to immigrate to the United States. At the Politburo discussion, KGB chairman Chebrikov proposed freeing one-third of political prisoners and bringing the figure to one-half later. This proposal was of the same nature as Andropov's plot to use Jews and dissidents as a bargaining chip in the détente negotiations during the 1970s. After 1986, the KGB began to reduce the number of arrests for "political crimes" and intensified instead its so-called prophylactic measures, that is, intimidation and blackmail of Soviet citizens who fell under suspicion.[128]

A major factor influencing Gorbachev and the Politburo at this time was the ongoing economic slump and the looming deficit. The initial programs for perestroika and improvement of the Soviet economy lay in ruins. Beginning in 1985, the USSR had to spend more hard currency than it was able to earn; this led to the double burden of a trade deficit as well as foreign debt[129]—a dangerous situation that had saddled the economies of Eastern European countries since the 1970s. Also, in the first two months of 1987, industrial production, in disarray from partial decentralization and other misguided experiments, plunged by 6 percent, with heavy and consumer industries suffering most. There was an 80 billion rubles gap between state revenues and expenditures. Gorbachev in his memoirs does not explain why the economic and financial situation had sharply deteriorated since he had come to power.[130]

Before fall 1986, rank-and-file Politburo members were not informed about the true figures of military expenditures, foreign assistance, and other secret budgetary items. The figures were shocking. In addition to the defense expenses that swallowed up 40 percent of the Soviet budget, the Soviet Union supported Central European allies and other numerous clients abroad. Politburo members learned with amazement that the annual "cost" of Vietnam was 40 billion rubles. Other clients were only marginally less expensive: Cuba cost 25 billion rubles, Syria cost 6 billion, and so on. Since the 1950s, the Soviets had sent to Iraq, Libya, and Syria great amounts of military equipment, including first-line tanks, aircraft, and missiles, but had never received payment for this equipment.[131]

The Soviet budget felt the burden of 67.7 billion rubles of the defense expenditures (16.4 percent of the budget). But the budget sustained even greater losses from the 1985 decision to invest an additional 200 billion rubles and hard currency into the modernization of the machine-building industries—a necessary investment but one that could not give any return soon. Meanwhile, the revenue from alcohol fell, and the last big source of revenue, the export of oil, continued to diminish, as oil prices plummeted from longtime highs to $12 a barrel in April 1986 and continued to fall. By 1987, the Soviet state had no other means to increase its revenues besides taxes and price increases. On October 30, 1986, Gorbachev said that the financial crisis "has clutched us by the throat." Yet he refused to balance the budget by raising consumer prices and reducing the state subsidies for food. Six months later, the Politburo learned that without price reform these subsidies alone would reach 100 billion rubles by 1990. Nevertheless, despite numerous discussions, preparations, and drafts, the price reform was never implemented. There were piecemeal measures, but all of them only aggravated the financial malaise. The reasons for Gorbachev's temporizing are not clear. It is obvious that he and the rest of the Politburo lacked even basic knowledge of macroeconomics. It is also possible that Gorbachev realized that drastic rises in prices would create turmoil in the society and undermine his domestic standing.[132]

The bleak economic and financial situation made détente and Soviet retrenchment look like an urgent necessity even in the eyes of the Politburo's conservatives. The Soviet Union simply could not afford further diplomatic gamesmanship. Gromyko was among those who urged the improvement of relations with Western countries without delay. In February 1987, Gromyko and Ligachev became vocal supporters of a "zero option" agreement with the United States to eliminate all intermediate-range missiles.[133]

In February 1987, Gorbachev was about to begin the third round of his peace offensive against Ronald Reagan. In advance of their next summit in Washington, he came up with more asymmetrical cuts in the Soviet military arsenal. During a meeting with Gorbachev late in the month, Italian prime minister Giulio Andreotti praised the Soviet leader for "boldly" agreeing to dismantle the intermediate-range missiles directed at Europe. Andreotti then encouraged Gorbachev "to take just another small step" and unilaterally cut Soviet short-range missiles. This "courageous step" in his opinion would undercut U.S. plans to deploy short-range missiles in Western Europe.[134] In their April meeting with George Shultz, Gorbachev and Shevardnadze accepted Reagan's "zero option" on intermediate ballistic missiles as the Politburo had decided. To everyone's surprise, Gorbachev and Shevardnadze told Schultz that the Soviet Union also would pledge to cut its new short-range missiles, the ss-23 ("Oka"). This proposal meant that the Soviet Union would dismantle many of its missiles that specifically targeted Western European territories. This was a minor, but highly significant, step past the boundaries of the pro-détente consensus outside the Politburo.[135] The military was aghast. It grumbled about the hasty squandering of Soviet strategic assets. As if to prove this point, Schultz pocketed Soviet concessions and left for home without giving anything back. Akhromeyev, however, was bound by his personal loyalty to Gorbachev. He, along with the rest of the military, chose to blame Shevardnadze for selling out to the Americans.[136]

Soon Gorbachev had a chance to reduce potential military resistance to his policies. In May 1987, Matthias Rust, a young West German pilot, flew a sport plane into the ussr from Finland and landed on Red Square. The bizarre "Rust affair" allowed Gorbachev to remove most of the old top brass, beginning with the minister of defense, Marshal Sergei Sokolov. Rust, after spending several months in the kgb Lubianka prison, quietly obtained amnesty. The Soviet leader handpicked a new minister of defense, Dmitry Yazov, a veteran of World War II and former head of the Far Eastern military district, who had little charisma or authority among the top brass. Gorbachev began to advocate "transparency and candor" on the issue of conventional arms in Europe, admitting a huge Soviet superiority of 27,000 tanks and almost 3.5 million soldiers. Simultaneously, the Soviet military began to implement the new military doctrine. The new doctrine of the Warsaw Pact, a carbon copy of the Soviet one, was adopted in July 1987. William Odom believes that the new policy replaced the old vision of war in Europe.[137] As a consequence, it also shook the ideological and psychological foundations of the Soviet military presence in Central Europe.

Meanwhile, with tacit encouragement from Alexander Yakovlev (who was in charge of media), as well as from Mikhail and Raisa Gorbachev, an informal network of the "men and women of the sixties," "enlightened" apparatchiks and intellectuals, and those who had been devoted to de-Stalinization and democratic change twenty years earlier began to grow and influence the public climate. Since 1986, these people had rapidly come to occupy strategic positions in the state-controlled media. Yakovlev's protégés would become the editors of some leading periodicals, among them Sergei Zalygin in *Novy Mir*, Vitaly Korotich in *Ogonek*, and Yegor Yakovlev in *Moscow News*. The "new thinkers" began publishing forbidden manuscripts, promoting anti-Stalinist films and novels, and criticizing the Brezhnev era of stagnation.

In the summer of 1987, Gorbachev revealed his intentions to a narrow circle, including Yakovlev and Chernyaev: he wanted to overhaul "the whole system—from economy to mentality." Chernyaev jubilantly recorded Gorbachev's words: "I would go far, very far."[138] By that time, Gorbachev already had nothing to fear from the conservative side, including the Politburo and the party nomenklatura. On the contrary, among the new cohort of party officials, people, among them Boris Yeltsin, head of the Moscow party organization, were beginning to grumble about Gorbachev's slow pace of domestic reforms. In November 1987, in his speech marking the seventieth anniversary of the Bolshevik Revolution, Gorbachev for the first time took up Khrushchev's criticism of Stalin, saying that there were still "blank pages" in Soviet history.[139] It was a turning point in the interaction between foreign policy innovations and domestic developments. From the early phase, with its emphasis on arms control and détente, Gorbachev moved on to the next phase in which he combined his peace offensive with Khrushchev's unfinished task of de-Stalinization. Chernyaev explains: "To achieve a success in foreign policy, we had to depose myths and dogmas of the confrontational ideology, and this had an impact—through mentality of the general secretary and the reformist mass media—on the entire intellectual environment of the society."[140]

The rapid ascendancy of this highly idealistic and reform-motivated "new thinking" did not end Gorbachev's baffling inconsistencies. On June 27, 1987, in his conversation with Robert Mugabe, the prime minister of Zimbabwe, Gorbachev described Soviet foreign policy philosophy in the same terms as Khrushchev would have used thirty years earlier. He concluded that "an increasing pressure has to be brought to bear on [Western countries]." On October 23, 1987, Gorbachev told Shultz that he would not come to Washington for a summit until Reagan renounced the SDI program. Simply signing a treaty on the reduction of intermediate-range nuclear forces (INF Treaty) would not be enough to justify the summit. The Soviet leader asked his group of inner advisers, including Shevardnadze, Yakovlev, Akhromeyev, Chernyaev, and deputy foreign minister Alexander Bessmertnykh, for advice. Some of them told him to wait until a new administration was in Washington and ready to deal with the SDI issue. Chernyaev, however, urged Gorbachev not to back out of the summit.[141]

Gorbachev's vacillations and his obsession with SDI could only add to the extreme skepticism about Soviet intentions within the Reagan administration and among neoconservatives in Washington. But the phenomenon of "new thinking" was not a public relations trick. Gorbachev moved on to ideas of radically transforming Soviet ideology and the political and economic systems and truly opening the Soviet Union to the world. Being realistic dictated caution, prudence, and a careful strategy, but Gorbachev was impatient. His radical reformism was driven by the deterioration of the Soviet economy and the financial crisis. But even more it was driven by romantic notions about international affairs and by his reformist abilities. Only a few in the Soviet leadership and political classes followed Gorbachev with reformist zeal and enthusiasm. The rest watched with tacit approval as Gorbachev's new foreign policy elevated Soviet international status to unprecedented heights and achieved substantial results in reducing Cold War tensions.

Soon, however, this approval was replaced by concern and dismay. The conservatives, the modernizers, and the military realized that the Soviet Union could ill afford its commitments in Central Europe, Afghanistan, and all over the world.[142] And they advocated cautious retrenchment to postpone the crumbling of the Soviet sphere of influence. In contrast, Gorbachev and the "new thinkers" began to proclaim a policy of noninterference in Central Europe. Soon they would be leaving Soviet allies completely to their own devices. Still, the Politburo majority, the KGB, and the military did not imagine that Gorbachev would be prepared to bring the Cold War to an end, at the cost of destruction of the Soviet external empire in Central Europe and fatal instability in the Soviet Union itself.

CHAPTER 10

GORBACHEV AND THE
END OF SOVIET POWER,
1988-1991

> In a word, the total dismantling of socialism as a world
> phenomenon has been proceeding. This is a reunification of
> mankind on the basis of common sense. And a common fellow
> from Stavropol [Gorbachev] set this process in motion.
> —Chernyaev, in his diary, October 5, 1989

It took three decades to turn the Soviet Union into a superpower, the main challenger of the supremacy of the United States in the world. But it took only three years for the Communist giant to disintegrate. For people who had come of age during the Cold War, the event was sudden and breathtaking. Those inclined to see the Cold War in apocalyptic terms as the struggle between good and evil concluded that it was Ronald Reagan and his administration that overthrew the great Satan of Communism. But most scholars and analysts conclude that the Soviet superpower met its end at the hands of its own leadership under the influence of new ideas, policies, and circumstances.[1] Canadian political scientist Jacques Lévesque, who wrote *The Enigma of 1989*, concluded: "Rarely in history have we witnessed the policy of a great power continue, through so many difficulties and reversals, to be guided by such an idealistic view of the world, based on universal reconciliation, and in which the image of the enemy was constantly blurring, to the point of making it practically disappear."[2]

It is a perennial human illusion to attribute great events to great causes. During the past century, scholars have tended to attribute transitions from one historical period to another to grand, impersonal forces: shifts in the balance of power, contradictions among states, revolutions, the rise of new ideologies and social movements, and so on. In the current scholarly climate, it has also become fashionable to highlight the micro-levels of history—the role and beliefs of the "common people," incremental changes in social life, and power as a phenomenon of everyday life. Between these two trends, the view that history is shaped by "great men" seems utterly discredited. Today, many historians are loathe to admit that the character of a personality in a position of power at a critical juncture can make a major difference in the course of history.

However, the figure of Mikhail Sergeievich Gorbachev proves this point. This energetic, handsome man with sparkling eyes and charming smile "did more than anyone else to end the Cold War between East and West," asserts British political scientist Archie Brown in his seminal study, *The Gorbachev Factor*.[3] It is worth quoting Anatoly Chernyaev, the most loyal and supportive of Gorbachev's assistants. Gorbachev, he claims, "was not 'a great man' as far as set of personal qualities was concerned." But he "fulfilled a great mission," and that is "more important for history."[4] A more critical Dmitry Volkogonov provides another, but also remarkable, estimate: Gorbachev "is a person of great mind, but with a weak character. Without this paradox of personality it is hard to understand him as a historical actor." Volkogonov admits that the "intellect, feelings, and will of Gorbachev" left a unique imprint on the Soviet collapse.[5]

The sources that aid in writing about Gorbachev are nearly all problematic. The same reservations apply to the retrospective observations of many of his critics. Some of them seem full of poison and viciousness, for example, the books of Valery Boldin (the person who was closest to Raisa Gorbachev) and of former prime minister Nikolai Ryzhkov. Still, such books—as well as the more measured writings of and interviews with KGB chief Vladimir Kryuchkov, Deputy General Secretary Yegor Ligachev, Vice President Gennady Yanaev, Deputy Foreign Minister Georgy Kornienko, Gorbachev's personal bodyguard Vladimir Medvedev, and many others—do reward careful reading.[6]

The observations of Gorbachev's friends present another kind of bias. Anatoly Chernyaev, Georgy Shakhnazarov, Vadim Medvedev, Andrei Grachev, and other Gorbachev aides and colleagues admit that their former boss made many mistakes and had weak spots but continue to admire the man and the ideas behind his policies.[7] The only exception is Karen Brutents, who concluded in his sharply critical memoirs that "Gorbachev made the end of the Cold War possible" but also "became an involuntary, unconscious liquidator of the Soviet Union."[8]

A more revealing source on Gorbachev's personality are minutes taken by his assistants at the Politburo sessions and the records of Gorbachev's conversations with foreign leaders and public figures, in part published, in part available in the Archive of the Gorbachev Foundation in Moscow. Finally, perhaps the most complicated source on Gorbachev's personality continues to be Gorbachev himself. It is not easy to glean evidence from Gorbachev's memoirs; they are so craftily opaque and carefully edited that only the best-trained reader can tease data from them. But, still, his memoirs and other recollections on his years in power do bear the strong imprint of his personality. Since he left the post of general secretary of the CPSU and presidency of the USSR, he has remained the same person, with unique behavior and a discourse that even today sets him apart from the rest of the Russian politicians.[9]

Both critics and admirers of Gorbachev inevitably come to a point at which they just scratch their heads and begin to talk about his personal "enigma." Dmitry Furman, a perceptive analyst of Russia and admirer of Gorbachev, concludes that "those six years of systematic dismantling" of the Cold War and Communism "were not an organic Soviet and Russian development. Rather, it was a contribution to history linked to Gorbachev's individuality."[10] Yegor Ligachev writes that politics "cannot explain the zigzags of the political course associated so closely with Gorbachev's name. There was an entire web of interrelated causes, including Gorbachev's personal qualities."[11]

To contend that Gorbachev was not a great statesman is not to denigrate or deny Gorbachev's historic contribution to the process of the peaceful end to the global bipolar confrontation. In fact, during the 1990s, Gorbachev had become so unpopular among his countrymen that a serious and unvarnished study of his personality and statesmanship can only contribute to dispelling the cloud of exaggerated rumors and mythical indictments that darken his reputation in Russia.

WOULD IT HAVE HAPPENED WITHOUT GORBACHEV?

The standard explanations for the end of the Cold War are important and necessary to describe, since they focus our attention on the crucial material, the political and intellectual settings in which Gorbachev's particular personality and leadership style wrought their powerful effect. According to the first standard explanation, advanced by scholars of international relations, by the mid-1980s the balance of power had shifted drastically in favor of the United States and the West. Relative decline offered the Soviets no alternative to a policy of imperial retrenchment and engagement with the powerful West. As soon as the Kremlin leaders perceived this power shift, they brought their behavior in line with reality.[12]

It is obvious, however, that reality, sobering as it was for the Kremlin, did not automatically dictate one set of perceptions (or "narrative" as a modern theorist would say). In the Kremlin, as everywhere else, the distance between reality and perceptions was great. And, most important, people in the Kremlin perceived more than one option by the mid-1980s.

The most dangerous option for the world and the Soviet Union itself was discussed by the aged Soviet leaders from 1981 to 1984 in response to their sense of threat from the military buildup and "aggressive" behavior of the Reagan administration. Yuri Andropov and Marshal Dmitry Ustinov contemplated emergency measures to mobilize the Soviet society and state for the task of preserving "strategic parity" with the United States in the all-out arms race. Though it is not clear how far the Kremlin was prepared to go in this direction,[13] the basis of its response was mistrust, fear, and reliance on deterrence by force. Even Gorbachev, when he first came to power, was under the influence of Andropov's opinion that no compromise could be reached while Reagan remained in the White House.[14]

Another option was unilateral, calibrated reductions of Soviet armed forces, similar to what the Kremlin carried out in the first years after Stalin's death. It did not mean bailing out of the arms race with the United States, but rather gaining "a breathing spell" in order to alleviate the burden of the military-industrial expenditures on the Soviet economy. This option, in contrast to the first one, corresponded to the desire for gradual reform of the Soviet centralized system but implied gradualism and maintaining a firm control over society and economic life. Until 1989, a majority of analysts in Washington suspected and feared that this was exactly what Gorbachev intended to do.[15] Indeed, some elements of this option were present in Gorbachev's arguments before the Politburo from 1986 to 1987 and became public after 1988 in the doctrine of "strategic sufficiency."

A third option was an "amicable agreement" with the West on the basis of mutual reductions of arms. This option was proposed at the end of World War II, among others, by Maxim Litvinov and became prominent after Stalin. Nikita Khrushchev and Leonid Brezhnev called it "peaceful coexistence" and adhered to it despite all the failures and frustrations in Soviet-American relations. At the core of this option was a Realpolitik not dissimilar to the Nixon-Kissinger strategy of the early 1970s. It aimed to preserve essential elements of Soviet imperial influence in the world, including strategic "parity" with the United States, the retention of Soviet allies abroad, and ideological support for international Communist and "progressive" movements. According to Chernyaev, Gorbachev, in his first years in office, believed that peaceful coexistence was the option of "common sense" and that socialism and capitalism "could coexist without interfering with each other."[16]

The key and frequently unrecognized point here is that *Gorbachev never pursued any of these options systematically.* While some domestic critics and Western policy makers might have thought he was following "peaceful coexistence" or "breathing spell" strategies, in fact, as I show below, he was doing something quite different and arguably far less coherent and calculated. This is recognized, ex post facto, by Gorbachev's loyalists and particularly by his critics, who even now continue to speak about it as a missed opportunity to take "a Chinese road."[17]

Soviet domestic structural decay and crisis are a second standard explanation for the end of the Cold War. Deterioration of the Soviet economy, ecology, and quality of everyday life—so-called stagnation under Brezhnev—as well as deep and growing problems of a multinational state, contrasted dramatically with the spectacular upsurge of the United States and Western Europe in the 1980s. By 1985, the USSR was a superpower only in the military sense. Under Gorbachev's leadership, Soviet domestic economic and financial systems deteriorated further and much faster. Some on the U.S. side, among them Secretary of State George Shultz and top CIA watcher Robert Gates, realized it was very advantageous for U.S. interests that the deepening crisis push the Soviet leadership to move unilaterally to meet American demands and conditions for the end of the confrontation.[18]

Even before Gorbachev, under Andropov and Chernenko, the old leadership of the Soviet Union agreed that a policy of détente and taming the arms race was imperative for the country's economy. Gorbachev seemed to agree with this. He is on record saying to the Politburo that this race will be "beyond our capabilities, and we will lose it, because we are at the limit of our capabilities. Moreover, we can expect that Japan and the FRG could very soon join the American potential. . . . If the new round begins, the pressure on our economy will be unbelievable."[19]

The "domestic structural" explanation is persuasive, but a closer look reveals that it, too, is incomplete. The important point is that the grave economic, financial, and state crisis began only between 1986 and 1988, and it kept growing worse because of Gorbachev's choices and policies. Of these, two were the most consequential. First, instead of relying on the most pragmatic elements of the party and state officialdom in restructuring of the country, Gorbachev tried to build up new political forces and movements while gradually diminishing the power of the party and of centralized state structures. Second, instead of taking unpopular economic measures such as price reforms and reduction of state subsidies within the framework of the existing political system, he encouraged a very rapid dismantling of this system. These choices led to political chaos and economic catastrophe after 1988. Gorbachev's "remedies" were killing the sick patient.[20]

Even with the economy and finances in steep decline, the Soviet Union still could hide its weak condition behind a respectable Potemkin facade and negotiate with the United States from a position of relative parity. After 1988, this situation drastically changed: Gorbachev's decision to launch radical political and state reforms, coupled with the removal of the party apparatus from economic life, created a most severe crisis of the state and produced centrifugal political forces that spun out of control within Soviet society. All this was tantamount to revolution, was visible to the world, and engulfed the Soviet leadership.

These policies essentially destroyed the Soviet capacity to act like a superpower on the international arena. The Soviet Union was left in no position to bail out its allies or to present itself as an equal partner to the United States in negotiations.

There are other aspects that also contradict the notion that domestic structural crisis was a primary determining factor in Gorbachev's motivation to end the Cold War quickly, and on the best available terms. First, Soviet negotiating behavior began to change drastically beginning in early 1987, before the crisis became grave and visible. Second, the Soviet Union continued, with the complete approval of Gorbachev and Shevardnadze, to pour billions of dollars into supplying military equipment to Cuba, Syria, Ethiopia, Vietnam, and other client countries during 1989, 1990, and even part of 1991, when Soviet coffers were already almost empty.[21] The American side tried to argue with Gorbachev to cut the pipelines to Castro, and radical Soviet reformers even proposed pursuing an alliance with Cuban anti-Castro émigrés in Miami. But Gorbachev never took these steps, although they would have earned the approval of many in the U.S. political establishment.

Many scholars and politicians convincingly contend that there was no way to reform the USSR without dismantling the old Soviet system. Still, it is possible to imagine a gradual transformation of the post-Stalinist Communist model into a post-Communist authoritarian model (as has been taking place in China). A leader supported by the pragmatic elements of the top party circles might have gradually privatized state property. The remarkable transformation of party secretaries and Communist ministers into bankers and rich oligarchs under Yeltsin prompted one observer to suggest that even under Gorbachev "the higher echelons of the party" would have been ready "to send to Hell at any moment the whole edifice of Marxism-Leninism, if such an act would only help them preserve their hierarchical positions and continue their careers."[22] Instead of co-opting the old bureaucratic elite, Gorbachev's chose a policy of leading Soviet society into "democracy" over the heads of the nomenklatura. This "populism" soon brought to the fore elements of the liberal and nationalist intelligentsia; however, almost immediately, the latter turned vehemently against the Soviet leader and began to support political separatism and incite social unrest. This, and the sabotage of the alienated party and state nomenklatura, left Gorbachev hanging without real political support. Denied political recognition and support at home, he increasingly looked for it abroad, from Western leaders.

A third standard explanation for the end of the Cold War is a shift of ideas within the Soviet leadership, both as a product of the longer-term erosion of Communist ideology and as a short-term by-product of glasnost of 1987–89. Some scholars focus on Gorbachev's "new thinking" as being a set of ideas that replaced the old Soviet mentality, in particular the core ideological thesis about class struggle and the inevitability of the world's division into two camps. As Robert English demonstrates in his book, the roots of new ideas about the world can be traced within the Soviet political establishment and intelligentsia as far back as the 1940s and 1950s. Some scholars point out that Gorbachev absorbed "new thinking" from various international sources and from his liberal-minded advisers.[23]

Indeed, the role of ideas in the changing Soviet international behavior was great. But even at the time, there was something bizarre about this role. To put it simply, Gorbachev took ideas too seriously. They played an excessive role in his behavior. They took precedence not only over the immediate demands of the negotiating process but also over the protection of state interests. The real importance was not in the ideas themselves but in the historical personality that espoused them and made them his own.

Again, the key evidence against the ideological explanation is that there were other scenarios under which the rejection of Communist ideology would have proceeded differently. First, the ideological revision could have been carried out more slowly, under more control from above. Gorbachev and his assistants allowed the process of glasnost to go on until it became a whirlwind of revelations that discredited the entire foundation of Soviet foreign policy and the regime itself. The emerging attitude among the intelligentsia (later shared by Gorbachev himself) was that of radical ideological revisionism. Some Moscow-based revisionists began to hold the Soviet Union solely and exclusively responsible for the Cold War. They began to consider the policies of the West to be purely reactive and dictated by the need to fight Stalin's Communist aggression and totalitarian threat. A more conservative approach (as, for instance, is practiced in China today) would have held historic revisionism in check and diminished its radicalizing pressure on foreign policy.

The rejection of the old ideology could have led to a pragmatic and flexible attitude, to a version of Realpolitik based less on lofty principles and ideas than on a modest and clear formulation of state interests. When Margaret Thatcher said in 1984 that one could do business with Gorbachev, she was particularly impressed with his citation from Lord Palmerston, who advocated basing foreign policy on "permanent interests."[24] But the basis of Soviet foreign policy in 1988–91 has been far removed from Palmerston's dictum. It has been highly idealistic and imbued with a messianic spirit. In mid-1987, Gorbachev wrote a book called *Perestroika: New Thinking for Our Country and the World*. It contained an image of international relations based on a just and democratic world order, in which the USSR would play a key role and the United Nations would reign supreme. Gorbachev replaced one messianic revolutionary-imperial idea that had guided Soviet foreign policy with another messianic idea—"that perestroika in the USSR was only a part of some kind of global perestroika, the birth of a new world order."[25]

New ideological motives need not have dictated a total rejection of the use of force and projection of power. For Gorbachev's predecessors and for most of his colleagues in the Politburo in 1985–88, the accumulation of strength, coercion, and the balance of power were even more important than Communist ideology. They cared about power and empire as much—if not more—as they did about the socialist perspective and proletarian internationalism. In his paradigm shift, Gorbachev rejected not only the Communist tenets of class struggle but also the entire post-Stalin logic of Soviet geopolitical interests, beginning with Central and Eastern Europe.

There is nothing intrinsic to the "new thinking" ideas themselves that necessitated Gorbachev's foreign policy and domestic choices. One could subscribe to the whole package of ideas and yet completely part ways with Gorbachev on the question of whether or when to start radical political reforms that inevitably led to the Soviet decline and disintegration. For most statesmen, ideas are tools, and to understand their impact on history one must examine how they are molded and manipulated by the human agents who espouse them. In Gorbachev's case, he clearly overreached when he attempted to mold Soviet and international realities according to his ideas of "new thinking."

There are few other examples in history of a leader in charge of a huge ailing state who willingly risked the geopolitical position of a great power and the very foundations of his political power for the sake of a moral global project. Even Lenin, Gorbachev's hero, compromised on "world revolution" in 1918 for the sake of staying in power. Gorbachev, however, did exactly the opposite. He made his priorities clear before his Politburo colleagues during the debate in March 1988 that resulted from the so-called Nina Andreeva letter.[26] He abandoned Andropov's course of conservative modernization and embarked on a more risky set of radical experiments in ideology and politics. This produced the growing polarization in his entourage. The majority in the Politburo, the Central Committee, and the state apparatus feared losing control over society and political life. They remembered the lessons of Khrushchev's de-Stalinization in 1956. Some began to grumble that Gorbachev wanted to destroy and give away everything that Stalin had built. The KGB chairman, Viktor Chebrikov, warned Gorbachev of a potentially disastrous meltdown of Soviet mentality under a barrage of revelations about the past. The spokesman of ideological conservatives, Yegor Ligachev, for the first time raised the specter of dissolution of the Communist bloc: "Arguably, we will muddle through, but there are socialist countries, the world Communist movement. What to do about them? History has become politics and, when we deal with it, we should think not only about the past, but also about the future."[27]

Gorbachev ridiculed his skeptical colleagues as panic-mongers. And Shevardnadze declared that "primitivism and intellectual narrow-mindedness had prevented Khrushchev from implementing to the end the line of the 20th Party Congress." The so-called Communist and working-class movement was largely a fiction, so there was not much to lose. As to the socialist bloc, he continued, "take for instance Bulgaria, take the old leadership of Poland, and take the current situation in the German Democratic Republic, in Romania. Is it socialism?"[28]

By the spring of 1989, it became obvious even to Gorbachev's closest assistants that the radical reappraisal of Soviet ideology and history, initiated from above, had triggered a political deluge from below. Gorbachev was irreversibly losing control over foreign and domestic events. In May 1989, Anatoly Chernyaev wrote in his private journal with anguish: "Inside me depression and alarm are growing, the sense of crisis of the Gorbachev Idea. He is prepared to go far. But what does it mean? His favorite catchword is 'unpredictability.' But most likely we will come to a collapse of the state and something like chaos."[29]

FATEFUL PERSONALITY

The previous chapter compared Gorbachev and Nikita Khrushchev. But this comparison should go even deeper. Russian scholar Natalya Kozlova studied the mentality of the Russian peasantry in the USSR. She found how the quick and violent demise of the "peasant civilization" led to breath-taking social and physical mobility, as young peasants moved to big cities and began making careers for themselves. New recruits to urban civilization were burning with the desire to leap from the "idiocy of village life" to the highest social status they could reach. The first cohort of such people was shaped by the 1930s and World War II. It had immense vitality, was ruthless and pragmatic, and believed in material tangible benefits. The second cohort came in the 1950s at the time of peace, during the final stages of Soviet urbanization and mass education. This cohort had an optimistic worldview, but also a naive belief in the "ideas" of cultured discourse and ideology, in comparison to sophisticated, cynical, double-thinking urbanites.[30] The common roots and differences of Khrushchev and Gorbachev should be sought there.

Arguably the central and most consequential feature of Gorbachev's personality was his remarkable *self-confidence and optimism*. His ability to bounce back was extraordinary. As an individual, Gorbachev possessed a very healthy ego and stable values. The political and social environments he lived in (the region of

Kuban Cossacks in the south of Russia, Moscow State University, and the Politburo itself, where he was by far the youngest member) fostered his healthy self-
esteem. In any case, he had an unflagging faith in his own capacities to succeed.

Flowing from this wellspring of essential optimism, admirers say, was Gorbachev's natural liberalism and democratic instincts. In Chernyaev's estimation,
Gorbachev's "natural democratic instincts had not been completely spoiled by
his long career in the party apparatus, although he acquired some 'pockmarks.'"
He allegedly suffered a genuine shock from observing the norms and mores of
the top political hierarchy when he moved to Moscow and joined the Politburo.
His democratic impulse, concludes Chernyaev, remained instrumental to his
actions, despite the many transgressions and dirty compromises he had been
involved in.[31]

A second key attitude, in the opinion of Gorbachev's supporters, was his
naïveté. One of his assistants, Georgy Shakhnazarov, recalled Gorbachev's "naive
belief in his colleagues' common sense." In Dmitry Furman's opinion, Gorbachev believed that the truth he discovered was "self-evident and that people
would grasp it. In the same way, Luther probably thought that his truths were so
obvious, that he could easily convince the Pope of them." Gorbachev's perestroika was a "reformation," and he needed the qualities of a preacher as he
sought to convert the pagans of Communism into a new, fairer, and better creed,
to help them move from the captivity of authoritarian regimes, militarism, and
pauperism.[32]

The life path of Gorbachev (as well as of his wife, Raisa) contributed to his
staunch belief in the "reformation" of Communism. He graduated from Moscow
State University and left for provincial Stavropol at the time of crisis for the
Stalinist creed and the development of romantic hopes for a Communism with "a
human face." He returned from the provinces to Moscow in the late 1970s, when
these romantic hopes were dead among the educated elites and increasingly
cynical party apparatchiks. Lenin remained Gorbachev's role model during his
first years in power. In Lenin's personality (rather, in his idealized, censored
image), Gorbachev saw the reflection of his own traits, in particular, feverish
belief in the power of revolutionary ideas, "historic" optimism, and unflagging
determination to muddle through social and political chaos. Even in early 1989,
Gorbachev confessed to Chernyaev that he mentally "asks for Lenin's advice."[33]

Critics see Gorbachev's self-confidence and democratic instincts in a completely different light. Ligachev argues that Gorbachev "did not have in his character a room for understanding" how difficult the reforms would be.[34] Gorbachev's chief of chancellery, Valery Boldin observes a profound psychological

gap between Gorbachev and the vast majority of the Soviet people. Gorbachev's security officer, Vladimir Medvedev, writes that "intellectual" Gorbachev, unlike patriarchal Brezhnev, felt uncomfortable with Soviet crowds and rather preferred talking to Westerners.[35]

Gorbachev's friends acknowledge how much Gorbachev's personality was at loggerheads with the mainstream of Russian and Soviet mentality. But they side with him, not with the people. Chernyaev, for instance, defines Soviet society as "a degraded population with give-me psychology." In the opinion of his friends, Gorbachev accomplished the Herculean feat of waking the society from the terrible stupor and slavery of Soviet totalitarianism. The rest, Chernyaev contends, was inevitable. Society turned out to be not worthy of the leader; the "new thinking" was ahead of its time. Given all this, Gorbachev could not really apply the brakes when Soviet society spun out of control, crushing everything in its way.[36]

Friends and foes alike highlight a key consequence of Gorbachev's essential optimism and naïveté: his "ad-hocism," his congenital lack of a long-range strategic plan, and his aversion to the practical details of governance. They all recognize that perestroika had no plan and that the "new thinking" was vague and could not be a practical guide for reforms. Gorbachev's favorite phrases, besides "unpredictability," were "let process develop" and "process of events is on the run" (protsessi poshli). In the judgment of Dmitry Furman, it was a continuation of his excessively positive view of people, particularly of Soviet people. "It always seemed to him that people could not help but be glad to organize their own life for themselves."[37] He had little doubt that it would be best to unleash social changes and then just wait while "processes" ran their course and provided the most sensible outcome.

Even his admirers admit that this feature of his psychology contributed to Gorbachev's chronic inability to chart a practical course for the state apparatus, to carry out a sustained and thought-through program of action, and to prevent psychological chaos and ideological breakdown in the society. Chernyaev's political memoirs reveal his frustration and nagging doubts about it. Gorbachev, he writes, failed to begin meaningful economic reforms when he still had the chance. He procrastinated endlessly on price reforms, letting the financial crisis grow to monstrous proportions. He let the Brezhnev-Andropov-Gromyko war in Afghanistan become "Gorbachev's war." And he let Boris Yeltsin take over the political initiative in 1990 and 1991 by breaking with the old discredited political order.[38] Still, his admirers stress that all this was not a crucial flaw. They argue that since nobody knew how to transform a totalitarian country, it could be done only by trial and error. Also, they argue, had Gorbachev accurately foreseen his task in all its complexity and danger, he simply could never have undertaken it.[39] This assessment of Gorbachev's abilities is based on the assumption that nobody could have reformed the Soviet system and Soviet empire. They could only be destroyed completely.

Ten years after he lost power, Gorbachev himself, in a candid discussion, agreed that there was "a lot of naiveté and utopianism" in his actions. But he said that he had deliberately run the risk of political destabilization since 1988 because he wanted to "wake up" the Soviet people. Otherwise, he said, "we would have shared the fate of Khrushchev," that is, the party nomenklatura would have removed Gorbachev from power.[40]

The critics deny that there was ever a serious challenge to Gorbachev's authority from party officials in 1988.[41] William Odom concludes that Gorbachev was "an inveterate schemer, a loquacious obfuscator, unable to anticipate the likely consequences of policies." Ligachev writes that "being too late, reacting too slowly to events was one of the most characteristic traits of Gorbachev's policies."[42] In an interview, he added: "When some controversial things happened, Gorbachev often reacted with delay. My explanation is that he wanted others to analyze what affected the society, was painful to the society. He wanted a ripe fruit to fall onto his lap, the one he could pick up. But often it was necessary to row against the tide. There were many instances in history when the leader remained in the minority, but turned out to be right. Gorbachev, unfortunately, lacked this quality."[43] Kryuchkov talks and writes about Gorbachev's "impulsiveness that is linked to his personality, to the traits of his abnormal character."[44]

The critics are convinced that another type of leader, with a stronger and steadier hand, would have made a huge difference. This hypothetical "other" could have brought about détente with the West and gradually transformed the Communist Party and the Soviet Union. And, critics argue, this could have been done without destroying the foundations of state power and without creating overall political and social chaos.

The self-image of Gorbachev as a leader is extremely important for understanding the end of the Cold War. It is linked to his goals and ideals, but at the same time it reflects his personal, intimate psychological "core" that allowed him to stick to these ideals and goals. In late October 1988, Gorbachev was preparing to proclaim his new beliefs to the world at the General Assembly of the United Nations. He told his brain trust of Shevardnadze, Yakovlev, Dobrynin, the new head of the International Department, Valentin Falin, and Chernyaev to prepare a speech that would respond to Churchill's famous speech at Fulton,

Missouri, in March 1946. It "should be an anti-Fulton—Fulton in reverse," he said. "We should present our worldview and philosophy based on the results of the last three years. We should stress the demilitarization and humanization of our thinking."[45]

Gorbachev modeled himself after the idealized Lenin, as opposed to Stalin, both in the sense of direction he gave to the Soviet Union and in the world arena. As the creator of the Soviet state and empire, Stalin barely differentiated his personality from his creations. He took the slightest challenge to them as a personal assault, and, vice versa, regarded any slight to his prestige and authority (particularly from foreigners) as an intolerable insult to the prestige of the USSR as a great power. Gorbachev did not feel a personal association with the Soviet state and empire in the form and shape he inherited from his predecessors. Later, he claimed that he did everything "to preserve the Union." In reality, however, he sought to unleash a revolution according to the ideas that he adopted and developed.

Gorbachev inherited from Stalin and Stalin's successors the office of the general secretary. But he had other priorities besides power, prestige, stability, and state interests. His first priority, as mentioned earlier, was the construction of a global world order on the basis of cooperation and nonviolence. This places Gorbachev, at least in his image of himself, in the ranks of such figures of the twentieth century as Woodrow Wilson, Mahatma Gandhi, and other prophets of universal principles. Most tellingly, perhaps, those figures did not excel as state-builders or statesmen.

Both Stalin and Gorbachev had enormous influence on the fate of the Soviet Union, even though, of course, the contrast between the statesmanship of the two cannot be greater. Stalin was, in his crude and bloody way, an architect of the Soviet Union and its external empire; his policies turned the country into a super-power. His favorite modus operandi was carving up spheres of influence, making these spheres totally impervious to the influence of and penetration by other great powers and imposing complete control over them through a combination of threats of force and devious manipulation of politics, both inside the USSR and in the countries under Soviet domination. As for Gorbachev, he resolutely refused to treat even the countries where Soviet troops were stationed as a Soviet sphere of influence. In fact, he meticulously observed a hands-off attitude toward the internal affairs of Central European countries. When Henry Kissinger, while on a visit in Moscow in January 1989, cautiously broached to Gorbachev an idea for a joint USSR-U.S. management of transformation in Central Europe, Gorbachev, as a preacher of "new thinking," was dismissive and even contemptuous.[46]

Stalin indoctrinated the entire Soviet state and society with extreme xenophobia; he regarded Western cultural influences as a mortal threat to his regime. Stalin was intolerant of different opinions, once he made up his own mind on any issue. He saw the slightest deviation from his "line" as an intolerable sign of dissent, or as posing the danger of chaos, or as a symptom of loss of control. He displayed a strong attraction to worst-case scenarios and suspected all Western statesmen and politicians, even those who sought to appease the USSR, of the worst anti-Soviet schemes. In contrast, Gorbachev did not have a trace of xenophobia or cultural hostility toward the West. He liked Westerners, respected Western statesmen of all creeds, and came to regard some of them as personal friends. He had a striking capacity for "best-case" thinking and began to act on assumptions of good faith, honesty, integrity, and fealty to agreements in international affairs.

In the opinion of his foreign admirers, Gorbachev was the first Soviet statesman who acted almost like a Western politician, a phenomenon that, given his background, they failed to comprehend at the time. To be sure, in his first years in power, he retained many standard Soviet political and ideological stereotypes of Western countries, particularly of the United States. But even as he treated Reagan and Kohl and their colleagues as adversaries, he was beginning to dismantle the iron curtain, first allowing free contact with foreigners for the select group of establishment intellectuals and officials, then opening the outside world for the rest of the society.

A typical example is the transformation of the idea of the "common European home." This idea, first used in 1985 and 1986 as a diplomatic tool to drive a wedge between the United States and other NATO countries, by 1989 was evoking public debates and becoming a synonym for a "return to Europe" and the rejection of Stalinist closed society. Gorbachev made this idea a cornerstone of his beliefs.[47] Sergei Tarasenko, a close assistant to Foreign Minister Shevardnadze, asserted that after mid-1988, "when we encountered domestic difficulties, we began to realize that we would be able to stay afloat for a while and even to preserve the status of great power only if we leaned on the United States. We felt that if we had stepped away from the U.S., we would have been pushed aside. We had to be as close as possible to the United States."[48]

As Gorbachev's admirers argue, this was not just a calculated policy. Dmitry Furman remarks that Gorbachev's Westernism was a dependency complex shared by other educated Russians. "For all Soviet people, including the higher echelons of the party," he writes, "the West has always been an object of longing. Trips to the West were the most important status symbol. There is nothing you can do about this; it is 'in the blood,' in the culture." Moreover, Gorbachev relished his huge personal success in the West, including in the United States. Gorbymania in the United States was the product of a natural mutual affinity between Gorbachev and Western public opinion.[49]

Chernyaev admires Gorbachev's ability to be on the same wavelength with Western leaders and people. He writes in his diary about Gorbachev's accomplishment in establishing a friendly relationship with West German chancellor Helmut Kohl. After all, he observed, the "new thinking" in foreign policy was not original or terribly new. What was new was that the leader of the Soviet system, himself conditioned by Soviet society, could so quickly break out of the Soviet mentality. When Chernyaev saw Gorbachev and Kohl conversing congenially, he "felt physically that we are entering a new world where class struggle, ideology, polarity and enmity are no longer determinate."[50]

Gorbachev's critics claim that Gorbachev's stunning personal success among West European and American audiences made his head swell. He began to put his friendly relations with foreign leaders ahead of state interests. Psychologically, they argue, Gorbachev turned to the West for recognition because his popularity at home began to sink precipitously as a result of the growing social and political chaos. As Valery Boldin sees it, "democratization began, but it suddenly took a wrong turn and not Gorbachev, but his arch-enemy Yeltsin became its leader. Then Gorbachev placed all his hopes on the West."[51] Also, the critics point out that Western advice played an ever-increasing and sinister role in diverting Gorbachev from the foreign and domestic policy course of 1985–87 toward a new course of radical political reforms.[52]

Soviet diplomats Anatoly Dobrynin and Georgy Kornienko are particularly blunt in stating that Gorbachev "frittered away the negotiating potential of the Soviet state" in exchange for ephemeral popularity and good relationships with Western statesmen. In Dobrynin's opinion, Western statesmen profited from Gorbachev's weaknesses. After 1988, Gorbachev was in a hurry to end the Cold War because he had a personal need to compensate for his declining prospects at home with breakthroughs in foreign policy. As a result, "Gorbachev's diplomacy often failed to win a better deal with the United States and its allies."[53] Kornienko believes that Gorbachev's excessive sensitivity to Western opinion and advice explained his hasty move to set up a new political system. Gorbachev the statesman was eager to replace the title of "chief of the Communist Party" with the internationally recognized title of "president of the Soviet Union."[54]

The records of Gorbachev's conversations with foreign leaders reveal beyond any doubt that after 1988, if not earlier, Westerners, from social democrats to anti-Communist conservatives, became perhaps the most crucial source of support for Gorbachev. In them he found the understanding and willingness to listen and, quite important, appreciation for the grandiose scope of his perestroika —the things he missed among his colleagues in the Politburo and even among his intellectual advisers.

This psychological dependence on the West is acknowledged by Gorbachev's admirers. Furman admits that "Gorbachev's attention was diverted to the West to the utmost degree. He clearly relaxed during his frequent trips, while in the country opposition and chaos grew." The same author rejects the notion that the West took advantage of Gorbachev and hastened the collapse of the USSR. But he deplores the fact that Gorbachev took so much of the Western advice uncritically. In his opinion, it would have been better for the country, and for the "correctly understood" interests of the West itself, "if Gorbachev had showed more indifference" toward the recommendations of American, German, and other European politicians.[55]

George Bush, Secretary of State James Baker, and the ambassador in Moscow, Jack Matlock, acknowledge that they had significant influence on Gorbachev but have denied that they had anything to do with his radical turn and the subsequent Soviet collapse. In his postmortem on the Soviet Union, Matlock wrote: "If it had been in the power of the United States and Western Europe to create a democratic union of the Soviet republics, they would have been delighted to do so."[56] It is obvious, however, that Gorbachev's passionate pro-Westernism contrasted with the reserved pragmatism of many of his counterparts. The American and Western policies toward the Soviet Union were based not on ideas, messianic projects, and personal affinity, but on geopolitical, economic, and military interests.

AVERSION TO THE USE OF FORCE

An additional feature of Gorbachev's personality that perplexed contemporaries and witnesses was his deep aversion to the use of force. To be sure, skepticism about military force was widely shared among "new thinkers."[57] It can also be regarded as a generational phenomenon that originated from the impact of World War II and was reinforced by the pacifist trends during the 1960s. Former Soviet foreign minister Andrei Gromyko, for example, privately called Gorbachev and his advisers "the Martians," for their ignorance of the laws of power politics. "I wonder how puzzled must be the US and other NATO countries," he confessed to his son. "It is a mystery for them why Gorbachev and his friends in the Politburo cannot comprehend how to use force and pressure for defending their state interests."[58]

Gorbachev personified the reluctance to use force. Indeed, for him it was less a lesson from experience than a fundamental part of his character. The principle of nonviolence was a sincere belief for Gorbachev—not merely the foundation of his domestic and foreign policies but one of his personal codes. His colleagues and assistants confirm that "the avoidance of bloodshed was a constant concern of Gorbachev" and that "for Gorbachev an unwillingness to shed blood was not only a criterion but the condition of his involvement in politics." Gorbachev, they observe, "by character was a man incapable not only of using dictatorial measures, but even of resorting to hard-line administrative means." The critics claim that Gorbachev "had no guts for blood," even when it was dictated by state interests.[59]

Gorbachev's renunciation of force was not an inevitable consequence of "new thinking" or liberal values. Liberals use force for liberal ends, and a substantial number of liberals and former dissidents would later come to believe that Gorbachev's absolutist rejection of force in the period from 1988 to 1991 was flawed and perhaps even immoral. Liberal philosopher Grigory Pomerants praised Gorbachev's decision to let go of Central Europe. But simultaneously, he said, Gorbachev "let go the forces of destruction"—forces of barbarism, ethnic genocide, and chaos—in the South Caucasus, Central Asia, and other areas of the Soviet Union. "The first duty of the state was to contain chaos," Pomerants admonished. Another critic, liberal-nationalist politician Vladimir Lukin, noted: "Firmness was necessary in such a country as Russia, not to mention the Soviet Union."[60]

As the Cold War was ending in Europe, the first fissures appeared in the Soviet Union—not a mere coincidence. In both cases, Gorbachev's predilections and personality played a major and necessary role. On the ideological level, the Soviet leader never separated the two goals, ending the Cold War and achieving the successful transformation of the Soviet Union. One of the staples of this was the idea of nonviolence, a product of Gorbachev's personal aversion to using force. After the tragedy in Tbilisi in April 1989 (Russian troops, at the request of the Georgian Communist leadership, used spades and gas against the nationalist rally and killed twenty-one Georgian civilians), Gorbachev declared a ban on the use of force, even though nationalist forces began to break the country apart. He said to the Politburo: "We have accepted that even in foreign policy force is to no avail. So especially internally—we cannot resort and will not resort to force."[61] Remarkably, Gorbachev thus renounced the authority to maintain order, a cornerstone of state sovereignty and the duty of the state leader. With a few exceptions, Gorbachev adhered to this peculiar principle tenaciously until his last day in power.

Western politicians, particularly Bush and Baker, understood this feature of

Gorbachev's statesmanship and successfully used it. At Malta, for instance, Bush suggested to Gorbachev a gentleman's agreement on the Baltic republics, where popular movements were beginning to demand complete independence from the USSR. This was a violation of a long-standing taboo in U.S.-Soviet relations, interference in the internal affairs of another superpower. Bush, however, found the correct approach. "I would like to have a fullest understanding of your approach to the Baltics," he said. "There should be no setbacks here. Perhaps it would be better to discuss this issue in a confidential way, since I would very much like to perceive the core of your thinking on this extremely complicated issue." Since the issue of the Baltic republics was presented in the context of concern for Gorbachev's "new thinking," to prevent setbacks for the U.S.-Soviet partnership for the sake of a new global order, Gorbachev readily agreed. As a result, there was an understanding that the Americans would refrain from any attempts to help the Baltic independence movement, while in return Gorbachev refrained from using force in dealing with the Baltic problem.[62]

Gorbachev himself, years after he lost power, continues to be an adamant believer in the nonuse of force. He regrets the cases when force was used against nationalists inside the USSR. Referring to these and other crisis situations (Armenian pogroms by an Azeri mob in the Azeri industrial town of Sumgait in February 1988, interethnic clashes in Nagorny Karabakh, bloodshed in Tbilisi in April 1989, more bloodshed in Baku in January 1990, crackdowns in Vilnius and Riga in January 1991), Gorbachev said: "There were many attempts to baptize me with blood. But they failed."[63] Essentially, Gorbachev agrees with what Ligachev said about him: "As far as the use of violence required to save people was concerned, Gorbachev resorted to it only when the last citizen in the country became convinced there was no other choice. It was a trait of Gorbachev's character."[64] Every time limited military force was used against nationalist crowds, on ambiguous and probably oral orders from Moscow, Gorbachev immediately stepped aside and left the military in the lurch, exposed to the fury of the nationalist and liberal media. This pattern had the double effect of paralyzing the Soviet army and strengthening the forces of those who wanted to destroy the Soviet Union.[65]

Gorbachev's decision to renounce the use of force in foreign and domestic policies as a matter of high principle was remarkable and unique in world history. Canadian scholar Jacques Lévesque writes that "the way the USSR separated itself from its empire and its own peaceful end" are linked and "may seem to be its most beneficial contributions to history."[66] But Gorbachev's principled nonviolence, so much appreciated in the West, was not likely to evoke admiration inside Russia. For all of his other roles, for his fellow countrymen Gorbachev was, first and foremost, the czar, the guarantor of their stability and livelihood—and of the very existence of the state. The clear inability and even refusal of Gorbachev to perform this role contributed to the sudden collapse of the Soviet Union and dislocation and misery for tens of millions of Russians and non-Russians.

GORBACHEV, THE PEACEFUL REVOLUTIONS OF 1989, AND GERMAN REUNIFICATION

The effect of this complex mix of character traits—optimism, naïveté, his tendency to act ad hoc, Westernism, and aversion to force—can be seen in the playing out of Soviet policies toward Eastern and Central Europe during the collapse of the Communist regimes and in Gorbachev's diplomacy leading up to German reunification. Critics and supporters point out that Gorbachev's foreign policy after 1987 was rarely discussed formally at the Politburo but instead only in a narrow circle of advisers. In conducting negotiations, Gorbachev relied on Foreign Minister Eduard Shevardnadze and also increasingly discussed issues "between four eyes," that is, directly with foreign leaders. The multi-institutional decision-making structures (the Defense Council, "the Big Five" commission that worked out proposals on arms reductions, the informal "alliance" of the KGB, and the Ministry of Defense) were often not in the loop. On Germany, one participant confirms, Gorbachev handled "all the negotiations virtually by himself or in tandem with Shevardnadze, sweeping aside professional diplomats and scarcely informing the Politburo."[67] In a word, although rejecting Stalin's legacy, Gorbachev used Stalin's power to monopolize vital policy decisions. Thus, Gorbachev's personal traits and his peculiarities as a statesman affected Soviet policy with remarkably few constraints.

In particular, Gorbachev's "anti-Stalin" personality had a lot to do with the peaceful (with the exception of Rumania and Yugoslavia) death of Communism in Eastern and Central Europe. The destabilization of Communist regimes there by the beginning of 1989, as the extensive research of Mark Kramer shows, was a direct consequence of the "spillover" effect of glasnost and reforms in the Soviet Union. As the regimes in Poland, Hungary, and then the GDR, Bulgaria, and Rumania, began to fall, the impact of these developments began to spill over into the Soviet Union, undermining Gorbachev's authority and weakening state and party controls.[68]

Why did Gorbachev and his advisers (but not all of the Politburo members and the military) decide to leave the Soviet Communist allies to their own devices, letting the developments in Central and Eastern Europe proceed without control from Moscow? The ideological factor of "new thinking" and Gorbachev's messianic goal of uniting North America, Europe, and the USSR were crucial. In late

January 1989, Gorbachev assigned the Politburo commission on foreign policy headed by Alexander Yakovlev to work with various agencies and think tanks on contingencies regarding future developments in Eastern and Central Europe. Yakovlev solicited a number of analytic papers from academic and state institutions. Most of them predicted an overall crisis in the alliance. There were frank conclusions that Soviet allies were already quietly rejecting socialism and were "in the powerful magnetic field of the West." One memorandum, written by Oleg Bogomolov and scholars from the Institute of Economics of the World Socialist System, concluded that if the ruling parties did not make concessions to the opposition forces, they faced a "political eruption." Other analysts predicted "a most acute social-political conflict with an unfathomable outcome." All the papers opposed any form of Soviet intervention in the region. The typical conclusion was that any political-military intervention did not guarantee success but might instead trigger a chain reaction of violence and the implosion of the Soviet bloc. The commission, however, did not solicit the opinion of the General Staff. These memoranda preached to the converted. Gorbachev and his "new thinkers" (Yakovlev, Shevardnadze, Chernyaev, Shakhnazarov) all believed that the Soviet invasion of Czechoslovakia in 1968 had been a terrible mistake, and they did not contemplate the use of Soviet troops under any circumstances.[69]

But all this does not fully explain the lack of Soviet *positive* involvement, that is, more vigorous attempts to coordinate actions with the reform-minded forces in the GDR, Poland, and Czechoslovakia, to provide them with material support and to refrain from unilateral measures that would accelerate the destabilization in the Warsaw Pact. Two domestic developments in the USSR help to explain Soviet passivity. The first was the preoccupation of Gorbachev and his entourage with the radical political and state reforms launched at the end of 1988. After this, the avalanche of domestic developments began to engulf the Gorbachev leadership. Gorbachev and his advisers, including those who were the "curators" and "watchers" of the situation in the Warsaw Pact, began to devote the lion's share of their time to writing memos and reports on preparations for the semi-free parliamentary elections in March 1989, on writing new legislation, and later on drafting Gorbachev's speeches and policies at the Congress of People's Deputies that opened in Moscow on May 25. The second development was a severe financial crisis. In January 1989, Gorbachev announced the reduction of Soviet forces in Central and Eastern Europe by 14 percent and cuts in the production of armaments by 19 percent. These measures reinforced his "anti-Fulton speech" at the United Nations on December 7, 1988. At the same time, they sprang from the leadership's desperate attempts to reduce state expenses. The Soviet leaders did not have the money to influence the events in Central and Eastern Europe and had to watch as the governments of these countries turned to the West for credits and other forms of support.[70]

Still, it is stunning, in retrospect, to observe how casually Gorbachev allowed the Soviet external empire in Central Europe to break away. On March 3, 1989, the chairman of the Council of Ministers of Hungary, Miklos Nemeth, informed Gorbachev of the decision "to completely remove the electronic and technological protection from the Western and Southern borders of Hungary. We have outlived the need for it, and now it serves only for catching citizens of Romania and the GDR who try to illegally escape to the West through Hungary." He added cautiously: "Of course we will have to talk to comrades from the GDR." The only words on the record from Gorbachev were: "We have a strict regime on our borders, but we are also becoming more open."[71]

This doctrine of noninvolvement and the lack of a viable strategy marked Soviet diplomacy during the critical months of the summer and fall of 1989, when developments in Central and Eastern Europe took a revolutionary turn. The cable traffic and other communications between Moscow and Warsaw at a critical moment, when the Poles voted for Solidarity to be their government on June 4, 1989, and particularly during the next two months when the issue of Wojciech Jaruzelski's presidency was at stake, is not yet available. Myaczyslaw Rakowski, a leading reformer in the Polish Communist Party, recalls that Gorbachev only called him to find out "what is going on." But he meticulously refrained from any specific advice or anything that could be interpreted as interference in Polish events.[72] On September 11, when the reform-minded Communist government of Hungary opened the borders for East Germans who wanted to flee to the FRG, Moscow kept pointedly silent. The resulting refugee crisis, when tens of thousands of East Germans rushed to Prague and Budapest, destabilized the regimes in those countries. On September 27–28, Shevardnadze, presumably on Gorbachev's instructions, met with his counterparts James Baker and Hans-Dietrich Genscher at the UN General Assembly in New York to discuss the growing crisis of East German refugees in Prague and Budapest. The result was that East German refugees were allowed to stay temporarily within the compounds of West German embassies in those cities.[73]

Gorbachev later claimed that by 1989 he was ready to withdraw all Soviet military forces from Central Europe but that he wanted to do it very gradually, largely because of domestic constraints not geopolitical realities. In Chernyaev's restatement of this thesis, the fear was that "once we start to withdraw troops, the howling begins: 'What did we fight for, what did millions of our soldiers die for in World War II? Are we renouncing all that?' For Gorbachev at that time those issues were very sensitive."[74]

Gorbachev was especially concerned about the positions of the Bush administration and the West German government. There was no consensus in Washington on Reagan's "romance" with Gorbachev. Robert Gates, Richard Cheney, and Brent Scowcroft dismissed "new thinking" as theatrics at best or as deception at worst. Even Soviet withdrawal from Afghanistan, completed by February 1989, did not convince them. Pragmatist and "realist" Scowcroft interpreted it as "cutting losses" and concluded: "Instead of changing, Soviet priorities seemed only to narrow."[75]

However, by the summer of 1989, Bush and Secretary of State James Baker concluded that they had to deal with Gorbachev. They also realized that his personality was crucial. "Look, this guy is perestroika," Bush said to the skeptical experts. He dismissed the analysis of the CIA's Soviet desk that indicated that Gorbachev was losing control over events and could not be a stable long-term partner. In July, Bush went to Poland and Hungary, where he supported Communist reformers and discouraged anti-Communist nationalists from rocking the boat. This trip and Bush's personal communications to Gorbachev assuaged the Soviet leader's fears.[76] In September 1989, Shevardnadze struck up an extraordinary friendship with Secretary of State James Baker and openly shared with him the domestic problems facing the Soviet leadership.[77]

The position of West Germany and its plans regarding the GDR also concerned Gorbachev. Aside from a handful of "new thinkers," the Soviet foreign policy and military establishment still treated the FRG with suspicion. However, by the end of 1988, Gorbachev had established excellent personal relations with Chancellor Helmut Kohl, once a bitter critic of the Soviet leader. This sparked a very rapid shift of Soviet foreign policy on the German Question—one Western scholar described it as nothing less than "a reversal of alliances." Simultaneous with the warming of ties with the FRG, GDR-Soviet relations entered a period of "cold peace." Gorbachev and Shevardnadze denied the East German leaders the leverage over Soviet foreign policy they had used so many times in the past.[78]

When Gorbachev came to West Germany for a visit on June 11–15, 1989, enthusiastic crowds greeted him in the streets. The Gorbymania of West Germans contrasted with the increasingly morose attitude of Soviet citizens toward their leader. Gorbachev's Westernism was also reinforced during his talks with Kohl. The Soviet leader believed he achieved his goal—ensuring that the chancellor became a supporter of Gorbachev's perestroika and his idea of bringing the Soviet Union into a "common European home." In return, he took a very tolerant stand when Kohl suggested joint interference in the affairs of the GDR in order to remove Honecker and encourage changes. Chernyaev contends that the joint FRG-USSR declaration deliberately singled out, from the principles and norms of international rights to be observed, the "respect for the right of national self-determination." It was a hint that the Soviet Union would not oppose by force changes in East Germany. At the same time, Kohl assured Gorbachev that he and his government did not want any destabilization of the GDR.[79] This informal understanding was crucial for the subsequent peaceful reunification of Germany.

But Kohl could not possibly have been neutral to the opportunities that the changes in Central and Eastern Europe provided to West German policy. On August 25, 1989, Kohl reached an understanding with the reformist leadership of Hungary to open the Hungarian-Austrian border to defectors from the GDR. In return, Hungary received 1 billion D-marks to cover its budget deficit. The details of this understanding, fateful for the GDR, have become known only recently.[80] It is still not known what intelligence Moscow received of the deal. When the Hungarian leadership sent a note to Shevardnadze about their agreement with the FRG (the monetary side of the deal was not mentioned), Shevardnadze only answered: "This is an affair that concerns Hungary, the GDR and the FRG."[81] In October, Honecker told Gorbachev that Nemeth received from the SPD a loan of 550 million D-marks on the condition that the "Hungarians opened a border with Austria."[82]

Gorbachev's reaction remains unknown. He and other "new thinkers" had been treating Erich Honecker as a reactionary relic since early 1987 when he began to voice opposition to Gorbachev's policies.[83] Central Committee secretary Vadim Medvedev, in charge of relations with socialist countries and ideology, was in the GDR in September 1989 and came back "with grave thoughts." His conclusion was that "the first thing one should have done—was to take a decision on the change of leadership [referring to Honecker]."[84] At the same time, the KGB in the GDR reported to Moscow on the lineup in the GDR leadership and indicated (without giving an explicit political recommendation) that the situation urgently dictated Honecker's removal.[85]

On October 5, 1989, Chernyaev wrote in his diary: "Gorbachev is flying to the GDR to celebrate its fortieth anniversary. He is very reluctant to go there. Today he called and said: I will not say a word in support of Honecker. But I will support the Republic and the revolution."[86] In fact, the Soviet leader did not take a clear stand during his stay in the GDR. Rather, as his behavior showed, he adhered to his policy of noninterference. Meeting with the East German leadership, he used cryptic language, saying that history punished those who delayed change. Also, at a public meeting in Berlin, he quoted the Russian diplomat and poet Fedor Tyutchev that "love" may be a stronger unifier than "iron and blood." Was this quote aimed at the West German leadership, as a warning against schemes of forced annexation of the GDR? Philip Zelikow and Condoleezza Rice read it this way: It was "a strange way for the leader of the Soviet Union to warn the FRG to respect the 'postwar realities.' "[87]

Vitaly Vorotnikov recorded the first impressions of this visit that Gorbachev shared with the Politburo. Gorbachev told his colleagues that Honecker was out of touch with reality and that a storm was brewing in the GDR. At the same time, he did not propose any specific measures nor discuss any possible implications for the USSR.[88] On October 16, East German leaders Willi Stoph, Egon Krenz, and Erich Mielke sent a messenger to Moscow to seek Gorbachev's support for removal of Honecker. Mielke, the head of Stasi, believed it was already too late for a managed transition of power. Instead of addressing the full Politburo, Gorbachev convened a conference in his office, which included Yakovlev, Medvedev, Kryuchkov, Ryzhkov, Shevardnadze, and Vorotnikov. Gorbachev proposed contacting Kohl and Bush. He also proposed that Soviet forces in the GDR "should behave calmly, without demonstrating force." Once Honecker finally stepped down, the new GDR leader, Egon Krenz, met with Gorbachev on November 1 to discuss the GDR's future. Gorbachev was shocked to learn that the GDR owed the West $26.5 billion and had a $12.1 billion deficit for 1989. He admitted to Krenz and later to his Politburo colleagues that without assistance from West Germany the Soviets could not "save" the GDR. Gorbachev approved the proposal of Krenz to reduce social tension in East Germany by allowing some travel to the West. Gorbachev and Krenz did not discuss in detail plans for the gradual removal of the Berlin Wall.[89]

The fall of the Berlin Wall on November 9, 1989, caught everyone in Moscow by surprise. The East German leaders, acting under growing public pressure and without any advice from Moscow, decided to allow the controlled movement of population between East and West Berlin. But this bungled attempt to open the safety valves triggered the political meltdown of the GDR. The events in Berlin caught Gorbachev, Shevardnadze, and other Kremlin leaders by surprise. The Soviet ambassador to the GDR, Vyacheslav Kochemasov, tried in vain to reach Gorbachev and Shevardnadze on a secure phone. As a senior official at the embassy recalls it, "The entire leadership was busy and nobody could find time for the GDR."[90] Gorbachev did not create any crisis commission to deal with the German Question. There were no substantive discussions of the German issue. The representatives of the military, as well as experts on Germany, were cut off from the decision-making process. Meanwhile, as Lévesque correctly concludes, the fall of the Wall doomed Gorbachev's grand design for gradual European reconciliation. Instead of patiently waiting for the Soviets and the West to construct "the common European home," the GDR, along with all the countries of Central Europe, "hurled itself through the Berlin Wall" to join the West.[91]

What was the Soviet leadership thinking on this fateful day? The available fragmentary minutes and recollections show that during a briefing with select colleagues in the Walnut Room on the eve of the Politburo session on November 9, Gorbachev shared his concerns about the political situation in Bulgaria and the separatist trends in Lithuania. The agenda of the Politburo included discussion on the time and agenda of the Second Congress of People's Deputies of the USSR and possible changes in the Constitution. Another big issue was the situation in Byelorussia, Latvia, Lithuania, and Estonia. This was part of a frantic search for palliatives to block the Baltic drive for political independence. Gorbachev remained optimistic, despite all indications: "Experience shows that even most avowed nationalists will not go far." He believed that the Baltic satellites could be kept in the Soviet sphere through economic incentives. Vorotnikov interjected: "If all that we say to the Balts became publicly known, there would be an explosion in Russia."[92]

These episodes highlight the ad hoc nature of Gorbachev's decision making and the impact of his optimistic and at the same time temporizing personality on Soviet policies. Even Gorbachev's admirer, Georgy Shakhnazarov, later called him a modern Fabius the Qunctator, a reference to a Roman politician notorious for his procrastination.[93] At work here were also two conflicting impulses within Gorbachev. On the one hand, he could not recognize that his vision of reform for Communism was doomed in Central Europe and East Germany. Gorbachev continued to believe that "the socialist base" would be "preserved," and these illusions helped him to ignore a torrent of alarmist voices and watch with sympathy the spectacular process of the dissolution of Communist regimes, first in Poland and Hungary and then in the GDR and the rest of Central Europe.[94]

On the other hand, Gorbachev did not have nor did he even seek to obtain in writing any agreement with the West to preserve Soviet "interests" in the region, such as preventing NATO expansion to the East. Dobrynin later fumed: "Able but inexperienced, impatient to reach agreement, but excessively self-assured and flattered by the Western media, Gorbachev and Shevardnadze were often outwitted and outplayed by their Western partners." Gorbachev in particular failed to state squarely and early enough Soviet terms for reunification (Germany's neutrality, demilitarization, compensation for withdrawal of Soviet troops). Instead, he temporized, played by ear, and yielded one position after another. Dobrynin returns to such features of Gorbachev as optimism, self-confidence, and the unbounded belief in "forces of history" as essentially good and reasonable. This, he argues, served him badly in international affairs, as he, in an increasingly desperate situation, held onto unwarranted expectations that he would, despite the odds, convince his Western counterparts as to the correctness of his initiatives. This "emotional makeup of a gambler," Dobrynin writes, was visible even in 1986 at the Reykjavik summit.[95]

The key lies in the interaction between Gorbachev's personality and his Western counterparts. After the fall of the Berlin Wall, the Bush administration quickly seized the initiative from the weakening hands of Gorbachev and played an active and stabilizing role in ending the Cold War in Europe. For Gorbachev, this was a very important development. Bush finally acted as he had promised to act when he was vice president, as an understanding and reassuring partner, following the model of Reagan's relationship with Gorbachev. On December 2 and 3, 1989, at the Malta summit, Bush and Gorbachev achieved what they had wanted to months before, a personal relationship of mutual trust and respect.[96]

It is remarkable, in retrospect, how much Bush, like Reagan before him, came to believe in Gorbachev as a person of common sense who would admit that the West had won the Cold War. In preparations for the summit, Bush told NATO secretary general Manfred Wörner on October 11 that the main thing was to persuade the Soviets to allow continued change in Central Europe and the GDR. When Wörner warned that Gorbachev would not let the GDR leave the Warsaw Pact, Bush wondered if he could persuade Gorbachev to let the Warsaw Pact go— to decide its military value was no longer essential. "That may seem naive," Bush said, "but who predicted the changes we are seeing today?"[97] One could hardly imagine any U.S. leader trying to persuade Stalin, Khrushchev, Brezhnev, or Andropov "to let go" of the Soviet sphere of influence in Europe.

Other members of the Bush team remained highly suspicious of Gorbachev's intentions. To them, it seemed so revolutionary and improbable that the Soviet leadership was renouncing its geopolitical ambitions that even a year after Malta they had lingering doubts and tried to convey them to the president. When Gorbachev joined the United States in a coalition against its longtime ally, Saddam Hussein, Bush, speaking to his advisers, vowed not to "overlook the Soviet desire for access to warm water ports."[98]

But there was a rare harmony between Bush and Gorbachev, as they talked at Malta in December 1989 one-to-one and almost effortlessly agreed on all the main issues at their first official summit. Bush startled Gorbachev by beginning the discussion with the issue of the "export of revolution" and the Soviet presence in Central America, instead of with Europe. The Americans were relieved when Gorbachev assured them that the Soviet Union "has no plans regarding spheres of influence in Latin America."[99] When the two leaders began to discuss the German Question, Gorbachev had an excellent opportunity to set the terms for the reunification of Germany and demand from Bush, in exchange for support for reunification, a firm commitment to the construction of "a common

European home" with the simultaneous dissolution of the two military-political blocs as part of a new security structure. Instead, he just came down hard on Kohl's "ten points" plan, seeing in it a move by the West German chancellor to swallow the GDR. In Gorbachev's words, this move "put in doubt whether the government of the FRG could be trusted. What would happen? Would a unified Germany be neutral, not belonging to military-political alliances, or a member of NATO? I think we should let everybody understand that it would be premature to discuss now one of the other scenarios." He then continued: "There are two German states, so history ordered. And let history now decide how the process should evolve and where it should lead to in the context of a new Europe and the new world."[100]

This was vintage Gorbachev, preferring to talk about principles on which a new global order and a "common European home" should be based rather than to haggle about the practicalities of a German settlement—again, a stark contrast with Stalin as statesman if one compares the record of the Malta summit with the records of Stalin's negotiations from 1939 to 1945. The Soviet dictator was a stubborn bulldog and sly fox simultaneously, fighting for every inch whenever Soviet state interests (in his view) were at stake and making "generous" concessions only when it suited his overall plan of negotiation. Stalin's foreign policy was imperialistic and very costly for his country, yet his negotiating techniques evoked grudging admiration from other imperialist masters, such as Winston Churchill and Anthony Eden. Gorbachev, by contrast, did not even try to elicit any specific agreements and promises from Bush. At that time, he obviously considered his "special relationship" with Bush as a priority. He was satisfied with Bush's assurances that he would not "dance on the Berlin Wall" and not "jump-start" the process of German reunification.

Various officials in Moscow—including the ambassador to the FRG, Yuli Kvitsinsky, and Eduard Shevardnadze—had been warning since November 1989 that the GDR was about to disappear and suggested a preemptive strategy: to put pressure on Kohl for the idea of confederation of the two states. Alternatively, Anatoly Chernyaev proposed to work toward "a new Rapallo," that is, to reach an early agreement with Kohl about German reunification linking it to Germany's commitment to a new pan-European security structure.[101]

But Gorbachev revealed no inclination for preemptive actions and Realpolitik deals, no matter how serious were their chances for success. For two crucial months, Soviet foreign policy regarding German reunification was adrift. Only by the end of January 1990, in preparation for the meeting of foreign ministers of the four great powers and two German states in Canada, did Gorbachev hold a policy-making workshop with his closest advisers. They accepted a "four-plus-two" formula for negotiations on German reunification. Gorbachev now finally admitted that the process would lead to reunification, but he still hoped against hope that the GDR could survive thanks to its own "perestroika." Gorbachev allegedly came to this conclusion due to false advice from some German experts who reflected the antireunification opinions of the West German social democrats. Although, in fairness, other experts had warned him very early on that the GDR would not sustain itself for long. Also the Soviet leader preferred to let the "two German states" take the lead in the settlement talks and later accepted with an easy heart the replacement of the "four-plus-two" formula with "two plus four."[102] Only in July 1990 did he take Chernyaev's advice and reach a unilateral settlement of the German Question with Kohl at Arkhyz, a resort in the North Caucasus. By that time, Gorbachev's negotiating hand was extremely weak; but even so, he never attempted to play his last card, that is, the presence of Soviet troops on German soil. No "new Rapallo" took place, and Gorbachev did not seek it, very much to the relief of the United States and other Western countries.

By contrast, there was a determined policy on the part of Kohl, supported by the Bush administration, to nudge history in the right direction at a rapid but coordinated pace. This coordinated policy, called by two young members of the Bush administration "a study in statecraft,"[103] helped produce the desired result: Germany became part of NATO, but the USSR did not get any firm commitments about the future structure of European security and Moscow's role in it.

GRAVE DIGGER OF SOVIET POWER

Gorbachev, in his determination to end the Cold War, had to wage two political campaigns: one aimed at the West and another at his own people. The main characteristics of his personality—tolerance for different opinions, idealism, a moralistic optimism, indecisiveness and procrastination, and a strong belief in common sense and the universalist interpretation of "all human values"—made him the darling of the West but the subject of near ostracism at home. For this reason, gradually the relationship between his foreign and domestic priorities was reversed. Initially, foreign policy was meant to overcome the international isolation of the USSR, to improve economic and trade relations with the West, and to wind down the arms race. But by 1987 and 1988, Gorbachev, increasingly alienated from the party nomenklatura and left without any real support in Soviet society, gave priority to the integration of the USSR into the world community. Accordingly, foreign policy became a determinant of domestic policy. His "new thinking" became a goal in itself, a substitute for a "normal" strategy of statesmanship. Gorbachev believed that his romantic schemes of common interests, nonuse of force, and the "common European home" amounted to a ticket for him and the USSR to join the community of "civilized nations."

Gorbachev's idealistic rush to bring the Soviet Union into the "common European home" made him the grave digger of Soviet power. After the Soviet "empire" in Central Europe had collapsed, the Soviet Union itself, "an affirmative action empire" of many old and new nationalities, became vulnerable.[104] The growing domestic anarchy, deepening economic crisis, rise of nationalist separatism, and imminent erosion of the existing state structures demanded action. Yet Gorbachev, as before, continued to rely on grassroots "processes" and believed that he would manage to forge a new democratic Soviet Union. His overconfidence again let him down, but this time the stake was not Soviet external power and influence in Central Europe but the fate of the Soviet Union itself. In 1987 and 1988, he adamantly refused to get rid of the recalcitrant Boris Yeltsin, who had already emerged as a major troublemaker and demagogic populist, by sending him as an ambassador to a small faraway country. "Do you take me for Brezhnev?" he indignantly retorted, when other "new thinkers" warned him that Yeltsin was ambitious and dangerous.[105] By 1991, Yeltsin had become the first popularly elected president of the Russian Federation and wanted to transform this republic from a nominal entity into the real base from which to challenge Gorbachev's power. Also, inexplicably for the "new thinkers," Gorbachev refused to run for popular elections as president of the Soviet Union, a fatal political mistake. He also kept the unreformed hard-liners Dmitry Yazov, Vladimir Kryuchkov, and Oleg Baklanov in charge of the army, the KGB, and the military-industrial complex.

On August 18, 1991, Gorbachev, his wife, Raisa, and his foreign policy assistant, Anatoly Chernyaev, were on vacation in the Crimea when the majority of Gorbachev's ministers took power into their hands. Their principal goal was to prevent the signing of a "Union treaty" between Gorbachev and the leaders of fifteen Soviet republics, a document that would have transformed the Soviet Union into a confederation. What ensued was a parody of the October 1964 coup that deposed Nikita Khrushchev. Tanks and troops flooded Moscow; Soviet citizens outside the capital and major cities hunkered down, waiting to see what would happen. But the ruling junta, all members of Gorbachev's government, seemed to lack the will to use violence and spill blood. They even failed to arrest Boris Yeltsin, the newly elected president of the Russian Federation. The coup leaders, led by KGB chairman Vladimir Kryuchkov (under the nominal leadership of Vice President Gennady Yanaev), later claimed that they wanted to convince Gorbachev to be on their side. Gorbachev, according to his own version, angrily refused and called them "criminals." For three days, the leader of a superpower was the prisoner of the KGB in his Crimean residence, Foros—the architects of the coup claimed he was "sick." Gorbachev and his wife had to rely on the news they received from a shortwave radio procured by his loyal bodyguards. Raisa Gorbachev was on the verge of a breakdown, apparently believing that she and her husband could be assassinated at any minute. She insisted on producing a tape (as proof that they were alive), and one of the housemaids managed to take it out of their Crimean palace, which was guarded by the KGB, in her underwear.[106]

By August 1991, Gorbachev had squandered much of the Soviet global power and his personal political authority. His chronic inability to choose a consistent course of economic and financial reform destroyed Soviet finances, ran up foreign debts, and put the huge country with colossal resources on the brink of default. The peace dividend from the disarmament and the end of the Cold War did not materialize. The domestic trade and distribution system ceased to function. The Soviet Union had not experienced such a situation before, even during World War II. It was this grave crisis that gave mass following to the national-separatist movements, above all, the one in the Russian Federation. Boris Yeltsin profited from this enormously.[107] Gorbachev was seen as a pathetic and procrastinating figure, hated and despised by many of his fellow countrymen and by former Soviet allies around the world. Intellectual and artistic elites abandoned Gorbachev (although he and his wife had cultivated and helped them so much) and enthusiastically supported the anti-Communist course and rhetoric of Boris Yeltsin. Even his partners, the Western statesmen who had benefited from the direction of his policy, did not come through, denying him the large subsidies for the already bankrupt Soviet budget that he asked for. In July 1991, Gorbachev, on the brink financially and politically, asked his George H. W. Bush to mobilize some sort of a Marshall Plan to help convert the Soviet economy into a market economy. This would have meant a pledge of dozens, perhaps hundreds, of billions of dollars. However, the fiscally conservative American president reacted coldly to Gorbachev's frantic pleas. The American economy was in recession, and the U.S. budget had no money for the USSR. Matlock concludes that Bush, despite all his sympathy for Gorbachev the politician, "seemed to be looking for reasons not to assist the Soviet Union rather than ways to do so." The fact that his Western friends abandoned the Soviet leader may have encouraged the hard-liners in Gorbachev's entourage to go ahead with plans for the coup.[108]

The meltdown of Gorbachev's personal power paralleled the meltdown of the state authority and the disorganization of the army and bureaucracies, as well as the collapse of the Soviet mentality, which wary conservatives had long warned about. The democratic nationalist movements in the Baltic republics, Georgia, Azerbaijan, and Armenia, undermined Soviet control there. And for the first time since 1956, a grassroots political movement swept through the capital and other major Russian cities. A sizable minority of the Russian people, perhaps up to 15 percent throughout the Soviet Union, with an even larger percentage of the population of Moscow and Leningrad, supported democratization. Still, the democratic movement in Russia did remain a minority, and Yeltsin, for all his popularity among the Russians, had few levers of power. It was a ridiculously inept coup that handed full power in the Russian Federation to Yeltsin and the minority of "democrats."

The resistance to the coup was the golden hour of the "men and women of the sixties." Together with younger people, students, businessmen, and intellectuals, they rushed to defend the Russian parliament, where Yeltsin stood in defiance of the Kremlin's hard-liners. The days of the August confrontation, capped by the day-and-night vigil around the parliament and the funerals of three young men who were accidentally run over by the armor sent into Moscow streets, produced the "second Russian revolution" and introduced the Russian national identity as a new political phenomenon. The international media, including CNN, beamed the image of a defiant Boris Yeltsin, standing on an armored troop carrier in front of the threatened Russian parliament, around the world. At the same time, the Soviet military, shattered and demoralized by the hasty withdrawal from Central Europe and by the storm of venomous criticism in the liberal media, felt extremely reluctant to use force and spill the blood of compatriots.[109] As the leaders dithered, the coup lost its momentum and collapsed like a house of cards. Pathetically, Kryuchkov, Yanaev, and other plotters flew to the Crimea, where they begged Gorbachev to pardon them and agreed to be arrested on the spot.

The fact that the active participants of this "revolution" never numbered more than 50,000 to 60,000 demonstrators does not diminish its significance. Most of the well-known figures from the Moscow cultural and intellectual elites opposed the coup and supported the "revolution." Soviet bureaucrats and the military abandoned Gorbachev in droves and went over to Yeltsin's camp. As the "new Russia," led by the impetuous Russian president, banned the Communist Party and separated itself from the Soviet Union, other non-Russian republics rushed toward independence as well. On December 8, in a state hunting lodge far from Moscow, Yeltsin and the Communist leaders of Ukraine and Belorussia decided to disband the Soviet Union.[110] One last time, Gorbachev refused to use force to remain in power, but by this time it was probably too late anyway. On December 25, 1991, the triumphant Yeltsin and his supporters forced Gorbachev out of his Kremlin office. A bit later, the Soviet flag went down the Kremlin mast one last time.

No doubt, the debates about Gorbachev's personality and his personal choices will continue for as long as Russia wavers between its need for a strong state, social stability, and prosperous economy, on the one hand, and the need to develop a dynamic, self-reliant civil society on the other. Perhaps a consensus on this question is impossible; in similar circumstances in the past the vision of liberal internationalists in Russia had differed sharply from the concerns of conservative advocates of the strong state, even the most "enlightened" ones. For instance, here is the opinion of one "enlightened" conservative, Russian count Sergei Trubetskoy, concerning Georgy Lvov, the first head of the Provisional Government after the abdication of Czar Nicholas II in February 1917. To a remarkable extent, it echoes the modern criticisms of Gorbachev. Trubetskoy wrote in exile from Paris in 1940:

> The populism [narodnichestvo] of Lvov was of a rather fatalistic nature. I am groping for proper words to characterize his belief in Russian people in general, in the common people in particular. He imagined them in false tones, as if through rosy glasses. "Do not worry," said Lvov to me on the eve of the first assault of the Bolsheviks in Petersburg in the summer of 1917. "We need not use force. Russian people do not like violence. . . . All will settle down by itself. All will turn out to be well. . . . People themselves will create from its wise instincts just and light forms of life." I was shocked by these words of the head of the government in those difficult minutes when he ought to take energetic actions. A true fighter in the matters of economy, in the affairs of the state he was some kind of a believer in non-violence under any circumstances.[111]

Another Russian émigré, Mikhail Geller, wrote a similar assessment of Gorbachev in a book on the history of Soviet society (edited by a former radical "democrat," Yuri Afanasyev): "Gorbachev continued to live in the world of illusions. He assuaged himself with chimerical schemes, in the belief that political zigzags would allow him to retain power, in fact, to aggrandize it." As to the decision to agree to reunification of Germany on Western terms: "The decision of Gorbachev was not an act of [a] statesman who carefully thought through the consequences of his step. Rather, it was an act of a gambler who believed that, if he sacrificed the GDR, he would get in return some aces that he would use at home. Gorbachev seemed to behave like a balloonist who, having discovered that his balloon was falling down, tosses overboard everything that one could find in the basket."[112]

Without Gorbachev (and Reagan and Bush as his partners), the end of the Cold War would not have come so quickly. Also without him, the rapid disintegration of the Soviet Union itself would not have occurred. At each stage of the Soviet endgame, Gorbachev made choices that destabilized the USSR and sapped its strength to act coherently as a superpower. And as this chapter has shown, those choices can be explained only by reference to Gorbachev's peculiar preferences and personality traits. A different person could have taken a very different course of action, and perhaps as a result the Soviet Union would not have collapsed as disastrously as it did, creating so many problems for the future. The peaceful and rapid end of the Cold War secured Gorbachev's place in international history. The unwitting destruction of the Soviet Union made him one of the most controversial figures in Russian history.

(EPILOGUE)

During the forty years that followed World War II, Soviet leaders and elites struggled to preserve and expand the great socialist empire that emerged out of this ordeal. After the historic victory over Nazi Germany, the majority of the Kremlin leaders, party elites, the military, the security police, and members of the military-industrial complex came to identify themselves with the idea of a great power with a central role in the world. The Russo-centric ideas among Russians in the Communist elites and the national feelings of non-Russians (for instance, in Georgia, Armenia, and Azerbaijan) became integrated into this new collective identity. Although terrible losses and material destruction during the war exhausted Soviet society and generated a yearning for a lasting peace and a better life, these same factors reinforced the growing mood among Soviet elites that the Soviet Union *should* and *could* be a global empire.

Documentary evidence on the Politburo's activities, as well as diplomatic and intelligence documents, reveal that the Kremlin recognized global realities of power and sought, above all, to build Soviet strength. At the same time, the Soviet socialist empire was constructed and defended in the name of revolutionary and anti-imperialist ideology. The promises of Leninist ideology—the global struggle against inequality, exploitation, and oppression; international solidarity with victims of racism and colonialism; radical improvement of the lives of the toiling masses—remained written on Soviet banners and in party platforms. The blend of geopolitical ambitions and Communist ideological promises—the revolutionary-imperial paradigm—guided Soviet international behavior throughout most of the Cold War. Soviet leaders from Stalin to Andropov, as well as the majority of the party elite, foreign policy officials, and security police agents—even the most cynical and pragmatic among them—were always obliged to justify their actions by using general ideological formulas and couching them in Marxist-Leninist jargon.

Joseph Stalin was the most murderous but also perhaps the most cynical and pragmatic of Soviet leaders. He was determined to consolidate the Soviet territorial and political gains made during World War II and to build an exclusive security buffer around the USSR. Until the fall of 1945, he was spectacularly successful: among his assets were the power of the Soviet army, the partnership with the United States and Great Britain, the devastation and weakness of Central European countries, the civil war in China, and the high prestige of the Soviet

Union as the primary force that crushed Nazism. Stalin hoped he could achieve his expansionist goals without antagonizing the United States. But the Americans soon proclaimed themselves the guarantors of the free world against Soviet expansion. The Soviet-American confrontation was, from the start, geopolitical and ideological, a clash between two forms of modernity, two ways of life, and two potentially global empires.[1]

The Cold War provided a powerful validation and justification for the Soviet revolutionary-imperial paradigm. Gradually it became clear that, given America's policies of containment and rollback of Communism, the Soviets had to either dismantle their empire or fight for it with all means at their disposal. Stalin was quick on the uptake: even before the Cold War began, he was seeking to restore his absolute control over Soviet elites and society and extend it over the countries of Eastern Europe. Massive state propaganda, capitalizing on popular feeling, created a wartime home front. Most members of the elites shared Stalin's perspective that the United States was preparing for another war. As before World War II, Stalin sought to consolidate Soviet elites and society with a series of increasingly murderous purges. Militarism, great power chauvinism, and xenophobia in Soviet society peaked in March 1953, when the Kremlin *vozhd* suddenly died.

Stalin's successors quickly concluded that the war with the United States was not inevitable. Acting collectively, they designed a "new foreign policy" with the objective of reducing tensions and ensuring a longtime "peaceful coexistence" between the Soviet Union and Western countries. However, the new evidence does not support the previously held views that the role of ideology declined after Stalin's death in favor of pragmatic state interests. In fact, the new Kremlin rulers and Soviet elites continued to subscribe to the revolutionary-imperial paradigm, which remained the core of their collective identity.

Several factors reinforced the strength of this identity. First, the collective leadership inherited a great empire from Stalin and was determined not to lose it. In addition to the memories of World War II, ideological and security considerations delegitimized any attempts to argue for Soviet withdrawal from Central Europe. For instance, by 1953, East Germany became in the eyes of Soviet leaders and elites the jewel and a hub of their empire in Central Europe, a valuable geopolitical and ideological asset that the Soviet Union had to maintain at any cost. The Kremlin also sought to maintain an alliance with China with generous assistance and by offering support of Chinese foreign policy ventures. The East German factor forced the Soviet Union to keep a huge military presence in Central Europe at all times, and the China factor constantly pushed the Kremlin to demonstrate its revolutionary credentials and loyalty to the common ideologi-

cal principles. Even after the Chinese leaders challenged the Kremlin's supremacy in the Communist camp, Soviet leaders vacillated between improving relations with the United States and restoring the Sino-Soviet ideological alliance.
They chose East-West détente, although at the same time, they sided with Chinese and Vietnamese Communists in the Vietnam War.

Second, Kremlin politics favored a leadership that combined flexibility with
toughness and pragmatism with ideological correctness. Khrushchev triumphed
over Beria and Malenkov, claiming that they were prepared to give away East
Germany to the West. And he prevailed over Molotov, arguing before the party
and state elites that Molotov's rigid diplomacy helped to unite Soviet enemies
instead of dividing them. Although Khrushchev publicly denounced Stalin, he
felt the need to prove he could cleanse the sins of Stalinism from Soviet Communism while selling it globally as an effective alternative to American capitalism.

Third, the economic and military power of the Soviet Union grew rapidly in
the years after Stalin's death. During the 1950s, the Soviet Union became the
second thermonuclear superpower after the United States. With the growing
power came the temptation to break through the American-made barriers of
containment around the Soviet empire and to force the United States and other
Western countries to accept an accommodation more favorable to Soviet state
interests. Simultaneously, the growth of Soviet capabilities, highlighted by the
launch of Sputnik in 1957 and by Yuri Gagarin in space in 1961, enormously
enhanced the attractiveness of the Soviet model of modernization among the
underdeveloped countries around the world.

Khrushchev's personal dynamism and ambitions and his periodic, albeit inconsistent, attempts to de-Stalinize the Soviet system and society became a major
engine behind changes in all areas of Soviet life and policies, including foreign
policy. At first, Khrushchev's energy and the "new foreign policy" allowed the
Soviets to make significant advances in the international arena. But Khrushchev's
passionate belief in the revolutionary-imperial paradigm, along with the confrontational logic of the Cold War, kept pushing him to tests of will against the
United States and other Western capitalist powers. Khrushchev believed that the
emerging military equilibrium between the Soviet and Western blocs would force
the Western powers to retreat globally. At the same time, he firmly believed that
Soviet Communism was the wave of the future. His obsession with the use of
nuclear brinkmanship and his ideological messianism explain why the "new
foreign policy" quickly changed its emphasis from tension-reduction and defensive pragmatic measures in Europe to risk-taking in Berlin and to exportation
of the Soviet economic and political model to the third world. In 1955 and
1956, Khrushchev and the collective leadership successfully destroyed American

plans to encircle the Soviet Union. From 1958 to 1962, however, Khrushchev was supporting so-called movements of national liberation and socialist regimes throughout the third world, from sub-Saharan Africa to Latin America. This trend culminated in Khrushchev's extraordinary and risky decision to protect Cuba by deploying Soviet missiles there in 1962. Only when Khrushchev was confronted with the immediate prospect of thermonuclear war did he retreat, sobered.

The Cuban crisis discredited the practice of nuclear brinkmanship and unrestrained ideological messianism. The new collective leadership that ousted Khrushchev in October 1964 discovered a safer way to promote Soviet interests: negotiations with Western powers and détente from the position of strength. In Leonid Brezhnev's view, supported by his lieutenants Gromyko and Andropov, détente with West Germany and agreements with the United States would be better for Soviet state interests and for the Soviet socialist empire than applying pressure on West Berlin and continuing the arms race with the United States. Brezhnev was crucial for détente in the Kremlin leadership. He was the first Soviet ruler who built his legitimacy among the elites and Soviet people not only as the advocate of the accumulation of strength and ideological toughness but also as a peacemaker. And he was, unlike Khrushchev, an effective, patient negotiator. Without Brezhnev, the "high" U.S.-Soviet détente of 1972–74 probably would never have taken place.

However, Brezhnev, despite his enormous power, was more a consensus seeker than a decision maker. And he, like his Politburo colleagues and the majority of his political generation, remained a prisoner of the revolutionary-imperial paradigm. Although Brezhnev and the Politburo renounced the use of military force for blackmail, they never felt they had enough of it. At the height of their nuclear capabilities, Soviet rulers and the military still believed that the United States remained superior and had policies aimed "at blackmailing them or else defeating the Soviet Union in a nuclear war—a mirror image of how American conservatives tended to view Soviet intentions."[2]

During the second half of the 1970s, Soviet security and foreign policies were guided not by a coherent strategy but rather by ideological and bureaucratic inertia and various factional and political interests. Despite the arms control negotiations with the United States, the massive Soviet military strategic buildup continued without interruption. And in the third world, especially in Africa, the Soviets again, as in the Khrushchev era, found themselves on a slippery slope of ideological-geopolitical expansionism, in a zero-sum game against the United States.

American neoconservatives claimed that détente was only a cover for the

Kremlin's drive toward military superiority and victory in the Cold War. They were wrong. Since Stalin's death Soviet society had been changing; during the 1960s and 1970s, Khrushchev's de-Stalinization and then Brezhnev's détente produced the first significant cracks in the Soviet home front. Soviet elites, beginning with the artistic and scientific intelligentsia and ending with some "enlightened" party apparatchiks, began to overcome the legacy of brutal violence and paranoid insecurity. The partial opening of the iron curtain and growing opportunities for international travel and exchange led to a slow diminishing of Soviet xenophobia, militarism, and ideological collectivism. Although the Soviet military, the KGB, and the military-industrial complex remained staunchly hard line, other bureaucracies began to lose their Stalinist edge. Among industrialists and economic managers, there had always been strong support for expanding trade and economic ties with Western countries. Among educated elites, the ability for comparative and free thinking began to grow. A recent study of the Soviet ideological landscape in the mid-1960s detected "a steep decline in the mobilization power of the Marxist-Leninist ideology and the consequent erosion of the ideological basis of the regime's legitimacy." A distinguished Russian scholar concluded in another study that by the early 1970s "the national dream that the Communist idea could be realized" was dashed to pieces. Instead of the "strong consensus" of the early 1960s, just one decade later there were "complete schisms" and "real conflicts" that "threatened the very existence of Soviet society."[3] This trend continued during the détente of the 1970s, and even during the early 1980s, and prepared the scene for the reforms of Mikhail Gorbachev.

Soviet ideology remained, in a bizarre way, part of the Soviet way of life, but instead of mobilizing, it produced duplicity, cynicism, and doubts. After the brutal suppression of the Prague Spring in 1968, even the most idealistic Soviet intellectuals lost interest in the ideological message of Communism. The political leadership, bureaucracies, and professional elites began to regard the official ideology as a ritual external to their real mind-set. Ideological dogma remained an instrument of regulating domestic political discourse and delineating domestic politics. It also remained a crucial part of the official collective identity, centered on great power chauvinism, while the increasingly nominal international Communist movement still validated Moscow's place at the world's center.

This book confirms the paramount importance of individual leaders in explaining Soviet international behavior. Stalin, in particular, controlled most crucial areas of policy making, especially state security, ideology, and military and foreign affairs. His monopoly of major decisions was striking in scope, but in the end this monopoly magnified the effect of his mistakes and miscalculations and contributed to the onset of the Cold War. Stalin's successors were much

lesser leaders. But their roles, too, were vital, as Khrushchev's nuclear brinkmanship and Brezhnev's contribution to détente demonstrated. The disintegration of
Brezhnev's personality, a result of his illness, contributed to the rapid decline of
U.S.-American détente and the growing arms race in Europe and, finally, to Soviet
intervention in Afghanistan in December 1979. This disastrous invasion was the
last major demonstration of the powerful inertia of the revolutionary-imperial
paradigm. The Soviet leaders, alarmed by the prospect of losing Afghanistan to
the United States (they underestimated the potential of Islamic fundamentalism),
resorted to the use of the Soviet army to bring about a change in leadership in
the country. They expected to withdraw troops after a few weeks or perhaps
months. Instead, they got bogged down there for almost a decade. The invasion
of Afghanistan gave a second wind to the U.S.-Soviet confrontation. It also was a
watershed in the history of the Soviet empire. The endless war against the Islamic
guerrillas began to undermine domestic support for Soviet expansionism.

In Washington, the Reagan administration hoped to use the Soviet predica-
ment in Afghanistan to force the Soviet Union into withdrawal from the third
world. It also applied pressure on Moscow to dissuade the Soviets from invading
Poland in 1980–81, when the Solidarity movement challenged the Communist
regime in that country. But economic, political, and military pressures from the
West only pushed the Kremlin to become a beleaguered fortress and to persevere.
Although Soviet leaders secretly renounced the use of military force in Poland,
this decision had little to do with American policies. They also preferred to risk
more losses in Afghanistan rather than suffer the humiliation of unconditional
withdrawal. In the end, the second wind of the Cold War only perpetuated the
Soviet confrontational stance and the anti-American component of the collective
identity of Soviet elites and the aging Politburo leadership.

It was Ronald Reagan's luck that his presidency coincided with generational
change in the Kremlin and the exit of the Old Guard. Mikhail Gorbachev was
the first Soviet leader since Stalin to reappraise drastically the relationship between ideology and Soviet security interests. From a Soviet apparatchik, Gorbachev evolved into an ideological statesman par excellence, but, instead of the
revolutionary-imperial paradigm, he came up with his own "new thinking"—a
vague messianic formula for integration of the world, an ideology that drew on
the ideals of democratized Communism, cherished two decades earlier by many
intellectuals of Gorbachev's generation. The general secretary ended up being
closer in substance to Western social democracy than to Marxism-Leninism.
Gorbachev wanted to reform the Communist Party, transform Soviet society, and
integrate the Soviet Union into "the common European home." He harbored,
however, a number of grand illusions. One was that the Soviet Union would grow

stronger after liberating itself from the Stalinist legacy and the shackles of the revolutionary-imperial paradigm. Second was that Western capitalist countries would help achieve this breathtaking project of merging Soviet reformist Communism with a democratic European socialism.

As was the case of previous Soviet leaders, Gorbachev's leadership played a crucial role in changing Soviet international behavior. At the end of 1988, Gorbachev publicly rejected the ideological rationales behind Stalin's foreign policy goals and renounced the use of force, the silence about past crimes, and the barriers of isolation that propped up the socialist empire. Within a year, this empire collapsed in Central and Eastern Europe. Two years later, the Soviet Union itself imploded and disintegrated into fifteen independent states.

There was a long road from Stalin to Gorbachev that prepared this amazing transformation. Above all, there was a declining will inside Soviet political and intellectual elites to risk a war. Stalin's successors began the shift from confrontation to détente in 1953. Khrushchev's pressure on the West from 1958 to 1962, for all its highly negative consequences, was not driven by purely aggressive aims; in his clumsy way, the Soviet leader wanted to convince the Western powers to end the Cold War on terms acceptable to the Soviet Union. Brezhnev, who had personal experience of World War II, was convinced that the Soviet people deserved a lasting peace. The implementation of détente policies required from the Brezhnev leadership, de facto, a surreptitious retreat from class warfare ideology to ideas of partnership and cooperation with Western powers, despite their capitalist natures. Brezhnev's détente provided an indispensable bridge from Stalin's quiet warmongering and Khrushchev's blustering to Gorbachev's ending of the Cold War.

Ideology, it should be stressed again, looms large in the history of the Cold War in general and in the story of the rise and fall of the Soviet empire in particular.[4] Ideological factors contributed to Soviet determination to confront the United States and expand Moscow's socialist empire, until it became truly global in the 1970s. Despite the decay of its belief system and growing cynicism, the Soviet leadership and elites continued to articulate its international behavior and security interests in both realist *and* ideological language. But the same ideological factors made the Soviet Union behave in peculiar, even bizarre, ways in the international arena. In particular, outdated or misguided ideological assumptions made Stalin inadvertently trigger the confrontation with the United States and later continue the Korean War. Different, but equally misconstrued, assumptions led Khrushchev, Brezhnev, and other Kremlin leaders to believe that it would be possible to negotiate a peaceful coexistence with the United States from the position of strength. Last, but not least, ideological factors contributed substantially to the Soviet downfall, as Gorbachev, in his messianic fervor, promoted the "new thinking" and rejected the use of force as the essential tool of power politics, even to preserve the state order. In the ultimate historical irony, the Soviet socialist empire, whose foundation was the ideology of revolutionary violence, perished by the ideology of nonviolence.

This book on Soviet international behavior brings out the extraordinary role and nature of American behavior in the Cold War. The United States never accepted the Soviet socialist empire in Central Europe and fought against all Soviet-supported revolutionary movements in Asia, Africa, and Central America. Unlike Western Europeans, Americans provided the USSR very little room for compromises and deals. With the exception of the 1960s and the time of Nixon-Kissinger détente, U.S. administrations insisted that the Soviets change their behavior and even their regime before any lasting accommodation could become possible. The American ideology of political freedom and market capitalism was every bit as global and messianic as Soviet Communist ideology. In this sense, the Cold War developed a zero-sum battle between the two messianic centers—imposing the bipolar confrontational logic onto the world and pushing other countries, movements, and ideologies to the sidelines.[5]

The United States emerged from this epic struggle as the only remaining superpower. But this book should serve as a caution to the Americans, who seem to draw triumphalist lessons from this victory and apply these lessons to foreign policy in other regions of the world. Some American politicians and pundits are too quick to claim that containment of Soviet Communism worked. Those who do so usually have even today only a very vague idea about the country that was the target of containment. Reagan's overzealous admirers continue to claim that his anti-Communist crusade and SDI won the Cold War. In retrospect, it is hard to see SDI as anything but a bit player in the finale of the confrontation. At the same time, Reagan played a vital role in the final stages of the superpowers' confrontation. He sensed a historic opportunity in his relationship with Gorbachev and finally seized on it. It was Reagan the peacemaker, negotiator, and supporter of nuclear disarmament, not the cold warrior, who made the greatest contribution to international history.[6]

The United States was also lucky to have an enemy that represented the ideological, economic, and political mirror image of Western capitalism. This enemy was the product of the European search for modernity. In other words, the Cold War was a competition between very distant cousins, who fought over the best way to modernize and globalize the world, not between the friends and foes of modernization and globalization. Some Western scholars and many Russians today believe that Russia had the great misfortune to be a testing ground for an especially vicious and violent means of modernization that promised a shortcut from economic and social backwardness to modernity and acculturation, rational planning, and social justice.[7] At first, the Soviet version of fast-track modernization granted the Soviet Union a victory in World War II, propelled it to superpower status, and won millions of supporters in the underdeveloped third world. Later, however, especially during the 1970s, it became obvious that the American model of modernization, with its political freedoms, private entrepreneurship, and allures of mass consumerism, was much more innovative and resourceful. With the help of the American model, Western Europe, Japan, and some other U.S. allies (although not all of them) emerged as societies with greater prosperity and quality of life than any in the Soviet bloc. Western Europeans managed to combine the benefits of market with social programs. The developed capitalist countries were also much more successful at economic and ultimately political integration than were the countries of the Soviet bloc.

What mattered in the end was the decline of Communist ideology inside the Soviet empire and among elites and the growing appeal of Western models of democracy and modernization. Contrary to Leon Trotsky's expectation in 1926 and Khrushchev's boasts in 1961, the world capitalist train ran at ever-faster speeds. It became gradually obvious to the leaders, elites, and general citizenry in the USSR that the train of Soviet socialism would never catch up with it; rather, it was lagging further and further behind, disastrously. This, in turn, undermined the validity of Soviet ideology and the imperial identity of the most "enlightened" segments of Soviet elites. If the Soviet road of modernization turned out to be not a fast track but a deadlock, why not change tracks? If the socialist empire was increasingly burdensome and generated "afghanistans" and bankrupt regimes in Central and Eastern Europe that needed to be propped up with Soviet subventions, why not abandon this empire? Gorbachev, with his false "new thinking," represented a futile, but historically understandable, closing of the circle: he wanted to integrate the Soviet anti-capitalist experiment with Western democracy. The rebellious cousin was knocking on the door of a distant cousin, asking for reconciliation.

However misguided, Gorbachev's "new thinking" ensured a peaceful end to one of the most protracted and dangerous rivalries in contemporary history. The colossal military power of the Soviet Union, amassed for decades, did not and could not compensate for its profound flaws—the erosion of ideological faith and political will in the Kremlin and among influential segments of Soviet elites. Gorbachev and those who supported him were not prepared to shed blood for the cause they did not believe in and for the empire they did not profit from. Instead of fighting back, the Soviet socialist empire, perhaps the strangest empire in modern history, committed suicide.

(NOTES)

Abbreviations

The following abbreviations are used throughout the notes.

AGF	Archive of the Gorbachev Foundation, Moscow
AMS	Archive of the Memorial Society, Moscow and St. Petersburg
APRF	Arkhiv Prezidenta Rossiyskoi Federatsii (Archive of the President of the Russian Federation), Moscow
AVPRF	Arkhiv vneshnei politiki Rossiyskoi Federatsii (Archive of Foreign Policy of the Russian Federation), Moscow
Brown	"Understanding the End of the Cold War, 1980–1987," oral history conference, Watson Institute, Brown University, Providence, R.I., May 7–10, 1998
CC	Central Committee
CPSU	Communist Party of the Soviet Union
CSA	Central State Archives, Sofia, Bulgaria
CSACH	Central State Archive of Contemporary History, Tbilisi, Georgia
CWIHP	Cold War International History Project, Woodrow Wilson International Center for Scholars, Washington, D.C.
d.	delo (file)
dok.	dokument (document)
f.	fond (collection)
FBIS-USR	Foreign Broadcasting Information Service, reports on the USSR
Fort Lauderdale	"Global Competition and the Deterioration of U.S.-Soviet Relations, 1977–1980," Harbor Beach Resort, Fort Lauderdale, Fla., March 23–26, 1995
FRUS	*Foreign Relations of the United States*
GAPPOD AzR	State Archive of Parties, Political Organizations, and Movements of the Azerbaijan, Baku, Azerbaijan
GARF	Gosudarstvenny Arkhiv Rossiyskoi Federatsii (State Archive of the Russian Federation), Moscow
inv.	inventory
Jachranka	"Poland, 1980–1982: Internal Crisis, International Dimensions," conference organized by the NSArch, the CWIHP, and the Institute for Political Studies of the Polish Academy of Sciences, Jachranka, Poland, November 8–10, 1997
KDB	Forthcoming collection of U.S. and Soviet documents on the Kissinger-Dobrynin back channel declassified by the U.S. State Department and the Ministry of Foreign Affairs of the Russian Federation

l.	list (page)
LC	Library of Congress, Manuscript Division, Washington, D.C.
Lysebu I	"U.S.-Soviet Relations and Soviet Foreign Policy towards the Middle East and Africa in 1970s," transcript of a workshop at Lysebu, Norway, October 1–3, 1994, edited by Odd Arne Westad (Oslo: Norwegian Nobel Institute, 1995)
Lysebu II	"The Intervention in Afghanistan and the Fall of Détente," transcript of a workshop at Lysebu, Norway, September 17–20, 1995, edited by David Welch, Svetlana Savranskaya, and Odd Arne Westad (Oslo: Norwegian Nobel Institute, 1996)
Musgrove I	"Salt II and the Growth of Mistrust," conference organized by the Carter-Brezhnev Project, sponsored by the Center for Foreign Policy Development of the Thomas J. Watson Jr. Institute for International Studies at Brown University and the NSArch, Musgrove Plantation, St. Simons Island, Georgia, May 6–9, 1994, edited by David Welch with Svetlana Savranskaya (Providence: Center for Foreign Policy Development, Brown University, 1994)
NARA	National Archives, College Park, Md.
NSArch	National Security Archive, George Washington University, Washington, D.C.
OHPECW	Oral History Project on the End of the Cold War, under the leadership of Dr. Oleg Skvortsov, transcripts at Institute of General History, Academy of Science, Moscow, and NSArch
op.	opis (inventory)
pap.	papka (folder)
per.	perechen (listing)
por.	portsia (portion)
PRO	Public Records Office, London
PUWP	Polish United Workers Party (Polish Communist Party)
RGALI	Rossiyski Gosudarstvenny Arkhiv Literatury i Iskusstva (Russian State Archive for Literature and Arts), Moscow
RGANI	Rossiisky Gosudartsvenny Arkhiv Noveishei Istorii (Russian State Archive for Contemporary History), Moscow
RGASPI	Rossiisky Gosudarstvenny Arkhiv Sotsialnoi i Politicheskoi Istorii (Russian State Archive for Social and Political History), Moscow
RRPL	Ronald Reagan Presidential Library, Simi Valley, Calif.
SAPMO-BArch	Stiftung Archiv der Parteien und Massenorganisationen der DDR im Bundesarchiv (Records of East Germany in German State Archives), Berlin
tetr.	tetrad (notebook)
TsADKM	Tsentralny Arkhiv Dokumentalnikh Kollektsii Moskvy (Central Archive of Documentary Collections of Moscow)

TsAODM	Tsentralny Arkhiv Obschestvennikh Dvizhenii Moskvy (Central Archive of Public Movements of Moscow)
TsKhDMO	Tsents Khranenia Dokumentov Molodezhnykh Organizatsii (Center for Storage of Documents of Youth Organizations), Komsomol Archives, Moscow
VKP(b)	All-Union Communist Party (Bolsheviks)

Preface

1. For various angles see Taubman, *Khrushchev*; Suri, *Power and Protest*; Wittner, *Resisting the Bomb* and *Toward Nuclear Abolition*.

2. The CWIHP (director, Christian F. Ostermann) and the NSArch (director, Thomas Blanton; research director, Malcolm Byrne) have coordinated such international projects during the past decade. For the impact of Communist allies and third world clients, see Harrison, *Driving the Soviets Up the Wall*; Weathersby, "Soviet Aims in Korea and the Origins of the Korean War"; Westad, *Global Cold War*.

3. Zubok and Pleshakov, *Inside the Kremlin's Cold War*.

Chapter One

1. Overy, *Russia's War*, 287. See also Beevor, *Fall of Berlin*.

2. The population of the USSR stood at 196.7 million in 1941; five years later the census found that 37.2 million were gone, dead, or no longer living in the country. The Nazi genocidal practices bear responsibility for most civilian casualties: 7.4 million were deliberately killed by the Nazis in Soviet-occupied territories, and 2.1 million died as slave labor in Germany and as prisoners in German camps. Krivosheev, *Rossiia i SSSR v voinakh XX veka*; Sokolov, "Cost of War," 172. See also Erickson, "Soviet War Losses," 256–58, 262–66; Kozol, "Price of Victory," 417–24.

3. The consistent view of the CIA in the postwar years was that "the state of the Soviet economy currently acts as a deterrent on the implementation of Soviet aggressive designs." Kuhns, *Assessing the Soviet Threat*, 82, 264.

4. I. Maisky and G. Arkadiev, "Guidelines to the Reparations Program of the USSR," AVPRF, f. 06, op. 7, pap. 18, d. 183, l. 9–10; N. Voznesensky to Stalin and Molotov, AVPRF, f. 06, op. 7, pap. 18, d. 181, 1.51; Zubkova, *Obshchestvo i reformi* and an updated version in translation, Ragsdale, *Russia after the War*, 20; Simonov, *Voienno-promishlennii kompleks*, 192.

5. Victor Kondratyev, "Paradoks frontovoi nostal'gii," *Literaturnaia gazeta*, May 9, 1990, cited in Senyavskaya, *Psykhologiia voini v XX veke*, 188.

6. See Linz, *Impact of World War II*; Barber and Harrison, *Soviet Home Front*; Zubkova, *Russia after the War*, 14–19; Thurston and Bonwetsch, *People's War*, 137–84.

7. English, *Russia and the Idea of the West*, 44.

8. Ehrenburg, *Liudi, godi, zhizn*, 7:711, 8:23; Mikoyan, *Tak bylo*, 513.

9. Beevor, *Fall of Berlin*, 421–23; Pomerants, *Zapiski gadkogo utenka*, 96–97; Barber and Harrison, *Soviet Home Front*, 209; English, *Russia and the Idea of the West*, 44–46.

10. Martin, *Affirmative Action Empire*.

11. Brandenberger, *National Bolshevism*, 55. See also Agursky, *Third Rome*.

12. Inozemtsev, *Frontovoi Dnevnik*, 181, 227.

13. John L. Gaddis perceptively observes that "thanks to Stalin and Hitler" Soviet people "came out of a culture of brutality with few parallels in modern history. Having been brutalized themselves, it did not occur to many of them that there was anything wrong with brutalizing others." *We Now Know*, 287.

14. This topic was a virtual taboo in historical studies until the 1990s; see Naimark, *Russians in Germany*; Beevor, *Fall of Berlin*, 28–31, 108–10; Anatoly S. Chernyaev, *Moia zhizn i moie vremia*, 132–33, 191–92; Slutsky, "Iz 'zapisok o voine'"; war letters of Viktor Olenev published in *Zavtra* 19 (1997); *Moskva Voennaia 1941–1945. Memuari i arkhivniie dokumenti* (Moscow: Mosgorarkhiv, 1995), 707.

15. Pomerants, *Zapiski gadkogo utenka*, 95, 202, 212.

16. Tumarkin, *Living and the Dead*, 88–89; author's personal observations during his visit to the Museum and Park of Victory in Moscow, July 2004.

17. Nekrasov, "Tragediia moiego pokoleniia," 8. See also on this point Grigorenko, *V podpolie mozhno vstretit tolko kris*, 288; Pomerants, *Zapiski gadkogo utenka*, 150; Aksyutin, "Why Stalin Chose Confrontation," 4; Zubkova, *Russia after the War*, 34.

18. Brodsky, *On Grief and Reason*, 3–21; Scherstjanoi, "Germaniia i nemtsi v pismakh krasnoarmeitsev vesnoi 1945 g.," 137–51; Slutsky, "Iz 'zapisok o voine,' " 48–51.

19. The strength of the Soviet army dropped by September 1946 from its peak of 12.5 million to 4.5 million. "Weekly Summary Excerpt, September 20, 1946, Effect of Demobilization on Soviet Military Potential," in Kuhns, *Assessing the Soviet Threat*, 83; memorandum of the CC Komsomol secretary N. M. Mikhailov to A. A. Kuznetsov, September 19, 1946, "O nekotorikh nedostatkakh politico-vospitatelnoi raboti v voiskakh, nakhodiaschikhsia za rubezhom SSSR," in Zubkova et al., *Sovetskaia zhizn*, 356–60; "Svergnut vlast nespravedlivosti," *Neizvestnaia Rossiia: XX vek* (Moscow: Mosgorarkhiv, 1993), 4:468–75; Pomerants, *Zapiski gadkogo utenka*, 210; Zinoviev, *Russkaia sudba*, 241.

20. See Chernyaev, *Moia zhizn*, 195, 208–10; Pomerants, *Zapiski gadkogo utenka*, 91, 154; Zubkova, *Obshchestvo i reformi*, 73.

21. Yakovlev, *Omut pamiati*, 50.

22. Zinoviev, *Russkaia sudba*, 245.

23. Ivnitsky, *Sud'bi Rossiiskogo Krest'anstva*, 420. Zubkova cites the ratio of women to men on collective farms in 1945 as 2.7:1. *Russia after the War*, 21.

24. Gudkov, "Otnosheniie k SShA v Rossii i problema antiamerikanizma," 42; Krylova: " 'Healers of Wounded Souls.' "

25. On prewar patriotism and militarism in Soviet society, see Brandenberger, *National Bolshevism*, 95–112; on the postwar mood in the army, see Chernyaev, *Moia zhizn*, 195.

26. Zubkova, *Obshchestvo i reformi*, 77–83.

27. Gudkov, *Negativnaia identichnost*, 34–37; Tumarkin, *Living and the Dead*.

28. P. Sudoplatov, A. Sudoplatov, J. Schecter, and L. Shecter, *Special Tasks*, 171; see also an expanded Russian version, Sudoplatov, *Razvedka i Kreml*, 206.

29. Mikoyan, *Tak bylo*, 513, 514; Grigorenko, *V podpolie*, 288.

30. Stalin, *Works*, 2:203.

31. Brooks, *Thank You, Comrade Stalin*, 188–91; Weiner, *Making Sense of War*; Miner, *Holy War*.

32. Slezkine, *Jewish Century*, 297. On the origins of the anti-Semitic campaign, see Kostyrchenko, *Out of the Red Shadow* (originally published in Russia in 1994).

33. See this point in Grigorenko, *V podpolie mozhno vstretit tolko kris*, 288–89; Miner, *Holy War*, 321.

34. Maisky to Molotov, January 11, 1944, AVPRF, f. 06, op. 6, pap. 14, d. 147, l. 3–40; *Istochnik* 4 (1995): 124–44.

35. Litvinov, "On the Prospects and Possible Foundation for Soviet-British Cooperation," AVPRF, f. 06, op. 6, pap. 14, d. 143, l. 53; memos of Litvinov in 1945, AVPRF, f. 06, op. 7, pap. 17, d. 175, l. 26–44, 52–65, 109–46, 161–64; Pechatnov, *Stalin, Ruzvelt, Trumen*, 239–57, 339.

36. RGASPI, f. 17, op. 128, d. 717, l. 90–97.

37. For example, see discussion at the All-Union Society for Cultural Ties Abroad (VOKS) of a trip of a group of Soviet officials to Czechoslovakia, June 29, 1945, RGASPI, f. 17, op. 128, d. 748, l. 110–40; Volokitina et al., *Vostochnaia Evropa*, 1:30–32; Malyshev's diary, March 28, 1945, *Istochnik* 5 (1997): 128; Chuev, *Sto sorok besed s Molotovim*, 90.

38. Montefiore, *Stalin*, 548–52.

39. P. N. Knyshevsky, *Dobycha. Taini germanskikh reparatsii* (Moscow: Soratnik, 1994), 20.

40. Rzheshevsky, *Stalin i Cherchill*, 494, 498–99; Maisky to Molotov et al., June 18, 1945, AVPRF, f. 06, op. 7, pap. 18, d. 182, l.32–35.

41. Brandenberger, *National Bolshevism*, 229.

42. Slezkine, "USSR as a Communal Apartment," 414–52.

43. Mgeladze, *Stalin*, 78–80.

44. Chuev, *Sto sorok besed*, 103–4.

45. Molotov's record of conversation with Roosevelt, May 29, Stalin to Molotov, cable of June 1, 1942, Stalin to Molotov, June 4, 1942, in Rzheshevsky, *Stalin i Cherchill*, 211–12, 244, 258–59; Rzheshevsky, *War and Diplomacy*, 94, 219.

46. The literature on this topic is large and growing. See Haynes and Klehr, *Venona*; Weinstein and Vassiliev, *Haunted Wood*; Eduard Mark, "Venona's Source 19," 10–31, esp. 14.

47. Stites, *Revolutionary Dreams*, 156–70; Fülop-Miller, *Mind and Face of Bolshevism*, 49; Parks, *Culture, Conflict, and Coexistence*, 21–46.

48. Mikoyan, *Tak bylo*, 300–315.

49. In 1944, according to Soviet official statistics, Lend-Lease accounted for 10 percent of Soviet GDP, or 45.6 billion rubles. The real contribution of American aid was much higher in specific crucial areas. For example, Lend-Lease gave the USSR 55 percent of its trucks and automobiles, 20.6 percent of tractors, 23 percent of machine tools, 42 percent of motor engines; it also provided 41 percent of its aluminum, 19 percent of zinc, 25 percent of nickel, 37 percent of mercury, 99 percent of tin, 57 percent of cobalt, 67 percent of molybdenum, 24.3 percent of stainless steel, 18 percent of aviation gasoline, 100 percent of natural rubber, 23.3 percent of ethylene spirit, and 38 percent of glycerin. Furthermore, American food, shoes, and Studebaker supplies helped the Soviet army to roll from Stalingrad to Berlin. Simonov, *Voienno-promishlennii kompleks*, 194.

50. Khrushchev, "Memuari Nikiti Sergeevicha Khrushcheva," 81; Schecter and Luchkov, *Khrushchev Remembers*, 85.

51. Parks, *Culture, Conflict, and Coexistence*, 86–87, 92, 95–96.

52. "Zapisnaia knizhka Marshala F. I. Golikova: Sovetskaia voennaia missia v Anglii i SSha v 1941 godu," *Novaia i noveishaia istoriia* 2 (2004): 82–118; author's conversation with Russian scientist Igor S. Alexandrov, New York, March 30, 2002. Both parents of Alexandrov traveled to the United States in the 1940s.

53. Troyanovsky, *Cherez godi i rasstoiania*, 56, 76.

54. Pechatnov, "Exercise in Frustration," 1–27.

55. On condescension see Costigliola, " 'Like Animals or Worse,' " 752–53; Costigliola, "I Had Come as a Friend," 103–28; "Zapisnaia knizhka Marshala F. I. Golikova," 100.

56. For expression of this mentality, see Ehrenburg, *Liudi, godi, zhizn*, 7:714.

57. Costigliola, "I Had Come as a Friend." On Soviet smuggling of American know-how and technological secrets, see Rhodes, *Dark Sun*, 94–102.

58. FRUS, 1945, 8:896–97.

59. When in July 1945, the Chinese minister of foreign affairs, Dr. Soong, asked Harriman to specify the language of some American concessions to Stalin, Harriman had to admit that "there had been no discussion of interpretation. The words were accepted as written." Navy cable, July 3, 1945, Harriman Collection, Special Files, box 180, LC; Gromyko, *Pamyatnoie*, 1:188–90.

60. Sudoplatov, *Razvedka i Kreml*, 265. This Russian version contains some additional information on Soviet preparations for Yalta, as compared with the American edition by Jerrold Schecter and Leona Schecter.

61. Pechatnov, "Big Three after World War II"; Zubok and Pleshakov, *Inside the Kremlin's Cold War*, 38.

62. Maisky's diary, AVPRF, Lichnii fond Maiskogo, op. 1, pap. 2, d. 9, l. 69, cited in Kynin and Laufer, *USSR and the German Question*, 1:701; Protocol no. 6 of the Litvinov Commission, AVPRF, f. 06, op. 6, pap. 14, d. 141, l. 23–24.

63. Aksyutin, "Why Stalin Chose Confrontation," 17.

64. Maisky to Molotov, draft of informational telegram to ambassadors and emissaries of the USSR, February 15, 1945, AVPRF, f. 017, op. 3, pap. 2, d. 1, l. 52–56, cited in Kynin and Laufer, *USSR and the German Question*, 1:608.

65. Stalin attributed the surrender of German forces in Italy to secret American-German bargaining behind his back and, most specifically, to the activities of Allen Dulles, the head of the OSS in Bern, Switzerland. For details see Smith and Agarossi, *Operation Sunrise*.

66. Montefiore, *Stalin*, 486.

67. Gromyko did not include recollections of this episode in his memoirs but shared them with his subordinates. See Troyanovsky, *Cherez godi i rasstoiania*, 129–30; and Semenov, "Ot Khrushcheva do Gorbacheva," 127. This author noticed the huge discrepancy when he read the memorandum of this conversation in Molotov's files at the Archive of Soviet Foreign Policy in 1988. For an interpretation that ignores Soviet memoir evidence, see Roberts, "Sexing up the Cold War," 105–26.

68. Powers, *Not without Honor*, 155–89; Hirshson, *General Patton*.

69. Mikoyan to Molotov, draft decision of GKO, June 24, 1945, AVPRF, f. 06, op. 7, pap. 45, d. 702. Mikoyan's draft was also circulated to Beria, Malenkov, Voznesensky, and Bulganin. On the deficit and war costs to the Soviet budget, see Simonov, *Voienno-promishlennii kompleks*, 187.

70. Molotov's instructions quoted in Pechatnov, "Averell Harriman's Mission to Moscow," 30.

71. The text of this cable was intercepted and later decoded by the American "Venona" project; see "The 1944–1945 New York and Washington-Moscow KGB Messages," Venona Historical Monograph no. 3 (Fort Meade, MD: National Security Agency, March 1996), 69–70. The cable contained names of other "reactionaries": Joseph C. Grew from the State Department, Senators Arthur Vandenberg and Tom Connally, Congressmen (Charles?) Eaton and (Sol?) Bloom, Admirals Ernest J. King and William D. Leahy, Generals (Brehon?) Somervell and George Marshall. It also characterized Averell Harriman as "one of the bitterest anti-Soviet propagandists." One of MGB's sources heard Harriman telling American journalists that "the USSR is aiming at world mastery and is trying to take up a dominating position at the [Berlin] conference."

72. Gusev to Moscow from London, May 18, 1945, cited in Rzheshevsky, *Stalin i Cherchill*, 524; the British plan for war with the USSR, dated May 22, 1945, was found in Churchill's personal files, PRO, CAB 120/161/55911, 1–29; information on GRU's reaction comes from author's interview with Mikhail A. Milstein, January 14, 1990, Moscow.

73. Dobrynin to Kissinger, in memorandum of conversation, July 20, 1970, SCF, 486, PTF, D/K 1970, 1, NARA.

74. Rieber, "Stalin," 1683–90.

75. Harriman, *Special Envoy to Churchill and Stalin*, 46; Kissinger, *Diplomacy*, 398. David Holloway writes that "the policy Stalin pursued was one of realpolitik." *Stalin and the Bomb*, 168.

76. On Litvinov's role and Soviet foreign policy in the 1930s, see Haslam, *Soviet Union and the Struggle for Collective Security in Europe*; Phillips, *Between the Revolution and the West*.

77. See Mastny, "Cassandra in the Foreign Office"; Tucker, *Stalin in Power*.

78. Stalin to Kaganovich and Molotov, September 2, 1935, in Khlevniuk et al., *Stalin i Kaganovich*, 545.

79. On Stalin's policies during Munich, see Lukes, *Czechoslovakia between Hitler and Stalin*. Lukes focuses on the aggressive and manipulative aspect of Soviet foreign policy.

80. Wohlforth, *Elusive Balance*, 33.

81. Chicherin to Lenin, August 18, 1921, in *Istochnik* 3 (1996): 55–56.

82. Pantsov, *Tainaia istoriia Sovetsko-kitaiskikh otnoshenii*, chaps. 6, 9, 10; Damie et al., *Komintern protiv faschizma*, 21–30.

83. Goldgeier, *Leadership Style and Soviet Foreign Policy*, 18–21; Tucker, *Stalin as Revolutionary*.

84. See more in Zubok and Pleshakov, *Inside the Kremlin's Cold War*, 19–25; see also many insights in Montefiore, *Stalin*.

85. Chuev, *Sto sorok besed*, 78, 82.

86. "Zapis besedi tov. Stalina s gruppoi angliiskikh leiboristov—deputatov parlamenta," October 14, 1947, CSACH, f. 1206, op. 2, d. 326d, l. 16.

87. More on this in Zubok and Pleshakov, *Inside the Kremlin's Cold War*, 16–17; Brandenberger and Dubrovsky, " 'People Need a Tsar,' " 879, 883–84.

88. Ilizarov, "Stalin"; Tarle, *Politika*, 7; Zelenov, "I. V. Stalin," 3–40.

89. Brandenberger and Dubrovsky, " 'People Need a Tsar,' " 880; Zelenov, "Kak Stalin kritikoval i redaktiroval konspekti shkolnikh uchebnikov po istorii," 3–30; Schecter and Luchkov, *Khrushchev Remembers*, 144.

90. Zubok and Pleshakov, *Inside the Kremlin's Cold War*, 13–15. More on the combination of ideological and geopolitical priorities in Soviet foreign policy can be found in Gould-Davies, "Rethinking the Role of Ideology," 92; Macdonald, "Formal Ideologies in the Cold War."

91. On the Churchill-Stalin talks in 1944, see record of conversation of Stalin with Churchill, October 14, 1944, *Istochnik* 4 (1995): 147; see also Records of the Meetings at the Kremlin, Moscow, October 9–October 17, 1944, Churchill Papers, 3/434/2, PRO; Gardner, *Spheres of Influence*, 208; Rzheshevsky, *Stalin i Cherchill*, 418–74, 499–506, 507.

92. Volokitina et al., *Vostochnaia Evropa*, 1:132–33.

93. Dimitrov, *Diary*, 357–58.

94. Chuev, *Sto sorok besed*, 92–93.

95. Stalin to the Yugoslavs, January 9, 1945, in Dimitrov, *Diary*, 352–53; "Notes of V. Kolarov from a meeting with J. Stalin," CSA, f. 147 B, op. 2, d. 1025, l. 1–6, provided by Jordan Baev to Stalin Collection, CWIHP; see also Stalin's milder but similar pronouncements in Volokitina et al., *Vostochnaia Evropa*, 1:130. For the background of events in Greece, see Iatrides, "Revolution or Self-Defense?" 3–17.

96. Chuev, *Sto sorok besed*, 67.

97. The growing historiography on Soviet intentions and behavior in Eastern Europe includes Naimark and Gibiansky, *Establishment of Communist Regimes in Eastern Europe*; Mastny, *Cold War and Soviet Insecurity*; Mark, "Revolution by Degrees"; Volokitina et al., *Vostochnaia Evropa*; Gibiansky, "Sowjetisierung Osteuropas"; Karner and Stelzl-Marx, *Rote Armee in Österreich*.

98. Volokitina et al., *Vostochnaia Evropa*, 1:28–29.

99. Schecter and Luchkov, *Khrushchev Remembers*, 100.

100. The views on Roosevelt's initiative and intentions in this instance remain polarized. See Gardner, *Spheres of Influence*; Perlmutter, *FDR and Stalin*.

101. Chuev, *Sto sorok besed*, 76.

102. Naimark, *Russians in Germany*, 385–90.

103. Author's interview with Boris Ponomarev, former head of the CC International Department, Moscow, July 15, 1991.

104. Kersten, *Establishment of Communist Rule in Poland*.

105. On the expulsion of Germans from Poland and Czechoslovakia and Stalin's role, see Naimark, *Fires of Hatred*, 108–38. On the divisions in Hungarian society, see Krisztian Ungvary, *The Siege of Budapest: One Hundred Days in World War II* (New Haven, Conn.: Yale University Press, 2005).

106. On the schemes of confederations, see Naimark and Gibiansky, *Establishment of Communist Regimes in Eastern Europe*; Gibiansky, "Ideia balkanskogo ob'edineniia i plani eie osu-

schestvleniia v 40-t godi XX veka"; Murashko and Noskova, "Stalin and the National-Territorial Controversies in Eastern Europe," 161–73.

107. The Poles had ample reasons to fear the worst. In 1937–38, 110,000 ethnic Poles, among them Communists, expats, and Soviet citizens of Polish origin, disappeared in the meat grinder of the Great Terror. In 1939–40, up to one and a quarter million former Polish citizens, among them Poles, Jews, Ukrainians, and Byelorussians, were deported to the Gulag and the Soviet interior. Tens of thousands died. At Stalin's order, the NKVD squads executed over 15,000 Polish POWs, mostly officers who surrendered to the Soviet army. See Petrov and Roginsky, " 'Polish Operation" of the NKVD," 12, 170–73; Lebedeva et al., Katyn; Chuev, Sto sorok besed, 78.

108. On October 17, 1944, the last day of the Stalin-Churchill talks about the future of Poland, Beria reported to Stalin that the head of SMERSH, Viktor Abakumov, would send "100 officers of SMERSH to prop up the counterintelligence of the [pro-Soviet] Polish Army." Beria himself sent "15 comrades through the channels of NKVD-NKGB to assist Polish state security." Also, 4,500 NKVD troops were dispatched to Poland. Volokitina et al., Vostochnaia Evropa, 1:83–84; NKVD i polskoie podpolye, 41–42; Bordyugov et al., SSSR-Polsha; Serov to Beria, March 21, 1945, GARF, f. 9401, op. 2, d. 94, l. 122–26; Volokitina et al., Vostochnaia Evropa, 1:72.

109. Hazard, Cold War Crucible, 29, 69, 74; Schuyler to Susaikov, March 6, 1945, AVPRF, f. 07, op. 10, pap. 24, d. 335, l. 32–33, in T. V. Volokitina et al., Tri vizita Vishinskogo v Bukharest, 86–92, 94–96, 98–100, 112–13, 107, 123.

110. Dimitrov, Diary, 352–53; "Notes of V. Kolarov from a meeting with J. Stalin," CSA, f. 147 B, op. 2, d. 1025, l. 1–6, collection of CWIHP; Volokitina et al., Vostochnaia Evropa, 1:128–29.

111. Gibiansky, "Stalin and Triest Confrontation of 1945," 49–57.

112. Pechatnov, "Allies Are Pressing on You."

113. See Hasegawa, Northern Territories Dispute and Russo-Japanese Relations, 1:59–73, esp. 69 and 71; Slavinsky, Yaltinskaia konferentsia i problema "severnikh territorii," 88; Leffler, Preponderance of Power, 87–88; Niu Jun, "Origins of the Sino-Soviet Alliance," 57.

114. Westad, Cold War and Revolution, 54–55.

115. Meetings of June 30, July 2, and July 7, 1945, Victor Hoo Papers, box 2, file "Sino-Soviet Relations, 1945–1946," Hoover Institute for War, Revolution, and Peace, Stanford, Calif. (provided by Dr. David Wolff to the CWIHP conference on Stalin, September 1999); Goncharov, Lewis, and Litai, Uncertain Partners, 3.

116. Stalin-Soong meeting, July 9, 1945, 18, Victor Hoo Papers, box 2, Hoover Institute for War, Revolution, and Peace, Stanford, Calif.

117. Zhang Shuguang and Chen Jian, Chinese Communist Foreign Policy, 29–32; Chen Jian, Mao's China and the Cold War, 27–28.

118. On July 18 Harriman in his summary on the Sino-Soviet talks noted that the issue of independence of the Mongolian People's Republic from China "goes beyond the strict interpretation of the Yalta agreement." However, he added, "it is not considered that the interests of the United States are adversely affected by this concession to the demands of the Soviet Government. "Yalta Agreement Affecting China," July 18, 1945, also the cable from Harriman

to the Secretary of State on July 7, 1945, box 180, Harriman Collection, LC; Liang Chin-tung, "Sino-Soviet Treaty of Friendship and Alliance of 1945," 382–90; Goncharov, Lewis, and Litai, *Uncertain Partners*, 5; Pechatnov, "Averell Harriman's Mission to Moscow," 34.

119. The most detailed study of this aborted operation is in Slavinsky "Soviet Occupation of the Kurile Islands," 62–64. The article is based on still-classified documents that Slavinsky was able to see in the Moscow branch of the Central Naval Archive.

120. Eisenberg, *Drawing the Line*, 105–7, 110–11, 182–83; Molotov to Dimitrov, August 6, 1945, in Dimitrov, *Diary*, 492; Hazard, *Cold War Crucible*, 114–15; Chuev, *Sto sorok besed*, 79.

121. Khariton and Smirnov, *Myths and Reality of the Soviet Atomic Project*, 64; author's interview with Igor Golovin, January 30, 1993, Moscow. Golovin told me that in the days following Hiroshima Soviet physicists from the Kurchatov laboratory were called every day to report to Soviet authorities on the nature of the new weapon.

122. Werth, *Russia at War*, 925; Holloway, *Stalin and the Bomb*, 127. Gromyko's son Anatoly cites his father as recalling that Hiroshima "set the heads of the Soviet military spinning. The mood in the Kremlin, in the General Staff was neurotic, the mistrust towards the Allies grew quickly. Opinions floated around to preserve a large land army, to establish controls over extended territories to lessen potential losses from atomic bombings. In other words, atomic bombing of Japan made us once again reappraise the meaning of the entire East European beachhead for the USSR." Gromyko, *Andrei Gromyko v labirintakh Kremlia*, 65.

123. The project was administered by a formidable group: Beria (chairman); head of the party secretariat, Georgy M. Malenkov; head of the State Planning Commission (Gosplan), Nikolai A. Voznesensky; minister of armaments, Boris L. Vannikov; two deputy ministers of the NKVD, Avraami P. Zaveniagin and Viktor A. Makhnev; as well as nuclear physicists Igor V. Kurchatov and Petr L. Kapitsa. New structures included the Scientific Technical Committee on atomic energy and the First Main Directorate (PGU) of the Council of Ministers. Kochariants and Gorin, *Stranitsi istorii iadernogo tsentra "Arzamas-16"*, 13–14.

124. See Alperovitz, *Atomic Diplomacy*.

125. There was a conspiracy of silence about the bomb in the Soviet leadership and bureaucracy. In December 1945 Litvinov wrote to Molotov: "I have always believed and believe now that, since any talks about the Atomic Bomb cannot produce positive results for us, the most beneficial stand for us is to pay complete indifference to this topic, to avoid speaking or writing about it, until we are asked." Litvinov to Molotov, December 8, 1945, AVPRF, f. 06, op. 8, pap. 125, d. 91, l. 4.

Chapter Two

1. See Hottelet's publication about this conversation in *Washington Post*, January 21–25, 1952; Mastny, "Cassandra in the Foreign Office." On Stalin-Litvinov disagreements and common ground see Zubok and Pleshakov, *Inside the Kremlin's Cold War*, 38–39.

2. Goncharov, Lewis, and Litai, *Uncertain Partners*, 4–5. This expectation is quite obvious in the memorandum of Solomon Lozovsky to Stalin on January 15, 1945, in Slavinsky, *Yaltinskaia konferentsia i problema "severnikh territorii,"* 86.

3. Stalin to Harriman, August 19, 1945, Special Files, box 182, Harriman Collection, LC;

Slavinsky, "Soviet Occupation of the Kurile Islands," 62–64; Hasegawa, *Northern Territories Dispute and Russo-Japanese Relations*, 1:63–64. For more detailed background see Hasegawa, *Racing the Enemy*.

4. Volokitina et al., *Vostochnaia Evropa*, 1:247–51; August 22 and 24, 1945, entries in Dimitrov, *Diary*, 380. On the British reaction see Hazard, *Cold War Crucible*, 117, 123.

5. August 30, 1945, entry in Dimitrov, *Diary*, 381.

6. For details see Alperovitz, *Atomic Diplomacy*.

7. Cable of September 13 from APRF, cited in Pechatnov, "Allies Are Pressing on You," 4.

8. Cable of September 21 from APRF, cited in Pechatnov, "Allies Are Pressing on You," 4; also Pechatnov, "Averell Harriman," 37.

9. Pechatnov, "Allies Are Pressing on You," 5.

10. Cable of September 22 from APRF, ibid., 5.

11. Cable of September 26 from APRF, ibid., 6. More on Stalin's struggle for control over Japan is in Pechatnov, "Averell Harriman," 35–42.

12. Notes on Stalin's statement during his meeting with a Bulgarian delegation, Moscow, August 30, 1945, CSA, f. 146B, op. 4, ae. 639, l. 20–28, provided by Jordan Baev to Stalin Collection, CWIHP.

13. Zubok and Pleshakov, *Inside the Kremlin's Cold War*, 97.

14. Pechatnov, "Allies Are Pressing on You," 6.

15. See Volokitina et al., *Vostochnaia Evropa*, 1:248–51, 280–87, 294–95; Harriman-Stalin meeting, October 25, 1945, Harriman Collection, Special Files, box 183, LC.

16. Leffler, *Preponderance of Power*, 47; on the American concept of "open" sphere of influence see Mark, "American Policy toward Eastern Europe."

17. Werblan, "Conversation between Wladyslaw Gomulka and Josef Stalin," 136.

18. Stalin to V. M. Molotov, G. M. Malenkov, L. P. Beria, A. I. Mikoyan, December 9, 1945, RGASPI, f. 558, op. 11, d. 99, l. 127; Khlevniuk et al., *Politburo TsK VKP(b) i Sovet Ministrov SSSR*, 201–2.

19. FRUS, 1945, 8:491–519; Taubman, *Stalin's American Policy*.

20. Schuyler diary cited in Hazard, *Cold War Crucible*, 152; December 23, 1945, entry in Dimitrov, *Diary*, 518.

21. Stalin's conversation with Bulgaria's chairman of Council of Ministers K. Georgiev, ministers P. Stainov and A. Yugov, and the emissary D. Mikhalchev, January 7, 1946, APRF, f. 45, op. 1, d. 252, l. 28–39, published in Volokitina et al., *Vostochnaia Evropa*, 1:357, 359, 360, 361. At that time Soviet intelligence reported on the increased Anglo-American attempts to encourage the Bulgarian opposition to resistance. See "Political Problems in Bulgaria and Romania Following Moscow Conference Decisions."

22. Dimitrov, *Diary*, 520, 521, 522–23.

23. Pechatnov saw the minutes of that meeting in Russian archives; see Levering, Pechatnov, Botzenhart-Viehe, and Edmondson, *Debating the Origins of the Cold War*, 121; Boterbloem, *Life and Times of Andrei Zhdanov*, 249–51.

24. Stalin's conversations with B. Bierut and E. Osubka-Morawski, May 24, 1946, in Volokitina et al., *Vostochnaia Evropa*, 1:458–59, 461, 462–63.

25. Niu Jun, "Origins of the Sino-Soviet Alliance," 55–56.

26. Chen Jian, *Mao's China and the Cold War*, 31–32.

27. Ledovsky, "Stalin i Chan Kai Shi."

28. "For the Visit of Jiang Jingguo," Solomon Lozovsky to Stalin and Molotov, December 29, 1945, document from APRF, published in Ledovsky, "Stalin i Chan Kai Shi," 108.

29. Record of conversation of Stalin with Jiang Jingguo, personal representative of Jiang Jieshi, December 30, 1945, document from APRF published in Ledovsky, "Stalin i Chan Kai Shi," 106, 108, 109–19; Chen Jian, *Mao's China and the Cold War*, 33.

30. Mao kept the Kremlin informed about his intentions to maintain armed forces for a future confrontation with the GMD government; see Ledovsky, "Stalin i Chan Kai Shi," 110; Chen Jian, *Mao's China and the Cold War*, 32.

31. Kuisong, "Soviet Factor and the CCP's Policy towards the United States," 26; Chen Jian, *Mao's China and the Cold War*, 34.

32. Westad, *Decisive Encounters*, 35.

33. The convention allowed the USSR to send its fleets through the straits in peacetime, but Turkey could shut them in time of war or if "threatened by aggression." Great Britain, France, Yugoslavia, Greece, and Bulgaria, as well as Germany and Japan, were among the signatories of the convention.

34. See "Beseda tov. Stalina i Molotova s ministrom inostrannikh del Turtsii Sarajoglu," Moscow, October 1, 1939, RGASPI, f. 558, op. 11, d. 388, l. 14–32; Molotov's notes with Stalin's instructions for November 1940 talks in Berlin, Volkogonov Collection, LC; "On the Eve"; "Zapis besedi tov. I. V. Stalina s Cherchillem," October 9, 1944, published in *Istochnik* 2 (2003): 50–51. For the best account of Soviet-Turkish relations, using Soviet archives, see Hasanli, *SSSR-Turtsiia*; Lavrova, *Chernomorskiie prolivi*, 42–77; Kochkin, "SSSR, Angliia, SShA i 'Turetskii krizis,'" 58–77.

35. Maxim Litvinov, "K voprosu o prolivakh," November 15, 1944, AVPRF, f. 06, op. 6, pap. 14, d. 143, l. 52; Miller to Dekanozov, January 15, 1945, AVPRF, f. 06, op. 7, pap. 57, d. 946, l. 6.

36. "K voprosu ob istorii sovetsko-turetskikh otnoshenii v 1944–1948 godakh," a review prepared by I. N. Zemskov for the Historic-Diplomatic Division of the Ministry of Foreign Affairs of the USSR, RGANI, f. KPK, "Delo Molotova," 13/76, 8:13. The best background from the Western side is in Kuniholm, *Origins of the Cold War in the Near East*, 257–64. See also FRUS, 1945, 1:1017–18.

37. In conversation with Akaky Mgeladze, Georgian party official, Marshal Fedor Tolbukhin, commander of Soviet troops in Bulgaria in 1944, said that he called Stalin twice to persuade him to attack Turkey. Mgeladze, *Stalin*, 61–62.

38. AVPRF, f. 129, op. 29, pap. 168, d. 22, l. 15–16, f. 06, op. 7, pap. 47, d. 758, l. 6–14, cited in Lavrova, *Chernomorskiie prolivi*, 77–78, and in Kochkin, "SSSR, Angliia, SShA i 'Turetskii krizis,'" 60.

39. Fromkin, *Peace to End All Peace*; Hasanli, *SSSR-Turtsiia*, 154–56; Melkonian, "Puti politicheskoi adaptatsii armianskoi diaspori"; S. Karapetian, minister of Foreign Affairs of the Armenian SSR, to G. A. Arutyunov, secretary of the NKK(b) Armenia, May 29, 1946, memoranda on the Armenian Question, Central Party Archive of Armenia, 'Special Files,' 1946.

40. Chuev, *Sto sorok besed*, 102–3; Zubok and Pleshakov, *Inside the Kremlin's Cold War*, 92–93; Lavrova, *Chernomorskiie prolivi*, 78.

41. Notes by V. Kolarov after his meeting with Stalin, January 28, 1945. Stalin's opinions on certain questions, CSA, f. 147 B, op. 2, d. 1025, l. 12, provided by Jordan Baev to Stalin Collection, CWIHP.

42. Kuniholm, *Origins of the Cold War in the Near East*, 262–65; Lavrova, *Chernomorskiie prolivi*, 84–85, 86; AVPRF, f. 017, op. 3, pap. 2, d. 2, l. 56, published in Kynin, *SSSR i Germanskii Vopros*, 1:608.

43. Taubman, *Stalin's American Policy*, 116–18; Chuev, *Sto sorok besed*, 103; Pechatnov, "Allies Are Pressing on You," 7–8.

44. Vladimirov to Dimitrov on December 27, 1944, in Dimitrov, *Diary*, 456; "K voprosu ob istorii sovetsko-turetskikh otnoshenii v 1944–1948 godakh," a review prepared by I. N. Zemskov for the Historic-Diplomatic Directorate of the Ministry of Foreign Affairs of the USSR, RGANI, f. KPK, "Delo Molotova," 13/76, 8:13.

45. Chuev, *Sto sorok besed*, 102–3; transcripts of the Plenum, July 11, 1955, RGANI, f. 2, op. 1, d. 161, l. 224.

46. Hasanli, *SSSR-Turtsiia*, 212–13, 296.

47. There were also two prominent Georgians in the Commissariat of Foreign Affairs: Sergei Kavtaradze and Vladimir Dekanozov. N. Khrushchev, *Khrushchev Remembers*, 295–96; Beria, *Beria, My Father*, 200–201.

48. Archive of the President of Georgia, Tbilisi, Georgia, f. 14, op. 19, l. 209, l. 27–29, 51–57; Hasanli, *SSSR-Turtsiia*, 216–21; author's interview with Davy Sturua, Tbilisi, August 20, 1999, in author's possession.

49. Hasanli, *SSSR-Turtsiia*, 250–51, 259–61, 271; *Izvestia*, December 16, 1945.

50. Stalin to Vinogradov, cable received in Ankara on December 7, 1945, RGASPI, f. 558, op. 11, d. 99, l. 117–18.

51. Hasanli, *Yuzhnii Azerbaijan*, 74, 421–22; for English version, see *At the Dawn of the Cold War: The Soviet-American Crisis over Iranian Azerbaijan, 1941–1946* (New York: Rowan and Littlefield, 2006). On Bagirov see Ismailov, *Vlast i Narod*; Scheid, "Stalin and the Creation of the Azerbaijan Democratic Party," 3.

52. Baibakov, *Ot Stalina do Eltsina*, 81, 83.

53. L. Beria to Stalin, "O mirovoi dobiche i zapasakh nefti," GARF, f. 9401 ("Special Dossier of Stalin"), op. 2, d. 66, l. 151–58.

54. Hasanli, *Yuzhnii Azerbaijan*, 35–71; report of M. J. Bagirov to Stalin, September 6, 1945, GAPPOD AzR, copy provided by Dr. Jamil Hasanli at NSArch.

55. Kennan to the State Department, November 7, 1944, FRUS, 1944, 5:470; Skrine, *World War in Iran*, 227; Abrahamian, *Iran between the Two Revolutions*, 210.

56. RGASPI, f. 17, op. 128, d. 176, l. 54–106, 121–66 and d. 819, l. 31–85, 155–229.

57. Politburo to Bagirov, July 6, 1945, GAPPOD AzR, f. 1, op. 89, d. 90, l. 4–5, copy provided by Dr. Jamil Hasanli at NSArch; see also Hasanli, *Yuzhnii Azerbaijan*, 74–78.

58. Information provided by Prof. Eldar Ismayilov at the international conference "Armenia, Azerbaijan, Georgia in the Cold War," Tsinandali, Georgia, July 8–9, 2002.

59. In 1920–21 the Red Army helped the separatist elements in northern Iran to set up "the Guilan Soviet Republic," which proclaimed autonomy from Tehran. The Kremlin sacrificed the separatists for the sake of a deal with the Shah Reza leadership in Tehran. The underlying motive of the Bolshevik leadership was to get rid of British influence in Iran. Jacobson, *When the Soviet Union Entered World Politics*, 63–67; Chaqueri, *Soviet Socialist Republic of Iran*, 426–29, 442–47; Abrahamian, *Iran between Two Revolutions*, 210, 218, 236–37. For Stalin's involvement, see Jakov Drabkin, et al., eds., *Komintern i ideia mirovoi revoliutsii. Dokumnenti* (Moscow: Nauka, 1998), 215–16.

60. L'Estrange Fawcett, *Iran and the Cold War*, 46; see also this point in Hasanli, *Yuzhnii Azerbaijan*, 86–87.

61. "Political Situation in Iran and the Measures to Develop a Democratic Movement," report of Ashurov to Fitin and Yemelyanov, December 30, 1945, with comments of Yemelyanov on January 19, 1946, and Bagirov on January 23, 1946, GAPPOD AzR, f. 1, op. 89, d. 113, l. 17–33, document provided by Dr. Jamil Hasanli at NSArch; reports of Artashes (Ovanesian), a Kremlin informer inside Tudeh, to the CC VKP(b), on September 21, 22, and 24, and October 5, 1945, RGASPI, f. 17, op. 128, l. 31–85. For more detail, see Hasanli, *Yuzhnii Azerbaijan*, 85–86, 88–135.

62. These hopes were not totally without foundation; there were signals that Great Britain might choose this option. Abrahamian, *Iran between Two Revolutions*, 222.

63. British ambassador in Tehran, Sir Reader Bullard, said to the Iranian chief of staff: "We were not going to declare war on Russia for that." Kuniholm, *Origins of the Cold War in the Near East*, 279; Ulam, *Expansion and Coexistence*, 426; Lytle, *Origins of the Iranian-American Alliance*, 149–51.

64. Transcripts of Molotov-Qavam's talks are in AVPRF, f. 06, op. 6, pap. 35, d. 547, l. 3–20 and d. 552, l. 14–32; the records of Stalin's conversations with Qavam are still inaccessible but their content can be reconstructed from other evidence; see Fatemi, *USSR in Iran*, 102–4; Hasanli, *Yuzhnii Azerbaijan*, 220–311.

65. Hasanli, *Yuzhnii Azerbaijan*, 423.

66. Kuniholm, *Origins of the Cold War*, 310–11, 314; Lytle, *Origins of the Iranian-American Alliance*, 161–63.

67. Chuev, *Sto sorok besed*, 103–4.

68. Quoted in Yegorova, " 'Iranskii krizis,' " 41.

69. Pechatnov, "Allies Are Pressing on You."

70. Ismailov, *Vlast i narod*, 276.

71. Mark, "War Scare of 1946," 400–406; see also his "Turkish War Scare of 1946," 112–26.

72. Mgeladze, *Stalin*, 61–62.

73. On February 13, 1947, the All-Union Society for Cultural Ties Abroad (VOKS), a state-funded "public organization" created by the Kremlin for cultivating friends and expanding Soviet influence abroad, reported to Molotov, Vyshinsky, and G. Alexandrov that VOKS had its branches in fifty-four countries in 1946 in comparison to only six in 1940. The number of the society's branches abroad had grown from 24 to 4,306, and its membership increased from

eight hundred to three million. RGASPI, f. 82, op. 2, d. 1013, l. 8. Also, in Italy and France the membership of Communist parties in 1946 numbered in the millions.

74. The NKGB report by Anatoly Gorsky to Vladimir Merkulov cited in Weinstein and Vassiliev, *Haunted Wood*, 283–85.

75. Weinstein and Vassiliev, *Haunted Wood*, 104–7; GRU must have "frozen" its agent network as well, for fear of exposure, since many GRU agents switched to NKGB networks after the purges of 1938. Since late 1945, GRU, as well as NKGB, was under the scrutiny of a special Politburo commission (consisting of Malenkov and Beria), which investigated the Gouzenko and Bentley cases. Author's interview with the former GRU official Mikhail A. Milstein, Moscow, January 20, 1990; Milstein, *Skvoz godi voin i nischeti: Vospominania voennogo razvedchika*, 78–99.

76. Levering et al., *Debating the Origins of the Cold War*, 114–19.

77. Werblan, "Conversation between Wladyslaw Gomulka and Josef Stalin," 136.

78. Gaddis, *We Now Know*, 196, 197, 292, 294.

79. Smyser, *From Yalta to Berlin*, 62–63; for geostrategic rationales behind U.S. foreign policy see Leffler, *Preponderance of Power*.

80. Chuev, *Sto sorok besed*, 86.

81. Stalin wrote in his cable on September 19, 1945: "Now the time has come to prepare some decisions that will most likely be made . . . on the Americans' initiative. There will be hard bargaining and attempts at a compromise." Cited in Zubok and Pleshakov, *Inside the Kremlin's Cold War*, 97.

82. Dimitrov, *Diary*, October 8, 1945, 506; Lundestad and Westad, *Beyond the Cold War*, 30–31.

83. For the documents on this episode see Khlevniuk et al., *Politburo TsK VKP(b) i Sovet Ministrov SSSR*, 195–202; Pechatnov and Chubarian, "Molotov 'the Liberal,'" 129–40; Naimark, "Cold War Studies," 1–15. For detailed analysis of this from the perspective of domestic politics see Gorlizki and Khlevniuk, *Cold Peace*, 21–23.

84. Pechatnov, "Allies Are Pressing on You," 11.

85. Ivan Maisky to V. M. Molotov, "Ob ekonomicheskoi politike SShA posle voini," November 14, 1945, AVPRF, f. 06, op. 7, pap. 18, d. 184, l. 38–75. Maisky addressed the memos exclusively to Molotov but sent him five copies of each document. Presumably, Molotov distributed them among the "four" leading Politburo members. A. Arutyunian to V. M. Molotov, "On the International Monetary Fund and the International Bank of Reconstruction and Development (spravka)," March 2, 1946, unsigned memorandum to V. Dekanozov, March 9, 1946, AVPRF, f. 06, op. 9, pap. 19, d. 225, l. 3–4, 16–17; on Voznesensky's position see Mikoyan, *Tak bylo*, 493–94.

86. Levering et al., *Debating the Origins of the Cold War*, 115; Chuev, *Sto sorok besed*, 88–89.

87. Stalin, *Works*, 15:2–3, 5–6, 15–16, 19–20. Stalin's editing of the speech is in Stalin Papers, RGASPI, f. 558, op. 11, d. 1127. On the speech see Resis, *Stalin, the Politburo, and the Onset of the Cold War*.

88. See this thesis in Tucker, *Soviet Political Mind*, 91; and Wohlforth, *Elusive Balance*, 63.

89. Zverev to Stalin, October 8, 1946, APRF, f. 3, op. 39, d. 18, l. 55, 56, published in *Istochnik* 5 (2001): 21–47; Bystrova, "Voienno-promishlennii kompleks SSSR," 242.

90. APRF, f. 3, op. 39, d. 18, l. 59, 60, 66, as published in *Istochnik* 5 (2001).

91. Stalin's draft of the article is in RGASPI, f. 558, op. 11, d. 1127; Stalin, interview in *Pravda*, March 14, 1946, in *Works*, 15:36–37; Pechatnov, "Fultonskaia rech Cherchillia," 91–92; Zubkova, "Mir mnenii sovetskogo cheloveka," 104–5; see also her "Stalin i obschestvennoie mneniie v SSSR, 1945–1953," in *Stalin i kholodnaia voina* (Moscow, 1998), 282.

92. Boterbloem, *Life and Times of Andrei Zhdanov*; Zubok and Pleshakov, *Inside the Kremlin's Cold War*, 112–19, 124.

93. Weekly Summary Excerpt, September 20, 1946, Effect of Demobilization on Soviet Military Potential, in Kuhns, *Assessing the Soviet Threat*, 83.

94. Khleviuk, *Politburo TsK VKP(b) i Sovet Ministrov SSSR 1945–1953*, 204–6. Reshetnikov, "Drama marshala Novikova," 3; I. N. Kosenko, "Zagadka 'aviatsionnogo dela,'" *Voenno-istoricheskii zhurnal* 6 (1994): 57–62, and 8 (1994): 54–66; Pikhoia, *Sovetskii Soiuz*, 45–47.

95. Naumov et al., *Georgii Zhukov*, 15–23; Pikhoia, *Sovetskii Soiuz*.

96. Maksimova, "Podslushali i rasstreliali," from the taped conversation between V. Gordov and his chief of staff, F. Rybalchenko, on December 28, 1946, and between Gordov and his wife, Tatyana, on December 31, 19465; Zubkova, *Obchestvo i reformi*, 52–53.

97. Maksimova, "Podslushali i rasstreliali," 5.

98. Chernyaev, *Moia zhizn*, 198; Khrushchev also criticized Stalin's "overweening arrogance" at that time, but this should be dismissed as an ex post facto reflection. See Khrushchev, "Memuari Nikiti Sergeevicha Khrushcheva," 80.

99. The scope of this drought was similar to the one that afflicted Soviet Russia in 1921–22, which also caused the death of millions from famine. N. Khrushchev, *Khrushchev Remembers*, 229. See also the official report of Soviet Gosplan, cited in Pikhoia, *Sovetskii Soiuz*, 18; Taubman, *Khrushchev*, 199–201.

100. By 1948 the state-owned stockpile of grain was 10.5 million tons; in 1952 it rose to 17.3 million, half of the entire meager breadbasket of the USSR. Without agricultural imports or the release of food from the state reserves, the Soviet Union faced immediate starvation. G. S. Zolotukhin to L. I. Brezhnev, "Spravka o zagotovkakh i raskhode zerna gosresursov v 1940–1977 selkokhoziaistvennikh godakh," Volkogonov Collection, reel 18, container 28, LC; Mikoyan, *Tak Bylo*, 526.

101. Levering et al., *Debating the Origins of the Cold War*, 115; Zubkova, *Sovetskaia zhizn*, 110–16, 497–503.

102. Mikoyan, *Tak bylo*, 517–19, 526.

103. From Sergei Kruglov and Roman Rudenko to Khrushchev, December 1953, Volkogonov Collection, box 28, LC.

104. *Izvestia*, July 16, 1992; Mikoyan, *Tak bylo*, 556–57. Mikoyan believes that Stalin could have "gotten rid of Zhukov as well" but Zhukov's national reputation deterred him.

105. Naimark, *Fires of Hatred*, 187. On the postwar refurbishing of Soviet elites and society along ethnic lines, see Weiner, *Making Sense of War*.

106. Chuev, *Sto sorok besed*, 272; on Jewish-Russian intermarriages during the 1920s see Slezkine, *Jewish Century*, 179–80.

107. RGASPI, f. 17, op. 125, d. 377, l. 1, 35, 36, and d. 378, l. 1–2, 76–85; on the attack against the Sovinformburo, see RGASPI, f. 17, op. 128, d. 870, l. 118–34. On Zhdanov's attitude toward Jewish predominance in Soviet cultural and propaganda institutions, see Kostyrchenko, *Tainaia politika*, 282, 290–91, 361–65; Slezkine, *Jewish Century*, 275, 301–5.

108. S. A. Vinogradov and B. E. Shtein to A. Y. Vyshinsky, March 15, 1948, and B. E. Shtein to A. Y. Vyshinsky, April 22, 1948, in Naumkin, *Blizhnevostochnii konflikt*, 1:29–30, 36–37; also Kolokolov et al., *Sovetsko-Izrailskie otnosheniia*, 1:276–86; Chuev, *Sto sorok besed*, 93–94.

109. Kolokolov et al., *Sovetsko-Izrailskie otnosheniia*, 1:276–86; Rucker, "Moscow's Surprise," esp. 20–23, 24–25.

110. Kostyrchenko, *Tainaia politika*, 388–91, 401–7, 422–48; Chuev, *Sto sorok besed*, 473.

111. Kostyrchenko, *Tainaia politika*, 401–7; Brent and Naumov, *Stalin's Last Crime*.

112. Hasanli, *SSSR-Turtsiia*, 387–403.

113. RGASPI, f. 17, op. 12, d. 83, l. 1–2, 87–89. I thank academician Grant Avetissian, director of the Institute of General History, Yeravan, Armenia, for bringing these documents to my attention.

114. Victor Berdinskikh, *Spetsposelentsy* (Moscow: Novoie literaturnoie obozvenie, 2005), 25–26.

115. Montefiore, *Stalin*, 597–98; Spravka ob osuzhdennikh po "leningradskomu delu," December 10, 1953, in *Politburo TsK VKP(b) i Sovet Ministrov*, 306.

116. Brandenberger, *National Bolshevism*, 224.

117. Gudkov, *Negativnaia identichnost*, 20–58; Shiraev and Zubok, *Anti-Americanism in Russia*.

118. Chernyaev, *Moia zhizn*, 203–6, 208.

119. Alexeyeva and Goldberg, *Thaw Generation*, 30–31.

120. Eimontova, "Iz Dnevnikov Sergeia Sergeevicha Dmitrieva," 147.

121. Holloway, *Stalin and the Bomb*, 163; author's interview with Alexandrov's son Igor, New York, November 2, 2004.

122. RGANI, f. 5, op. 39, d. 12, l. 23, 28, 61–66, 67.

123. On empires, see Duverger, *Concept d'Empire*; Miles, "Roman and Modern Imperialism"; Abernethy, *Dynamics of Global Dominance*; Lieven, *Empire*; Ferguson, *Empire*.

Chapter Three

1. Eisenberg, *Drawing the Line*.

2. Chuev, *Sto sorok besed*, 95; Israelyan, *Na frontakh kholodnoi voini*, 60.

3. Loth, *Stalin's Unwanted Child*, 7–12, 170–74; Kramer, "Soviet Union and the Founding of the German Democratic Republic," 1132; Smyser, *From Yalta to Berlin*, 32; Creuzberger, *Die sowjetische Besatzungsmacht und das politische System des SBZ*; Wettig, *Bereitschaft zu Einheit in Freiheit?*; Filitov, "SSSR i Germanskii vopros," 223–56.

4. Naimark, *Russians in Germany*.

5. Maisky's diary, January 5, 1943, AVPRF, published in Kynin and Laufer, SSSR i *Germanskii vopros*, 2:701.

6. Semenov, "Ot Khrushcheva do Gorbacheva," 110.

7. On views of the primacy of economic interests in 1945, see Eisenberg, "Old Cold War," 802–3; Laufer, "Stalin and German Reparations," 23.

8. Maisky's diary, February 6, 1945, as cited in Rzheshevsky, *Stalin i Cherchill*, 499; Koval, "Na postu zamestitelia Glavnonachal'stvuiushchevo SVAG."

9. Koval, *Poslednii Svidetel*, 63; also his "Zapiski," 126, 142–43, 144–45; Laufer, "Stalin and German Reparations," 11–12.

10. See the impressive volume of documentation on the plans regarding Germany created by the special commissions on the peace treaties (the Voroshilov commission), on reparations (the Maisky commission), and on the planning of the postwar world (the Litvinov commission), in Kynin and Laufer, SSSR i *Germanskii vopros*, vol. 1.

11. Naimark, *Fires of Hatred*, 108–38; Kynin and Laufer, SSSR i *Germanskii vopros*, 2:66–67.

12. "Proidet desiatok let i eti vstrechi ne vosstanovish uzhe v pamiati" (Diary of Vyacheslav Malyshev), record of March 28, 1945, *Istochnik* 5 (1997): 128; cable from Molotov to Soviet ambassador to London Fedor Gusev, March 24, 1945, published in Kynin and Laufer, SSSR i *Germanskii vopros*, 1:626; Kynin, "Anti-Hitler Coalition and the Post-War Settlement in Germany," 100.

13. Koval, "Zapiski," 143.

14. Zubok and Pleshakov, *Inside the Kremlin's Cold War*, 48; Gaddis, *We Now Know*, 116. One source was Djilas, *Conversations with Stalin*, 153–54, about the meeting of the Yugoslav Communists with Stalin on May 26–27, 1946. Stalin allegedly said: "All of Germany must be ours, that is, Soviet, Communist." Yet the notes of the meeting from the Yugoslav archives have no mention of this statement; see Arhiv Josipa Broza Tita, Fond Kabinet Marsala Jugoslavije, I-1/7, l. 6–11, original manuscript, translated into Russian by L. Gibiansky, CWIHP. On the meeting of June 4, 1945, see Badstübner and Loth, *Wilhelm Pieck*, 50–52, SAPMO-BArch, NL 36/ 629, 62–66.

15. Semenov recalls episodic intrigues against him on the part of the secret police officials Abakumov, Serov, and Kruglov; his position as Stalin's emissary, as well as Molotov's "ears and eyes" in Germany, invoked jealousy and hostility on their part. Semjonow, *Vom Stalin bis Gorbatschow*, 279–81.

16. Sokolovsky, besides his administrative and coordinating experience in the general staff during World War II, was well educated. He also could quote by heart from the Bible and recite Goethe's "Erlkönig." See Semjonow, *Vom Stalin bis Gorbatschow*, 216.

17. Kynin and Laufer, SSSR i *Germanskii vopros*, 2:19–22; Semjonow, *Vom Stalin bis Gorbatschow*, 207, 218. Semenov's memoirs overlook this problem and grossly inflate his authority and access to Stalin.

18. Record of conversation of Stalin with Churchill, October 9, 1944, 10 P.M. (transcribed by V. Pavlov), *Istochnik* 2 (2003): 52.

19. "Discussion in the USSR of American Proposal to Conclude a Treaty of Disarmament and Demilitarization of Germany (1945–1947)," *Mezhdunarodnaia zhizn* 8 (1996): 70–71.

20. Zhukov to CC VKP(b), May 24, 1946, in "Discussion in the USSR," 73.

21. Kynin and Laufer, SSSR i Germanskii vopros, 2:517–24, 543–51, 574–82. The summary mentioned the opinions of Politburo members A. A. Andreev, K. E. Voroshilov, M. I. Kalinin, L. M. Kaganovich, N. M. Shvernik, A. J. Vyshinsky, V. G. Dekanozov, K. V. Novikov, L. A. Govorov, and N. N. Voronov. The same summary resurfaced in the well-known "Novikov telegram" from the Soviet embassy in the United States to Moscow in September 1946; see Jensen, Origins of the Cold War, 3–67.

22. Kynin and Laufer, SSSR i Germanskii vopros, 2:477.

23. Ibid., 2:452–53, 473–75; Zhukov, Sokolovsky, and Semenov to V. M. Molotov (undated), in "Discussion in the USSR," 76. This memo was probably written after February but before May 1946.

24. Department of State Bulletin 15 (September 15, 1946): 496; Leffler, Preponderance of Power, 119–20.

25. Kynin and Laufer, SSSR i Germanskii vopros, 2:693–703.

26. Badstübner and Loth, Wilhelm Pieck, 68.

27. Semenov, "Ot Khrushcheva do Gorbacheva," 85, 117.

28. Influential SMAG officials included Col. Sergei Tyulpanov in charge of the division of political information and propaganda; Alexander Kotikov, the military commander of Berlin; D. Dubrovsky, P. Kolesnichenko, and V. Sharov as procurators in various East German Länder; and Pavel Maletin and Konstantin Koval in charge of finances and economic affairs, including dismantling and reparations. Bokov, Vesna Pobedy, 391–94.

29. At first, the political adviser's authority and influence on Soviet policy making in Germany was severely limited. Semenov commanded a modest staff, in contrast to the enormous SMAG apparatus. Stalin did not even meet him once in 1946, while SMAG leadership had direct channels to the supreme party leadership and various departments of the CC. Semenov, a civilian, had to deal with the cohort of the decorated marshals, generals, and colonels, veterans of recent battles—a daunting challenge.

30. On the "enigma" of Tyulpanov's influence and his decline, see Naimark, Russians in Germany, 327–52; Bordiugov, Chrezvychainii vek Rossiiskoi istorii, 236–46. For more on the influence of the "Zhdanovites" and their fall, see Gorlizki and Khlevniuk, Cold Peace; and Boterbloem, Life and Times of Andrei Zhdanov, esp. 269, 273, 286–88.

31. Kynin and Laufer, SSSR i Germanskii vopros, 2:24; Koval, Poslednii svidetel, 59, 278.

32. Serov to Beria, transmitted by Beria to Stalin's secretary, A. N. Poskrebishev, on October 20, 1946, RGASPI, f. 558, op. 11, d. 732, l. 50–51.

33. Kynin and Laufer, SSSR i Germanskii vopros, 2:34–35; Werblan, "Conversation between Wladyslaw Gomulka and Josef Stalin," 137; Koval, Poslednii svidetel, 333; Naimark, Russians in Germany, 48–49, 189–90; information of S. Agamirov, veteran of the Wismuth project, Voronezh, July 1, 2002.

34. Cited in Eisenberg, Drawing the Line, 182.

35. Naimark, Russians in Germany, 150–51; Semjonow, Von Stalin bis Gorbatschow, 237–39.

36. Badstübner and Loth, Wilhelm Pieck, 33; Bokov, Vesna Pobedy, 403–4.

37. Naimark, Russians in Germany, 327–29; Kramer, "Soviet Union and the Founding of the

German Democratic Republic," 1100; RGASPI, f. 17, op. 128, d. 1091, l. 43–54; also Bonwetsch and Bordjugov, "Stalin und die SBZ," 279–303.

38. Chuev, *Sto sorok besed*, 45–46.

39. Record of conversation of Stalin with W. Pieck, O. Grotewohl, W. Ulbricht, M. Fechner, and F. Oelssner (meeting was attended by Molotov, Suslov, and Semenov), January 31, 1947, APRF, f. 45, inv. 1, d. 303, l. 7, l. 8–11, as cited in Volkov, "German Question as Stalin Saw It," 7–8; see also Volkov, *Uzloviie problemi noveishei istorii stran Tsentralnoi i Yugo-Vostochnoi Evropi*.

40. Semjonow, *Vom Stalin bis Gorbatschow*, 253–54.

41. Naimark, *Russians in Germany*, 394; Semjonow, *Vom Stalin bis Gorbatschow*, 254–57.

42. RGASPI, f. 17, op. 128, d. 1091, l. 43–54, published in Bonwetsch and Bordjugov, "Stalin und die SBZ," 294–301; Volkov, "German Question as Stalin Saw It," 8.

43. Naimark, *Russians in Germany*, 467; see also Scherstjanoi, "Political Calculation and the Interpretation of Western Positions," 5; Semjonow, *Vom Stalin bis Gorbatschow*, 262–63.

44. See the cables from AVPRF published in *Novaia i noveishaia istoriia* 2 (March–April 1993): 14–15.

45. Molotov's cable is cited in Vladimir O. Pechatnov, "The Soviet Union and the Outside World, 1944–1953," in *The Cambridge History of the Cold War*, ed. Melvin P. Leffler and Odd Arne Westad (New York: Cambridge University Press, forthcoming); Cable from the CC VKP(b) to Georgy Dimitrov and the Communist leadership of Bulgaria, July 8, 1947, CSA, f. 146, op. 4, d. 639, NSArch.

46. "Stalin, Czecholoslovakia, and the Marshall Plan: New Documentation from Czechoslovak Archives," *Bohemia: Zeitschrift für Geschichte und Kultur der bömischen Länder* 32, no. 1 (1991): 133–44; record of Stalin's conversation with the Czechoslovak government delegation on the issue of their position regarding the Marshall Plan and the prospects for economic cooperation with the USSR, July 9, 1947, in Volokitina et al., *Vostochnaia Evropa*, 1:672–75.

47. Report of N. V. Novikov, as quoted in his *Vospominaniia diplomata*, 394.

48. For more details see Zubok and Pleshakov, *Inside the Kremlin's Cold War*, 114, 125–33.

49. Boterbloem, *Life and Times of Andrei Zhdanov*, 321–22.

50. More in Adibekov et al., *Soveschaniia Kominforma*, esp. xiv–xxi, 3–20; Gibiansky, "Sovetskiie tseli v Vostochnoi Evrope v kontse vtoroi mirovoi voiny i v perviie poslevoennie gody," 197–215.

51. Kramer, "Soviet Union and the Founding of the German Democratic Republic," 1101–2; Thoss, *Volksarmee schaffen ohne Geschrei*.

52. Maier, *Dissolution*; Bordiugov, Kosheleva, and Rogovaia, SVAG, 115–16; Bordiugov, *Chrezvychainii vek Rossiiskoi istorii*, 204–7.

53. Smyser, *From Yalta to Berlin*, 75–76; Narinsky, "Soviet Policy and the Berlin Blockade," 5–8; Volkov, "German Question as Stalin Saw It," 10.

54. This discussion is based on Laufer, "UdSSR und die deutsche Währungsfrage," 460–71.

55. Ibid., 483.

56. Gibiansky, "Soviet Bloc and the Initial Stage of the Cold War," 112–34.

57. M. Kostylev to Moscow, March 24, 1948, APRF, f. 3, op. 3, d. 198, l, 55–58; V. Molotov

to M. Kostylev, March 26, 1948, APRF, f. 3, op. 3, d. 198, l. 59, cited and analyzed in Zaslavsky, *Lo Stalinismo e la Sinistra Italiana*, esp. 84–85; see also Aga-Rossi and Zaslavsky, *Togliatti e Stalin*.

58. Pechatnov, *Stalin, Ruzvelt, Truman*, 527–50.

59. Smyser, *From Yalta to Potsdam*, 87; Laufer, "UdSSR und die deutsche Währungsfrage," 474–85.

60. I thank Michael Thumann (*Die Zeit*), Dr. Michael Lemke (Zentrum für Zeitgeschichte, Potsdam), and Dr. Hans Seit (Ost-Europa Institute, Berlin) for stimulating conversations that informed these conclusions.

61. Naimark, *Russians in Germany*, 129–40; Goedde, *GIs and Germans*, esp. 85–86, 203–10.

62. Record of conversation of Stalin with a group of English Labourites—deputies of the Parliament, October 14, 1947, CSACH, f. 1206, op. 2, d. 326, l. 14, 15, 16.

63. Volkov, "Za sovetami v Kreml," 9–25; Volkov, "German Question as Stalin Saw It," 11.

64. Record of conversation between Stalin and W. Pieck, O. Grotewohl, W. Ulbricht, F. Oelssner, December 18, 1948, AVRP, f. 45, inv. 1, d. 303, l. 57–58, published by A. D. Chernev, *Istoricheskii arkhiv* 5 (2002): 5–23.

65. Pechatnov, "The Soviet Union and the Outside World"; Harrison, *Driving the Soviets Up the Wall*, 18.

66. Gorlizki and Khlevniuk, *Cold Peace*, 75, 76–78. Molotov's successor was Andrei Vyshinsky, Stalin's sycophantic henchman, the prosecutor during the Great Trials of 1936–38. Vaksberg, *Stalin's Prosecutor*; Westad, *Global Cold War*, 66; remarks from Stalin's conversation with Kim Il Sung in Moscow in April 1950, quoted from *DPRK Report* (Moscow), 23 (March–April 2000).

67. Chuev, *Sto sorok besed*, 104.

68. On the poor treatment of and lack of assistance to Vietnamese Communists until 1949, see Duiker, *Ho Chi Minh*, 420–22; Olsen, "Changing Alliances," 26–28, 37–39.

69. Zubok, " 'To Hell with Yalta!' "; Westad, *Brothers in Arms*.

70. For different interpretations of the Sino-Soviet talks, see Shen Zhihua, "Stolknoveniie i uregulirovanie interesov v protsesse peregovorov o kitaisko-sovetskom Dogovore 1950 goda," 126–29; Ledovsky, "Stalin, Mao Tsedun i koreiskaia voina 1950–1953 godov," 81–86; Zubok and Pleshakov, *Inside the Kremlin's Cold War*, 58–62; Chen Jian, *Mao's China and the Cold War*, 52–53.

71. On the road toward the Korean War, see Weathersby, "To Attack or Not to Attack," and also her "Should We Fear This?," 15; Bajanov, "Assessing Politics of the Korean War," 40–42; Ledovsky, "Stalin, Mao Tsedun i koreiskaia voina 1950–1953 godov," 93–85.

72. Leffler, *Preponderance of Power*, 361–90; Hitchcock, *France Restored*, 134–47.

73. Documents of the Ministry of Foreign Affairs of the USSR (the secretariat of the minister and the 3rd European [German] Department) clearly indicate that the Soviet leadership and diplomats knew well in advance about the content of those agreements from intelligence (although some, like Andrei Gromyko, feared disinformation) and discussed, in internal correspondence, the existence of "secret military clauses" in the treaties of Bonn. Memo of Gromyko to Stalin, January 21, 1952, in AVPRF, f. 07, op. 25, pap. 13, d. 144, l. 27; memo of the 3rd Department to Stalin, February 26, 1953, on the position of the Soviet

government with regard to the "European community of coal and steel," in AVPRF, f. o84, op. 11, pap. 275, d. 51, l. 3. See also Ruggenthaler, "Novyie sovetskie dokumenti"; Ruggenthaler, *Stalins grosser Bluff.*

74. RGASPI, f. 558, op. 11, d. 62, l. 71–72. This cable was found and published by Ledovsky, "Stalin, Mao Tsedun i koreiskaia voina 1950–1953 godov," 96–97.

75. Cable from Stalin to Kim Il Sung (via Shtykov), October 8 [7?], 1950, from APRF, f. 45, op. 1, d. 347, l. 65–67, found and translated by Alexander Mansourov; record of conversation between Stalin and Zhou Enlai, August 20, 1952, both documents published in *CWIHP Bulletin*, no. 6–7 (Winter 1995/96): 13, 116.

76. Steven Zaloga writes that by 1953 only 847 long-range Tu-4 bombers had been were built. They were much poorer than American B-29s, from which they had been copied. The Soviet Air Force, concludes Zaloga, "was capable of little more than harassment attacks against the United States." Zaloga, *Kremlin's Nuclear Sword*, 15.

77. Dobrynin, *In Confidence*, 525; Cristescu, "Ianuarie 1951," 15–23.

78. I do not have access to the text of this decision, but it was quoted in the memorandum from the Foreign Ministry (signed by A. A. Gromyko) to Molotov on January 21, 1952, AVPRF, f. 07, op. 25, pap. 13, d. 144, l. 28. Ruggenthaler, "Novyie sovetskie dokumenti," 20.

79. Naimark, *Russians in Germany*, 470; Harrison, *Driving the Soviets Up the Wall*, 4.

80. AVPRF, f. 07, op. 25, pap. 13, d. 144, l. 27–29. More facts on the Soviet treatment of the GDR as a political instrument are in Loth, "Origins of Stalin's Note," 66–89.

81. Hitchcock, *France Restored*, 167; Soutou, "France et les notes sovietique," 261–73; Wettig, "Stalin-Note vom 10 Marz 1952: Antwort auf Elke Scherstjanoi," 862–65; also his *Bereitschaft zu Einheit in Freiheit.* My views on Stalin's policies in Austria rely on the well-documented research of Karner, Ruggenthaler, and Stelzl-Marx in *Die Rote Armee in Österreich*; also Karner and Ruggenthaler, "Stalin und Österreich: Sowjetische Österreich-politik 1938 bis 1953" (a research paper, 2006); and comments from the discussions during the workshop "Begann der Kalten Krieg in Österreich?" organized by Lüdwig Boltzmann Institut in Graz, Austria, May 20, 2006.

82. Copy of document from APRF, f. 45, inv. 1, d. 303, l. 168–69, Volkogonov Collection, LC; also Pieck's notes of final discussion on April 7, 1952, in Badstübner and Loth, *Wilhelm Pieck*, 396.

83. Volkov, "German Question as Stalin Saw It"; an excerpt also published by Narinsky, "Stalin and the SED leadership," 34–35, 48.

84. Copy of document from APRF, f. 45, pap. 1, d. 303, l. 187, Volkogonov Collection, LC.

85. Dijk, "Bankruptcy of Stalin's German Policy," 19.

86. Official Soviet figures are from memorandum of Vladimir Semenov to Molotov, "Spravka po germanskomu voprosu," May 5, 1953, AVPRF, f. 082, op. 41, pap. 271, d. 19, l. 37–38.

87. Khrushchev's speech at the July 1953 Plenum reveals that the Kremlin leadership was fully aware of the catastrophic situation. Naumov and Sigachev, *Lavrentii Beria*, 93–94.

88. The best Soviet estimates on this are in a memorandum from General Fadeikin, prepared at the request of Lavrenty Beria for the CC Presidium on May 18, 1953, printed in

CWIHP Bulletin, no. 10 (March 1998): 74–78; also "On the Measures to Ameliorate the Political Situation in the GDR," attachment to the decision of the Council of Ministers on June 2, 1953, no. 7576-rs, published in Naumov and Sigachev, *Lavrentii Beria*, 55.

89. Naumov, "Cold War," 3–5. Western authorities never learned about these plans. Zaloga, *Kremlin's Nuclear Sword*, 12–21.

90. On the "affairs" see Khleviuk, *Politburo TsK VKP(b)*, 342–97; Thome, "Stalin, Beria, and Mingrelian Affair." On Stalin's bizarre obsession with the discussion on linguistics and other scientific discussions, see Pollock, *Stalin and the Soviet Science Wars*.

91. See Richter, "Reexamining Soviet Policy," 671–91; Wettig, "Befinnende Umorientierung der sowjetischen Deutschland-Politik im Frühjahr und Sommer 1953," 495–507; Ostermann, " 'This is not a Politburo, But a Madhouse,' " 61–110; Ostermann, *Uprising in East Germany*; Scherstjanoi, "Sowjetische Deutschlandpolitik nach Stalins Tod 1953," 497–549; Scherstjanoi, "In 14 Tagen werden Sie vielleicht schon keinen Staat mehr haben," 907–37; Kramer, "Early Post-Stalin Succession Struggle and Upheavals in East-Central Europe," 3–55; Harrison, *Driving the Soviets Up the Wall*, chap. 1.

92. It is noteworthy in this regard that on April 26, 1953, Molotov sent "a package" of three documents to the members of the Collegium of Foreign Ministry and to Semenov. First was the memo of Jakov Malik and Grigory Pushkin, "Proposals on the German Question"; second, Malik's memo, "Proposals on the Austrian Question"; third, Pushkin's memo, "Proposals on the Iranian Question." AVPRF, f. 082, op. 41, pap. 271, d. 19, l. 1.

93. Schecter and Luchkov, *Khrushchev Remembers*, 100–101.

94. Richter, "Reexamining Soviet Policy," 676.

95. Molotov's speech on July 2, 1953, at the CC CPSU Plenum, in Naumov and Sigachev, *Lavrentii Beria*, 101.

96. "Zapiska po germanskomu voprosu," April 18, 1953, from Pushkin and Gribanov to Molotov, AVPRF, f. 082, op. 41, pap. 271, d. 18, l. 15.

97. Naumov and Sigachev, *Lavrentii Beria*, 219, 220.

98. Ibid., 243. See the volume and intensity of deliberations on the German Question in memorandum of the Committee of Information (KI), "On the Western Powers' Policy Regarding the German Question," April 18, 1953, AVPRF, f. 082, op. 41, pap. 271, d. 18, l. 13–29; Pushkin and Gribanov to Molotov on April 21, 1953, AVPRF, f. 082, op. 41, pap. 271, d. 18, l. 30–43; "Predlozheniia po germanskomu voprosu," April 24, 1953, from Malik and Pushkin to Molotov, AVPRF, f. 082, op. 41, pap. 271, d. 19, l. 20–30; "O nashikh dalneiskhikh meroprikatikhakh po germanskomu voprosu," April 28, 1953, from Malik, Semenov, Pushkin, and Gribanov to Molotov, AVPRF, f. 082, op. 41, pap. 271, d. 18, l. 44–47; "Spravka po Germanskomu voprosu," from [undecipherable] to Semenov, May 5, 1953, AVPRF, f. 082, op. 41, pap. 271, d. 19, l. 31–38.

99. The experts also suggested inviting the GDR leadership to Moscow for a first official visit. In the economic field, the memo recommended "transfer under GDR custody of German factories that worked as joint stock companies under the GUSIMZ" (Chief Directorate for Soviet Property Abroad), "Zapiska po germanskomu voprosu," April 18, 1953, from Pushkin and Gribanov to Molotov, AVPRF, f. 082, op. 41, pap. 271, d. 18, l. 15.

100. Vladimir Semenov became the head of the third European Directorate of the Foreign Ministry (on Germany). He recalled in his memoirs that he wrote his proposals together with his SMAG colleague, Marshal Vasily Sokolovsky, who at that time was the head of the General Staff. Semjonow, *Vom Stalin bis Gorbatschow*, 290; "Zapiska po germanskomu voprosu," May 2, 1953, from Semenov to Molotov, AVPRF, f. 082, op. 41, pap. 271, d. 18, l. 54–55, 58.

101. "O dalneishikh meropriiatiiakh Sovetskogo pravitelstva po germanskomu voprosu" (written before May 4 1953), AVPRF, f. 06, op. 12, pap. 16, d. 259, l. 45–46; on "an exchange of views that took place" at the Presidium, see Molotov's memo to Malenkov, Beria, Khrushchev, and Mikoyan, May 8, 1953, AVPRF, f. 06, op. 12, pap. 16, d. 259, l. 48, 49–55; "Proekt ukazanii tt. Chuikovu i Semenovu," March 18, 1953, with cover note from V. Molotov to the CPSU Presidium, AVPRF, f. 06, op. 12, pap. 18, d. 283 (obtained and translated by Hope Harrison).

102. Beria, *Beria, My Father*, 262; Mikoyan, *Tak bylo*, 581–84; Naumov and Sigachev, *Lavrentii Beria*, 17–66. The earlier version of my interpretation is in Zubok and Pleshakov, *Inside the Kremlin's Cold War*, 156–57; Zubok, " 'Unverfroren und grob in der Deutschlandfrage,' " 32–34. For a different interpretation of Beria's and Malenkov's roles, see Kramer, "Early Post-Stalin Succession Struggle."

103. Semjonow, *Vom Stalin bis Gorbatschow*, 290; Semenov's diary, May 31, 1964, in *Novaia i noveishaia istoriia* 3 (2004): 112.

104. Sudoplatov et al., *Special Tasks*, 363–65; expanded Russian version in Sudoplatov, *Tainaia zhizn generala Sudoplatova*, 2:369–70. Some of Beria's actions are difficult to explain. For instance, he recalled the top representatives of Soviet secret services in the GDR back to Moscow and proposed recalling most secret police advisers within the structures of the East German state, except for the Soviet advisers at the MfS (the Ministry of Security) of the GDR. According to Beria's deputy, the MVD representatives in the GDR stayed in Moscow "for three months," that is, since April, waiting for reorganization of their apparatus. See the speech of Sergei Kruglov after Beria's arrest at the July 1953 Plenum, in Naumov and Sigachev, *Lavrentii Beria*, 155.

105. Report no. 44/B, Beria to the CC CPSU Presidium, May 6, 1953, Archiv Sluzhbi vneshnei razvedki (SVRA), pap. 2589, vol. 7, d. 3581, quoted in Murphy, Kondrashev, and Bailey, *Battleground*, 156–58.

106. See *Neues Deutschland*, May 7, 1953, 3; Sudoplatov, *Tainaia zhizn generala Sudoplatova*, 370.

107. "Protokol No. 8, zasedaniya Prezidiuma TsK KPSS ot 14 maya 1953 goda," RGANI, f. 3, op. 10, d. 23, l. 41, cited in Kramer, "Early Post-Stalin Succession Struggle," 24–25.

108. Unsigned draft of the Foreign Ministry, "O dalneishih merakh sovetskogo pravitelstva po germanskomu voprosu," May 8, 1953, AVPRF, f. 06, op. 12, pap. 16, d. 259, l. 39–46.

109. Semenov, "Po voprosu o predotvrascheniia ukhoda naseleniia iz GDR v Zapadniiu Germaniu," May 15, 1953, AVPRF, f. 0742, op. 41, pap. 271, d. 92, l. 99–102.

110. Naumov and Sigachev, *Lavrentii Beria*, 98.

111. The earlier reconstruction of this can be found in Zubok and Pleshakov, *Inside the Kremlin's Cold War*, 160–61; Molotov's speech on July 2, 1953, at the CC CPSU Plenum in Naumov and Sigachev, *Lavrentii Beria*, 102, 103.

112. Mikoyan, *Tak bylo*, 584; Beria's letter to Malenkov from prison, July 1, 1953, APRF, f. 3, op. 24, d. 463, l. 165, published in *Istochnik* 4 (1994): 5 and in Naumov and Sigachev, *Lavrentii Beria*, 73; see also my English translation *CWIHP Bulletin*, no. 10 (March 1998): 99.

113. Wettig, *Bereitschaft zu Einheit in Freiheit?*; remarks and exchange among Alexei Filitov, Gerhard Wettig, and Elke Scherstjanoi at the conference "The Crisis Year 1953 and the Cold War in Europe," Potsdam, November 1996; Kramer, "Early Post-Stalin Succession Struggle," 28.

114. As Semenov recalled, Beria "read his draft on German policy that was fundamentally different from the one that was in my pocket. To deceive Beria, Khrushchev proposed to accept his draft. Molotov made a sign to me to remain silent. 'Agree, agree,' joined the audience in the room. I returned to the Foreign Ministry crestfallen." Semjonow, *Vom Stalin bis Gorbatschow*, 291.

115. "O merakh po ozdorovleniiu politichsekoi obstanovki v GDR," Prilozheniie k rasporiazheniiu Soveta Ministrov SSSR ot 2 iiunia 1953 f. No. 7578-pc., APRF, f. 3, op. 64, d. 802, l. 153–61, in Naumov and Sigachev, *Lavrentii Beria*, 55–59.

116. "O merakh," in Naumov and Sigachev, *Lavrentii Beria*, 58, 59.

117. There were demonstrations and strikes on May 3 in Plovdiv and Khaskovo, Bulgaria, and on June 1–2 in Plzen, Czechoslovakia, that evoked serious concerns in Moscow. Kramer, "Early Post-Stalin Succession Struggle," 15–22; Ostermann, *Uprising in East Germany*.

118. "Lavrenti Beria: 'Tcherez 2–3 goda ia krepko ispravlius' (Pisma L. P. Berii iz tiuremnogo bunkera, 1953)," *Istochnik* 4 (1994): 5; compare with *CWIHP Bulletin*, no. 10 (March 1998): 99; see also Herrnstadt, *Das Herrnstadt-Dokument*, 59.

119. Zapiska ministra vnutrennikh del SSSR S. Kruglova v TsK KPSS G. Malenkovu s preprovozhdeniiem soobscheniia otvetstvennikh rabotnikov MVD SSSR Fedotova i Fadeikina, July 9, 1953, APRF, f. 3, op. 64, d. 925, l. 156–65, copy provided to CWIHP by Leonid Reshin at NSArch.

120. Naumov and Sigachev, *Lavrentii Beria*, 97, 102–3; Stenografichsekii otchet o Plenume Ts KPSS, January 31, 1955, RGANI, f. 2, op. 1, d. 127, l. 65–66.

121. "Iz dnevnika Yakova Malika 30 iiunia 1953, Zapis Besedi s Premier-Ministrom Velikobritanii Cherchillem, June 3, 1953," published in *Istochnik* 2 (2003) (note that the record of the conversation with Churchill, found in the Politburo archives, has been dated June 30, that is, after Beria's arrest); on the dismissal of Churchill in Washington, see Immerman, " 'Trust in the Lord but Keep Your Powder Dry,' " 36–41.

122. The letter, dated July 1, was found in APRF, f. 3, op. 24, d. 463, l. 170–1700b, published in Naumov and Sigachev, *Lavrentii Beria*, 407; Sudoplatov, *Tainaia zhizn generala Sudoplatova*, 2:372–74. On Pierre Cot see Andrew and Mitrokhin, *Sword and the Shield*, 108–9; Smyser, *From Yalta to Berlin*, 128.

123. For exhaustive documentation on this episode see Ostermann, *Uprising in East Germany, 1953*.

124. Sudoplatov, *Tainaia zhizn generala Sudoplatova*, 2:372–74.

125. V. Sokolovsky, V. Semenov, P. Yudin, "O sobitiiakh 17–19 iiunia 1953 v Berline i v GDR i nekotorie vivodi iz etikh sobitii," June 24, 1953, AVPRF, f. 06, op. 12a, pap. 5, d. 301, l. 1–51,

published in excerpts in Christian Ostermann, "New Documents on the East German Uprising of 1953," *CWIHP Bulletin*, no. 5 (Spring 1995): 10–21.

126. Malenkov's notes at the CC Presidium where Beria was arrested, "K resheniiu voprosa o Beria," Protocol no. 10 of June 26, 1953, in Naumov and Sigachev, *Lavrentii Beria*, 69–70; Mikoyan, *Tak bylo*, 565–66; Zubok and Pleshakov, *Inside the Kremlin's Cold War*, 140–55.

127. See the transcripts of the Plenum, published in Naumov and Sigachev, *Lavrentii Beria*, 93–94, 207, 353.

128. Zapiska ministra vnutrennikh del SSSR S. Kruglova, July 9, 1953, APRF, f. 3, op. 64, d. 925, l. 156–65.

129. Naumov and Sigachev, *Lavrentii Beria*, 97, 189–90; see also Stickle, *Beria Affair*, 22–23, 134–35.

130. In Austria, for instance, on June 9, 1953, Soviet authorities stopped searching and checking people and goods crossing the demarcation line between the Soviet and Western zones. Also, they stopped media censorship in the Soviet zone and returned radio broadcasting facilities to the Austrian state. There was also a decision that from August 1953 Austria would stop paying the costs of the Soviet troops stationed on its territory. The last group of Austrian POWs returned home. After Beria's arrest these "goodwill" gestures were still implemented, but only half-heartedly. Michail Prozumenscikov, "Nach Stalins Tod. Sowjetische Österreich-Politik 1953–1955," in Karner et al., *Die Rote Armee in Österreich*, 733–34.

131. Semjonow, *Vom Stalin bis Gorbatschow*, 297; memo of Pushkin to Vyshinsky on July 9, 1953, AVPRF, f. 82, op. 41, pap. 280, d. 93, l. 63–68, published in *CWIHP Bulletin*, no. 10 (March 1998): 105. For more information on the Herrnstadt-Zeissner "faction" and Ulbricht's moves, see Harrison, *Driving the Soviets Up the Wall*, 42–43.

132. On the Day X in the GDR, see Bezymensky, "Kto i kak gotovil v Germanii den' Iks," 22–26; Zubok, "Soviet Intelligence and the Cold War," 465.

Chapter Four

1. Troyanovsky, "Making of Soviet Foreign Policy," 213–14.

2. Immerman, " 'Trust in the Lord but Keep Your Powder Dry' "; Trachtenberg, *Constructed Peace*, 132–45; Mitrovich, *Undermining the Kremlin*; Brooks, "Stalin's Ghost."

3. See Fursenko et al., *Prezidium TsK KPSS*; and Bekes, Byrne, and Rainer, *1956 Hungarian Revolution*. On the domestic-foreign nexus see Richter, *Khrushchev's Double Bind*; Brooks, "Stalin's Ghost"; Taubman, *Khrushchev*, chaps. 10–14.

4. The circle of "oligarchs" included the members of Stalin's Presidium before October 1952: Klement Voroshilov, Nikolai Bulganin, Lavrenty Beria, Lazar Kaganovich, Nikita Khrushchev, Georgy Malenkov, Anastas Mikoyan, and Vyacheslav Molotov. Matvei Saburov and Mikhail Pervukhin were junior members of that group.

5. See Mikoyan, *Tak Bylo*, 555–58, 572–74; Khlevniuk et al., *Prezidium TsK VKP(b) i Sovet Ministrov SSSR*; October 1952 Plenum files are in RGANI, f. 2, op. 1, d. 21–22; for substantive recollections on Stalin's speech in October 1952, see Simonov, "Glazami cheloveka moego pokoleniia," 96–99.

6. Gorlizki and Khlevniuk, *Cold Peace*, 6; Chuev, *Sto sorok besed*, 471; Mikoyan, *Tak bylo*, 584.

7. See Protocol no. 105, Presidium session on January 31, 1955, in Fursenko et al., *Prezidium TsK KPSS*, 1:37.

8. Eimontova, "Iz Dnevnikov Sergeia Sergeevicha Dmitrieva," 160.

9. Zubok, "CPSU Plenums, Leadership Struggles, and Soviet Cold War Politics," 28–33; notes of V. A. Kochetov, editor in chief of *Literaturnaia gazeta*, around 1955, RGALI, f. 634, op. 4, d. 1516, l. 13.

10. *Izvestia*, August 9, 1953; peasants' income increased from 13 billion rubles in 1953 to 25 billion rubles in 1954. Stenographic report of the meeting of party members of the Supreme Soviet of the USSR, February 8, 1955, APRF, f. 52, op. 1, d. 285, l. 1–34, published in *Istochnik* 6 (2003); Mikoyan, *Tak Bylo*, 518; Aksyutin, *Khrushchevskaia "ottepel" i obschestvenniie nastroeniia v SSSR v 1953–1964 gg*, 53–57.

11. Sakharov, *Vospominaniia*, 230; Holloway, *Stalin and the Bomb*, 337.

12. On the rivalry between Malenkov and Khrushchev in this area see Elena Zubkova, "Rivalry with Malenkov," 78–81; Mikoyan, *Tak bylo*, 599–600; Taubman, *Khrushchev*, 262–63.

13. Barsukov, "Rise to Power," 52; Taubman, *Khrushchev*, 258–64.

14. See Presidium sessions on January 22 and 31, 1955, in Fursenko et al., *Prezidium TsK KPSS*, 1:35–38.

15. Plenum of January 25–31, 1955, Protocol no. 7, RGANI, f. 2, op. 1, d. 127, l. 45; *CWIHP Bulletin*, no. 10 (March 1998): 34–35; Khrushchev, "Memuari Nikiti Sergeevicha Khrushcheva," 70.

16. See remarks of Bulganin, Pervukhin, and Voroshilov in Fursenko et al., *Prezidium TsK KPSS*, 1:37, 887; also stenographic report of the meeting of party members of the Supreme Soviet of the USSR, February 8, 1955, APRF, f. 52, op. 1, d. 285, l. 1–34, published in *Istochnik* 6 (2003).

17. The CC Presidium, Protocols no. 66, December 20, 1954, and no. 106, February 7, 1955, in Fursenko et al., *Prezidium TsK KPSS*, 1:29–31, 40.

18. Zubkova, "Rivalry with Malenkov," 76; Fursenko et al., *Prezidium TsK KPSS*, 1:36–72.

19. Fursenko et al., *Presidium TsK KPSS*, 1:29–31.

20. On the background of the Soviet-Austrian talks see Stourzh, *Um Einheit und Freiheit*; also Bischof, *Austria in the First Cold War*, 130–49.

21. Zubok, "Soviet Foreign Policy in Germany and Austria," 21–24. Also Mastny, "NATO in the Beholder's Eye," 61–62.

22. See the comments to the Presidium session, May 19, 1955, in Fursenko et al., *Prezidium TsK KPSS*, 1:41, 888–90.

23. *CWIHP Bulletin*, no. 10 (March 1998): 43.

24. Troyanovsky, "Making of Soviet Foreign Policy," 214; Molotov's speech at the CC CPSU Plenum, July 9, 1955, RGANI, f. 2, op. 1, d. 173, l. 3; Molotov refers here to the episode in 1948 when Gomulka was ousted from the post of the general secretary of the PUWP and later arrested for "nationalist deviationism." For details and documents see Volokitina et al., *Vostochnaia Evropa*, 1:505–11.

25. The Plenum of the CC CPSU, July 9, 1955, RGANI, f. 2, op. 1, d. 172, l. 76, 87; *CWIHP Bulletin*, no. 10 (March 1998): 29, 38.

26. At the Presidium session on May 25, Voroshilov and Molotov spoke against the use of this subterfuge. Bulganin said, "Then they will [criticize] Stalin." See remarks of Bulganin and Mikoyan, Presidium sessions, May 19 and 23, 1955, in Fursenko et al., *Prezidium TsK KPSS*, 1:43, 45, 46.

27. RGANI, f. 2, op. 1, d. 173, l. 4.

28. Khrushchev, "Memuari Nikiti Sergeevicha Khrushcheva," 82, 84, 85; RGANI, f. 2, op. 1, d. 173, l. 40; *Istoricheskii arkhiv* 4 (1993): 77.

29. Quotations from Immerman, " 'Trust in the Lord but Keep Your Powder Dry,' " 48–49.

30. Troyanovsky, "Nikita Khrushchev and the Making of Soviet Foreign Policy," 38.

31. Prozumenscikov, "Nach Stalins Tod," 750.

32. Alexandrov-Agentov, *Ot Kollontai*, 93; see also Troyanovsky, "Nikita Khrushchev and the Making of Soviet Foreign Policy," 7.

33. Alexandrov-Agentov, *Ot Kollontai*, 93, 94.

34. Stenograficheskaia zapis zasedania Prezidiuma TsK KPSS po voprosu "O direktivakh sovetskoi delegatsii v Komitete desiati po razoruzheniiu," February 1, 1960, in Fursenko et al., *Prezidium TsK KPSS*, 1:424.

35. Vojtech Mastny believes that the Kremlin leadership had even more far-reaching aims: to "trade off" the Warsaw Pact for NATO in the future talks on common European security. "Following the dissolution of the phantom Eastern alliance along with the real Western one while leaving Moscow's network of bilateral military treaties with its dependencies intact, such a system would have allowed the Soviet Union, as its strongest member, to become the arbiter of European security." Mastny, "NATO in the Beholder's Eye," 66. In my opinion, Soviet goals were more straightforward.

36. Zubok, "Soviet Foreign Policy in Germany and Austria"; Prozumenscikov, "Nach Stalins Tod," 747–51.

37. Alexandrov-Agentov, *Ot Kollontai*, 93, 94.

38. Khlevniuk et al., *Stalin i Kaganovich*, 159–63; Zubok and Pechatnov, "Stalin and the Wall Street" (unpublished manuscript).

39. Interviews with Oleg Troyanovsky, Moscow, May 6, 1994; author's conversation with Rostislav Sergeev, Moscow, May 14, 1994.

40. Caute, *Dancer Defects*, 411; Adzhubei, *Krushenie illuzii. Vremia v sobitiakh i litsakh*, 128–35.

41. Zubok, "Nebo nad sverkhderzhavami," 47–55.

42. A closer look at Kremlin politics suggests that in 1955 Molotov stood virtually alone (although Kaganovich and Voroshilov joined him on some issues) among the Kremlin oligarchs in his doubts about and sometimes opposition to the "new foreign policy." See Fursenko et al., *Prezidium TsK KPSS*, 1:35–158.

43. Protokol no. 184. Zasedaniie 30 janvaria 1956. Exchange of opinions on the draft report of the CC CPSU to the Twentieth Party Congress, in Fursenko et al., *Prezidium TsK KPSS*, 1:90, 92.

44. Taubman, *Khrushchev*, xvii–xx.

45. Ibid., 330. Khrushchev's speech at the conference of the Leningrad city and regional apparatus, May 8, 1954, APRF, f. 52, op. 1, d. 398, l. 222–38; the stenographic report of the Presidium meeting on July 1, 1959, in Fursenko et al., *Prezidium TsK KPSS*, 1:256–87.

46. Troyanovsky, "Nikita Khrushchev and the Making of Soviet Foreign Policy," 5.

47. British prime minister Anthony Eden presented his plan at the Berlin conference of foreign ministers in January–February 1954. The essence of the Eden Plan was to call for free elections throughout Germany and to form an all-German government that would negotiate a peace treaty with the four occupying powers. The united Germany would be free to choose or reject alignment with either the East or the West. See Dockrill, "Eden Plan and European Security," 162–89; see also Varsori, "Gouvernement Eden et l'Union Sovietique."

48. "On the positions of the governments of the United States, Britain and France on the German question with regard to the upcoming conference of the leaders of governments of the four powers," Committee of Information (KI), memorandum, June 1955, AFPRF, f. 595, op. 6, por. 51, d. 769, d. 51, l. 29–47; "The positions of Western powers with regard to creation of a system of collective security in Europe with regard to the upcoming conference of the leaders of governments of the four powers," AFPRF, f. 898, op. 6, d. 769, l. 48–63; RGANI, f. 89, per. 70, dokument 7, l. 6.

49. RGANI, f. 89, per. 70, dokument 7, l. 6. Soviet estimates were largely correct; see Antonio Varsori on British aims and Collette Barbier on French aims at Geneva, in Bischof and Dockrill, *Cold War Respite*, 75–116.

50. Khrushchev, "Memuari Nikiti Sergeevicha Khrushcheva," 69; FRUS, 1955–57, 5:259, 417–18; Richter, *Khrushchev's Double Bind*, 71; Taubman, *Khrushchev*, 349–53.

51. Immerman, " 'Trust in the Lord but Keep Your Powder Dry,' " 49.

52. Memorandum of discussion at the 256th meeting of the National Security Council, Washington, July 28, 1955, in FRUS, 1955–57, 5:534.

53. Georgy Kornienko, then a senior analyst of the committee, was in Geneva as a member of this on-site intelligence group. Interview with author, April 16, 1990, Moscow.

54. Prados, "Open Skies and Closed Minds," 224–25, 232–33; see also Rostow, *Open Skies*.

55. FRUS, 1955–57, 5:534.

56. Dobrynin, *In Confidence*, 38.

57. More in Smirnov and Zubok, "Nuclear Weapons after Stalin's Death," 16; see also FRUS, 1955–57, 5:413.

58. "Zapis besedi N. A. Bulganina s Poslom KNR v SSSR Liu Qiao," March 19, 1955, RGANI, f. 5, op. 30, d. 116, l. 19; Eimontova, "Iz Dnevnikov Sergeia Sergeevicha Dmitrieva," *Otechesvennaia istoriia* 1 (2000): 161.

59. Adenauer believed that the summit of great powers would fail to reach agreement on German unity. The trip to the Soviet Union was for him a tactical move to prevent the rise of neutralist sentiments in West Germany. See Schwarz, *Die Ära Adenauer*, and the same author's edited volume, *Entspannung und Wiedervereinigung*; Conze, "No Way Back to Potsdam," 209–10. The Soviets were well informed about Adenauer's motives. See, for instance, a memo from Pavel Naumov, *Pravda*'s correspondent in West Germany, July 3, 1955, which Khrushchev and Bulganin read on July 20, when the Geneva summit started, in RGANI, f. 5, op. 30, d. 114, l. 176–77.

60. Similar arguments are in Harrison, *Driving the Soviets Up the Wall*, 47–48, 53–57.

61. Fursenko et al., *Prezidium TsK KPSS*, 1:900; for more details see Zubok, "Multi-Level Dynamics of Moscow's German Policy."

62. Protocol no. 168 of the Presidium session, November 6, 1957, and November 7, 1958, Fursenko et al., *Prezidium TsK KPSS*, 1:58–60, 900.

63. Kolokolov et al., *Sovetsko-Izrailskie otnosheniia*, 2:430–36; "O meropriiatiakh SShA po prevrashcheniiu Izrailia v voienny platsdarm na Blizhnem Vostoke," KI to Stalin on September 19, 1952, AVPRF, f. 595, op. 6, por. 8, d. 769, l. 74–87.

64. Naumkin, *Blizhnevostochnii konflikt*, 1:114, 139–41, 148, 149–56, 170–71, 180–81; KI to Stalin on the situation in Egypt on December 9, 1952, AVPRF, f. 595, op. 6, por. 8, d. 569, l. 45–48; KI to the CC Presidium on Nasser, March 8, 1954, AVPRF, f. 595, d. 769, l. 25.

65. Zubok, "Soviet Intelligence and the Cold War," 466–68.

66. Mlechin, *MID: Ministri inostrannikh del*, 335–36; Sakharov, *Vospominania*, 247.

67. Information of the Department of the Near and Middle East of the Foreign Ministry of the USSR, July 18, 1955, in Naumkin, *Blizhnevostochnii konflikt*, 1:306–7; see also 301, 328, 333–34, 335, 340–44, 365–67.

68. Gaiduk, *Confronting Vietnam*, 15–16; Olsen, "Changing Alliances," 65–66.

69. See Qiang Zhai, *Dragon, the Lion, and the Eagle*, 175; on the U.S. strategic view of the crisis, see Chang, *Friends and Enemies*, 129–42; Zubok and Pleshakov, *Inside the Kremlin's Cold War*, 217–18.

70. Westad, *Global Cold War*, 69; Fursenko, *Presidium TsK KPSS*, 1:154–55, 162–63; "USSR-PRC (1949–1983), Documents and Materials, Part I, 1949–1963" (Moscow: Historical-Diplomatic Division of the Ministry of Foreign Affairs of the USSR, Moscow, 1985), AVPRF, 145–46, 147–48; Negin and Smirnov, "Did the USSR Share Its Atomic Secrets with China?" 303–17.

71. Chen Jian, *Mao's China and the Cold War*, 167–69. In July 1955 during the annual air show the Soviets were desperate to impress Western military attachés. They used a ruse of flying the only available wing of ten M-4 bombers three times over the field. Zaloga, *Kremlin's Nuclear Sword*, 24.

72. FRUS, 1955–57, 5:416.

73. See the record of conversation of Soviet ambassador Pavel Yudin with Mao Ze-dong on March 8 and May 25, 1955, from AVPRF, translated and published by Wingrove, "Mao's Conversations with the Soviet Ambassador," 28, 35–41.

74. Chen Jian, *China's Road to the Korean War*, 42–43; Chen Jian, *Mao's China and the Cold War*, 63.

75. Chang, *Friends and Enemies*, 137; Qiang Zhai, *Dragon, the Lion, and the Eagle*, 173–74.

76. Eimermacher et al., *Doklad N. S. Khrushcheva o kulte lichnosti*; Nikolai Barsukov, "Kak sozdavalsia 'zakritii doklad Khrushcheva," *Literaturnaia Gazeta*, February 21, 1996; Roy Medvedev and Vladimir Naumov, "XX s'ezd: taina zakrytogo zasedaniia," *Vechernii klub*, February 26, 1996; Aksyutin and Pyzhikov, "O podgotovke zakrytogo doklada N. S. Khrushcheva XX s'ezdu KPSS v svete novikh dokumentov," 107–17.

77. On Pospelov's reaction see Mikoyan, *Tak bylo*, 592.

78. Mikoyan, *Tak bylo*, 594; "Iz rabochei protokolnoi zapisi zasedaniia Prezidiuma TsK

KPSS," February 9, 1956, and Stenogramma Plenuma TsK KPSS, February 13, 1956, in Eimermacher et al., *Doklad N. S. Khrushcheva o kulte lichnosti*, 234–37, 241–43.

79. Yakovlev, *Omut pamiati*, 116.

80. Troyanovsky commented in his book that one such clash during the Geneva summit "negatively affected an important state business." Troyanovsky, *Cherez godi i rasstoiania*, 189; Alexandrov-Agentov, *Ot Kollontai*, 95.

81. Chuev, *Kaganovich, Shepilov*, 342, 352.

82. "O povedenii sovetskikh diplomatov," report to the CC CPUS by writer Boris Polevoi, who was a member of the delegation, RGALI, f. 631, op. 26, d. 3826, l. 9–10.

83. Presidium session, August 11, 1956, Protocol no. 32, in Fursenko et al., *Prezidium TsK KPSS*, 1:156–57.

84. Chuev, *Kaganovich, Shepilov*, 352; Fursenko and Naftali, *Khrushchev's Cold War*, 101–6.

85. Fursenko et al., *Prezidium TsK KPSS*, 1:156–59, 162–63; Mlechin, *MID: Ministri inostrannikh del*, 343; undelivered speech of Vladimir Semenov at the June 1957 Plenum CC CPSU, in Kovaleva et al., *Molotov, Malenkov, Kaganovich*, 678.

86. For a different view see Narinsky, "Sovetskii Soiuz i Suetskii krizis 1956 goda," 54–66.

87. Fursenko et al., *Prezidium TsK KPSS*, 2:359–62.

88. Presidium minutes for July 9 and 12 and October 4, 20, and 21, 1956, in Fursenko et al., *Prezidium TsK KPSS*, 1:149, 168, 173–75; Granville, *First Domino*, 121–23. The Presidium decided to convene an emergency meeting of the Communist parties of all other countries, members of the Warsaw Treaty Organization. There were also ominous phrases in Malin's notes about "preparing a document" and "creating a committee" that leave room for various interpretations. Sergo Mikoyan claims he heard his father, Khrushchev, and other leaders discussing a military invasion of Poland (his report at an international workshop in Saratov, Russia, July 3, 2001). On the Polish side see Gluchowski, *Soviet-Polish Confrontation of October, 1956*.

89. Chen Jian, *Mao's China and the Cold War*, 146–48. This paragraph is also based on the documents made public by Leo Gluchowski, on file at NSArch.

90. The declaration's text was published by *Pravda*, October 31, 1956. On the Hungarian and other sources related to the Hungarian revolution, see the briefing book "Hungary and the World, 1956: The New Archival Evidence," organized in Budapest on September 26–29, 1996, by the NSArch, the CHWIP, and the Institute for the History of the 1956 Hungarian Revolution.

91. Fursenko et al., *Prezidium TsK KPSS*, 1:180, 181, 185, 188–90; Kramer, "New Evidence on Soviet Decision-Making," 389–92.

92. On the Chinese role see Fursenko et al., *Prezidium TsK KPSS*, 1:178–79, 188–89; Chen Jian, *Mao's China and the Cold War*, 150–57.

93. Fursenko et al., *Prezidium TsK KPSS*, 1:1988–91.

94. Ibid., 1:191–92; Kramer, "New Evidence on Soviet Decision-Making," 393.

95. Mark Kramer and Johanna Granville emphasize more the factors of the Suez crisis and "spillover" effect. See Kramer, "New Evidence on Soviet Decision-Making," 369–71; and Granville, *First Domino*. Alexander Stykalin, however, acknowledges that the opinion of the CCP, Palmiro Togliatti, and other Communist leaders, had a last-minute impact on Kremlin

decision making. See his *Prervannaia revoliutsia*; Gluchowski, "Khrushchev, Gomulka, and the 'Polish October,'" 1, 38–49.

96. Malin notes, October 28, 1956, in Fursenko et al., *Prezidium TsK KPSS*, 1:186, 191.

97. Yakovlev, *Omut pamiati*, 117.

98. On the position of Tito and Gomulka see Granville, *First Domino*, 100–121.

99. Mikoyan, *Tak Bylo*, 604; Malin notes, November 4, 1956, in Fursenko et al., *Prezidium TsK KPSS*, 1:202.

100. On the Chinese version of events see Shi Zhe, "At the Side of Mao Ze-dong and Stalin: Shi Zhe's Memoirs," translated by Chen Jian (quoted with his permission); Chen Jian, *Mao's China and the Cold War*, 158–62; Zubok, "'Look What Chaos in the Beautiful Socialist Camp!'" 153.

101. Zhou Enlai's observations on the Soviet Union, January 24, 1957, translated and published by Zhang Shuguang and Chen Jian, "Emerging Disputes between Beijing and Moscow," 153–54; see also remarks of Deng Xiaoping to the Soviet delegation at the meeting in Moscow, July 5–20, 1963, copy found at SAPMO-BArch, JIV 2/207 698, S. 75. According to Chen Jian, Mao in several internal speeches emphasized that Khrushchev and his colleagues had abandoned not only "the banner of Stalin" but also "the banner of Lenin." It was China's turn and duty to pick up that banner. Chen Jian, *Mao's China and the Cold War*, 158–62.

102. Molotov's remark at the June 1957 Plenum, in Kovaleva et al., *Molotov, Malenkov, Kaganovich*, 131.

103. Kovaleva et al., *Molotov, Kaganovich, Malenkov*, 128; *Pravda*, November 19 and 23, 1956; Khrushchev's speech at Varna, May 16, 1962, published in *Istochnik* 6 (2003): 136; on the reasons behind Tito's contradictory actions see Granville, "Tito and the 'Nagy Affair,'" 23–57; Rainer, *Nagy Imre*, 2:347. On Khrushchev's reaction to Tito's turnabout see Tischler, "Poland's October and the 1956 Hungarian Revolution."

104. Letter from Antonina Peterson to Shepilov, May 3, 1957, letter from engineer M. Petrygin to the CC CPSU, January 25, 1957, letter from Colonel P. Nesterov to Khrushchev, January 30, 1957, RGANI, f. 5, op. 30, d. 189, l. 1–6, 29–30, and d. 190, l. 142–62.

105. Mikoyan, *Tak bylo*, 599, 602.

106. "Posledniaia 'antipartiinaia' gruppa. Stenograficheskii otchet iiunskogo (1957) plenuma TsK KPSS," *Istoricheskii arkhiv* 3, 4, 5, 6 (1993), and 1, 2 (1994); for the unedited versions of the same materials, see Kovaleva et al., *Molotov, Malenkov, Kaganovich*.

107. *Istoricheskii arkhiv* 3 (1993): 74–75.

108. *Istoricheskii arkhiv* 4 (1993): 27, 29.

109. *Istoricheskii arkhiv* 3 (1993): 79.

110. See comparison between the two groups in Mikoyan, *Tak Bylo*, 604.

111. Naumov et al., *Georgii Zhukov*, 297, 425; Fursenko et al., *Presidium TsK KPSS*, 1:252, 263–64, also comments on 1011–12; Dobrynin, *In Confidence*, 37–38. For Zhukov's criticism of Khrushchev see Taubman, *Khrushchev*, 314.

112. Naumov et al., *Georgii Zhukov*, 379.

113. Zubok, "Soviet Intelligence and the Cold War," 453–72.

114. Troyanovsky, "Making of Soviet Foreign Policy," 216.

Chapter Five

1. This chapter draws on the article I coauthored with Hope S. Harrison, "Nuclear Education of Nikita Khrushchev." I thank Professor Harrison for her permission to use fragments of our joint publication for this book.

2. See Weart, *Nuclear Fear*.

3. Zaloga, *Kremlin's Nuclear Sword*, 21. The "New Look" strategy of the Eisenhower administration was adopted in 1953. It put an emphasis on nuclear means of deterring the Soviet threat, which was reflected in the deployment of nuclear weapons of all kinds and ranges in Western Europe for the purpose of "massive retaliation" to Soviet aggression. At the end of 1957 Eisenhower, trying to soften the shock of Sputnik in Western Europe, announced the deployment of IRBM missiles in the NATO countries willing to host them. See Bundy, *Danger and Survival*, 245–55; and Trachtenberg, *History and Strategy*, 138–39, 156–62, and 202.

4. On the scholarly debate regarding the stabilizing effect of nuclear weapons, see Mearsheimer, "Nuclear Weapons and Deterrence in Europe," 19–46; Gaddis, "Long Peace," 99–142; Gaddis, Gordon, May, and Rosenberg, *Cold War Statesmen Confront the Bomb*.

5. On this flaw of the U.S. "containment" doctrine, see Logevall, "Bernath Lecture," 475–84.

6. V. B. Adamsky, in Lebedev, *Andrei Sakharov*, 31. A recent account of the Soviet side of the strategic arms race is in Zaloga, *Kremlin's Nuclear Sword*. Also, on the Soviet hydrogen project as taking a distinctly different route from the American one, see Holloway, *Stalin and the Bomb*, 294–319.

7. See Ryabev, ed., *Atomnii Projekt SSSR: Dokumenti i Materiali*, vol. 2, book 1, 639–43; Marshal Alexander Vasilevsky to Stalin on the preparatory protection measures from atomic and biological weapons, September 12, 1950, copy of the handwritten document, Volkogonov Collection, LC.

8. Transcript of July 3, 1953, CC CPSU Plenum, *Izvestia TsK KPSS* 2 (1991): 166–70.

9. N. Khrushchev, *Khrushchev Remembers*, 68; S. Khrushchev, *Nikita Khrushchev: Krizisi i raketi*, 1:45; S. Khrushchev, *Nikita Khrushchev and the Creation of a Superpower*; G. Goncharov, "Khronologiia," 247; Sakharov, *Memoirs*, 180–81; Holloway, *Stalin and the Bomb*, 324.

10. Zubok and Smirnov, "Moscow and Nuclear Weapons," 1, 14–18.

11. On the enormous impact of that test on world public opinion, see Holloway, *Stalin and the Bomb*, 337.. See also Weisgall, *Operation Crossroads*, 302–7; York, *Advisors*, 85–86; Hewlett and Holl, *Atoms for Peace and War*, 168–82.

12. G. Goncharov, "Khronologiia," 249.

13. "Danger of Atomic War and President Eisenhower's Proposal," memorandum of V. Malyshev to N. Khrushchev, April 1, 1954, RGANI, f. 5, op. 126, d. 126, l. 38.

14. Ibid., l. 39, 40, 41; see also Zubok and Smirnov, "Moscow and Nuclear Weapons," 14–15. The physicists might have communicated their concerns orally to the leadership, at least to Malenkov, before putting them in writing.

15. For Malenkov's speech, see *Pravda*, March 13, 1954; for Mikoyan's speech, see *Kommunist* (Yerevan), March 12, 1954.

16. *Pravda*, April 27, 1954.

17. Volkov and Kolesova, "Soviet Reaction to U.S. Nuclear Policy," 6–9.

18. S. Khrushchev, *Nikita Khrushchev: Krizisi i raketi*, 1:45; the excerpts from this classified film were later used in many documentaries, including "Scientific Director: The Life of Yuli B. Khariton," produced in Moscow in the 1990s; Vlasov, "Desiat' let riadom s Kurchatovym," 42; Holloway, *Stalin and the Bomb*, 307; Heikal, *Sphinx and Commissar*, 129. Italics for emphasis added.

19. S. Khrushchev, *Nikita Khrushchev: Krizisi i raketi*, 1:62–67.

20. Zubok and Pleshakov, "The Soviet Union," in Raynolds, *Origins of the Cold War in Europe*, 71.

21. "Turnir dlinoi v tri desiatiletiia," *Istoricheskii arkhiv* 2 (1993): 58–67.

22. Wittner, *Resisting the Bomb*, 23–25, 105–6; Sakharov, *Memoirs*, 194–95; Holloway, *Stalin and the Bomb*, 316–17.

23. "Zapis besedy G. K. Zhukova s Prezidentom SShA Eizenkhauerom," July 20, 1955, RGANI, f. 5, op. 30, d. 116, l. 122–23, published in Naumov et al., *Georgii Zhukov*, 38–40; the American version of the meeting is in FRUS, 1955–57, 5:408–18.

24. *Pravda*, February 15, 1956.

25. Sergei Khrushchev recollects an episode when he accompanied his father on a visit to see the missiles under construction at Korolev's firm "around January 1956." Khrushchev asked Dmitry Ustinov, then head of the military-industrial commission of the Council of Ministers, how many bombs would suffice "to knock out England." When Ustinov said "five," Khrushchev allegedly said: "Terrible power. The last war was bloody, but with charges like this one it becomes simply impossible." S. Khrushchev, *Nikita Khrushchev: Krizisi i raketi*, 1:103; *Pravda*, November, 18, 1955; Holloway, *Stalin and the Bomb*, 343.

26. *Pravda*, February 15, 1956.

27. Rosendorf, "John Foster Dulles' Nuclear Schizophrenia," 83; and Erdmann, " 'War No Longer Has Any Logic Whatever,' " 98–110. Dobrynin, *In Confidence*, 38; "Conference of First Secretaries of Central Committees of Communist and Workers Parties of Socialist Countries for the Exchange of Views on Questions Related to the Preparation and Conclusion of a German Peace Treaty, August 3–5, 1961," *CWIHP Bulletin*, no. 3 (Fall 1993): 60. On Khrushchev's learning from John Foster Dulles and his "duel" with the Dulles brothers, see Zubok and Pleshakov, *Inside the Kremlin's Cold War*, 190–91; and Zubok, "Inside the Covert Cold War," 25–27.

28. Taubman, *Khrushchev*, 359–60; transcript of the June 1957 CC CPSU Plenary meeting, *Istoricheskii arkhiv* 4 (1993): 36; Immerman, *John Foster Dulles and the Diplomacy of the Cold War*. Indeed, from 1957 on, John Foster Dulles began to have serious doubts about the practicability of his "massive retaliation" doctrine, since, as he once put it, "a nuclear exchange between the U.S. and the USSR could make all of the Northern Hemisphere uninhabitable or, in any event, risky to inhabit." Memorandum of conversation at National Security Council (NSC) meeting, April 7, 1958, NSArch. I thank William Burr for bringing this document to my attention.

29. It is not clear what Khrushchev knew about Clausewitz's ideas. The Soviet General

Staff, however, always held the Prussian theorist in high regard. Clausewitz's legacy was always part of the party ideological exegesis because Friedrich Engels had admired his views on war and Lenin commented on it, too. In 1947 Stalin returned to Clausewitz to confirm that he had foreseen the Marxist-Leninist idea that "there is a direct connection between war and politics, that politics generates war, and that war is continuation of politics by violent means." Stalin, "Otvet tovarischu Razinu," February 23, 1946, Bolshevik 3, 1947. See also Soviet publication of Clausewitz, O voine (Moscow: Voenizdat, 1941); and Kokoshin, Soviet Strategic Thought.

30. Pravda, May 14, 1957; transcript of the June 1957 CC CPSU Plenum, Istoricheskii arkhiv 4 (1993): 5.

31. Presidium meeting on February 1, 1960, in Fursenko et al., Prezidium TsK KPSS, 1:424.

32. Gosplan statistics demonstrated that in 1958 the missiles took up only 8.5 percent of the total expenditure of equipment by the Ministry of Defense. In 1959 this share almost tripled, to 21.5 percent. In 1962 it rose to almost 44 percent. Simonov, Voienno-promishlennii kompleks, 247; S. Khrushchev, Nikita Khrushchev: Krizisi i raketi, 1:384; P. L. Podvig, ed., Strategicheskoie iadernoie vooruzheniie Rossii (Moscow: IzdAt, 1998); Bystrova, "Sovetskii voennii potentsial perioda "kholodnoi voini" v amerikanskikh otsenkakh," 132–36; see also the data of the Center for the Study of Disarmament, Energy, and Ecology at the Moscow Institute for Physics and Technology at <http://www.armscontrol/ru>.

33. Engerman, "Romance of Economic Development and New Histories of the Cold War," 29–42; Taubman, Khrushchev, 364–65, 480.

34. Simonov, Voienno-promishlennii kompleks, 249–50, 303, 307; <http://www.vriitf.ru/begin.phtml>; Viktoriia Glazyrina, "Krasnoiarsk-26: A Closed City of the Defense-Industry Complex," in Barber and Harrison, Soviet Home Front, 196; Ladyzhenskii, "Krasnoiarsk-26," 125–51.

35. This would have meant that the access routes from West Germany to West Berlin could then pass under Ulbricht's jurisdiction. The Western powers feared that the GDR regime would close those routes, which would then put the West in a difficult quandary: to withdraw from West Berlin or go to war. On the idea of renouncing the 1945 agreements on Germany, see Fursenko et al., Presidium TsK KPSS, 1:338–39.

36. Troyanovsky, "Making of Soviet Foreign Policy," 221; Burr, "Eisenhower's Search for Flexibility."

37. See Adomeit, Soviet Risk-Taking and Crisis Behavior; Schick, Berlin Crisis; Catudal, Kennedy and the Berlin Wall Crisis; Slusser, Berlin Crisis of 1961; Beschloss, Crisis Years; Harrison, Driving the Soviets Up the Wall, 114. Adenauer and Defense Minister Franz-Joseph Strauss indeed sought the nuclearization of West Germany. See Kosthorst, Brentano und die deutsche Einheit, 137–43; on the issue of West German nuclearization, see Kelleher, Germany and the Politics of Nuclear Weapons, 43–49; and Trachtenberg, History and Strategy, 252–53.

38. S. Khrushchev, Nikita Khrushchev: Krizisi i raketi, 416; Hope Harrison, Driving the Soviets Up the Wall, 116–17. In November-December 1958, Soviet medium-range missiles were deployed, on Khrushchev's order, to the newly built posts in East Germany, to support his threats. Uhl and Ivkin, "Operation Atom," 299–307.

39. Wittner, Resisting the Bomb, 278–80; Fursenko et al., Prezidium TsK KPSS, 1:252.

40. Stenograficheskaia zapis zasedaniia Prezidiuma TsK KPSS po voprosu "O direktivakh sovetskoi delegatsii v Komitete desiati po razoruzheniiu," February 1, 1960, Fursenko et al., *Prezidium TsK KPSS*, 1:423–24, 427, 431, 432, 434–35.

41. On the tension inside Khrushchev, see Taubman, *Khrushchev*, 423–39.

42. Zubok, "Khrushchev's 1960 Troop Cut," 416–20; Nichols, *Sacred Cause*, 71–83; Hansen, *Correlation of Forces*, 67.

43. "Report of the CC CPSU Presidium to the Central Committee, no later than October 14, 1964," *Istochnik* 2 (1998): 112.

44. *Military Thought* had been copied by Penkovsky and passed to the CIA. They were declassified and released in June 1992 and are available at NSArch.

45. Sokolovskii, *Military Strategy*. Interview with Lt. Gen. Valentin Larionov (who participated in writing *Military Strategy*), Moscow, May 29, 1991; Valentin Larionov, "Tiazhkii put poznaniia (Iz istorii iadernoi strategii)," unpublished manuscript, 9–10 (courtesy of Valentin Larionov).

46. On the background of the Mao-Khrushchev feud, see Zubok and Pleshakov, *Inside the Kremlin's Cold War*, 210–35; Chen Jian, *Mao's China and the Cold War*, 64–67; Taubman, *Khrushchev*, 336–42, 389–95, 470–71. On nuclear cooperation, see Yuli Khariton and Yuri Smirnov, "Otkuda vzialos i bilo li nam neobkhodimo iadernoie oruzhiie," *Izvestia*, July 21, 1994, 5; Negin and Smirnov, "Did the USSR Share Its Atomic Secrets with China?," 303–17.

47. N. Khrushchev, *Khrushchev Remembers*, 467–68; Schecter and Luchkov, *Khrushchev Remembers*, 147–50; Fursenko et al., *Presidium TsK KPSS*, 1:326–27.

48. Li Zhisui, *Private Life of Chairman Mao*, 270–71; CC CPSU to CC CCP, letter of September 27, 1958, published in *CWIHP Bulletin*, no. 6–7 (Winter 1995/96): 219, 226–27; Zubok, "Khrushchev-Mao Conversations," 243–72.

49. Negin and Smirnov, "Did the USSR Share Its Atomic Secrets with China?," 311–12; Troyanovsky, "Making of Soviet Foreign Policy," 229.

50. Taubman, *Khrushchev*, 393–95.

51. For possible scenarios of the Kremlin debates in March–April 1960, see Oleg Grinevsky, *Tysiacha i odin den Nikity Sergeevicha*, 154–64; Taubman, *Khrushchev*, 454–55.

52. On the background of the U-2 affair and Khrushchev's actions during 1960, see Zubok and Pleshakov, *Inside the Kremlin's Cold War*, 202–9; Taubman, *Khrushchev*, 442–79; Israelyan, *Na frontakh kholodnoi voini*, 76.

53. Davidson, Mazov, and Tsypkin, *SSSR i Africa, 1918–1960*, 99; Mirsky, "Polveka v mire vostokovedenia," 130.

54. Taubman, *Khrushchev*, 474–77; Khrushchev to the CC Presidium, October 10, 1960, *Istochnik* 6 (2003): 116–17.

55. See more details in Taubman, *Khrushchev*, 491, 495; Dobrynin, *In Confidence*, 44.

56. Protocol no. 331, session of the CC CPUS Presidium on May 26, 1961, and "Vyskazyvaniia N. S. Khrushcheva v khode zasedaniia Prezidiuma TsK KPSS ob obmene mneniiami k vstreche tov. Khrushcheva N. S. s Kennedy v Vene," May 26, 1961, in Fursenko et al., *Prezidium TsK KPSS*, 1:498–99, 502–3.

57. Korol, "Upushchennaiia vozmozhnost," 102–3.

58. Beschloss, *Crisis Years*, 330.

59. On KGB-GRU reports on U.S. plans of attack, the first of them on June 29, 1960, see Fursenko, "Neobychnaia sudba razvedchika G. N. Bolshakova," 94–95. Conference of first secretaries of CC, August 3–5, 1961, translated excerpts in the *CWIHP Bulletin*, no. 3 (1993): 60.

60. Harrison, *Driving the Soviets Up the Wall*, 116, 164, 195; Tismaneanu, *Stalinism for All Seasons*, 144, 163, 167, 177–81. In July 18, 1961, Penkovsky said to his CIA handlers that "if we consider today's situation, the Soviet Army is not ready for any widespread war." Penkovsky's debriefings, July 18–19, 1961, 14, NSArch; Schecter and Deriabin, *Spy Who Saved the World*, 205–13.

61. Zubok, "Inside the Covert Cold War," 26–27.

62. This decision is inferred from the document cited by the retired Gen. Maj. Vadim Makarevsky, "O premiere N. S. Kruscheve, marshale G. K. Zhukove i generale I. A. Plieve," *Mirovaia ekonomika i mezhdunarodniie otnosheniia* 8–9 (1994): 193; Lebedev, *Andrei Sakharov*, 602–3; Adamsky and Smirnov, "Soviet 50-Megaton Test in 1961," 3, 19–20.

63. Fursenko, *Rossiia i mezhdunarodniie krizisi*, 248–49, 252–53; Fursenko and Naftali, *Khrushchev's Cold War*, 372–75; Harrison, *Driving the Soviets Up the Wall*, 178–86; Khrushchev's notes on the German Question, December 11, 1961, *Istochnik* 6 (2003): 123–27.

64. *XXII S'ezd Kommunisticheskoi Partii Sovetskogo Soiuza. Stenograficheskii otchet* (Moscow: Gospolitizdat, 1992), 2:571–72.

65. On the Checkpoint Charlie episode, see Troyanovsky, "Making of Soviet Foreign Policy," 233, and Khrushchev's explanation to the Presidium on January 8, 1962, in Fursenko et al., *Prezidium TsK KPSS*, 1:546; Fursenko, *Rossiia i mezhdunarodniie krizisi*, 243–44; and Fursenko and Naftali, *Khrushchev's Cold War*, 403–4. For a less sanguine interpretation of the tank confrontation, see Falin, *Bez Skidok na obstoiatelstva*, 88–89; Falin, *Politische Erinnerungen*, 345–46; and Garthoff, "Berlin 1961."

66. "Stenograficheskaia zapis zasedaniia Prezidiuma TsK KPSS po voprosu o pozitsii Pravitelstva SSSR na dalneishikh peregovorakh s pravitelstvami SShA, Anglii i Frantsii po germanskomu voprosu," January 8, 1962, in Fursenko et al., *Prezidium TsK KPSS*, 1:545, 547.

67. Naftali, "NATO, the Warsaw Pact and the Rise of Détente"; see Naftali's comments also at <http://www.cia.gov/csi/books/watchingthebear/article06.html>.

68. Fursenko et al., *Prezidium TsK KPSS*, 1:536–37; Sakharov, *Sakharov Speaks*, 33.

69. The discussion about how serious the threat of war was never stops. For recent polemics, see Kramer, "Tactical Nuclear Weapons, Soviet Command Authority, and the Cuban Missile Crisis"; Blight, Allyn, and Welch, "Kramer vs. Kramer," 40, 41, 42–46, 47–50; Lebow and Stein, *We All Lost the Cold War*, 94–109.

70. Ulam, *Expansion and Coexistence*, 668–72.

71. Blight, Allyn, and Welch, *Cuba on the Brink*, 348.

72. Fursenko and Naftali, *"One Hell of a Gamble,"* 170–71, 182–83; Taubman, *Khrushchev*, 406, 414, 531–32.

73. On the evidence from the U.S. archives about American covert planning to invade Cuba and carry out other subversive actions against Cuba, see Hershberg, "Before 'The Missiles of October.'"

74. There was genuine mass enthusiasm among Soviet citizens when Fidel Castro visited the Soviet Union *after* the Cuban missile crisis, in spring 1963. Castro himself observed "how deeply the question of the Cuban Revolution had penetrated the feelings of the Soviet people. We simply could not begin to understand how they [Soviet leaders] would be able to face the enormous impact, the explosive and uncontrollable impact that news of a U.S. invasion of Cuba would have on the Soviet people." Blight and Brenner, *Sad and Luminous Days*, 63.

75. Ibid., 38; Fursenko and Naftali, *"One Hell of a Gamble,"* 167–70.

76. Fursenko and Naftali assume that Khrushchev's decision was based not on specific intelligence reports about U.S. activities against Cuba but on his misreading of political messages from the White House. Fursenko and Naftali, *"One Hell of a Gamble,"* 152–53, 156–60, 176–77.

77. Quotation from minutes of meeting of the Special Group on Operation MONGOOSE, October 4, 1962, attended by Robert Kennedy, Lyndon Johnson, Roswell Gilpatric, General Maxwell Taylor, General Lansdale, CIA director McCone, and others, and memorandum of meeting of CIA's McCone with the president, August 23, 1962, in Blanton et al., *Primary Source Documents*.

78. Troyanovsky, "Making of Soviet Foreign Policy," 234. Soviet sources on the strategic balance are ambiguous. One author claims that 48 ICBMs could reach the United States from Soviet territory in fall 1962. Fursenko gives the number as 20. The number of U.S. ICBMs at the time stood at, at a minimum, 93, and there were rockets and medium-range bombers deployed on bases in Europe and Asia. A. P. Leutin, "V pogone za paritetom (Iz istorii amerikano-sovetskoi gonki iadernikh vooruzhenii)," in *Sovetskoie obshchestvo: budni kholodnoi voini: Materialy "kruglogo stola,"* ed. V. S. Lelchuk (Moscow-Arzamas: IRI-RAN-AGPI, 2000), 91; Fursenko and Naftali, *Khrushchev's Cold War*, 429–31; Fursenko, *Rossiia i mezhdunarodniie krizisi*, 338. The independent American think tank, the National Resources Defense Council, asserts that by 1962 the Soviet Union had 36 ICBMs and 72 ballistic missiles on atomic submarines. The United States had 203 ICBMs and 144 submarine-based missiles. The U.S. Strategic Air Command had 1,306 long-range bombers; the Soviet Union had only 138. The data are from <http://www. nrdc.org/nuclear/nudf/datainx.asp/>.

79. Fursenko and Naftali, *"One Hell of a Gamble,"* 179–80.

80. Protocol no. 32, Presidium session on May 21, 1963, in Fursenko et al., *Prezidium TsK KPSS*, 1:556; Garthoff, *Reflections on the Cuban Missile Crisis*, 12–17; Hansen, "Soviet Deception in the Cuban Missile Crisis."

81. Uhl and Ivkin, " 'Operation Atom,' " 299–304.

82. Raul Castro's recollection on January 23, 1968, at the plenary meeting of the Central Committee of the Cuban Communist Party, in Blight and Brenner, *Sad and Luminous Days*, 43.

83. Fursenko and Naftali, *"One Hell of a Gamble,"* 191–92; General Nikolai Leonov to author, conversation at Cuban conference, Havana, October 12, 2002.

84. Memorandum of Rodion Malinovsky and Matvei Zakharov to Khrushchev, June 24, 1962, Deployment of Soviet Forces to Cuba, Volkogonov Collection, LC, printed in *CWIHP Bulletin*, no. 11 (Winter 1998): 254–56.

85. N. P. Kamanin, *Skrytii kosmos*, vol. 1 (Moscow: Infortekst-IF, 1997), 174–75.

86. *Neizvestnaia Rossiia. XX vek. Kniga 3* (Moscow: Istoricheskoie nasledie, 1993), 229–56, cited in Adamsky and Smirnov, "Moralnaia otvetstvennost uchenikh i politicheskikh liderov v iadernuiu epokhu," 334–35.

87. Sakharov, *Vospominaniia*, 294; Adamsky and Smirnov, "Moralnaia otvetstvennost uchenikh i politicheskikh liderov v iadernuiu epokhu," 335–37.

88. Fursenko and Naftali, *"One Hell of a Gamble,"* 195, 232; Taubman, *Khrushchev*, 553–56.

89. Protocol no. 60, Presidium session on October 22, 1962, in Fursenko et al., *Prezidium TsK KPSS*, 1:617; Fursenko, *Rossiia i mezhdunarodniie krizisi*, 358–59; Fursenko and Naftali, *Khrushchev's Cold War*, 467–74.

90. This information has been repeatedly confirmed by General Anatoly Gribkov, a representative of the Soviet General Staff in Cuba before and during the crisis; see, for example, Cuban conference, October 11–13, 2002, Havana, and author's conversations with Gribkov at conference, October 12, 2002. Gribkov and Smith, *Operation Anadyr*, 183.

91. Recollections of Captain Ryurik Ketov in Cherkashin, *Povsednevnaia zhizn rossiiskikh podvodnikov*, 143, 146; Mozvogoi, *Cuban Samba of the Quartet of Foxtrots*.

92. Telegram from Dobrynin to the USSR Foreign Ministry, October 24, 1962, in Blanton et al., *Primary Source Documents*; Protocol no. 61, Presidium session on October 25, 1962, in Fursenko et al., *Prezidium TsK KPSS*, 1:621–22.

93. Letter from chairman Khrushchev to President Kennedy, FRUS, 1961–63, 6:178–81; Fursenko and Naftali, *"One Hell of a Gamble,"* 275–77; Israelyan, *Na frontakh kholodnoi voini*, 81–82.

94. For the texts of Dobrynin's and others' accounts of the meeting, see Hershberg, "Anatomy of a Controversy," 75, 77–80.

95. Blight, Allen, and Welch, *Cuba on the Brink*, 361–65; Schecter and Luchkov, *Khrushchev Remembers: The Glasnost Tapes*, 177; exchange of cables between Khrushchev and Castro is printed in *Cuba on the Brink*, 481–91.

96. Fursenko et al., *Prezidium TsK KPSS*, 1:569; Trostnik—Pavlovu, October 27, 1962, declassified cable from APRF, in Blanton et al., *Primary Source Documents*.

97. Troyanovsky, "Caribbean Crisis," 147–57; author's interview with Troyanovsky, March 2, 1993, Washington, D.C. On Castro's and the Cubans' furious reactions, see Blight and Brenner, *Sad and Luminous Days*, 49–56.

98. Trostnik—tovarischu Pavlovu, a telegram on November 20, 1962, declassified cable from AVRF, in Blanton et al., *Primary Source Documents*.

99. Minutes of conversation between the delegations of the Czechoslovak Communist Party (CPCz) and the Communist Party of the Soviet Union (CPSU), the Kremlin, October 30, 1962, from Central State Archive, Archive of the CC Communist Party of Czechoslovakia (Prague), Antonin Novotny, Kuba, box 193, provided by Oldrich Tuma and translated by Linda Mastalir, in Blanton et al., *Primary Source Documents*.

100. Mikoyan, *Tak Bylo*, 606.

101. See the discussion of this by Thomas S. Blanton, "Cuban Missile Crisis: 40 Years Later," *Washington Post*, October 16, 2002; see also Sagan, *Limits of Safety: Organizations, Accidents, and Nuclear Weapons*.

102. Troyanovsky, "Making of Soviet Foreign Policy," 238–39.

103. Shelest, *Da ne sudimi budete*, 161.

104. Fursenko et al., *Prezidium TsK KPSS*, 2:569; Fursenko and Naftali, *Khrushchev's Cold War*, 470.

105. Israelyan, *Na frontakhi*, 82–83; Fursenko and Naftali, *"One Hell of a Gamble,"* 301–2, 307–8.

106. Author's summary of the presentations of and informal communications with the ex-Soviet veterans of the crisis at the Conference on the Caribbean Crisis of 1962, Moscow, September 27–29, 1994.

107. Taubman, *Khrushchev*, 579; Castro's recollection of his trip to the USSR, in Blight and Brenner, *Sad and Luminous Days*, 63–65; author's notes from the Cuban conference, October 11–13, 2002, where Castro confirmed his impressions.

108. Sakharov, *Memoirs*, 204; on Kurchatov's "enlightening" diplomacy, see Smirnov and Zubok, "Nuclear Weapons after Stalin's Death," 16; Evangelista, "Soviet Scientists and Nuclear Testing"; Wittner, *Resisting the Bomb*, 278–80.

109. On the multiple levels and channels of the test ban negotiations, see Bunn, *Arms Control by Committee*, 26–35. Adamsky, in Lebedev, *Andrei Sakharov*, 38–39; see also Sakharov, *Vospominaniia*, 307–8. On the larger role of transnational scientific communities, see Evangelista, "Soviet Scientists and Nuclear Testing."

110. Stenograficheskaia zapis zasedaniia Prezidiuma TsK KPSS, April 25, 1963, in Fursenko et al., *Prezidium TsK KPSS*, 1:705, 706; S. Khrushchev, *Nikita Khrushchev: Krizisi i raketi*, 2:458.

111. Khrushchev's sensitivity to Chinese criticism at that time is acknowledged by CC insiders. Arbatov, *System*, 95; Burlatsky, *Khrushchev and the First Russian Spring*, 185–86.

112. N. Khrushchev, "Present International Situation and the Foreign Policy of the Soviet Union," report to session of USSR Supreme Soviet, December 12, 1962, in *Current Digest of the Soviet Press* 14, no. 52 (January 23, 1963): 3; Protocol no. 107, Presidium session on July 23, 1963, in Fursenko et al., *Prezidium TsK KPSS*, 1:734; see also Mastny, *Documentation on the PPC of Warsaw Treaty Organization in Moscow*; Bunn, *Arms Control by Committee*, 37. On the Chinese nuclear program, see Lewis and Litai, *China Builds a Bomb*.

113. Seaborg and Loeb, *Kennedy, Khrushchev, and the Test Ban*, 239; Kohler to the Department of State, Moscow, July 18 and 19, 1963, FRUS, 1961–63, 7:808, 814; Burr and Richelson, "Chinese Puzzle"; Zubok, " 'What Chaos in the Beautiful Socialist Camp!' " 152–62.

114. Selvage, "Warsaw Pact and Nuclear Nonproliferation," 10.

115. For Malinovsky's report see Kamanin's diary on February 8, 1963, in his *Skrytii kosmos*, 220; on the "restoration" of more traditional military policies and doctrine after Khrushchev's New Look "revolution," see Nichols, *Sacred Cause* 84–86.

Chapter Six

1. For absence of any mention of the crisis see Nagibin, *Dnevnik*, 151–59; Samoilov, *Podennie zapisi*, 1:306–18; Chukovskaia, *Zapiski ob Anne Akhmatovoi*, 2:531–67.

2. Caute, *Dancer Defects*, 1.

3. On American attitudes and expectations see Whitfield, *Culture of the Cold War*; Hixson, *Parting the Curtain*; Major and Mitter, "East Is East and West Is West?" 1–22; May, *Homeward Bound*; Farber, *Age of Great Dreams*; Dudziak, *Cold War Civil Rights*.

4. Volkov, *Intellektualnyi sloi v sovetskom obschestve*, 30–31, 126–27.

5. Zubkova, *Russia after the War*, 175.

6. See Bushnell, " 'New Soviet Man' Turns Pessimist," 179–85.

7. A brief discussion of the transformation of Soviet society from "totalitarian" to "post-totalitarian" can be found in Kenez, *History of the Soviet Union*.

8. Cohen, *Rethinking the Soviet Experience*, 128–34; Zaslavsky, *Neo-Stalinist State*; Vail and Ghenis, *1960-e*; English, *Russia and the Idea of the West*. On the nonliberal groups see Dunlop, *New Russian Revolutionaries*; Yanov, *Russian New Right*; Laqueur, *Black Hundred*.

9. Suri, *Power and Protest*.

10. Brandenberger, *National Bolshevism*, 224–25. I prefer to stress the "imperial" and not the "national" component in Stalinist ideology and mass culture.

11. Pollock, "Conversations with Stalin on Questions of Political Economy"; Ilizarov, "Stalin."

12. Zezina, *Sovetskaia khudozhestvennaia intelligentsiia*, 97; Paperny, *Kultura Dva*; Gromov, *Stalin: Vlast i Iskusstvo*.

13. Dobrenko, *Making of the State Writer*; Gromov, *Stalin. Vlast i iskusstvo*, 149.

14. Kurchatov's personal note from the Archive of the Kurchatov Institute, published in Smirnov, "Stalin and the Atomic Bomb," 128–29; Negin and Goleusova, *Soviet Atomic Project*; Mikhailov and Petrosiants, *Creation of the First Soviet Nuclear Bomb*.

15. Kostyrchenko, *Out of the Red Shadow*; by the same author, *Tainaia politika Stalina. Vlast i antisemitizm*. Kostyrchenko denies that Stalin had ever planned Jewish deportation; other authors, however, refer to secondary sources in support of this. See G. Kostyrchenko, "Deportatsiia-Mistifikatsiia," *Lechaim* (September 2002). For an opposite view, see Taubkin and Lyass, "O statie Kostyrchenko." On the longer-term consequences of the Stalinist anti-Semitic campaign, see Slezkine, *Jewish Century*, 310–11, 335–37.

16. Eimontova, "Iz Dnevnikov Sergeia Sergeevicha Dmitrieva" (May 25, 1949 and March 26, 1954), *Otechestvennaia istoriia* 3 (1999): 152, 164, and 4 (1999): 122.

17. "Dnevnik kommuni 33," July 9, 1960, TsADKM, f. 193, op. 1, d. 1, tetr. 1959–61, l. 219–20 (this is a collective diary of a group of educated reform-minded Russians); Taubman, *Khrushchev*, 306–10, 384; Tvardovsky, "Iz rabochikh tetradei," 135–40; K. Eimermacher in introduction to Afanasiev et al., *Ideologicheskiie komissii TsKh KPSS, 1958–1964*, 7.

18. Zezina, *Sovetskaia khudozhestvennaia intelligentsiia*, 131.

19. See Shlapentokh, *Soviet Intellectuals and Political Power*.

20. Spechler, *Permitted Dissent in the USSR*; Frankel, "*Novy Mir*"; Woll, *Real Images*; Faraday, *Revolt of the Filmmakers*.

21. Consider, for example, the reaction of Italian Communists during their conversation with Khrushchev, Relazione della delegazione Pajetta, Negarville, Pellegrino ad Direzzione del Partito, July 18, 1956, in the Archive of the Italian Communist Party, Fondazione Gramsci, Rome, Italy.

22. Stenogramma zakritogo partsobraniia partorganizatsii moskovskikh pisatelei, izdatelstva "Sovetskiii pisatel," Litfonda SSSR i Pravleniia SP SSSR, March 29, 1956, TsAODM, f. 8132, op. 1, d. 5, l. 106–98, and d. 6, l. 1–138; Taubman, *Khrushchev*, 283.

23. Eimontova, "Iz Dnevnikov Sergeia Sergeevicha Dmitrieva," 4 (1999): 166.

24. Gennady Kuzovkin, "Partiino-komsomolskiie presledovaniia po politicheskim motivam v period rannei 'ottepeli,'" in *Korni Travi*, 100–124.

25. Taranov, "Raskachaem Leninskiie Gori!" 99–101.

26. Iofe, "Politicheskaia oppozitsia v Leningrade," 212–15; Iofe, "Novie etiudi ob optimizme: Sbornik statei i vistuplenii" (1998), 98–99, AMS, St. Petersburg; Mikhail Trofimenkov, "'Malenkii Budapesht' na Ploschadi Isskustv: Ermitazh, Picasso, 1956 . . .," *Smena*, January 26, 1990.

27. RGANI, f. 5, op. 30, d. 141, l. 13–15, 67–68; Bukovsky, *To Build a Castle*, 109.

28. RGANI, f. 5, op. 30, d. 236. The letter was addressed to writer Yuri Zbanatski, who sent it to the CC CPSU on January 2, 1957.

29. Vitalii Troyanovsky, "Chelovek Ottepeli," in Fomin, ed., *Kinematograf ottepeli*, 31; Woll, *Real Images*, 41.

30. Brumberg, *Russia under Khrushchev*, 428; interview with Vladlen Krivosheev, a correspondent in the early 1960s for *Izvestia*, May 19, 1999, Moscow.

31. Orlova, *Vospominaniia o neproshedshem vremeni*, 227; cited in Zezina, *Sovetskaia khudozhestvennaia intelligentsiia*, 170.

32. Interview with Marat Cheshkov, *Voprosi istorii*, 4 (April 1994): 118–19; interview with Marat Cheshkov, September 28, 1992, by T. Kosinova, Oral History Collection, AMS, Moscow and St. Petersburg.

33. Bovin, *XX vek kak zhizn*, 54–55.

34. Meeting of Politburo of CPSU, July 12, 1984, published in *CWIHP Bulletin*, no. 4 (Fall 1994): 81.

35. Grigorenko, *V podpolie mozhno vstretit tolko kris*, 312–15.

36. See the stenographic report of the meeting of the editorial board of *Literaturnaia Gazeta* on October 18, 1956, RGALI, f. 634, op. 4, d. 1271; Bobkov, *KGB i Vlast*, 144–45; also Erik Kulavig, "Evidence of Public Dissent in the Khrushchev Years," in Bryld and Kulavig, *Soviet Civilization between Past and Present*, 85–86.

37. Boris Pustyntsev in Tatiana Kosinova, "Sobitiia 1956 g. v Polshe glazami Sovetskikh dissidentov," in *Korni Travi*, 194.

38. *Literaturnaia Gazeta*, November 22 and 24, 1956.

39. See official reports to the CC CPSU published in "Studencheskoie brozheniie v SSSR (konets 1956)," *Voprosi istorii* 1 (1997): 2–23.

40. Zezina, "Shokovaia terapia; ot 1953–go k 1956 godu," 133.

41. RGANI, f. 5, op. 39, d. 12, l. 23, 28, 61–66, 67, 161–217.

42. V. F. Afiani and N. G. Tomilina, eds., *Boris Pasternak i Vlast, 1956–1972: Dokumenti* (Moscow: ROSSPEN, 2001); Evgeny Pasternak and Elena Pasternak, *Zhizn Borisa Pasternaka: Dokumentalnoie povestvovaniie* (St. Petersburg: Zvezda, 2004), 436–84.

43. Report of the Ministry of Internal Affairs of the USSR, May 13, 1958, GARF, f. 9041, d. 498, l. 37–38.

44. Garthoff, *Journey through the Cold War*, 30–31.

45. On the changing landscape of visual propaganda, see Kenez, *Cinema and Soviet Society*.

46. Brodsky, "Spoils of War," in his *On Grief and Reason*, 3–21.

47. Aksenov, *In Search of Melancholy Baby*.

48. Yurchak, *Everything Was Forever, Until It Was No More*, 170–75; Garthoff, *Journey through the Cold War*, 32.

49. Joseph Brodsky, "Spoils of War," in his *On Grief and Reason*, 13–14.

50. L. Ilyichev, A. Romanov, G. Kazakov to the CC CPSU, August 6, 1958, "O glushenii inostrannikh radiostantsii," RGANI, f. 5, op. 30, d. 75, l. 165–67.

51. Starr, *Red and Hot*; Caute, *Dancer Defects*, 441–61; Kozlov, *Kozel na sakse*, 76–96.

52. Transcripts of the Preparatory Commission for the Festival, TsKhDMO, f. 3, op. 15, d. 11, l. 18.

53. The extent of Khrushchev's involvement is unclear. See Adzhubei, *Krusheniie Illuzii*, 186.

54. On these preparations and preorganized events, TsKhDMO, f. 3, op. 15, d. 136. See also daily reports of the Komsomol and the Ministry of Interior on the festival, TsAODM, f. 4, op. 104, d. 31 and GARF, f. 9401, op. 2, d. 491. I was denied access to KGB reports on the Festival that are stored at TsAODM.

55. Kozlov, *Kozel na sakse*, 102.

56. Ibid., 100–101.

57. Bukovsky, *To Build a Castle*, 139; interview with Maya Turovskaya, June 25, 2000, Moscow.

58. Short summary of the talks with the GDR Party-Governmental Delegation on June 9, 1959, AVPRF, f. 0742, op. 4, pap. 31, d. 33, l. 86–87, translated and published by Hope Harrison in *CWIHP Bulletin*, no. 11 (Winter 1998): 212.

59. Gorbachev and Mlynar, *Conversations with Gorbachev*.

60. Fitzpatrick, Rabinowitch, and Stites, *Russia in the Era of Nep*; Jeffrey Brooks, *Thank You, Comrade Stalin*; Gerovitch, *From Newspeak to Cyberspeak*; Eimontova, "Iz Dnevnikov Sergeia Sergeevicha Dmitrieva," *Otechestvennaia istoriia* 5 (1999): 169; Adzhubei, *Krusheniie illuzii*, 130–34.

61. *Literaturnaia Gazeta*, February 28, 1957, and March 23, 1957.

62. More on this split is in Nikolai Mitrokhin, *Russkaia Partiia*.

63. For the background see Shiraev and Zubok, *Anti-Americanism in Russia*, 7–24.

64. Nikolai Barsukov, "Kommunisticheskiie illuzii Khrushcheva: o razrabotke tretiei programmy partii," and "Mysli vslukh: zamechaniia N. S. Khrushcheva na proekt tretiei programmy KPSS," cited in Taubman, *Khrushchev*, 509–11.

65. Adzhubei, *Krusheniie illuzii*, 135–36.

66. *Komsomolskaia Pravda*, May 19, 1960; recollections of Boris Grushin, in Batygin and Yarmoliuk, *Rossiiskaia sotsiologiia shestidesiatikh godov v vospominaniiakh i dokumentakh*, 208–9.

67. Woll, *Real Images*, 84–86.

68. Zinoviev, *Russkaia sud'ba*, 327–30.

69. Interview with Eligiusz Liasota, November 3, 1992, Oral History Collection, AMS, Moscow.

70. Interview with Marat Cheshkov, Moscow, September 21, 1992, by T. Kosinova, Oral History Collection, AMS, Moscow and St. Petersburg.

71. Batygin and Yarmoliuk, *Rossiiskaia sotsiologiia shestidesiatikh godov*, 48.

72. Chernyaev, *Moia zhizn*, 238.

73. On this mood see Vail and Ghenis, *1960-e*, 12–18.

74. Grachev, *Gorbachev*, 29.

75. English, *Russia and the Idea of the West*, 72; Grushin, in Batygin and Yarmoliuk, *Rossiiskaia sotsiologia shestidesiatikh godov*, 211–13. Most of the "Prague circle" then plunged into Soviet politics, but some, including Grushin, Tatiana Motroshilova, Merab Mamardashvili, E. A. Arab-Ogli, and Yuri Zamoshkin, became innovative scholars and thinkers.

76. Vail and Ghenis, *60-e*, 103, 263.

77. Simonov, *Voienno-promishlennii kompleks*, 273–76; Vladimirov, *Rossiia bez prikras i umolchanii*, 124–25.

78. Krementsov, *Stalinist Science*, 8–9; Gerovitch, *From Newspeak to Cyberspeak*, 3, 299.

79. Negin and Smirnov, "Did the USSR Share Its Atomic Secrets with China?" 303–4.

80. Davidson et al., *SSSR i Afrika*, 198, 251.

81. Stenographic record of the speech by S. P. Pavlov, Secretary of the CC VLKSM, about his trip to Cuba, January 25, 1961, TsKhDMO, f. 1, op. 5, d. 782, l. 38–39.

82. Leonov, *Likholetie*, 52.

83. TsKhDMO, f. 1, op. 5, d. 782, l. 51–52.

84. Konchalovsky, *Nizkie istini*, 115.

85. TsKhDMO, f. 1, op. 5, d. 824, l. 172.

86. Gorbachev, *Zhizn i reformi*, 1:155–68; Grachev, *Gorbachev*, 56.

87. RGANI, f. 2, op. 1, d. 416, l. 9–11, translation and comments by author in the *CWIHP Bulletin*, no. 8–9 (Winter 1996–97): 416–12.

88. RGANI, f. 5, op. 30, d. 456, l. 66.

89. Friedberg, *Decade of Euphoria*, 306–10; Wittner, *Resisting the Bomb*, 282.

90. Woll, *Real Images*, 39–41, 72–74, 80–81, 88–91, 96–98, 118–22, 139–41.

91. Wittner, *Resisting the Bomb*, 282; Voznesensky's interview to the French magazine *Candide* in RGANI, f. 5, op. 55, d. 46, l. 33; Dedkov, " 'Kak trudno daiutsia iniie dni,' " 184; Alex Adamovich, "Patsifizm Shestidesiatnikov," in Pavlova, *Dolgii put rossiiskogo patsifizma*, 323.

92. Wittner, *Resisting the Bomb*, 23–25, 105–6; Sakharov, *Vospominaniia*, 257–58; Sakharov, *Sakharov Speaks*, 31.

93. Galay, "Soviet Youth and the Army," 17–20.

94. Soldatenkov, *Vladimir Visotsky*, 56.

95. Voinovich, *Life and Extraordinary Adventures of Private Ivan Chonkin*.

96. For background see Martin, *Affirmative Action Empire*, 1–27, 432–61.

97. Slezkine, *Jewish Century*, 310–11, 335–37.

98. Solzhenitsyn, *Dvesti let vmeste*, 411–31.

99. Samoilov, *Podennie zapisi*, 1:268.

100. See this point in Slezkine, *Jewish Century*, 335–36, 338–45; Agursky, *Pepel Klaasa*, 27.

101. Stenographic copy of Romm's speech (attached to the correspondence in Ilyichev's file), RGANI, f. 5, op. 5, d. 51, l. 24, 30.

102. Lipkin, *Zhizn i sudba Vasiliia Grossmana*, 60–61, 94–95; Vail and Ghenis, *60-e*, 299–301.

103. "In 1956 I was indignant at Israel for splitting world public opinion in the days of the Budapest crisis," recalled Grigory Pomerants, in *Zapiski*, 321.

104. Recollections of Arseny Berezin, then a young Leningrad physicist and participant in the festival; interview with author in Alexandria, Virginia, November 15, 2000.

105. TsAODM, f. 4, op. 104, d. 31, l. 8–9, 67, 81, 110.

106. Brudny, *Reinventing Russia*, 36–56, esp. 36–37. Among the Russian nationalists was Alexander Solzhenitsyn, but also writer Vladimir Soloukhin, artist Ilya Glazunov, poet Stanislav Kunyaev, and critic Vadim Kozhinov. Mitrokhin, *Russkaia Partiia*, 204–11.

107. On the antagonism between the cosmopolitan socialists and Russian nationalists, see Solzhenitsyn, *Dvesti let vmeste*, 436–48. On pro-Zionist sympathies, see Morozov, *Evreiskaia emigratsiia v svete novikh dokumentov*.

108. Eimontova, "Iz Dnevnikov Sergeia Sergeevicha Dmitrieva" (March 3, 1961), *Otechestvennaia istoriia* 6 (1999): 76.

109. Yevgeny Yevtushenko, *Volchii passport* (Moscow: Vagrius, 1998), 280–81, 296–98.

110. KGB's report to the CC, December 11, 1965, RGANI, f. 5, op. 30, d. 462, l. 250.

111. Alexeyeva and Goldberg, *Thaw Generation*, 117–38; Bovin, *XX vek kak zhizn*, 150–57; Max Hayward, ed., *On Trial: The Soviet State versus "Abram Terz" and "Nikolai Arzhak"* (New York: Harper and Row, 1966).

Chapter Seven

1. A useful discussion on this is in Westad, "Fall of Détente and the Turning Tides of History," 4–33.

2. Analysts of détente, mostly diplomats and political scientists, list several developments that brought about Soviet-American rapprochement. A most important development, they agree, was the rapid growth of Soviet strategic capabilities in the late 1960s, coupled with the severe internal crisis in the United States. They also note the crisis in the Communist bloc after the Soviet invasion of Czechoslovakia in 1968 and the Sino-Soviet border clashes in 1969. They point to the growing problems of the Soviet autarchic model of economic development and the increasing Soviet need for Western investments and technology. Finally, they see the origins of détente in the initiatives of Western leaders, such as "triangular diplomacy" by Richard Nixon and Henry Kissinger in the United States and Ostpolitik by Willy Brandt and Egon Bahr. See Hanhimäki, *Flawed Architect*; Isaacson, *Kissinger*; Baring, *Machtwechsel*; Haftendorn, *Security and Détente*; Nelson, *Making of Détente*.

3. Gelman, *Brezhnev Politburo and the Decline of Détente*; Anderson, *Public Politics in an Authoritarian State*.

4. "Report of the CC CPSU Presidium to the Central Committee, no later than October 14, 1964," *Istochnik* 2 (1998): 102–25, cited on p. 113.

5. Ibid., 113–14.

6. In Brezhnev's personal notes for the Politburo in October 1964, he jotted down and underlined: "the Polyansky report" and then "About the report of com. Suslov for the Plenum (to distribute)." These were two options for the Plenum the conspirators discussed. They chose the second, and Suslov delivered his much less specific version of anti-Khrushchev critique. Volkogonov, *Sem Vozhdei*, 2:83.

7. The group that deposed Khrushchev included Politburo members L. I. Brezhnev, G. I. Voronov, A. P. Kirilenko, A. N. Kosygin, N. V. Podgorny, D. S. Polyansky, M. A. Suslov, N. M. Shvernik, V. V. Grishin, L. N. Efremov, K. T. Mazurov, V. P. Mzhavanadze, P. E. Shelest, and Sh. P. Rashidov and CC secretaries and department heads Yu. V. Andropov, P. N. Demichev, L. F. Ilyichev, V. I. Polyakov, B. N. Ponomarev, N. G. Ignatov, and A. N. Shelepin. Of them only Andropov, Shelepin, Ponomarev, and to a certain extent Suslov were experts on international affairs.

8. Mikoyan, *Tak Bylo*, 619.

9. See the transcripts of Glassboro meetings in FRUS, 1964–68, 14:514–56; on Kosygin's foreign policy activities, see recollections of Oleg Troyanovsky (who, in 1964–66, was his foreign policy adviser) in his *Cherez godi i rasstoyaniia*, 267, 269–74; Alexei Voronov, "Na nive vneshnei politiki," in *Premier izvestnii i neizvestnii*, 57–63.

10. Alexandrov-Agentov, *Ot Kollontai*, 168.

11. According to most memoir recollections, this "faction" included KGB's head Semichastny, Polyansky, Moscow party leader Nikolai Yegorychev, and Nikolai Mesyatsev. Vladimir Semichastny in his memoirs categorically denied that such a group had ever existed. *Bespokoinoie serdtse*, 375, 389–90.

12. On "the hostile-isolationist identity," see English, *Russia and the Idea of the West*, 120–22.

13. The materials from Stalin's meeting with the authors of a textbook on the political economy of socialism in April 1950, RGASPI, f. 17, op. 133, d. 41, l. 20–25, cited in Pollock, *Politics of Knowledge*, 182. For similar views, see the diary of Vladimir Semenov, *Novaia i Noveishaia istoriia* 4 (July–August 2004): 96–97.

14. English, *Russia and the Idea of the West*, 121–22; Zubok and Pleshakov, *Inside the Kremlin's Cold War*, 177–79.

15. On the neo-Stalinist backlash and the mood among the intelligentsia, see Alexeyeva and Goldberg, *Thaw Generation*, 116–46; Samoilov, *Podenniie zapisi*, 2:15–16; Tvardovsky, "Rabochie tetradi 60-kh godov," 165.

16. Taubman, *Khrushchev*, 508–11; English, *Russia and the Idea of the West*, 72–73, 122; Arbatov, *System*, 85–86; Arbatov, *Zatianuvsheesia vyzdorovlenie (1953–1985 gg.) Svidetelstvo sovremennika*, 45; Burlatsky, *Vozhdi i sovetniki. O Khrusheve, Andropove i ne tolko o nikh*, 257; Bovin, *XX vek kak zhizn*, 144–47.

17. Arbatov, *System*, 115.

18. Gaiduk, *Confronting Vietnam*, 203–4, 207.

19. Gaiduk, *Soviet Union and the Vietnam War*, 8–9, 17–21, 28–30, 37–38, 40, 54–55, 58. Gaiduk believes that the removal of Khrushchev only intensified the process of a reappraisal of Soviet policy toward Vietnam but was "not the starting point" of this reappraisal (19). I

attribute more significance to Khrushchev's ouster. True, the North Vietnamese held the initiative in escalating the conflict and forced Moscow to come along. It is hard to imagine Khrushchev standing aloof when Americans bombed Vietnam. At the same time it would have been more difficult for the North Vietnamese to drag the USSR into supporting their cause under Khrushchev.

20. Author's interview with Fedor Mochulsky, councilor at the Soviet embassy in Beijing at the time, Moscow, June 20, 1992; Elizavetin, "Peregovori Kosygina i Chou Enlaia v Pekinskom Aeroportu," 54; Bovin, XX vek kak zhizn, 131–32; Karnow, Vietnam, 427. On the background and bad memories of the Soviet-Sino-Vietnamese collaboration, see Gaiduk, Confronting Vietnam; and Olsen, "Changing Alliances."

21. For the background, see Logevall, Choosing War.

22. Georgi Kornienko, then head of the U.S. desk in the Foreign Ministry, remarked on the harmful spillover of the Vietnam War into Soviet-American relations, in his Kholodnaia voina, 123.

23. Dobrynin, Sugubo doveritelno, 127; Igor Ognetov (former councilor at the Soviet embassy in Hanoi), "Tonkinskii intsident i Sovetskaia pomosch Vietnamu," 97–98; FRUS, 1964–68, 14:233–59.

24. On the position of Brezhnev and Gromyko, see Dobrynin, In Confidence, 140, 143; see also Gaiduk, Soviet Union and the Vietnam War, 48.

25. Mikoyan, Tak Bylo, 619–20.

26. Bovin, XX vek kak zhizn, 134; Mikoyan, Tak bylo, 620.

27. Andropov, KGB to the CC CPSU, November 17, 1967, published in Morozov, Evreiskaia emigratsiia, 60–61.

28. Kornienko, Kholodnaia voina, 130–35.

29. Shelest, Da Ne Sudimy Budete, 283–84.

30. Dobrynin, In Confidence, 160–62; Bovin, XX vek kak zhizn, 160.

31. Dobrynin, In Confidence, 162–67; Kornienko, Kholodnaia voina, 124–27; author's interview with Kornienko, Moscow, March 15, 1990; Savelyev and Detinov, Big Five, 7–9.

32. Brezhnev's notes since 1944 were a jumbled collection of "illiterate phrases and unintelligible expressions." Volkogonov, Sem Vozhdei, 2:11.

33. Ibid.

34. Leonid Zamyatin's recollections in Mlechin, Predsedateli KGB: Rassekrechenniie sudbi, 439; see the same point in Adzhubey, Krusheniie illiuzii, 309–10; Grigorenko, V podpol'e mozhno vstretit tolko krys, 268.

35. Alexandrov-Agentov, Ot Kollontai, 112–13; also his interview in Sovershenno sekretno 6 (1992): 8.

36. Arbatov, Zatianuvsheesia vyzdorovleniie, 45; English, Russia and the Idea of the West, 122.

37. Viktor Sukhodrev told about the "Sermon on the Mount" at Musgrove I, transcript. A version of Brezhnev's sermon is taken from memorandum of conversation of W. Averell Harriman with Brezhnev, June 4, 1974, Special Files, box 586, Harriman Collection, LC.

38. Bovin, XX vek kak zhizn, 138, 139; see Protocol no. 137, Presidium session on March 20, 1964, in Fursenko et al., Prezidium TsK KPSS, 820.

39. Information from KGB general Nikolai Leonov to author at the conference on the Cuban missile crisis, Havana, October 12, 2002; on Brezhnev's criticism of Khrushchev, see diary of Anatoly Chernyaev, January 1, 1976, NSArch.

40. Bovin, *XX vek kak zhizn*, 256–57.

41. Mikoyan, *Tak Bylo*, 619; Semichastny, *Bespokoinoie serdtse*, 352.

42. Brezhneva, *World I Left Behind*, 38; Chazov, *Zdorovie i Vlast*, 85; Alexandrov-Agentov, *Ot Kollontai*, 118; "Dnevnik kommuni 33," TsADKM, f. 193, op. 1, d. 3, l. 156.

43. This information head of the regional KGB, L. Stupak, reported to Ukrainian first secretary Petr Shelest; see Shelest's diary, December 5, 1966, *Da ne sudimi budete*, 266.

44. Arbatov, *System*, 245–48; Bovin, *XX vek kak zhizn*, 254–55.

45. Kevorkov, *Tainii Kanal*, 127; Alexandrov-Agentov, *Ot Kollontai*, 116, 250; Burlatsky, *Vozhdi i sovetniki*, 149; Chazov, *Zdorovie i vlast*, 14–15.

46. P. Rodionov, *Znamia* 8 (August 1989): 194–95; Shelest in *Leonid Brezhnev v vospominaniiakh, razmishleniiakh, suzhdeniiakh*, 223–24; Alexandrov-Agentov, *Ot Kollontai*, 257, 259.

47. Shelest, *Da ne sudimi budete*, 219–20; Adzhubei, *Krusheniie illuzii*, 312; Savelyev and Detinov, *Big Five*, 16; Kornienko, "On the ABM Treaty," a lecture at the Institute of U.S. and Canada Studies, Moscow, November 15, 1989, notes in the personal archive of author.

48. On Grechko, see *Red Star*, October 18, 2003; and S. Khrushchev, *Nikita Khrushchev: Krizisi i raketi*, 2:417–29. On Ustinov, see Zalessky, *Imperia Stalina*, 455; Alexandrov-Agentov, *Ot Kollontai*, 268; Kevorkov, *Tainii kanal*, 234–37.

49. Savelyev and Detinov, *Big Five*, 9–11.

50. Holloway, *Soviet Union and the Arms Race*, 58–59; Zaloga, *Kremlin's Nuclear Sword*, 103, 118–41.

51. Chernyaev, *Moia zhizn*, 305.

52. Bovin, *XX vek kak zhizn*, 141, 145–46. On the struggle for Brezhnev's soul, see Arbatov, *System*, 127–30; Chernyaev, *Moia zhizn*, 259–60.

53. Chernyaev, *Moia zhizn*, 305.

54. Alexandrov-Agentov, *Ot Kollontai*, 68; see a profile of Gromyko in Mlechin, *MID: Ministri inostrannikh del*, 352–442.

55. Dobrynin, *In Confidence*, 640.

56. Ibid., 642; author's interviews with Georgy Kornienko, Moscow, December 10, 1996.

57. The most comprehensive documentary collection on the crisis is in Navratil, *Prague Spring, 1968*.

58. RGANI, f. 5, op. 60, d. 309, l. 58–72, as cited in Pikhoia, *Sovetskii Soiuz*, 321. The documents from the Czech archives on this issue are corroborating but inconclusive. See Mastny, " 'We Are in a Bind,' " 230–50; Chernyaev, *Moia zhizn*, 265.

59. Suri, *Power and Protest*, 199–200; Shelest, *Da ne sudimi budete*, 287, 330, 337, 396–97; Alexandrov-Agentov, *Ot Kollontai*, 146–47; Chernyaev, *Moia zhizn*, 264; see also Pikhoia, *Sovetskii Soiuz*, 303 and 336.

60. Nikolai Shmelev, "Curriculum vitae," *Znamia-plus*, 1997/98, 112; Pikhoia, *Sovetskii Soiuz*, 301–26; Navratil, *Prague Spring, 1968*, 114–25, 132–43, 158–59, 212–33, 336–38.

61. Alexandrov-Agentov, *Ot Kollontai*, 112–13; Shelest, *Da ne sudimi budete*, 363, 368, 384–85.

62. Pikhoia, *Sovetskii Soiuz*, 326–40.

63. Minutes of the Politburo session, July 19, 1968, cited in Pikhoia, *Sovetskii Soiuz*, 327.

64. Medvedev, *Neizvestni Andropov*, 106–7, 114.

65. Excerpts from an assessment of the course of foreign policy and the state of Soviet-American relations, September 16, 1968 (approved by the Politburo), in Dobrynin, *In Confidence*, 643.

66. Kvitsinsky, *Vremia i sluchai*, 278.

67. Bovin, *XX vek kak zhizn*, 194–95.

68. Navratil, *Prague Spring, 1968*, 547–63; Kramer, "Ukraine and the Soviet-Czechoslovak Crisis of 1968," 234–47.

69. Evidence on the watershed role of the 1968 invasion for Soviet intellectuals is galore. See Bovin, *XX vek kak zhizn*, 193; Chernyaev, *Moia zhizn*, 266; Alexeyeva and Goldberg, *Thaw Generation*, 216; Arbatov, *Zatianuvsheesia vyzdorovleniie*, 143; English, *Russia and the Idea of the West*, 110–15, esp. 114.

70. Chernyaev, *Moia zhizn*, 268, 272, 292.

71. Goncharov and Usov, "Peregovori A. N. Kosygina i Chou Enlaia v Pekinskom Aeroportu," 41, 43; Kuisong, "Sino-Soviet Border Clash," 21–52.

72. Alexandrov-Agentov, *Ot Kollontai*, 216–17; Semichastny, *Bespokoinoie*, 328.

73. Kissinger, *Years of Upheaval*, 233; Burr and Richelson, "Whether to 'Strangle the Baby in the Cradle,'" 67–71.

74. Alexandrov-Agentov, *Ot Kollontai*, 217.

75. Goncharov and Usov, "Peregovori A. N. Kosygina i Chou Enlaia" (recollections of A. Elizavetin and the editors' comments), 54–56, 57–58; see also the continuation of these recollections in *Problemi Dalnego Vostoka* 1 (1993): 118.

76. Kvitsinsky, *Vremia i sluchai*, 226.

77. Alexandrov-Agentov, *Ot Kollontai*, 184; Kvitsinsky, *Vremia i sluchai*, 272.

78. Falin, *Bez skidok na obstoiatelstva. Politicheskiie vospominania*, 127.

79. "Iz dnevnika Semenova," January 27, 1969, *Novaia i noveishaia istoriia* 4 (July–August 2004): 91; Kvitsinsky, *Vremia i sluchai*, 264–71; Sarotte, *Dealing with the Devil*, 31–32.

80. Chazov, *Zdorovie i vlast*, 90.

81. Sarotte, *Dealing with the Devil*, 34–35; Kevorkov, *Tainii kanal*, 24–25.

82. Kevorkov, *Tainii kanal*, 58–64.

83. Bahr, *Zu meiner Zeit*, 284–338; Sarotte, *Dealing with the Devil*, 77–84.

84. On the American side of the story, see Garthoff, *Détente and Confrontation*, 279–87; Kissinger, *White House Years*, 406–7, 801–3, 809–10; Hanhimäki, *Flawed Architect*, 85–91; Burr, *Kissinger Transcripts*, 11, 44. See also the KDB.

85. Kevorkov, *Tainii kanal*, 95–96; Alexandrov-Agentov, *Ot Kollontai*, 189–91. For the West German perspective, see Brandt, *Erinnerungen*, 206–10.

86. Bovin, *XX vek kak zhizn*, 245–46; Kvitsinsky, *Vremia i sluchai*, 276–77.

87. Molotov to Chuev, July 12, 1976, in Chuev, *Sto sorok besed*, 116. Yitzhak Brudny exaggerates Brezhnev's support of Russian nationalists and asserts, on the basis of very inconclusive evidence, that he promoted the policy of their "inclusion" into the state cultural establish-

ment. On the contrary, Brezhnev's policies evoked growing criticism from the nationalists. Brudny, *Reinventing Russia*, 70–93; Laqueur, *Black Hundred*; Semanov, *Brezhnev*.

88. Diary of Chernyaev, January 1, 1976, NSArch. See also stenographic minutes of a conference with Brezhnev on December 16, 1975, cited in Brutents, *Tridtsat let*, 279.

89. Bovin, *XX vek kak zhizn*, 213–14, 229–30.

90. Nelson, *Making of Détente*, 101.

91. Kevorkov, *Tainii kanal*, 95.

92. Bovin, *XX vek kak zhizn*, 256–57.

93. Savelyev and Detinov, *Big Five*, 9–11.

94. The first SALT team included Deputy Foreign Minister Vladimir Semenov, head of the U.S. Department of the Foreign Ministry Georgy Kornienko, head of the scientific council to the Military-Industrial Commission Alexander Shchukin, representative of Radio Ministry Peter Pleshakov, Generals Nikolai Ogarkov and Nikolai Alexeiev, and representative of the First Chief Directorate of the KGB Vladimir Pavlichenko. See Saveliev and Detinov, *Big Five*, 9, 12; author's interview with Kornienko, December 22, 1989, Moscow; "Iz dnevnika Semenova," *Novaia i noveishaia istoriia* 4 (July–August 2004):101.

95. Dobrynin, *Sugubo doveritelno*, 184, 216–17.

96. Memorandum of conversation of the Ambassador of the USSR to the USA A. F. Dobrynin with Kissinger, Assistant to President Nixon, July 12, 1969, RGANI, f. 5, op. 61, d. 558, l. 92–105, translated and published in *CWIHP Bulletin*, no. 3 (Fall 1993): 64.

97. Dobrynin, *Sugubo doveritelno*, 206; see also KDB.

98. Hersh, *Price of Power*, 376; Garthoff, *Détente and Confrontation*, 245–63; Ross, *Negotiating Cooperation*, 17–54; Burr, *Kissinger Transcripts*, 12–13; Alexandrov-Agentov, *Ot Kollontai*, 217.

99. Alexandrov-Agentov, *Ot Kollontai*, 218; Dobrynin, *Sugubo doveritelno*, 214–15.

100. Kevorkov, *Tainii kanal*, 97–107.

101. On the background and events of the 1971 Indian-Pakistani war, see Kissinger, *White House Years*, 842–918; Nixon, RN, 525–31; Garthoff, *Détente and Confrontation*, 295–322; a much briefer account from the Soviet perspective is in Alexandrov-Agentov, *Ot Kollontai*, 218–20.

102. Garthoff, *Détente and Confrontation*, 300–301; Hanhimäki, *Flawed Architect*, 161, 171, 179–84; Alexandrov-Agentov, *Ot Kollontai*, 242; Arbatov, *System*, 195.

103. Kissinger, *White House Years*, 1113–22, 1154, 1176–91; Dobrynin, *Sugubo Doveritelno*, 228–29.

104. Chernyaev recorded one such call from Kosygin to Brezhnev on March 9, 1972, *Moia zhizn*, 285.

105. Alexandrov-Agentov, *Ot Kollontai*, 222–23.

106. Ibid., 221, 226; Georgy Kornienko's account gives this impression in *Kholodnaia voina*, 144–45.

107. According to American records, Brezhnev said to Kissinger, "You and I can accomplish much together between the two of us. Maybe we should just abolish our Foreign Offices." Kissinger responded, "We on our side have already taken steps in that direction. Now we need a reduction of Gromyko." Brezhnev then said, "If I see a glum look on President

Nixon's face, I will tell him a couple of stories to cheer him up." Kissinger remarked that Gromyko "looks a bit like the President." These jocular remarks are missing in the Soviet records of the conversation. Memorandum of Brezhnev-Kissinger conversation, April 22, 1972, NARA; record of conversation of Brezhnev with the special assistant of the U.S. president, Henry Kissinger, April 22, 1972, KDB.

108. KDB; Sukhodrev, *Iazik moi—drug moi*, 263.

109. Alexandrov-Agentov, *Ot Kollontai*, 221; KDB.

110. Alexandrov-Agentov, *Ot Kollontai*, 223–24; Dobrynin, *Sugubo Doveritelno*, 233.

111. Shelest diary's entries on October 10–25, 1969, and January 8, 1972, *Da ne sudimi budete*, 437–38, 496.

112. Dobrynin, *Sugubo Doveritelno*, 233–34.

113. Hanson, *Rise and Fall of the Soviet Economy*, 122–23.

114. Diary of Chernyaev, April 6, 1972, NSArch.

115. Alexandrov-Agentov, *Ot Kollontai*, 210; Kissinger on Smirnov, in *White House Years*, 1234. On Brezhnev's priority investments into agriculture, especially in the Russian Federation, see Brudny, *Reinventing Russia*, 58–59; "Iz dnevnika Semenova," April 18 and May 31, 1972, *Novaia i noveishaia istoriia* 4 (July–August 2004): 104–5.

116. Alexandrov-Agentov, *Ot Kollontai*, 223–24.

117. Kissinger, *White House Years*, 1138; see also his *Years of Upheaval*, 231.

118. Alexandrov-Agentov, *Ot Kollontai*, 224.

119. Sukhodrev, *Iazik moi—drug moi*, 269; Alexandrov-Agentov, *Ot Kollontai*, 225, 232.

120. Memorandum of conversation between Brezhnev and Harriman, June 4, 1974, Brezhnev's office, the Kremlin, Harriman Collection, Special Files, box 586, LC.

121. Sukhodrev in Musgrove I, transcript, 14–16.

122. Nelson, *Making of Détente*, 32–39.

123. Kissinger, *White House Years*, 1138; see also his *Years of Upheaval*, 231.

124. Olshanskaia, "Kiseleva, Kishmareva, Tyuricheva," 9–27; Kozlova, "Krestianskii syn: Opyt issledovaniia biografii," 112–23.

125. Chernyaev, *Moia zhizn*, 290.

126. Gelman, *Brezhnev Politburo and the Decline of Détente*.

127. Bahr, *Zu meiner Zeit*, 420.

Chapter Eight

1. The most detailed and thoroughly documented description of Soviet policies in Afghanistan in 1978–79 is by Garthoff in *Détente and Confrontation*; see also Cordovez and Harrison, *Out of Afghanistan*; Westad, "Prelude to Invasion." See also the Russian accounts: Lyakhovsky, *Tragediia*, and the updated version, *Plamia Afghana*; Kornienko, *Kholodnaiia voina*, 188–209; Gai and Snegirev, "Vtorzheniie," 3–4; Gareev, "Pochemu i kak mi voshli v Afghanistan," 17–23; Gankovsky, "Kto, gde, kogda prinial resheniie o vvode sovetskikh voisk v Afghanistan?" 2–9.

2. Cordovez and Harrison, *Out of Afghanistan*, 14.

3. See Ouimet, *Rise and Fall of the Brezhnev Doctrine*; Kramer, "Soviet Deliberations during the Polish Crisis," 10; Mastny, "Soviet Non-Invasion of Poland"; Voronkov, "Sobitiia 1980–1981 v Polshe. Vzgliad so Staroi ploschiadi"; materials from Jachranka.

4. Mastny, "Soviet Non-Invasion of Poland," 14, 34.

5. Westad, *Fall of Détente*; Kornienko, *Kholodnaia voina*, 164–86; Dobrynin, *Sugubo doveritelno*, 487–94.

6. Dobrynin, *Sugubo doveritelno*, 245.

7. Minutes of CC CPSU Secretariat, November 20, 1972, Volkogonov Collection, LC.

8. Alexandrov-Agentov, *Ot Kollontai*, 193–95.

9. Ibid., 232.

10. Kissinger, *Years of Upheaval*, 233, 274–86; Garthoff, *Détente and Confrontation*, 376–86; see also his *Journey through the Cold War*, 283. On China see the memorandum of conversation between Brezhnev and Nixon at San Clemente, California, June 23, 1973, NARA, copies at NSArch.

11. Garthoff, *Détente and Confrontation*, 1135–37; see also his *Journey through the Cold War*, 282–85.

12. Garthoff, *Journey through the Cold War*, 285; Alexandrov-Agentov, *Ot Kollontai*, 193–95.

13. See Kissinger, *Ending the Vietnam War*; Hanhimäki, *Flawed Architect*, 341–44.

14. Diary of Chernyaev, March 9, 1975, NSArch.

15. Memorandum of conversation between Brezhnev and Kissinger, September 13, 1972, NARA, on file at NSArch.

16. Report of the 5th Department of the KGB, May 9, 1973, published in Morozov, *Evreiskaia emigratsiia v svete novikh dokumentov*, 169.

17. See Buwalda, *They Did Not Dwell Alone*; Goldberg, *Jewish Power*, 167–74.

18. One can read more on this in Hunt, *Ideology and U.S. Foreign Policy*; Ninkovich, *Wilsonian Century*; Smith, *America's Mission*; Mead, *Special Providence*; Stephansson, "Cold War Considered as a U.S. Project," 52–67.

19. Chernyaev, a member of Brezhnev's speechwriters' circle and sensitive to manifestations of anti-Semitism, never noticed a trace of it in Brezhnev's behavior and remarks. Interview with author, Moscow, January 4, 2003.

20. "K voprosu o viezde za granitsu lits evreiskoi natsionalnosti," minutes of the Politburo, March 20, 1973, *Istochnik* 1 (1996): 156; see also Morozov, *Evreiskaia Emigratsiia*, 164–68.

21. "K voprosu o viezde za granitsu," *Istochnik* 1 (1996): 158.

22. Dobrynin, *Sugubo doveritelno*, 492.

23. Brudny, *Reinventing Russia*, 108, 111, 112, 113.

24. Ibid., 156; Kissinger, *Years of Upheaval*, 252. There is nothing on these details in Dobrynin's memoirs.

25. Among them were Jackson's assistant Richard Perle, Jeane Kirkpatrick, editor of the Jewish intellectual journal *Commentary* Norman Podhoretz, Max K. Kampelman, Eugene V. Rostow, and Paul Wolfowitz.

26. Roy Medvedev in "Dissidenti o dissidentstve," *Znamia* 9 (September 1997): 183; Pontuso, *Solzhenitsyn's Political Thought*, 143, 149–57.

27. Bovin, *XX vek kak zhizn*, 257–58.

28. Kevorkov, *Tainii kanal*, 169–72.

29. Vasily Aksenov and Leonid Borodin, in "Dissidenti o dissidentstve," *Znamia* 9 (September 1997): 164–65, 170–71; Morozov, *Evreiskaia emigratsiia*, 190–91, 213; Pearson, *Solzhenitsyn*; Scammell, *Solzhenitsyn*; Scammell, *Solzhenitsyn Files*; *Kremlevsky samosud: Sekretniie dokumenti Politburo o pisatele A. Solzhenitsyne*.

30. Memorandum from N. Shchelokov, "On the Solzhenitsyn Question," October 7, 1971, minutes of a Politburo Session, March 30, 1972, minutes of the CC Meeting, April 13, 1972, all in Scammell, *Solzhenitsyn Files*, 161–63, 164, 185–87, 194–97, 199–210, 221–22, 256–57.

31. Solzhenitsyn, *Oak and the Calf*; Carlisle, "Solzhenitsyn and the Secret Circle," 27–33; Medvedev, *Neizvestny Andropov*, 143.

32. Minutes of the Politburo, January 7, 1974, Volkogonov Collection, LC; Scammell, *Solzhenitsyn Files*, 283–92.

33. Kevorkov, *Tainii kanal*, 169–72.

34. Ibid., 174–76; letter from Y. Andropov to L. Brezhnev, February 7, 1974, in Scammell, *Solzhenitsyn Files*, 342–44.

35. Dobrynin, *Sugubo doveritelno*, 333; author's conversation with Dobrynin, Oslo, September 20, 1995.

36. Israelyan, *Inside the Kremlin*; also Vinogradov, *Diplomatiia: Liudi i Sobitiia*, 201–72; Kirpichenko, *Iz arkhiva razvedchika*; Dobrynin, *Sugubo doveritelno*, 268–79; Kornienko, *Kholodnaia Voina*, 160–64; Alexandrov-Agentov, *Ot Kollontai*, 203–6; Garthoff, *Détente and Confrontation*, 404–46; Lebow and Stein, *We All Lost the Cold War*; Ginor, "Under the Yellow Arab Helmet Gleamed Blue Russian Eyes," 127–57.

37. Dobrynin, *Sugubo doveritelno*, 244; Garthoff, *Détente and Confrontation*, 1135–37; Garthoff, *Journey through the Cold War*, 282–85.

38. Dobrynin, *Sugubo doveritelno*, 261; Hanhimäki, *Flawed Architect*, 281–82, 305–6.

39. Syrian president Hafiz Assad informed the Soviet ambassador in Damascus, Nuritdin Mukhitdinov, about the war plan. Also, the Soviet leadership learned about the time of the attack a few days ahead, probably through intelligence sources. Israelyan, *Inside the Kremlin*, 10–11, 15–18.

40. Ibid., 26, 99.

41. Memorandum of conversation, March 18, 1974, among Kissinger, Helmut Sonnenfeld, Arthur Hartman, William Hyland, and Lawrence S. Eagleburger, in Burr, *Kissinger Transcripts*, 225.

42. Israelyan, *Inside the Kremlin*, 10–11, 95, 125–26, 128, 168; Dobrynin, *Sugubo doveritelno*, 266–83; Kornienko, *Kholodnaia voina*, 160–64; Alexandrov-Agentov, *Ot Kollontai*, 203–6; Kissinger's account is in his *Years of Upheaval*, 450–613.

43. Andropov to Brezhnev, October 19, 1973, Volkogonov Collection, LC.

44. Israelyan, *Inside the Kremlin*, 165–66; Dobrynin, *Sugubo doveritelno*, 273; Alexandrov-Agentov, *Ot Kollontai*, 204.

45. Dobrynin, *Sugubo doveritelno*, 274; Alexandrov-Agentov, *Ot Kollontai*, 204–6; minutes of the Politburo session on October 25, 1973, cited in Israelyan, *Inside the Kremlin*, 179–81.

46. Garthoff, *Détente and Confrontation*, 428; Israelyan, *Inside the Kremlin*, 182–86; Hanhimäki, *Flawed Architect*, 310, 315–16.

47. See the opposite conclusion in Hanhimäki, *Flawed Architect*, 328–30.

48. Israelyan, *Inside the Kremlin*, 188; Dobrynin, *Sugubo doveritelno*, 277–78.

49. See Chernyaev's November 1973 secondhand note of Brezhnev-Gromyko conversation on this issue in his *Moia Zhizn*, 301.

50. Expression of KGB general Leonid Shebarshin, cited in Westad, *Fall of Détente*, 132.

51. Meeting with Soviet ambassador Anatoly Dobrynin in the Oval Office, December 26, 1973, from Henry A. Kissinger to President's File, copy at NSArch; Dobrynin, *Sugubo doveritelno*, 280–83, 291–92; Alexandrov-Agentov, *Ot Kollontai*, 233; Sukhodrev, *Iazik moi—drug moi*, 315.

52. The KGB sources asserted that Brandt was a victim of intrigues within the SPD, in Kevorkov, *Tainii kanal*, 177–87; Bahr, *Zu meiner Zeit*, 261–62; Smyser, *From Yalta to Berlin*, 267–70; Chazov, *Zdorovie i Vlast*, 87.

53. Chazov, *Zdorovie i vlast*, 75.

54. Sukhodrev, *Iazik moi—drug moi*, 288–89, 290.

55. Andropov to Brezhnev, October 29, 1973, Volkogonov Collection, reel 16, container 24, LC.

56. Volkogonov cited the evidence that Brezhenv may have received some pills from Andropov, in *Sem Vozhdei*, 99–100.

57. Chazov, *Zdorovie i vlast*, 85, 112–13, 116–17; Arbatov, *System*, 192; diary of Chernyaev, October 10 and 24, 1975, NSArch.

58. Podvig, *Strategicheskoie iadernoie vooruzheniie Rossii*, also available at <http://www.armscontrol.ru>; Zaloga, *Kremlin's Nuclear Sword*, 171–77.

59. Savelyev and Detinov, *Big Five*, 3.

60. Discussion on this question took place at Musgrove I.

61. Garthoff, *Journey through the Cold War*, 331–32; Cahn, *Killing Detente*; Zaloga, *Kremlin's Nuclear Sword*, 177.

62. Dobrynin, *Sugubo doveritelno*, 336.

63. Sukhodrev, *Iazik moi—drug moi*, 309; for a version of this conversation with different participants, see Dobrynin, *Sugubo doveritelno*, 259–60.

64. Memorandum of conversation, Brezhnev-Kissinger, October 26, 1974, published in Burr, *Kissinger Transcripts*, 345–54; Kissinger, *Years of Renewal*, 277–79.

65. Dobrynin, *Sugubo doveritelno*, 315; memorandum of conversation, Brezhnev-Ford meeting, November 23, 1974, on board a train between Vozdvizhenka Airport and Okeanskaya Sanatorium near Vladivostok, 2:30 P.M., NSArch.

66. Kissinger, *Years of Renewal*, 288–90; the authors of Gorbachev's proposal were Deputy Foreign Minister Georgy Kornienko and Deputy Head of the Chief Operational Department of the General Staff general Sergei Akhromeyev, members of the panel of experts ("little five") in Vladivostok; see Savelyev and Detinov, *Big Five*, 37.

67. Dobrynin, *Sugubo doveritelno*, 315; Kornienko, *Kholodnaia voina*, 157–58.

68. Kornienko, *Kholodnaia Voina*, 158; author's interview with Kornienko, Moscow, November 23, 1989; Nikolay Detinov at Musgrove I; Kissinger, *Years of Renewal*, 297.

69. "Intelligence Community Experiment in Competitive Analysis. Soviet Strategic Objectives: An Alternative View" (Team-B report), December 1976, NSArch; see also Pipes, *Vixi*, 134–42.

70. Kissinger, *Years of Renewal*, 302–7; Dobrynin, *Sugubo doveritelno*, 320–22, 327; Hanson, *Rise and Fall of the Soviet Economy*, 123.

71. Chazov, *Zdorovie i vlast*, 127–28; Sheludko, in *Leonid Brezhnev v vospominaniiakh, razmishleniiakh, suzhdeniiakh*, 320–23; diary of Chernyaev, March 2 and September 11, 1975, NSArch.

72. Diary of Chernyaev, October 10 and 24, 1975, NSArch.

73. Unofficial minutes of Brezhnev's remarks on December 16, 1975, recorded in Karen Brutents, *Tridtsat let*, 270–71; another record of the same remark is in the diary of Chernyaev, January 2, 1976, NSArch.

74. Alexandrov-Agentov, *Ot Kollontai*, 236–37; Dobrynin, *Sugubo doveritelno*, 335, 492.

75. See Lysebu I; see also Fort Lauderdale.

76. Oleg Troyanovsky on Andropov's reaction, in Fort Lauderdale, 12.

77. Davidson et al., *SSSR i Afrika*, 132, 198–99.

78. Westad, *Global Cold War*, chapter 3.

79. Anatoly Dobrynin and Oleg Troyanovsky in Fort Lauderdale, 8, 11.

80. Brutents, *Tridtsat let*, 325; Davidson et al., *SSSR i Afrika*, 251–303.

81. Davidson et al., *SSSR i Afrika*, 220–21.

82. *Istochnik* 2 (1998): 114–20.

83. Brezhnev-Kissinger memorandum of conversation, April 22, 1972, Kissinger Papers, NARA.

84. Westad, "Moscow and the Angolan Crisis," 20. In 1991–92, Westad gained access to the documents of the former CC of the CPSU. These documents were later reclassified.

85. Ibid., 20.

86. Karen Brutents in Fort Lauderdale, 22, 23.

87. On Gorshkov see Chipman, "Admiral Gorshkov and the Soviet Navy."

88. Hewett, *Open for Business*, 12; Pikhoia, "Pochemu raspalsia SSSR?" 16–17 <www.sgu.ru/faculties/historical/ sc.publication/historynewtime/cold_war/1.php>.

89. On the "little deal," see Millar, "Little Deal," 694–706; Derluguian, "Tale of Two Cities," 47–48; author's correspondence with Georgy Derluguian (in author's archives). The value of overseas jobs among the Soviet public grew dramatically during the 1970s.

90. Garthoff, *Journey through the Cold War*, 295.

91. Diary of Chernyaev, May 13, 1974, NSArch; Lysebu I, 33.

92. Kissinger, *Years of Renewal*, 818.

93. Kornienko in Lysebu I, 78.

94. Westad, "Moscow and the Angolan Crisis," 21.

95. Gleijeses, *Conflicting Missions*; see also his "Havana's Policy in Africa," 5–8.

96. Blight and Brenner, *Sad and Luminous Days*.

97. Recollections of Georgi Shakhnazarov in Fort Lauderdale, 39–40.

98. The first contact occurred between Agostino Neto and Che Guevara in 1965; see Gleijeses, "Havana's Policy in Africa," 7.

99. Kornienko, *Kholodnaia voina*, 166.

100. Arbatov, *System*, 194–95; on the orthodox position of the troika and their pressure on Brezhnev after the Helsinki Conference, see Chernyaev, *Moia zhizn*, 317; Dobrynin, *Sugubo doveritelno*, 359.

101. Kornienko, *Kholodnaia voina*, 167–68; Kornienko's interview with author, Moscow, November 23, 1989, and March 15, 1990; Westad, "Moscow and the Angolan Crisis," 24, 30–31; Lysebu I, 32; Garthoff, *Détente and Confrontation*, 566–67; Gleijeses, "Havana's Policy in Africa," 271–72.

102. Garthoff, *Détente and Confrontation*, 586.

103. Kornienko, *Kholodnaia voina*, 167–68; Karen Brutents made this point in Lysebu I, 47.

104. Brenner and Blight, "Cuba, 1962," 81–85; Westad, "Moscow and the Angolan Crisis," 25–27.

105. Garthoff, *Détente and Confrontation*, 581, cites Kissinger's address from *Department of State Bulletin* 74 (April 5, 1976): 428; Westad, "Moscow and the Angolan Crisis," 28–29.

106. Anatoly Dobrynin in Fort Lauderdale, 44–45; Dobrynin, *Sugubo doveritelno*, 383.

107. I saw several profiles of Brzezinski composed in fall 1976–early 1977 by the analysts of the Institute for the U.S. and Canada Studies, Soviet Academy of Sciences; also Chernyaev, *Moia zhizn*, 298; Dobrynin, *Sugubo doveritelno*, 409.

108. Alexeyeva and Goldberg, *Thaw Generation*, 288–89; RGANI, f. 89, op. 25, doc. 44.

109. Kornienko, *Kholodnaia voina*, 170–72; diary of Chernyaev, January 9 and 15, 1977, NSArch.

110. In fall 1976, neoconservatives and leading critics of détente and SALT organized the Committee on Present Danger. They denounced the Vladivostok framework as one that gave advantages to the Soviet Union, particularly in the "throw-weight" of superheavy intercontinental missiles, the ones for which the United States had no match. Members of the Carter administration, especially Secretary of Defense Harold Brown and Undersecretary William Perry, had their own concerns about growing numeric superiority of Soviet strategic and conventional forces. On Nitze's influence, see Brzezinski in Musgrove I, transcript, 48–49; Njolstad, *Peacekeeper and Troublemaker*.

111. Brzezinski in Musgrove I, transcript, 56–57; Njolstad, "Keys of Keys?" 37–40; Njolstad, *Peacekeeper and Troublemaker*, 43–46.

112. Kissinger, *Years of Renewal*, 856–59; Garthoff, *Détente and Confrontation*, 596–99; interview with author, Moscow, November 23, 1989, and March 15, 1990; also cited in Westad, "Fall of Détente," 12; Dobrynin, *Sugubo doveritelno*, 391; Brezhnev to Carter, February 4, 1977, published in *CWIHP Bulletin*, no. 5 (1995); Kornienko, *Kholodnaia voina*, 173; journal of Dobrynin, record of conversation with Secretary of State Vance, March 21, 1977, NSArch; Viktor Starodubov in Musgrove I, transcript, 74; Brezhnev's diary, March 18, 1977, Volkogonov Collection, LC.

113. Vance in Musgrove I, transcript, 62; diary of Chernyaev on his reading of the transcript of Soviet-American talks, April 1, 1977, NSArch.

114. See discussion among Harold Brown, Zbigniew Brzezinski, Nikolai Detinov, Viktor Starodubov, and Dobrynin in Musgrove I, transcript, 27–37.

115. Record of conversation between A. A. Gromyko and U.S. Secretary of State C. Vance, May 31, 1978, New York, provided in February 1994 by the Russian government to the Carter-Brezhnev Project, NSArch.

116. Dobrynin in Musgrove I, transcript, 66, 80–81; Dobrynin, *Sugubo doveritelno*, 397; KGB to the CC, March 18, 1977, RGANI, f. 89, per. 18, dok. 63.

117. Dobrynin in Musgrove I, transcript, 136; see also his *Sugubo doveritelno*, 395–96.

118. Carter's instructions to Brzezinski, May 17, 1978, NSArch; see also Fort Lauderdale, 145–46. For the discussion on China, see the minutes of Security Coordinating Council on Horn of Africa, March 2, 1978, NSArch. The detailed description of Brzezinski's visit is in his memoirs, *Power and Principle*, 208–15; see also Garthoff, *Détente and Confrontation*, 705–6, 770–78; memorandum of conversation between W. Averell Harriman and Ambassador Dobrynin at luncheon, N Street, March 3, 1978, Harriman Collection, LC.

119. Record of Gromyko-Vance conversation, May 31, 1978, and speech of Com. L. I. Brezhnev at the Politburo Session of the CC CPSU concerning several issues of international relations, extract from Protocol no. 107 of the session of the Politburo of the CC CPSU of June 8, 1978, RGANI, f. 89, per. 34, dok. 1, l. 7; "Soviet-American Relations in the Contemporary Era," RGANI, f. 89, per. 76, dok. 28, l. 1–2.

120. Transcripts of the Vienna summit, June 16–18, 1979, NSArch; Dobrynin, *Sugubo doveritelno*, 422–27; Sukhodrev, *Iazik moi—drug moi*, 344–45.

121. Garthoff, *Journey through the Cold War*, 285. The best historical background of Soviet involvement in Afghanistan is Lyakhovsky, *Plamia Afgana*, 11–46.

122. Kornienko, *Kholodnaia voina*, 190; Kalugin and Montaigne, *First Directorate*, 230–33; Mitrokhin, "KGB in Afghanistan."

123. Kalugin and Montaigne, *First Directorate*, 232.

124. Westad, "Road to Kabul," 123–24.

125. Transcript, meeting of the CPSU Politburo, "About the Sharpening of the Situation in the Democratic Republic of Afghanistan and Our Possible Moves," March 17–19, 1979, RGANI, f. 89, per. 25, dok. 1.

126. Ibid.

127. Karen Brutents supports this version in *Tridsat Let*, 465.

128. Record of meeting of A. N. Kosygin, A. A. Gromyko, D. F. Ustinov, and B. N. Ponomarev with N. M. Taraki, March 20, 1979, RGANI, f. 89, per. 14, dok. 26; record of conversation of L. I. Brezhnev with N. M. Taraki, March 20, 1979, RGANI, f. 89, per. 14, dok. 25.

129. "Our Future Policy in Connection with the Situation in Afghanistan," April 1, 1979, Gromyko, Andropov, Ustinov, and Ponomarev to the CC CPSU, translation in *CWIHP Bulletin*, no. 3 (Fall 1993): 67–69; U.S. intelligence estimate on Soviet advisers leaked to the *New York Times*, April 13, 1979.

130. Gai and Snegirev, "Vtorzheniie," 204–8. The cable is dated September 13, 1979, and quoted by Dobrynin from his notes, Lysebu II, 89; Westad, *Fall of Détente*, 129–30.

131. Chazov, *Zdorovie i vlast*, 152; diary of Chernyaev, December 20, 1979, NSArch. Alexandrov made this remark to Karen Brutents. In his memoirs, however, Brutents makes no reference to this fact.

132. Kevorkov, *Tainii kanal*, 243.

133. On the hostage crisis and the American response to it, see Farber, *Taken Hostage*; on Soviet fears, see Valentin Varennikov in Lysebu II, 73; Brutents, *Tridsat Let*, 477.

134. The text of Andropov's personal letter to Brezhnev and the content of his (and Ustinov's) briefing of Brezhnev in early December 1979 was found by Ambassador Anatoly Dobrynin; see Lysebu II, 91–93; and Westad, *Fall of Détente*, 134–35.

135. Quoted by Dobrynin, Lysebu II, 91–93; cited in Westad, *Fall of Detente*, 135.

136. This reconstruction is based on the discussions at Lysebu, Musgrove, and Fort Lauderdale and on private conversations between the author and Soviet veterans during those conferences.

137. Dobrynin, Lysebu II, 91–93; Westad, *Fall of Détente*, 135; the "last straw" argument is in Lyakhovsky, *Plamia Afghana*, 123.

138. Lyakhovsky, *Tragediia*, 109; Lyakhovsky, *Plamia Afghana*, 121; Varennikov, Lysebu II, 85–86.

139. Alexandrov-Agentov, *Ot Kollontai*, 246–47; Dobrynin's testimony in Westad, *Fall of Détente*, 141–42.

140. Diary of Chernyaev, December 30, 1979, NSArch.

Chapter Nine

1. On the danger of confrontation with the declining Soviet Union, see Gray, "Most Dangerous Decade," 16, 18, 24, 25; Brzezinski, *Grand Failure*, 99, 100, 254–55.

2. U.S. intelligence estimates until 1985 understated the burden of military expenses on the Soviet economy and grossly exaggerated the Soviet GDP. But more important than wrong numbers were the attitudes of all Soviet experts in the intelligence community. They just could not imagine that the Warsaw Pact and the Soviet Union itself might one day fall apart. See the materials and discussions of the conference "U.S. Intelligence and the End of the Cold War," Bush Presidential Conference Center, College Station, Texas, November 19–20, 1999.

3. For the background and description of Polish events, see Ouimet, *Rise and Fall of the Brezhnev Doctrine*, chaps. 4–6; see also Musatov, *Predvestniki buri*; Gribkov, "Doktrina Brezhneva i pol'skii krizis nachala 80-kh godov"; Shakhnazarov, *Tsena Svobody*. Leonid Zamyatin, then head of the CC Department for International Information, told me about the Polish "underground" in an interview in Moscow, January 16, 1995. On Soviet fears about the Polish Catholic Church, see Andrew and Mitrokhin, *Sword and the Shield*, 513–14.

4. Voronkov, "Sobitiia 1980–1981 v Polshe," 109.

5. Session of the CPSU CC Politburo, April 2, 1981, quoted in Kramer, "Soviet Deliberations during the Polish Crisis," 24–34, 100–101.

6. Dobrynin, In Confidence, 500.

7. Author's minutes at Jachranka.

8. Leonov, Likholetie, 212; Pavlov, Bylem rezydentem KGB w Polsce, 28, as cited in Voronkov, "Sobitiia 1980–1981 v Polshe," 98.

9. Dobrynin, In Confidence, 500; see also recollections of two other witnesses of this discussion, General Anatoly Gribkov and Georgy Shakhnazarov; author's minutes at Jachranka.

10. Kania, Zatrzymac konfrontacje, 91, as cited in Mastny, "Soviet Non-Invasion of Poland," 15. The Soviet version of Brezhnev's reply is in Voronkov, "Sobitiia 1980–1981 v Polshe." Voronkov, then at the CC International Department, heard about this from his colleague who interpreted at the meeting.

11. Voronkov, "Sobitiia 1980–1981 v Polshe," 105; minutes of the Politburo session, January 22, 1981, NSArch; author's interview with Leonid Zamyatin, Moscow, January 16, 1995.

12. Voronkov, "Sobitiia 1980–1981 v Polshe," 106.

13. The meeting took place on March 4, 1981; see Voronkov, "Sobitiia 1980–1981 v Polshe," 110. Voronkov interpreted at the meeting.

14. Cited in Voronkov, "Sobitiia 1980–1981 v Polshe," 107.

15. Ibid., 113.

16. Diary of Chernyaev, August 10, 1981, NSArch.

17. Shubin, Istoki Perestroiki, 1:63; Gorbachev, "Andropov," 24; Pikhoia, Sovetskii Soiuz, 414.

18. Ouimet, Rise and Fall of the Brezhnev Doctrine, 88.

19. Diary of Chernyaev, February 9 and March 1, 1980. NSArch.

20. Brezhnev's letter to Honecker (also duplicated with letters to other Central European Communist rulers), November 4, 1980, SAPMO-BArch, J IY 2/202, Akt 550; on the reaction of Central European leaders, see Kubina and Wilke, "Hart und kompromisslos durchgreifen," 140–95. See also Tuma, "Czechoslovak Communist Regime and the Polish Crisis"; Tischler, "Hungarian Party Leadership and the Polish Crisis"; Baev, "Bulgaria and the Political Crises."

21. Session of the CPSU Politburo, December 10, 1981, NSArch; Voronkov, "Sobitiia 1980–1981 v Polshe," 119; Jaruzelski's comments, in author's minutes at Jachranka. See more in Kramer, "Soviet Deliberations during the Polish Crisis," 160–61, and his "Jaruzelski, the Soviet Union, and the Imposition of Martial Law in Poland," 5–39.

22. Minutes of CPSU Politburo, December 10, 1981, cited in Kramer, "Soviet Deliberations during the Polish Crisis," 165; Volkogonov, Sem Vozhdei, 2:99–101; Leonov, Likholetie, 212.

23. Ouimet, Rise and Fall of the Brezhnev Doctrine, 243.

24. On the costs see Shubin, Istoki Perestroiki, 9. Shubin cites the figures obtained by G. Urushadze in the Kremlin archives.

25. On Reagan's reaction, see Thatcher, Downing Street Years, 253. Kuklinski defected to the United States shortly before the coup; see Kramer, "Colonel Kuklinski and the Polish Crisis," 48–59.

26. Schweizer, Victory; see also Schweizer, Reagan's War; Weinberger, In the Arena.

27. Pravda, April 23, 1982, cited in Garthoff, Great Transition, 62.

28. Andrew and Gordievsky, Comrade Kryuchkov's Instructions, 67, 69; declassified evidence

on RYAN is analyzed in Fischer, *Cold War Conundrum*, 4–5; Akhromeyev and Kornienko, *Glazami Marshala i Diplomata. Kriticheskii Vzgliad na Vneshniuiu Politiku SSSR do i posle 1985 goda*, 14; Dobrynin, *In Confidence*, 522.

29. Dobrynin, *In Confidence*, 482; *Pravda*, June 16, 1982, and July 12, 1982; Ustinov, *Otvesti ugrozu iadernoi voini*, 7; Garthoff, *Great Transition*, 56, 77.

30. Fischer, *Cold War Conundrum*, 9–10; General Vladimir Slipchenko's remarks at Brown, author's notes; Andrew and Gordievsky, *Comrade Kryuchkov's Instructions*, 69–85.

31. Gates, *From the Shadows*, 265, 266; Robert MacFarlane's remarks at Brown, author's notes; FitzGerald, *Way Out There in the Blue*.

32. Velikhov, "Nauka rabotaet na bezyadrnii mir," 50–51; Sagdeev, *Making of a Soviet Scientist*, 261–62, 273; Nikolai Detinov's remarks, Brown, author's notes; Akhromeyev and Kornienko, *Glazami Marshala i Diplomata*, 19–20; Evangelista, *Unarmed Forces*, 238–42.

33. Gorbachev, "Andropov," 18, 25; see also Volkogonov, *Sem Vozhdei*, 2:139–43.

34. Pechenev, *Gorbachev: k vershinam vlasti*, 54; Akhromeyev and Kornienko, *Glazami Marshala i Diplomata*, 32–33; on the public reaction see Volkogonov, *Sem Vozhdei*, 2:143.

35. Reagan to Andropov, July 11, 1983, and Andropov to Reagan, August 27, 1983, Executive Secretariat NSC, Head of the State file: USSR: Andropov, box 38, RRPL; Alexandrov-Agentov, *Ot Kollontai*, 282–83; Dobrynin, *In Confidence*, 523, 530–32.

36. For the American side of the story of KAL-007, see Pearson, *KAL 007*. For the discussion in the Kremlin, see the minutes of the Politburo on September 2, 1983, in Pikhoia, *Sovetskii Soiuz*, 438–41; also Akhromeyev and Kornienko, *Glazami Marshala i Diplomata*, 44–45, 49–50.

37. Dobrynin, *In Confidence*, 540.

38. Lt. Col. Stanislav Petrov, the duty officer at the air defense early-warning center at Serpukhov-15, believed it was a false alarm and decided against passing on the warning and triggering a nuclear alert. Had he done the opposite, "it is quite possible that the Kremlin would have launched a nuclear-missile strike" based on the false alert; see Zaloga, *Kremlin's Nuclear Sword*, 201.

39. Information from the CC CPSU to the leaders of the Warsaw Pact, copy sent to general secretary of the SED Erich Honecker, probably December 1 or 2, 1983, NSArch.

40. Information from the CC CPSU to the leaders of the Warsaw Pact (another draft), around December 1, 1983, NSArch.

41. Akhromeyev and Kornienko, *Glazami Marshala i Diplomata*, 51.

42. Oleg Grinevsky's remarks at Brown, author's notes.

43. The group that produced the framework consisted of Secretary of State George Schulz, National Security Adviser Robert C. McFarlane, NSC assistants Jack Matlock and Rick Burt, and Jeremy Azrael. See Jack Matlock, memorandum for Robert C. McFarlane, February 24, 1984, "U.S.-Soviet Relations: 'Framework' Paper," Matlock Papers, box 23, RRPL. See also Matlock, *Reagan and Gorbachev*, 75–87; and *Autopsy on an Empire*, 84–86.

44. Gromyko's words from Grinevsky's diary, entry of January 16, 1984, cited at Brown, author's notes. Also at Brown, Chernyaev stated that the CC International Department "did not comprehend" the meaning of Reagan's January 1984 speech.

45. Dobrynin, *In Confidence*, 482.

46. Author's personal observations during his lecturing tours around the Soviet Union in 1984–86; see also Gorbachev, "Otkrovennyi dialog o perestroike," *Izvestia*, April 29, 1990, cited in English, *Russia and the Idea of the West*, 189.

47. Minutes of the Politburo CC CPSU, July 12, 1984, translated and published in the *CWIHP Bulletin*, no. 4 (Fall 1994): 81; Pribitkov, *Apparat*, 67–70; English, *Russia and the Idea of the West*, 186–91.

48. *Izvestia*, April 29, 1990. Indirect defense-related costs include the costs of military-industrial production, scientific programs, intelligence, etc. The figure of 40 percent appeared in Gorbachev, *Zhizn i reformi*, 1:334.

49. The version on the "debates" is in English, "Sources, Methods, and Competing Perspectives," 286; Fischer, *Cold War Conundrum*, 27; Vorotnikov, *A bylo eto tak*, 59–62; Akhromeyev and Kornienko, *Glazami Marshala i Diplomata*, 17.

50. "O rezhime raboti chlenov, kandidatov v chleni Politburo TsK KPSS, sekretarei TsK KPSS i zamestitelei Predsedatelia Soveta Ministrov SSSR," Politburo decision, March 24, 1983, Volkogonov Collection, LC; Pribitkov, *Apparat*, 128–29.

51. Gorbachev, *Zhizn i reformi*, 1:264.

52. Reddaway, "Khrushchev and Gorbachev," 321–24; Zubok and Pleshakov, *Inside the Kremlin's Cold War*, 175–79; Chernyaev, "Fenomen Gorbacheva v kontekste liderstva," 51–53. On Gorbachev as a transitional leader and innovator, see Glad and Shiryaev, *Russian Transformation*.

53. Taubman, *Khrushchev*, 648.

54. Historical evidence does not support the later arguments that Gorbachev was elected by a narrow margin and had to conceal his radical reformist potential from the conservatives. For these arguments, see Brown, *Gorbachev Factor*, 69, 84, 122–23; Ligachev, *Inside Gorbachev's Kremlin*, 69, 72–78; Pikhoia, *Sovetskii Soiuz*, 448–49; Pechenev, *Gorbachev: K vershinam vlasti*, 110. Gorbachev's memoirs describe the smooth process; *Zhizn i reformi*, 1:265–70. See also minutes of the Politburo on March 11, 1985, *Istochnik o* (1993): 34–75.

55. Gorbachev's acceptance speech on March 11, 1985, *Istochnik o* (1993): 74–75; Pikhoia, *Sovetskii Soiuz*.

56. Vorotnikov, *A bylo eto tak*, 66–67; Pikhoia, "Pochemu raspalsia SSSR?" 18.

57. Gorbachev, *Zhizn i reformi*, 1:336–37, 338–42. Recent scholarship confirms that Gorbachev and his "team" took over Andropov's disciplining campaign; see Pikhoia, *Sovetskii Soiuz*, 454, 456, 457–63.

58. Akhromeyev and Kornienko, *Glazami Marshala i Diplomata*, 55–56, 86–89; Savelyev and Detinov, *Big Five*, 31–53, 83–84.

59. Gorbachev, *Zhizn i reformi*, 2:7.

60. Ibid., 1:288–89. Later, when Gorbachev became immersed in domestic crises and problems, he began to delegate foreign affairs to Shevardnadze. On Shevardnadze's role, see McGiffert Ekedahl and Goodman, *Wars of Eduard Shevardnadze*.

61. Gromyko, *Andrei Gromyko v labirintakh Kremlia*, 133–37.

62. English, *Russia and the Idea of the West*, 212, 330; Matlock, *Reagan and Gorbachev*, 214.

63. On the origins of the "new thinking," see English, *Russia and the Idea of the West*; English, "Road(s) Not Taken," 256–57; Yakovlev, *Muki prochteniia bytiia. Perestroyka: nadezhdy i realnosti*, 181, 188.

64. This group included, among others, Georgy Arbatov, Yevgeny Velikhov, Anatoly Chernyaev, Georgy Shakhnazarov, Abel Aganbegyan, and Tatyana Zaslavskaia. See Brown, *Gorbachev Factor*, 97–103; on the early role of Arbatov and Velikhov, see Chernyaev, *Shest Let s Gorbachevim*, 23–24 (see also English version, *My Six Years with Gorbachev*); Sagdeev, *Making of a Soviet Scientist*, 266; English, *Russia and the Idea of the West*, 201–2.

65. Chernyaev, *Shest Let s Gorbachevim*, 41; Arbatov, *System*, 321–22.

66. Diary of Chernyaev, November 11, 1982, NSArch; Sagdeev, *Making of a Soviet Scientist*, 268–69.

67. Gorbachev, *Zhizn i reformi*, 1:36–37, 42–51.

68. Perhaps earlier, during 1984, Gorbachev had to deal sporadically with nuclear issues when he informally chaired the Politburo and Secretariat sessions while Chernenko was hospitalized.

69. Information on Oleg Skvortsov based on his interview with Oleg Baklanov, at the conference on the end of the Cold War organized by the Mershon Center, Ohio State University, October 15–16, 1999.

70. Mikhail Gorbachev in an interview with Yuri Smirnov, August 23, 1994, Moscow, in *Science and Society: History of the Soviet Atomic Project*, 333.

71. Gates, *From the Shadows*; for a partisan's account of the "crusade," reflecting its spirit, see Schweizer, *Reagan's War*.

72. Matlock, *Reagan and Gorbachev*, 113–22. Anatoly Chernyaev, Gorbachev's foreign policy assistant since January 1996, learned about the four-part framework document from Matlock only in 1997.

73. On the pressure from below to quit in Afghanistan and the position of the intellectual advisers, see the excerpts from Chernayev's diary dated April 4, June 20, and October 17, 1985, *Svobodnaia Mysl* 11 (2002): 39–41; Gorbachev, *Zhizn i reformi*, 1:276; Kornienko, *Kholodnaia voina*, 197–99.

74. Gorbachev's letters to Reagan, March 24, June 22, and September 12, 1985, Executive Secretariat of the NSC, Head of State File: USSR: Gorbachev, box 40, RRPL.

75. Dobrynin, *Sugubo doveritelno*, 92, 622–23. In the Russian edition of his memoirs, Dobrynin gives an almost complete text of the draft guidelines that the Politburo approved with some modifications.

76. Gorbachev, *Zhizn i reformi*, 2:15; diary of Chernyaev, notes of Gorbachev's talk on November 27, 1985, NSArch. Gorbachev's words about Reagan to the Politburo are in Dobrynin, *Sugubo doveritelno*, 655; Sagdeev, *Making of a Soviet Scientist*, 271.

77. Chernyaev, "Fenomen Gorbacheva v kontekste liderstva," 57.

78. Gorbachev, *Zhizn i reformi*, 1:293.

79. Chernyaev, *Shest Let s Gorbachevim*, 152.

80. English, *Russia and the Idea of the West*, 210.

81. Gorbachev, *Political Report*; Garthoff, *Journey through the Cold War*, 348–450.

82. Diary of Chernyaev, March 20, 1986, NSArch.

83. Garthoff, *Journey through the Cold War*, 350; Gates, *From the Shadows*, 349–68; Bearden and Risen, *Main Enemy*. More then ten years later Chernyaev admitted that he still did not understand the reasons for such a hostile and mistrustful reaction by the U.S. leadership to Soviet signals; see his remarks, Brown; also Tannenwald, *Understanding the End of the Cold War*.

84. Remarks of Robert McFarlane on SDI, Brown; Tannenwald, *Understanding the End of the Cold War*.

85. Politburo session, April 15, 1986, notes of Anatoly Chernyaev, AGF, f. 2, op. 1.

86. Diary of Chernyaev, March 20 and April 3, 1986, NSArch.

87. Reagan to Gorbachev, undated, November 1985, after Geneva summit, Executive Secretariat of the NSC, Head of State File: USSR: Gorbachev, box 40, RRPL.

88. Akhromeyev and Kornienko, *Glazami Marshala i Diplomata*, 72; General Vladimir Slipchenko's remarks and author's notes, Brown; Tannenwald, *Understanding the End of the Cold War*; Politburo session, March 24, 1986, notes of Anatoly Chernyaev, AGF, f. 2, op. 1; Sagdeev, *Making of a Soviet Scientist*, 272.

89. Gorbachev's thoughts about ending the nuclear moratorium, March 24, 1986, in the presence of the KGB's Viktor Chebrikov, Shevardnadze, the head of the Military-Industrial Commission Lev Zaikov, Dobrynin, Alexander Yakovlev, Vladimir Medvedev, and Chernyaev. Chernyaev's notes, NSArch.

90. Yaroshinska, *Chernobyl*; Politburo minutes of April 28, April 29, and May 5, 1986, in *Istochnik* 5 (1996): 87–103.

91. English, *Russia and the Idea of the West*, 215–16.

92. Akhromeyev and Kornienko, *Glazami Marshala i Diplomata*, 98–99. Jack Matlock reports that the same transformation happened to Yazov, Soviet minister of defense since May 1987, in *Autopsy on an Empire*, 137.

93. Chernyaev et al., *V Politbiuro TsK KPSS*, 43; Chernyaev's notes of the CC Politburo meeting, July 3, 1986, a copy on file at the NSArch.

94. Record of the speech in Gorbachev, *Godi Trudnikh Reshenii*, 48, 50.

95. Author's notes of Grinevsky's remarks, Brown; Tannenwald, *Understanding the End of the Cold War*.

96. English, *Russia and the Idea of the West*, 212.

97. "Zapis besedi M. S. Gorbacheva s prezidentom F. Mitteranom," July 7, 1986, AGF.

98. Chernyaev, *Shest Let s Gorbachevym*, 137–38.

99. "Zapis besedi M. S. Gorbacheva s bivshim prezidentom SShA R. Niksonom," July 17, 1986, AGF.

100. Chernyaev et al., *V Politbiuro TsK KPSS*, 66, 77, 96, 103, 169.

101. Gorbachev, *Zhizn i reformi*, 1:306.

102. For the best background on this, see Matlock, *Reagan and Gorbachev*, 197–202.

103. Gorbachev to Reagan, September 15, 1986, Executive Secretariat of the NSC, Head of State File: USSR: Gorbachev, box 40, RRPL.

104. The only source is Akhromeyev, who does not give the date but indicates that the draft of the new doctrine was ready soon after Reykjavik, which means that the military started working on it *before* the summit; see Akhromeyev and Kornienko, *Glazami Marshala i Diplomata*, 121, 125.

105. Thatcher, *Downing Street Years*, 470–71; Gorbachev, *Zhizn i reformi*, 2:26–27.

106. Politburo sessions on October 4 and 8, 1986, notes of Anatoly Chernyaev, AGF, f. 2, op. 1.

107. "Zapis besedi M. S. Gorbacheva s prezidentom F. Mitteranom," July 7, 1986, AGF; Brown, *Gorbachev Factor*, 226.

108. "Ustanovki Gorbacheva gruppe po podgotovke Reikjavika," Chernyaev's notes, October 4, 1986, NSArch.

109. Records of Gorbachev-Reagan conversations at Reykjavik, October 11–12, 1986, published in *Mirovaia ekonomika i mezhdunarodniie otnosheniia* 4, 5, 7, 8 (1993); partially translated in FBIS-USR-93-087, July 12, 1993, 1–6, and FBIS-USR-93-113, August 30, 1993, 1–11.

110. Gorbachev-Reagan conversations at Reykjavik, a morning conversation on October 11, 1986, *Mirovaia ekonomika i mezhdunarodniie otnosheniia* 4 (1993): 81–83.

111. Shultz, *Turmoil and Triumph*, 760, 765.

112. Reagan-Gorbachev conversations at Reykjavik, a meeting in the afternoon of October 12, 1986, *Mirovaia ekonomika i mezhdunarodniie otnosheniia* 8 (1993): 68–78; the U.S. record is still not declassified but is cited in Shultz, *Turmoil and Triumph*, 767–73; Matlock, *Reagan and Gorbachev*, 229. For a critical view on the American background, see FitzGerald, *Way Out There in the Blue*.

113. On the latter point, see Matlock, *Reagan and Gorbachev*, 232–38.

114. Chernyaev's notes of Gorbachev's thinking about Reykjavik, October 12, 1986, AGF.

115. Gorbachev, *Zhizn i reformi*, 2:27; Akhromeyev, Kornienko, *Glazami Marshala i Diplomata*, 120; Dobrynin, *In Confidence*, 606.

116. Gorbachev, *Zhizn i reformi*, 1:312, 348.

117. Meeting, December 1, 1986, "O direktivakh delegatsii SSSR na peregovorakh po SNV v Zheneve," Chernyaev's notes, NSArch.

118. Ibid.

119. Ibid.; Akhromeyev and Kornienko, *Glazami Marshala i Diplomata*, 127.

120. Meeting, December 1, 1986, "O direktivakh delegatsii SSSR na peregovorakh po SNV v Zheneve," Chernyaev's notes, NSArch.

121. Vladimir Kryuchkov interview with Oleg Skvortsov, October 13 and December 7, 1998, OHPECW.

122. Chernyaev, *Shest Let s Gorbachevym*, 69; Chernyaev, "Fenomen Gorbacheva v kontekste liderstva," 50–51, 53; Dobrynin, *Sugubo doveritelno*, 653.

123. Cordovez and Harrison, *Out of Afghanistan*; see also Crile, *Charlie Wilson's War*.

124. Kornienko, *Kholodnaia voina*, 200–203; Chernyaev's notes and Vadim Medvedev's notes of Politburo discussions, January 21–22, February 28, May 7, May 21–22, 1987.

125. Cordovez and Harrison, *Out of Afghanistan*, 246–48.

126. See the records of Gorbachev's conversation with Fidel Castro, March 2, 1986, with Mengistu Haile Mariam on April 17, 1987, and with Rajiv Ghandi on July 2–3, 1987, AGF.

127. Matlock, *Autopsy on an Empire*, 106. The jamming of Munich-based and consistently anti-Communist Radio Liberty continued.

128. Chernyaev's impression was that Gorbachev stopped regarding the human rights issue as a concession to foreign policy needs only when he decided to change the political system of the USSR in the spring of 1988 (remarks in a conversation with author, Providence, R.I., May 8, 1998). KGB reports on 1985, 1986, 1987, NSArch; see also Garthoff, "KGB Reports to Gorbachev," 224–44.

129. Pikhoia, " Pochemu raspalsia SSSR?"

130. Gorbachev, *Zhizn i reformi*, 1:346, 349, 351.

131. These numbers are mentioned by Gorbachev and other Politburo members, according to Chernyaev's notes at the Politburo meetings of May 29, October 23, and December 1, 1986, NSArch.

132. For Soviet defense expenditures, see the calculations of economists Yu D. Masliukov and E. S. Glubokov, in Minaiev, *Sovetskaia voiennaia moshch ot Stalina do Gorbacheva*, 105–6; Politburo meetings, October 30, 1986, and April 23, 1987, Chernyaev's notes, NSArch. See also Ryzhkov, *Desiat let velikikh potriasenii*, 184–92; Vorotnikov, *A bylo eto tak*, 130–31, 164–68; Chernyaev et al., *V Politbiuro TsK KPSS*, 102–3, 169–72. On the Politburo's lack of preparedness to deal with the crisis, see Gaidar, *Gibel imperii*, 235–46, 306, 310–11.

133. Politburo meeting, February 26, 1987, Chernyaev's notes, NSArch.

134. Record of conversation between Gorbachev and Andreotti, February 27, 1987, AGF.

135. Politburo meeting, February 23 and 26, 1987, Chernyaev's notes, NSArch; on Gorbachev's ideas of trying "to oust the maximum possible number of American troops from Western Europe," Dobrynin, *In Confidence*, 570, and *Sugubo doveritelno*, 607.

136. See Akhromeyev and Kornienko, *Glazami Marshala i Diplomata*, 130–33. Another much-criticized "mistake" and "concession" was Gorbachev's agreement at the Washington summit in December 1987 to dismantle SS-20 missiles in Asia (deployed as a counterbalance to American and Chinese nuclear weapons); see Dobrynin, *Sugubo doveritelno*, 656–57. A different interpretation is in Gorbachev, *Zhizn i reformi*, 2:35–49; Shultz, *Turmoil and Triumph*, 889–95.

137. Chernyaev's minutes at the Defense Council, May 8, 1987, AGF; Odom, *Collapse of the Soviet Military*, 112–14. Odom erroneously dated the change as the fall of 1987, when Gorbachev published his book *Perestroika*.

138. Chernyaev, "Fenomen Gorbachev v kontekste liderstva," 53.

139. I was at that time a researcher at the Institute for U.S. and Canada Studies in Moscow, and I remember that many at that institute took this speech as a clear signal to revise thinking on Soviet domestic and foreign policies.

140. Chernyaev, *Shest Let s Gorbachevim*, 191.

141. This paragraph is based on the recollections of Gorbachev's interpreter, Igor Korchilov, in his *Translating History*, 35, 42–43.

142. Compare with Ouimet, *Rise and Fall of the Brezhnev Doctrine*, 7.

Chapter Ten

1. See, for example, Lebow, "Long Peace," 249–77; Gaddis, "International Relations Theory," 5–58; Wohlforth, "Realism and the End of the Cold War," 91–129; Hopf, "Getting the End of the Cold War Wrong," 202–8; Risse-Kappen, "Did 'Peace Through Strength' End the Cold War?" 162–88; Tannenwald and Wohlforth, "Role of Ideas," 3–12; English, "Sociology of New Thinking," 43–80.

2. Lévesque, Enigma of 1989, 252.

3. Brown, Gorbachev Factor, 317. For other works emphasizing Gorbachev's personality, see Greenstein, "Reagan and Gorbachev"; and Matlock, Reagan and Gorbachev.

4. Chernyaev, "Fenomen Gorbacheva v kontekste liderstva"; see also his Shest Let s Gorbachevim and 1991 god.

5. Volkogonov, Sem Vozhdei, 2:322–23. An account of intellectual debates on Gorbachev's role can be found in Guerra, Urss, 131–60.

6. Boldin, Krusheniie pedestala; Ligachev, Zagadka Gorbacheva; Vorotnikov, A bylo eto tak; Ryzhkov, Desiat let velikikh potriasenii; Ryzhkov, Perestroika; Kryuchkov, Lichnoie delo; Leonov, Likholetie; Medvedev, Chelovek za spinoi; Shenin, Rodinu ne prodaval; Akhromeyev and Kornienko, Glazami marshala i diplomata; Kornienko, Kholodnaia voina; Falin, Politische Erinnerungen; Pechenev, Gorbachev; Pechenev, Vzlet i padeniie Gorbacheva; Gromyko, Andrei Gromyko v labirintakh Kremlia; Yeltsin, Ispoved na zadannuiu temu; Dobrynin, In Confidence, and the Russian edition, Sugubo doveitelno. Also, I used transcripts of the interviews with Soviet officials in OHPECW.

7. Chernyaev, "Fenomen Gorbacheva v kontekste liderstva"; see also his Shest Let s Gorbachevim and his 1991 god; Shakhnazarov, Tsena Svobody; Medvedev, V komande Gorbacheva; Medvedev, Raspad; Yakovlev, Predisloviie, obval, posleslovie; Shevardnadze, Moi vybor v zaschitu demokratii i svobody; Grachev, Dalshe bez menya; Grachev, Kremlevskaia khronika; Palazhchenko, My Years with Gorbachev and Shevardnadze. In addition to these sources, I used the materials of the "oral history conferences" on the end of the Cold War, with the participation of some of the same figures. See Tannenwald, Understanding the End of the Cold War and "End of the Cold War in Europe."

8. Brutents, Nesbyvsheesia, 651.

9. Gorbachev, Zhizn i reformi, vols. 1 and 2; Gorbachev, Avgustovskii putch; Gorbachev, Dekabr-91. See also his conversation with Russian intellectuals in his Perestroika.

10. Furman, "Fenomen Gorbacheva," 62.

11. Ligachev, Inside Gorbachev's Kremlin, 126, 128. The literal translation of the Russian title of this work is "Gorbachev Enigma."

12. See Brooks and Wohlforth, "Economic Constraints and the End of the Cold War," 273–309.

13. Oleg Grinevsky, senior Soviet arms negotiator, contends that the Kremlin even considered fall-back plans to repeat "the Cuban scenario" of 1962 by responding to U.S. deployment of Pershings in West Germany with equally provocative deployments of Soviet arms in the immediate vicinity of the United States. Grinevsky, "Understanding the End of the Cold War." Georgy M. Kornienko believes that this is a figment of Grinevsky's imagination. Telephone conversation between author and Kornienko, Moscow, June 29, 2002.

14. Chernyaev in Grinevsky, "Understanding the End of the Cold War," 77–78.

15. Gates, *From the Shadows*, 330–34, 335–40.

16. Chernyaev in Grivensky, "Understanding the End of the Cold War," 78.

17. Obviously, "the Chinese road" was not the term the Soviets used in the 1980s. At that time the scope and direction of the economic reforms introduced by Deng Xiaoping in 1978 were still not clear.

18. Gates, *From the Shadows*, 385–88, 439; Shultz, *Turmoil and Triumph*, esp. 765; Bush and Scowcroft, *World Transformed*; see also the analysis in Garthoff, *Great Transition*.

19. Politburo meetings, October 4 and 8, 1986, Chernyaev's notes, AGF, f. 2, op. 1.

20. Michael Ellman and Vladimir Kantorovich convincingly conclude that "the USSR was killed, against the wishes of its ruler, by politics, not economics. The immediate cause of death, the dissolution of the Union, was the result of the chain of events set in motion by Gorbachev starting in 1985." *Destruction of the Soviet Economic System*, 26, 22–23, 165–69. See also their "Collapse of the Soviet System." This conclusion is corroborated by Gaidar, *Gibel imperii*.

21. Documents on Soviet assistance to these countries from RGANI, f. 89, are available at NSArch.

22. Furman, "Fenomen Gorbacheva," 70–71.

23. Brown, *Gorbachev Factor*, 59, 220–30.

24. Oral communication of Geoffrey Howe, in Strober and Strober, *Reagan*, 327.

25. Furman, "Fenomen Gorbacheva," 71.

26. In early March 1988, the newspaper *Soviet Russia* published a feature article by "a professor from Leningrad," Nina Andreeva, under the title "I Cannot Forsake My Principles." It quickly became a manifesto of the forces that opposed the radicalization of reforms. Some Poliburo members, including Yegor K. Ligachev, encouraged this process. Gorbachev was at the time on a trip abroad, but when he returned, he addressed the issue at the Politburo and used the "Andreeva affair" as an occasion to rout conservative forces.

27. Politburo meeting, March 24–25, 1988, Chernyaev's notes, AGF, f. 2, op. 1.

28. Politburo meeting, March 24–25, 1988, Chernyaev's notes, NSArch.

29. Chernyaev, *1991 god*, 15–16.

30. Kozlova, *Gorizonti povsednevnosti Sovetskoi epokhi*.

31. Chernyaev, "Fenomen Gorbacheva v kontekste liderstva," 52.

32. Shakhnazarov, *Tsena Svobody*, 47; Furman, "Fenomen Gorbacheva," 66; see also Vladimir Shemyatenkov, deputy head of the Cadre Department of the CC CPSU in 1985–88, who implies that Gorbachev was too good for Soviet society. Interview with Shemyatenkov by Oleg Skvortsov, Moscow, November 18, 1998, OHPECW.

33. Chernyaev, *Shest Let s Gorbachevim*, 278, 280.

34. Interview with Ligachev by Oleg Skvortsov, Moscow, December 17, 1998, OHPECW.

35. Medvedev, *Chelovek za spinoi*, 214–15, 225; interview with Valery Boldin by Oleg Skvortsov, Moscow, February 24, 1999, OHPECW.

36. Chernyaev, "Fenomen Gorbacheva v kontekste liderstva," 59.

37. Furman, "Fenomen Gorbacheva," 65–67.

38. Chernyaev, "Fenomen Gorbacheva v kontekste liderstva," 56; see also his *Shest Let s Gorbachevim*, 241, 343.

39. Furman, "Fenomen Gorbacheva," 67.

40. *Perestroika desiat let spustia*, 102–3; Gorbachev's last words give credibility to the version of Ligachev and Boldin about the post-1986 political confrontation between Gorbachev and the party cadres—that it was the result of political liberalization and democratization of the Soviet regime.

41. This important debate cannot be resolved on the basis of today's scholarship. It is true that when Gorbachev introduced "elements of democracy" into the party he made it possible for the CC Plenums to oust him from power. But Gorbachev then and much later (even in 1990) was able to prevail quite decisively over his critics inside the party.

42. Odom, "Sources of 'New Thinking' in Soviet Politics," 150; Ligachev, *Inside Gorbachev's Kremlin*, 128.

43. Interview with Ligachev by Oleg Skvortsov, Moscow, December 17, 1998, OHPECW.

44. Interviews with Kryuchkov by Oleg Skvortsov, Moscow, October 13 and December 7, 1998, OHPECW.

45. Chernyaev's notes, October 31, 1988, AGF; see also Palazhchenko, *My Years with Gorbachev and Shevardnadze*, 103–4.

46. He told the Politburo on January 21, 1989, that Kissinger hinted at the idea of a USSR-USA condominium over Europe. "We should also work on this range of issues," Gorbachev concluded, "but in such a way that it would not leak," so that Europeans would not see it as "an effort at conspiracy between the USSR and the USA over Europe." Chernyaev's notes, AGF. Chernyaev believes that Gorbachev was not interested in Kissinger's proposal. "End of the Cold War in Europe," 158–59.

47. Rey, " 'Europe Is Our Common Home,' " 33–65.

48. Interview with Sergei Tarasenko by Oleg Skvortsov, Moscow, March 19, 1999, OHPECW.

49. For the crucial role of isolation in the Soviet regime's stability, see Connor, "Soviet Society," 43–80; Furman, "Fenomen Gorbacheva," 68, 70–71.

50. Chernyaev, *1991 god*, 11–12.

51. Interview with Valery Boldin by Oleg Skvortsov, Moscow, February 24, 1999, OHPECW; Ligachev, *Inside Gorbachev's Kremlin*, 126, 127.

52. Dobrynin, *In Confidence*, 624–27.

53. Ibid., 627.

54. Kornienko's personal communication to author, Moscow, October 18, 1996.

55. Furman, "Fenomen Gorbacheva," 71–72.

56. Matlock, *Autopsy on an Empire*, 16, 672.

57. Lévesque, *Enigma of 1989*, 252; see also Bennett, *Condemned to Repetition?*

58. Gromyko, *Andrei Gromyko v labirintakh Kremlia*, 182, 184.

59. Interviews with Alexander Yakovlev and Andrei Grachev cited by Archie Brown in *Gorbachev Factor*, 383–84; Yegorov, *Out of a Dead End into the Unknown*; Shakhnazarov, *Tsena Svobody*, 147.

60. *Perestroika desiat let spustia*, 29–30, 60.

61. Chernyaev's and Medvedev's notes at the Politburo, May 11, 1989. Discussion of memorandum of six Politburo members on the situation in the Baltic Republics, AGF, f. 4, op. 1; see also Veber, *Soiuz mozhno bilo sokhranit*, 52, 55.

62. Soviet record of the Malta Summit, AGF, f. 4, op. 1; Zelikow and Rice, *Germany Unified and Europe Transformed*, 129.

63. *Perestroika desiat let spustia*, 19.

64. Interview with Yegor Ligachev by Oleg Skvortsov, Moscow, December 17, 1998, OHPECW.

65. See Odom, *Collapse of the Soviet Military*.

66. Lévesque, *Enigma of 1989*, 2.

67. Interview with Ligachev by Oleg Skvortsov, Moscow, December 17, 1998, OHPECW; on the process of cutting off "conservative" elements, party structures, and other bureaucratic players from the foreign policy field, see McGiffert Ekedahl and Goodman, *Wars of Eduard Shevardnadze*, 71–98.

68. Kramer, "Collapse of East European Communism," pt. 1, 178–256, and pt. 2, 3–64.

69. The texts of all the memoranda are at NSArch; Lévesque, *Enigma of 1989*, 68–90; Shakhnazarov, *Tsena Svobody*, 369.

70. See Vladislav Zubok, "New Evidence on the Soviet Factor in the Peaceful Revolution of 1989," *CWIHP Bulletin*, no. 12/13 (Fall/Winter 2001): 10; Gaidar, *Gibel imperii*, 245.

71. Record of conversation between M. S. Gorbachev and member of the CC of the Hungarian Socialist Workers' Party and chairman of the Council of Ministers of the People's Republic of Hungary, Miklos Nemeth, March 23, 1989, Chernyaev's notes, NSArch.

72. Author's conversation with Rakowski on April 8, 1999, at the conference on the anniversary of the Polish 1989 Roundtable, organized by the University of Michigan, Ann Arbor. Rakowski also told Lévesque that Gorbachev refused to see him in Moscow for consultations. See Lévesque, *Enigma of 1989*, 125.

73. There is intriguing evidence on that in the memoirs of the last Soviet ambassador to the GDR, Vyacheslav Kochemasov; see his *Meine letzte Mission*, 168–69. Kochemasov claims it was his own decision to order the Soviet military commander to refrain from interference during the crucial confrontation at Leipzig; Sergei Tarasenko informed on Shevardnadze's activities in New York at Musgrove I, transcript, 98.

74. Musgrove I, transcript, 79.

75. Bush and Scowcroft, *World Transformed*, 135.

76. Quoted by Talbott and Beschloss, *At the Highest Levels*, 73–100. See, for example, the analytical paper of Fritz Ermarth, chairman of the National Intelligence Council, CIA, "The Russian Revolution and the Future Russian Threat to the West," May 18, 1990, declassified and posted by Ermarth on the Johnson Russia List, Center for Defense Information, June 30, 1999 <http://www.cdi.org/russia/johnson/>. See also "Rising Political Instability under Gorbachev: Understanding the Problem and Prospects for Resolution, an Intelligence Assessment," Directorate of Intelligence, April 1989, and "Gorbachev's Domestic Gambles and Instability in the USSR, an Intelligence Assessment," September 1989, both documents declassified by Freedom of Information Act request, NSArch. Bush and Scowcroft stress that

Bush's meetings in Poland played a crucial role in brokering the dangerous political standoff between Jaruzelski and Solidarity. *World Transformed*, 117–23. This is fully supported by Jaruzelski himself; see his memoir, *Les chaines et le refuge*, 337; Lévesque, *Enigma of 1989*, 123.

77. Baker, *Politics of Diplomacy*, 144–52; Bush and Scowcroft, *World Transformed*, 173.

78. On the Soviet-FRG relations before Kohl's visit, see Smyser, *From Yalta to Berlin*, 304–13, 316.

79. Third conversation of M. S. Gorbachev with chancellor of the FRG, H. Kohl (one-to-one), Bonn, June 14, 1989, notes of Chernyaev, provided by Chernyaev to NSArch.

80. Conversations of Chancellor Kohl and Foreign Minister Genscher with President Nemeth and Foreign Minister Horn, Palais Gymnich, August 25, 1989, published in Küsters and Hoffmann, *Dokumente zur Deutschlandpolitik*, 377–82.

81. Interview of Laszlo Kovacs by Jacques Lévesque, Budapest, May 2, 1992, cited in *Enigma of 1989*, 153.

82. Gorbachev's conversation with Honecker, October 7, 1989, AGF, provided by Chernyaev to NSArch.

83. Medvedev, *Raspad*, 171; notes of Chernyaev, October 5, 1989, AGF, f. 2, op. 2.

84. Medvedev, *Raspad*, 191.

85. Kuzmin, *Khrushcnie GDR*, 112–13.

86. Notes of Chernyaev, October 5, 1989, AGF, f. 2, op. 2; Vladislav Zubok, "New Evidence on the Soviet Factor in the Peaceful Revolution of 1989," *CWIHP Bulletin*, no. 12/13 (Fall/Winter 2001): 13; Chernyaev et al., *V Politbiuro TsK KPSS*, 524.

87. Zelikow and Rice, *Germany Unified and Europe Transformed*, 83.

88. Vorotnikov, *A bylo eto tak*, 301, 304–5.

89. Ibid., 308.

90. The most comprehensive account is in Hertle, *Chronik des Mauerfalls*, 233–37; see also Igor Maksimychev, "Berlinskaia stena: Eio padeniie glazami ochevidtsa," *Nezavisimaia gazeta*, November 10, 1993; Kochemasov, *Meine letzte Mission*, 185; Kuzmin, *Kruscheniie GDR*, 60.

91. Lévesque, *Enigma of 1989*, 162–65.

92. Vorotnikov, *A bylo eto tak*, 311–18; Veber, *Soiuz mozhno bilo*, 75–77.

93. Shakhnazarov, *Tsena Svobody*, 353.

94. Lévesque, *Enigma of 1989*, 83, 178–81, 255. Soviet ambassadors and intelligence chiefs in Central European capitals, as well as some well-informed Soviet visitors (for example, Vadim Zagladin, who traveled to Czechoslovakia in July 1989), warned Moscow repeatedly of the grave situation. At the same time, nobody could have predicted what direction and character the revolutions in Central Europe would take.

95. Dobrynin, *In Confidence*, 627–28, 630–31, 642; author's personal communication with Dobrynin, Moscow, June 18, 1999; see also Kornienko, *Khodnaia voina*, 261–68.

96. Baker, *Politics of Diplomacy*, 144–52; Bush and Scowcroft, *World Transformed*, 173.

97. Record of the meeting cited in Zelikow and Rice, *Germany Unified and Europe Transformed*, 398–99.

98. Bush and Scowcroft, *World Transformed*, 317.

99. Soviet record of conversation with U.S. president George Bush (one-to-one conversa-

tion), December 2, 1989, AGF. Pavel Palazhchenko, who interpreted for this conversation, told the author about Gorbachev's startled reaction; see also Bush and Scowcroft, *World Transformed*, 165.

100. Soviet record of conversation with U.S. president George Bush (one-to-one conversation), December 2, 1989, AGF.

101. This term stems from the bilateral treaty, signed by Germany and the Soviet Union in Rapallo, Italy, in 1922, behind the backs of the European great powers.

102. Kvitsinsky, *Vor dem Sturm*, 16–17; Zelikow and Rice, *Germany Unified and Europe Transformed*, 124–25; record of the meeting on Germany at the CC CPSU, January 28, 1990, diary of Chernyaev, NSArch.

103. Zelikow and Rice, *Germany Unified and Europe Transformed*.

104. On the internal Soviet "empire" and the reasons for its instability, see Zaslavsky, "Nationalism and Democratic Transition in Postcommunist Societies," 99–119; see also his "Collapse of Empires"; Tuminez, "Nationalism, Ethnic Pressures, and the Breakup of the Soviet Union," 81–136.

105. Author's conversation with Georgy Shakhnazarov, November 9, 1997, Jachranka, Poland.

106. For details, see Chernyaev, *1991 god*, 186–207; see also *Putch: khronika trevozhnikh dnei*.

107. The best study of this collapse is Gaidar, *Gibel imperii*, chaps. 6 and 7, esp. 318, 332, 344.

108. Matlock, *Autopsy of an Empire*, 551–59; Brown, *Gorbachev Factor*, 291.

109. Odom, *Collapse of the Soviet Military*; Taylor, "Soviet Military and the Disintegration of the USSR," 17–66.

110. Matlock, *Autopsy of an Empire*, 612–47; Dunlop, *Rise of Russia and the Fall of the Soviet Empire*. For the best Russian analysis, see Pikhoia, *Sovetskii Soiuz*.

111. Trubetskoy, *Minuvshee*, 109, 110.

112. Afanasyev, *Sovetskoie obshchestvo*, 2:560, 562.

Epilogue

1. See this point in Westad, *Global Cold War*, 4, 396–97.

2. *Parallel History Project of NATO and the Warsaw Pact: Annual Report, 2003*, 9.

3. Brudny, *Reinventing Russia*, 58; Grushin, *Chetyre zhizni Rossii v zerkale oprosov obshchestvennogo mneniia*, 843, 876.

4. See Nuti and Zubok, "Ideology," 73–110.

5. See Logevall, "Bernath Lecture," 475–84.

6. Vladislav Zubok, "Reagan the Dove: Soft Power," *New Republic*, June 21, 2004, 11–12.

7. This point is eloquently expressed in Malia, *Soviet Tragedy*, 50–78.

(BIBLIOGRAPHY)

Archival Sources

Archive of Foreign Policy of the Russian Federation, Moscow

Archive of the Gorbachev Foundation, Moscow

Archive of the Italian Communist Party, Fondazione Gramsci, Rome

Archive of the Memorial Society (Memorial), Moscow and St. Petersburg

Archive of the President of Georgia, Tbilisi, Georgia

Archive of the President of the Russian Federation, Moscow

Center for Storage of Documents of Youth Organizations (Komsomol Archives), Moscow

Central Archive of Documentary Collections of Moscow

Central Archive of Public Movements of Moscow

Central Party Archive of Armenia, Yerevan

Central State Archive of Contemporary History, Tbilisi, Georgia

Cold War International History Project, Woodrow Wilson International Center for Scholars, Washington, D.C.

Hoover Institute for War, Revolution, and Peace, Stanford, California

Library of Congress, Manuscript Division, Washington, D.C.

    Averell W. Harriman Collection

    Dmitry Volkogonov Collection

National Archives, College Park, Maryland

National Security Archive, George Washington University, Washington, D.C.

Public Records Office, London

Records of East Germany in German State Archives, Berlin

Ronald Reagan Presidential Library, Simi Valley, California

Russian State Archive for Contemporary History, Moscow

Russian State Archive for Literature and Arts, Moscow

Russian State Archive for Social and Political History, Moscow

State Archive of Parties, Political Organizations, and Movements of the Azerbaijan, Baku, Azerbaijan

State Archive of the Russian Federation, Moscow

State Archives of Armenia, Yerevan, Armenia

Published Documents

Adibekov, Grant M., et al., eds. *Soveschaniia Kominforma, 1947, 1948, 1949. Dokumenti i materiali*. Moscow: ROSSPEN, 1998.

Afanasiev, E. S., V. Yu. Afiani, L. A. Velichanskaia, Z. K. Vodopianova, et al., eds. *Ideologicheskiie komiissi TsKh KPSS, 1958–1964: Dokumenti*. Introduction by Karl Eimermacher. Moscow: ROSSPEN, 1998.

Bekes, Csaba, Malcolm Byrne, and Janos Rainer, eds. *The 1956 Hungarian Revolution: A History in Documents*. Budapest: Central European University Press, 2003.

Blanton, Thomas, Peter Kornbluh, Svetlana Savranskaya, and Malcolm Byrne, eds. *Primary Source Documents for an International Conference, "The Cuban Missile Crisis: A Political Perspective after 40 Years," Palacio de Convenciones, La Habana, Cuba, October 11–13, 2002*. Unpublished.

Bordyugov, Gennady, L. Kosheleva, and L. Rogovaia, eds. *SVAG. Upravleniie propagandy i S. I. Tyulpanov. 1945–1949 godi*. Moscow: Rossiia molodaia, 1994.

Bordyugov, Gennady, Gennady Matveev, Adam Kosetski, and Andjei Packowski, eds. *SSSR-Polsha. Mekhanizmi podavleniia, 1944–1949*. Moscow: AIRO XX, 1995.

Damie, V., et al. *Komintern protiv faschizma. Dokumenti*. Moscow: Nauka, 1999.

Davidson, Apollon, Sergei Mazov, and Georgy Tsypkin. *SSSR i Afrika. 1918–1960: Dokumentirovannaia istoriia vzaimootnoshenii*. Moscow: Institute of General History, 2002.

Eimermacher, Karl, Vitali Afiani, M. Yu. Prozumenschikov, et al., eds. *Doklad N. S. Khrushcheva o kulte lichnosti Stalina na XX s'ezde KPSS. Dokumenti*. Moscow: ROSSPEN, 2002.

Fursenko, A. A., ed. *Prezidium TsK KPSS 1954–1964 Chernoviie protokolnie zapisi zasedanii. Stenogrammi. Postanovlenia*. Vol. 1. Moscow: ROSSPEN, 2003.

Khlevniuk, Oleg, et al., eds. *Politburo TsK VKP(b) i Sovet Ministrov SSSR 1945–1953*. Moscow: ROSSPEN, 2002.

Kolokolov, B. L., E. Bentsur, et al., eds. *Sovetsko-Izrailskie otnosheniia. Sbornik dokumentov*, vol. 1, 1941–1953. Moscow: Mezhdunarodnie otnoshenia, 2000.

Kovaleva, N., A. Korotkov, S. Melchin, et al., eds. *Molotov, Malenkov, Kaganovich, 1957: Stenographic Report of the June Plenum of the CC CPSU and Other Documents*. Moscow: Mezhdunarodnii Fond "Demokratiia," 1998.

Kremlevsky samosud. Sekretniie dokumenti Politburo o pisatele A. Solzhenitsyne. Moscow: Rodina, 1994.

Küsters, Hans Jürgen, and Daniel Hoffmann, eds. *Dokumente zur Deutschlandpolitik: Deutsche Einheit: Sonderedition aus den Akten des Bundeskanzleramtes 1989/90*. Munich: R. Oldenbourg Verlag, 1998.

Naumkin, V. V., ed. *Blizhnevostochnii Konflikt 1947–1956. Iz dokumentov arkhiva vneshnei politiki Rossiiskoi Federatsii*. Vols. 1–2. Moscow: Mezhdunarodnii Fond "Demokratiia," 2003.

Naumov, Vladimir, Mikhail Prozumenschikov, et al., eds. *Georgii Zhukov. Stenogramma oktiabr'skogo (1957) plenuma TsK KPSS i drugiie dokumenti*. Moscow: Mezhdunarodnii Fond "Demokratiia," 2001.

Naumov, Vladimir, and Yuri Sigachev, eds. *Lavrentii Beria. 1953: Stenogramma iulskogo plenuma TsK KPSS i drugiie dokumenti*. Moscow: Mezhdunarodnii Fond "Demokratiia," 1999.

Navratil, Jaromir, Malcolm Byrne, Peter Kornbluh, et al., eds. *The Prague Spring, 1968: A National Security Archive Documents Reader*. Budapest: CEU Press, 1998.

Relich, Simon, and Gennady Kostyrchenko, eds. *Evreiskii Antifashistskii Komitet v SSSR 1941–1948: Dokumental'naia istoriia*. Moscow: Mezhdunarodnie otnoshenniia, 1996.

Ryabev, L. D., ed. *Atomnii Projekt SSSR: Dokumenti i Materiali*, vol. 2. *Atomnaia bomba 1945–1954*. Kniga 1. Compiled by G. A. Goncharov. Sarov: RFNC-VNIIEF, 1999.

Veber, Alexander B., ed. *Soiuz mozhno bylo sokhranit. Belaia kniga. Dokumenti i fakti o politike*

M. S. Gorbacheva po reformirovaniiu i sokhraneniiu mnogonatsionalnogo gosudarstva. Moscow: Gorbachev-Fond/Aprel-85, 1995.

Volokitina, T. V., D. A. Yermakova, G. P. Murashko, et al., eds. *Tri vizita A. Y. Vyshinskogo v Bukharest (1944–1946). Dokumenti rossiiskikh arkhivov.* Moscow: ROSSPEN, 1998.

Secondary Sources

Abernethy, David B. *The Dynamics of Global Dominance: European Overseas Empires, 1415–1980.* New Haven, Conn.: Yale University Press, 2001.

Abrahamian, Evrand. *Iran between the Two Revolutions.* Princeton, N.J.: Princeton University Press, 1982.

Adamsky, Viktor B., and Yuri N. Smirnov. "Moralnaia otvetstvennost uchenikh i politicheskikh liderov v iaderniiu epokhu." In *Science and Society: History of the Soviet Atomic Project (40's–50's): Proceedings of the International Symposium at Dubna, May 14–18, 1996.* Moscow: Izdat, 1997.

——. "Soviet 50-Megaton Test in 1961." *CWIHP Bulletin,* no. 4 (Fall 1994).

Adomeit, Hannes. *Soviet Risk-Taking and Crisis Behavior: A Theoretical and Empirical Analysis.* Boston: George Allen and Unwin, 1982.

Adzhubei, Alexei. *Krusheniie Illuzii: Vremia v sobitiiakh i litsakh.* Moscow: Interbuk, 1991.

Afanasyev, S., V. Yu. Afiani, L. Velichanstaka, Z. Vodopianova, and E. Kochubei, eds. *Ideologicheskie komissii TsK KPSS 1958–1964: Dokumenti.* Moscow: ROSSPEN, 1998.

Afanasyev, Yuri, ed. *Sovetskoie obschestvo: vozniknoveniie, razvitie, istoricheskii final.* Vol. 2. Moscow: Rossiiskii gosudarstvennii gumanitarnii universitet, 1997.

Aga-Rossi, Elena, and Victor Zaslavsky. *Togliatti e Stalin. Il PCI e la politica estera staliniana negli archivi di Mosca.* Rome: Il Mulino, 1997.

Agursky, Mikhail. *Pepel Klaasa. Razryv.* Jerusalem: URA, 1996.

——. *The Third Rome: National Bolshevism in the USSR.* Boulder, Colo.: Westview, 1987.

Akhromeyev, Sergei F., and Georgi M. Kornienko. *Glazami Marshala i Diplomata. Kriticheskii Vzgliad na Vneshniuu Politiku SSSR do i posle 1985 goda.* Moscow: Mezhdunarodniie Otnosheniia, 1992.

Akinsha, Konstantin, and Grigorii Kozlov. *Beautiful Loot: The Soviet Plunder of Europe's Art Treasures.* With Sylvia Hochfield. New York: Random House, 1995.

Aksenov, Vassily. *In Search of Melancholy Baby.* New York: Random House, 1987.

Aksyutin, Yuri. *Khrushchevskaia "ottepel" i obschestvenniie nastroeniia v SSSR v 1953–1964 gg.* Moscow: ROSSPEN, 2004.

——. "Why Stalin Chose Confrontation Rather Than Cooperation with the Wartime Allies after the Victory? Some Socio-Psychological Aspects of the Cold War Origins." Paper presented at conference "The New Evidence on the Cold War." Moscow, January 12–15, 1993.

Aksyutin, Yuri, and Alexandr Pyzhikov. "O podgotovke zakrytogo doklada N. S. Khrushcheva XX s'ezdu KPSS v svete novikh dokumentov." *Novaia i noveishaia istoriia* 2 (2002).

Alexandrov-Agentov, Alexander M. *Ot Kollontai do Gorbacheva. Vospominaniia.* Moscow: Mezhdunarodniie otnosheniia, 1994.

Alexeyeva, Ludmilla, and Paul Goldberg. *The Thaw Generation: Coming of Age in the Post-Stalin Era.* Pittsburgh: University of Pittsburgh Press, 1990.

Alperovitz, Gar. *Atomic Diplomacy: Hiroshima and Potsdam—The Use of the Atomic Bomb and the American Confrontation with Soviet Power.* Boulder, Colo.: Pluto Press, 1994.

Anderson, Richard D., Jr. *Public Politics in an Authoritarian State: Making Foreign Policy during the Brezhnev Years.* Ithaca, N.Y.: Cornell University Press, 1993.

Andrew, Christopher, and Oleg Gordievsky. *Comrade Kryuchkov's Instructions: Top Secret Files on KGB Foreign Operations, 1975–1985.* Stanford, Calif.: Stanford University Press, 1994.

Andrew, Christopher, and Vasily Mitrokhin. *The Sword and the Shield: The Mitrokhin Archive and the Secret History of the KGB.* New York: Basic Books, 1999.

Arbatov, Georgy. *The System: An Insider's Life in Soviet Politics.* New York: Times Books, 1992.

——. *Zatianuvsheiesia vizdorovleniie (1953–1985). Svidetelstvo sovremennika.* Moscow: Mezhdunarodnie otnosheniia, 1991.

Badstübner, Rolf, and Wilfried Loth, eds. *Wilhelm Pieck: Aufzeichnungen zur Deutschlandpolitik, 1945–1953.* Berlin: Akademie-Verlag, 1994.

Baev, Jordan. "Bulgaria and the Political Crises in Czechoslovakia (1968) and Poland (1980/81)." *CWIHP Bulletin,* no. 11 (Winter 1998).

Bahr, Egon. *Zu meiner Zeit.* Munich: Carl Blessing Verlag, 1996.

Baibakov, Nikolai K. *Ot Stalina do Eltsina.* Moscow: GazOil Press, 1998.

Bajanov, Evgeny. "Assessing Politics of the Korean War, 1949–1951." *CWIHP Bulletin,* nos. 6–7 (Winter 1995/96).

Baker, James A., III. *The Politics of Diplomacy: Revolution, War, and Peace, 1989–1992.* With Thomas M. DeFrank. New York: G. P. Putnam's, 1995.

Barber, John, and Mark Harrison. *The Soviet Home Front, 1941–1945: A Social and Economic History of the USSR in World War II.* London: Longman, 1991.

Baring, Arnulf. *Machtwechsel: Die Ära Brandt-Scheel.* Stuttgart: Deutsche Verlags-Anstalt, 1982.

Barsukov, Nikolai. "The Rise to Power." In *Nikita Khrushchev: Fresh Perspectives on the Last Communist,* edited by William Taubman, Sergei Khrushchev, and Abbott Gleason. New Haven, Conn.: Yale University Press, 2000.

Batygin, G. S., and C. F. Yarmoliuk. *Rossiiskaia Sotsiologiia Shestidesiatikh Godov v Vospominaniiakh i Dokumentakh.* St. Petersburg: Russian Christian Humanitarian Institute, 1999.

Bearden, Milton, and James Risen. *The Main Enemy: The CIA's Final Showdown with the KGB.* New York: Random House, 2003.

Beevor, Antony. *The Fall of Berlin 1945.* New York: Viking, 2002.

Bennett, Andrew. *Condemned to Repetition? The Rise, Fall, and the Reprise of Soviet Russian Military Interventionism, 1973–1996.* Cambridge, Mass.: Massachusetts Institute of Technology Press, 1999.

Beria, Sergo. *Beria, My Father: Inside Stalin's Kremlin.* Edited by Françoise Thom. London: Duckworth, 2001.

Beschloss, Michael. *The Crisis Years: Kennedy and Khrushchev, 1960–1963.* New York: Edward Burlinghame Books, 1991.

Bezymensky, Lev. "Kto i kak gotovil v Germanii den' Iks." *Novoe Vremya* 27 (July 1953).

Bischof, Günter. *Austria in the First Cold War, 1945–55*. New York: St. Martin's, 1999.

Bischof, Günter, and Saki Dockrill, eds. *Cold War Respite: The Geneva Summit of 1955*. Baton Rouge: Louisiana State University, 2000.

Blight, James G., Bruce J. Allyn, and David A. Welch. *Cuba on the Brink: Castro, the Missile Crisis, and the Soviet Collapse*. New York: Pantheon Books, 1993.

——. "Kramer vs. Kramer." *CWIHP Bulletin*, no. 3 (Fall 1993).

Blight, James G., and Philip Brenner. *Sad and Luminous Days: Cuba's Struggle with the Superpowers after the Missile Crisis*. New York: Rowman and Littlefield, 2002.

Bobkov, Philip. *KGB i Vlast*. Moscow: Veteran MP, 1995.

Bokov, Fedor. *Vesna Pobedy*. Moscow: Mysl, 1985.

Boldin, Valery. *Krusheniie pedestala: Shtrikhi k portretu M. S. Gorbacheva*. Moscow: Respublika, 1995.

Bonwetsch, Bernd, and Gennadij Bordjugov. "Stalin und die SBZ: Ein Besuch der SED Führung in Moskau vom 30. Januar–7. Februar 1947." *Vierteljahrshefte für Zeitgeschichte* 42, no. 2 (1994): 279–303.

Bordiugov, Gennady. *Chrezvychainii vek Rossiiskoi istorii: chetyre fragmenta*. St. Petersburg: Dmitri Bulanin, 2004.

Boterbloem, Kees. *The Life and Times of Andrei Zhdanov, 1896–1948*. Montreal: McGill-Queen's University Press, 2004.

Bovin, Alexander. *XX vek kak zhizn. Vospominaniia*. Moscow: Zakharov, 2003.

Brandenberger, David. *National Bolshevism: Stalinist Mass Culture and the Formation of Modern Russian National Identity, 1931–1956*. Cambridge, Mass.: Harvard University Press, 2002.

Brandenberger, D. L., and A. M. Dubrovsky. " 'The People Need a Tsar': The Emergence of National Bolshevism as Stalinist Ideology, 1931–1941." *Europe-Asia Studies* 50 (1998).

Brandt, Willy. *Erinnerungen*. Berlin: Siedler Verlag, 1989.

Brenner, Philip, and James G. Blight. "Cuba, 1962: The Crisis in Cuban-Soviet Relations: Fidel Castro's Secret 1968 Speech." *CWIHP Bulletin*, no. 5 (Spring 1995).

Brent, Jonathan, and Vladimir P. Naumov. *Stalin's Last Crime: The Plot against the Jewish Doctors, 1948–1953*. New York: HarperCollins, 2003.

Brezhneva, Luba. *The World I Left Behind: Pieces of the Past*. New York: Random House, 1995.

Brodsky, Joseph. *On Grief and Reason: Essays*. New York: Farrar, Straus, Giroux, 1995.

Brooks, Jeffrey. "Stalin's Ghost: Cold War Culture and the U.S.-Soviet Relations." In *After Stalin's Death: The Cold War as International History*, edited by Klaus Larres and Kenneth Osgood. New York: Rowman and Littlefield, 2003.

——. *Thank You, Comrade Stalin! Soviet Public Culture from Revolution to Cold War*. Princeton, N.J.: Princeton University Press, 2000.

Brooks, Stephen G., and William C. Wohlforth. "Economic Constraints and the End of the Cold War." In *Cold War Endgame: Oral History, Analysis, Debates*, edited by William C. Wohlforth. University Park: Pennsylvania State University Press, 2003.

Brown, Archie. *The Gorbachev Factor*. Oxford: Oxford University Press, 1996.

Brudny, Itzhak. *Reinventing Russia: Russian Nationalism and the Soviet State, 1953–1991*. Cambridge, Mass.: Harvard University Press, 1998.

Brumberg, Abraham, ed. *Russia under Khrushchev: An Anthology from Problems of Communism*. New York: Praeger, 1962.

Brutents, Karen. *Nesbyvsheesia. Neravnodushnie zametki o perestroika*. Moscow: Mezhdunarodniie otnosheniia, 2005.

———. *Tridtsat let na staroi ploschadi*. Moscow: Mezhdunarodniie otnosheniia, 1998.

Bryld, Mette, and Erik Kulavig, eds. *Soviet Civilization between Past and Present*. Viborg, Denmark: Odense University Press, 1998.

Brzezinski, Zbigniew. *The Grand Failure: The Birth and Death of Communism in the Twentieth Century*. London: Macdonald Books, 1989.

———. *Power and Principle: Memoirs of the National Security Advisor, 1977–1981*. New York: Farrar, Straus, Giroux, 1983.

Bukovsky, Vladimir. *To Build a Castle: My Life as a Dissenter*. New York: Viking Press, 1977.

Bundy, McGeorge. *Danger and Survival*. New York: Random House, 1988.

Bunn, George. *Arms Control by Committee: Managing Negotiations with the Russians*. Stanford, Calif.: Stanford University Press, 1992.

Burlatsky, Fedor. *Khrushchev and the First Russian Spring: The Era of Khrushchev through the Eyes of His Advisor*. London: Weidenfeld and Nicolson, 1991.

———. *Vozhdi i sovetniki. O Khruschehve, Andropove i ne tolko o nikh*. Moscow: Politizdat, 1990.

Burr, William. "Eisenhower's Search for Flexibility: Strategy and Diplomacy during the Berlin Crisis, 1958–1960." Paper presented at the conference "The Second Berlin Crisis." Woodrow Wilson Center for International Scholars, Washington, D.C., May 1993.

———, ed. *The Kissinger Transcripts: The Top Secret Talks with Beijing and Moscow*. New York: New Press, 1998.

Burr, William, and Jeffrey T. Richelson. "A Chinese Puzzle." *Bulletin of Atomic Scientists* 53, no. 4 (July–August 1997).

———. "Whether to 'Strangle the Baby in the Cradle': The United States and the Chinese Nuclear Program, 1960–1964." *International Security* 3 (Winter 2000–2001).

Bush, George, and Brent Scowcroft. *A World Transformed*. New York: Alfred A. Knopf, 1998.

Bushnell, John. "The 'New Soviet Man' Turns Pessimist." In *The Soviet Union since Stalin*, edited by Stephen F. Cohen, Alexander Rabinowitch, and Robert Sharlet. Bloomington: Indiana University Press, 1980.

Buwalda, Petrus. *They Did Not Dwell Alone: Jewish Immigration from the Soviet Union, 1967–1990*. Washington, D.C.: Woodrow Wilson Center Press, 1997.

Bystrova, I. V. "Sovetskii voennii potentsial perioda "kholodnoi voini" v amerikanskikh otsenkakh." *Otechestvennaia istoriia* 2 (2004).

———. "Voienno-promishlennii kompleks SSSR v 1920-e–1980-egg.: ekonomicheskie aspekti razvitia." In *Ekonomicheskaia istoriia Ezhegodnik*, edited by L. I. Borodkin and Yu. A. Petrov. Moscow: ROSSPEN, 2003.

Cahn, Anne. *Killing Detente: The Right Attacks the CIA*. University Park: Pennsylvania State University Press, 1998.

Carlisle, Olga Andreyev. "Solzhenitsyn and the Secret Circle." In *Under the New Sky: A Reunion with Russia*, by Olga Andreyev Carlisle. New York: Ticknor and Fields, 1993.

Catudal, Honore. *Kennedy and the Berlin Wall Crisis: A Case Study of the U.S. Decision-Making.* Berlin: Berlin-Verlag, 1980.

Caute, David. *The Dancer Defects: The Struggle for Cultural Supremacy during the Cold War.* New York: Oxford University Press, 2003.

Chang, Gordon H. *Friends and Enemies: The United States, China, and the Soviet Union, 1948–1972.* Stanford, Calif.: Stanford University Press, 1990.

Chaqueri, Cosroe. *The Soviet Socialist Republic of Iran, 1920–1921: Birth of the Trauma.* Pittsburgh: University of Pittsburgh Press, 1995.

Chazov, Evgeni. *Zdorovie i Vlast: Vospominaniia 'kremlyovskogo vracha.* Moscow: Novosti, 1992.

Chen Jian. "Beijing and the Hungarian Crisis of 1956." Paper presented at the conference "The Soviet Union, Germany, and the Cold War: New Evidence from Eastern Archives." Essen, Germany, June 28–30, 1994.

———. *China's Road to the Korean War: The Making of the Sino-American Confrontation.* New York: Columbia University Press, 1994.

———. *Mao's China and the Cold War.* Chapel Hill: University of North Carolina Press, 2001.

Chen Jian, and David L. Wilson. "All Under the Heaven Is Great Chaos: Beijing, the Sino-Soviet Border Clashes, and the Turn toward Sino-American Rapprochement, 1968–1969." *CWIHP Bulletin*, no. 11 (Winter 1998).

Cherkashin, Nikolai. *Povsednevnaia zhizn rossiiskikh podvodnikov.* Moscow: Molodaia Gvardiia, 2000.

Chernyaev, Anatoly S. "Fenomen Gorbacheva v kontekste liderstva." *Mezhdunarodnaia zhizn* 7 (1993).

———. *Moia zhizn i moie vremia.* Moscow: Mezhdunarodniie otnosheniia, 1995.

———. *My Six Years with Gorbachev.* Translated and edited by Robert D. English and Elizabeth Tucker. University Park: Pennsylvania State University Press, 2000.

———. *1991 god: Dnevnik pomoshnika prezidenta SSSR.* Moscow: Terra-Respublika, 1997.

———. *Shest Let s Gorbachevim. Po dnevnikovim Zapisiam.* Moscow: Progress-Kultura, 1993.

Chernyaev, A., with V. Medvedev, A. Veber, eds. *V Politbiuro TsK KPSS . . . Po zapisiam, Anatolia Chernyaeva, Vadima Medvedeva, Georgia Shakhnazarova (1985–1991).* Moscow: Gorbachev Fond, Alpina Business Books, 2006.

Chipman, Donald. "Admiral Gorshkov and the Soviet Navy." <http://www.airpower .maxwell.af.mil/airchronicles/aureview/1982/jul-aug/chipman.html>.

Chuev, Felix. *Kaganovich, Shepilov.* Moscow: Olma Press, 2001.

———. *Molotov Remembers. Iz dnevnika F. Chueva.* Moscow: Terra, 1991.

———. *Sto sorok besed s Molotovim.* Moscow: Moskovskii rabochii, 1990.

Chukovskaia, Lydia. *Zapiski ob Anne Akhmatovoi.* Vol. 2. Moscow: Soglasiie, 1997.

Cohen, Stephen F. *Rethinking the Soviet Experience: Politics and History since 1917.* New York: Oxford University Press, 1985.

Connor, Walter D. "Soviet Society, Public Attitudes, and the Perils of Gorbachev's Reforms." *Journal of Cold War Studies* 5, no. 5 (2003).

Conze, Eckart. "No Way Back to Potsdam: The Adenauer Government and the Geneva

Summit." In *Cold War Respite: The Geneva Summit of 1955*, edited by Günter Bischof and Saki Dockrill. Baton Rouge: Louisiana State University, 2000.

Cordovez, Diego, and Selig S. Harrison. *Out of Afghanistan: The Inside Story of the Soviet Withdrawal*. New York: Oxford University Press, 1995.

Costigliola, Frank. " 'I Had Come as a Friend': Emotion, Culture, and Ambiguity in the Formation of the Cold War." *Cold War History* (August 2000).

——. " 'Like Animals or Worse': Narratives of Culture and Emotion by U.S. and British POWs and Airmen behind Soviet Lines, 1944–1945." *Diplomatic History* 28 (November 2004).

Creuzberger, Stefan. *Die sowjetische Besatzungsmacht und das politische System der SBZ*. Cologne-Weimar: Böhlau, 1996.

Crile, George. *Charlie Wilson's War: The Extraordinary Story of the Largest Covert Operation in History*. New York: Atlantic Monthly, 2003.

Cristescu, C. "Ianuarie 1951: Stalin decide inarmarea Romanei." *Magazin Istoric* 10 (Bucharest) (1995).

Dedkov, Igor. " 'Kak trudno daiutsia iniie dni': Iz dnevnikovikh zapisei 1953–1974." *Novy Mir* 4 (1996).

Derluguian, Georgy. "A Tale of Two Cities." *New Left Review* 3 (May/June 2000).

Detinov, Nikolai, and Alexander Savelyev. *The Big Five: Arms Control Decision-Making in the Soviet Union*. Westport, Conn.: Praeger, 1995.

Dijk, Ruud van. "The Bankruptcy of Stalin's German Policy, 1949–1953." Paper presented at the conference "Stalin and the Cold War." Yale University, New Haven, Conn., September 24–25, 1999.

Dimitrov, Georgi. *The Diary of Georgi Dimitrov, 1933–1949*. Introduced and edited by Ivo Banac. New Haven, Conn.: Yale University Press, 2003.

Djilas, Milovan. *Conversations with Stalin*. Translated by Michael B. Petrovich. New York: Harcourt, Brace and World, 1962.

Dobrenko, Evgeny. *The Making of the State Writer: Social and Aesthetic Origins of Soviet Literary Culture*. Stanford, Calif.: Stanford University Press, 2001.

Dobrynin, Anatoly. *In Confidence: Moscow's Ambassador to America's Six Cold War Presidents (1962–1986)*. New York: Random House, 1995.

——. *Sugubo doveritelno. Posol v Vashingtone pri shesti prezidentakh SShA (1962–1986 gg.)*. Moscow: Avtor, 1997.

Dockrill, Saki. "The Eden Plan and European Security." In *Cold War Respite: The Geneva Summit of 1955*, edited by Günter Bischof and Saki Dockrill. Baton Rouge: Louisiana State University, 2000.

Dudziak, Mary. *Cold War Civil Rights: Race and the Image of American Democracy*. Princeton, N.J.: Princeton University Press, 2000.

Duiker, William J. *Ho Chi Minh*. New York: Hyperion, 2000.

Dunlop, John B. *New Russian Revolutionaries*. Belmont, Mass.: Nordland, 1976.

——. *The Rise of Russia and the Fall of the Soviet Empire*. Princeton, N.J.: Princeton University Press, 1995.

Duverger, Maurice, ed. *Le Concept d'Empire*. Paris: Presses Universitaires de France, 1980.

Ehrenburg, Ilya. *Liudi, godi, zhizn*. Vol. 7 in *Sobraniie sochinenii v vosmi tomakh*. Moscow: Khudozhestvennaia literatura, 2000.

Eimontova, R. G. "Iz Dnevnikov Sergeia Sergeevicha Dmitrieva." *Otechestvennaia istoriia* 3–6 (1999), 1–6 (2000).

Eisenberg, Carolyn. *Drawing the Line: The American Decision to Divide Germany, 1944–1949*. Cambridge: Cambridge University Press, 1996.

———. "The Old Cold War." Review of *No Exit: America and the German Problem, 1943–1954*, by James McAllister. *Diplomatic History* 28, no. 5 (November 2004).

Elizavetin, A. "Peregovori Kosygina i Chou Enlaia v Pekinskom Aeroportu." *Problemi Dalnego Vostoka* 1 (1993).

Ellman, Michael, and Vladimir Kantorovich. "The Collapse of the Soviet System and the Memoir Literature." *Europe-Asia Studies* 49 (March 1997).

———. *The Destruction of the Soviet Economic System: An Insider's History*. New York: M. E. Sharpe, 1998.

"The End of the Cold War in Europe, 1989: 'New Thinking' and New Evidence." Transcript of the Proceedings of the Musgrove Conference on the Openness in Russia and Eastern Europe Project, Musgrove Plantation, St. Simon's Island, Ga., May 1–3, 1998, prepared by Svetlana Savranskaya under the auspices of the National Security Archive, George Washington University.

Engerman, David C. "The Romance of Economic Development and New Histories of the Cold War." *Diplomatic History* 28, no. 1 (January 2004).

English, Robert D. "The Road(s) Not Taken: Causality and Contingency in Analysis of the Cold War's End." In *Cold War Endgame: Oral History, Analysis, Debates*, edited by William C. Wohlforth. University Park: Pennsylvania State University Press, 2003.

———. *Russia and the Idea of the West: Gorbachev, Intellectuals, and the End of the Cold War*. New York: Columbia University Press, 2000.

———. "The Sociology of New Thinking: Elites, Identity Change, and the End of the Cold War." *Journal of Cold War Studies* 7, no. 2 (Spring 2005).

———. "Sources, Methods, and Competing Perspectives on the End of the Cold War." *Diplomatic History* 23, no. 2 (Spring 1997).

Erdmann, Andrew P. N. " 'War No Longer Has Any Logic Whatever': Dwight D. Eisenhower and the Thermonuclear Revolution." In *Cold War Statesmen Confront the Bomb: Nuclear Diplomacy since 1945*, edited by John Lewis Gaddis et al. New York: Oxford University Press, 1999.

Erickson, John. "Soviet War Losses: Calculations and Controversies." In *Barbarossa: The Axis and the Allies*, edited by J. Erickson and D. Dilks. Edinburgh: Edinburgh University Press, 1994.

Evangelista, Matthew. "Soviet Scientists and Nuclear Testing, 1954–1963." Paper presented at the conference "The New Evidence on the Cold War." Moscow, January 12–15, 1993.

———. *Unarmed Forces: The Transnational Movement to End the Cold War*. Ithaca, N.Y.: Cornell University Press, 1999.

Falin, Valentin. *Bez Skidok na obstoiatelstva. Politicheskiie vospominania*. Moscow: Respublika-Sovremennik, 1999.

——. *Politische Erinnerungen*. Translated from Russian into German by Heddy Pross-Weerth. Munich: Drömer Knaur, 1993.

Faraday, George. *Revolt of the Filmmakers: The Struggle for Artistic Autonomy and the Fall of the Soviet Film Industry*. University Park: Pennsylvania State University Press, 2000.

Farber, David. *The Age of Great Dreams: America in the 1960s*. New York: Hill and Wang, 1994.

——. *Taken Hostage: The Iran Hostage Crisis and America's First Encounter with Radical Islam*. Princeton, N.J.: Princeton University Press, 2004.

Fatemi, Faramarz S. *The USSR in Iran*. Cranbury, N.J.: A. S. Barnes, 1980.

Ferguson, Niall. *Empire: The Rise and Demise of the British World Order and the Lessons for Global Power*. New York: Basic Books, 2003.

Filitov, Alexei M. "SSSR i Germanskii vopros: povorotniie punkti (1941–1961)." In *Kholodnaia voina 1945–1963: Istorichestkaia retrospective*, edited by Natalia Yegorova and Alexandr Chubarian. Moscow: Olma Press, 2003.

Fischer, Ben B. *A Cold War Conundrum: The 1983 Soviet War Scare*. An Intelligence Monograph. Langley, Va.: Center for the Study of Intelligence, September 1997.

Fomin, V. I., ed. *Kinematograf ottepeli. Dokumenti i svidetelstva*. Moscow: Materik-Alfa, 1998.

FitzGerald, Frances. *Way Out There in the Blue: Reagan, Star Wars, and the End of the Cold War*. New York: Simon and Schuster, 2000.

Fitzpatrick, Sheila, Alexander Rabinowitch, and Richard Stites, eds. *Russia in the Era of Nep: Explorations in Soviet Society and Culture*. Bloomington: Indiana University Press, 1991.

Frankel, Edith Rogovin. *"Novy Mir": A Case Study in the Politics of Literature, 1952–1958*. New York: Cambridge University Press, 1981.

Friedberg, Maurice. *A Decade of Euphoria: Western Literature in Post-Stalin Russia, 1954–1964*. Bloomington: Indiana University Press, 1977.

Fromkin, David. *A Peace to End All Peace: The Fall of the Ottoman Empire and the Creation of the Modern Middle East*. New York: Owl Books, 2001.

Fülop-Miller, Réné. *The Mind and Face of Bolshevism: An Examination of Cultural Life in the Soviet Union*. Translated by F. S. Flint and D. F. Tait. New York: Harper and Row, 1965.

Furman, Dmitry. "Fenomen Gorbacheva." *Svobodnaia Misl* 11 (Moscow) (1995).

Fursenko, A. A. "Neobychnaia sudba razvedchika G. N. Bolshakova." *Novaia i noveishaia istoriia* 4 (2005).

——. *Rossiia i mezhdunarodniie krizisi. Seredina xx veka*. Moscow: Nauka, 2006.

Fursenko, A. A., et al., eds. *Prezidium TsK KPSS 1954–1964 Chernoviie protokolnie zapisi zasedanii. Stenogrammi. Postanovlenia*. Vol. 1. Moscow: ROSSPEN, 2003.

Fursenko, Alexander, and Timothy Naftali. *Khrushchev's Cold War: The Inside Story of an American Adversary*. New York: W. W. Norton, 2006.

——. *"One Hell of a Gamble": Khrushchev, Castro, and Kennedy, 1958–1964*. New York: W. W. Norton, 1997.

Gaddis, John Lewis. "International Relations Theory and the End of the Cold War." *International Security* 17 (Winter 1992/93).

——. "The Long Peace: Elements of Stability in the Postwar International System." *International Security* 10, no. 4 (Spring 1986).

——. *We Now Know: Rethinking Cold War History.* New York: Oxford University Press, 1996.

Gaddis, John Lewis, Philip H. Gordon, Ernest R. May, and Jonathan Rosenberg, eds. *Cold War Statesmen Confront the Bomb: Nuclear Diplomacy since 1945.* New York: Oxford University Press, 1999.

Gai, David, and Vladimir Snegirev. "Vtorzheniie." *Znamia* 3–4 (Moscow) (March–April 1991).

Gaidar, Yegor. *Gibel imperii. Uroki dlia sovremennoi Rossii.* Moscow: ROSSPEN, 2006.

Gaiduk, Ilya V. *Confronting Vietnam: Soviet Policy toward the Indochina Conflict, 1954–1963.* Stanford, Calif.: Stanford University Press, 2003.

——. *The Soviet Union and the Vietnam War.* Chicago: Ivan R. Dee, 1996.

Gaiduk, Ilya, Natalia Yegorova, and Alexander Chubarian, eds. *Stalin i kholodnaia voina.* Moscow: Institute of General History, 1998.

Galay, Nikolai. "Soviet Youth and the Army." *Bulletin of the Institute for the Study of the USSR* (Munich) (February 1963).

Gankovsky, Yuri. "Kto, gde, kogda prinial resheniie o vvode sovetskikh voisk v Afghanistan?" *Azia i Afrika segodnia* 5 (1994).

Gardner, Lloyd C. *Spheres of Influence: The Great Powers Partition Europe, from Munich to Yalta.* Chicago: Ivan R. Dee, 1993.

Gareev, Makhmut. "Pochemu i kak mi voshli v Afghanistan." *Orientir* 6 (Moscow) (1994).

Garthoff, Raymond. "Berlin 1961: The Record Corrected." *Foreign Policy* 84 (Fall 1991).

——. *Détente and Confrontation: American-Soviet Relations from Nixon to Reagan.* Rev. ed. Washington, D.C.: Brookings Institution Press, 1994.

——. *The Great Transition: American-Soviet Relations and the End of the Cold War.* Washington, D.C.: Brookings Institution Press, 1994.

——. *A Journey through the Cold War: A Memoir of Containment and Coexistence.* Washington, D.C.: Brookings Institution Press, 2001.

——. "The KGB Reports to Gorbachev." *Intelligence and National Security* 11, no. 2 (April 1996).

——. *Reflections on the Cuban Missile Crisis.* Washington, D.C.: Brookings Institution, 1987.

Gates, Robert M. *From the Shadows: The Ultimate Insider's Story of Five Presidents and How They Won the Cold War.* New York: Simon and Schuster, 1996.

Gelman, Harry. *The Brezhnev Politburo and the Decline of Détente.* Ithaca, N.Y.: Cornell University Press, 1984.

Gerovitch, Slava. *From Newspeak to Cyberspeak: A History of Soviet Cybernetics.* Boston: Massachusetts Institute of Technology Press, 2002.

Gibiansky, Leonid. "Ideia balkanskogo ob'edineniia i plani eie osuschestvleniia v 40-t godi XX veka." *Voprosi istorii* 11–12 (2001).

——. "Sovetskiie tseli v Vostochnoi Evrope v kontse vtoroi mirovoi voiny i v perviie poslevoennie gody: spori v istoriografii i problemy izucheniia istochnikov." *Russian History—Histoire Russe* 29, nos. 2–4 (2002): 197–215.

——. "The Soviet Bloc and the Initial Stage of the Cold War: Archival Documents on Stalin's Meetings with Communist Leaders of Yugoslavia and Bulgaria, 1946–1948." *CWIHP Bulletin,* no. 10 (March 1998).

——. "Sowjetisierung Osteuropas—Character und Typologie." In *Sowjetisierung und Eigenständigkeit in der SBZ/DDR (1945–1953)*, edited by Michael Lemke. Cologne: Böhlau, 1999.

——. "Stalin and Triest Confrontation of 1945: Behind the Scene of the First Cold War International Crisis." In *Stalin i kholodnaia voina*, edited by Ilya Gaiduk, Natalia Yegorova and Alexander Chubarian. Moscow: Institut vseobshchei istorii, 1998.

Ginor, Isabella. " 'Under the Yellow Arab Helmet Gleamed Blue Russian Eyes': Operation Kavkaz and the War of Attrition." *Cold War History* 1 (October 2002).

Glad, Betty, and Eric Shiraev, eds. *The Russian Transformation: Political, Sociological, and Psychological Aspects*. New York: St. Martin's Press, 1999.

Gleijeses, Piero. *Conflicting Missions: Havana, Washington, and Africa, 1959–1976*. Chapel Hill: University of North Carolina Press, 2002.

——. "Havana's Policy in Africa, 1959–1976: New Evidence from Cuban Archives." *CWIHP Bulletin*, nos. 8–9 (Winter 1996/97).

Gluchowski, L. W. "Khrushchev, Gomulka, and the 'Polish October.' " *CWIHP Bulletin*, no. 5 (Spring 1995).

——. *The Soviet-Polish Confrontation of October, 1956: The Situation in the Polish Internal Security Corps*. With Edward Nalepa. CWIHP working paper no. 17 (1997).

Goedde, Petra. *GIs and Germans: Culture, Gender, and Foreign Relations, 1945–1949*. New Haven, Conn.: Yale University Press, 2003.

Goldberg, J. J. *Jewish Power: Inside the American Jewish Establishment*. Reading, Mass: Addison-Wesley, 1996.

Goldgeier, James M. *Leadership Style and Soviet Foreign Policy*. Baltimore: Johns Hopkins University Press, 1994.

Golovanov, Yaroslav. "Beseda na Dache." *Komsomolskaya Pravda*, 30 September 1989.

Goncharov, German A. "Khronologiia osnovnikh sobitii istorii sozdaniia vodorodnoi bombi v SSSR i SShA." In *Science and Society: History of the Soviet Atomic Project (40's–50's): Proceedings of the International Symposium at Dubna, May 14–18, 1996*. Moscow: Izdat, 1997.

Goncharov, Sergei N., John W. Lewis, and Xue Litai. *Uncertain Partners: Stalin, Mao, and the Korean War*. Stanford, Calif.: Stanford University Press, 1993.

Goncharov, Sergei N., and Victor Usov, eds. "Peregovori A. N. Kosygina i Chou Enlaia v Pekinskom Aeroportu." *Problemi Dalnego Vostoka* 5 (Moscow) (1992).

Gorbachev, Mikhail. "Andropov: Novii generalnii sekretar deistvuiet." *Svobodnaia Mysl* 11 (1995).

——. *Avgustovskii putch: Prichiny i Sledstviya*. Moscow: Novosti, 1991.

——. *Dekabr-91: Moya pozitsiia*. Moscow: Novosti, 1992.

——. *Godi Trudnikh Reshenii*. Moscow: Alfa-Print, 1993.

——. *On My Country and the World*. New York: Columbia University Press, 2000.

——. *Perestroika i novoie myshlenie dlia nashei strani i dlia vsego mira*. Moscow: Politizdat, 1987.

——. *Political Report of the CPSU Central Committee to the 27th Party Congress*. Moscow: Novosti, 1986.

——. *Zhizn i reformi*. 2 vols. Moscow: Novosti, 1995.

Gorbachev, Mikhail, and Zdenek Mlynar. *Conversations with Gorbachev.* Introduction by Archie Brown. New York: Columbia University Press, 2001.

———. "Dialog o perestroike, 'Prazhskoi vesne' i o sotsializme." Unpublished manuscript, 1994. Courtesy of Robert D. English.

Gorlizki, Yoram, and Oleg Khlevniuk. *Cold Peace: Stalin and the Soviet Ruling Circle, 1945–1953.* New York: Oxford University Press, 2004.

Gorodnitsky, Alexandr. "Vos'memsia za ruki, druzia." *Dossier of the Literary Gazette: Bards,* no. 11 (1992).

Gould-Davies, Nigel. "Rethinking the Role of Ideology in International Politics during the Cold War." *Journal of Cold War Studies* 1 (Winter 1999).

Grachev, Andrei. *Dalshe bez menya. Ukhod Prezidenta.* Moscow: Progress: Kultura, 1994.

———. *Gorbachev.* Moscow: Vagrius, 2001.

———. *Kremlevskaia khronika.* Moscow: EKSMO, 1994.

Granville, Johanna. *The First Domino: International Decision Making during the Hungarian Crisis of 1956.* College Station: Texas A&M University Press, 2004.

———. "Tito and the 'Nagy Affair.'" *East European Quarterly* 32, no. 1 (1998).

Gray, Colyn S. "The Most Dangerous Decade: Historic Mission, Legitimacy, and Dynamics of the Soviet Empire in the 1980s." *Orbis* 25, no. 1 (Spring 1981).

Greenstein, Fred I. "Reagan and Gorbachev: What Difference Did They Make?" In *Retrospective on the End of the Cold War,* edited by William Wohlforth. Baltimore: Johns Hopkins University Press, 1996.

Gribkov, Anatoly I. "Doktrina Brezhneva i pol'skii krizis nachala 80-kh godov." *Voenno-istoricheskii zhurnal* 9 (1992).

Gribkov, A., and W. Smith. *Operation Anadyr: U.S. and Soviet Generals Recount the Cuban Missile Crisis.* Chicago: Edition q, 1994.

Grigorenko, Petr. *V podpolie mozhno vstretit tolko kris.* Moscow: Zvenia, 1997.

Grinevsky, Oleg. *Tysiacha i odin den Nikity Sergeevicha.* Moscow: Vagrius, 1998.

———. "Understanding the End of the Cold War, 1980–1987." Provisional transcript of Oral History Conference, Brown University, May 7–10, 1998. Translated and transcribed by Jeffrey W. Dillon. Edited by Nina Tannenwald.

Griscom, Robert. "Report on Soviet Youth." *Ladies Home Journal,* February 1957.

Gromov, Evgenii. *Stalin: Vlast i Iskusstvo.* Moscow: Respublika, 1998.

Gromyko, Anatoly. *Andrei Gromyko v labirintakh Kremlia: Vospominaniia i razmyshleniia syna.* Moscow: IPO Avtor, 1997.

———. *Pamyatnoe.* 2 vols. Moscow: Gospolitizdat, 1988.

Grushin, Boris. *Chetyre zhizni Rossii v zerkale oprosov obshchestvennogo mneniia. Zhizn 2-ia. Epokha Brezhneva (Chast 2).* Moscow: Progress-Traditsiia, 2006.

Gudkov, Lev. *Negativnaia identichnost. Ocherki, 1997–2002.* Moscow: Novoie literaturnoie obozreniie—VTSIOM-A, 2004.

———. "Otnosheniie k SShA v Rossii i problema antiamerikanizma." *Russian Public Opinion Monitor* 58, no. 2 (2002).

Guerra, Adriano. *Urss. Perché è crollata. Analisi sulla fine di un impero.* Rome: Editori Riuniti, 2001.

Haftendorn, Helga. *Security and Détente: Conflicting Priorities in German Foreign Policy.* New York: Praeger, 1985.

Hanhimäki, Jussi. *The Flawed Architect: Henry Kissinger and American Foreign Policy.* New York: Oxford University Press, 2004.

Hansen, James. *Correlation of Forces: Four Decades of Soviet Military Development.* New York: Praeger, 1987.

———. "Soviet Deception in the Cuban Missile Crisis." *Studies of Intelligence* 46, no. 1 (2002).

Hanson, Philip. *The Rise and Fall of the Soviet Economy.* London: Pearson Education, 2003.

Harriman, Averell. *Special Envoy to Churchill and Stalin, 1941–46.* New York: Random House, 1975.

Harrison, Hope. *Driving the Soviets Up the Wall: Soviet-East German Relations, 1953–1961.* Princeton, N.J.: Princeton University Press, 2003.

Hasanli, Jamil P. *The Place Where the Cold War Began: Southern Azerbaijan, 1945–1946.* Baku: Muterjim, 1999.

———. "Soviet Policy in the Iranian Azerbaijan, 1945–1946: The First Crisis of the Cold War." Paper presented at the international conference "Georgia, Armenia, and Azerbaijan in the Cold War: New Archival Evidence." Tsinandali, Georgia, July 8–9, 2002.

———. *SSSR-Turtsiia: Poligon kholodnoi voiny.* Baku: Adilogli, 2005.

———. *Yuzhnii Azerbaijan. Nachalo kholodnoi voini.* Baku: Adilogli, 2003.

Hasegawa, Tsuyoshi. *The Northern Territories Dispute and Russo-Japanese Relations.* Vol. 1 of *Between War and Peace, 1697–1985.* Research Series no. 97. Berkeley: University of California, 1998.

———. *Racing the Enemy: Stalin, Truman, and the Surrender of Japan.* Cambridge, Mass.: Harvard University Press, 2005.

Haslam, Jonathan. *The Soviet Union and the Struggle for Collective Security in Europe, 1933–39.* London: Macmillan, 1984.

Haynes, John Earl, and Harvey Klehr. *Venona: Decoding Soviet Espionage in America.* New Haven, Conn.: Yale University Press, 1999.

Hazard, Elizabeth W. *Cold War Crucible: United States Foreign Policy and the Conflict in Romania, 1943–1953.* New York: Columbia University Press, 1996.

Heikal, Mohamed. *Sphinx and Commissar: The Rise and Fall of Soviet Influence in the Arab World.* London: Collins, 1978.

Herrnstadt, Rudolf. *Das Herrnstadt-Dokument: Das Politbüro der SED und die Geschichte des 17. Juni 1953.* Edited by Nadja Stulz-Herrnstadt. Hamburg: Rowohlt, 1990.

Hersh, Seymour. *The Price of Power: Kissinger in the Nixon White House.* New York: Summit Books, 1983.

Hershberg, James G. "Anatomy of a Controversy: Anatoly F. Dobrynin's Meeting with Robert F. Kennedy, Saturday, 27 October 1962." *CWIHP Bulletin,* no. 5 (Spring 1995).

———. "Before 'The Missiles of October': Did Kennedy Plan a Military Strike against Cuba?"

In *The Cuban Missile Crisis Revisited*, edited by James A. Nathan. New York: St. Martin's, 1992.

Hertle, Hans-Hermann. *Chronik des Mauerfalls. Die dramatischen Ereignisse um den 9. November 1989.* Berlin: Ch. Links Velag, 1996.

Hewett, E. A. *Open for Business: Russia's Return to the Global Economy.* With Clifford G. Gaddy. Washington, D.C.: Brookings Institution, 1992.

Hewlett, Richard G., and Jack M. Holl. *Atoms for Peace and War, 1953–1961: Eisenhower and the Atomic Energy Commission.* Berkeley: University of California Press, 1989.

Hirshson, Stanley P. *General Patton: A Soldier's Life.* New York: HarperCollins, 2002.

Hitchcock, William I. *France Restored: Cold War Diplomacy and the Quest for Leadership in Europe, 1944–1954.* Chapel Hill: University of North Carolina Press, 1998.

Hixson, Walter L. *Parting the Curtain: Propaganda, Culture, and the Cold War, 1945–1961.* New York: St. Martin's, 1997.

Holloway, David. *Stalin and the Bomb: The Soviet Union and Atomic Energy, 1939–1956.* New Haven, Conn.: Yale University Press, 1994.

Hopf, Ted. "Getting the End of the Cold War Wrong." *International Security* 18 (Fall 1993).

Hoskings, Geoffrey. *Russia: People and Empire.* Cambridge, Mass: Harvard University Press, 1997.

Hunt, Michael H. *Ideology and U.S. Foreign Policy.* New Haven, Conn.: Yale University Press, 1987.

Iatrides, John O. "Revolution or Self-Defense? Communist Goals, Strategy, and Tactics in the Greek Civil War." *Journal of Cold War Studies* 7, no. 3 (Summer 2005).

Ilizarov, Boris. "Stalin. Shtrikhi k portretu na fone ego biblioteki i arkhiva." *Novaia i noveishaia istoriia* 3–4 (2000).

Immerman, Richard. " 'Trust in the Lord but Keep Your Powder Dry': American Policy Aims at Geneva." In *Cold War Respite: The Geneva Summit of 1955*, edited by Günter Bischof and Saki Dockrill. Baton Rouge: Louisiana State University, 2000.

——, ed. *John Foster Dulles and the Diplomacy of the Cold War: A Reappraisal.* Princeton, N.J.: Princeton University Press, 1989.

Inozemtsev, Nikolai. *Frontovoi Dnevnik.* Moscow: Nauka, 2005.

Iofe, Veniamin. "Politicheskaia oppozitsia v Leningrade, 1950–1960-kh." *Zvezda* 7 (July 1997).

Isaacson, Walter. *Kissinger: A Biography.* New York: Simon and Schuster, 1992.

Ismailov, Eldar. *Vlast i Narod, 1945–1953.* Baku: Adilogli, 2003.

Israelyan, Viktor. *Inside the Kremlin during the Yom Kippur War.* University Park: Pennsylvania State University Press, 1996.

——. *Na frontakh kholodnoi voini. Zapiski sovetskogo posla.* Moscow: Mir, 2003.

Ivnitsky, N. A., ed. *Sud'bi Rossiiskogo Krest'anstva.* Moscow: RGGU, 1996.

Jacobson, Jon. *When the Soviet Union Entered World Politics.* Berkeley: University of California Press, 1994.

Jaruzelski, Wojciech. *Les chaines et le refuge: Memoires.* Paris: Jean-Claude Lattes, 1992.

Jensen, Kenneth M., ed. *Origins of the Cold War*. Rev. ed. Washington, D.C.: U.S. Institute of Peace Press, 1994.

Jervis, Robert. "Stalin, an Incompetent Realist." *National Interest* (Winter 1997/98).

Kalugin, Oleg, and Fen Montaigne. *The First Directorate*. New York: St. Martin's, 1994.

Kamanin, N. P. *Skrytii kosmos*. Vol. 1. Moscow: Infortekst-IF, 1997.

Kania, Stanislaw. *Zatrzymac konfrontacje*. Warsaw: BGW, 1991.

Karner, Stefan, Peter Ruggenthaler, and Barbara Stelzl-Marx, eds. *Die Rote Armee in Österreich. Sowjetische Besatzung, 1945–1955. Beiträge*. Vienna: Oldenbourg Verlag, 2005.

Karnow, Stanley. *Vietnam: A History*. New York: Penguin, 1997.

Kelleher, Catherine. *Germany and the Politics of Nuclear Weapons*. New York: Columbia University Press, 1975.

Kenez, Peter. *Cinema and Soviet Society from the Revolution to the Death of Stalin*. New York: I. B. Tauris, 2001.

——. *A History of the Soviet Union from the Beginning to the End*. Cambridge: Cambridge University Press, 1999.

Kersten, Krystyna. *The Establishment of Communist Rule in Poland, 1943–1948*. Translated by John MacGiel and Michael H. Bernhard. Berkeley: University of California Press, 1991.

Kevorkov, Vyacheslav. *Tainii Kanal*. Moscow: Gea, 1997.

Khariton, Yuli, and Yuri Smirnov. *Myths and Reality of the Soviet Atomic Project*. Russian Federal Nuclear Center: Arzamas-16, 1994.

Khlevniuk, O. V., R. U. Davis, L. P. Kosheleva, E. A. Ris, and L. A. Rogovaia. *Stalin i Kaganovich. Perepiska. 1931–1936*. Moscow: ROSSPEN, 2001.

Khrushchev, Nikita. *Khrushchev Remembers: The Last Testament*. Translated and edited by Strobe Talbott. Boston: Little, Brown, 1971.

——. "Memuari Nikiti Sergeevicha Khrushcheva." *Voprosi istorii* (1990–1995).

Khrushchev, Sergei. *Nikita Khrushchev and the Creation of a Superpower*. University Park: Pennsylvania State University Press, 2000.

——. *Nikita Khrushchev: Krizisi i raketi*. 2 vols. Moscow: Novosti, 1994.

Kirpichenko, Vadim A. *Iz arkhiva razvedchika*. Moscow: Mezhdunarodniie otnosheniia, 1993.

Kissinger, Henry. *Diplomacy*. New York: Simon and Schuster, 1994.

——. *Ending the Vietnam War: A Personal History of America's Involvement in and Extrication from the Vietnam War*. New York: Touchstone, 2002.

——. *White House Years*. Boston: Little, Brown, 1982.

——. *The Years of Renewal*. New York: Simon and Schuster, 1999.

——. *The Years of Upheaval*. Boston: Little, Brown, 1982.

Klehr, Harvey, and John Earl Haynes. *Venona: Decoding Soviet Espionage in America*. New Haven, Conn.: Yale University Press, 1999.

Knyshevsky, P. N. *Dobycha. Taini germanskikh reparatsii*. Moscow: Soratnik, 1994.

Kochariants, S. G., and N. N. Gorin. *Stranitsi istorii iadernogo tsentra "Arzamas-16."* Arzamas-16: VNIIEF, 1993.

Kochemasov, Vyacheslav. *Meine letzte Mission*. Berlin: Dietz, 1994.

Kochkin, N. V. "SSSR, Angliia, SShA i 'Turetskii krizis' 1945–1947 gg." *Novaia i noveishaia istoriia* 3 (May–June 2002).

Kokoshin, Andrei A. *Soviet Strategic Thought, 1917–91.* Cambridge, Mass.: Massachusetts Institute of Technology Press, 1998.

Konchalovsky, Andrei. *Nizkie istini.* Moscow: Sovershenno Sekretno, 1998.

Korchilov, Igor. *Translating History.* New York: Scribner's, 1997.

Kornienko, Georgy M. *Kholodnaia voina: Svidedelstvo eie uchastnika.* Moscow: Mezhdunarodniie otnosheniia, 1994.

Korni Travi: Sbornik Statei Molodikh Istorikov. Moscow: Zvenia, 1996.

Korol, V. E. "The Price of Victory: Myths and Realities." *Journal of Slavic Military Studies* 9 (1996).

———. "Upushchennaiia vozmozhnost. Vstrecha Khrushcheva i Kennedy v Vene v 1961 g." *Novaiia i noveishaia istoriia* 2 (1992).

Kosenko, I. N. "Enigma of 'Aircraft Affair.' " *Voenno-istoricheskii zhurnal* 6 (1994).

Kosthorst, Daniel. *Brentano und die deutsche Einheit: die Deutschland—und Ostpolitik des Aussenministers im Kabinett Adenauer, 1955–1961.* Düsseldorf: Droste, 1993.

Kostyrchenko, Gennadi V. *Out of the Red Shadow: Anti-Semitism in Stalin's Russia.* New York: Prometheus Books, 1995.

———. *Tainaia politika Stalina. Vlast i anti-Semitism.* Moscow: Mezhdunarodniie otnosheniia, 2001.

Kotkin, Stephen. *The Magnetic Mountain: Stalinism as a Civilization.* Berkeley: University of California Press, 1995.

Kotz, David, and Fred Weir. *Revolution from Above: The Demise of the Soviet System.* London: Routledge, 1997.

Koval, Konstantin I. "Na postu zamestitelia Glavnonachal'stvuiushchevo SVAG, 1945–1949 gg." *Novaia i noveishaia istoriia* 3 (1987).

———. *Poslednii Svidetel. "Germanskaia Karta" v Kholodnoi Voine.* Moscow: ROSSPEN, 1997.

———. "Zapiski upolnomochennogo GKO na territorii Germanii." *Novaia i noveishaia istoriia* 3 (1994).

Kozakov, Mikhail. *Avtorskaia kniga.* Moscow: Vagrius, 1997.

Kozlov, Alexei. *Kozel na Sakse.* Moscow: Vagrius, 1998.

Kozlova, N. N. *Gorizonti povsednevnosti Sovetskoi epokhi. Golosa iz khora.* Moscow: Institute of Philosophy, 1996.

———. "Krestianskii syn: Opyt issledovaniia biografii." *Socis* 6 (1994).

Kozol, V. E. "The Price of Victory: Myths and Realities." *Journal of Slavic Military Studies* 9 (March 1996).

Kramer, Mark. "The Collapse of East European Communism and the Repercussions within the Soviet Union." Pts. 1 and 2. *Journal of Cold War Studies* 5, no. 4 (2003); 6, no. 4 (2004).

———. "Colonel Kuklinski and the Polish Crisis, 1980–1981." *CWIHP Bulletin*, no. 11 (Winter 1998).

———. "The Early Post-Stalin Succession Struggle and Upheavals in East-Central Europe:

Internal-External Linkages in Soviet Policy Making (Part 1)." *Journal of Cold War Studies* 1, no. 1 (Winter 1999).

———. "Jaruzelski, the Soviet Union, and the Imposition of Martial Law in Poland: New Light on the Mystery of December 1981." *CWIHP Bulletin*, no. 11 (Winter 1998).

———. "New Evidence on Soviet Decision-Making and the 1956 Polish and Hungarian Crises." *CWIHP Bulletin*, nos. 8–9 (Winter 1996/97).

———. "Soviet Deliberations during the Polish Crisis, 1980–1981." CWIHP working paper no. 1. Washington, D.C.: Woodrow Wilson International Center for Scholars, April 1999.

———. "The Soviet Union and the Founding of the German Democratic Republic: 50 Years Later—A Review Article." *Europe-Asia Studies* 51, no. 6 (1999).

———. "Tactical Nuclear Weapons, Soviet Command Authority, and the Cuban Missile Crisis." *CWIHP Bulletin*, no. 3 (Fall 1993).

———. "Ukraine and the Soviet-Czechoslovak Crisis of 1968 (Part 1): New Evidence from the Diary of Petro Shelest." *CWIHP Bulletin*, no. 10 (March 1998).

Krementsov, Nikolai. *Stalinist Science.* Princeton, N.J.: Princeton University Press, 1997.

Krivosheev, G. F., ed. *Rossiia i SSSR v voinakh XX veka. Poteri vooruzhennikh sil. Statisticheskoie issledovaniie.* Moscow: Olma-Press, 2001.

Krylova, Anna. " 'Healers of Wounded Souls': The Crisis of Private Life in Soviet Literature and Society, 1944–46." *Journal of Modern History* 73 (June 2001): 307–31.

Kryuchkov, Vladimir. *Lichnoie Delo.* 2 vols. Moscow: Olimp, 1996.

Kubina, Michael, and Manfred Wilke, eds. *"Hart und kompromisslos durchgreifen": The SED contra Polen, 1980/81: Geheimakten der SED-Fürung über die Unterdrückung der polnischen Demokratiebewegung.* Berlin: Akademie Varlag, 1995.

Kuhns, Woodrow J., ed. *Assessing the Soviet Threat: The Early Cold War Years.* Langley, Va.: Center for the Study of Intelligence, 1997.

Kuisong, Yang. "The Sino-Soviet Border Clash of 1969: From Zhenbao Island to Sino-American Rapprochement." *Cold War History* 1 (2000).

———. "The Soviet Factor and the CCP's Policy towards the United States." *Chinese Historians* 5, no. 1 (Spring 1992).

Kuniholm, Bruce. *The Origins of the Cold War in the Near East.* Princeton, N.J.: Princeton University Press, 1980.

Kuzmin, Ivan N. *Khrushcnie GDR: Istoria. Posledstviia.* Moscow: Nauchnaia kniga, 1996.

Kvitsinsky, Yuli. *Vremia i sluchai: zametki professionala.* Moscow: Olma-Press, 1999.

———. *Vor dem Sturm: Errinerungen eines Diplomaten.* Translated by Hilde and Helmut Ettinger. Berlin: Siedler, 1993.

Kynin, Georgy. "The Anti-Hitler Coalition and the Post-War Settlement in Germany." *Mezhdunarodnaia zhizn* 8 (1995).

Kynin, G., and J. Laufer, eds. *SSSR i Germanskii vopros 1941–1949.* Vols. 1–2. Moscow: Mezhdunarodniie otnosheniia, 2000.

———. *The USSR and the German Question, 1941–1945.* Vols. 1–2. Moscow: Mezhdunarodniie otnosheniia, 1996.

Ladyzhenskii, Jakov. "Krasnoiarsk-26." *Druzhba Narodov* 6 (1996).

Laqueur, Walter. *The Black Hundred: The Rise of the Extreme Right in Russia*. New York: HarperCollins, 1993.

Laufer, Jochen. "Stalin and German Reparations, 1941–1953." Paper presented at the conference "Stalin and the Cold War." Yale University, New Haven, Conn., September 24–25, 1999.

——. "Die UdSSR und die deutsche Währungsfrage, 1944–1948." *Vierteljahrshefte für Zeitgeschichte* 3 (July 1998).

Lavrova, Tatiana V. *Chernomorskiie prolivi (Istoricheskii ocherk)*. Rostov-on-Don, 1997.

Lebedev, P. N., ed. *Andrei Sakharov: Facets of a Life*. Hong Kong: Edition Frontières, 1991.

Lebedeva, N. S., N. A. Petrosova, et al. *Katyn. Plenniki neobiavlennoi voini. Dokumenti i materiali*. Moscow: Mezhdunarodnii fond "Demokratiia," 1999.

Lebow, Richard Ned. "The Long Peace, the End of the Cold War, and the Failure of Realism." *International Organization* 48 (Spring 1994).

Lebow, Richard Ned, and Janice Gross Stein. *We All Lost the Cold War*. Princeton, N.J.: Princeton University Press, 1994.

Ledovsky, A. V. "Stalin i Chan Kai Shi. Tainaia poezdka syna Chana v Moskvu v dekabre 1945–janvare 1946." *Novaia i noveishaia istoriia* 4 (July–August 1996).

——. "Stalin, Mao Tsedun i koreiskaia voina 1950–1953 godov." *Novaia i noveishaia istoriia* 5 (September–October 2005).

Leffler, Melvyn P. *A Preponderance of Power: National Security, the Truman Administration, and the Cold War*. Stanford, Calif.: Stanford University Press, 1992.

Leonov, Nikolai S. *Likholetie*. Moscow: Mezhdunarodniie otnosheniia, 1995.

L'Estrange Fawcett, Louise. *Iran and the Cold War: The Azerbaijan Crisis of 1946*. Cambridge: Cambridge University Press, 1992.

Levering, Ralph B., Vladimir O. Pechatnov, Verena Botzenhart-Viehe, and C. Earl Edmondson. *Debating the Origins of the Cold War: American and Russian Perspectives*. New York: Rowman and Littlefield, 2002.

Lévesque, Jacques. *The Enigma of 1989: The USSR and the Liberation of Eastern Europe*. Berkeley: University of California Press, 1997.

Lewis, John, and Xue Litai. *China Builds a Bomb*. Stanford, Calif.: Stanford University Press, 1988.

Liang Chin-tung. "The Sino-Soviet Treaty of Friendship and Alliance of 1945: The Inside Story." In *Nationalist China during the Sino-Japanese War, 1937–1945*, edited by Paul K. T. Sih. Hicksville, N.Y.: Exposition Press, 1977.

Lieven, Dominic. *Empire: The Russian Empire and Its Rivals*. New Haven, Conn.: Yale University Press, 2001.

Ligachev, Yegor. *Inside Gorbachev's Kremlin*. Boulder, Colo.: Westview Press, 1992.

——. *Zagadka Gorbacheva*. Novosibisk: Interbuk, 1992.

Linz, S. J., ed. *The Impact of World War II on the Soviet Union*. Totowa, N.J.: Rowman and Allanheld, 1985.

Lipkin, Semyon. *Zhizn i sudba Vasiliia Grossmana. Proschaniie*, by Anna Berzer. Moscow: Kniga, 1990.

Li Zhisui. *The Private Life of Chairman Mao: The Memoirs of Mao's Personal Physician*. New York: Random House, 1994.

Logevall, Frederik. "Bernath Lecture: A Critique of Containment." *Diplomatic History* 28 (September 2004).

——. *Choosing War: The Lost Chance for Peace and the Escalation of War in Vietnam*. Berkeley: University of California Press, 1999.

Loth, Wilfried. "The Origins of Stalin's Note of 10 March 1952." *Cold War History* 2 (January 2004).

——. *Stalin's Unwanted Child: The Soviet Union, the German Question, and the Founding of the GDR*. Translated by Robert F. Hogg. London: Macmillan, 1998.

Lukes, Igor. *Czechoslovakia between Hitler and Stalin: The Diplomacy of Edvard Benes in the 1930s*. New York: Oxford University Press, 1996.

Lundestad, Geir, and Odd Arne Westad, eds. *Beyond the Cold War: New Dimensions in International Relations*. New York: W. W. Norton, 1982.

Lyakhovsky, Alexander. *Plamia Afghana*. Moscow: Vagrius, 1999.

——. *Tragediia i doblest Afghana*. Moscow: GPI Iskona, 1995.

Lytle, Mark Hamilton. *The Origins of the Iranian-American Alliance, 1941–1953*. New York: Holmes and Meier, 1987.

Macdonald, Douglas J. "Formal Ideologies in the Cold War: Toward a Framework for Empirical Analysis." In *Reviewing the Cold War: Approaches, Interpretations, Theory*, edited by Odd Arne Westad. London: Frank Cass, 2000.

Maier, Charles S. *Dissolution: The Crisis of Communism and the End of East Germany*. Princeton, N.J.: Princeton University Press, 1997.

Major, Patrick, and Rana Mitter. "East Is East and West Is West? Towards a Comparative Socio-Cultural History of the Cold War." *Cold War History* 1 (October 2003).

Maksimova, Ella. "Podslushali i rasstreliali." *Izvestia*, 16 July 1992.

Malashenko, Yevgeni. "Operatsiia Vikhr." *Voenno-istoricheskii zhurnal* 11 (1993).

Malenkov, G. *O moyem otse Georgii Malenkove*. Moscow: Tekhnoekos, 1992.

Malia, Martin. *The Soviet Tragedy: A History of Socialism in Russia, 1917–1991*. New York: Free Press, 1994.

Mark, Eduard. "American Policy toward Eastern Europe and the Origins of the Cold War, 1941–1946: An Alternative Interpretation." *Journal of American History* 68 (September 1981).

——. "Charles E. Bohlen and the Acceptable Limits of Soviet Hegemony in Eastern Europe: A Memorandum of 18 October 1945." *Diplomatic History* 3 (Spring 1979).

——. "Revolution by Degrees: Stalin's National-Front Strategy for Europe, 1941–47." CWIHP working paper no. 31. Washington, D.C.: Woodrow Wilson International Center for Scholars, 2000.

——. "The Turkish War Scare of 1946." In *Origins of the Cold War: An International History*, edited by Melvyn Leffler and David Painter. New York: Routledge, 2005.

——. "Venona's Source 19 and the 'Trident' Conference of May 1943: Diplomacy or Espionage?" *Intelligence and National Security* 13, no. 2 (Summer 1998).

——. "The War Scare of 1946 and Its Consequences." *Diplomatic History* 21, no. 3 (Summer 1997).

Martin, Terry D. *The Affirmative Action Empire: Nations and Nationalism in the Soviet Union, 1923–1939*. Ithaca, N.Y.: Cornell University Press, 2001.

Mastny, Vojtech. "The Cassandra in the Foreign Office." *Foreign Affairs* 54 (January 1976).

——. *Cold War and Soviet Insecurity: Stalin Years*. New York: Oxford University Press, 1996.

——. *Documentation on the PPC of Warsaw Treaty Organization in Moscow, July 26, 1963*. <http://www.isn.ethz.ch/php/documents/collection_3/PCC_texts/ed_note_63.htm>.

——. "NATO in the Beholder's Eye: Soviet Perceptions and Policies, 1949–1956." CWIHP working paper no. 35. Washington, D.C.: Woodrow Wilson International Center for Scholars, March 2001.

——. *Russia's Road to the Cold War: Diplomacy, Warfare, and the Politics of Communism, 1941–1945*. New York: Columbia University Press, 1973.

——. "The Soviet Non-Invasion of Poland, 1981." CWIHP working paper no. 233. Washington, D.C.: Woodrow Wilson International Center for Scholars.

——. "'We Are in a Bind': Polish and Czechoslovak Attempts at Reforming the Warsaw Pact, 1956–1969." *CWIHP Bulletin*, no. 11 (Winter 1998).

Matlock, Jack F., Jr. *Autopsy on an Empire: The American Ambassador's Account of the Collapse of the Soviet Union*. New York: Random House, 1995.

——. *Reagan and Gorbachev: How the Cold War Ended*. New York: Random House, 2004.

May, Elaine Tyler. *Homeward Bound: American Families in the Cold War Era*. New York: Basic Books, 1988.

McGiffert Ekedahl, Carolyn, and Melvin A. Goodman. *The Wars of Eduard Shevardnadze*. University Park: Pennsylvania State University Press, 1997.

Mead, Walter Russell. *Special Providence: A History of U.S. Foreign Policy*. New York: Century Foundation, 2001.

Mearsheimer, John J. "Nuclear Weapons and Deterrence in Europe." *International Security* 9, no. 3 (Winter 1984/1985).

Medvedev, Roy A. *Lichnost i epokha: politicheskii portret L. I. Brezhneva*. Vols. 1–2. Moscow: Novosti, 1991.

——. *Neizvestni Andropov: Politicheskaia biografiia Yuriia Andropova*. Moscow: Prava Cheloveka, 1999.

Medvedev, Roy A., and Dmitry Ermakov. "'Seryi kardinal': M. A. Suslov, politicheskii portret." Moscow: Izd-vo Respublika, 1992.

Medvedev, Vadim. *Raspad: kak on nazreval v 'mirovoi sisteme sotsializma.'* Moscow: Mezhdunarodniie otnosheniia, 1994.

——. *V komande Gorbacheva: Vzgliad iznutri*. Moscow: Bylina, 1994.

Medvedev, Vladimir. *Chelovek za spinoi*. Moscow: Russlit, 1994.

Melkonian, Eduard. "Puti politicheskoi adaptatsii armianskoi diaspori." Presentation at the international conference "Georgia, Armenia, and Azerbaijan in the Cold War: New Archival Evidence." Tsinandali, Georgia, July 8–9, 2002.

Mgeladze, Akaky. *Stalin, kakim ia ego znal: stranitsi nedavnego proshlogo*. Tbilisi: n.p., 2001.

Mikhailov, V., and A. Petrosiants, eds. *The Creation of the First Soviet Nuclear Bomb.* Moscow: Energoatomizdat, 1995.

Mikoyan, Anastas. *Tak bylo. Razmyshleniia o minuvshem.* Moscow: Vagrius, 1999.

Miles, G. "Roman and Modern Imperialism." *Comparative Studies in Society and History* 32 (1990).

Millar, James R. "The Little Deal: Brezhnev's Contribution to Acquisitive Socialism." *Slavic Review* 4 (Winter 1985).

Milstein, Mikhail. *Skvoz godi voin i nischeti. Vospominania voiennogo razvedchika.* Moscow: ITAR-TASS, 2000.

Minaiev, A. V. ed. *Sovetskaia voiennaia moshch ot Stalina do Gorbacheva.* Moscow: Voiennii parad, 1999.

Miner, Steven Merritt. *Between Churchill and Stalin: The Soviet Union, Great Britain, and the Origins of the Grand Alliance.* Chapel Hill: University of North Carolina Press, 1988.

——. *Holy War: Religion, Nationalism, and Alliance Politics, 1941–1945.* Chapel Hill: University of North Carolina Press, 2003.

Mirsky, G. I. "Polveka v mire vostokovedenia." *Vostok* 6 (1996).

Mitrokhin, Nikolai. *Russkaia Partiia. Dvizheniie russkikh natsionalistov v SSSR. 1953–1985 godi.* Moscow: Novoie literaturnoie obozrenie, 2003.

Mitrokhin, Vasily. "KGB in Afghanistan." CWIHP working paper no. 40. Washington, D.C.: Woodrow Wilson International Center for Scholars, 2002.

Mitrovich, Gregory. *Undermining the Kremlin: America's Strategy to Subvert the Soviet Bloc, 1947–1956.* Ithaca, N.Y.: Cornell University Press, 2000.

Mlechin, Leonid. *MID. Ministri inostrannikh del. Romantiki i tsiniki.* Moscow: Tsentrpoligraf, 2001.

——. *Predsedateli KGB: Rassekrechenniie sudbi.* Moscow: Tsentrpoligraf, 1999.

Montefiore, Simon Sebag. *Stalin: The Court of the Red Tsar.* New York: Alfred A. Knopf, 2004.

Morozov, Boris. *Evreiskaia Emigratsiia v svete novikh dokumentov.* Tel Aviv: Ivrus, 1998.

Mozvogoi, Alexander. *The Cuban Samba of the Quartet of Foxtrots: Soviet Submarines in the Caribbean Crisis of 1962.* Moscow: Military Parade, 2002.

Murashko, Galina P., and Albina F. Noskova. "Stalin and the National-Territorial Controversies in Eastern Europe, 1945–1947." *Cold War History* 1, no. 3 (April 2001).

Murphy, David E., Sergei A. Kondrashev, and George Baily. *Battleground Berlin: CIA vs. KGB in the Cold War.* New Haven, Conn.: Yale University Press, 1997.

Musatov, Valerii L. *Predvestniki buri: Politichestkiie krizisy v Vostochnoi Evrope.* Moscow: Nauchnaia kniga, 1996.

Naftali, Timothy. "NATO, the Warsaw Pact, and the Rise of Détente, 1965–1972." Talk at international conference "NATO, the Warsaw Pact, and Détente, 1965–73." Dobbiaco, Italy, September 26–28, 2002.

Nagibin, Yuri. *Dnevnik.* Moscow: Knizhnii Sad, 1996.

Naimark, Norman. "Cold War Studies and New Archival Materials on Stalin." *Russian Review* 61 (January 2002): 1–15.

——. *Fires of Hatred: Ethnic Cleansing in Twentieth-Century Europe.* Cambridge, Mass.: Harvard University Press, 2001.

———. *Russians in Germany: A History of the Soviet Zone of Occupation, 1945–1949*. Cambridge, Mass.: Harvard University Press, 1995.

Naimark, Norman, and Leonid Gibiansky, eds. *The Establishment of Communist Regimes in Eastern Europe, 1944–1949*. Boulder, Colo.: Westview, 1997.

Narinsky, Mikhail. "Sovetskii Soiuz i Suetskii krizis 1956 goda. Novye Dannie." *Novaia i noveishaia istoria* 2 (March–April 2004).

———. "Soviet Policy and the Berlin Blockade, 1948." Paper presented at the conference "The Soviet Union, Germany, and the Cold War, 1949–1952: New Evidence from Eastern Archives." Essen, Germany, June 28–29, 1994.

———. "Stalin and the SED Leadership, 7 April 1952: 'You Must Organize Your Own State.' " *CWIHP Bulletin*, no. 4 (Fall 1994).

———. "The USSR and the Berlin Crisis, 1948–1949." Paper presented at the conference "The Soviet Union and Europe in the Cold War, 1943–1953." Cortona, Italy, September 23–24, 1994.

Naumkin, V. V., ed. *Blizhnevostochnii Konflikt 1947–1956. Iz dokumentov arkhiva vneshnei politiki Rossiiskoi Federatsii*. Moscow: Mezhdunarodnii Fond "Demokratiia," 2003.

Naumov, Vladimir P. "The Cold War: On the Brink of Nuclear Catastrophe." Paper presented at the conference "Stalin and the Cold War." Yale University, New Haven, Conn., September 24–25, 1999.

Naumov, Vladimir P., et al., eds. *Georgy Zhukov. Stenogramma oktiabr'skogo (1957) plenuma TsK KPSS i drugiie dokumenti*. Moscow: Mezhdunarodnii fond "Demokratiia," 2001.

Negin, E. A., and L. Goleusova, eds. *The Soviet Atomic Project: The End of the Atomic Monopoly—How It Happened*. Nizhni Novgorod: Arzamas-16, 1995.

Negin, E. A., and Yu. N. Smirnov. "Did the USSR Share Its Atomic Secrets with China?" In *Science and Society: History of the Soviet Atomic Project (40's–50's): Proceedings of the International Symposium at Dubna, May 14–18, 1996*. Moscow: Izdat, 1997.

Nekrasov, Viktor. "Tragediia moiego pokoleniia." *Literaturnaia gazeta*, April 25, 1990.

Nelson, Keith L. *The Making of Détente: Soviet-American Relations in the Shadow of Vietnam*. Baltimore: Johns Hopkins University Press, 1995.

Neumann, Iver B. *Russia and the Idea of Europe: A Study of Identity and International Relations*. London: Routledge, 1996.

Newhouse, John. *Cold Dawn: The Story of SALT*. New York: Holt, Rinehart and Winston, 1973.

Nichols, Thomas M. *The Sacred Cause: Civil-Military Conflict over Soviet National Security, 1917–1992*. Ithaca: Cornell University Press, 1993.

Ninkovich, Frank. *The Wilsonian Century: U.S. Foreign Policy since 1900*. Chicago: Chicago University Press, 1999.

Niu Jun. "The Origins of the Sino-Soviet Alliance." In *Brothers in Arms: The Rise and Fall of the Sino-Soviet Alliance, 1945–1963*, edited by Odd Arne Westad. Washington, D.C.: Woodrow Wilson Center Press; Stanford, Calif.: Stanford University Press, 1998.

Nixon, Richard. *RN: The Memoirs of Richard Nixon*. New York: Grosset and Dunlap, 1978.

Njolstad, Olav. "Keys of Keys? SALT II and the Breakdown of Détente." In *The Fall of Détente:*

Soviet-American Relations during the Carter Years, edited by Odd Arne Westad. Oslo: Scandinavian University Press, 1997.

——. *Peacekeeper and Troublemaker: The Containment Policy of Jimmy Carter, 1977–1978*. Oslo: Norwegian Institute for Defence Studies, 1995.

Noskova, A. F., ed. NKVD i polskoie podpolye, 1944–1945 *(Po "Osobym Papkam" I. V. Stalina)*. Moscow: Institut slavianovedeniia i balkanistiki RAN, 1994.

Novikov, N. V. *Vospominaniia diplomata, 1938–1947*. Moscow: Politizdat, 1989.

Nuti, Leopoldo, and Vladislav Zubok. "Ideology." In *Cold War History*, edited by Saki R. Dockrill and Geraint Hughes. New York: Palgrave Macmillan, 2006.

Odom, William E. *The Collapse of the Soviet Military*. New Haven, Conn.: Yale University Press, 1998.

——. "The Sources of 'New Thinking' in Soviet Politics." In *The Last Decade of the Cold War: From Conflict Escalation to Conflict Transformation*, edited by Olav Njolstad. New York: Frank Cass, 2004.

Ognetov, Igor. "Tonkinskii intsident i Sovetskaia pomosch Vietnamu." *Mezhdunarodnaia zhizn* 5 (1999).

Olsen, Mari. "Changing Alliances: Moscow's Relations with Hanoi and the Role of China, 1949–1964." Ph.D. diss., University of Oslo, 2004.

Olshanskaia, E. M. "Kiseleva, Kishmareva, Tyuricheva" (The Diary of Kiseleva). *Novy Mir* (February 1991).

"On the Eve." *International Affairs* 7 (July 1991).

Origins of the Cold War: The Novikov, Kennan, and Roberts "Long Telegrams" of 1946. Washington, D.C.: United States Institute of Peace, 1991.

Orlova, Raisa. *Vospominaniia o neproshedshem vremeni*. Ann Arbor, Mich.: Ardis, 1983.

Ostermann, Christian. "New Documents on the East German Uprising of 1953." *CWIHP Bulletin*, no. 5 (Spring 1995).

——. " 'This Is Not a Politburo, But a Madhouse': The Post-Stalin Succession Struggle, Soviet Deutschlandpolitik, and the SED." *CWIHP Bulletin*, no. 10 (March 1998).

——, ed. *Uprising in East Germany, 1953: The Cold War, the Germany Question, and the First Major Upheaval behind the Iron Curtain*. Budapest: Central European University Press, 2001.

Ouimet, Matthew J. *The Rise and Fall of the Brezhnev Doctrine in Soviet Foreign Policy*. Chapel Hill: University of North Carolina Press, 2003.

Overy, Richard. *Russia's War: A History of the Soviet War Effort, 1941–1945*. New York: Penguin, 1997.

Palazhchenko, Pavel. *My Years with Gorbachev and Shevardnadze: The Memoir of a Soviet Interpreter*. University Park: Pennsylvania State University Press, 1997.

Pantsov, Alexei V. *Tainaia istoriia Sovetsko-kitaiskikh otnoshenii. Bolsheviki i kitaiskaia revolutsiia (1919–1927)*. Moscow: Muravei-Gaid, 2001.

Paperny, Vladimir. *Kultura Dva*. Moscow: Novoie literaturnoie obozreniie, 1996.

Parallel History Project of NATO and the Warsaw Pact: Annual Report, 2003.

Parks, J. D. *Culture, Conflict, and Coexistence: America-Soviet Cultural Relations, 1917–1958*. Jefferson, N.C.: McFarland, 1983.

Pavlov, Vitaly. *Bylem rezydentem KGB w Polsce.* Warsaw: BGW, 1994.

Pavlova, T. A., ed. *Dolgii put rossiiskogo patsifizma. Ideal mezhdunarodnogo i vnutrennego mira v religiozno-filosofskoi i obshchestvennoi mysli Rossii.* Moscow: Institut vseobshchei istorii, 1997.

Pearson, David E. *KAL 007: The Cover-up.* New York: Summit Books, 1987.

Pearson, Joseph. *Solzhenitsyn: A Soul in Exile.* Grand Rapids, Mich.: Baker Book House, 2001.

Pechatnov, Vladimir. " 'The Allies Are Pressing on You to Break Your Will': Foreign Policy Correspondence between Stalin and Molotov and Other Members of the Politburo, September 1945–December 1946." CWIHP working paper no. 26. Washington, D.C.: Woodrow Wilson International Center for Scholars, September 1999.

——. "Averell Harriman's Mission to Moscow." *Harriman Review* 14 (July 2003).

——. "The Big Three after World War II: New Documents on Soviet Thinking about Postwar Relations with the United States and Great Britain." CWIHP working paper no. 13. Washington, D.C.: Woodrow Wilson International Center for Scholars, July 1995.

——. "Exercise in Frustration: Soviet Foreign Propaganda in the Early Cold War, 1945–47." *Cold War History* 1 (January 2001).

——. "Fultonskaia rech Cherchillia." *Istochnik* 1 (1998).

——. *Stalin, Ruzvelt, Trumen: SSSR i SShA v 1940kh gg. Dokumentalnie ocherki.* Moscow: Terra, 2006.

Pechatnov, Vladimir, and Alexander Chubarian. "Molotov 'the Liberal': Stalin's 1945 Criticism of His Deputy." *Cold War History* 1 (August 2000).

Pechenev, Vadim. *Gorbachev: K vershinam vlasti: Iz teoretiko-memuarnykh razmyshlenii.* Moscow: Gospodin narod, 1991.

——. *Vzlet i padeniie Gorbacheva; Glazami ochevidtsa.* Moscow: Respublika, 1996.

Perestroika desiat let spustia (aprel 1985–aprel 1995). Moscow: April-85 Publishing House, 1995.

Perlmutter, Amos. *FDR and Stalin: A Not So Great Alliance.* Columbia: University of Missouri Press, 1993.

Perry, John Curtis, and Constantine Pleshakov. *The Flight of the Romanovs: A Family Saga.* New York: Basic Books, 1999.

Petrov, Nikita, and Arseny Roginsky. "The 'Polish Operation' of the NKVD, 1937–9." In *Stalin's Terror: High Politics and Mass Repression in the Soviet Union,* edited by Barry McLaughlin and Kevin McDermott. New York: Palgrave Macmillan, 2003.

Phillips, Hugh D. *Between the Revolution and the West: A Political Biography of Maxim M. Litvinov.* Boulder, Colo.: Westview, 1992.

Pikhoia, Rudolf G. "Pochemu raspalsia SSSR?" In *Konets kholodnoi voini: noviie fakti i aspekti,* edited by V. M. Zubok, S. Y. Shenin, and A. A. Shubin. Saratov: Nauchnaia kniga, 2004.

——. *Sovetskii Soiuz: Istoriia vlasti, 1945–1991.* 2nd expanded ed. Novosibirsk: Sibirskii khronograf, 2000.

Pipes, Richard. *Vixi: Memoirs of a Non-Belonger.* New Haven, Conn.: Yale University Press, 2003.

Podvig, P. L., ed. *Strategicheskoie iadernoie vooruzheniie Rossii.* Moscow: Izdat, 1998.

Polikovskaia, Lyudmila. *Mi predchuvstvie . . . predtecha . . . Ploschad Maiakovskogo 1958–1965.* Moscow: Zvenia, 1997.

"Political Problems in Bulgaria and Romania Following Moscow Conference Decisions, Sofia—Moscow, January 8, 1946." Venona Historical Monograph no. 5. Fort Mead, Md.: National Security Agency, October 1996.

Pollock, Ethan. "Conversations with Stalin on Questions of Political Economy." CWIHP working paper no. 33. Washington, D.C.: Woodrow Wilson International Center for Scholars, 2001.

——. *Stalin and the Soviet Science Wars.* Princeton, N.J.: Princeton University Press, 2006.

Pomerants, Grigory. *Zapiski gadkogo utenka.* Moscow: Moskovski rabochii, 1998.

Pontuso, James F. *Solzhenitsyn's Political Thought.* Charlottesville: University Press of Virginia, 1990.

Powers, Richard Gid. *Not without Honor: The History of American Anticommunism.* New York: Free Press, 1995.

Prados, John. "Open Skies and Closed Minds: American Disarmament Policy at the Geneva Summit." In *Cold War Respite: The Geneva Summit of 1955,* edited by Günter Bischof and Saki Dockrill. Baton Rouge: Louisiana State University, 2000.

Premier izvestnii i neizvestnii: Vospominaniia o A. N. Kosygine. Moscow: Respublika, 1997.

Pribitkov, Viktor. *Apparat. 390 dnei i vsia zhizn Genseka Chernenko.* Moscow: Molodaia Gvardia, 2002.

Prizel, Ilya. *National Identity and Foreign Policy: Nationalism and Leadership in Poland, Russia, and Ukraine.* Cambridge: Cambridge University Press, 1998.

Prozumenscikov, Michail. "Nach Stalins Tod." In *Die Rote Armee in Österreich. Sowjetische Besatzung, 1945–1955. Beiträge,* edited by Stefan Karner, Peter Ruggenthaler, and Barbara Stelzl-Marx. Vienna: Oldenbourg Verlag, 2005.

Putch. Khronika trevozhnikh dnei. Moscow: Progress, 1991.

Qiang Zhai. *The Dragon, the Lion, and the Eagle: Chinese-British-American Relations, 1949–1958.* Kent, Ohio: Kent State University Press, 1994.

Rainer, M. János. *Nagy Imre, 1953–1958.* 2 vols. Budapest: 1956-os Intezet, 1999.

Reddaway, Peter. "Khrushchev and Gorbachev: An American View." In *Nikita Khrushchev,* edited by William Taubman, Sergei Khrushchev, and Abbott Gleason. New Haven, Conn.: Yale University Press, 2000.

Reshetnikov, Vasily. "Drama marshala Novikova." *Krasnaia zvezda,* June 5, 1993.

Resis, Albert. *Stalin, the Politburo, and the Onset of the Cold War, 1945–1946.* Carl Beck Papers in Russian and East European Studies no. 701. Pittsburgh, Penn.: University of Pittsburgh Press, 1988.

——, ed. *Molotov Remembers: Inside Kremlin Politics: Conversation with Felix Chuev.* Chicago: Ivan Dee, 1993.

Rey, Marie-Pierre. " 'Europe Is Our Common Home': A Study of Gorbachev's Diplomatic Concept." *Cold War History* 2 (January 2004).

Rhodes, Richard. *Dark Sun: The Making of the Hydrogen Bomb.* New York: Simon and Schuster, 1995.

Richter, James. *Khrushchev's Double Bind: International Pressures and Domestic Coalition Politics.* Baltimore: Johns Hopkins University Press, 1994.

——. "Reexamining Soviet Policy towards Germany in 1953." *Europe-Asia Studies* 45, no. 4 (1993).

Rieber, Alfred. "Stalin: Man of the Borderlands." *American Historical Review* 106 (December 2001).

Risse-Kappen, Thomas. "Did 'Peace through Strength' End the Cold War? Lessons from INF." *International Security* 16 (Summer 1991).

Roberts, Geoffrey. "Sexing up the Cold War: New Evidence on the Molotov-Truman Talks of April 1945." *Cold War History* 3 (April 2004).

Rosendorf, Neal. "John Foster Dulles' Nuclear Schizophrenia." In *Cold War Statesmen Confront the Bomb: Nuclear Diplomacy since 1945*, edited by John Lewis Gaddis et al. New York: Oxford University Press, 1999.

Ross, Robert R. *Negotiating Cooperation: The United States and China, 1969–1989*. Stanford, Calif.: Stanford University Press, 1995.

Rostow, Walt W. *Open Skies: Eisenhower's Proposal of July 21, 1955*. Austin: University of Texas Press, 1982.

Rucker, Laurent. "Moscow's Surprise: The Soviet-Israeli Alliance of 1947–1949." CWIHP working paper no. 46. Washington, D.C.: Woodrow Wilson International Center for Scholars, 2005.

Ruggenthaler, Peter. "Novyie sovetskie dokumenti k note Stalina ot 10 marta i k avstriiskomu 'kratkomu dogovoru' ot 13 marta 1952g." Unpublished paper.

——. *Stalins grosser Bluff: Die Geschichte der Stalin-Note in Dokumenten der sowjetischen Führung*. Schriftenreihe der Vierteljahreshefte für Zeitgeschichte, vol. 95. Munich: 2007.

Ryzhkov, Nikolai I. *Desiat Let Velikikh Potriasenii*. Moscow: Kniga, Prosvescheniie, Miloserdie, 1996.

——. *Perestroika: Istoriya predatelstv*. Moscow: Novosti, 1992.

Rzheshevsky, Oleg. *Stalin i Cherchill. Vstrechi. Besedi, diskussii. Dokumenti, kommentarii 1941–1945*. Moscow: Nauka, 2004.

——, ed. *War and Diplomacy: The Making of the Grand Alliance: Documents from Stalin's Archives*. Amsterdam: Harwood Academic, 1996.

Sagan, Scott. *The Limits of Safety: Organizations, Accidents, and Nuclear Weapons*. Princeton, N.J.: Princeton University Press, 1993.

Sagdeev, Roald. *The Making of a Soviet Scientist: My Adventures in Nuclear Fusion and Space from Stalin to Star Wars*. New York: John Wiley, 1994.

Sakharov, Andrei. *Memoirs*. New York: Alfred A. Knopf, 1990.

——. *Sakharov Speaks*. New York: Alfred A. Knopf, 1974.

——. *Vospominaniia*. New York: Chekhov Press, 1990.

Samoilov, David. *Podennie zapisi*. Vols. 1-2. Moscow: Vremia, 2002.

Sarotte, M. E. *Dealing with the Devil: East Germany, Détente, and Ostpolitik, 1969–1973*. Chapel Hill: University of North Carolina Press, 2001.

Savelyev, Alexander G., and Nikolay N. Detinov. *The Big Five: Arms Control Decision-Making in the Soviet Union*. Translated by Dmitry Trenin. Edited by Gregory Varhall. Westport, Conn.: Praeger, 1995.

Scammell, Michael. *Solzhenitsyn: A Biography.* New York: W. W. Norton, 1984.

———, ed. *The Solzhenitsyn Files: Secret Soviet Documents Reveal One Man's Fight against the Monolith.* Chicago: Edition q, 1995.

Schecter, Jerrold L., and Peter S. Deriabin. *The Spy Who Saved the World: How a Soviet Colonel Changed the Course of the Cold War.* New York: Scribner's, 1992.

Schecter, Jerrold L., and Vyacheslav V. Luchkov, eds. *Khrushchev Remembers: The Glasnost Tapes.* Boston: Little, Brown, 1990.

Scheid, Fernande. "Stalin and the Creation of the Azerbaijan Democratic Party in Iran, 1945." *Cold War History* 1 (October 2001).

Scherstjanoi, Elke. "Germaniia i nemtsi v pismakh krasnoarmeitsev vesnoi 1945 g." *Novaia i noveishaia istoriia* 2 (2002).

———. "In 14 Tagen werden Sie vielleicht schon keinen Staat mehr haben." *Deutschlandarchiv* 31 (1998).

———. "Political Calculation and the Interpretation of Western Positions as a Topic: Research into Stalin's Policy toward Germany." Paper presented at the conference "Stalin and the Cold War." Translated by CWIHP. Yale University, New Haven, Conn., September 24–25, 1999.

———. "Die Sowjetische Deutschlandpolitik nach Stalins Tod 1953: Neue Dokumente aus dem Archiv des Moskauer Aussenministeriums." *Vierteljahrshefte fur Zeitgeschichte* 3 (July 1998).

Schick, Jack. *The Berlin Crisis, 1958–1962.* Philadelphia: University of Pennsylvania Press, 1971.

Schulzinger, Robert D. *Henry Kissinger: Doctor of Diplomacy.* New York: Columbia University Press, 1989.

Schwarz, Hans-Peter. *Die Ära Adenauer, 1949–1957: Gründerjahre der Republik 1919–1957.* Vol. 2 of *Geschichte der Bundesrepublik.* Stuttgart: DVA/Brockhaus, 1981.

———, ed. *Entspannung und Wiedervereinigung: Deutschlandpolitische Vorstellungen Konrad Adenauers 1955–1958.* Vol. 2 of *Rhöndorfer Gespräche.* Stuttgart: Belser, 1979.

Schweizer, Peter. *Reagan's War: The Epic Story of His Forty Year Struggle and Final Triumph over Communism.* New York: Doubleday, 2002.

———. *Victory: The Reagan Administration's Secret Strategy That Hastened the Collapse of the Soviet Union.* Boston: Atlantic Monthly, 1996.

Science and Society: History of the Soviet Atomic Project (40's–50's). Proceedings of the International Symposium at Dubna, May 14–18, 1996. Moscow: Izdat, 1997.

Seaborg, Glenn T., and Benjamin S. Loeb. *Kennedy, Khrushchev, and the Test Ban.* Berkeley: University of California Press, 1981.

Selvage, Douglas. "The Warsaw Pact and Nuclear Nonproliferation, 1963–1965." CWIHP working paper no. 33. Washington, D.C.: Woodrow Wilson International Center for Scholars, April 2001.

Semanov, Sergei. *Brezhnev: Pravitel 'Zolotogo Veka'.* Moscow: Veche, 2002.

Semenov, V. S. "Ot Khrushcheva do Gorbacheva. Iz dnevnika V. S. Semenova." *Novaia i noveishaia istoriia* 3, 4 (2004).

Semichastny, Vladimir. *Bespokoinoie serdtse.* Moscow: Vagrius, 2002.

Semjonow, Wladimir S. *Von Stalin bis Gorbatschow: Ein halbes Jahrhundert in diplomatischer Mission, 1939–1991.* Berlin: Nicolai, 1995.

Senyavskaya, Yelena S. *Psykhologiia voini v XX veke. Istoricheskii opit Rossii.* Moscow: ROSSPEN, 1999.

Shakhnazarov, Georgii. *Tsena Svobody: Reformatsiia Gorbachev glazami ego pomoshchnika.* Moscow: Rossika Zevs, 1993.

Shelest, Petr E. *Da ne sudimi budete. Dnevnikoviie zapisi, vospominaniia chlena Politburo TsK KPSS.* Moscow: Edition q, 1995.

Sheludko, V., ed. *Leonid Brezhnev v vospominaniiakh, razmishleniiakh, suzhdeniiakh.* Rostov-on-Don: Pheonix, 1998.

Shenin, Oleg. *Rodinu ne prodaval.* Moscow: Paleyia, 1994.

Shen Zhihua. "Stolknoveniie i uregulirovanie interesov v protsesse peregovorov o kitaisko-sovetskom Dogovore 1950 goda." *Problemi Dalnego Vostoka* 4 (2002).

Shevardnadze, Eduard. *Moi vybor v zaschitu demokratii i svobody.* Moscow: Tnovosti, 1991.

Shiraev, Eric, and Vladislav Zubok. *Anti-Americanism in Russia: From Stalin to Putin.* New York: Palgrave, 2000.

Shlapentokh, Vladimir. *Soviet Intellectuals and Political Power: The Post-Stalin Era.* London: I. B. Tauris, 1990.

Shubin, Alexandr. *Istoki Perestroiki, 1978–1984.* Vol. 1. Moscow: Academy of Sciences, 1997.

Shultz, George P. *Turmoil and Triumph: My Years as Secretary of State.* New York: Scribner's, 1993.

Sidorova, L. A. *Ottepel v Istoricheskoi Nauke: Sovetskaia istoriografiia pervogo poslestalinskogo desiatiletiia.* Moscow: Pamiatniki istoricheskoi misli, 1997.

Simonov, Konstantin. "Glazami cheloveka moego pokoleniia. Razmishleniia o I. V. Staline." *Znamia* 4 (1988): 96–99.

———. *Razniie dni voini. Dnevnik pisatelia, 1942–1945.* Moscow: Izvestia, 1981.

Simonov, Nikolai. *Voienno-promishlennii kompleks SSSR v 1930–1950 godi.* Moscow: ROSSPEN, 1996.

Skrine, C. *World War in Iran.* London: Constable, 1962.

Slavinsky, Boris. "Soviet Occupation of the Kurile Islands and the Plans of Conquest of Northern Part of Hokkaido." *Znakomtes—Yaponiia* 1 (1993).

———. *Yaltinskaia konferentsia i problema "severnikh territorii": sovremennoe dokumentalnoie pereosmisleniie.* Moscow: TOO Novina, 1996.

Slavkin, Viktor I. *Pamyatnik neizvestnomy stilyage.* Moscow: Artist-Rezhisser-Teatr, 1996.

Slezkine, Yuri. *The Jewish Century.* Princeton, N.J.: Princeton University Press, 2004.

———. "The USSR as a Communal Apartment, or How a Socialist State Promoted Ethnic Particularism." *Slavic Review* 53, no. 2 (1994): 414–52.

Slusser, Robert M. *The Berlin Crisis of 1961: Soviet-American Relations and the Struggle for Power in the Kremlin, June–November 1961.* Baltimore: Johns Hopkins University Press, 1973.

Slutsky, Boris. "Iz 'zapisok o voine.'" *Ogonyok* 17 (April 1995).

Smirnov, Yuri. "This Man Has Done More Than All of Us." In *Andrei Sakharov: Facets of a Life*, edited by P. N. Lebedev. Hong Kong: Edition Frontières, 1991.

———. "Stalin and the Atomic Bomb." *Voprosi istoriii estestvoznaniia i tekhniki* 2 (1994).

Smirnov, Yuri, and Vladislav Zubok. "Nuclear Weapons after Stalin's Death: Moscow Enters the H-Bomb Age." *CWIHP Bulletin*, no. 4 (Fall 1994).

Smith, Bradley F., and Elena Agarossi. *Operation Sunrise: The Secret Surrender*. New York: Basic Books, 1979.

Smith, Tony. *America's Mission: The United States and the Worldwide Struggle for Democracy in the Twentieth Century*. Princeton, N.J.: Princeton University Press, 1994.

Smyser, W. R. *From Yalta to Berlin: The Cold War Struggle over Germany*. New York: St. Martin's, 1999.

Snegirev, Gai I. "Vtorzheniie." *Znamia* 3 (1989).

Sokolov, B. V. "The Cost of War: Human Losses for the USSR and Germany, 1939–1945." *Journal of Slavic Military Studies* 9, no. 1 (March 1996).

Sokolovskii, V. D., ed. *Military Strategy*. Translated by Herbert S. Dinerstein, Leon Goure, and Thomas W. Wolfe. Englewood Cliffs, N.J.: Prentice-Hall, 1963.

Soldatenkov, Petr. *Vladimir Visotsky*. Moscow: Olimp, 1999.

Solzhenitsyn, A. I. *Dvesti let vmeste*. Part 2. Moscow: Russkii put, 2002.

———. *The Oak and the Calf: Sketches of Literary Life in the Soviet Union*. Translated by Harry Willetts. New York: Harper and Row, 1980.

Soutou, Georges-Henri. "La France et les notes sovietique de 1952 sur l'Allemagne." *Revue de L'Allemagne* 20, no. 3 (July–September 1988).

Spechler, Dina R. *Permitted Dissent in the USSR: "Novy Mir" and the Soviet Regime*. New York: Praeger, 1982.

Stalin, Joseph. *Works*. Edited by Robert H. McNeal. 15 vols. Stanford, Calif.: Stanford University Press, 1967.

Starr, S. Frederick. *Red and Hot: The Fate of Jazz in the USSR, 1917–1980*. Oxford: Oxford University Press, 1983.

Steininger, Rolf. *Eine vertane Chance: Die Stalin-Note vom 10. März 1952 und die Wiedervereinigung Deutschlands*. Berlin: Dietz, 1985.

Stent, Angela E. *Russia and Germany Reborn*. Princeton, N.J.: Princeton University Press, 1999.

Stephansson, Anders. "The Cold War Considered as a U.S. Project." In *Reinterpreting the End of the Cold War: Issues, Interpretations, Periodizations*, edited by Federico Romero and Silvio Pons. London: Frank Cass, 2005.

Stickle, D. M., ed. *The Beria Affair*. New York: Nova Science, 1992.

Stites, Richard. *Revolutionary Dreams: Utopian Vision and Experimental Life in the Russian Revolution*. New York: Oxford University Press, 1989.

Stourzh, Gerald. *Um Einheit und Freiheit: Staatsvertrag, Neutralität und das Ende der Ost-West-Besetzung Österreichs 1945–1955*. 4th ed. Vienna: Böhlau, 1998.

Strober, Deborah Hart, and Gerald S. Strober. *Reagan: The Man and His Presidency*. Boston: Houghton Mifflin, 1998.

———. *The Reagan Presidency: An Oral History of the Era*. Washington D.C.: Brasseys, 2003.

Stykalin, Alexander. *Prervannaia revoliutsia: Vengerskii krizis 1956 goda i politika Moskvy.* Moscow: Novii khronoraf, 2003.

Sudoplatov, Andrei. *Tainaia zhizn generala Sudoplatova: Pravda i vimisli o moem otse.* Vol. 2. Moscow: Sovremennik-Olma Press, 1998.

Sudoplatov, Pavel. *Razvedka i Kreml. Zapiski nezhelatelnogo svidetelia.* Moscow: Geia, 1996.

Sudoplatov, Pavel, Anatoli Sudoplatov, Jerrold L. Schecter, and Leona P. Schecter. *Special Tasks: The Memoirs of an Unwanted Witness, a Soviet Spymaster.* Boston: Little, Brown, 1995.

Sukhodrev, Viktor. *Iazik moi—drug moi: Ot Khrushcheva do Gorbacheva.* Moscow: Olimp-AST, 1999.

Suri, Jeremi. *Power and Protest: Global Revolution and the Rise of Détente.* Cambridge, Mass.: Harvard University Press, 2003.

Talbott, Strobe, and Michael Beschloss. *At the Highest Levels: The Inside Story of the End of the Cold War.* Boston: Little, Brown, 1993.

Tannenwald, Nina, ed. *Understanding the End of the Cold War, 1980–87: An Oral History Conference, Brown University, May 7–10, 1998.* Translated and transcribed by Jeffrey W. Dillon, Watson Institute, Brown University, Providence, R.I., May 1999.

Tannenwald, Nina, and William C. Wohlforth. "The Role of Ideas and the End of the Cold War." *Journal of Cold War Studies* 7, no. 2 (Spring 2005).

Taranov, Evgeny. " 'Raskachaem Leninskiie Gori!': Iz istorii 'volnodumstva' v Moskovskom Universitete (1955–1956)." *Svobodnaia Mysl* 10 (1993).

Tarle, Evgeny. *Politika: Istoriia territorialnykh zakhvatov.* 15th–20th century. Moscow: Eksmo-Press, 2001.

Taubkin, David, and Fedor Lyass. "O statie Kostyrchenko." *Zametki o Evreiskoi Istorii* 22 (2003), <http:// www.berkovich-zametki.com>.

Taubman, William. *Khrushchev: The Man and His Era.* New York: W. W. Norton, 2003.

——. *Stalin's American Policy: From Entente to Détente to Cold War.* New York: W. W. Norton, 1982.

Taubman, William, Sergei Khrushchev, and Abbott Gleason, eds. *Nikita Khrushchev.* New Haven, Conn.: Yale University Press, 2000.

Taylor, Brian D. "The Soviet Military and the Disintegration of the USSR." *Journal of Cold War History* 5, no. 1 (Winter 2003): 17–66.

Thatcher, Margaret. *The Downing Street Years.* New York: HarperCollins, 1993.

Thome, Françoise. "Stalin, Beria, and Mingrelian Affair." Paper presented at the international conference "Georgia, Armenia, and Azerbaijan in the Cold War: New Archival Evidence." Tsinandali, Georgia, July 8–9, 2002.

Thornton, Richard C. *The Nixon-Kissinger Years: Reshaping America's Foreign Policy.* 2nd rev. ed. St. Paul, Minn.: Paragon House, 2001.

Thoss, Bruno, ed. *Volksarmee schaffen—ohne Geschrei! Studien zu den Anfängen einer verdeckten Aufrüstung in der SBZ/DDR, 1947–1952.* Munich: R. Oldenbourg Verlag, 1995.

Thurston, Robert W., and Bernd Bonwetsch. *The People's War: Responses to World War II in the Soviet Union.* Urbana: University of Illinois Press, 2000.

Timasheff, Nicholas. *The Great Retreat: The Growth and Decline of Communism in Russia.* New York: E. P. Dutton, 1946.

Tischler, Janos. "The Hungarian Party Leadership and the Polish Crisis of 1980–1981." *CWIHP Bulletin*, no. 11 (Winter 1998).

——. "Poland's October and the 1956 Hungarian Revolution: Gomulka's Intercession with Khrushchev on Behalf of Imre Nagy: Excerpt from the Records of the Discussions Conducted between the Party and Government Delegation of the Polish People's Republic and the Party and Government Delegation of the Soviet Union, May 24–25, 1957." <http://www.rev.hu/html/en/studies/1956/interconn.htm>.

Tismaneanu, Vladimir. *Stalinism for All Seasons: A Political History of Romanian Communism.* Berkeley: University of California Press, 2003.

Trachtenberg, Marc. *A Constructed Peace: The Making of the European Settlement, 1945–1963.* Princeton, N.J.: Princeton University Press, 1999.

——. *History and Strategy.* Princeton, N.J.: Princeton University Press, 1991.

Troyanovsky, Oleg A. "The Caribbean Crisis: A View from the Kremlin." *International Affairs* 4–5 (Moscow) (1992).

——. *Cherez godi i rasstoiania. Istoriia odnoi semyi.* Moscow: Vagrius, 1997.

——. "The Making of Soviet Foreign Policy." In *Nikita Khrushchev: Fresh Perspectives on the Last Communist*, edited by William Taubman, Sergei Khrushchev, and Abbott Gleason. New Haven, Conn.: Yale University Press, 2000.

——. "Nikita Khrushchev and the Making of Soviet Foreign Policy." Paper presented at the Khrushchev Centenary Conference. Brown University, December 1–3, 1994.

Trubetskoy, Sergei E. *Minuvshee.* Moscow: DEM, 1991.

Tucker, Robert C. *The Soviet Political Mind: Stalinism and Post-Stalin Change.* Rev. ed. New York: W. W. Norton, 1971.

——. *Stalin as Revolutionary, 1879–1929: A Study in History and Personality.* New York: W. W. Norton, 1973.

——. *Stalin in Power: The Revolution from Above.* New York: W. W. Norton, 1990.

Tuma, Oldrich. "The Czechoslovak Communist Regime and the Polish Crisis, 1980–1981." *CWIHP Bulletin*, no. 11 (Winter 1998).

Tumarkin, Nina. *The Living and the Dead: The Rise and Fall of the Cult of World War II in Russia.* New York: Basic Books, 1995.

Tuminez, Astrid S. "Nationalism, Ethnic Pressures, and the Breakup of the Soviet Union." *Journal of Cold War Studies* 5, no. 4 (2003).

Tvardovsky, Alexander. "Iz rabochikh tetradei (1953–1960)." *Znamia* 8 (July 1989).

——. "Rabochie tetradi 60-kh godov." *Znamia* 4 (April 2002).

Uhl, Matthias, and Vladimir I. Ivkin. " 'Operation Atom': The Soviet Union's Stationing of Nuclear Missiles in the German Democratic Republic." *CWIHP Bulletin*, nos. 12–13 (Fall–Winter 2001).

Ulam, Adam. *Expansion and Coexistence: Soviet Foreign Policy, 1917–1973.* 2nd ed. New York: Holt, Rinehart and Winston, 1974.

Ustinov, D. F. *Otvesti ugrozu iadernoi voini.* Moscow: Politizdat, 1982.

Vaksberg, Arkady. *Stalin's Prosecutor: The Life of Andrei Vyshinsky.* New York: Grove Press, 1991.

Varsori, Antonio. "Le gouvernement Eden et l'Union Sovietique, 1955–1956: de l'éspoir à la disillusion." *Relations Internationales* 71 (Autumn 1992).

Velikhov, Evgeny P. "Nauka rabotaet na bezyadrnii mir." *Mezhdunarodnaia zhizn* 10 (1988).

Venona Historical Monograph no. 3. Fort Mead, Md.: National Security Agency, March 1996.

Vinogradov, V. M. *Diplomatiia: Liudi i Sobitiia. Iz zapisok posla.* Moscow: ROSSPEN, 1998.

Vladimirov, Leonid. *Rossiia bez prikras i umolchanii.* Frankfurt: Possev-Verlag, 1969.

Vlasov, N. A. "Desiat' let riadom s Kurchatovym." In *Vospominaniia ob akademike I. V. Kurchatove,* edited by M. K. Romanovsky. Moscow: Nauka, 1983.

Voinovich, Vladimir. *The Life and Extraordinary Adventures of Private Ivan Chonkin.* Translated by Richard Lourie. Chicago: Northwestern University Press, 1995.

Volkogonov, Dmitry. *Sem Vozhdei: Galereia liderov SSSR.* Vol. 2. Moscow: Novosti, 1995.

———. *Stalin: Triumph and Tragedy.* New York: Prima Lifestyles, 1996.

Volkov, Alexander, and Marina Kolesova. "Soviet Reaction to U.S. Nuclear Policy (1953–1962)." Paper presented at the conference "The New Evidence on the Cold War." Moscow, January 12–15, 1993.

Volkov, S. V. *Intellektualnyi sloi v sovetskom obschestve.* Moscow: Fond Razvitie, 1999.

Volkov, Vladimir. "German Question as Stalin Saw It, 1947–1952." Paper presented at the conference "Stalin and the Cold War." Yale University, New Haven, Conn., September 24–25, 1999.

———. *Uzloviie problemi noveishei istorii stran Tsentralnoi i Yugo-Vostochnoi Evropi.* Moscow: Indrik, 2000.

———. "Za sovetami v Kreml. Zapis besedy I. V. Stalna s rukovoditeliami SEPG. Mart 1946." *Istoricheskii arkhiv* 2 (2002).

Volokitina, T. V., T. Islamov, G. Murashko, A. Noskova, et al., eds. *Vostochnaia Evropa v dokumentakh rossiiskikh arkhivov.* Vol. 1, 1944–1948 (Moscow-Novosibirsk: Sibirsky khronograf, 1997). Vol. 2, 1949–1953 (Moscow-Novosibirsk: Sibirsky khronograf, 1998).

Volokitina, Tatiana, Galina Murashko, Albina Noskova, and Tatiana Pokivailova. *Moskva i Vostochnaia Evropa. Stanovleniie politicheskikh rezhimov sovetskogo tipa, 1949–1953, Ocherki istorii.* Moscow: ROSSPEN, 2002.

Voronkov, Vladimir I. "Sobitiia 1980–1981 v Polshe. Vzgliad so Staroi ploschiadi." *Voprosi istorii* 10 (1995).

Vorotnikov, Vitalii. *A bylo eto tak: Iz dnevnika chlena Politbyuro TsK KPSS.* Moscow: Sovet veteranov knigoizdaniya SI-MAR, 1995.

Wail, Peter, and Alexander Ghenis. *1960-e: Mir Sovetskogo Cheloveka.* 2nd ed. Moscow: Novoie Kulturnoie Obozreniie, 1998.

Weart, Spencer R. *Nuclear Fear: A History of Images.* Cambridge, Mass: Harvard University Press, 1988.

Weathersby, Kathryn. "Should We Fear This? Stalin and the Danger of War with America." CWIHP working paper no. 39. Washington, D.C.: Woodrow Wilson International Center for Scholars, July 2002.

———. "Soviet Aims in Korea and the Origins of the Korean War, 1945–1950: New Evidence from Russian Archives." CWIHP working paper no. 8. Washington, D.C.: Woodrow Wilson International Center for Scholars, November 1993.

———. "To Attack or Not to Attack: Stalin, Kim Il Sung, and the Prelude to War." CWIHP Bulletin, no. 5 (1995).

Weinberger, Caspar. In the Arena: A Memoir of the 20th Century. Washington, D.C.: Regnery, 2001.

Weiner, Amir. Making Sense of War: The Second World War and the Fate of the Bolshevik Revolution. Princeton, N.J.: Princeton University Press, 2001.

Weinstein, Allen, and Alexander Vassiliev. The Haunted Wood: Soviet Espionage in America—The Stalin Era. New York: Random House, 1999.

Weisgall, Jonathan M. Operation Crossroads: The Atomic Tests at Bikini Atoll. Annapolis, Md.: Naval Institute Press, 1994.

Werblan, Andrzej. "The Conversation between Wladyslaw Gomulka and Josef Stalin." CWIHP Bulletin, no. 11 (1998).

Werth, Alexander. Russia at War, 1941–1945. London: Pan Books, 1964.

Westad, Odd Arne. Brothers in Arms: The Rise and Fall of the Sino-Soviet Alliance, 1945–1963. Washington, D.C.: Woodrow Wilson Center Press; Stanford, Calif.: Stanford University Press, 1998.

———. Cold War and Revolution: Soviet-American Rivalry and the Origins of the Chinese Civil War, 1944–1946. New York: Columbia University Press, 1993.

———. Decisive Encounters: The Chinese Civil War, 1946–1950. Stanford, Calif.: Stanford University Press, 2003.

———. "The Fall of Détente and the Turning Tides of History." In The Fall of Détente: Soviet-American Relations during the Carter Years, edited by Odd Arne Westad. Oslo: Scandinavian University Press, 1997.

———. The Global Cold War: Third World Interventions and the Making of Our Times. New York: Cambridge University Press, 2005.

———. "Moscow and the Angolan Crisis, 1974–1976: A New Pattern of Intervention." CWIHP Bulletin, nos. 8–9 (Winter 1996/97).

———. "Prelude to Invasion: The Soviet Union and the Afghan Communists, 1978–1979." International History Review 16, no. 1 (Canada) (February 1994).

———. "The Road to Kabul: Soviet Policy on Afghanistan, 1978–1979." In The Fall of Détente: Soviet-American Relations during the Carter Years, edited by Odd Arne Westad. Oslo: Scandinavian University Press, 1997.

———. "Secrets of the Second World: The Russian Archives and the Reinterpretation of the Cold War History." Diplomatic History 21 (Spring 1997).

———, ed. The Fall of Détente: Soviet-American Relations during the Carter Years. Oslo: Scandinavian University Press, 1997.

Wettig, Gerhard. "Die befinnende Umorientierung der sowjetischen Deutschland-Politik im Frühjahr und Sommer 1953." Deutschland Archiv 28, no. 5 (May 1995).

———. Bereitschaft zu Einheit in Freiheit? Die Sowjetische Deutschland-Politik, 1945–1955. Munich: Olzog, 1999.

———. "Die Stalin-Note vom 10 Marz 1952: Antwort auf Elke Scherstjanoi." *Deutschland Archiv* 25 (August 1992).

———. "Zum Stand der Forschung über Berijas Deutschland-Politik." *Deutschland Archiv* 26 (1993).

Whitfield, Stephen J. *The Culture of the Cold War*. Baltimore: Johns Hopkins University Press, 1991.

Wingrove, Paul. "Mao's Conversations with the Soviet Ambassador, 1953–1956." CWIHP working paper no. 36 (April 2002).

Wittner, Lawrence S. *Resisting the Bomb: A History of the World Nuclear Disarmament Movement, 1954–1970*. Stanford, Calif.: Stanford University Press, 1997.

———. *Toward Nuclear Abolition: A History of the World Nuclear Disarmament Movement, 1971 to the Present*. Stanford, Calif.: Stanford University Press, 2003.

Wohlforth, William C. *The Elusive Balance: Power and Perceptions during the Cold War*. Ithaca, N.Y.: Cornell University Press, 1993.

———. "Realism and the End of the Cold War." *International Security* 19 (Winter 1994/95).

———, ed. *Cold War Endgame: Oral History, Analysis, Debates*. University Park: Pennsylvania State University Press, 2003.

———, ed. *Retrospective on the End of the Cold War*. Baltimore: Johns Hopkins University Press, 1996.

Wolff, David. *To the Harbin Station: The Liberal Alternative in Russian Manchuria, 1898–1914*. Stanford, Calif.: Stanford University Press, 1999.

Woll, Josephine. *Real Images: Soviet Cinema and the Thaw*. New York: I. B. Tauris, 2000.

Yakovlev, Alexander. *Muki prochteniia bytiia. Perestroyka: nadezhdy i realnosti*. Moscow: Novosti, 1991.

———. *Omut pamiati*. Moscow: Vagrius, 2000.

———. *Predisloviie, obval, posleslovie*. Moscow: Novosti, 1992.

Yanov, Alexander. *The Russian New Right*. Berkeley: University of California Press, 1978.

Yaroshinska, Alla. *Chernobyl: The Forbidden Truth*. Lincoln: University of Nebraska Press, 1995.

Yegorov, Vladimir. *Out of a Dead End into the Unknown: Notes on Gorbachev's Perestroika*. Chicago: Edition 9, 1993.

Yegorova, Natalia. " 'Iranskii krizis,' 1945–1946 gg." *Novaia i noveishaia istoriia* 3 (May–June 1994).

Yegorova, Natalia, and Alexandr Chubarian, eds. *Kholodnaia voina 1945–1963: Istorichestkaia retrospektive*. Moscow: Olma Press, 2003.

Yeltsin, Boris. *Ispoved na zadannuiu temu*. Moscow: PIK, 1990.

Yevtushenko, Yevgeny. *Volchii passport*. Moscow: Vagrius, 1998.

York, Herbert F. *The Advisors: Oppenheimer, Teller, and the Superbomb*. Stanford, Calif.: Stanford University Press, 1989.

Yurchak, Alexei. *Everything Was Forever, Until It Was No More: The Last Soviet Generation*. Princeton, N.J.: Princeton University Press, 2006.

Zalessky, K. A. *Imperia Stalina: Biograficheskii entsiklopedicheskii slovar*. Moscow: Veche, 2000.

Zaloga, Steven. *The Kremlin's Nuclear Sword: The Rise and Fall of Russia's Strategic Nuclear Forces, 1945–2000.* Washington, D.C.: Smithsonian Institution Press, 2002.

Zaslavsky, Victor. "Collapse of Empires: The Soviet Union." In *After Empire*, edited by Karen Barkley and Mark von Hagen. Boulder, Colo.: Westview, 1997.

——. "Nationalism and Democratic Transition in Postcommunist Societies." *Daedalus* (Spring 1992).

——. *The Neo-Stalinist State: Class, Ethnicity, and Consensus in Soviet Society.* Armonk, N.Y.: M. E. Sharpe, 1982.

——. *Lo Stalinismo e la Sinistra Italiana. Dal mito dell'Urss alla fine del communismo 1945–1991.* Rome: Mondadori, 2004.

Zelenov, M. V. "Joseph Stalin's 'On Engels's article "The Foreign Policy of Tsarist Russia"' and Ideological Preparation for the World War." *Voprosi istorii* 7 (July 2002): 3–40.

——. "Kak Stalin kritikoval i redaktiroval konspekti shkolnikh uchebnikov po istorii (1934–1936 godi)." *Voprosi istorii* 6 (2004).

Zelikow, Philip, and Condoleezza Rice. *Germany Unified and Europe Transformed: A Study in Statecraft.* Cambridge, Mass.: Harvard University Press, 1995.

Zezina, Marina R. "Shokovaia terapia; ot 1953-go k 1956 godu." *Otechestvennaia istoriia* 3 (1995).

——. *Sovetskaia khudozhestvennaia intelligentsiia i vlast v 1950-e–1960-e godi.* Moscow: Dialog-MGU, 1999.

Zhang Shuguang and Chen Jian, "The Emerging Disputes between Beijing and Moscow: Ten Newly Available Chinese Documents, 1956–58." *CWIHP Bulletin*, nos. 6–7 (Winter 1995).

——, eds. *Chinese Communist Foreign Policy and the Cold War in Asia: Documentary Evidence.* Chicago: Imprint Publications, 1996.

Zhukov, Georgi. *Vospominania i razmyshleniia.* 2 vols. Moscow: Olma Press, 2002.

Zinoviev, Alexander. *Russkaia sudba: ispoved otschepentsa.* Moscow: ZAO Tsentrpoligraf, 1999.

Zubkova, Elena. "Mir mnenii sovetskogo cheloveka." *Otechesvennaia istoriia* 4 (1998).

——. *Obshchestvo i reformi 1945–1965.* Moscow: Rossiia molodaia, 1993.

——. "The Rivalry with Malenkov." In *Nikita Khrushchev: Fresh Perspectives on the Last Communist,* edited by William Taubman, Sergei Khrushchev, and Abbott Gleason. New Haven, Conn.: Yale University Press, 2000.

——. *Russia after the War: Hopes, Illusions, and Disappointments, 1945–1957.* Translated by Hugh Ragsdale. Armonk, N.Y.: M. E. Sharpe, 1998.

——. "Stalin and Public Opinion in the USSR." In *Stalin i kholodnaia voina,* edited by Ilya Gaiduk, Natalia Yegorova, and Alexander Chubarian. Moscow: IVI RAN, 1997.

Zubkova, Elena, et al., eds. *Sovetskaia zhizn 1945–1953.* Moscow: ROSSPEN, 2003.

Zubok, Vladislav M. "CPSU Plenums, Leadership Struggles, and Soviet Cold War Politics." *CWIHP Bulletin*, no. 10 (March 1998).

——. "Inside the Covert Cold War: The KGB vs. the CIA, 1960–1962." *CWIHP Bulletin*, no. 4 (Fall 1994).

——. "The Khrushchev-Mao Conversations, 31 July–3 August 1958 and 2 October 1959." *CWIHP Bulletin*, nos. 12–13 (Fall/Winter 2001).

——. "Khrushchev's 1960 Troop Cut: New Russian Evidence." *CWIHP Bulletin*, nos. 8–9 (Winter 1996/1997).

——. " 'Look What Chaos in the Beautiful Socialist Camp!' Den Xiaoping and the Sino-Soviet Split, 1956–1963." *CWIHP Bulletin*, no. 10 (March 1998).

——. "The Multi-Level Dynamics of Moscow's German Policy from 1953 to 1964." In *Re-Viewing the Cold War: Domestic Factors and Foreign Policy in the East-West Confrontation*, edited by Patrick M. Morgan and Keith L. Nelson. Westport, Conn.: Praeger, 2000.

——. "Nebo nad sverkhderzhavami." *SShA: ekonomika, politika, ideologiya* 7 (July 1990).

——. "Soviet Foreign Policy in Germany and Austria and the Post-Stalin Succession Struggle, 1953–1955." Paper prepared at the conference "The Soviet Union, Germany, and the Cold War, 1945–1962: New Evidence from Eastern Archives." Essen, Germany, June 28–30, 1994.

——. "Soviet Intelligence and the Cold War: The 'Small' Committee of Information, 1952–1953." *Diplomatic History* 19, no. 3 (Summer 1995).

——. " 'To Hell with Yalta!': Stalin Opts for a New Status Quo." *CWIHP Bulletin*, nos. 6–7 (Winter 1995/96).

——. " 'Unverfroren und grob in der Deutschlandfrage': Berija, der Nachfolgestreit nach Stalins Tod und die Moskauer DDR-Debatte im April–Mai 1953." In *1953—Krisenjahr des Kalten Krieges in Europa*, edited by Christoph Klessmann and Bernd Stöver. Cologne: Böhlau, 1999.

——. " 'What Chaos in the Beautiful Socialist Camp!': Deng Xiaoping and Sino-Soviet Relations, 1956–1963." *CWIHP Bulletin*, no. 10 (March 1998).

Zubok, Vladislav M., and Hope Harrison. "The Nuclear Education of Nikita Khrushchev." In *Cold War Statesmen Confront the Bomb*, edited by John Lewis Gaddis, Philip H. Gordon, Ernest R. May, and Jonathan Rosenberg. London: Oxford University Press, 1999.

Zubok, Vladislav M., and Constantine Pleshakov. *Inside the Kremlin's Cold War: From Stalin to Khrushchev*. Cambridge, Mass.: Harvard University Press, 1996.

——. "The Soviet Union." In *The Origins of the Cold War in Europe*, edited by David Raynolds, 53–76. New Haven: Yale University Press, 1994.

Zubok, Vladislav M., S. Y. Shenin, and A. A. Shubin, eds. *Konets kholodnoi voini: noviie fakti i aspekti*. Saratov: Nauchnaia kniga, 2004.

Zubok, Vladislav M., and Yuri Smirnov. "Moscow and Nuclear Weapons after Stalin's Death." *CWIHP Bulletin*, no. 4 (1994).

(INDEX)

317, 325, 331; and Cold War end, 329, 330

Chervonenko, Stepan, 197

Cheshkov, Marat, 169

China, xxiii, 18, 31; under Guomindang, 25–26; treaty with USSR, 26, 79, 110, 137; and nuclear program, 152; fears of USSR, 210; and U.S. "China card," 257–58. *See also* Manchuria; Sino-Soviet relations; Xinjiang

Chinese Communist Party (CCP), 25, 26, 35, 36

Chuikov, Vasily, 82, 83

Churchill, Winston, 16, 26, 88; and Eastern Europe, 23; Fulton speech, 34, 53; and Stalin's death, 91, 98

Cinema: impact of American, 172–73; and de-Stalinization, 178, 184

Clausewitz, Carl von, 130, 378–79 (n. 29)

Cold War: "domestic" in USSR, 50, 56–60; as cultural warfare, 163, 171, 175–76; explanation of end of, 305–10; and modernization, 344–45

"Collective leadership." *See* Kremlin leadership

Cominform (Informational Bureau of the Communist Parties), 73

Conferences and summits: Tehran (1943), 37; Bretton Woods (1944), 51; London (1945), 31–32; Moscow (1945), 33, 40; Potsdam (1945), 16, 26; San Francisco (1945), 39; Yalta (1945), 9, 11, 14, 38; Paris (1946), 60; Moscow (1947), 72; Geneva (1954), 111; Geneva (1955), 106–8, 111; Paris (1960), 138; Vienna (1961), 140; Moscow (1972), 221–22; Vladivostok (1974), 243–45; Vienna (1979), 257, 258; Geneva (1985), 284; Reykjavik (1986), 292, 293; Malta (1989), 320, 328. *See also* Yalta

Connally, Tom, 67

Cot, Pierre, 91

Council for Mutual Economic Assistance (COMECON or CMEA), 78. *See also* Eastern and Central Europe: Soviet economic support of

Cuba, 299; Soviet forces in, 144–46; interventions in Africa, 251–53; "brigade crisis" in, 263

Cuban missile crisis, 143–50; impact on Soviet policies, 193–94, 199, 203, 243, 339

Cuban revolution, 143; impact on USSR, 182–83, 382 (n. 74)

Czechoslovakia, 90, 110, 180; eviction of Germans in, 64; and Marshall Plan, 73; Communist coup in, 75; Prague Spring and Soviet invasion in, 190, 191, 207–8

Daniel, Yuli, 190

Daniloff, Nicholas, 291

"Death to the Spies" (SMERSH). *See* Secret police

Defense Council, 98, 220, 277, 283, 296, 321

Dekanozov, Vladimir, 68

Derluguian, Georgy, 250

De-Stalinization, 166–67, 340; during World War II, 6; and foreign policy, 94, 99, 102–3, 104, 164, 174; and Khrushchev, 112, 168; and Cold War consensus, 164, 170–71, 177, 191; and Iron Curtain, 172, 183; and 1957 World Youth Festival in Moscow, 174–77; and decline of militarism, 183–84, 186; stopped under Brezhnev, 190; under Gorbachev, 281, 282, 286, 298, 301

Détente, xxv, 192–93, 216, 217–18, 389 (n. 2); criticism of, 192; and invasion of Czechoslovakia, 209; opposition to, 213–14, 219–20, 224, 245; European security and cooperation conference, 214, 229, 237, 243, 245; and back channel, 216, 255; Soviet goals in, 220, 223, 247

Dimitrov, Georgy, 8, 20, 30, 34

Germany: Soviet occupation of, 9, 32, 63–
64; demilitarization of, 31, 65–66; Ger-
man Question, 62, 87, 89, 93, 106, 132,
142, 143, 329–30; and currency reform,
75; and 1952 Stalin note, 82–83; and
1955 Eden Plan, 107, 373 (n. 47)
Gilpatric, Roswell, 140, 141
Ginzburg, Alexander, 255
Ginzburg, Vitaly, 124
Goldgeier, James, 18
Golikov, Fedor, 12
Golikov, V. A., 197, 206
Gomulka, Wladyslaw, 33, 114, 115, 371 (n. 24)
Gonzalez, Felipe, 290
Gorbachev, Mikhail, xxv, 3, 167, 170, 180,
209, 273, 277; and "new thinking," xxv,
280–81, 285–86, 294, 296, 298, 307–9,
312, 321, 330, 341; and Khrushchev, 178,
311; and foreign travel, 183, 316; background and character of, 278, 282–83,
304–5, 311–12, 313, 316–19, 327, 330;
economic reforms of, 279–80, 290–91;
early reforms of, 279–80, 301; and
nuclear arms, 282–93 passim; opposition to violence, 282–83, 318–19; and
SDI, 284, 285, 287, 292, 293; and
Afghan war, 284, 297, 313; and Reagan,
284–85, 291–93; inconsistencies of,
287, 301, 306; and glasnost, 289, 301;
and financial crisis, 291, 299, 322, 332;
and military, 295–96, 300, 320; radical
reformism of, 301, 302, 307–9; and
party cadres, 301, 308, 412 (n. 40);
debate about role of, 304–5, 334–35;
and Stalin, 315, 316, 321, 329; and
"common European home," 316, 324,
326, 328–29, 331; and German reunification, 317, 324–26, 327, 328–30;
loses control, 322, 332–33; and Yeltsin,
331, 333; and coup, 331–32
Gorbachev, Raisa, 170, 180, 183, 281, 301,
331, 332

Gordov, Vasily, 54, 55, 59
Gorshkov, Sergei, 249
Gottwald, Klement, 80
Gouzenko, Igor, 47
Great Britain, 113, 114, 123, 194, 244
Grechko, Andrei, 145, 202, 215, 219, 220–
21, 245, 251
Greece, 21, 75
Grinevsky, Oleg, 410 (n. 13)
Gromyko, Andrei, 13–14, 137, 140, 152, 194,
200, 258, 297; as Khrushchev's foreign
minister, 121–22; supports détente, 197,
206–7, 213; and human rights, 237, 256;
and Reagan, 276; supports Gorbachev,
277; and "new thinking," 294–95, 318
Grotewohl, Otto, 90
Gulag, 165, 166
Gusev, Fedor, 16

Hammarskjold, Dag, 248
Harriman, Averell, 17, 26, 34, 152, 222, 258;
and Stalin, 32–33
Harrison, Hope, 82, 133
Harrison, Selig S., 228
Hasanli, Jamil, 39, 44
Honecker, Erich, 212, 241, 324, 325–26
Hopkins, Harry, 11, 46
Hottelet, Richard C., 29
Human rights: and Helsinki Final Act, 237,
254; and Carter's policy, 254–55; and
Gorbachev, 298
Hungary, 102; revolution in and Soviet inva-
sion of, 115–18, 170; opening of borders,
323, 325
Hussein, Saddam, 328

Ideology (Soviet), 77, 100, 180; and Leninism, 49, 61, 170, 198, 336; and domestic
controls, 53, 165; and nuclear threat,
128; and romanticism, 169–70; and
decolonization, 181–82, 182–83; and
"socialism with a human face," 190, 191;

Sakharov, Andrei, 97, 110, 124, 143, 237; and nuclear arms, 124, 128, 146, 151, 185; exiled, 227; return from exile, 298

SALT (Strategic Arms Limitations Treaty). *See* Arms control

Samoilov, David, 187

Sarper, Selim, 37

Scheid, Fernande, 41

Schlesinger, James, 245

Scowcroft, Brent, 324

Secret police (Soviet): and terror, 4, 55; in East Germany, 65; reforms after Stalin, 87, 97. *See also* KGB

Semenov, Vladimir, 65, 87, 88, 368 (n. 100); as Stalin's commissar in Germany, 65, 68, 363 (n. 29); as high commissioner in Germany, 90, 91, 93; as SALT negotiator, 215, 220, 394 (n. 94)

Semichastny, Vladimir, 194

Serov, Ivan, 9, 23, 97, 119

Shakhnazarov, Georgy, 178, 180, 215, 327

Shakhurin, Alexei, 53

Shcharansky, Nathan, 237, 255

Shchelokov, Nikolai, 233, 235

Shebarshin, Leonid, 248

Shelepin, Alexander, 194, 195, 197, 204

Shelest, Petro, 207, 218, 219

Shepilov, Dmitry, 113, 114, 116, 119, 171; and Middle East, 110

Shevardnadze, Eduard, 280, 281, 311, 321; and Afghan war, 297; and end of Soviet empire, 323, 325, 329; friendship with Baker, 324

Shishlin, Nikolai, 205

Shostakovich, Dmitry, 187

Shultz, George, 274, 275, 293, 300

Shvernik, Nikolai, 104

Simonov, Konstantin, 60–61, 167, 169, 171, 184

Sino-Soviet relations: under Khrushchev, 110–11, 136–37, 138, 151; Soviet assistance to China, 111, 132, 181–82, 337–

38; under Brezhnev, 197, 198, 209–10. *See also* China; Manchuria; Xinjiang

Sinyavsky, Andrei, 185, 190

Slavsky, Efim, 151

Slezkine, Yuri, 7, 9

Smirnov, Leonid, 221, 243

Smyser, W. R., 49

Socialist Unity Party of Germany (SED), 64, 74

Sokolov, Sergei, 297, 300

Sokolovsky, Vasily, 65, 69, 91, 146, 362 (n. 16); and nuclear strategy, 135

Solidarity. *See* Poland

Solzhenitsyn, Alexander, 163, 189, 234; expelled from USSR, 235–37

Soong, T. V., 25–26, 350 (n. 59)

South Africa, 253

South Caucasus: nationalism in, 10, 40, 336; and Turkey, 37; deportations from, 58; and collapse of USSR, 320, 332

Soviet Control Commission (in Germany), 82, 89, 91

Soviet elites: and jingoism, 5, 170–71; and anti-Americanism, 11–12, 59, 60–61, 176, 197, 215, 223, 341; and nuclear fears, 27–28, 125, 128, 150, 185, 271; and Russification, 56, 104; and Party Plenums, 86, 100; and memories of Nazi attack, 106; and xenophobia, 113; on foreign policy, 120, 213–14, 219–20; and "enlightened" apparatchiks, 164, 178–79, 191, 205–6, 214, 282; privileges of, 165, 166; and invasion of Czechoslovakia, 209, 322; and détente, 213–14; support Yeltsin, 332, 333

Soviet intelligence. *See* Intelligence

Soviet military, 53, 81, 153; early criticism of Stalin by, 54; nuclear plans and arms of, 126–27, 135–36, 145–46, 147, 153; Khrushchev's cuts in, 135; in Cuban missile crisis, 145, 147, 151; under Brezhnev, 242–43, 249; Chernobyl impact on, 288–89; Gorbachev's reforms of, 295–96; and collapse of USSR, 320, 333

Soviet Military Administration in Germany (SMAG), 64–65, 68, 75, 82, 363 (n. 28)

Soviet military-political doctrine, 104, 215, 272, 292, 295, 296, 300, 306

Soviet society: impact of World War II on, 2–3, 4, 6; impact of Western and American culture on, 12, 172, 175, 177, 185, 190, 225; student unrest in, 117, 167–71; "spillover" effect in, 117, 168–69, 209, 266; fear of war in, 128, 276; and Cuban revolution, 143; social and demographic changes in, 163–64, 186; and Cold War consensus, 164, 277

Sputnik, 123, 131, 175, 377 (n. 3)

Stalin, Joseph, xxiv, 86, 336–37; and Roosevelt, 11, 14; background of, 16–21; as "realist," 17, 19, 336–37; foreign policy of, 20, 37–38, 40, 43, 76; and "socialist empire," 21, 43, 48, 315; and nuclear arms, 30–32, 34; and Eastern Europe, 32, 33; and Turkey, 37–40; and nationalism, 39, 63, 70–71, 77; and Iran, 40–45; and domestic mobilization and repressions, 50, 52, 53–55, 165; and Bretton-Woods system, 51; and strategic reserves, 55, 360 (n. 100); and Jews, 56–57; and Germany, 62, 63, 64–65, 70–71, 74, 77–78, 82–83; health problems of, 68, 83; and Yugoslavia, 73–74; and Italy, 76; and Korean War, 78–81; and China, 79, 80–81; and war preparations, 81, 85; xenophobia of, 103, 281; compared to successors, 105, 315, 316, 321, 329; and cadres, 195–96

Starodubov, Viktor, 243

Stevenson, Adlai, 150

Strategic Defense Initiative (SDI), 272, 287, 292, 293, 343; Soviet reaction to, 273, 284, 287

Strategic Rocket Forces (RVSN), 131, 145

Sturua, Davy, 39

Sudoplatov, Pavel, 6, 88

Sukhodrev, Viktor, 202, 220

Suri, Jeremi, 164

Suslov, Mikhail, 136, 137, 140, 196, 197; as top ideologist, 200, 204, 219, 232; and Polish crisis, 266

Syria, 110, 199–200, 299

Taiwan, 111, 136–37

Taraki, Nur Mohammad, 259, 260, 261, 262

Tarasenko, Sergei, 316

Taubman, William, 97, 143, 278

Thatcher, Margaret, 290, 309

Thaw. See De-Stalinization

Tito, Josip Broz, 24, 74; and Khrushchev, 118–19. See also Yugoslavia

Togliatti, Palmiro, 76, 375 (n. 95)

Tolbukhin, Fedor, 45, 356 (n. 37)

Trade, USSR-U.S., 229, 231, 233, 245–46

Trapeznikov, Sergei, 197, 206

Tripolitania (Libya), 38–39

Troyanovsky, Alexander, 12

Troyanovsky, Oleg, 101, 122, 137, 150

Trubetskoy, Sergei, 334

Truman, Harry, 14, 30, 35; and containment of USSR, 44, 46, 49

Turkey, 8, 10, 45, 57; Turkish Straits, 36–38; Soviet plans in, 36–39; U.S. missiles in, 123, 129, 147–48, 149, 150

Tvardovsky, Alexander, 16, 171, 176

Tyulpanov, Sergei, 68–69, 363 (n. 28)

Ukraine, 5, 7, 9, 10; deportations from, 60; and anti-Semitism, 187

Ulbricht, Walter, 67, 70, 83–84, 88, 141, 207, 211, 212; criticized by Soviets, 90–92

United Nations, 31, 55, 134, 139; and Gorbachev, 309, 314

United States: and intelligence on USSR, 2, 53, 205, 265, 271, 400 (n. 110); and Grand Alliance, 11–16; and containment of USSR, 24, 30, 33, 44, 46, 80, 129; and China, 26, 35, 216; and nuclear arms and fears, 27, 123, 131, 153; and occupation of Japan, 30; cooperation with Great Britain, 34, 42; ideological worldview of, 49, 234, 343; strategic superiority of, 125, 140, 144; and arms control, 125, 198, 200; and Cuban revolution, 144; neoconservatives in, 153, 192, 223, 234, 255, 257, 339–40, 400 (n. 110); and Vietnam War, 193; interventions by, 199, 274

USSR: as empire, xxiii, 61, 336; collapse of, xxv, 303, 319, 327, 331–33, 344; surrounded by U.S. bases, 66, 101, 123; appeal in third world, 131, 179, 247; and Africa, 139

Ustinov, Dmitry, 27, 151, 170, 202, 251, 274, 276, 277, 378 (n. 25); background of, 204–5; and Afghanistan, 262–64; and Solidarity, 267

Vance, Cyrus, 254, 256–57
Vandenberg, Arthur H., 67
Van Dijk, Ruud, 84
Vanik, Charles, 232
Varennikov, Valentin, 262, 297
Vassiliev, Alexander, 47
Velikhov, Evgeny, 273, 287
Vietnam: Vietnam War, 197–99, 217–18, 219–20; Communist leadership in, 198; U.S. defeat in, 250, 251; Soviet economic assistance to, 299
Vinogradov, S. A., 40
Visotsky, Vladimir, 186
Voinovich, Vladimir, 186
Volkogonov, Dmitry, 201, 304
Voroshilov, Klement, 22, 57, 112, 115, 119
Vorotnikov, Vitaly, 326, 327
Voznesensky, Andrei, 185

Voznesensky, Nikolai, 51, 58, 354 (n. 123)
Vyshinsky, Andrei, 22, 24, 67, 82, 185, 189, 365 (n. 66)

Wallace, Henry, 47, 76
Warsaw Treaty Organization (Warsaw Pact) (WTO), 102, 115, 117, 140, 152, 207, 208, 372 (n. 35); and Polish crisis, 266, 267, 270; disintegration of, 322
Watergate scandal, 239, 246; Soviet perception of, 241
Weinberger, Caspar, 271, 275, 283
Weinstein, Allen, 47
Westad, Odd Arne, 111
West Berlin. See Berlin
West Germany, 86, 101, 194, 292; creation of, 67, 74–75, 77; and "economic miracle," 85; relations with USSR, 108, 217; and nuclear arms, 133; and Ostpolitik, 210–11
White Russia. See Byelorussia
World Bank, 51
World War II: impact on Soviet society, xxiv, 2–3, 4, 6, 337; Soviet losses in, 1–2, 347 (n. 2); Soviet wartime plans, 8

Xinjiang, 25, 35, 42

Yakovlev, Alexander, 5, 180, 209; and glasnost, 201; as Gorbachev's adviser, 281–82, 296; and Eastern Europe, 322
Yalta: Yalta-Potsdam framework, 21, 25, 26, 29, 31, 49, 81, 82, 134; Declaration of Liberated Europe, 22, 30, 237; and Far East, 35–36, 79, 350 (n. 59); and Germany, 65, 74
Yanaev, Gennady, 331
Yazov, Dmitry, 300, 331
Yeltsin, Boris, 301, 313; as president of Russia, 331, 332, 333
Yevtushenko, Yevgeny, 182, 187, 189
Yudin, Pavel, 91, 115

Yugoslavia, 91; as Soviet ally, 24; split with USSR, 73, 76, 100–101; after Stalin, 99, 118

Zagladin, Vadim, 180, 205, 414 (n. 94)
Zakharov, Matvei, 145, 153
Zaloga, Steven, 123
Zamyatin, Leonid, 267
Zaslavsky, Victor, 76
Zaveniagin, Avraami, 93, 124, 354 (n. 123)

Zelikow, Philip, 325
Zhdanov, Andrei, 22, 34, 53, 59
Zhou Enlai, 112, 118, 198, 210
Zhukov, Georgy, 1, 9, 26; demotion of, 54, 121; in Germany, 65, 66; as Khrushchev's ally, 98, 99, 119; and Eisenhower, 106, 107, 128–29
Zinoviev, Alexander, 5
Zubkova, Elena, 99, 164
Zverev, Arseny, 51

(THE NEW COLD WAR HISTORY)

Vladislav M. Zubok, *A Failed Empire: The Soviet Union in the Cold War from Stalin to Gorbachev* (2007).

Stephen G. Rabe, *U.S. Intervention in British Guiana: A Cold War Story* (2005).

Christopher Endy, *Cold War Holidays: American Tourism in France* (2004).

Salim Yaqub, *Containing Arab Nationalism: The Eisenhower Doctrine and the Middle East* (2003).

Francis J. Gavin, *Gold, Dollars, and Power: The Politics of International Monetary Relations, 1958–1971* (2003).

William Glenn Gray, *Germany's Cold War: The Global Campaign to Isolate East Germany, 1949–1969* (2003).

Matthew J. Ouimet, *The Rise and Fall of the Brezhnev Doctrine in Soviet Foreign Policy* (2003).

Pierre Asselin, *A Bitter Peace: Washington, Hanoi, and the Making of the Paris Agreement* (2002).

Jeffrey Glen Giauque, *Grand Designs and Visions of Unity: The Atlantic Powers and the Reorganization of Western Europe, 1955–1963* (2002).

Chen Jian, *Mao's China and the Cold War* (2001).

M. E. Sarotte, *Dealing with the Devil: East Germany, Détente, and Ostpolitik, 1969–1973* (2001).

Mark Philip Bradley, *Imagining Vietnam and America: The Making of Postcolonial Vietnam, 1919–1950* (2000).

Michael E. Latham, *Modernization as Ideology: American Social Science and "Nation Building" in the Kennedy Era* (2000).

Qiang Zhai, *China and the Vietnam Wars, 1950–1975* (2000).

William I. Hitchcock, *France Restored: Cold War Diplomacy and the Quest for Leadership in Europe, 1944–1954* (1998).